THE UNEXTINGUISHED HEARTH

Shelley and His Contemporary Critics

Marianne Hunt's bust of Shelley is the only one based upon a personal study of the poet during his life. Her husband, Leigh Hunt, is said to have considered it a startling likeness; Trelawny, on the other hand, considered it bad. In some respects it harmonizes with contemporary portraits, sketches, and descriptions; in others, particularly the mouth and chin, it clashes with them. Robert Browning once owned a replica of it. It is now owned by Dr. Abraham S. Wolf Rosenbach, to whose kindness I am indebted for the photograph here used. An etching from this bust, slightly idealized, appeared in 1910 in H. Buxton Forman's Letters of E. J. Trelawny. *Whether an accurate likeness or not, this bust suggests a decided possibility that the usually printed likenesses are considerably sentimentalized.*

The
Unextinguished Hearth

Shelley and His Contemporary Critics

By

Newman Ivey White

1966

OCTAGON BOOKS, INC.

New York

Copyright 1938 by Duke University Press

Reprinted 1966
by special arrangement with Duke University Press

OCTAGON BOOKS, INC.
175 FIFTH AVENUE
NEW YORK, N.Y. 10010

LIBRARY OF CONGRESS CATALOG CARD NUMBER: 66-18033

Printed in U.S.A. by
NOBLE OFFSET PRINTERS, INC.
NEW YORK 3, N. Y.

TO THE MEMORY OF THE LATE

THOMAS J. WISE, ESQ.

A FRIEND OF MANY SCHOLARS

PREFACE

This book is the outgrowth of a yet unfinished study of the development of Shelley's reputation. The amount of previously unknown contemporary interest in Shelley, together with the fact that most of the known reviews have never been reprinted, soon convinced me that the publication in one volume of all that was ever printed about Shelley during his lifetime would radically revise the current romantic idea of Shelley as an oppressed, misunderstood and (contradictorily) ignored genius. The present volume does reprint practically every obtainable known contemporary review or article dealing with Shelley,[1] and it either reprints or lists every obtainable incidental contemporary mention that could be found during an intermittent search lasting several years. One or two items known to have existed I have been unable to locate, and there are doubtless a few items that have been overlooked even though the effort was made to examine every volume of every periodical which might contain literary comment. Such omissions, however, cannot affect the result. I feel confident that this volume furnishes for the first time a sure basis for sound conclusions as to what Shelley's contemporaries really thought of him.

Perhaps one may be allowed to feel that affording the material for setting a great poet in his proper relation to contemporary opinion is sufficient justification for the somewhat lengthy and grubby labor it entails— even sufficient justification for publishing. Should this be considered too narrow an object, I hope I may claim that in attaining it I have also provided materials for a truer understanding of the relations of the other Romantic poets to the times in which they lived, and have made it possible to think of reviewing during the Regency as something a little different from wanton and stupid assassination. This last, at least, should justify the ways of scholarship to reviewers.

Scholarly reviewers, on the other hand, may feel that the headings I have given the various items are intrusive and that the quotations from Shelley's poems should be reprinted as in the original articles. The headings are to appease the "general reader"—if there is any; and the quotations are too bulky to be brought within reasonable book limits. Omitting them really does sacrifice, for the casual reader, one very important impression that he should receive—namely, that through the hundreds of lines that were quoted by the periodicals any reader of the reviews in Shelley's day could obtain a very good idea of both the best and the worst of his poetry without ever having seen a volume of it. I have followed

[1] Except several newspaper notices of Shelley in Ireland and Wales, which are omitted because they are available in the Julian edition of Shelley, and the Irish items also in D. F. M. MacCarthy's *The Early Life of Shelley*.

general practice in modernizing the spelling, except that I have preserved original spellings of Shelley's name.

The universal anonymity of reviewing in the early nineteenth century makes the identification of all reviewers a matter of sheer impossibility. It was a difficult matter even at the time, as Shelley's mistakes about the identity of Quarterly reviewers testify. I have spent considerable time trying to trace down such slight clews as occasionally presented themselves, with what slender results is quite evident. The publication of the reviews will, it is hoped, lead to further identifications.

I am generally indebted to several books and articles without which I should probably have missed some of the items here included, but my principal reliance has been an examination, index by index, and page by page, of all available periodicals and miscellaneous contemporary sources. I have also investigated all references I have found in books and articles about Shelley. Some brief newspaper notices mentioned in Dowden's biography of Shelley, practically all the contemporary Oxford and Irish items quoted in MacCarthy's *The Early Life of Shelley*, two or three Leigh Hunt items cited in Professor Peck's biography of the poet or in Professor Walter Graham's article;[2] and three or four items each first cited in H. B. Forman's *The Shelley Library*, T. J. Wise's *A Shelley Library* or Professor S. C. Chew's *Byron—His Fame and After-Fame*, I should probably have missed had I depended solely upon my investigation of contemporary sources. Some half dozen items I *did* miss were listed and described by Professor George L. Marsh in his article, "The Early Reviews of Shelley,"[3] which appeared while I was editing my materials for publication. Two of these were reviews of *Rosalind and Helen* identical or partly identical with that here given from The Commercial Chronicle, one was the unusually interesting obituary notice in The Paris Monthly Review, and the remainder were incidental comments. To these may be added two incidental comments from The Literary Chronicle contributed by an anonymous reviewer of Professor Graham's article in The London Times Literary Supplement for January 2, 1930, and two or three brief items given me by Professor Alan Lang Strout.

While the appearance of Professor Marsh's valuable article dashed my hopes of being the first to publish findings of which I imagined myself the only discoverer, the close coincidence of the results independently obtained confirms my confidence that the list is now practically complete.

I am indebted to Professor Walter Edwin Peck for the suggestion of several items that I might not otherwise have located, and to Professor Marsh for information about The Paris Monthly Review and for permission to reprint two items from his article. The late Roger Ingpen very kindly read and commented upon a part of my manuscript. To Mr. Ingpen, Miss Addie Frances Rowe, and my colleague, Mr. Wil-

[2] "Shelley's Debt to Leigh Hunt and *The Examiner*," PMLA, March, 1925 (40: 185-192).

[3] In Modern Philology, August, 1929 (27: 73-95).

liam Blackburn, I am indebted for assistance in procuring copies of several items not accessible to me at the time and for the verification or completing of several references.

Principally, however, I am indebted to my wife, whose industrious co-labor during several months of intensive reading materially shortened my own researches and first called many items to my attention.

I am also indebted to the following libraries for valued courtesies: The Harvard Library, The Library of the British Museum, The Library of Congress, The Bibliotheque Nationale, The Yale Library, The Library of the City of New York, The Public Library of the City of Boston, The Library of the Massachusetts Historical Association, The Athenaeum Library, and The Duke University Library. Grants from the Research Council of Duke University have aided me greatly in the collection of materials.

N. I. W.

TABLE OF CONTENTS

Frontispiece: Marianne Hunt's Bust of Shelley.

PAGE

Preface.. vii

CHAPTER

I. INTRODUCTION: SHELLEY AND CONTEMPORARY CRITICS..... 3

II. THE JUVENILE PERIOD..................................... 29

ORIGINAL POETRY BY VICTOR AND CAZIRE...................... 29

The Literary Panorama Chuckles 29
(The Literary Panorama, October, 1810)

The British Critic Condemns............................... 31
(The British Critic, April, 1811)

"Downright Scribble" 32
(The Poetical Register for 1810-1811)

ZASTROZZI, A ROMANCE 33

The Gentleman's Magazine Detects Merit.................... 33
(The Gentleman's Magazine, etc., September, 1810)

The Critical Review Exposes Corruption.................... 33
(The Critical Review, etc., November, 1810)

ST. IRVYNE, OR THE ROSICRUCIAN............................. 35

The British Critic Condemns Again........................ 35
(The British Critic, January, 1811)

Laconic Sarcasm 35
(The Literary Panorama, February, 1811)

The Anti-Jacobin Review Functions as Moralist............ 36
(The Anti-Jacobin Review, etc., January, 1812)

A Fellow Collegian Exposes the Author.................... 38
(The Anti-Jacobin Review, etc., February, 1812)

THE NECESSITY OF ATHEISM, AND A DECLARATION OF RIGHTS....... 39

Blasphemy and Sedition Revived........................... 39
(The Brighton Magazine, May, 1822)

III. QUEEN MAB... 45

FIRST SIGNIFICANT ENCOURAGEMENT........................... 45
(The Theological Enquirer, etc., March, 1815, and following)

FIRST PRAISE OF THE PIRATED EDITION BY THE RADICALS........... 52
(John Bull's British Journal, March 11, 1821)

FIRST PRAISE OF THE PIRATED EDITION BY THE LIBERALS.......... 53
(London Magazine and Theatrical Inquisitor, March, 1821)

THE LITERARY GAZETTE SEEKS TO DISCRIMINATE................. 55
(The Literary Gazette, etc., May 19, 1821)

CHAPTER   PAGE

THE MONTHLY MAGAZINE DENIES QUARTER.................... 60
    (The Monthly Magazine, June 1, 1821)

A LIBERAL WEEKLY LAMENTS WASTED GENIUS................. 61
    (The Literary Chronicle and Weekly Review, June 2, 1821)

A RADICAL SEEKS SHELTER................................ 62
    (William Clark's *Reply to . . . Queen Mab*, 1821)

RICHARD CARLILE OFFERS A NEW PIRACY.................... 95
    (The Republican, February 1, 1822)

PIRATED EDITIONS DISCRIMINATED......................... 97
    (The Republican, December 27, 1822)

WICKEDNESS IS PUT DOWN................................. 98
    (The Investigator, etc., 1822)

IV. THE ALASTOR VOLUME TO THE COURT OF CHANCERY 105

"SUBLIME OBSCURITY" 105
    (The Monthly Review, etc., April, 1816)

"PROFOUND STUPIDITY" 105
    (The British Critic, May, 1816)

"MORBID IMAGINATION" 106
    (The Eclectic Review, October, 1816)

THE EXAMINER PROPHESIES AND PRAISES.................... 108
    (The Examiner, December 1, 1816, and January 19, 1817)

SHELLEY IN COURT 109
    (The Examiner, January 26, 1817)

BLACKWOOD'S UNEARTHS PROMISE.......................... 110
    (Blackwood's Edinburgh Magazine, November, 1819)

V. THE REVOLT OF ISLAM 117

THE EXAMINER PRAISES AT LENGTH........................ 117
    (The Examiner, February 1 and 22, and March 1, 1818)

THE MONTHLY MAGAZINE NOTES BRIEFLY.................... 124
    (The Monthly Magazine, etc., March, 1818)

LEIGH HUNT AS A HANDICAP.............................. 124
    (The Quarterly Review, May 1818, and The British Critic,
       July, 1818)

BLACKWOOD'S PRAISES AND CONDEMNS...................... 125
    (Blackwood's Edinburgh Magazine, January, 1819)

MORE PRAISE AND CENSURE............................... 132
    (The Monthly Review, March, 1819)

THE QUARTERLY PASSES SENTENCE......................... 133
    (The Quarterly Review, April, 1819)

LEIGH HUNT TO THE DEFENCE............................. 143
    (The Examiner, September 26 and October 3 and 10, 1819)

CHAPTER   PAGE

VI. ROSALIND AND HELEN 151

    THE EXAMINER EXPLAINS AND PRAISES 151
        (The Examiner, May 9, 1819)

    A DISAPPROVING QUARTET 153
        (The Commercial Chronicle, London Chronicle, Gentleman's
          Magazine, and New Times, June, 1819)

    BLACKWOOD'S ENCOURAGES GENIUS 158
        (Blackwood's Edinburgh Magazine, June, 1819)

    IMMORAL GENIUS CONDEMNED 164
        (The Monthly Review, October, 1819)

VII. THE CENCI 167

    THE EXAMINER PROMISES A REVIEW 167
        (The Examiner, March 19, 1820)

    THE MONTHLY MAGAZINE IS DISGUSTED 167
        (The Monthly Magazine, etc., April, 1820)

    "A DISH OF CARRION" 168
        (The Literary Gazette, etc., April 1, 1820)

    A COCKNEY WITH POSSIBILITIES 171
        (London Magazine and Monthly Critical and Dramatic
          Review, April 1820)

    THE THEATRICAL INQUISITOR IS PLEASED 176
        (The Theatrical Inquisitor, etc., April, 1820)

    THE NEW MONTHLY ADMIRES AND DOUBTS 181
        (The New Monthly Magazine, May, 1820)

    MORE ADMIRATION AND DOUBT 185
        (The Edinburgh Monthly Review, May, 1820)

    GREAT GENIUS AND BASE MORALS 188
        (The London Magazine, May, 1820)

    THE INDICATOR EXPLAINS AND PRAISES 197
        The Indicator, July 19 and 26, 1820)

    GENIUS POORLY EMPLOYED 203
        (The Monthly Review, February, 1821)

    CAUTIOUS ADMIRATION 206
        (The Independent, February 17, 1821)

    ILL-WRITTEN BLASPHEMY 210
        (The British Review, etc., June, 1821)

VIII. PROMETHEUS UNBOUND 217

    A WORK OF IRREGULAR GENIUS 217
        (The London Magazine, June, 1820)

    RIGHTEOUS WRATH FROM THE LITERARY GAZETTE 217
        (The Literary Gazette, etc., September 9, 1820)

    HIGH GENIUS AND EVIL PRINCIPLES 225
        (Blackwood's Edinburgh Magazine, September, 1820)

CHAPTER   PAGE

"A Vast Wilderness of Beauty".. 231
    (London Magazine and Monthly Critical and Dramatic
      Review, September and October, 1820)

Provincial Praise and Censure.. 236
    (The Lonsdale Magazine, November, 1820)

Obscurity, Impiety, and Genius.. 238
    (The Monthly Review, February, 1821)

"Drivelling Prose Run Mad".. 240
    (The Quarterly Review, October, 1821)

IX. General and Incidental Comment in 1820 and 1821 .. 251

The Best of the Cockneys... 251
    (The Honeycomb, August 12, 1820)

Hesitant Dislike.. 255
    (The Dublin Magazine, etc., November, 1820)

Enthusiastic Praise 258
    (The London Magazine and Theatrical Inquisitor, February, 1821)

Vegetarianism Revived 263
    (The London Magazine and Theatrical Inquisitor, July, 1821)

Moderate Appreciation 269
    (The Retrospective Review, 1820)

Hazlitt Pronounces 269
    ("Essay on Paradox and Commonplace," 1821)

Passing Comment from The London Magazine 271
    (The London Magazine, January and April, 1821)

A Voice from Eton... 272
    (The Etonian, August, 1821)

The Champion Explains... 272
    (The Champion, December 23, 1821)

X. Epipsychidion 275

The Gossip Mixes Praise and Censure................................. 275
    (The Gossip, June 23, 1821)

The Gossip Enjoys Shelley's Style................................... 276
    (The Gossip, July 14, 1821)

Christopher North Detects the Author................................ 281
    (Blackwood's Edinburgh Magazine, February, 1822)

A Foreign Notice 284
    (The Paris Monthly Review, March, 1822)

XI. Adonais and Hellas.. 285

"Transcendant Merit" 285
    (The Literary Chronicle and Weekly Review, December 1, 1821)

Nonsense and Impiety.. 286
    (The Literary Gazette, etc., December 8, 1821)

Blackwood's Blows Up.. 289
    (Blackwood's Edinburgh Magazine, December, 1821)

CHAPTER PAGE

THE EXAMINER PRAISES AND COUNTER-ATTACKS................... 298
(The Examiner, July 7, 1822)

A POOR SPECIMEN OF GENIUS................................ 303
(The General Weekly Register, etc., June 30, 1822)

XII. GENERAL AND MISCELLANEOUS COMMENT IN 1822........ 309

LEIGH HUNT FIGHTS BACK................................... 309
(The Examiner, January 20, and June 9, 16, and 23, 1822)

A GENERAL ESTIMATE 315
The Album, July, 1822)

APROPOS OF THE LIBERAL................................... 316
(Blackwood's Edinburgh Magazine, March, 1822; The Examiner,
October 13, 1822; The Country Literary Chronicle, etc., Octo-
ber 26, 1822; The Council of Ten, November, 1822; and The
Edinburgh Magazine, etc., November, 1822)

XIII. SHELLEY'S DEATH...................................... 321

ACCOUNT IN THE EXAMINER................................. 321
(August 4, 1822)

ACCOUNT IN THE MORNING CHRONICLE........................ 321
(August 12, 1822)

OBITUARY NOTICE IN THE COUNTRY LITERARY CHRONICLE........ 322
(August 10, 1822)

COMMENT IN THE JOHN BULL............................... 322
(August 19, 1822)

COMMENT IN THE REPUBLICAN.............................. 325
(August 16, 1822)

COMMENT IN THE BRITISH LUMINARY........................ 325
(August 18, 1822)

AN OBITUARY DEFENCE IN THE PARIS MONTHLY REVIEW......... 326
(August, 1822)

OBITUARY NOTICE IN THE GENTLEMAN'S MAGAZINE............ 329
(September, 1922)

OBITUARY NOTICE IN THE MONTHLY MAGAZINE................ 330
(September, 1822)

OBITUARY NOTICE IN THE NEW MONTHLY MAGAZINE............ 330
(October, 1822)

OBITUARY NOTICE IN THE DRAMA.......................... 331
(December, 1822)

LEIGH HUNT DEFENDS THE DEAD........................... 335
(The Examiner, November 3, 1822)

INCIDENTAL NOTICES IN REVIEWS OF ELEGIES.............. 336
(The Literary Chronicle and Weekly Review, October 12; The
Eclectic Review, November, 1822; The Monthly Magazine,
October, 1822; The Gentleman's Magazine, supplement to
1822)

CHAPTER   PAGE

XIV. POEMS INSPIRED BY SHELLEY 339
    ODE TO THE AUTHOR OF QUEEN MAB. By F.................... 339
        (The Theological Inquirer, July, 1815)
    SONNET TO THE AUTHOR OF THE REVOLT OF ISLAM. By Horace Smith 340
        (The Examiner, February 8, 1818)
    TO PERCY SHELLEY ON THE DEGRADING NOTIONS OF
        DEITY. By Leigh Hunt............................... 340
        (Leigh Hunt's Foliage, 1817)
    TO THE SAME. By Leigh Hunt............................. 341
        (Leigh Hunt's Foliage, 1817)
    STANZAS ADDRESSED TO PERCY BYSSHE SHELLEY. By Bernard Barton.. 341
        (Poems, by Bernard Barton, 1820)
    SONNET TO THE AUTHOR OF THE REVOLT OF ISLAM. By Arthur Brooke 343
        (The Examiner, November 5, 1820)
    THE SPIRIT OF THE STORM. By Leigh Cliffe.................... 344
        (The London Magazine and Theatrical Inquisitor, January, 1821)
    THE ATHEIST. By C... 344
        (The Literary Gazette, etc., June 2, 1821)
    ON MR. SHELLEY'S POEM "PROMETHEUS UNBOUND"................. 345
        (John Bull, February 4, 1822)
    ON THE DEATH OF MR. SHELLEY. By B........................ 345
        (The Examiner, August 25, 1822)
    ELEGY ON THE DEATH OF SHELLEY. By F...................... 346
        (The Bard, November 16, 1822)
    ELEGY ON THE DEATH OF PERCY BYSSHE SHELLEY. By Arthur Brooke 348
        (1822)
    VERSES ON THE DEATH OF PERCY BYSSHE SHELLEY. By Bernard Barton 352
        (1822)
    ON THE DEATH OF PERCY BYSSHE SHELLEY. By J. N.............. 357
        (The Hermes, December 14, 1822)

XV. A CHRONOLOGICAL SUMMARY, 1810-1822.................. 359

XVI. A SUMMARY BY PERIODICALS AND OTHER PUBLICATIONS
    IN WHICH SHELLEY IS NOTICED, 1819-1822 377

THE UNEXTINGUISHED HEARTH

I

INTRODUCTION: SHELLEY AND CONTEMPORARY CRITICS

IN THE YEAR 1820 a popular quip went the rounds of English literary circles: "*Prometheus Unbound;* it is well named, for who would take the trouble to bind it." At about the same time an English traveler in Italy who met Shelley in a post-office exclaimed, "What, are you that damned atheist Shelley!"—and straightway knocked him down. The two stories seem somewhat inconsistent. The one implies that English criticism was utterly indifferent to Shelley; the other, that any Tom, Dick, or Harry could recognize him at once as a threat to religion and society. Shelley himself seems to support both these irreconcilable inferences, for he speaks in his letters of not expecting *Prometheus Unbound* to sell beyond twenty copies and also of the odium in which he is held.

It is one of the commonplaces of literary histories that Shelley was largely ignored and entirely misunderstood by contemporary reviewers. The reviews of Shelley and Keats which are commonly quoted have fully established the conviction that no reviewers were so dull, so unfair, and vindictive as those of the early nineteenth century.[1] This view is tenable only so long as we continue to take a part for the whole. No biographer or critic of Shelley has ever judged his relations with contemporary criticism against a background of complete knowledge of what was published about him during his lifetime. Several very significant reviews of Shelley have apparently been entirely unknown between the time of their original publication and their appearance in this volume. Not more than eight or ten contemporary criticisms have ever been reprinted. Perhaps half of the criticisms in this volume have been mentioned before 1929, but no biographer or editor of Shelley has ever given evidence of having read more than a very few of them. Everyone has generalized about the treatment Shelley received from the reviewers, but the conclusions have been based more on Shelley's own estimate and on that of his friends than upon a close study of the reviews themselves. Shelley, with Chatterton and Keats in mind, easily fitted himself into the same role with them. His friends, who were finally to gain the victory in the ten years' struggle between conservative distrust and liberal enthusiasm which was to decide Shelley's posthumous reputation, all thought of him as the victim of hatred and misunderstanding. The tradition was established before Shelley himself was fully established. Once it had been established, the easiest and most natural course was to adhere to it. Biographers and critics all had greater

[1] For Keats and the periodicals of his time, see article of that title by George L. Marsh and Newman I. White in Modern Philology, August, 1934 (33: 37-53).

fish to fry than the comparatively insignificant one of testing this tradition for accuracy.

It would be trifling to charge anyone with negligence for the persistence of this inaccurate and unfair tradition. There is ample support for the traditional point of view in the materials readily available, and there was enough of this material to have rendered the conclusions sound, in nine cases out of ten. Biographers and critics simply forgot, because the whole subject was beyond their immediate purpose, that in an era of changing opinions the documents must be examined more fully and carefully than in a more settled period. The same conclusion which this examination will reach, on the basis of all the documents now available, can be reached in essence by a careful study of all the reviews in Blackwood's Edinburgh Magazine, which has always been at hand. That conclusion is that Shelley's contemporary critics were not blind to his genius, but merely afraid of it. If they were stupid beyond the amount of stupidity inherent in normal human nature, it was the stupidity of fear and not of blindness. Whether or not these fears were really stupid in the position in which England stood between 1815 and 1822 is a matter not to be lightly judged. If we must judge them, let it be with some faint recollections of how our own similar stupidities have embellished the record of the recent post-war decade.

To see the matter justly, we must first assemble all the documents. We must then consider them in their relation to the general conditions prevailing among early nineteenth-century periodicals, with their critical inheritances, and their special tendencies as shaped by the political, moral, and social fears of the times. Shelley's poetry and conduct must be viewed in conflict with this background. Finally, though not absolutely essential, it will be useful to consider Shelley's opinions of his reviewers, since his own incomplete and not altogether just conclusions have been a powerful factor in forming the general opinion after the triumph of his reputation.

A few years before Shelley began writing, the principal reviews, with one exception, were running satisfactorily in grooves worn smooth by the eighteenth century. The Monthly Review, to which Goldsmith had earlier lent some quality, was now no longer written with as much care and impartiality as Dr. Johnson once conceded it, but its mediocre Whig conventionality still carried considerable weight. Its veteran Tory rival, The Critical Review, had also lost influence since the days of Smollett, but was still one of the most important reviews. The British Critic, organ of High Church orthodoxy and dullness, had just inspired Edward Copleston's witty *Advice to a Young Reviewer*. The Anti-Jacobin Review and Magazine, the only one of the lot that was a product of the new era, was a somewhat inferior offspring of the old Anti-Jacobin, or Weekly Review, too often substituting savagery for wit. Mediocre as they were, these were the principal reviews at the beginning of the nineteenth century.

The founding of The Edinburgh Review in 1802 began a revolution in journalism and lifted reviews, for the first time, to the level of criticism.

Reviews in The Edinburgh were practically free from the almost universal dominance of the publishers and were written by able writers who had a real knowledge of the subject. Though the periodical was an organ of the New Whigs, its reviews were only mildly biased by party considerations. A few exceptions may be granted. The motive for reviewing Keats favorably may not have been so much admiration for Keats as taking advantage of an opportunity to embarrass the Tory reviewers. Byron's *Hours of Idleness* probably was noticed mainly because it seemed to offer a good rod with which to chastise presumptuous young aristocrats. Shelley may have been pointedly ignored because to notice him favorably would seem to be endorsing atheism and so furnish the Tories with ammunition against The Edinburgh. Scott might have been praised a little more heartily had he been a Whig. Party prejudice, however, was not a glaring fault in The Edinburgh, as even some of the radicals admitted. Its principal fault, as its treatment of Wordsworth exemplifies, was inelasticity of taste. It failed to realize that the standards of literary judgment were being materially altered from those of the eighteenth century. It regarded as a mere presumptuous colt the gray mare that was to be accepted as the better horse. Had the revolution in poetry failed to succeed, The Edinburgh would still be regarded as an almost infallible critic.

The enormous success won and merited by The Edinburgh Review brought about the establishment of The Quarterly Review in 1809. The men who wrote for The Quarterly were fully as well informed as those who wrote for The Edinburgh. The names of Scott and Southey certainly carried as much weight in contemporary opinion as those of Sidney Smith and Jeffrey. If today The Edinburgh seems superior, it is mainly because it was less prejudiced and because the prejudices of The Quarterly were exercised against authors who are favored by our own prejudices. In the early nineteenth century, however, the prejudices of The Quarterly had the weight of the Tory government and the Church of England behind them and were endorsed by the majority of respectable Englishmen. Able as The Edinburgh was, The Quarterly probably exerted a greater influence on English opinion during the time that Shelley's poems were being reviewed. This influence, which played up to the popular fears and prejudices of the decade, was almost incredible. One sturdy Briton quoted by Tennyson's father ranked The Quarterly next to the Bible. Hazlitt testified to its power when he complained that one review in The Quarterly absolutely stopped the sales of one of his books. Leigh Hunt offers testimony of another sort when he ignores all other enemies to assail The Quarterly alone for its attacks on Hunt and Keats. Byron and Shelley acknowledged it when they solemnly supposed that a Quarterly review could kill not only a book, but a genuine poet.

Blackwood's Edinburgh Magazine, established in 1817, was the ablest and most influential monthly magazine, but it never approximated the influence of the two great quarterlies. Its undeniably great ability and wit were offset by its recklessness, which got it into libel suits from the beginning and which deprived it of the sober authority wielded by the two quarterlies.

Leigh Hunt's The Examiner was in general no more than fearlessly liberal in tone, but in its day was regarded as decidedly radical. It is important in the literary criticism of the times mainly because it championed several writers like Hazlitt, Keats, and Shelley; but it was not so largely devoted to literature as the other periodicals discussed, and exercised at the time no particular influence upon literary criticism.

Side by side with these creations of the new age were a number of more conventional periodicals, mostly monthlies. A considerable proportion of them had been established in the eighteenth century and continued the old methods of reviewing. Their reviews were principally either of the informational Monthly Review type, depending largely on summaries, or of the more vigorously opinionated Critical Review type, running largely to excerpts, with appreciation or condemnation. The reviewers were all anonymous, nor would their names have meant much if printed. The few monthlies, like The London Magazine and Blackwood's, which sometimes employed really able reviewers, were on the whole far behind the two quarterlies in learning and ability.

The new periodicals founded before the third decade of the century were mainly mediocre. Their criticism belonged mainly to the old models and was not greatly influenced by the substantiality of the criticism in the quarterlies or the vivacity of Blackwood's. The foundation of The London Magazine in 1820, by giving the Cockneys recognition and combatting the arrogance of Blackwood's (with its haughty nickname of "Maga"), did something for catholicity. Its reviews and those of the other London magazines connected with it were better and more tolerantly written, but they were written upon essentially the same critical principles (where there were any) as those of the other monthlies. The general elevation of reviewing to something like its present imperfect status was to be accomplished in the third and fourth decades of the century, when the temper of the times made it a more feasible possibility and the liberals and radicals finally secured able and humane, instead of merely vigorous, writers for such new periodicals as The Athenaeum, The Westminster Review, and The Spectator.

The various weeklies, semiweeklies, and semimonthlies, many of which were only incidentally interested in literature, followed the general trend. In the early 1820's, however, there was a considerable outbreak of ephemeral journals in many of which party virulence affected the critical tone more than in most of the older periodicals. Many of these journals ran for only a few issues, but some were of longer duration. Few were primarily interested in literature. William Hone, Theodore Hook, William Benbow, and Richard Carlile were mainly interested in literature only insofar as it promoted or retarded radicalism or Toryism. One or two of their periodicals, like Hook's John Bull, could write with a certain sparkle; all could write recklessly and ferociously, and nearly all at one time or another suffered from the libel laws. The charge made by Leigh Hunt and Hazlitt that it was necessary only for The Examiner to praise a young author in order for The Quarterly to assassinate him was even more true of the crop of Tory journals that sprang up in the early 1820's. The radicals were only a shade better in this regard, and they were certainly a shade worse in innate ability (even if rarely practiced) to appreciate literature for its own sake. A good example of how these journalists made literature play second fiddle to political animosities is furnished by some of the comment on Shelley's death quoted in this volume. The John Bull (violently Tory) seizes upon the sympathetic account of Shelley's death in The Morning Chronicle (progressive Whig) and uses it to demonstrate how dangerous to the British constitution are such journals as The Morning Chronicle, and, incidentally, Carlile's The Republican. The British Luminary (mildly radical) quotes John Bull's account, with a sarcastic comment on journals that attack cant and yet practice it—but with no attention at all to Shelley. The Republican (violently radical) simply quotes the article from The British Luminary as a means of discrediting John Bull. Shelley is here rather a pawn than a poet. Even Leigh Hunt's repeated defence of Shelley and Keats, though undoubtedly sincere in its personal aspect, serves also a plain political purpose of attacking an enemy who has overreached himself.

Since the political factor was so important in criticism during the first three decades of the nineteenth century, it would be well to take a glance at the general milieu of the critics before attempting to isolate the principles that governed their criticism. The hysteric horror of republicanism that Burke helped to foster in the closing years of the eighteenth century had largely died down during the long years of Napoleonic warfare, but it prepared the ground for the later outbreak following Waterloo. The imprisonment of Sir Francis Burdett in 1810 was a sufficient indication that anything savoring of radical utterance was too dangerous for the times. With the peace a number of dangers loomed up at once. Labor unrest due to the displacement of workers by machines was complicated by demobilization. Commercial and agricultural depression, industrial overproduction, famine, and high taxation called loudly for the overdue reforms toward which Pitt had been looking when stopped by the wars—all this at a time when the Tory rulers of England were hand in glove with the Continental rulers who wanted a return to Bourbonism. To their minds any concession was an invitation to revolution. The prevalence of government spies who were in some cases *agents provocateurs,* the mounting number of prosecutions for blasphemy and treason, and the increasing desperation of the working classes produced a really dangerous situation. The alarming suspension of the right of habeas corpus, the Cato Street Conspiracy, and the Manchester Massacre increased both the desperation of the workers and the fear of the government.

The crisis of this uneasiness came in 1819, at the time of the Manchester Massacre, when at least nine people were killed and 418 injured in an attack by yeomanry and regular soldiers upon a peaceable assembly of radicals being addressed near Manchester by "Orator" Hunt. The investigation of this tragedy was notoriously biased and unfair. To Tories like Lord Grenville the occurrence was mainly an occasion to warn the Lords that the nation was "inundated with inflammatory and poisonous publications" and "deluged with sedition and blasphemy." Shelley wrote his white-hot *Masque of Anarchy*, which Leigh Hunt feared to publish; but numerous other radical protests were published, including several by Leigh Hunt. It was moved in Parliament to appoint a committee to inquire into the state of the country. Shelley earnestly warned his friends, the Gisbornes, of the insecurity of their money invested in the public funds: "An additional army of 11,500 men has received orders to be organized. Everything is preparing for a bloody struggle." The two ablest radical journals of the period, Cobbett's Political Register and Leigh Hunt's Examiner, are crowded with the details of suffering and injustice pressing upon both the agricultural and manufacturing laborers. The Edinburgh Monthly Review for January, 1820 (to single out one Whig utterance from many similar ones of all parties) in an article entitled "On the State of the Country" regarded the country as practically facing revolution: "A fierce collision appears to have been meditated betwixt all that a virtuous citizen holds sacred and the fearful errors of revolution—a distemper of unexampled malignity had seized the public mind." Such expressions were not mere feverish outgrowths of the Manchester Massacre. As early as 1816 at a meeting in London presided over by the Lord Mayor, it was stated that England faced "either bloody revolution . . . or a military despotism."[2]

In 1821 came the exciting trial of Queen Caroline, with its renewed radical outbursts and its violent demonstrations against the ministers of the government. The situation began slowly to calm down into a less dangerous reform agitation when Castlereagh committed suicide in 1822 and was succeeded by the somewhat more tolerant Canning.

It was during these seven years (1816-1822) of anticipated revolution that every single volume published during the poet's lifetime under the name of Percy Bysshe Shelley appeared and received the attention of reviewers.

Immorality and irreligion had accompanied the French Revolution and had caused a large part of the conservative antipathy to it. They were sure signs of rottenness in the state. Hence the Society for the Prevention of Vice, with its numerous prosecutions, and its hearty support by the respectable middle classes. Acute liberal observers like Sydney Smith did not fail to point out that its operations were really class oppressions, a fact which made the radicals bitter against it from the first. Its great power while it lasted attests the determination of the responsible classes to keep England

---

[2] See the article by Prof. A. Stanley Walker, in PMLA, March, 1925 (40: 128-164), entitled "Peterloo, Shelley and Reform."

free from atheism and immorality. England had escaped the French Revolution and "Boney" only by the grace of God. It was mainly by the grace of godliness, to judge from many printed utterances, that it was to escape the radical aftermath. The cause of church and state had always been one, and the deep conservative fear to which Burke had so powerfully appealed was once more alert and panicky. Byron's domestic scandal drove him out of the country. Newspapers and journals of every description bristled with stern alarm over the spread of atheism. There were even a number of rather ridiculous warnings against the spread of seduction. The poet laureate, who had already written for The Quarterly Review an article on the spread of sedition and atheism, sounded a general official alarm in the preface to his *A Vision of Judgment*. A Satanic School of poetry now existed, commanding some of the most powerful pens in the kingdom and apparently devoted to spreading atheism and immorality. The witty scorn of Byron's reply won him an easy victory with posterity, but the numerous echoes of Southey's alarm in the press of the day show that the overwhelming preponderance of respectable opinion was on his side.

Tom Paine and his apostle, Richard Carlile, were bitterly denounced by the pulpit and the press all over Great Britain. The radicals celebrated Paine's birthday; the conservatives burned him in effigy. For publishing blasphemous matter, principally Paine's *The Age of Reason* and Palmer's *Principles of Nature*, Richard Carlile underwent a series of convictions between 1817 and 1834 that cost him nearly ten years in prison and thousands of pounds in fines, seizures, and deterioration of property. The second sentence imposed on him (1819) was a £1,500 fine, three years in prison, and £1,200 security for good behavior *for life*, the imprisonment to continue as long as fines and securities were unpaid. This savage sentence was matched by the treatment of his wife for publishing *The Age of Reason*. Carlile had read the entire book to the jurors as his defence, and his wife, exercising her legal right to publish an account of his trial, had published the book as a part of Carlile's speech in his defence. This did not save her from a fine of £500, one year in prison, and the exaction of £1,200 security for seven years' good behavior. These sentences were the subject of much radical and some Whig protest. W. J. Fox preached a sermon against them, but his sermon was disapproved by the congregation and the public. Even the partially liberal-minded Crabb Robinson, who attended Carlile's trial, seemed to think he received full justice. It is significant of the temper of the times that Shelley's long indignant letter against Carlile's treatment was prudently withheld from publication by Leigh Hunt, who was also too prudent to publish Shelley's indignant poem on the Manchester Massacre until ten years after the poet's death. It cannot be doubted that as an experienced and courageous radical Hunt had cogent and justifiable reasons for such suppressions.

The effect of these prejudices on the policies and professions of the periodicals is conspicuously apparent. The Quarterly was a semi-official organ of established religion. The British Review and London Critical

Journal described itself as "decidedly religious." The New Monthly Magazine was established, in the words of its first editor, "to counteract the pernicious and anarchical designs of sedition and infidelity." The Investigator set as its main purpose the exposure of religious and moral corruption. The Hermes proclaimed in its introductory editorial, "We respect religion and morality as the palladium of our country." The John Bull displayed a Holy Bible at the masthead of a journal whose first function was to justify George IV and besmirch Queen Caroline.

Journals expressing radical views in religion and politics were discouraged not only by libel prosecutions but by special applications of the newspaper stamp act against which Henry Hetherington later waged such spectacular warfare. It was notorious that the government applied this act especially against radicals and winked at conservative violators. In the 1820's a whole crop of cheap periodicals arose in which political and religious discussion was entirely eschewed, in order to escape the application of this law. The Mirror, a very popular journal for workingmen, stated in its millennial edition that it began in 1822, in consequence of acts passed that year against journals that expressed religious and political opinions, and that its policy had been to steer clear of both these fields.

There is nothing to indicate that the Regency period was blessed with more than a moderate or even meager amount of actual, practical religion. Yet there has never been a time since journalism developed in England when the press was so concerned about religious defection, or public opinion so severe on atheists. Shelley asserted that only those deists were prosecuted who would otherwise be considered enemies of the existing regime, and claimed to know certain Tory deists among the prosecutors. Undoubtedly religion had become more of a Tory appanage than the early saints had anticipated. Even the most hypocritical prosecution, however, had a secure foundation in the honest consternation of the average Englishman. In his opinion something indispensable to his whole social inheritance was threatened with destruction by reckless meddlers.

Thus, during the years when Shelley's books were receiving their first reviews the English periodical press was dominated by a religious fear and bigotry unprecedented in its history. This feeling was closely allied with a fear of political revolution that was more panic-stricken and therefore more unscrupulous than the similar fear of a "red menace" a hundred years later. At the very moment of publication, Shelley's poems flew straight in the face of two almost hysterical fears.

A glance through the literary journals of this troubled period will reveal at once how greatly the special fears of the times warped criticism in the direction of considering literature largely from an unliterary point of view. "Poetry, after all, if pursued as an end, is but child's play," said The Eclectic Review (September, 1820) in condemning Keats. The reviews of Shelley here collected are in themselves sufficient to prove that poetry was criticized only secondarily as literature. Evidence abounds elsewhere in the periodicals and in contemporary criticisms outside of the periodicals.

Even the Romantic victims of this distorted critical point of view were not entirely guiltless of similar prejudices and practices. The greatest Romantic critics won their reputations largely on their criticism of older writers, particularly the Elizabethans, but Charles Lamb disapproved of Shelley almost as much as Southey did, and on similar grounds. Scott, despite his great humanity, campaigned against Catholic emancipation and countenanced John Bull and The Quarterly and Blackwood's reviewers. Byron's critical point of view was wholly the traditional one. Wordsworth's first recorded pronouncement on Shelley—a brusque "Won't do" —is an almost ridiculous echo of certain memorable words once applied to Wordsworth himself by the critical narrowness of the age; Shelley's estimate of Keats was slightly tinged with traditionalism and his treatment of Wordsworth with radical prejudice; while Hazlitt, the greatest of them all in ability to criticize his contemporaries, could trade personal buffets with Gifford on more than even terms and could not praise the Waverley novels without regarding their conservatism as almost a curse to humanity.

Thus we have, in the best critics of the age, touches of the lack of complete poise which in ordinary reviewers appeared more grossly. The excess is evidently of two kinds, a down-at-heels literary traditionalism inherited from eighteenth-century critical practice, and an extreme social, religious, and political fear born of their own age. Both are omnipresent in the reviews of the day.

Despite the fact that the eighteenth century had laid the groundwork for Romantic criticism, the vast majority of reviewers in the early nineteenth century were as stubbornly unaware of the fact that theirs was the Romantic Age as the ancients were that they were ancients. The common practice of taking the waning influence of Pope as an index of change leads easily to a misapprehension. Though "the infallibility of Pope Alexander" was questioned even in the eighteenth century, it was not really safe to challenge his authority within a hundred years of his death. Bowles asserted Pope to be a second-rater, but Byron voiced the majority sentiment when he trounced him for it. Keats was much worse mauled for the same offense. Even later, Robert Browning's father was disturbed because young Robert wrote so differently from Pope. As late as 1831 the Reverend George Croly, in the introduction to *Croly's Beauties of the English Poets,* says that among the English poets after Dryden, "Pope still retains the pre-eminence." The quarterlies differed from the eighteenth-century reviewers more in quality than in fundamental principles. The principles on which Jeffrey condemned Wordsworth were the same principles on which Wordsworth would have been condemned in the eighteenth century. The great majority of periodicals were simply eighteenth-century survivals or their imitators and continued a tradition very little changed except inasmuch as the fear of revolution intensified elements already existing.

In the matter of subservience to the booksellers, early nineteenth-century reviewers were considerably more free than their predecessors, but enough special damning and puffing persisted to transmit the custom to later times. Henry Colburn's letters, as quoted in Lady Sydney Morgan's *Memoirs*, show plainly how the publisher of the early eighteen-twenties expected to control reviews. "I am intimately acquainted with the editors," he wrote (speaking of The Examiner, New Times, and John Bull), "and advertising with them a great deal keeps them in check." In its issue of May 4, 1822, The Gazette of Fashion and Magazine of Literature, etc., presented a burlesque notice in which a Blackwood's reviewer offered to trade favorable reviews with an Edinburgh reviewer, and another in which a critic advertises "puffing and duffing by the page, column or yard, on reasonable terms." A few years later a sensational journal appropriately entitled The Wasp (October 28, 1826) printed an article on Modern Criticism in which it claimed that reviewing was a nefarious practice "propped up by ignorant conceit, presumptuous ignorance, and glaring pretence" and described "that useful race of men called Helots," hungry and out-at-elbows, who frequented publishing houses and wrote reviews for and against at the price of a dinner. A satirical poem by T. W. Coller entitled *The Battle of Oblivion, or Criticism and Quackery* (1831) was commended by The Day (Glasgow, January 6, 1832) for denouncing the venality of reviewers in the following lines:

> The Critic—alias advertising sage
> Ne'er reads the work, but scans the title page,—
> Runs o'er his base "Retainer Book" to find
> The Author's talents, tact, and strength of mind;
> Then dashes off the quaint, the kingly "We,"
> And measures out his fustian by his fee!

The same charge is made in a department called "Political and Literary Commentary" in Bennet's Glasgow Magazine for August, 1832: "You are no doubt aware that certain of the Reviews are the property of booksellers. Of some of these it is broadly asserted that they are made the mere vehicles for puffing such works into notice as the capital of the Review proprietors may happen to be invested in." Such charges, however, are much more frequent in the decade after Shelley's death than in the actual years when his poems were first published. It is true that in his youthful contacts with the reviewers Shelley proceeded on the assumption of their venality and that when Shelley's works were appearing Coleridge charged The Edinburgh Review with occasional reviews actuated by other than purely literary motives, while Leigh Hunt and others pointedly charged The Quarterly with especial lenience to Byron, whose publisher also published The Quarterly. A study of the periodicals themselves, however, suggests a strong probability that during the particularly nervous seven years in which Shelley's acknowledged volumes appeared, this heritage of the eighteenth-century status of reviewing temporarily yielded place to party spirit and fear for the state of the country.

There were of course signs of the dawn of a new critical point of view and of a consciousness that poetry was entering a new age. Coplestone's *Advice to a Young Reviewer* (1807) was a powerful ironic satire on current reviewing practices, but it went unheeded by the reviewers. Two or three similar satires occur before 1822, the best of which is a review of *Macbeth* in the first number of Ollier's Literary Miscellany (1820), beginning:

Quare—Tragedy or melodrama?

It consists of a dance of hobgoblins—the murder of a Scotch king—the elevation of a murderer to the throne—a ghost with his throat cut from ear to ear—a lady walking in her chemise—and the murderer's death! This last is good: poetic justice. The following are pleasant specimens of the style. We select them sincerely from the first page alone:

> "When the hurly burly's done
> When the battle's lost *and* won!" etc.

The clearest and best analysis of the weakness of current criticism occurs in Coleridge's *Biographia Literaria,* but even Coleridge is insufficiently aware of the strength of eighteenth-century tradition when he implies that Jeffrey's criticisms of Wordsworth are based wholly on personal whim, to the exclusion of philosophic principles.

Just as Coplestone's satire was not the only sign of impatience with the old criticism, so Wordsworth's prefaces were not alone in recognizing a change in poetry itself. The anonymous author of *The Modern Parnassus; or the New Art of Poetry* (1814) points out in his preface that the age is a new and flourishing age of poetry, with new ideas, and cites Wordsworth and Southey. In March, 1820, The New Monthly Magazine published an article entitled "What is Poetry?," by M. N., showing both a consciousness of a change and doubt of its value: "On the right hand and on the left I hear that Pope was not a poet . . . that he had nothing of a poet's fire. This fire is all the rage, but unfortunately, in the attempts at kindling a fire from green materials, the world of poetry is now as much distinguished by smoke." The dominance of the new ideas in poetry was not yet fully established with a majority of the poets themselves, much less with their reviewers.

A study of the periodicals of any age, however, always reveals the fact that literary tastes and prejudices change much less rapidly than is supposed by the literary historians who write after the change has been accomplished. The eighteenth century may have "blown out its brains" with the French Revolution, but its criticism (with or without the brains) survived long afterwards. The consciousness of change was but a slowly widening trickle in comparison with the main stream of opinion. Far more numerous are the discussions of contemporary poetry or articles on the nature of poetry, like Byron's letters on Pope and Peacock's *The Four Ages of Poetry,* which show no consciousness that poetry is undergoing a significant change. Jeffrey's attacks on Wordsworth's innovations in diction and subjects were based not so much on personal whimsy as on the eighteenth-century legacy of decorum. They were echoed, on the same basis, by Byron in *English Bards and Scotch Reviewers* (1809) and years later (1818-1824) in *Don Juan*. Between the terminal dates of Byron's attacks may be mentioned a number of similar ones exclusive of reviews. *Modern Poets, A Dialogue in Verse* (1813) sneers at Wordsworth and longs for the discipline and restraint of earlier poetry. *The Modern Parnassus, or the New Art of Poetry* (1814) arraigns Wordsworth's theories as absurd. *Childe Harolde's Monitor—Including Hints to Other Contemporaries* (1818) satirizes Wordsworth in both the text and the notes. Numerous contemporary. parodies are based implicitly on the same principle; e.g., James Smith's in *Rejected Addresses* (1812) and an anonymous versifier's (James Hogg's) in *The Poetic Mirror, or the Living Bards of Great Britain* (1816). The latter of these prompted The Augustan Review (December, 1816) to several pages condemning the silliness of Wordsworth and his associates. The point of view was far too prevalent to sustain Coleridge's charge of personal whim against Jeffrey. Rather it indicated a "philosophic principle" which Coleridge overlooked—the old principle of decorum, intuitive, unstated, and perhaps mistakenly applied, as Wordsworth himself argued in his letter to John Wilson defending *The Idiot Boy*.

On similar principles both the theory and practice of Leigh Hunt and Keats were condemned—not to mention Shelley at this point. Not only did these writers violate decorum of language and subject, but they substituted for the old ethical and didactic emphasis of poetry a bewildering looseness of fancy and imagination. Most of the reviewers still read *Rasselas* and were of Imlac's persuasion as to the dangers of imagination. In the reviews of Shelley quoted in this volume the numerous particulars of "absurdities" may be overdone on account of other prejudices, but they represent an honest difficulty in the face of a new poetic technique, and they were applied to other poets whose imagery was of the newer order, though naturally to none so much as to Shelley. "The business of a poet," as explained by Imlac to Rasselas, very fairly expresses the creed of early nineteenth-century reviewers. This was "to examine, not the individual, but the species; to remark general properties and large appearances: he does not number the streaks of the tulip, or describe the different shades in the verdure of the forest. He is to exhibit, in his portraits of nature, such prominent and striking features as recall the original to every mind; and must neglect the minuter discriminations." It was the same thesis as that announced by Pope in more general terms in his preface to *An Essay on Man*. Incidentally, the remainder of Imlac's disquisition is curiously like Shelley's view as expressed in his *Defence of Poetry*—and curiously unlike the views implied by Shelley's practice. The idea of the poet as a rare soul and his properly qualified reader as another is implicit in much of Shelley's practice and that of his Romantic contemporaries. This idea which has reached such grotesque development with some twentieth-century poets, was a very genuine source of suspicion to the traditionalist reviewers of the early Romantic poets.

The most striking characteristic of reviewing during Shelley's later life was the strong political and moral bias of the critics. The critical journals of the eighteenth century furnish numerous examples of the same bias, but without the intensifying fear which made it almost a mania during the Regency. We have already seen how this fear affected the general tone and policy of the periodicals; it only remains to show how strongly it affected the theory and practice of literary criticism.

From the publication of the first canto of *Childe Harold's Pilgrimage* the mixture of moral with literary judgment may be seen in a large proportion of the numerous reviews and articles that followed the Byronic melodrama like a spotlight. Thomas Moore made his initial bow to a stinging moral rebuke for which a duel was the only salve. The essentially political and literary animosity to Leigh Hunt was buttressed by appeals to moral prejudice because a few of his poems depicted with suspicious sympathy situations not sanctioned by the English church. "It is a fact of very melancholy import that the poetry—we may say the literature of the present hour, is become the ally of immorality, infidelity, and political disaffection," mourned The British Review and London Critical Journal, reviewing Byron in August, 1818. "Immorality, infidelity, and political disaffection" became an unholy Trinity, as powerful, and as mystically inseparable as the theological one. Southey, the ablest poet laureate between Dryden and Wordsworth and one of the most adequate of all the laureates as a spokesman of his times, made the matter almost an official crusade in the preface to his *Vision of Judgment* (1821). To him the "monstrous combinations of horrors and mockery, lewdness and impiety, with which English poetry has in our days first been polluted" required that the age should "regard the morals more than the manner of a composition." Says the anonymous author of *The Press, or Literary Chit-Chat* (1822) in his preface, "I am not wont to be timid or suspicious, but when we see impious ribaldry and profane obscenity openly written—openly published— and openly displayed in our libraries, what thinking mind but must tremble for the consequences?"—followed by a blushing hint of the consequences: "The cestus of virtue is daily becoming more loose. If not speedily tightened it will fall off altogether." To the author of *A Critique on The Liberal* (1822) the duties of a critic in such a situation are unpleasant, but clear: "But when, on the other hand, the slightest tendency to immorality and impiety pollutes a book, then no wit, no humor, nor all the elegant and splendid ornaments that genius can impart, ought to preserve it from the severest lash of criticism. . . . Criticism should be alert when any man, however humble in talent, assails the pillars that support society; but when men high in literary fame abuse their talents in composing writings of such a tendency, it becomes every man to rally round those supporters of the community, those moral and religious principles which, if eradicated from the minds of our youth, their loss must be followed by the downfall of the empire." In the same year another conservative booklet, *Revolutionary Causes with a Brief Notice of Some Late Publications,* deplored the revolutionary tendency of literature and praised The Quarterly's assault on *Prometheus Unbound* as a defence of society against "atheistical poets."

The same sentiments are expressed by Nathan Drake in his *Evenings in Autumn* (two volumes, 1822) beginning a long appreciation of Bernard Barton:

"It must ever be a subject of deep regret with those who know and feel how effective an agent like Poetry may be rendered in furthering the great interests of morality and religion . . . to behold an art thus honored in the past, and consecrated, as it were, upon the altar of our God, prostituted, as it often has been in the present age, to the worst and most debasing purposes of scepticism and impiety. Of all the instances of wickedness and folly which have sullied and degraded the history of our species, perhaps the most revolting, and, were it not for the desolation it inflicts, the most worthy of derision and contempt, is that of him who . . . endeavors to strip himself and his fellow creatures of every hope which rests beyond the grave"—continuing at some length, and quoting Southey's preface to *A Vision of Judgment* to the same effect.

"From the beginning to the end," writes the Reverend T. F. Dibdin, F.R.S., A.S., in the preface to his *The Library Companion*, etc. (1824), "I have never lost sight of what I consider to be the most material object to be gained from a publication of this nature, namely, the imparting of a *moral feeling* to the gratification of a *literary taste*."[3] Similar passages could be quoted from other prefaces and reviews of the period, but enough has already been given to establish the preponderance of morality and political and religious orthodoxy in the literary criticism of the years in which Shelley's books appeared.

After 1822 this bias waned at first sharply, and then gradually, to its present status. For, as a writer somewhat unctuously remarked in The Spirit and Manners of the Age (February 18, 1826): "Since that period [the early 1820's] more than one mighty but errant soul has been swept into eternity, and most of the bards that remain to us strike the harps of harmlessness and innocence, and many even those of piety." A writer in The Liverpool Repository of Literature, etc., for August, 1826, explained "The Present Popularity of Novel Writing" partly by the "removal of a great deal of puritanical austerity"; and other critics pointed to the growth of such liberal reviews as The Westminster Review as an alleviating influence.

While this obsession was at its height, however, it undoubtedly joined hands with the political tension to increase the tendency to purely personal attacks in criticisms. This tendency, brought over from the eighteenth century, was already strong enough in 1817 to elicit Coleridge's classic definition of the proper bounds of personal criticism. The limitless personalities of Blackwood's Edinburgh Magazine increased the tendency and brought Blackwood's and many another magazine of the Regency into libel

---

[3] His italics.

actions, in addition to providing grounds for several duels. Condemnation of Hunt, Keats, and Shelley on personal grounds was general. To the earnest fears of many reviewers during the years of greatest panic, any means of suppressing danger seemed justifiable. Thus The Literary Gazette, etc., in reviewing *Queen Mab* justifies a personal attack probably written "by a powerful clerical pen" by saying that the enormity of Shelley's moral offence calls for any possible means of suppression.

Thus far we have confined ourselves to the critical fears and antagonisms of the period. Its complacencies and approbations are fully as illustrative of the temper of criticism, and powerfully reinforce the conclusions already deducible. In various contemporary anthologies, articles on the state of poetry, literary satires, and reviews of favorite poets, we find what the age really preferred, while the grounds for the preference dovetail most strikingly with the grounds for antipathies already discussed.

The well-known poetic preferences of Byron in *English Bards and Scotch Reviewers* (1809) are no more an indication that critically he was a child of the eighteenth century than that he was very much in touch with his own. Both his preferences and antipathies are faithfully echoed by numerous poems and articles which bear no evidence that their opinions depend on Byron's. *Modern Poets, A Dialogue in Verse* (1813) praises Byron, Crabbe, and Scott, and attacks the Lakers. *The Modern Parnassus,* etc. (1814) praises Byron, Scott, and Southey, and attacks Wordsworth. Of all the poets who come to Apollo's board in Leigh Hunt's *The Feast of the Poets* (1814) only Campbell, Moore, Scott, and Southey are admitted —Crabbe being left in the kitchen and Wordsworth being both praised and censured. *Sortes Horatianae, A Poetical Review of Poetical Talent* (1814) regrets the death of Mrs. Tighe, but wishes Southey and Coleridge transported to America, and finds Wilson too "pretty," Crabbe tedious, and Scott of no lasting value. James Hogg's parody collection, *The Poetic Mirror, or The Living Bards of Britain* (1816), includes only Byron, Hogg, Scott, Southey, Wilson, and Wordsworth. Charles Hughes Terrot's anonymous *Common Sense, a Poem* (Edinburgh, 1819) praises Joanna Baillie, Campbell, Crabbe, Felicia Hemans, Moore, and Southey while condemning Byron morally, slighting Wordsworth and Coleridge, and scorning "the Cockney School." David Carey's *The Beauties of the Modern Poets,* etc. (1820) presents a "Modern Temple of Fame" in the following order: Campbell, Byron, Scott, Moore, Southey, Wordsworth, Rogers, James Montgomery, Crabbe, Wilson, Colman, and Dibdin. The Album (July, 1822) in an article on the Augustan Age in England, considers the greatest poets of the age to be Byron, Crabbe, Campbell, Moore, Scott, Wordsworth, Coleridge, Southey, Milman, Proctor, and Rogers; and mentions Shelley. The Metropolitan Literary Journal, etc. (1824) contains a series of "Lectures on Poetry Delivered at the Metropolitan Institution in May and June, 1823, by the Honorary Secretary" in which Bloomfield, Bowles, Byron, Coleridge, Moore, Proctor, Southey, Alaric Watts, and Wordsworth are approvingly mentioned and quoted. Richard Ryan's three-volume *Poetry and Poets: Being a Collection of the Choicest Anecdotes Relative to the Poets of Every Age and Nation*, etc. (1826) considers that the contemporaries most worthy of favorable notice are Bernard Barton, Robert Bloomfield, James Montgomery, John Keats (who surprisingly receives a strongly appreciative sketch), and Henry Kirke White. The list could be extended further, showing a growing fondness for Mrs. Hemans, the two Montgomerys, and Bernard Barton. As late as 1845 the second edition of David Grant's *The Beauties of the Modern British Poets Systematically Arranged* (Aberdeen) contains for Shelley and Keats only two chaste "beauties" each, while James and Robert Montgomery, Bernard Barton, Mrs. Hemans, John Clare, and Crabbe are all well represented.

It needs only a brief backward glance to interpret the significance of these preferences. Except for Byron, practically all those preferred are writers of good moral character who wrote constantly in support of morality, religion, and government. Except for Wordsworth, practically every one of them wrote a poetic style only slightly modified from that of the eighteenth century. Such Romantic writers as are chosen seem to be chosen for the strong non-Romantic qualities they possess. Rebels of all kinds—political, moral, theological, and stylistic—are conspicuously absent.

The poets most extensively praised in the periodicals of the 1820's and early 1830's were Bernard Barton, James and Robert ("Satan") Montgomery, and Mrs. Felicia Dorothea Hemans. The quarterlies, Blackwood's, and The London Magazine paid less attention to them than did the numerous second-rate magazines. The Edinburgh Review eventually did most efficiently demolish Robert Montgomery, at the hands of Macaulay. A few reviewers did hint that Bernard Barton was more pious than poetic. Of the lot, only James Montgomery and Mrs. Hemans would be considered even fourth-rate poets by any modern critic, yet the prevalence of their praise in the periodicals shows that they were the favorite poets of the English middle-class reading public. Of all the poets of the day, they were also the most religious, the most moral, the most contented with good old England as it was or had been, and the least inclined to innovations in poetic diction, imagery, or materials. Therein lies the secret of an otherwise amazing phenomenon. A display of some of their admired inanities as specimens of poetic taste in the 1820's would provide a truly overwhelming climax, but would call for more resolution than either the reader or the present writer could muster.

When we come at length to the treatment accorded Shelley by his contemporaries, there are some factors which are made sufficiently clear by merely collecting and arranging the criticisms.

Here we may well pause in our generalizations for a glance at the actual figures. The first volume of poems that Shelley published under his own name appeared in 1816, the last in 1822. The years 1816 to 1822 include the whole of his public life as an author of definite name and personality. For these seven years the totals are as follows: fourteen publications by Shelley himself, including separate poems printed with his name or initials and excluding anonymous or pseudonymous publications; sixty-seven reviews, excluding reviews of books not openly acknowledged by Shelley; forty miscellaneous notices, including personal comment, obituaries, and quotations of poems with Shelley's name attached; about one hundred briefer, incidental comments including notice of works issued or in press, Ollier's rare advertisements, and digressions in articles not primarily devoted to Shelley; and twenty poems about Shelley. The poems range from a single stanza in one poem to two works that were published as independent volumes and include eight republications which are here counted because for most readers they were new. For similar reasons several reviews or articles that appeared serially have been counted once for each appearance. The grand total is about two hundred and forty items concerned with Shelley in seven years. These items appeared in seventy-three different periodicals and eleven books and pamphlets, three of which were devoted to Shelley exclusively. Any attempt to distinguish the attitudes of the different periodicals toward Shelley would depend largely on the subjective bias of the critic; the present writer classifies sixteen as predominantly unfriendly, fourteen as predominantly friendly, and the remainder as either colorless or too mixed to be placed definitely in either category.

The bulk, variety, and range of this material and the particular significance of some of it, especially the poems, should abolish forever the absurd supposition that Shelley was ignored. Even today, with our far more numerous organs of criticism, a yearly average of about ten reviews and more than one poem during the whole of his publishing career would be unusual publicity for a poet whose subjects were avowedly unpopular. Among his Romantic contemporaries, only Byron and possibly Moore and Scott received as much attention as Shelley during these years; Wordsworth, Coleridge, Keats, and Landor received far less.

By examining a chronological arrangement of all the materials now available it is possible for the first time to obtain a view of Shelley's relations with the public, unwarped by what his earlier protagonists thought or wished us to think. His early anonymous publications drew more attention than they deserved, but are insignificant because their connection with Percy Bysshe Shelley was unknown until three of them were revived in the light of his later notoriety. The remarkable recognition of his anonymous genius by The Theological Inquirer failed to attract any attention. The *Alastor* volume, almost devoid of political and religious radicalism, was treated rather badly because Shelley's imagination and technique were too free for the prevailing modes; but there is no evidence of particular animus in the attitude.

The reception of *The Revolt of Islam* (1818) emphasizes the first great handicap that Shelley encountered in his relations with the public. Its outspoken radicalism was alone sufficient to array all conservative feeling against it, but the open association with Leigh Hunt which appeared at the same time made Shelley's radicalism appear much more than merely philosophic. Leigh Hunt, one of the most notorious radicals in England, introduced Shelley to the reading public in his article on Young Poets. A few months before *The Revolt of Islam* appeared, Hunt bestowed lavish praise on Shelley, as a radical, in two sonnets published in a volume which was certain to draw Tory denunciations and which was dedicated to Shelley. The Examiner printed extracts from the poem, a long review in three instalments, and a sonnet by Horace Smith praising the author. When The Quarterly attacked, Leigh Hunt defended. In 1820 Shelley dedicated *The Cenci* to Leigh Hunt. It was evident to every reviewer that they were two of a kind and that the same treatment accorded Hunt should be extended to Shelley. Gallant as Leigh Hunt's long championship of Shelley seems today, it was certainly more disastrous than beneficial during Shelley's lifetime.

By this time also the tragedy of Shelley's domestic life was made known through the Chancery hearings of 1817. Some of his unpopularity was probably due to this knowledge, but not so much at this time, apparently, as later, in 1822.

In 1820 and 1821 it appeared that Shelley might succeed with the reviewers in spite of these handicaps. Then came *Adonais*, as an open declaration of war against reviewers, and the project of The Liberal. Leigh Hunt and Shelley were to join hands more closely and unite with Byron, who had recently added *Don Juan* to the offence of *Manfred* and *Cain*. At the same time the revival of *Queen Mab* by the radicals showed exactly what a dangerous person Shelley was. The union of the three to produce, not poems, but practical journalism, was a danger calling for universal condemnation, and no quarter. Shelley was overwhelmed in a storm of conservative abuse which obliterated the somewhat more tolerant attitude of the previous year. So far as the respectable people of England were concerned, he was done for. His radical friends, almost as much as his radical writings and actions, had ruined his chance for contemporary fame. The infamy which was not his fame, however, was the seed of a growing radical appreciation. In the years following his death this appreciation contributed importantly toward keeping Shelley's name alive until the growing power of liberalism and better poetic standards effected his recognition as one of the great poets of his century.[4]

Fear, rather than indifference, was the significant characteristic of Shelley's conservative reviewers. Far from being unknown and neglected, he was known and feared. The treatment he received was not freakish or particularly personal. It was the natural and logical outgrowth of the times. There were three especial dangers almost universally feared by the reviewers—the change to a new poetic expression, political radicalism, and

[4] The contribution of radicals toward the growth of Shelley's posthumous reputation has been partly dealt with by the present writer in two articles: "Shelley and the Practical Radicals of the Early Nineteenth Century," in the South Atlantic Quarterly, July, 1930 (29: 248-261), and "Literature and the Law of Libel," etc., in Studies in Philology, January, 1925 (22: 34-47).

moral and theological radicalism. Shelley alone represented every one. Wordsworth's radical theories of poetry were balanced by political and moral conservatism. Keats kept clear of theology and politics, and was radical only in his associates and his poetic practice. Even Hunt had no flagitious moral history and was not a foe to Christianity. Byron, radical both theologically and politically, fell far short of Shelley's radicalism in both particulars and was conservative in criticism and poetic technique. His known moral offenses, in the eyes of the times, were less reprehensible than Shelley's. Wordsworth was in theory much more radical in his view of poetry than Shelley, but his actual style was nearer to that of the eighteenth century than Shelley's, and his use of an idiot boy as a subject was hardly a more serious violation of traditional decorum than Shelley's use of incest. It might be said, therefore, that Shelley was not only the sole poet who ran counter to all the particular prejudices of Regency criticism, but that in each case his offense was greater that that of any of the others.

The really remarkable phenomenon, in the light of the times, is that Shelley received any favorable criticism at all, beyond that of the radical propagandists. Much of the more violently radical appreciation, like much of the violently conservative denunciation, has little literary significance, since to these reviewers Shelley was much less a poet than a symbol. Beyond this, however, there remains a surprisingly large amount of favorable criticism based largely on the real poetic value of his work. The obvious explanation is a very hopeful one for those who wish to believe that literary merit depends for recognition on something besides mere accident. Under circumstances almost perfectly adapted for his obliteration, the genuine appreciation that Shelley received is a testimony both to the strength of genius and to the innate *in*ability of criticism to be totally blind to it.

The strongest proof that Shelley's genius was recognized (because, as we have seen, they had the most compelling reasons for denying it) comes from the Tories rather than from his professed friends. There were really two Tory attitudes toward Shelley, only the less significant of which has been sufficiently recognized. There was the utter, all-inclusive denunciation represented by such periodicals as The Quarterly, John Bull, and The Investigator; and there was the equally emphatic condemnation, accompanied by a frank recognition of his poetic powers, best typified by Blackwood's. In every one of its notices of Shelley, Blackwood's never failed to make vigorous assaults on his principles. At the same time it recognized and championed his genius from the very first, until John Wilson's absorption in his Edinburgh professorship coincided with Shelley's publication of *Adonais* and the association to publish The Liberal. Others then took Shelley in hand and displayed an uncompromisingly inimical attitude. Since practically all writers who have noticed Blackwood's criticism of Shelley have overlooked the significance of the praise,[5] it would be well

[5] Since these lines were written the subject has been excellently discussed in Mr. Alan Lang Strout's "*Maga*, Champion of Shelley," Studies in Philology, January, 1932 (29: 95-119).

here to notice these reviews somewhat more in detail than would otherwise be advisable.

In reviewing *The Revolt of Islam* (January, 1819) Blackwood's finds that Shelley has "a powerful and vigorous intellect," though he is "weak and worthless" as a philosopher. As a poet he is "strong, nervous, and original, well entitled to take his place near to the great creative masters" of the age. Hitherto he has not been much reviewed because competent critics who recognize his genius fear to give currency to his ideas. "Mr. Shelly [*sic*] has displayed his possession of a mind intensely poetical, and of an exuberance of poetic language, perpetually strong and perpetually varied. In spite, moreover, of a certain perversion in all his modes of thinking, which, unless he gets rid of it, will ever prevent him from being acceptable to any considerable or respectable body of readers, he has displayed many glimpses of right understanding and generous feeling which must save him from the unmingled condemnation even of the most rigorous judges. His destiny is entirely in his own hands; if he acts wisely it cannot fail to be a glorious one; if he continues to pervert his talents—their splendor will only contribute to render his disgrace the more conspicuous. Mr. Shelly [*sic*], whatever his errors may have been, is a scholar, a gentleman and a poet, and he must therefore despise from his soul the only eulogies to which he has hitherto been accustomed—paragraphs from The Examiner and sonnets from Johnny Keats. He has it in his power to select better companions; and if he does so he may very securely promise himself abundance of better praise."

Blackwood's next notice of Shelley, a fourteen-column review of *Rosalind and Helen* in June, 1819, begins, "We have already expressed our belief that Mr. Shelley is a true poet and that it will be his own fault if his name does not hold a conspicuous place in the literature of his country." We see "in this highly gifted man much to admire—nay, much to love—but much also to move to pity and to sorrow. For what can be more mournful than the degradation of youthful genius involving in its fall virtue, respectability and happiness?" Though Shelley has hitherto been little noticed, Blackwood's says it proposes to support genius and hopes Shelley will not long need its support. After three columns of reprobation of his principles it concludes that these faults are not fundamental to his genius and that when he shakes them off he will "take his place not far from the first poets of his time" and "his fame will yet be a glorious plant."

It is a testimony to the genuineness of Blackwood's interest in Shelley that its next review (November, 1819) goes back to *Alastor,* which had been three years off the press. This it does frankly as an encouragement to "those who, like us, cherish high hopes of this gifted but wayward young man." The review concludes with three columns on the unfair and inadequate criticism Shelley has received and condemns The Quarterly reviewer at length as "a dunce rating a man of genius." "It is not in the power of all the critics alive to blind one true lover of poetry to the splendor of Mr. Shelley's genius." Shelley should be encouraged "to walk onward to his high destiny" by the knowledge that there is in England a strong love of genius which will pardon its possessor much extravagance and error. Therefore let Shelley "come forth—in his strength, conquering and to conquer. Let his soul watch his soul and listen to the voice of its own noble nature—and there is no doubt that the future will make amends for the past, whatever its errors might have been—and that the poet may yet be good, great, and happy."

The next review is of *Prometheus Unbound*, in September, 1820. This review has been misrepresented by quoting only the first half of the following sentence: "In short, it is quite impossible that there should exist a more pestiferous mixture of blasphemy, sedition and sensuality than is visible in the whole structure and strain of this poem—which nevertheless, and notwithstanding all the detestation its principles excite, must and will be considered by all that read it attentively as abounding in poetical beauties of the highest order—as presenting many specimens not easily to be surpassed of the moral sublime of eloquence—as overflowing with pathos, and most magnificent in description." "But the truth of the matter is this," it adds later on, "and it is impossible to conceal it were we willing to do so, that Mr. Shelley is destined to leave a great name behind him, and that we, as lovers of true genius, are most anxious that this name shall ultimately be pure as well as great." After its usual vigorous condemnation of Shelley's principles, the review concludes with the most optimistic hope that Blackwood's ever expressed; namely, that Shelley would "learn to fear God and honor the King"!

Three of these reviews were almost certainly written by Christopher North, a poet himself, and less out of sympathy than most reviewers with the new poetic practices. They show beyond a doubt not only a firm conviction of Shelley's great genius, but a friendly desire to convert him to conservatism. They even promise him "more and better praise" if he will reform.

Many of the same sentiments were expressed by other reviews less friendly to Shelley. The Edinburgh Monthly Review acknowledges Shelley's great genius and rich and lively imagination in *The Cenci*, states frankly that its high opinion of Shelley's powers is the reason why it says so much of their perversion, and remarks on the "foolish timidity" of other reviewers "which prevents them from doing justice to the genius at the same time that they inflict due chastisement on the errors of this remarkable young man." This reviewer also promises a bright future for Shelley, "were he to choose and manage his themes with some decent measure of regard for the just opinions of the world." The Album (July, 1822) makes a similar conditional promise of universal popularity. In the years 1819, 1820, and 1821 nineteen reviews appeared in Tory and Whig periodicals in which Shelley's genius is clearly acknowledged while (in most cases) his principles are condemned. This does not include any praise by radical friends or periodicals, or general or miscellaneous articles in which the same admission occurs. Bernard Barton's poem in 1820 was another effort to convert erring genius.

Many of the reviews which contain these admissions are in the main decidedly unfriendly to Shelley. Inimical as some of the reviewers were, they could not help perceiving the extraordinary qualities of this "misguided young man." And so we come again to the conclusion that it was fear, and not dullness, that motivated Shelley's more unfriendly critics. The very frenzy of the worst denunciations is an index to the reviewer's real opinion of Shelley's powers. The reviewers themselves were not incapable of seeing this truth. Shelley "sacrificed a fine genius at the shrine of infidelity," said The Literary Chronicle and Weekly Review (October 12, 1822), and was "consequently dangerous in the proportion that his talents were splendid."

One of the noblest things ever said about the relations of poets and critics was Shelley's statement in the last year of his life, that a poet must be judged by a jury of his compeers, impanelled from all time. It would be odious to pronounce this merely a "defence complex," but it would be misleading not to consider that his previous experience had some share in generating it. Shelley did not think it derogatory of Byron, for example, that his present fame

—bent
Over his head, a living monument.

His own early career shows a curious, almost ludicrously practical interest in reviewers and public opinion. This interest possibly explains why works not intrinsically worth a review sometimes received two or three. Two months before Zastrozzi was published, Shelley wrote to his cousin Edward Graham that the publisher would "take no trouble with the reviewers," hence, "let everything proper be done about the venal villains and I will settle with you when we meet at Easter." "Pouch the reviewers," he concludes. He italicizes the pouch. Ten pounds should be about right, though "the British Review is the hardest, let that be pouched well." A little later, when he is bringing out Posthumous Fragments of Margaret Nicholson, he writes Graham, "I shall possibly send you the abuse to-day, but I am afraid that they will not insert it." Whether Shelley was himself to write the abuse of his own book and pay for its insertion is not quite clear; it is evident, however, that he regarded abuse as good publicity and was willing to furnish it himself.

In those days the jury need not necessarily be impanelled from all time. A little corruption of the jury even, in a good cause, was expedient. And the contempt of court, even while seeking its favorable verdict, is mildly amusing.

Mr. Denis Florence MacCarthy has shown, in his Shelley's Early Life, that the poet's Irish adventure received a surprising amount of attention from the Dublin press. We do not know that any of this was produced by the methods formerly employed, but we do know that Shelley was greatly pleased with the sketch of himself published in The Dublin Weekly Messenger, which he exultingly sent to Godwin and Elizabeth Hitchener, requesting the latter to "insist or make them [the Sussex papers] insert the account of *me*." The probable author of this sketch was John Lawless ("a valuable man") who was later charged by a journalistic contemporary with fleecing Shelley, and for whom Shelley tried to raise a loan of £250.

It may have been Shelley's narrow escape in Barnstaple that helped the youthful enthusiast to add to his knowledge some of that "understanding" which kindly Walter Scott had already suggested as desirable. At any rate, that highly dangerous poem, *Queen Mab*, was not shouted from the housetops. It was not even published, but was hand-circulated among a chosen few, with Shelley's name in most cases carefully cut out of the title-page. Not more than seventy copies got abroad between its first appearance and the year in which it was pirated. Nevertheless, the poem *was* published, after a fashion, in a way to avoid prosecution. The series of articles in The Theological Enquirer and Polemical Magazine (1815) signed F. furnishes a glowing description and analysis of the poem and quotes over six hundred lines, to which the editor adds another passage and a convenient pseudonymous correspondent another, making a total of just about a third of the entire poem. The actionable lines are omitted and Shelley's name is not mentioned. Considering that the magazine is at the same time reprinting Shelley's *Refutation of Deism* and a correspondent's answer to it, also a poem to the author of *Queen Mab*, all this interest in an author who is never named becomes significantly mysterious. It is improbable that Shelley wrote any of these items himself, but he certainly knew the authors (and all others who owned copies of *Queen Mab*) and he was very likely privy to the whole scheme. It must be remembered in this connection that he himself published the note on vegetarianism as *A Vindication of Natural Diet* in the same year (1813) in which *Queen Mab* appeared; and three years later, in the *Alastor* volume, an excerpt from *Queen Mab* entitled *Superstition*, and part of *The Daemon of the World*, which was a rehandling of *Queen Mab*. The episode of The Theological Inquirer fits in too well with Shelley's previous and subsequent methods of reaching the public not to have some connection with them. Shelley was by this time not so anxious to put Percy Bysshe Shelley before the world, but he was quite anxious that the world should listen to *Queen Mab*.

After his elopement with Mary Godwin, Shelley seemed to scorn the opinions of reviewers. Occasionally his letters to his publishers, the Olliers, hinted more interest in contemporary opinion than he admitted, but his inquiries about reviews generally protested (like the lady, a little "too much") that he was only interested in those that condemn him. He *was* interested in condemnation—too much so to be entirely consistent with his professed indifference to reviewers. When a Quarterly reviewer engaged in belaboring Leigh Hunt's *Foliage* digressed for a moment to assail Shelley, the victim wrote Hunt that the assault "makes me melancholy," and devoted about half his letter to further comment on the article. He wrote Peacock (April 6, 1819), "As to the Reviews, I suppose there is nothing but abuse; and this is not hearty or sincere enough to amuse me." He informed Ollier in July, 1819, that he would not own *The Cenci*, until it has been successfully acted, after which he might utilize its celebrity. "My great stimulus in writing is to have the approbation of those who feel kindly toward me," he wrote to Leigh Hunt on August 15, 1819, in expressing his appreciation of Hunt's friendly review of *Rosalind and Helen*. Ollier informed Shelley that The Quarterly was to review *The Revolt of Islam*, and Shelley directed him (September 6, 1819) to send the article by mail and the rest of the review by parcel, in order to avoid delay. "Of course it gives me a certain degree of pleasure to know that anyone likes my writings; but it is objection and enmity alone that rouses my *curiosity*." The italics are Shelley's. Is this unnecessary explanation of a natural interest not suggestive of what the psychologists call a defense mechanism?

The Quarterly's attack occupies most of a letter which Shelley wrote to the Olliers (October 15, 1819) in which he defended himself and ridiculed the reviewer. Some of the ridicule he repeated in his next letter to Charles Ollier (December 15, 1819). The English traveler who (according to Medwin) saw Shelley reading this review in Delesert's Reading Rooms in Florence must have reported rather accurately when he said that Shelley burst into "convulsive laughter" and closed the book "with an hysteric laugh." He drafted part of a letter to the editor of The Quarterly on the subject, and rejoiced in his next letter to Charles Ollier (December 15, 1819) that Blackwood's had administered a rebuke to The Quarterly reviewer. The Blackwood's reviewer, he thought, must be a friend in disguise. "If any of the Reviews abuse me, cut them out and send them," he directed the Olliers (March 6, 1820). "If they praise, you need not trouble yourself. I feel ashamed, if I could believe that I should deserve the latter; the former, I flatter myself, is no more than a just tribute." "If Hunt praises me," he added, "send it, because that is another character of things." Who else, in Shelley's view at the time, would have been likely to praise him?

Mr. Gisborne sent Shelley a batch of reviews of *The Cenci*. Shelley's comment on them to the Olliers (January 20, 1821) shows that "though some of them . . . are written with great malignity" they afforded him moderate encouragement. A friendly notice sent by Ollier (probably that in The Retrospective Review) proved pleasing to Shelley and he inquired as to its authorship—as he had done in the case of the only other friendly review he noticed, Blackwood's review of *The Revolt of Islam*. In June, 1822, Shelley wrote to John Gisborne expressing "supreme indifference" to such books as John Watkins's *Memoirs of the Life and Writings of Lord Byron, with Some of His Contemporaries*, which contained several passages unfavorable to Shelley. Yet he wrote to Trelawny on the same day (June 18), "I am curious to hear of this publication about Lord Byron and the Pisa circle. I hope it will not annoy him; as to me, I am supremely indifferent." Either curiosity or indifference would have been comprehensible, but the two together suggest that contemporary opinion interested Shelley even while he persuaded himself that it did not.

The real state of affairs appears more plainly with the publication of *Adonais*. Shelley begged Leigh Hunt (January 25, 1822) to say what effect was produced by *Adonais*. "My faculties are shaken to atoms, and torpid. I can write nothing; and if *Adonais* had no success, and excited no interest, what incentive can I have to write?" Yet in the lines following this very plain statement of the truth, he reasserted that indifference to reviews which is inconsistent with it: "The man must be enviably happy whom reviews can make miserable. I have neither curiosity, interest, pain, nor pleasure in anything, good or evil, they can say of me. I feel only a slight disgust, and a sort of wonder that they presume to write my name." Both the assumed indifference and the implied confession he repeated to John Gisborne, the former on April 10, 1822, and the latter on April 17, as follows: "I write little now. It is impossible to compose except under the strong excitement of an assurance of finding sympathy in what you write. Imagine Demosthenes reciting a Phillipic to the waves of the Atlantic. Lord Byron is in this respect fortunate. He touched a chord to which a million hearts responded, and the coarse music which he produced to please them, disciplined him to the perfection to which he now approaches."

This is the whole record, as revealed by Shelley's letters. His poems tell a similar story. In two short poems, *Lines to a Critic* (1817) and *Lines to a Reviewer* (1820), he protested his indifference to the critic's hate. *Adonais*, however, is the most overwhelming chastisement ever inflicted on reviewers by English poetry. Previous to its composition Shelley was by no means an unqualified admirer of Keats' poetry. His personal connection with Keats was rather slight. Although Shelley's hatred of oppression was so great that the conception of Keats as a victim of tyranny would undoubtedly have been sufficient to account for the poem, yet there seems to be a personal feeling in it not quite explicable on this basis alone. The explanation is not so difficult, in the light of the letters just examined. Shelley himself was a victim of critical oppression, as Keats and Chatterton had been. For himself, he sedulously professed an indifference which he tried vainly to experience. Hatred and revenge were contrary to his avowed creed; hence he could not retaliate as Byron did. But for Keats, he could speak feelings otherwise suppressed. Temporary identification with Keats would have been practically inevitable under the circumstances. In the significantly long passage on himself he even describes himself as a pathetic poet overcome by the weight of the superincumbent hour "who in another's fate now wept his own."

The youth who thought the opinions of reviews so important that they should be bought was a very different person from the mature poet who wrote *Prometheus Unbound* and *Adonais*, but he was not so different in his attitude toward reviews and public opinion as his later utterances would persuade us—and himself. How could he be? The function of the poet was to reach the ear of mankind, for the improvement of humanity. It was scarcely his function, though it might be his mournfully Romantic fate, to be an unappreciated Chatterton. If the reviews opposed him, public opinion would condemn him for a while, possibly forever; and he would be frustrated for a while, if not forever. The most powerful reviews did oppose him; in his own opinion the opposition was practically unanimous. And Shelley answered repeatedly that he was utterly indifferent to their assaults. It was the very natural expression of a wounded spirit, but not of an indifferent one. Shelley could not have been indifferent without being false to the whole purpose of his poetry.

In the end, what does it all come to? Shelley in Italy, conscious that he was writing some of the great poetry of the age, hoping that the world would listen. "The world should listen then, as I am listening now." A few radicals and a few genuine lovers of poetry already beginning to scatter the ashes of the "unextinguished hearth" which its owner feared desperately might be extinguished already. Shelley apparently ignorant of them—spring still far behind. The dominant opinion in a nervous, irascible, insulted little island, shouting in almost grotesque panic that it would not hear, and listening because of the determination not to do so. Hysteric laughter in Delesert's Reading Rooms in Florence; exaggerated scorn in Murray's back parlor in London. A disastrous past combining with the unpropitious accidents of the present to blight the one opportunity for contemporary honor. Shelley giving unconscious evidence of a normal, human respect for the power of opinion through the very excess of his scornful utterances. His enemies giving unconscious evidence of respect through the excessive vociferation of their scorn. Mary, more of a worldling, urging some of the concessions the critics would have been glad to welcome. Shelley unwilling and perhaps unable to bend—"How, my dear Mary, are you critic-bitten?" In the epilogue, the triumph of Romantic poetry and Romantic criticism—the *deus ex machina* unexpected of all the actors, arriving in a Promethean car of the hour, about two decades late for the Prometheus who had been drowned at sea.

As applied to the Prometheus who survived in his poems, all this carries a curious suggestion of Shelley's favorite image of the conflict between the Serpent of righteousness and the Eagle of oppression, with the Serpent always defeated, yet sure to be victorious in the end. Viewed in this light, Shelley's struggle for fame and influence may be regarded as a triumph of indomitable, half-mystical faith. But there is a broader, blunter conclusion which Shelley's story should suggest even to the skeptical materialist. Genius *is* valid and vital. It is an extremely difficult thing for reviewers either to ignore or obliterate a really great genius.

II

THE JUVENILE PERIOD

ORIGINAL POETRY BY VICTOR AND CAZIRE

The Literary Panorama Chuckles

[From The Literary Panorama, October, 1810 (8: 1063-1066).[1] This respectable but undistinguished monthly refused to consider the pseudonymous youthful poet and romancer as anything more than a joke. Before its incorporation with The New Monthly Magazine, which continued its interest in Shelley, it quoted from his first two acknowledged volumes.]

Surely modern poets are the most unhappy of men! Their imaginations are perpetually haunted with terrors. While others are congratulating themselves on a beautiful day, and basking in the enlivening rays of the sun, these votaries of the Muse of misery see nothing but glooms, and listen to the pealing thunder, distant or near, as fancy dictates, "not loud but deep." In the evening "black whirlwinds," and "yelling fiends" beset them on every side, in spite of the golden beams of the declining sun, or the cheerful azure of a cloudless day. At night,—ghosts,—hobgoblins,—shadowy forms, death, devils, disaster, and damnation dance around them, in dire dismay, till their "souls are chilled,"—their "blood is frozen,"—their "heart sinks within them," and miserable they are, to be sure! At length they commit their sorrows to paper; they publish, and the public are enraptured with their sufferings. Well, after all, the Fairy people for our money! There was something *so* blithesome and gay in the gambols of the elfin crew "that frisked in the frolicsome round"; something *so* equitable in their rewards and punishments! We who might confidently expect to find "sixpence in one of our shoes," while lubber louts intent on mischief might be pinch'd and pull'd without mercy,—we regret the change. Willingly would we renounce all the phantoms and spectres of Monk Lewis and Mrs. Radcliffe, to enjoy a rencounter with a ring of these lightly tripping dancers, whether by moon light, or star light. But alas!

> Farewell rewards and fairies,
>   Good housewives now may say;
> For now foul sluts in dairies
>   Do fare as well as they!

As sung the witty Bishop Corbet, long ago. Now, under the fascination of these cheerful ideas, what can we say to such terrific meteors of song as those which flit before us in these poems? e.g.

[1] Here, as hereinafter, I omit the original heading when it consists merely of the usual statement of title, author, size, price, publisher, and date.

Horror covers all the sky,
   Clouds of darkness blot the moon
Prepare, for mortal thou must die,
   Prepare to yield thy soul up soon.

Fierce the tempest raves around,
   Fierce the volleyed lightnings fly,
Crashing thunder shakes the ground,
   Fire and tumult fill the sky.—

Hark! the tolling village bell,
   Tells the hour of midnight come,
Now can blast the powers of Hell,
   Fiend-like goblins now can roam.

So, so; we cannot be frightened by a spectre without a tempest, it seems: certainly all poets of feeling will allow that a tempest affords a delightful opportunity for strong painting, glowing description, and the full range of fine compound epithets: intermingled with blue lightning, chilling blasts, howling storms, sulphurous clouds, and black marble tombs; or gaping graves, as the case may be.

Can any thing possibly be finer—that is, more terrific—that is—ahem! —than the following?—

The night it was bleak the fierce storm raged around,
The lightnings blue firelight flashed on the ground,
Strange forms seemed to flit,—and howl tidings of fate,
As Agnes advanced to the sepulchre gate.—

The youth struck the portal,—the echoing sound
Was fearfully rolled midst the tombstones around,
The blue lightning gleamed o'er the dark chapel spire,
And tinged were the storm clouds with sulphurous fire.

Still they gazed on the tombstone where Conrad reclined,
Yet they shrank at the cold chilling blast of the wind,
When a strange silver brilliance pervaded the scene,
And a figure advanced—tall in form—fierce in mien.

A mantle encircled his shadowy form,
As light as a gossamer borne on the storm,
Celestial terror sat throned in his gaze,
Like the midnight pestiferous meteors blaze.

Spirit.

Thy father, Adolphus, was false, false as hell,
And Conrad has cause to remember it well,
He ruined my Mother, despised me his son,
I quitted the world ere my vengeance was done.

I was nearly expiring—'twas close of the day,—
A demon advanced to the bed where I lay,
He gave me the power from whence I was hurled,
To return to revenge, to return to the world,—

Now Adolphus I'll seize thy best loved in my arms,
I'll drag her to Hades, all blooming in charms,
On the black whirlwind's thundering pinions I'll ride,
And fierce yelling fiends shall exult o'er thy bride.

He spoke and extended his ghostly arms wide,
Majestic advanced with a swift, noiseless stride,
He clasped the fair Agnes—he raised her on high,
And clearing the roof sped his way to the sky—

All was now silent,—and over the tomb,
Thicker, deeper, was swiftly extended a gloom,—
Adolphus in horror sank down on the stone,
And his fleeting soul fled with a harrowing groan.

December 1809.

December! What a dismal ditty for Christmas! no, Sir: —

    ever 'gainst that Season
Wherein our Saviour's birth is celebrated,
  —————————no spirit dares stir abroad;
The nights are wholesome, then; no planets strike,
No fairy takes, no witch hath power to charm,
So hallow'd and so gracious is the time!

However, we must not part with our poets unkindly; we adopt their
own good wishes (*numberless* though they be) in their own words and
verses:

May misfortunes, dear Girl, ne'er thy happiness cloy,
May thy days glide in peace, love, comfort, and joy,
May thy tears with soft pity for other woes flow,
Oh dear! what sentimental stuff I've written,
Only fit to tear up and play with a kitten.
Now adieu, my dear—, I'm sure I must tire,
For if I do, you may throw it into the fire,
So accept the best love of your cousin and friend,
Which brings this nonsensical rhyme to an end.[1]

The British Critic Condemns

[From The British Critic, April, 1811 (37: 408-409). To this conservative
monthly both the pseudonymous juvenile Shelley and the acknowledged author of
Alastor are worthless writers mainly on account of literary rather than moral
offences. The latter, however, may account for its failure to review any of Shelley's
more radical volumes.]

When we ventured to say that poetical taste and genius abound in the
present day, we by no means intended to assert, that we always meet with
either the one or the other. Miserable, indeed, are the attempts which we
are often doomed to encounter; so miserable somtimes that it seems quite

[1] These lines are from a poem written by Shelley's sister Elizabeth to Shelley's cousin
and sweetheart, Harriet Grove.—N.I.W.

wonderful how any individuals fancying themselves able to write should be so far behind their contemporaries. One of the unknown authors of this volume begins by complaining, most sincerely, we are convinced, of the difficulty of writing grammatically, but there is another difficulty, which seems never to have entered the lady's head (if a lady!)—that is, the difficulty of writing *metrically*. In this she is still less successful than in the other, and does not seem at all to suspect it. The verse intended to be used is that of "The Bath Guide," and so it is *sometimes;* but sometimes also not. For example—

> This they friendly will tell, and n'er make you blush,
> With a jeering look, taunt, or an O fie! tush!
> Then straight all your thoughts in black and white put,
> Not minding the *if's*, the *be's*, and the *but's.*—P. 6.

Again.

> My excuse shall be humble, and faithful, and true
> *Such as I fear can be made but by few.*—P. 7.

This *humble* and *faithful* lady lays claim *only* to "sense, wit, and grammar!" Yet she tells her friend:—

> Be not a coward, shrink not a tense,
> But read it all over, *and make it out sense.*
> *What a tiresome girl!*—pray soon make an end.—P. 9.

This last line, if not measure, contains at least truth in the first part, and a reasonable wish in the second.

Two epistles, in this exquisite style, begin the volume, which is filled up by of songs of sentimental nonsense, and very absurd tales of horror. It is perfectly clear, therefore, that whatever we may say in favour of the poetry of this time, such volumes as this have no share in the commendation. One thing may be said in its favour, that the printer has done his task well; would he had been employed on something better! If he has taste as well as skill, he must dread the names of Victor and Cazire.

"Downright Scribble"

[From The Poetical Register, and Repository of Fugitive Poetry for 1810-1811. Published in 1814, under *Criticisms 1811*, p. 617. Brief and cursory as it is, this review is of average length and quality for The Poetical Register.]

There is no "original *poetry*" in this volume; there is nothing in it but downright scribble. It is really annoying to see the waste of paper which is made by such persons as the putters-together of these sixty-four pages. There is, however, one consolation for the critics who are obliged to read all this sort of trash. It is, that the crime of publishing is generally followed by condign punishment, and in the chilling tones of the booksellers, when, to the questions of the anxious rhymer, how the book sells, he answers that not more than half a dozen copies have been sold.

ZASTROZZI, A ROMANCE

The Gentleman's Magazine Detects Merit

[From The Gentleman's Magazine and Historical Chronicle, September, 1810 (80: 258, part 2). This is the only one of the early reviews that suggests Shelley's instructions to Graham to "pouch the reviewers." Except for the borrowed review of *Rosalind and Helen* it is the only volume of Shelley's ever reviewed by The Gentleman's Magazine, though he did shock its conservatism, in the last year of his life, into incidental denunciation.]

A short, but well-told tale of horror, and, if we do not mistake, not from an ordinary pen. The story is so artfully conducted that the reader cannot easily anticipate the denouement, which is conducted on the principles of moral justice: and, by placing the scene on the Continent, the Author has availed himself of characters and vices which, however useful in narratives of this description, thank God, are not to be found in this country.

The Critical Review Exposes Corruption

[From The Critical Review and Annals of Literature, November, 1810 (21: 329-331). This is the only work by Shelley reviewed in The Critical Review, which ceased to exist in 1817. However, it did print, anonymously, the only review ever published by Shelley.]

Zastrozzi is one of the most savage and improbable demons that ever issued from a diseased brain. His mother, who had been seduced by an Italian nobleman by the name of Verezzi, and left by him in wretchedness and want, conjures her son on her death bed, to avenge her wrongs on Verezzi and his progeny forever! Zastrozzi fulfills her diabolical injunctions, by assassinating her seducer; and pursues the young Verezzi, his son, with unrelentless and savage cruelty. The first scene which opens this *shameless* and disgusting volume represents Verezzi in a damp cell, chained to the wall.

His limbs, which not even a little straw kept from the rock, were fixed by immense staples to the flinty floor; and but one of his hands was left at liberty to take the scanty pittance of bread and water which was daily allowed him.

This beautiful youth (as he is described), is released from his confinement by the roof of the cell falling in during a most terrific storm. He is then conducted, though in a raging fever, by the emissaries of the fiend-like Zastrozzi to the cottage of an old woman which stands on a lone heath, removed from all human intercourse. From this place he contrives to escape, and we find him at another old woman's cottage near Passau. Here he saves the life of Mathilda, La Contessa di Laurentini, who, in a fit of desperation and hopeless love for the Adonis Verezzi, plunges herself into the river. The author does not think proper to account to his readers when and how these two persons had become acquainted, or how Verezzi could know the unbounded and disgusting passion which Mathilda entertains for him. It is vaguely intimated that Verezzi loves, and is beloved by, Julia Marchesa di Strobazzo, who is as amiable as Mathilda is diabolical; but we are left to conjecture how the connection between Zastrozzi and Mathilda is brought about. But these inconsistencies need not surprise us, when we reflect that a more discordant, disgusting, and despicable performance has not, we are persuaded, issued from the press for some time. Verezzi accompanies Mathilda to Passau, with whom he remains, and by whom he is informed of the death of Julia. This intelligence throws him into another fever; on his recovery, Mathilda conveys him to a castella of her own, situated in the Venetian territory. Here she practices every art and assumes all the amiable appearances and fascinating manners she is mistress of, which she thinks most likely to wean Verezzi from his fondness for the memory of Julia, and to inspire him with an affection for herself. But all her arts prove fruitless, till Zastrozzi suggests the scheme of affecting to assassinate Verezzi, when Mathilda is to interpose and make him believe that she saves his life. Verezzi, who is a poor fool, and anything but a man, falls into the snare, forgets his Julia, indulges a vicious passion for Mathilda, which the author denominates love, but which is as far removed from that exalted passion as modesty is from indecency, and deserves a name which we shall not offend our readers by repeating. Revelling in an inordinate and bestial passion, of which the fiend Mathilda is the object, he discovers that Julia still lives. This causes momentary regret, but awakens the jealousy of Mathilda, which he calms by the most indelicate professions, and whilst he is about to drink a goblet of wine to the happiness of his infamous paramour, Julia glides into the room. Verezzi is instantly seized with a frenzy, and stabs himself. Mathilda is rendered furious by this death-blow to her criminal gratifications.

"Her eyes scintillated," (a favorite word with the author, which he introduces in almost every page) "with fiend-like expression. She advanced to the lifeless corpse of Verezzi, she plucked the dagger from his bosom, it was stained with his life's blood, which trickled fast from the point to the floor, she raised it on high, and imperiously called upon the God of nature to doom her to endless torments should Julia survive her vengeance."

She is as good as her word; she stabs Julia in a thousand places; and, with exulting pleasure, again and again buries her dagger in the body of the unfortunate victim of her rage. Mathilda is seized by the officers of justice, as well as Zastrozzi, who confesses that he had planned the whole business, and made Mathilda the tool by which he satiated his revenge.

The story itself, and the style in which it is told, are so truly contemptible, that we should have passed it unnoticed, had not our indignation been excited by the open and barefaced immorality and grossness displayed throughout. Mathilda's character is that of a lascivious fiend, who dignifies vicious, unrestrained passion by the appellation of love.

Does the author, whoever he may be, think his gross and wanton pages fit to meet the eye of a modest young woman? Is this the instruction to be instilled under the title of a romance? Such trash, indeed, as this work contains, is fit only for the inmates of a brothel. It is by such means of corruption as this that the tastes of our youth of both sexes become vitiated, their imaginations heated, and a foundation laid for their future misery and dishonour. When a taste for this kind of writing is imbibed, we may bid farewell to innocence, farewell to purity of thought, and all that makes youth and virtue lovely.

We know not when we have felt so much indignation as in the perusal of this execrable production. The author of it cannot be too severely reprobated. Not all his "scintillated eyes," his "battling emotions," his "frigorific torpidity of despair," nor his "Lethean torpor," with the rest of his nonsensical and stupid jargon, ought to save him from infamy, and his volume from the flames.

St. Irvyne; or The Rosicrucian

The British Critic Condemns Again

[From The British Critic, January, 1811 (37:70-71).]

"Red thunder-clouds, borne on the wings of the midnight whirlwind, floated at first athwart the crimson-coloured orbit of the moon; the rising fierceness of the blast, sighed through the stunted shrubs, which bending before its violence, inclined towards the rocks whereon they grew: over the blackened expanse of heaven, at intervals, was spread the blue lightning's flash; it played upon the granite heights, and with momentary brilliancy, disclosed the terrific scenery of the Alps; whose gigantic, and misshapen summits, reddened by the transitory moon-beam, were crossed by black fleeting fragments of the tempest-cloud."

The above is the first sentence of this Romance, by "a gentleman of Oxford." Some readers will, perhaps, be satisfied, and will proceed no further. They who do, will find the Cavern of Gil Blas with very little variation of circumstance, a profusion of words which no dictionary explains, such as *unerasible, Bandit, en-horrored*, descriptions wilder than are to be found in Radcliffe, and a tale more extravagant than the St. Leon of Godwin.

Would that this gentleman of Oxford had a taste for other and better pursuits, but as we presume him to be a *young gentleman*, this may in due time happen.

Laconic Sarcasm

[From The Literary Panorama, February, 1811 (9: 252-253). This sarcastic "review" consists entirely of four excerpts, to which the reviewer contributes captions.]

St. Irvyne, or the Rosicrucian: a Romance, by a gentleman of the University of Oxford.

How to Begin a Romance. A.D. 1811

Here follows a long paragraph from the novel, beginning, "Red thunder-clouds . . ." and ending, ". . . hot and sulphurous thunder-blast."

How to End a Romance. A.D. 1811

Two excerpts are quoted under this head, the first beginning, "It was night, all was still . . ." and ending ". . . he entered the vault"; and the second beginning, "For a time the novelty of his situation . . ." and ending ". . . rushed into the vault."

Conclusion

One excerpt is quoted, beginning, "Deeper grew the gloom of the cavern . . ." and ending ". . . a dateless and hopeless eternity of horror."

The Anti-Jacobin Review Functions as Moralist

[From The Anti-Jacobin Review and Magazine, etc., January, 1812 (41: 69-72). Though something like "Jacobinism" was later a popular reason for assailing Shelley, this rather inferior successor to the old Anti-Jacobin paid him no attention after 1812.]

Had not the title-page informed us that this curious "Romance" was the production of "a gentleman," a freshman of course, we should certainly have ascribed it to some "Miss" in her teens; who, having read the beautiful and truly poetic descriptions, in the unrivalled romances of Mrs. Ratcliffe [sic], imagined that to admire the writings of that lady, and to imitate her style were one and the same thing. Here we have *description run mad;* every uncouth epithet, every wild expression, which either the lexicographer could supply, or the disordered imagination of the romance-writer suggest, has been pressed into the service of "the Rosicmeian" [sic]. Woe and terror are heightened by the expressions used to describe them. Heroes and heroines are not merely distressed and terrified, they are "enanguished" and "enhorrored."

Nor are the ordinary sensations of *joy* or even *delight,* sufficient to gratify such exalted beings. No, when the hero was pleased, not only did he experience "a transport of delight"; *burning ecstasy revelled through his veins; pleasurable coruscations were emitted from his eyes.* Even hideous sights acquire an additional deformity under the magic of this "gentleman's" pen. We read of "a form more hideous than the imagination is capable of portraying, whose proportions, gigantic and deformed, were seemingly blackened by the *inerasible traces of the thunderbolts of God.*"

From one who, disdaining the common forms and modes of language, aims at sublimity both of thought and expression, a slavish subjection to the vulgar restrictions of grammar, a tame submission to the *Jus et Norma loquendi* cannot reasonably be extracted. Exalted genius ever spurns restraint; and the mind accustomed to indulge in "a train of labyrinthic meditations" cannot very well bear up under the trammels of common sense.

Were he, however, only enthusiastic and nonsensical, we should dismiss his book with contempt. Unfortunately he has subjected himself to censure of a severer cast. In the fervor of his illustrations he is, not infrequently, impious and blasphemous. And his notions of *innocence* and *virtue* are such as, were they to pass current in the world, would soon leave society without one innocent or virtuous being. His two heroines are represented as women of rank, family, and education; yet one of them, Megalina, is made to fall in love at first sight with a member of a company of banditti, residing in a cave in the Alps, who had just robbed and murdered her father. And to this man, who is the hero of the piece, she surrenders herself, without a struggle, and becomes his mistress. The other heroine, Eloise, who has had a religious education, and who has just buried her mother, also falls in love at first sight with a man wholly unknown to her, and whom she had seen under very suspicious circumstances. To him she, also, surrenders her virgin charms; lives with him as his mistress, becomes pregnant by him; then leaves him and becomes the mistress of another stranger.

Yet, under these circumstances, the reader is insulted with the assertion, that "her soul was susceptible of *the most exalted virtue and expansion.*" Fitzeustace, the man with whom she lives, at length proposes to take her with him to England, when the following dialogue occurs between them.

"But before we go to England, before my father will see us, it is necessary that we should be married—nay, do not start, Eloise; I view it in the light that you do; I consider it an human institution and incapable of furnishing that bond of union by which, alone, can intellect be conjoined; I regard it as but a chain, which, although it keeps the body bound, leaves the soul unfettered: it is not so with love. But still, Eloise, to those who think like us, it is at all events harmless; 'tis but yielding to the prejudices of the world wherein we live, and procuring moral expediency, at a slight sacrifice of what we believe to be right."

"Well, well, it shall be done, Fitzeustace," resumed Eloise, "but take the assurance of my promise that I cannot love you more."

"They soon agreed on a point of, in their eyes, such trifling importance,[2] and arriving in England, tasted that happiness which love and *innocence* alone can give. Prejudice may triumph for a while, but *virtue* will be eventually the conqueror."

His penetration must be deeper than any to which we can form pretensions, who can discover in this denouement, any thing bearing the most distant resemblance to the triumph of virtue. It exhibits, however, a tolerably fair criterion by which the standard of the writer's intellectual powers, and his peculiar system of ethics, may be estimated.

A third female character, Olympia, a young lady of the first rank in

---

[2] Eloise, be it observed, is a Catholic, and must therefore have been taught to regard marriage, not as a "human institution" but as a *sacrament*. (Reviewer's footnote.)

Genoa, is introduced for no other imaginable purpose than to increase the reader's contempt and abhorrence of the sex. She, setting aside all dignity and decorum, as well as every feature of virtue, seeks at night the residence of a man whom she believes to be married and courts prostitution. He, however, who has never restrained his passions in any one instance, during his whole life, and who for their gratification has committed the most enormous crimes, suddenly displays a virtue wholly foreign from his disposition and character, and resolutely resists the most powerful temptation presenting itself under the most alluring form. Olympia, thus unable to become a prostitute, commits suicide.

But 'tis not surprising that the writer, who can outrage nature and common sense in almost every page of his book, should libel a sex, of whom, we suppose, he has no knowledge, but such as may be collected in the streets or in a brothel.

Of his hero, Wolfstein, and *his* mistress, Megalina, he disposes in a very summary way. The latter is found dead in the vaults of the Castle of St. Irvyne; though how she came there we are not informed. To these vaults Wolfstein repairs for the purpose of being taught the secret of obtaining eternal life. Here the Devil himself "borne on the pinions of hell's sulphurous whirlwind," appears to him and calls on him to deny his Creator. Wolfstein refuses; then, "blackened in terrible convulsions, Wolfstein expired; over him had the power of hell no influence."—*Why* he was made to expire, and *why* hell had no power over him, we are left to conjecture. Wolfstein, be it observed, had lived in the habitual commission of atrocious crimes, and died an impenitent sinner.

Of such a rhapsody we have, perhaps, said too much. But it is a duty due from critics to the public to mark every deviation from religious and moral principle with strong reprobation; as well as to deter readers from wasting their time in the perusal of unprofitable and vicious productions, as to check silly and licentious writers at an early period of their literary career. If this duty were performed with greater punctuality, the press would be more purified than it is. As to this Oxford gentleman, we recommend him to the care of his tutor, who, after a proper *jobation* for past folly, would do well, by *imposition*, to forbid him the use of the pen until he should have taken his *bachelor's degree*.

A Fellow Collegian Exposes the Author

[From The Anti-Jacobin Review and Magazine, etc., February, 1812 (41: 221), entitled "Salutary Attention to Morals in the University of Oxford."]

To the Editor of the Anti-Jacobin Review

SIR,—I am happy to say that your excellent review now begins to be much more properly appreciated, and particularly at this University, where it is gaining ground rapidly. Of late I attribute this to your very excellent critique on the Oxford University Romance, St. Iroyne [*sic*], on the subject of which I now trouble you with these few lines. This iniquitous and absurd romance is attributed to the pen of a very young gentleman, who I understand is heir to a title and a landed estate of ten thousand a year, which he will, if he lives, be in possession of very soon. And this reputed author was not long after the publication of this romance, expelled from the University, in consequence of the freedom with which he avowed his singularly wicked sentiments. He had a companion in the college, who was expelled at the same time. These facts appear to have been kept out of all public prints, but I think their promulgation will do good, as they will at once hold out a warning to others, and prove to the world, that a vigilant eye is still kept in this University over improprieties of conduct,

Your well-wisher

AN OXFORD COLLEGIAN.

OXFORD UNIVERSITY, Feb. 8th, 1812.

Report says that our ex-collegian, on being discountenanced by his friends, ran off with a young lady of no fortune, to Scotland, after a very sudden acquaintance, and has married her. I presume in revenge!

THE NECESSITY OF ATHEISM AND A DECLARATION OF RIGHTS

Blasphemy and Sedition Revived

[From The Brighton Magazine, May, 1822 (1: 540-545). The fact that this magazine turns back ten years and devotes five pages to a "review" of two works which totalled only fourteen pages is striking evidence that in 1822 the conservative press regarded Shelley seriously and hesitated at nothing to discredit him.]

The name of Percy Bysshe Shelley is not prefixed to these tracts, but they are well known to be the production of his pen; and we have selected them in our first notice of his works, as with them he commenced his literary career. In this view they are extraordinary, not as efforts of genius, but as indications of that bold and daring insubordination of mind, which led the writer, at a very early age, to trample both on human and divine authority. The Necessity of Atheism contains a distinct negation of a Deity; and the Declaration of Rights is an attempt to subvert the very foundations of civil government. Were not the subject far too grave for pleasantry, we might amuse ourselves with the idea of a stripling, an undergraduate, commencing hostilities against heaven and earth, and with the utmost self-satisfaction exulting that he has vanquished both.

Some of our readers are aware, that for the first of these performances, (after every persuasion from his superiors to induce him to retract it had been urged in vain,) Mr. Shelley was expelled from college; and that for posting up the second on the walls of a provincial town, his servant was imprisoned; and, from these facts, they may perhaps imagine that they are remarkably effective engines of atheism and democracy. But, in truth, they are below contempt,—they rather insult than support the bad cause to which they are devoted.

To maintain the Necessity of Atheism is, perhaps, the wildest and most extravagant effort of a perverted understanding; and to consider this as achieved by a mere boy in thirteen widely printed pages of a duodecimo pamphlet, is to conceive the performance of a miracle more stupendous than any recorded in the Scriptures. Had we not of late been accustomed to witness the arrogance and presumption of impiety; had not the acuteness of our sensibility been somewhat deadened by familiar acquaintance with the blasphemies of the school in which this young man is now become a professor, we could not trust our feelings even with a remote reference to his atrocious, yet most imbecile, production. It is difficult, on such a subject, to preserve the decorum of moral tolerance, and to avoid a severity of indignation incompatible with the office of Christian censors.

Mr. Shelly [sic] oddly enough denominates belief a passion; then he denies that it is ever active; yet he tells us that it is capable of excitement, and that the degrees of excitement are three. But lest we should be suspected of misrepresentation, Mr. Shelly [sic] shall speak for himself.

The senses are the sources of all knowledge to the mind, consequently their evidence claims the strongest assent. The decision of the mind, founded upon our experience derived from these sources, claims the next degree; the experience of others, which addresses itself to the former one, occupies the lowest degree. Consequently, no testimony can be admitted which is contrary to reason; reason is founded on the evidence of our senses.

Every proof may be referred to one of these three divisions; we are naturally led to consider what arguments we receive from each of them, to convince us of the existence of a Deity.

These sentences embrace a page of the pamphlet, and immediately succeed a general introduction occupying eight more; and, of course, the whole investigation is despatched in less than four. Its result is summed up in the following words:

From this it is evident, that having no proofs from any of the three sources of conviction, the mind cannot believe the existence of a God. It is also evident, that as belief is a passion of the mind, no degree of criminality can be attached to disbelief. *They only are reprehensible who willingly neglect to remove the false medium through which their mind views the subject.* It is almost unnecessary to observe, that the general knowledge of the deficiency of such proof cannot be prejudicial to society. Truth has always been found to promote the best interests of mankind. Every reflecting mind must allow that there is no proof of the existence of a Deity.

Such is the jargon of the new philosophy. "The satanic school" maintains, that belief cannot be virtuous; yet, that it may be reprehensible, and therefore vicious; and that the greatest crime of which a rational creature can be guilty, is to admit the being of a God. Such is the logic of Mr. Shelly. To discuss the question at issue between atheists and theists with such a writer, would be extreme folly; nor should we have drawn from oblivion this extravagant freak of his boyhood, had he not by subsequent writings, and at a matured period of his life, avowed the same sentiments, and obtruded them upon the world with an effrontery unexampled in the annals of impiety. But on this strange intellectual and moral phenomenon we shall take occasion to offer a few remarks. In what light are we to consider the intellectual qualities and attainments of an individual, who denies the existence of a Deity, on the supposition that he has discovered a great and momentous truth? But he has explored the universe, and not only cannot find a God, but can demonstrate the impossibility of his existence. How surprisingly great must be his understanding! how stupendous and overpowering his knowledge! For as this is a fact that requires demonstration, no inferior degree of evidence can be admitted as conclusive. What wondrous Being then presents himself before us in all the confidence of absolute persuasion, founded on irrefragable evidence, declaring that there is no God? And how has he grown to this immense intelligence? Yesterday he was an infant in capacity, and humble; and now he is invested with the attributes of the very Divinity whose existence he denies. "For unless this man is omnipresent, unless he is at this moment in every place in the universe, he cannot know but there may be in some place manifestations of a Deity, by which even *he* would be overpowered. If he does not know absolutely every agent in the universe, and does not know what is so, that which is so may be God. If he is not in absolute possession of all the propositions that constitute universal truth, the one which he wants may be, that there is a God. If he cannot, with certainty, assign the cause of all that he perceives to exist, that cause may be God. If he does not know everything that has been done in the immeasurable ages that are past, some things may have been done by a God. Thus, unless he knows all things, that is, precludes another Deity, by being one himself, he cannot know that the Being whose existence he rejects does not exist. But he must know that he does not exist, else he deserves equal contempt and compassion for the temerity with which he firmly avows his rejection, and acts accordingly."[3] As, however, no individual can presume that he has attained this alarming superiority above his fellow-creatures; as the necessity of atheism has never been proved; but in every case where it has been pretended, it has been the result of some peculiar conjunction of disastrous influences, we are constrained to infer that the atheist must be the victim of a mental obliquity, of a strange perversion of the understanding, which renders him incapable of comprehending the laws of evidence, and the principles of right and reason.

There are certain principles on which, with a few anomalous exceptions, all men are agreed. The foundation of all reasoning concerning being and events, for instance, is a supposed or acknowledged connexion between cause and effect. By cause is meant that something, be it what it may, which produces, or causes to produce, existence, or any change of existence, and without which the existence or the change would not have been. It is universally admitted, that we have no knowledge of any existence, or any change, which has taken place without a cause. The human mind, under whatever circumstances of culture or neglect, has

[3] Foster's Essays. (Reviewer's footnote.)

acknowledged, in the clearest manner, and in every way of which the subject is susceptible, the inseparable nature of this connexion. We learn it from experience, and in two ways—by the testimony of our senses, and by the inspection of our minds. We cannot realize the fact, that no existence or change can take place without a cause. The man who begins by denying what is so self-evident, discovers an incapacity to reason. He holds nothing in common with the rest of mankind, and no absurdity can be greater than to attempt to argue with him. Indeed, he cannot pursue an argument on the subject without a practical refutation of the principle he assumes. In speaking, he exhibits *himself* as the cause of all the words uttered by him, and of the opinions he would communicate; and, in the act of arguing, admits you to be a similar cause. If his body be not a cause, and your eyes another, you cannot see him; if his voice and your ears be not causes, you cannot hear him; if his mind and yours be not causes, you cannot understand him. In a word, without admitting the connexion between cause and effect, you can never know that he is arguing with you, or you with him. But the sophistry which leads to Atheism, denies this first principle of all reasoning, and betrays a mental perversion, which utterly disqualifies for sober and rational investigation.

And with this sturdy rejection of everything like evidence on the subject of a Deity, it is remarkable that Atheists are the most credulous of mankind. There is no absurdity which the human mind, in the very spirit of extravagance, has been capable of inventing, which they have not gravely maintained. The dogmas of Atheism are the most melancholy exhibition of weakness which has ever degraded the human understanding. And we are warranted in affirming, that Atheism, *in all its forms*, is a specimen of the most absolute credulity. The three grand schemes of existence, which it has devised, to get rid of the idea of one glorious, intelligent Creator; namely, that things have existed in an eternal series; that their existence is casual; and that all distinct, or separate, beings owe their existence to the powers and operations of matter; have been refuted by direct demonstrations; they have been unanswerably proved not only to be false, but to be impossible. What then can we think of the mental capacities of him, who goes on quietly with his faith in these hypotheses, and resolves to believe, in defiance of demonstration and impossibility?

But the source of Atheism is the heart rather than the head; and it is a moral phenomenon of the most portentous and appalling character. It is the child of depravity, bearing all the worst features of its parent. A tree is known by its fruits; reason never produced such a monster as Atheism; it is to be traced to the indisposition of the heart to acknowledge the existence of a Creator. He that hates the control, and dreads the inspection, judgment, and retribution of his Maker, finds no refuge from anxiety and alarm so safe, as the belief that there is no God.

To us there is something fearful and even terrific in the state of mind which can delight in the renunciation of a Deity—which can derive satisfaction from the feeling, that the infinite Spirit is gone, that the only solid foundation of virtue is wanting; which can enjoy pleasure in renouncing that system of doctrine of which a God is the great subject, and that train of affections and conduct of which He is the supreme object. The idea of a God seems essential to every pleasurable and sublime execution; without it we can conceive of nothing glorious, nothing delightful. And, could it once be exploded, in one view it would diminish to insignificance the range of thought, the circle of enjoyment. The absence of God would cover the face of nature with funereal gloom; and, he that should first make the fatal discovery, according to our apprehension, would be at once and forever the most miserable being in the universe. He would evince no eagerness to communicate the dismal search; on the contrary, he would envy his fellow-creatures the pleasant delusion which sustained their virtue, and encouraged their hope.

But "Truth," says Mr. Shelly, "has always been found to promote the best interests of mankind." We admit the proposition, and therefore maintain that that which is subversive of their best interests, cannot be truth. We may confidently ask, in what possible way can Atheism secure the well-being of society?

If we grant that the belief in a Deity operates as a very slight restraint on vice, in individual cases where the character has become utterly depraved, yet its general influence must be mighty, interwoven as it is with the whole civil and social economy of man. It must act powerfully as an incentive to whatever is good, and as a check to whatever is evil; and, it can only fail in particular instances of atrocious obduracy. But, what offences against himself or his fellow-creatures, may not an Atheist perpetrate with conscious impunity, without regret, and without a blush? What protection can his principles afford to confiding innocence and beauty? What shall deter him from dooming an amiable and lovely wife to penury, to desolation, and an untimely grave? What shall make seduction and adultery criminal in his eyes, or induce him when she is in his power, to spare the victim of unhallowed and guilty passions? What can he know of honour, of justice, and integrity? What friend will he not betray? What tradesman will he not defraud? What enemy will he not pursue to utter destruction? What lawless gratification will he not indulge, when its indulgence does not compromise his personal safety. Who, we may ask, are those that set the decencies of life at defiance, that laugh at virtue, and riot in epicurean debauchery? Are they not the base apostates from God, who boast of their impiety, and write themselves "Atheists" to their own disgrace, and the scandal of the country that gave them birth? These are the questions which we put to what was once a conscience in the breast of Mr. Shelly, with little hope, however, that they will rouse this benumbed and long-forgotten faculty, to any thing like feeling. It is well for mankind that the life of the Atheist is so just a comment upon his creed, and that none can feel a wish to join his standard, but he who has become an alien from virtue, and the enemy of his species.

We had intended to indulge in further observations, and to bring the principles of the declaration of rights more prominently and distinctly before our readers; but for the present we shall forbear. A government founded on Atheism, or conducted by Atheists, would be the greatest curse the world has ever felt. It was inflicted for a short season, as a visitation on a neighboring country, and its reign was avowedly and expressly the reign of terror. The declarers of rights, intoxicated by their sudden elevation, and freed from every restraint, became the most ferocious tyrants; and, while they shut up the temples of God, abolished his worship, and proclaimed death to be an eternal sleep, they converted, by their principles and spirit, the most polished people of Europe into a horde of assassins; the seat of voluptuous refinement, of pleasure and of arts, into a theatre of blood.

With an example so recent and so fearfully instructive before our eyes, it is not probable that we shall be deluded by Mr. Shelly or any of his school; the splendours of a poetical imagination may dazzle and delight, and they may prove a mighty engine of mischief to many who have more fancy than judgment; but they will never impose upon the sober and calculating part of the community; they will never efface the impression from our minds, that Atheism is an inhuman, bloody, and ferocious system, equally hostile to every useful restraint, and to every virtuous affection; that having nothing above us to excite awe, or around us to awaken tenderness, it wages war with Heaven, and with earth: its first object is to dethrone God; its next to destroy man. With such conviction the enlightened and virtuous inhabitants of Great Britain will not surely be tempted to their fate by such a rhapsody as the following, with which Mr. Shelley concludes his Declaration of Rights, and with which we take our leave of him:

Man! thou whose rights are here declared, be no longer forgetful of the loftiness of thy destination. Think of thy rights; of those possessions which will give thee virtue and wisdom, by which thou mayest arrive at happiness and freedom. They are declared to thee by one who knows thy dignity; for every hour does his heart swell with honourable pride, in the contemplation of what thou mayest attain; by one who is not forgetful of thy degeneracy, for every moment brings home to him the bitter conviction of what thou art.

Awake!—Arise!—or be forever fallen.

III

QUEEN MAB

FIRST SIGNIFICANT ENCOURAGEMENT

[From The Theological Inquirer, or Polemical Magazine, March, April, May, July, 1815 (pp. 34-39; 105-110; 205-209; 358-362), under the title *Queen Mab*. One might almost suspect that this puzzling and ably written magazine existed mainly for Shelley's benefit. All discussion and quotation carefully avoid betraying the anonymous author of *Queen Mab* and *A Refutation of Deism*, yet six of the eight numbers issued give him prominent attention. That Shelley was fully cognizant of and connived at this clever exploitation of his work is hardly to be doubted.

The story told by F., who signs the series of articles on *Queen Mab*, sounds a trifle strange. Shelley might well have sent a copy to Kotzebue, who, F. claims, recommended the book to him in the summer of 1814; but the six copies bought with such seeming ease by F. in Berlin, seem rather surprising. Shelley printed only 250 copies in 1813. Only 170 copies were disposed of before December, 1822, when Richard Carlile bought all that were left; namely, 180 copies. The contributions of F. are presumably distinct from the reprinting of *A Refutation of Deism*, which bears no signature or comment and makes no mention of Shelley's name. The fact that this reprint corrects most of the errors of Shelley's edition led Mr. Bertram Dobell (The Athenaeum, March 7, 1855, p. 313) to suspect that Shelley himself had some hand in it. And then, strangely suggestive of Shelley's early methods of stimulating discussion, there is a letter signed Mary Anne which takes issue with the *Refutation*. Mary Anne is not wholly convincing as a genuine antagonist. The *Refutation* itself is an example of Shelley's peculiar methods at the time, for its real aim, of course, is to support deism. Mr. Dobell, in the article already cited, conjectured that F. might be James Laurence, author of *The Empire of the Nairs*, and then seemed to find an indication elsewhere in the journal that F. was Fare, or Fair. It might be possible to identify F. by means of the various mediocre poems throughout the journal bearing the signature F., but so far I have been unable to do so. Curiously, the Preface to the so-called first American edition of *Queen Mab* (1821) concludes with "An Ode to the Author of Queen Mab," signed R. C. F., which is identical with the one originally signed F.; and the author of the ode is mentioned as a friend of the present editor, who signs himself Pantheist. There is also a prose extract from The Theological Inquirer, outlining the plot. Thus the two principal mysteries about *Queen Mab*, the origin of its first criticism and the origin of the "first American" edition, seem to converge on each other. It seems probable also that F. knew Shelley—rather well, too, considering Shelley's prudence in circulating *Queen Mab*—and wrote with his connivance. Nowhere in the periodical is Shelley mentioned by name.

The identity of F. may be guessed at with some plausibility after F. is identified with R. C. F. In March, 1817, Shelley directed his publishers to send a copy of *A Proposal for Putting Reform to the Vote* to "Sir R. Ferguson, M.P." General Sir Ronald Crawford Ferguson, though one of Wellington's generals and a member of

Parliament during the Regency, was well known at the time as a liberal, a consistent supporter of Catholic emancipation, and all other measures of civil and religious liberty. I can find no evidence to connect him with the non-Shelleyan poems signed F. in The Theological Inquirer. Another possibility is a brother of Sir Ronald Crawford Ferguson, about whom I have so far been able to find only that he was a radical M.P. and that his first initial is R. A more remote possibility still is Robert Cutlar Fergusson, prominent as a radical M.P. shortly after Shelley's death, but resident in India during the period immediately in question. Before leaving England he was an associate of the Earl of Thanet, and some time after the appearance of F.'s poems in The Theological Enquirer, poems signed F. but not demonstrably by the same author, appeared in The Thanet Magazine.]

To the Editor of the Theological Inquirer

SIR,

Observing in your prospectus, that it is your intention occasionally to insert criticisms on books connected with the subjects proposed, and also to give an account of scarce and valuable works in the different departments you have laid down, I take the liberty of informing you that during an excursion on the Continent, in the last summer, the celebrated Kotzebue put into my hands an English poem, which he doubted if I had seen in my own country, as he considered it too bold a production to issue from the British press. He spoke of it in the highest terms of admiration; and though I had not time then to peruse it, I afterwards purchased six copies of it at Berlin and have been amply repaid by the pleasure it has afforded me. I would send you a copy to reprint in your journal; but am afraid, notwithstanding the freedom, candour, and impartiality you seem to aim at, that you would be intimidated from the publication, as our press is at present too much shackled to give vent to the many important truths it contains. I shall, however, attempt a description of this poem, and extract such passages as will serve to give a faint idea of the whole, though, I am sorry to say, I shall be under the necessity of omitting some of its greatest beauties. The author has made fiction, and the usual poetical imagery, the vehicles for his moral and philosophical opinions. It is entitled *"Queen Mab,"* and the attributes of that celebrated personage form the machinery of a work, in which the delightful creations of fancy and the realities of truth unite to produce an indelible impression on the mind.

The fairy descends in her chariot, and hovering over this earth, confers on the soul of a beautiful female (Ianthe) the glorious boon of a complete knowledge of the past, the present, and the future; the body is lulled to sleep, the soul ascends the fairy car, and they take their flight through the immeasurable expanse of the universe. Arrived at the palace of the "Queen of Spells," the spirit is led by her to the "overhanging battlement," and thence beholds the inexpressible grandeur of that multitude of worlds, among which this earth (to which her attention is especially directed) is but an insignificant speck. The fairy then proceeds to point out the ruined cities of ancient time, and her sublime descriptions, with the reflections naturally suggested by the pomp and decay of grandeur, and the rise and fall of empires, will form some of the most interesting of those extracts which I design to introduce.

Having reviewed the deeds of ages past, the fairy then expatiates on the systems of present existence; and here the author's opinions, conveyed through the lips of his visionary instrument, are bold to the highest pitch of daring; this, however, is not the theatre for their discussion; to state and to applaud would be dangerous, and to condemn would be ungenerous, while a restricted press allows not of open defence.

The doctrine of *Necessity*, abstruse and dark as the subject is generally believed, forms a leading consideration in this poem, and is treated with a precision of demonstration, and illumined with a radiance of genius, far beyond expectation itself:

> The present and the past thou hast beheld;
> It was a desolate sight.

And the fairy then lifts the veil of an imaginary futurity, and presents to the delighted spirit the prospect of a state of human perfection, which affords illimitable range for the erratic wanderings of poetic ardour: here the fairy and the spirit revel in all the luxury of hope and joy; and having contemplated awhile with virtuous satisfaction the happy scene thus opened to mortal conception, the former declares her task completed, and conveys the latter to her earthly tenement, which her anxious lover is watching with impatient ardor for its resuscitation.

The reflections in the commencement of the poem over the inanimate body of Ianthe, are remarkably impressive. . . .

> [*Quotes Canto I, lines 19-36*]

The approach of Queen Mab is thus powerfully described:

> [*Quotes Canto I, lines 45-58*]

The description of the fairy's appearance, as

> —Leaning gracefully from th' etherial car,
> Long did she gaze, and silently,
> Upon the slumbering maid.

is introduced in the following sublime strain of exclamation:

> Oh! not the visioned poet in his dreams,
> When silvery clouds float through the wildered brain,
> When every sight of lovely, wild and grand
> Astonishes, enraptures, elevates,
> When fancy at a glance combines
> The wondrous and the beautiful,—
> So bright, so fair, so wild a shape
> Hath ever yet beheld,
> As that which reigned the coursers of the air,
> And poured the magic of her gaze
> Upon the maiden's sleep.

Her address to the soul of Ianthe, and its effects, are marked with the most vivid beauties of poetry. . . .

[*Quotes Canto I, lines 114-156*]

In answer to the spirit's natural inquiry of astonishment at the new feeling which pervades her, the fairy proceeds to explain her own state of being. . . .

[*Quotes Canto I, lines 167-187*]

The magic power of this command operates instantaneously:

> The strains of earth's immurement
> Fell from Ianthe's spirit;
> They shrank and brake like bandages of straw
> Beneath a wakened giant's strength.

Satan's passage through chaos, in Milton, sublime as it is, sinks into comparative insignificance, when considered with the description of the fairy and the spirit's course through the immensity of the universe; it is lengthy, but a short extract or two will justify my opinion. . . .

[*Quotes Canto I, lines 222-248*]

The reflections on this imposing scene, with which the first part of the poem (which is in nine divisions) concludes, must not be omitted. . . .

[*Quotes Canto I, lines 264-277*]

If, Mr. Editor, you mark your approbation of this correspondence by inserting it, I shall continue my selections from a work, the whole of which there is but small probability of the present generation becoming acquainted with. I am, Sir,

Your well-wisher, F.

[April, 1815]

Mr. Editor,

As you have gratified me, and (I trust) the public, by inserting my first selection of specimens from "Queen Mab," I shall continue to point out what appear to me its principal excellencies; proud of the opportunity of homaging the shrine of genius, and delighted to cull flowers from the luxuriant garden of a rich poetic imagination.

The description of the Fairy Queen's palace is introduced in a manner peculiarly calculated to arrest the attention. . . .

[*Quotes Canto II, lines 1-21*]

The light step of beauty has been frequently the subject of fanciful description. Scott, in his *Lady of the Lake*, has it:

> Ev'n the light hare-bell raised its head
> Elastic from her airy tread.

But the following is a more sublime picture:

> The Fairy and the Spirit
> Entered the Hall of Spells:
> Those golden clouds
> That rolled in glittering billows
> Beneath the azure canopy
> With the ethereal footsteps trembled not.

In the view of the "countless and unending orbs" of the universe, this earth is described as:

> —a little light
> That twinkled in the misty distance;
> None but a spirit's eye
> Might ken that rolling orb.

The tombs of the lovely, the good, and the great, have always afforded a fruitful source of reflection to the sensitive mind; even the gibbet of the criminal excites a sigh for the perversion of human ability.

But over the records of mighty nations, fallen beneath the mad blow of the conqueror's ambition; or decayed by the consumptive influence of moral corruption; the sensibilities take a wider and more dignified scope for meditation; and although the disordered relations of man are thus martialled in dreadful array before the shrinking perception, so as to produce a transient emotion of despair in the bosom of the philanthropist, yet is the glow of patriotism ultimately benefited, and every virtue strengthened and improved. . . .

> [*Quotes Canto II, lines 109-181*]

The author's favorite doctrine of the eternity of matter is thus forcibly illustrated and insisted upon. . . .

> [*Quotes Canto II, lines 211-243*]

Adverting to the rottenness of certain established systems of government, and the patient and wonderful endurance of man, the Fairy indignantly proceeds. . . .

> [*Quotes Canto III, lines 106-117*]

How nobly contemptuous is the tone of the inquiry which follows a deprecation of the evils of tyranny, and a fond prophecy of a period when

> Falsehood's trade
> Shall be as hateful and unprofitable
> As that of truth is now.

> [*The quotation continues through lines 138-149 of Cento III.*]

That the author is a powerful advocate of *Necessity* is evinced by the following extract. . . .

> [*Quotes Canto III, lines 214-240*]

Alas! how little is there in the present aspect of the world and its institutions, to warrant a hope of the speedy consummation of this anticipated
state of perfection! yet does the eye of innocence receive with grateful
delight the feeble ray thus stealing through the crevice of its persecuted-
being's dungeon.   F.

[May, 1815]

The following description of a fine night in winter will strike the
reader with a forcible sense of admiration.

[*Quotes Canto IV, lines 1-19*]

Further on, the author imagines the quiet of this scene destroyed by
the tumult and horror of war.

[*Quotes Canto IV, lines 33-69*]

The Fairy, in a strain of indignant inquiry into the moral causes which
produce the scenes of horror and devastation depicted above, asks. . . .

[*Quotes Canto IV, lines 89-104*]

The demon of trade, that enemy of virtue, that monster whose breath
chills the ardor of sensibility, and drives the shivering soul to the inmost
corner of distrustful reserve, is an object of our author's most powerful
indignation.

[*Quotes Canto V, lines 44-63*]

How lamentably true the following picture of the evils resulting from
the love of gain.

[*Quotes Canto V, lines 166-196*]

An episode, founded on the celebrated legend of the wandering Jew,
forms a prominent feature in the admirable poem under analysis. The
fairy thus expresses herself.

[*Quotes Canto VII, lines 59-82*]

This is that supposititious character, who, for insulting Christ on his way
to the place of execution, is said to be condemned to a restless existence
on earth till the day of judgment; the vengeful acrimony of his disposition,
naturally produced by this severe decree, pervades the whole of his long
harrangue to the fairy and the spirit, so as to render it imprudent to submit
it here; but the reader must be gratified by the sublime and impressive
manner of its conclusion.

[*Quotes Canto VII, lines 254-275*]

If, in this division of the poem, which describes the systems of the
present, I have confined myself to extracts characteristic, by their power of
fancy and beauty of description, of the author's ability as a poet; and have

not produced those indications that he is a philosopher of the first rank, with which the volume abounds, it must be attributed to the boldness of his sentiments, which, in this country, where the freedom of the press is little more than an empty name, it would be hazardous to disseminate.

[July, 1815]

Now it is that the visionary golden age bursts in full splendour on the luxurious imagination of our poet: and this favorite theme of all bards is treated in a manner which covers former descriptions with insignificance, its effects on the Spirit are rapturous.

[*Quotes Canto VIII, lines 11-40*]

The concluding simile is inexpressibly beautiful; nor does an extensive poetical reading furnish me with any reason to doubt its originality. It is not to the blooming vales of Tempé, to the golden groves of Arcadia; or to any other favorite spot that our poet confines the happiness of his mental vision; the whole earth is the work of renovation, and the desert and the deep alike are resigned to the desirable influence.

[*Quotes Canto VIII, lines 70-87*]

The sublime and faultless fabric of his conception being perfected, the poet exclaims with rapturous gratulation,

[*Quotes Canto IX, lines 1-55*]

The following are striking, but, alas! unhoped-for changes:

[*Quotes Canto IX, lines 93-129*]

Thus, Mr. Editor, have I endeavoured, like Mahomet and St. John, to give your readers a faint idea of the paradise to which I have been admitted; surely my selections must interest the soul of fancy, the heart of feeling, to such a degree, that the energies of resolution will be impelled with increased force to the accomplishment of that great object the complete freedom of the press in matters of public opinion. For the reflection must occur that this is only one of the numerous productions of genius which have perished in the bud, which have been destroyed in the womb by its oppressive restrictions.

The copious and elegant notes to the poem, it is not within my design to call your attention to.

A Paine, a Voltaire, and a Volney, have written to teach man his dignity; they have conveyed the voice of Reason to the unprejudiced ear, and have seemed monuments of fame in the gratitude of future ages, but it was reserved for the author of Queen Mab to show, that

"The poet's eye, in a fine frenzy rolling,"

might soar to other and to nobler objects than the domes of superstition, and the heaven of priestly invention, and to prove the justice of Milton's beautiful ejaculation;

> How charming is divine philosophy!
> Not harsh and crabbed as dull fools suppose,
> But musical as is Apollo's lute,
> And a perpetual feast of nectared sweets
> Where no crude surfeit reigns.

F.

FIRST PRAISE OF THE PIRATED EDITION
BY THE RADICALS

[From John Bull's British Journal, March 11, 1821 (no. 3, p. 22), under the title, Queen Mab, a Poem, by Percy Bysshe Shelley, Esq. During the eight years between Shelley's first printing of the poem and its piratical publication by William Clark in 1821 the poem had had only a limited circulation and had not been connected with Shelley's name until the Chancery hearings in 1817, when it was introduced as evidence by the Westbrooks. Had they desired to bring an indictment for blasphemy against Shelley at this time, there is no doubt but that they could have had him fined and imprisoned. Writers about the malevolence of Eliza Westbrook might well give her credit for this much restraint. The Chancery hearings undoubtedly attracted some radical attention to the poem and associated it with Shelley's name. In 1821 Clark's piracy and Shelley's published protest completed the association and began one of the most important influences upon Shelley's reputation. William Benbow, publisher of John Bull's British Journal, was a notorious radical and piratical publisher, who later published several Shelley piracies over his own name, and who in this very year was publishing Paine's *Theological Works* secretly. He was quite possibly the clandestine publisher of the so-called first American edition of *Queen Mab*, the Preface of which quotes an extract from The Theological Inquirer outlining the poem, just as the present review is almost entirely quoted from its obscure predecessor of six years before.]

As the name of this poet is now become familiar to the literary world, in consequence of the animadversions his "Revolt of Islam," "The Cenci," a tragedy, and "Prometheus," a lyrical drama, have given rise to in the magazines and Reviews, they may perhaps feel interested in an account of a poem, written and printed (for private circulation only), but never published, some years since. It contains thoughts and sentiments so bold, no bookseller has hitherto ventured to publish it; but that is no reason why some of its beauties should not be made known to our readers. The author has made fiction and suitable poetical imagery the vehicles of his moral and philosophic opinions. The attributes of Queen Mab form the machinery of a work in which the delightful creations of fancy, and the realities of truth, unite to produce an indelible impression on the mind.

[*The remainder of this review is identical with the first instalment of F.'s review in The Theological Inquirer, except that F.'s opening and closing remarks are omitted, together with the last twenty-seven lines of F.'s longest quotation, and one of the quotations is introduced by a close paraphrase of F.'s language instead of the identical sentences.*]

FIRST PRAISE OF THE PIRATED EDITION BY THE LIBERALS

[From The London Magazine and Theatrical Inquisitor, March, 1821 (3:278-281). This liberal "Cockney" magazine took over the friendly attitude toward Shelley assumed by its predecessor, The London Magazine and Monthly Critical and Dramatic Review. Together they make the most sympathetic, complete, and capable acknowledgment of Shelley's greatness made by any periodical during his lifetime, except The Examiner, which was a special pleader. The expiration of this periodical in 1821 was undoubtedly a setback to the development of Shelley's reputation.]

Queen Mab is a poem, written (as we understand) by Mr. Shelley when at Oxford, and is one of the earliest of his productions. The sentiments contained in it gave considerable offense to the learned heads of the University, and entailed on the author some unpleasant consequences. With these, however, we have nothing to do at present. Our business is with the poetical merits of the work. With the speculative tenets of the writer we shall not intermeddle. If his opinions are palpably absurd and false, they must fall by their own absurdity and falsehood; and discussion could serve no other purpose than to invest them with an importance they do not intrinsically possess. As to the private scandal from which some critics have borrowed pungency and attraction for their disquisitions, we utterly disclaim it; we can neither conceive its connection with criticism, nor its propriety from the pen of a reviewer.

The prominent features of Mr. Shelley's poetical character are energy and depth. He has not the tenderness and delicacy of some living poets, nor the fertile and soaring imagination of others. In the former he is surpassed very far indeed by Barry Cornwall, nor does he approach in the latter to Coleridge, or even to Keats. But he has an intense and overwhelming energy of manner, and if he does not present us with many original conceptions, his turn of thought, as well as expression, is strongly indicative of original genius. We apprehend, indeed, that the peculiar charm of Shelley's writing is derived from that complete conviction which he evidently entertains of the justness and importance of all he asserts. This feeling, whether a man's opinions be right or wrong, communicates a force and pointedness to diction, and an interest to composition, which mere labour can never bestow. All Mr. Shelley's thoughts are feelings. He instantly communicates to his reader the impression made upon his own mind, and gives it, even in our apprehension, all the vividness and strength with which it struck his own fancy. His figures, it is true, are often disproportioned, often terrific; but they burst upon us from the canvas in all the energy of life and motion. This gives interest to his sketches, even where the colouring is coarse, and the drawing deficient in exactitude.

Queen Mab opens with some fine reflections upon sleep and death, and allusions to a maid termed Ianthe, apparently dead. Her the poet describes as all that was pure and lovely. He proceeds to tell us that a rushing noise is heard where the body lay, and soon the fairy queen makes her appearance in a radiant car, arrayed in all the lightness and splendour of poetical decoration. She addresses the spirit of Ianthe—she declares herself to be acquainted both with the past and the future, and that it is permitted her "to rend the veil of mortal fraility," and to inform the human spirit how it may best accomplish those purposes for which it received its being. That this is a privilege granted only to pure sinless spirits like Ianthe's. She accordingly invites her to avail herself of it immediately, and ascend the car with her. The spirit complies, and they proceed upon their journey to the palace of the fairy. They pass by innumerable suns and worlds, and at length terminate their etherial voyage upon the very boundaries of this universe. The description of this voyage, and of the palace of her fairy majesty, is highly splendid and poetical. When arrived there, Queen Mab declares the purpose of their journey, presents the spirit with a view from the eternal battlements of her palace, of the immense universe stretched below. She takes a review of the past; dwells upon the glories and disgraces of mankind as exhibited in history: upon their crimes, their infatuations, their prejudices, and the absurdity of all received opinions and institutions. She then opens a vista of the future, clad in all the splendid anticipations of perfectibility. She tells how crime, tyranny, and war shall cease: how swords shall be turned into plough-shares, and spears into pruning-hooks; and how, in spite of the doleful predictions of Mr. Malthus, the increase of population, consequent on such state, will only tend to the increase of happiness and virtue. Thus the fairy's task is ended: she restores the spirit to its fleshy tabernacle; and we discover, at the conclusion, that Ianthe was not dead, but had slept, and that all was a dream!—The poetical excellence of this work may be judged from the following extracts. . . .

[*Quotes I, 144-156; I, 264-277; II, 225-243; III, 138-169*]

Our readers, we think, will agree with us in pronouncing, that none but a man of genius could write this. At the same time it must be confessed, that the poem possesses many of the faults of a young writer, and a few of the affectations of that school with which the author has been classed, but from whose restrictions we trust he will soon completely emancipate himself. We cannot conclude this article without earnestly exhorting Mr. Shelley to undertake something truly worthy of his great powers—something that can be read by the generality of mankind—something divested of those peculiar associations which render him at present so unpopular. Let him remember, that the most effectual mode of combating prejudice is not by direct and violent opposition, but by gentleness and inteneration. We would also tell him, that a genius like his was formed for mankind—that his home is the universe; and that he will not fulfil his high destiny by contracting himself within the narrow limits of a circle of friends, whose standard of literary excellence is regulated by certain conventional ideas peculiar to themselves. It is not thus that his writings will acquire that extension and permanence that alone can render them truly beneficial to mankind, and productive of immortality to their author.

THE LITERARY GAZETTE SEEKS TO DISCRIMINATE

[From The Literary Gazette and Journal of Belles Lettres, May 19, 1821 (no. 226, pp. 305-308). This influential weekly was one of Shelley's most consistent assailants and did all in its power to counteract the influence of his writings. It did, however, make some show of acknowledging his genius, though it seems never to have made an effort, as Blackwood's did, to reform him.

This is the only review in The Literary Gazette with which Shelley's letters show him to be acquainted. In his letter of August 9, 1821, he says to Mary apropos of the scandalous story believed of them by the Hoppners, that "this is evidently the source of the violent denunciations of the Literary Gazette." Certainly the hint about "incestuous relations" in the footnote may refer to Shelley's rumored relations with Claire Clairmont, but they may also refer only to the stories afloat about the association of Byron, the Shelleys, and Claire at Geneva in 1816.]

The mixture of sorrow, indignation, and loathing, with which this volume has overwhelmed us, will, we fear, deprive us of the power of expressing our sentiments upon it, in the manner best suited to the subject itself, and to the effect which we wish our criticism to have upon society. Our desire is to do justice *to* the writer's genius, and *upon* his principles: not to deny his powers, while we deplore their perversion; and above all, when we lay before our readers the examples of his poetry, to warn them against the abominable and infamous contagion with which in the sequel he poisons these splendid effusions. We have doubted whether we ought to notice this book at all; and if our silence could have prevented its being disseminated, no allusion to it should ever have stained the Literary Gazette. But the activity of the vile portion of the press is too great to permit this hope,[1] and on weighing every consideration presented to our minds, we have come to the conclusion to lay, as far as we are able, the bane and antidote before the public. Queen Mab has long been in limited and private circulation, as a duodecimo; and the first two or three cantos, under the title of The Demon of the World, were reprinted at the end of a poem called Alastor; as was also the principal note against Christianity in a detached pamphlet. Though the hellish ingredients, therefore, are now for the first time brought together into one cauldron, they have, like those of the evil beings in Macbeth, previously disgusted the world in forms of separate obsceneness.

We have spoken of Shelley's genius, and it is doubtless of a high order; but when we look at the purposes to which it is directed, and contemplate the infernal character of all its efforts, our souls revolt with tenfold horror at the energy it exhibits, and we feel as if one of the darkest of the fiends had been clothed with a human body, to enable him to gratify his enmity against the human race, and as if the supernatural atrocity of his hate were only heightened by his power to do injury. So strongly has this impression

[1] As this is a book of so blasphemous a nature, as to have no claim to the protection of copy-right, it may be published by Scoundrels at all prices, to destroy the moral feeling of every class of the community. In the present instance the author has not, we imagine, been consulted. (Reviewer's footnote.)

dwelt upon our minds that we absolutely asked a friend who had seen this individual, to describe him to us—as if a cloven foot, or horn, or flames from the mouth, must have marked the external appearance of so bitter an enemy to mankind. We were almost disappointed to learn that the author was only a tall, boyish looking man, with eyes of unearthly brightness, and a countenance of the wildest cast: that he strode about with hurried and impatient gait, and that a perturbed spirit seemed to preside over all his movements. It is not then in his outward semblance but in his inner man, that the explicit demon is seen; and it is a frightful supposition, that his own life may have been a fearful commentary upon his principles[2]— principles, which in the balance of law and justice, happily deprived him of the superintendance of his infants, while they plunged an unfortunate wife and mother into ruin, prostitution, guilt, and suicide.

Such, alas! are the inevitable consequences of the fatal precepts enforced in this publication, which spares not one grace, one good, one ornament, nor one blessing, that can ameliorate our lot on earth; which wages exterminating war against all that can refine, delight or improve human kind; which ridicules every thing that can contribute to our happiness here, and boldly tries to crush every hope that could point to our happiness hereafter.

As we shall, however, have to say something of these matters in detail, we shall now turn to the review of Queen Mab.

The rhythm is of that sort which Mr. Southey employed so forcibly in his Thalaba, and other poems; and it is no mean praise to observe, that in his use of it, Mr. Shelley is not inferior to his distinguished predecessor. The first Canto opens with great beauty, in the same way as Thalaba.

[*Quotes Canto I, lines 1-113*]

This is genuine poetry; and in an almost equal strain does the author proceed through forty pages, when he lapses into metaphysics of the worst kind, and becomes at once prosaic and unintelligible. The story, or vehicle for spreading his atrocious opinions, is thus framed. Mab releases the soul of Ianthe from her body, and they pass together, namely, the spirit and the fairy, to an empyreal region, where the mortal globe is made to submit its elements to the enquiry of the freed soul, and the superior being explains, according to Mr. Shelley's ideas, the depravity of the existing system, and shapes out a new moral, or rather immoral world, in millennial perspective. Of course, the spirit is delighted to find that there are to be no restraints on the passions, no laws to curb vice, no customs to mark with reprobation the grossest indulgence in sensuality and crime: that in the

---

[2] We are aware, that ordinary criticism has little or nothing to do with the personal conduct of authors; but when the most horrible doctrines are promulgated with appalling force, it is the duty of every man to expose, in every way, the abominations to which they irresistibly drive their odious professors. We declare against receiving our social impulses from a destroyer of every social virtue; our moral creed, from an incestuous wretch; or our religion, from an atheist, who denied God, and reviled the purest institutes of human philosophy and divine ordination, did such a demon exist. (Reviewer's footnote.)

revocated order, chastity in women, and honour in men, are to be unknown or despised: and in fine, that in the perfected creation there are to be no statesmen, no priests, no king, no God!

The pure enlightened spirit of Ianthe then returns instructed to its corporeal frame, and finds some Henry kneeling by her bedside, to begin the practice of these holy precepts.

The ascent to the visionary abode of Mab is however a piece of splendid composition.

[*Quotes Canto I, lines 199-277*]

Thus ends the first Canto; and the second opens in nearly as sublime a strain; but speedily degenerates into affectation and bombast. New-coined words, and a detail in what may well be styled nonsense verses succeed, and the author becomes what he would call "meaningless," ever and anon exclaiming, "how wonderful," as if he were himself surprized at his own absurdities. The Mosaic account of creation is, as might be anticipated, treated with ridicule; and we are given to understand that instead of an Almighty Providence, the Creator of the Universe with all the "rolling orbs," was a certain power whose appellation is NECESSITY. The attributes of this Necessity are not very definite; but Mr. Shelley supposes it is enough to know and to believe that they were the cause of all nature, and are the universal soul of his precious system. And this leads us to Canto 3, in which the present wickedness and future destiny of man are unfolded. Were it turned to aught but the vilest of purposes, there might be much of excellent writing selected from this part; with which, as we have already noticed, the beauty of the poem as a poem dies. For example, the following reflections on the instability of sublunary things is finely shaped to draw a virtuous moral from; but the author only lays it as the foundation for his engine to cast a fiercer desolation among mankind.

> Where is the fame
> Which the vain-glorious mighty of the earth
> Seek to eternize? Oh! the faintest sound
> From time's light footfall, the minutest wave
> That swells the flood of ages, whelms in nothing
> The unsubstantial bubble. Aye! to-day
> Stern is the tyrant's mandate, red the gaze
> That flashes desolation, strong the arm
> That scatters multitudes. To-morrow comes!
> That mandate is a thunder-peal that died
> In ages past; that gaze, a transient flash
> On which the midnight closed, and on that arm
> The worm has made his meal.

We shall now quote what appears to us to be the noblest piece of poetry which the author ever imagined; and having done him that justice, refrain from further example, except in so far as may be necessary to show, that however gifted with talents, he has only heaped coals of fire upon his head by their perversion, and is a writer to be shunned, loathed, and execrated by every virtuous mind, as dangerous to the ignorant and weak, hateful to the lovers of social felicity, and an enemy to all that is valuable in life, or hopeful in eternity. The passage alluded to follows.

[*Quotes Canto IV, lines 1-70*]

We are afraid that we may be obnoxious to censure, for giving nearly all the brilliant parts of this poem, as they may excite a desire to peruse the whole; but our object in so doing (besides that truth demands it, and that we cannot help indulging a slight hope that the fiend-writer may yet be struck with repentance) is, that in our pages all that curiosity could long for might be gratified, and the impious volume whence we derive these extracts, be allowed to fall into oblivion, with all its deep pollutions and horrid blasphemies. For having selected the poetical beauties from the first four cantos, we have now, at page 42, reached the doctrinal inculcations of the author, which are heavy and inexplicable, having nothing to recommend them, if their heresies do not; nothing to induce any one to read them, unless he is prompted by a desire to see how daringly, as well as stupidly, a man can outrage every good feeling of the human heart, try to make life a chaos of sin and misery, and fling his filth against Omnipotence. But even if there are those whom curiosity would prompt to this, let them, we adjure them, be satisfied with what follows. The fairy instilling her poisons, thus speaks of that balm of afflicted souls, the Christian faith—

> Twin-sister of religion, selfishness!
> Rival in crime and falsehood, aping all
> The wanton horrors of her bloody play.
>
>   *   *   *
>
> How ludicrous the priest's dogmatic roar!
> The weight of his exterminating curse,
> How light! and his affected charity,
> To suit the pressure of the changing times,
> What palpable deceit!—but for thy aid,
> Religion! but for thee, prolific fiend,
> Who peoplest earth with demons, hell with men,
> And heaven with slaves!
> Thou taintest all thou lookest upon.[3]

And what substitute have we for piety, good-will to man, religion, and a God? The answer of this incarnate driveller is, a "Spirit of Nature! . . .

[*Continues the quotation, Canto VI, lines 197-219*]

The utter annihilation of every enjoyment which man can have on earth—the black catalogue of woes, to which so dreadful a creed as this must tend—the blank and dismaying prospect which it opens to the revolting sense—all the idiotcy of its conception, and all the villany of its avowal

---

[3] This is the beginning of the mixture of poetry, bombast, and blasphemy, entitled an Ode to Superstition, in 'Alastor.' (Reviewer's footnote.)

—deprive us of words to speak our detestation of its author. But the blaster of his race stops not here: in the very next page—we tremble while we transcribe it—he desperately, insanely asserts—

THERE IS NO GOD.

Miserable worm! Pity pleads for thee; and contempt, disgust, and horror, are tempered by compassion for thy wretched infirmity of mind. But an overwhelming passion rises when we gaze on the hideous blasphemy of thy more prolix commentary on this detestable text. We hardly dare copy it; but it is our duty to show to what monstrous extent the author carries his impious profanation.

[*Quotes Canto VII, lines 26-44*]

We cannot proceed: pages of raving atheism, even more atrocious than what we have quoted, follow; and the blasphemer revels in all the pruriency of his disordered and diabolical fancy. For men like the writer, when they are known to exist, there are no terms of infamy sufficiently strong. We may therefore say, in the mild language of Bentley, that as "no atheist, as such, can be a true friend, an affectionate relation, or a loyal subject," we leave to his conscience, at some awakened hour, this contemner of every thing that is good, this sapper of every thing that is sacred,—this demoniac proscriber of his species, and insolent insulter of his Maker.

To observe that extreme madness[4] and contradiction are notorious in every paragraph, is not enough; it is the bounden duty of those to whom the conservation of public morals is entrusted, to prohibit the sale of this pernicious book—

Deny the curst blasphemer's tongue to rage,
And turn God's fury from an impious age.

It is hardly worth while to ask how a theorist of Mr. Shelley's class would act in the relations between man and man. It can hardly be doubted but his practice would square with his principles, and be calculated to disturb all the harmonies of nature. A disciple following his tenets, would not hesitate to debauch, or, after debauching, to abandon any woman: to such, it would be a matter of perfect indifference to rob a confiding father of his daughters, and incestuously to live with all the branches of a family whose morals were ruined by the damned sophistry of the seducer; to such it would be sport to tell a deserted wife to obtain with her pretty face support by prostitution; and, when the unhappy maniac sought refuge in self-destruction, to laugh at the fool while in the arms of associate strumpets. For what are the ties of nature, what are the pangs of humanity, to them? They are above the idle inventions of tyrants and priests—the worthless restrictions of "morals, law, and custom,"—the delusions of virtue, and the ordinances of a deity. The key to their heaven is in the annexed lines.

[*Quotes Canto IX, lines 76-90*]

[4] Ex. gr. the following jargon:—(*Reviewer's footnote—Quotes Canto IV, lines 139-151*).

Promiscuous intercourse of the sexes, and individual "courage of soul," to despise every thing but the gratification of its own appetites: this is the millenium promised by the votaries of Shelley, and the worshippers of the god Necessity!

The notes are worthy of the poem; and it is said that those distinguished by an ☞ are the production of a noble lord, who once lived in unrestrained intimacy with the author, and partook of the pleasures of his free mode of testifying to the sincerity of his professed opinions. One of these is a dialogue between Vice and Falsehood; very proper interlocutors, for Falsehood says. . . .

[*Quotes Note IV, lines 49-53 and 89-108*]

Another has the following political illustration of the new philosophy.

English reformers exclaim against sinecures,—but the true pension-list is the rentroll of the landed proprietors: wealth is a power usurped by the few, to compel the many to labour for their benefit. The laws which support this system derive their force from the ignorance and credulity of its victims: they are the result of a conspiracy of the few against the many, who are themselves obliged to purchase this pre-eminence by the loss of all real comfort.

The domestic relations are of the same character.

[*Quotes Note V, paragraphs 2 and 4 and the first four and last two sentences of paragraph 6*]

Need we go farther to justify what we have said respecting this most infamous publication? We will not stain our pages with another line; and we trust to Heaven, that in discharging as painful and difficult a duty as ever fell upon a Review, we may be pardoned if we have acted unwisely, since we are sure we have acted conscientiously.

THE MONTHLY MAGAZINE DENIES QUARTER

[From The Monthly Magazine and British Register, June 1, 1821 (51: 460-461). The Monthly, from the number of its reviews and incidental comments, seems to have been somewhat interested in Shelley; but for a periodical considered radical enough to have The New Monthly set up as a corrective, its attitude toward Shelley is surprisingly stern. Its owner, Sir Richard Phillips, had himself been sentenced for publishing Paine's *The Age of Reason*.]

A poem entitled *Queen Mab*, by Mr. Percy Bysshe Shelley, was printed and distributed among his friends, about seven years ago; but has at length been published. The text of the work is in measured lines, of unequal length, which being divided into parcels, by means of Roman numerals, have the appearance of so many odes, but without rhyme. It is in the Thalaba style, which has been so bepraised by the poetasters of the present day. "He," says Dr. Johnson, "that thinks himself capable of astonishing, may write blank verse; but these that hope only to please, must condescend to rhyme." The Author before us does, indeed, endeavour to *astonish*, by the extravagance of his paradoxes, and the incongruity of his metaphors; and may, therefore, claim the right to print his lines of such various lengths as may suit his own whim or the taste of his compositor. It is a continuous declamation without either "rhyme or reason," and the speaker may pause where he will without injury to the sense or interruption to the monotonous flow of the harangue. The notes occupy much more space than the text; and consist chiefly of extracts from various authors, in favour of Atheism, the equalization of property, and the unrestrained intercourse of the sexes! The French, Latin, and Greek passages, which were left in their original dress in the gratuitous edition, are here translated for the benefit of the mere English reader. Advocates, as we are, for a very extended freedom of the press, we fear commenting further on this work, lest we should, unintentionally, assist in that *powerful* criticism, to which, we fear, it will soon be subjected. We have observed, of late, a seeming design to lure the unwary author to his destruction. The public journals, not even ex-cepting the Quarterly Review, have lauded Mr. Shelley as a poet,—as a genius of the highest order! The other panders of corruption speak of his "powerful talents"! What can all this flattery mean, if it be not to decoy the witless bird, and to catch him in the snare? Either this is the case, or our Critics are a set of dunces, who cannot distinguish between sublimity and bombast,—between poetry and "prose run mad."

A LIBERAL WEEKLY LAMENTS WASTED GENIUS

[From The Literary Chronicle and Weekly Review, June 2, 1821 (no. 107, pp. 344-345). Although The Literary Chronicle was friendly to Shelley and seems to have had some special connection with him in its publication of *Adonais*, it illustrates the fact that Shelley's moral and religious radicalism went too far for some who ad-mired him on other grounds.]

Mr. Shelley furnishes one of the most striking and melancholy in-stances of the perversion, or rather prostitution of genius, that we ever met with. With talents that, if properly directed, might have made him uni-versally admired and esteemed, he has made such a total wreck of his character, that he has not only armed society against him, but has almost put himself out of the pale of human laws. While we cannot but feel some portion of pity for a man of enlarged intellectual powers thus de-basing himself, we feel disgust at his licentious and incestuous principles, and horror at his daring impiety; and his very name—

> Comes over our memory,
> As doth the raven o'er th' infected house,
> Boding to ill.

The history of the poem of 'Queen Mab' is as curious as the subject is impious. Whether, when it was first written some years ago, a trader in blasphemy was not to be found, or that the author felt some dread at the injury a general diffusion of his work might occasion, we know not, but it was only circulated privately among the author's friends; it was afterwards, we believe, printed in the *Theological Enquirer;* and the first three cantos also appeared under the title of *The Demon of the World;* the notes being printed in a separate pamphlet. The whole are now, for the first time, brought together, and, as it would appear, without the knowledge of the author; the poem contains much powerful writing and many beautiful passages; but these make but a miserable atonement for the principles which it inculcates. The author is an avowed Atheist, who would shake off all laws, human and divine, and have a society rioting in lust and incest, and, as he himself terms it,—

> Unchecked by dull and selfish chastity.

We shall not quote another line from this baneful production, and shall only observe, that the private life of Mr. Shelley is said to be in unison with his principles; and that—

> His own example strengthens all his laws;
> And he's himself the *monster* that he draws.

Of the character of this poem, we might have been spared the labour of criticism, since a court of equity deemed its principles such, that the author ought not to be intrusted with the guardianship of his own children, of which he was in consequence deprived.

A man of Mr. Shelley's cultivated mind, cannot but possess strong feelings, and he must sometimes reflect on the ruin he has brought on himself, and on the probable injury he may have done to society; if he does so reflect, he must have a hell in his own conscience, which will torture him more severely than even the scorn of society and the abhorrence of all good men; and to that we consign him, sincerely wishing that this may be his only punishment, and that it may never be aggravated by the consciousness of having destroyed the happiness of others, either by his precept or example.

A RADICAL SEEKS SHELTER

REPLY TO THE ANTI-MATRIMONIAL HYPOTHESIS AND SUPPOSED ATHEISM OF PERCY BYSSHE SHELLEY AS LAID DOWN IN QUEEN MAB

[Printed and published by William Clark in 1821. On July 14, 1821 (p. 448) The Literary Chronicle announced *An Answer to Queen Mab* as in the press. Its authorship is unknown. Neither Clark nor his radical former friend and employer, Richard Carlile, seems quite capable of its tone or literary finish. The dissent from Shelley's views on matrimony coincides with Carlile's later dissent from these views, but Carlile accepted and rejoiced in Shelley as a declared atheist, whereas the present treatise seeks to show that Shelley's atheism is not real. The latter argument is thus capable of being considered an advance defence against a prosecution for blasphemous libel. Clark, who had just published *Queen Mab,* was notoriously timid and shifty when it came to taking the consequences. Before his trial he offered to surrender all unsold copies, and during his trial he cited the *Reply* as evidence that his purpose was not to advance Shelley's ideas. The second and third sentences of the prefatory letter, the concluding paragraph of Chapter I, and much of Chapter II seem to have been written in anticipation of just such use. Clark also surrendered all unsold copies and in his second piracy of Queen Mab omitted all supposedly blasphemous passages. For the robust scorn which his timidity excited in Richard Carlile, see the later excerpts from The Republican.

Lacking any specific evidence, the best pure guess at the authorship of this ably-written little book seems to be William Johnson Fox, later one of Browning's first encouragers and a leader in reform activities in the eighteen-thirties and forties. Fox was already a remarkably able dialectician and had only recently published his sermon On the Duties of Christians toward Deists, in which he bespoke toleration for Richard Carlile. His liberal Monthly Repository was the only monthly magazine to notice Clark's trial for publishing Queen Mab, and the notice was unusually full and friendly. Possibly Leigh Hunt, who was later connected with The Monthly Repository, also had some slight connection with the present publication, though he could hardly have written it himself. A letter from Horatio Smith to Shelley, quoted in Shelley and Mary, speaks of Clark's piracy and mentions seeing Clark coming from Leigh Hunt's house.]

To the
Publisher of Queen Mab

You have probably thought yourself conferring a benefit on the literary world, by the re-publication of Queen Mab. I say the literary world; for the splendid edition you have published, plainly indicates you did not intend to circulate it among those whom a certain portion of the press would call the "rabble readers." I do not dispute your motives; and I can readily agree that the glittering, though frequently illusive, beauties of the poem deserve preservation. As far as he wages war against positive errors of religion, and government, it is not my purpose to endeavour to confute his principles; but since he attacks an institution which I conceive to be the bond of the social union, I cannot allow the opportunity to pass without entering a decided protest against his anti-matrimonial hypothesis. He will have other, and abler opponents, on other topics; and perhaps on this;— but lest no one should accept his challenge of defiance to matrimony, I appeal to your impartiality, for the publication of the following pages.

I have also wandered into some analysis of what I think erroneously called his Atheistical tenets. I am aware Bacon says that "Atheism "leaves a man to sense, to philosophy, to natural "piety, to laws, to reputation:"— but I am not inclined to think that these principles leave a man to Atheism. However I am bold to say that Mr. Shelley is not an Atheist:—and were he to persist in an avowal of such a creed, I would say with Shakespeare:—

> *I would not hear your enemies say so;*
> *Nor shall you do mine ear that violence,*
> *To make it truster of your own report,*
> *Against yourself.*

THE AUTHOR.

CHAPTER I

ANTI-MATRIMONIAL THESIS OF QUEEN MAB

It is as common for great powers of imagination to lead writers into error, as for great natural powers to exhaust themselves, in useless feats, or ridiculous exploits. Nor does this detract from the value of such powers. The vigour necessary to give effect to the exertions of either body or mind, can as readily be ill as well employed. It may be confined to the beaten road, where it will the more readily reach its goal; or it may climb the precipice, or descend into the abyss, and destroy its energy without accomplishing any desirable object. Some without wings, it is true, will attempt to fly; but the consequences are not so lamentable, as where those who have the strongest pinions attract the public gaze, by soaring into unknown regions, and find their powers fail at so perilous a height.

Queen Mab is a glittering, rather than a splendid oddity. Much of what it would merit as a poem, is lost in the want of originality. The Fairy is the spirit of Volney's Ruins, trimly dressed for a new character. The execution of the design will bear no comparison with that of the work from which it is evidently copied; though it cannot be denied that the varying illustrations are given in an exalted strain of poetry. The scorn of slavery, and the contempt of slaves:—the hatred of hypocrisy, and the eager pursuit of truth and happiness, even where they are not to be found:—the indignation which tyranny excites; and the forcible contrast of its own wretchedness, whilst it makes others wretched:—even the enthusiastic dream of unattainable perfection, with which the poem closes:—all interest us strongly in favor of the writer's *wishes* for the happiness of the human species; but this only increases our regret that he should have directed them to a path, in which it would be ever sought in vain.

I am one of those who do not expect, nor even wish, that man should be completely changed in his nature, which would be a necessary prelude to this anticipated perfection. While he supposes himself about to confer upon humanity an ideal superiority over its present existence, he proposes in fact to create a *new world*, and to people it with a *new race!* It will be seen that he carries this idea, not merely to the extermination of all the aberrations of passion, but to the improvement of the face of nature. The "wastes of frozen billows," "hurled by *everlasting* snow storms round the poles," are to be "unloosed"; and "fragrant zephyrs," from "spicy isles," are to "melodize with man's blest nature there." The deserts of Arabia, are to

> . . . teem with countless rills and shady woods,
> Corn-fields, and pastures, and white cottages.

The wonders of Pope's Messiah, from which much of this matter, and all the ideas seem gathered, as those of the Messiah from Virgil and the prophets, are to be realized in this *new world:*—for

. . . where the startled wilderness beheld
A savage conqueror stained in kindred blood;
A tigress sating with the flesh of lambs
The unnatural famine of her toothless cubs,
Whilst shouts and howlings through the desert rang,
Sloping and smooth the daisy-spangled dawn,
Offering sweet incense to the sun-rise, smiles
To see a babe before his mother's door,
   Sharing his morning's meal
With the green and golden basilisk,
   That comes to lick his feet!

Every ocean is "to teem" with islands, at such convenient distances, that the sailor may not see as now:

Morning on night, and night on morning rise,
Whilst still no land to greet the wanderer spreads
Its shadowy mountains on the sun-bright sea.

These agreeable resting places will of course supersede the necessity of ships, and destroy all the dangers of navigation. The Venetian gondola, to harmonious music, over the ever placid wave, and with ever-favouring breezes, will serve all the purposes of marine intercourse; and remove the necessity of those perilous adventures in which our enterprising sailors are now embarked in the frozen regions of the north. Nay, he boldly tells us "all things are to be *re-created*." No storms are to deface the beauties of nature, and no excess of evil passion is to disturb the happiness of man!

What influence on this re-creation, by any possibility, can have the *conduct of man?* The *apparent* object of the poem, is to point out the baneful effects of superstition, vice, tyranny, and falsehood; to attribute the countless ills that curse humanity, to the bad passions, the mistaken self-interests, and the ignorance of men:—to call them, by the precepts of reason and virtue, to a proper sense of their own dignity; and to a consideration of the means of happiness which they have neglected. What has this to do with the *material world?*—with a reversal, or total change of the laws of nature; with studding the Atlantic with islands, or transferring the perfumes of Arabia to replace the dissolved ice-bergs of the pole? Could a universe of Shelleys, with all the sensibility, and virtue, which he recommends, effect the slightest change in the laws that govern the material world?—Could they transform a shower of snow into a halo of sunbeams—or bid the chilling breezes of the north blow as mildly as Italian zephyrs? out of respect to the "naked beauties" of Ianthe!

Virtue may overcome the severity of nature—and bloom as freshly and as vigorously beneath the frigid, or the burning, as the temperate zone. It is with reason Gray indignantly asks:—

Need we the influence of the northern star,
To still our souls, or string our nerves to war?
And where the face of nature laughs around,
Must sickening virtue fly the tainted ground?

Unmanly thought! No seasons can controul,
No fancied zone can circumscribe the soul;
Who conscious of the source from whence she springs,
By reason's light, on resolution's wings,
Spite of her frail companion, dauntless goes,
Through Lybia's deserts, and through Zembla's snows!
All little wants, all low desires refine,
And raise the mortal to a height divine?

This is placing things in a true light. The end of virtue is to despise those obstacles, which it cannot remove—to make that conducive to its splendour, which it is necessary to conquer:—not to change the face of nature, which is impossible; but to render nature, as it is, subservient, and conducive, to the happiness of humanity.

My principal object is to show that Mr. Shelley's scheme of sexual intercourse is not adapted either to the well-being, or the existence of Society, in a world like this; and I have deemed it just to show, that while he recommends it, as a great improvement, he does not take into consideration, any such world as ours; but a world purely ideal, which has scarcely any foundation in his own imagination. I say scarcely any foundation;— for if he had possessed decided and clear ideas upon the subject, he would not have confounded the contradictory ideas of a new world, and a reformation of the manners of the old! When his new world was created, it would have been ample time to lay down such a thesis of intercourse; if the creator of such new world had not spared Mr. Shelley the necessity of devising means for the supreme felicity of his creatures!

I believe every rational being will agree with Pope, that—

In the scale of reasoning life 'tis plain,
There must be somewhere such a rank as man;
And all the question, wrangle e'er so long,
Is only this, if God has placed him wrong?

The theory of Mr. Shelley is, that God has created knaves, and fools, instead of men: and he would have us believe that to get rid of the folly and knavery, would be to introduce a species superior to man; and a new modification of the external and material world, to suit his new order! The object of other philosophers, (admitting Mr. Shelley to be one) is to realize the philosophical idea of what man ought to be in the development of his reason;—Mr. Shelley is not satisfied with this; but would entrench upon the ideal world for a species of fabulous angles, of "faultless monsters, which the "world ne'er saw," to people his new regions.

All this, as a mere theory may amuse the volatile, and those who seek only amusement; and though useless, I will not call it dangerous. It is a common principle with man, to seek abroad for felicity, while it lies within his reach. Overlooking it at home, and not finding it elsewhere, he flies to the clouds, and is content to fancy, what, but for a most unfortunate sensibility, would court his actual enjoyment, without labour or research.

But when Mr. Shelley addresses himself directly to society, and deliberately proposes to loosen the keystone of its arch, he ceases to be "madly wild," and bcomes actually dangerous. His proposal to realize Mahomet's paradise on earth, is not merely an error. However disinterested the author of such a proposal might be, avails nothing. A child, with the most innocent intention in the world, might carry a torch amongst combustibles, and produce the most dreadful conflagration. He who should succeed in persuading society to cut the gordian knot of marriage, would do more towards the demoralization of his species, and the extinction of science, than all the tyrants, and all the hypocrites who ever lived. It is with these impressions, I propose to analyze his scheme of sexual intercourse.

In the poem itself, his ideas are not fully developed: though his conclusions are sufficiently palpable. The first passage to which it is necessary to refer, is in page forty-eight, of your edition, when speaking of the mischievous venality which the spirit of commerce, and the love of riches, has produced, he says:—

> *Even love is sold;*—the solace of all woe,
> Is turned to deadliest agony; old age
> Shivers in selfish beauty's loathing arms,
> And youth's corrupted impulses prepare
> A life of horror from the blighting bane
> Of commerce.

To the first four words of this quotation, is appended a note of some length, in which he enters more in detail into the subject of our difference. Before I proceed to this, let me remark, that the expression "even love is sold," in the text of his dissertation, is *a fallacy:*—and he himself demonstrates it to be such, when he adds that "old age shivers in *selfish beauty's* loathing arms!" In the instance he has offered, it is *not love* that is the object of *sale,* but "selfish beauty"; which whether *sold,* or *given,* affords no reason for his hypothesis. A better reasoner than Mr. Shelley has said—

> Judges and senates may be bought for gold;
> Esteem, and *love,* were *never* to be *sold!*

It is hardly to be presumed, if the institution of marriage were abolished, that mercenary beauty would not dispose of itself to the *best advantage;* and to hazard the proposition that a yearly, a monthly, or a diurnal sale, of such selfish charms, would better the condition of society, would be to hazard the probability of universal ridicule. Extinguish the *mercenary motive,* and good would be effected. Were not beauty venal, it would not prostitute itself to what it abhorred, either for a long, or a short period; but where the venality exists, it would be unnecessary to contend that it is wisely limited in its power of setting itself up for sale.

Mr. Shelley says "Law pretends even to govern the indisciplinable wanderings of passion, to put fetters on the clearest deductions of reason, and, by appeals to the will, to subdue the involuntary affections of our nature." In the instance selected for the illustration of this description of the law, it does no such thing. In too many instances, I confess, laws have put fetters on the deductions of reason; but in the institution of marriage, I can perceive no such manacling;—nor do they pretend to *govern* the passions; because it is quite evident they cannot govern them. I do not understand how "appeals to the will," are to subdue "our involuntary affections." Laws *appeal* to nothing; still less would they appeal to the *will*—and least of all would they appeal to *our wills*, against our *involuntary affections*. General laws are meant to regulate our conduct to each other, within certain rules; that the confidence necessary for the social union may be maintained. A principle laid down by the law, is promulgated as a general rule; and in the confidence that this rule will be respected by all; or that if violated, society will punish the violator, it is recognized as a general principle of action. Law speaks only to the judgment. The laws relative to the institution of marriage have probably less effect than any other species of law;—on account of those passions which they cannot control, and which they fear to punish. On *man* they are seldom considered binding. His caprice, or his passion, is continually despising, and overleaping them:—but though they are not so binding upon man, as their nature should require, they are still in some measure the protection of WOMAN; and, in any state of society, form almost the only protection she can receive from the social law. The rights of men are to a certain extent secured, because man fears man; and dreads to do wrong, lest the wrong should be amply revenged. But man does not fear woman; and it is only in his sense of *honour*, that she has any security, beyond the respect which is ensured her by the name of wife! The marriage law secures her rank in society; renders that protection an obligatory duty where it would not be voluntarily performed; and, in the absence of affection, compels man in some measure to be just!

What protection against distress, misery, infancy, and old age, would the scheme of Mr. Shelley confer on woman? "Love," says he, "is inevitably consequent on the perception of loveliness." This is not true, in the sense in which love is here employed. Every man does not love every woman in whom he perceives loveliness. It could not even be a consequence of inculcating the idea, that man like the butterfly should pass from flower to flower, and revel in the sweets of every beauty; for nature would mock his powers of enjoyment, by the endless renewals of loveliness and beauty, with which she would deride his sated appetite. But to inculcate this idea would be to sacrifice every sensation, which

Fill the languid pause with finer joy!

It would be to brutalize man, and to degrade woman—to fill the earth with such worthless beings as seek all pleasure in mere sensual gratifications; and such females as minister to the pleasure of man without any participation in his gross delights.

The old tale that "love withers under constraint; that its very essence is liberty; that it is compatible neither with obedience, jealousy, nor fear:" —is as ridiculous as untrue. Whilst love exists, it *feels* no restraint. It is perfectly immaterial whether it be enclosed with flowery hedges, or massy walls. With no wish to stray from its bower, it cares not whether the boundary be near or distant. It cannot become impatient of restraint; and when that impatience is felt, love has already vanished. Love has no preference for liberty, for it chooses its bondage. It delights to serve; finds service perfect freedom; and its essence, so far from being liberty, is the most decided slavery:—

> The sweetest bondage it is true,
> That ever human slavery knew,
> But it is bondage still!

Obedience is too tame an epithet, for its anxiety to serve. Its jealousy, lest any one should presume to share its service, is so notorious as to be proverbial; and its fear is as excessive as its fondness. Really, Mr. Shelley, from his practice, ought to have known the divinity better. It may be allowed this writer, that love is "*most* pure, *most* perfect, and *most* unlimited, where its votaries live in confidence, equality, and unrestraint." But there are a thousand intermediate degrees before we reach this superlative definition:—and at each of them a man might do well to pause, and ask himself whether by changing the shrine, his devotion would be more acceptable to the deity, or better calculated to ensure happiness to himself.

"How long then ought the sexual connection to last?" asks Mr. S. The laws of society say, that without *moral*, or physical cause, be shewn against it, it ought to last during the lives of the parties! They endeavour to prevent individuals from choosing companions, until they are *capable* of forming a correct judgment of themselves, and the partners they are about to choose. They declare that one female alone can be recognized as the wedded wife of one man. They declare that he who selects a woman is bound to maintain and to protect her; and if he neglect his duty, the laws endeavour to enforce it. The laws have nothing to do with love, or affection. Where they exist, the civil laws are *mere* formalities; and the bonds are neither felt nor heeded. Where they do not exist, or where they have existed, and exist no longer, the laws step in to protect the female, as far as their authority can interfere; and to secure her rights as a member of society. No law binds, or could bind, parties to a cohabitation which they abhorred. No law professes to do this. Marriages are virtually dissolved, and the individuals separate, when the yoke becomes unbearable to either party; and the laws only provide, as far as they can, that society shall not suffer wrong, nor the weaker party endure more than the evils of separation, by the caprice, the inconstancy, or the guilt of man!

By *love* our author seems only to mean, the ungovernable emotion, which beauty first awakens in the bosom of maturing manhood. This furious impulse is of the most evanescent description. Satiety succeeds to enjoyment; and for the *same person,* the same maddening sensation can seldom, if ever, be again awakened. While that individual continued to be an object of the affections, the sensation could be awakened for no other; but is this furor alone worthy of the name of love? Is it to be constantly excited for some *new object,* that it may be continually in existence? and are fresh victims to be periodically sacrificed to this inordinate avarice of beauty? which would then become a greater curse than the avarice of gold! Suppose all men acting in this mode, they would cut each other's throats, as fast as they destroyed the happiness of the female portion of society. Murder and debauchery would be the "twin fiends of desolation"; and the imagined paradise of Queen Mab, would become in verity the worst of hells.

Woman can never be raised upon the stage of this bustling world, into an equality with man. Her very virtues, her beauties, her excellencies, forbid it. Beauty is the universal object of desire; and what men desire, they will obtain, by any means in their power. Women have no intuitive knowledge to discover the truth of affection, from its dissembled counterfeit. Prone to believe "what seems but fair," how are they to detect the guile that lurks beneath the specious promise of the flatterer's tongue! What security have they for the reality of an affection? or if real, that it might last the passing of a single moon? It is proposed to hold out to every man, the idea of obtaining as many women as he could deceive; and of abandoning with impunity those whom he has betrayed into affection for so dishonourable a wretch. The author of Queen Mab complains of the state of society! It may be bad enough; but this method of mending it, would be to replace the noisy puppies that infest our streets, by tigers and hyenas.

We now arrive at some of the most senseless and absurd jargon, that ever affected sensibility reduced to language—if that may be called language, which inverts its purpose, and *confounds,* instead of *assisting,* the understanding. I must quote the words, or I should be considered as creating shadows, for the purpose of dispelling them. He says—"if happiness be the object of morality, of all human unions and disunions; if the worthiness of every action is to be estimated by the quantity of pleasurable sensation it is calculated to produce, then the connection of the sexes is so long sacred, as it contributes to the comfort of the parties, and is naturally dissolved, when its evils are greater than its benefits. There is nothing *immoral* in this separation. *Constancy has nothing virtuous in itself,* independently of the pleasure which it confers, and partakes of the *temporizing spirit of vice,* in proportion as it endures tamely moral defects of magnitude in the object of its indiscreet choice. Love is free: To promise for ever to love the same woman, is not less absurd than to promise to believe the same creed: such a vow, in both cases, excludes us from all enquiry. The language of the votarist is this.—'The woman I now love may be infinitely inferior to many others; the creed I now profess may be a mass of errors and absurdities; but I exclude myself from all future information as to the amiability of the one, and the truth of the other, resolving blindly, and in spite of conviction, to adhere to them.'—Is this the language *of delicacy,* and *reason?*—Is the love of such a frigid heart of more worth than its belief?"

It is said Mr. Shelley was *very young* when he wrote this; and it would require the apology of a nonage when the pen and the hand had as little intercourse, as these rhapsodies have connection with the head, or the heart. That happiness, in the sense here implied, is the object of *morality,* is preposterous. Morality points out the strict line of duty. The leading object is *justice*—and it does not leave man at liberty, to seek his own happiness at the expense of the well being, or the peace of others. Man sighs for the possession of woman:—he engages her affections: fixes all her hopes and chance of happiness upon his constancy:—but he has already enjoyed her—his palled appetite wanders after more tempting, because more novel, charms;—and in this new code of morals, he may say—"I am no longer happy in your society,—happiness was my object in the union. I must now seek it in disunion, and fresh engagements. I am extremely sorry:—my comfort requires a separation. Adieu!" What must he be, who could hold this language to an affectionate, astonished, deceived, and broken-hearted woman? Men may be often false;—may often forget the vows sworn at the altar, and venture to taste "forbidden fruits:" but to make falsehood a creed, villainy a profession, and injustice a moral duty, is a measure of guilt, for which language has no adequate expression.

An affection cannot be supposed to expire at the *same moment,* between individuals of opposite sexes. We have a thousand instances, in which the love of woman has survived coldness, treachery, desertion, insult, and privation—where it still clung to the father of the children, when it could no longer be felt for the husband of the wife:—and suppose the fondness of woman undiminished, at the moment when man finds it a "moral duty" to abandon her, in search of "happiness," and "comfort." Is there, *then,* nothing *immoral,* nothing *criminal,* in devoting the deserted object of this injustice, to a life of wretchedness—the more acute, as it admits of no alleviation; and which is heightened by the convenient "morality," which permits the object of her solicitude to seek his own "happiness," by reducing all who will trust his falsehood to the same desperate condition. "When the evils of the connection of the sexes, ARE greater than its benefits," separation necessarily ensues; but so attractive, so necessary, is woman; such are the endearing and lasting ties which the relations of husband and wife, father, mother, and children, weave around the heart, that it is not in the power of many evils to overbalance the advantages of that connection. While "passions are the elements of life," the discordance of temper, and the strife of opposing wills, amid the varied incidents of life, will agitate the mental and moral atmosphere, as nature is agitated by the winds; but as destructive convulsions are of rare occurrence; so is it almost as rarely that the evils of the matrimonial state are felt to surpass its advantages. Fathers and mothers are often dissatisfied with their children; and frequently with cause; yet it is seldom we hear any wish they were childless; and when the wish is expressed by the tongue, the heart is not always ready to concur. Bachelors laugh at marriage, and then marry:—husbands rail at matrimony; and wish they were again single:—that, should fate listen to them, they may marry again! Even Mr. Shelley has been married *twice*,[5] after having had an opportunity, at least, of trying the preponderating blessings of his novel scheme. Whatever authority his own example might have given to his precepts, is entirely lost. Perhaps it would not be assuming too much, to say that his experience has made him a convert to matrimony. Should this be the case, he owes society the duty of recording his conversion.

If *justice* be *virtue*, constancy is virtue. Even supposing that a man should sacrifice his happiness, by his constancy, has he not *sworn* that he will be constant? Will he adopt the paltry subterfuge, that he did not know what he was about to promise? Will he plead his folly, to excuse his caprice? I am not speaking of the matrimonial law—but, suppose it entirely abrogated, such an oath, or a promise which ought not to be considered less binding than an oath, must be the preliminary means of obtaining woman. The marriage would not be less real, in the eye of reason, if the priest were absent, and the law annulled. The union would still have all the force of a solemn contract. No woman would surrender herself to the pleasures of a libertine, avowedly on the tenure of his good liking. Even Mr. Shelley does not assert the abolition of formal marriages "would lead to promiscuous intercourse." Then the contract must be made between the parties; and does he mean to say, that either would, or ought to reserve the right of separation, when caprice should suggest the convenience of change? Would it be less dishonorable to break such an engagement, than any other? At any rate, should not *both* concur in such separation, before it could be deemed just? This brings us back to the present condition of affairs. Where both agree to separate, the law is useless. It cannot compel cohabitation; and if it impose any privations upon parties, their mistaken judgment is the cause. Society must protect itself:—and the squabbles of a few individuals cannot be considered. The lesser evil must be endured to prevent the greater. In our author's new world, these things may be managed better;—but we must wait for its re-creation; and in the mean time be as comfortable as we can.

"Constancy has nothing virtuous in itself, independently of the pleasure it confers!" Indeed, Mr. Shelley! Such language would only be in character with a selfish boy, who would engross the honey-pot to himself, until it made him sick. Is there nothing virtuous in a constancy, which would sacrifice its own pleasure, to *avoid giving pain* to a woman, who had placed all her hopes of happiness in that constancy? Is *self* to be the ever-

---

[5] I forbear indulging in any commentary upon the conduct of Mr. Shelley, as contrasted with his written principles; because rumour has adopted slanders, and exaggerated facts. (Reviewer's footnote.)

lasting, and only thought? Is man never to remember there are other creatures in existence, whose well-being ought to be consulted, as well as his pleasure? The nonsense about "moral defects of magnitude," is puerile in the extreme. Both law, and reason, allow of separation for just cause; —the object of Mr. Shelley's theory is to shew that separation for *any* cause, or *any* caprice, is justifiable! This is the point at issue between him and the world.

"To promise for ever to love the *same woman,* is not less absurd, than to promise to believe the same creed!" Good, now! Mr. Shelley, your reason? Were this pressed hard upon you, you would probably with Falstaff exclaim, "If reasons were as plenty as black-berries, I would not give you one upon compulsion!" A *woman* resemble a religious creed! When I promise to believe a creed, I promise only that I will believe it, until its falsehood is pointed out. The variest fanatic has this conditional reservation. It is the nature of such promises; and they cannot be otherwise made, or construed. It may be difficult, or impossible, to convince a fanatic; but he does not tell you he would maintain his creed, *if it were* proved false. He holds it, because he is satisfied it cannot be proved false. He does *not* admit "the creed he professes *may* be a mass of errors and absurdities"; so far from it, he would go to the stake for the contrary opinion, that it was impossible it should contain either error, or absurdity. Nor does any votary of love admit, "the woman he then loves *may* be infinitely inferior to many others." In the points of preference which determine his choice, he must, on the contrary, contend she is *superior* to all others:—and if he be *competent to judge,* while those excellencies remain, his reasons for preference will continue. He selects that woman who most promises to realize his ideas of happiness!—Surely woman has the same reason to urge in her behalf, on which Othello reposes his confidence in Desdemona—"she had her eyes and chose him"! To plead for an allowance, on the part of want of judgment, is well enough in a boy, who may wish to change his plaything; but it is unworthy of a man, who ought to be better acquainted with his feelings, and his reason. Could man replace woman in the advantageous situation, in which he found her:—could he restore her charms untasted, her bloom unchanged, her affections uninjured;—even then her *consent* would be necessary to give any colouring of justice to a separation; but in the impossibility of this,— with certain loss, and absolute injury to her;—after having rendered her less desirable to others, to throw her from himself, in search of other charms to ruin and betray, on the pretence of promoting his own "comfort," is a proposition that has more of the devil in it, than of the man.

Where marriages are unhappy, he says they make *hypocrites,* or *open enemies.* There may be tempers with whom perfect happiness, or even comparative comfort, is not to be expected. But here, perhaps the institution of marriage has its advantages. Such spirits would be unquiet every where, and in any species of intercourse. In some cases the passionate excess of love subsides into rational esteem, and calm affection. In others, affection nearly evaporates, and esteem alone remains. In others, the union is cemented by a respect for the ordinary decorums of life, and an anxiety for the welfare of an offspring. In some few, the temper breaks out into open violence against all forms, and principles; and all duties are neglected. But it is for Mr. Shelley to shew that in the state of unbridled *liberty*, on the part of man, for this must be the effect of his theory, *greater hypocrisy* would not be resorted to, for the purpose of *betraying* the individuals than is now employed to deceive the world—that *greater enmity* would not arise from the *desertions* of those who were betrayed, than arises now from the impossibility of dissolving the marriage tie! What brother, what father, would suffer a daughter, or a sister, to be abandoned, at the caprice of a two-legged ape of manhood, who thought he saw a brilliant butterfly at a distance, which his "morality" taught him he might have some pleasure in running down? It would be an absolute duty for every one interested in the honor, and happiness of woman, to wear swords, not "for fashion's sake," but to teach those who approached them, they were not to be injured with impunity.

Mr. S. says the children of unfortunate marriages are "nursed in a systematic school of ill humour, violence, and falsehood." Allow this to be the case, though the whole are rarely combined, would it mend the matter, to nurse them in the school of their mother's injuries; to be brought up to consider one of the authors of their existence, as the destroyer of the other's peace? Or to nurse them in the school of hatred towards a step-father, whose harshness and injustice might implant the bitterest principles of revenge? Or, if taken from the mother, at the period of the separation, to be nursed in the school of contemptuous neglect, by a step-mother? Or, not to be nursed in any school, but left to gather what weeds they might chance to select, on the wild common of bandoned nature?

It is strange that in condemning hypocrisy, as a fruit of unhappy marriages, he should propose *hypocrisy* as a means of perpetuating his *ad libitum* connexions. Yet so it is; for he says, "if this connexion were put upon a *rational* basis, each would be assured that habitual ill temper would terminate in separation; and would check *(disguise)* this vicious and dangerous propensity"! This is little more than saying, that a harlot would be extremely civil, lest she should not be sufficiently rewarded. It is somewhat curious too, that even in his "recreated world," the scene of "absolute perfection," when every natural evil should have vanished; he does not expect to *get rid* even of "*habitual* ill temper";—his only hope is to *disguise* it lest it should be punished! The fancies of this brilliant dreamer are not made of more substantial stuff, than the dreams of less favoured mortals.

As he proceeds, he gets bolder:—and he has reason for it. Being so deeply entangled in the web of sophistry, his only hope of effect, is to wrap fold on fold, in the desperate chance of entangling his readers. He tells us, that "*prostitution is the legitimate offspring of marriage, and its accompanying errors!*" One would have thought, from his hypothesis, that prostitution should be hailed as the *natural means* by which the *political evils* of *marriage* were to be remedied. Instead of speaking of prostitution as *an evil*, he should have contended for it as a *comparative good*, as far as it extends;—and lamented that it was not a universal practice, instead of a partial one. What is prostitution, but a *promiscuous* intercourse; and what but promiscuous intercourse of the sexes does Mr. Shelley recommend? Man is to seek whatever is lovely—to remain no longer attached to one object than while he finds it convenient; and to change as often as his judgment or his caprice sets before him a "lovelier object." His theory is, that enjoyment alone should be aimed at; and that every *man* is at perfect liberty to pursue every variety of enjoyment. He says, indeed, towards the close of his note, "I by no means *assert* that the intercourse would be promiscuous"; but it is quite evident, whatever Mr. Shelley may choose to assert, that to this "it must come at last." The reasons against promiscuous intercourse he is able to perceive. The "relation of parent to child," which should render the sexual union of "long duration, and marked above all others with generosity and self-devotion," is the justification of the marriage laws; for the history of *man* sufficiently proves that, without an obligation, the great majority of fathers might abandon their children, as readily as they cast from their bosoms the deluded, trusting females, who have been the instruments of their pleasures. Look at the world! Does any *gentleman* think himself at all obliged to notice either the objects, or the fruits of his illicit intercourse? In all cases of *seduction*, we may see what would be the *effects* of the abolition of marriage. There it is, in effect, *abolished* inasmuch as it is *disregarded*; and there is no law to compel any observance of it. The love, in many instances, is probably *mutual*. Rank may forget its authority, and wealth its influence, for the moment. Man sighs, vows, and betrays:—woman believes, confides, and is undone. The treasure is rifled; and the robber hastes on the high-road of pleasure to make other victims. The institution of marriage *checks*, though it does not eradicate this evil. It takes care, at least, that part of the female sex shall be, in some degree, protected from the caprice of the *lords* of the creation. It takes care that some portion of the rising generation shall be properly provided for. It lessens the evils of prostitution, and seduction; though it cannot annihilate them, while interest and inclination are encouraged at the expence of justice. There is now a multitude of women, whom licentiousness *dare* not approach with its contaminating lust. The protection afforded to women by fathers, brothers, and friends, in some compensation for the evident partiality of the laws to man. Still too many females fall a sacrifice to infamy, without being guilty of any crime, but that of trusting to the honor of some villain:—and yet it is gravely proposed to subject every woman to dependance on that honor, as a remedy for the evil! Infatuation never put forth a more gross absurdity. Impudence never advanced a more daring violation of reason.

How is prostitution to be diminished by reducing the world into a general brothel? Suppose, by some singular chance, a male and female Shelley

happened to meet each other, entangled by a variety of other engagements
—the male Shelley with a wife and children—the female Shelley with a
husband and family. Of course, they would recognise each other immediately as the "loveliest specimens" of "creation." That "love is
inevitably consequent upon loveliness," is an article of the new code. Of
course, the female Shelley must love the male Shelley; and the male the
female! The female must at once abandon all previous love and regard
for her first husband, and transfer them to the "lovelier object." The
memory of all past endearments must pass away, to make room for new
sensations. Her children must be abandoned, as well as her duty forgotten.
The new impulse will awaken new desires, and to satisfy them she must
break through all engagements. Her husband may not have exchanged his
affections. He may not have seen a "lovelier object";—and may be left
broken-hearted and despairing, at the wreck of his happiness. Nevertheless, the male Shelley, heedless of the happiness he destroys, has a right
to consult his own. His own wife he is tired of, and seeing a "lovelier
object," his soul expands, and his arms are outstretched to receive her.
His wife is left to wait also "for a lovelier object," and to hopeless
misery, if her affections remain undiminished. To be sure the *lovely*
beings who thus desert all duties, may leave their families behind them,
for the consolation of those who are deserted; as they may have a
fresh offspring to provide for, from their newer loves! And thus *double
adultery* would be the *remedy* for *prostitution!* It is easy to perceive that
such a picture might be much heightened. Instead of the two *loveliest*
objects of the species meeting, while entangled with single engagements,
it might be after a series of transfers from lovely, to lovelier, and lovelier,
and lovelier still; until the embraces of a moderately decorous courtezan of
the present age, would be comparative purity, to the numerous debaucheries
through which the loveliest of the species had wallowed, in their progress
to each other's arms. Modern sensibility may not be shocked at this; but
I am certain old fashioned morality would startle at the mere proposal of
such a system.

It is singular that Mr. Shelley should pretend to any respect for the
happiness and well-being of woman, while laying down a code that would
tear from her all the security she has of being treated as a rational creature.
He affects to lament, that "Women, for no other crime than having followed the dictates of a natural appetite, are driven from society." Does he
not perceive that it is not the law, but the *individual man*, (on whom Mr.
Shelley would confer still more power to treat woman thus barbarously)
who drives her from society? It is not the law which compels a man to
support the woman he has married, that shuts prostitutes out of the pale
of society. It is the *want of laws* to compel every man to support, as
respectably as his means allow, those whom he has seduced. Seduction with
impunity, which Mr. Shelley would *render universal*, is the *evil* that ought
to be cured. Society does not "declare war against the prostitute";—she
is first *seduced*, and then *driven*, to declare war against society. She who

has yielded herself to one man, becomes less desirable to others. Is it this feeling that Mr. Shelley would eradicate? Would he contend that delicacy on this point is entirely misplaced—that

> beauty should be kind to all who love?

If this be his object, the sensibility of which he boasts is not very acute. But this opinion it is the less necessary to impugn; as the feelings of the great majority of the world will ever be arrayed against it; and there is no fear of such notions becoming current. Whatever gratification the most profligate father in existence might feel in endless debauchery, he would shrink from the propagation of its tenets in his own family. There is something so beautiful in decency and virtue, that the vilest wretches are anxious their children should be, what they cannot hope to be themselves.

The evils of prostitution are extreme:—and are the more to be regretted, as they certainly spring, in a great measure, from the want of laws, which *man* has neglected to frame, lest his gratifications should be limited;—and from certain principles, not embodied into laws, but which are inculcated in such a manner as to render them more operative than laws. Thus, it is considered *disgraceful* for a *gentleman* to degrade himself by a marriage with a poor, fond, deluded woman, whose all of happiness and hope has been sacrificed for his amusement—whose life has been rendered miserable and infamous by his treachery and falsehood—whose reputation, tainted by him, is held cheaply by all besides. The father of an illegitimate child feels no shame at the knowledge that his offspring is abandoned to all the evils of poverty, or the temptations of guilt. A small sum paid to the parish compensates for the crime, and annihilates the necessity of feeling. It is ONLY an illegitimate child; and whether a miserable existence be terminated by the hangman, or by disease engendered by distress, is immaterial to the *gentleman* father! What becomes of the mother, is a matter of still less consideration with the seducer. She is old enough to work. The parish does not insist upon a maintenance for her; and the fine feelings of our *gentleman* are not in the slightest degree affected by the knowledge, that premature old age has wasted that beauty to the grave, which was once an object of the highest desire. Is it to such a race as this, that the honor, and happiness, of the whole female race, should be trusted without some better security, than the chance of being beloved while no fairer object of loveliness should tempt the licensed senses to fresh enjoyment! With the volume of unspeakable misery before us, which the vagrant disposition of man occasions to that part of the female world with which he can sport at pleasure, would it be wise, or prudent, or just, to subject the *whole* to his unbridled passions?—to break down all the fences which morality and reason have established, to enable man to enjoy a few additional moments of rapture, purchased at the price of so much agony to woman?[6]

---

[6] It would be here out of place to enter into any examination of the defence usually set up by wealth and cunning for the seduction of ignorance, and poverty. But I cannot refrain

Upon this question, Mr. Shelley takes not into the account any consideration of the happiness or advantage of the female. She is the mere instrument of male gratification—the passive and unconsulted medium of his transports. If this were not evident from the fact that such unlimited license would only be available to man, it would be found in his simile between *love,* and *belief.* A woman, he says, may be rejected, when another more lovely appears;—as a creed may be dismissed, when it is shewn to be inferior to another. The argument, of course, supposes the *lady* as *insensible* and indifferent as the *creed!* No mischief is done to the creed, by the desertion:—*ergo,* says Mr. Shelley, no mischief could be done to the lady, by an abandonment. The creed cannot feel slighted;—*ergo,* the lady ought not to feel herself insulted. The creed is not rendered the less eligible to other admirers;—*ergo,* the lady is in the same situation, and remains as desirable to others, as before! The creed is only a series of sentences, well or ill put together:—*ergo,* the lady is only a beautiful human form, with no mind, no affections, no feelings, no rights! The creed is a mere combination of the letters of the alphabet, which combination may be changed at the pleasure of the party;—*ergo,* the lady is only an ornament, which may be changed, on the slightest variation of taste on the part of the lover! Is it necessary to waste any time, in the refutation of such contemptible, but yet such dangerous opinions! The least degree of reflection would fortify the weakest mind against their adoption; but, unfortunately they are addressed to the senses upon a subject on which they never reflect. The passions hurry us along, and in their fury leave us no time for thought. The pleasure tempts too strongly. Every natural impulse swells the tide of passion:—and men rarely awaken to remorse, until the power of doing wrong is exhausted, or the evil is irreparable. This is the weak point, "where most our reason fails us:" and it is therefore the paramount duty of every author to encrease, and not to diminish the defences. With writers who propose to change existing institutions, this precaution, and this duty, are the most imperious. Who would attempt to stop the current of a rapid stream, without providing a safe channel for the reception of its diverted waters?

A man, whose reason is collected, and whose passions have had time to cool, may read the reveries of Queen Mab, upon this head, without any danger; but to the juvenile mind of either sex, the possible evils are so extensive, and so palpable, as naturally to alarm all who are anxious for the happiness of woman, or the peace of man! What is meant by the expression, that "*Chastity* is a *monkish* and *evangelical superstition:*—a

---

from remarking, that the ignorance, low birth, and want of affluence, which pride insists are sufficient reasons for declining to form matrimonial connections;—ought to be still stronger reasons for the punishment of seduction in the severest manner; for surely it is most criminally despicable, to endeavour to render these disqualifications the means of triumph over female virtue, which already are of sufficient disadvantage to the parties, without the addition of infamy superadded, by those who urge them as objections against their elevation to respectability. (Author's footnote.)

greater foe to *natural temperance,* even than unintellectual sensuality; it strikes at the root of all domestic happiness, and consigns more than half of the human race to misery, that some few may monopolize according to law"! Is the author of such sentiments anxious to qualify himself for Bedlam? Does he envy the felicitous ravings of incurable lunatics? I have heard that *celibacy* is a monkish superstition: and I can believe it injurious to the interests of society; but chastity and celibacy have no necessary connection with each other! On such a topic, it is hardly possible to enlarge. One can only shudder at the insult offered to decency, morality, and justice. He himself seems to shrink from his proposition, when he denies supposing that *promiscuous intercourse* would follow the abolition of marriage; but he must have contemplated a promiscuous intercourse, when he pronounced this outrageous anathema against chastity:—and again when he says—"Young men, excluded by the *fanatical idea* of chastity, from the society of *modest* and accomplished women, associate with vicious and miserable beings, &c." How can *modesty* be separated from the idea of *chastity?* How could it escape the grossest rhapsodist, that the *vicious* and *miserable* beings to whom he alludes, have become so from the loss of that *chastity,* of which he would deprive modest and accomplished women? Would he have his modest and accomplished women visited for the same purposes, and treated in the same manner, as the vicious and miserable outcasts of society? If Mr. Shelley dare answer *yes*—what door would be ever opened to receive him, which a father, a husband, or a brother, could shut in his face?

That such opinions are not now maintained by him, I would earnestly hope; but they remain uncontradicted; and he cannot be ignorant that they are in circulation as his opinions. That the work has not been on public sale, for some years, has probably rather added to its circulation; for it is certain that a work which cannot be obtained without difficulty, is not only more extensively read, from the impulse which curiosity affords; but it is read with more eagerness, and attention, than it would otherwise be. Young men, in particular, almost *devour* the contents of such works. They fear no other opportunity may be afforded for the perusal:—copies are made of detached passages:—they are talked of with rapture, as hidden novelties, and circulated from hand to hand, with inconceivable rapidity. What is trifling in itself is thus elevated into importance. The faults of a performance are overlooked, and its merits over-rated. To suppress any work, in the present state of society, I am convinced is utterly impossible; and any attempt to do so, only increases what mischief there may be.—A work openly sold, is open to reply; and the antidote may be circulated with the poison. But where suppression is attempted, the poison circulates alone, with as much rapidity, and with tenfold effect. I scarcely ever met with a young reader who had not carefully studied Paine's Rights of Man, and Age of Reason, during the period of their nominal suppression. Since they have been comparatively easy to be procured, I know many who have bought, but never read them. I therefore think you have rendered the doctrines less pernicious by an open publication, than they have been in their silent, though not less extensive, wanderings through private circles; with all the additional importance that mystery and curiosity could confer upon them.—The good sense of the public mind can determine for itself. The collision of opinion produced by discussion is favorable to correct decisions: and that which is subjected to an open test, is less likely to influence weak or inexperienced minds improperly, than what is addressed to them in secret, and comes recommended by prohibition.

CHAPTER II

ON THE SUPPOSED ATHEISM OF QUEEN MAB

I SHALL NOW trouble you with a few comments, on what is called the Atheism of Mr. Shelley.—When reduced to its nature, and stripped of the mystic veil, in which he endeavours to shroud it, it will be found as harmless, as it appears monstrous. His muse has the effect of a magic lanthorn. It is only the light, situation, and medium, through which we view his paradoxes, that render them so alarming. The very terrible creations of the lanthorn are deceptions produced from the most ordinary, and least formidable materials; and attract our attention from what they seem to be, not what they are:—so the illusions of Mr. Shelley startle us, because their real nature is disguised in the exaggeration of description. To dispel these shadows, however, is of comparatively little importance. What concerns our practice, comes home to the bosoms and business of us all; but our opinions may be indulged in more excursive flights;—and if the world of realities be not disturbed by the fictions of our dreamers, we may pardon them for building their castles in the air; and either giving, or denying,

. . . to airy nothing
A local habitation and a name!

Of the fairies of his own creation, Mr. Shelley may dispose as he pleases:—either by gift, by lottery, or by sale:—but while he cannot make the present race of human beings better, it is not to be endured that he should make them worse, by recommending the *extension* of an acknowledged evil, as a means of securing the general good! This he has done by recommending the abolition of the marriage ceremony; but when he recommends atheism, he offers a chalice to the lips of which the wise and the good will refuse to drink, while the vicious and the ignorant will fear to taste.

An ordinary reader of the first cantos would believe him a profound theist. His first allusion to this subject, is an appeal to the *Spirit of Nature*, in p. 12, at the close of the first canto, in which he has borrowed the same idea of divinity which Pope adopts:—as of a spirit that—

Lives through all life, extends through all extent.

After describing the scene to which the Fairy conducts the soul of Ianthe, he declares it to be the fitting temple for the Spirit of Nature; while nevertheless the lightest leaf, the meanest worm, are equally instinct with the eternal breath. In p. 16, we have the epithets of "changeless nature," and "eternal nature's law," as regulating the eloquent harmony of the "circling systems." At p. 19, we have an appeal to "the poor man's God," to sweep from the face of the earth something which displeases Mr. Shelley. Then we are asked, what must have been the nature of the being who taught that

> . . . the God
> Of Nature and benevolence had given
> A special sanction to the trade of blood?

The close of the second Canto gives us some peculiar reasoning, and singular opinions—such as that every atom of the earth was once living man—that every drop of rain had circulated in human veins—that cities had, at one or other period, covered the surface of the globe—and that insects think, feel, and live like man:—but no glimpse of atheism. In pages 30, and 31, we have the following stanza, in which a bold and just comparison is made with that Being, whose existence he afterwards denies:—

> Spirit of nature, no!
> The pure diffusion of thy essence throbs
> Alike in every human heart:
> Thou aye erectest there
> Thy throne of power unappealable:
> Thou art the judge beneath whose nod,
> Man's brief and frail authority
> Is powerless as the wind,
> That passeth idly by.
> Thine the tribunal which surpasseth
> The shew of human justice,
> *As* GOD *surpasseth man!*

Who would have imagined, from such language, he could ever arrive at the startling proposition, *"there is no God!"* In the following stanza, p. 31, we have man unconsciously fulfilling the will of the Spirit of Nature! In p. 35, we are asked—

> . . . Hath Nature's soul,
> That *formed this world* so beautiful; that *spread*
> Earth's lap with plenty, and life's smallest chord
> Strung to unchanging unison; that gave
> The happy birds their dwelling in the grove;
> That yielded to the wanderers of the deep
> The *lovely silence* of the unfathom'd main;
> And fill'd the meanest worm that crawls in dust
> With spirit, thought, and love:—on man alone,
> Partial in causeless malice, wantonly
> Heaped ruin, vice, and slavery; *his soul*
> Blasted with withering curses; placed afar

> The meteor happiness, that shuns his grasp,
> But serving on the frightful gulph to glare,
> Rent wide beneath his footsteps?
> Nature! No?

Who would not suppose that this was intended to "vindicate the ways of God to man"? rather than to afford any reason for supposing the author was about to deny the existence of a God? Setting aside the Pythagorean notion, that every worm has "spirit, *thought*, and love," this stanza might have been written by Bishop Porteus. So far from denying the existence of spirit, and adopting the doctrine of annihilation, which atheism proclaims, he contends that *all is spirit!*

> Throughout this varied and eternal world,
> *Soul is the only element.* The *block*,
> That for uncounted ages has remained
> The moveless pillar of a mountain's weight,
> Is *active, living spirit! Every grain*
> Is *sentient*, both *in unity* and *part*,
> And the *minutest atom* comprehends
> A world of loves and hatreds!

We may smile at this; but *want* of *faith* cannot be attributed to the man who could form such a thesis. If there be no mistake in this matter, we should really treat the cuttings of our toes, and the parings of our finger nails, with more ceremony than to throw them behind the fire, since they comprehend many "worlds of loves and hatreds!" To be sure, when they are reduced to ashes, they remain atoms still, and the loves and hatreds may be only *purified* by the ordeal. The process by which the *sentient* principle was infused into them, after they were clipped, or filed off, would be a curious matter for Queen Mab to explain, when she next visits the earth:—or perhaps they are quite *independent* atoms; and while growing on the toe or finger nails, have each their separate "loves and hatreds" to themselves!

After this adoption and extension of the doctrine of Pythagoras, we are distinctly told that *"man is of* SOUL *and* BODY"; which conveys some little contradiction to the doctrine that every *atom* is *sentient*, and that the block basis of a mountain is a living and entire spirit;—but poets must not be measured by too strict rules. In either case, we have arrived at nothing like atheism yet.

At the commencement of the sixth Canto, we find it questioned, whether "the *universal* spirit" will not "re-vivify" this "wild and miserable world," which is most emphatically called in the peculiar style of Calvinistic energy a *"withered limb of heaven!"* And answering the question in the affirmative, he seems to prophesy of the Millennium, for he says:—

> How sweet a scene will earth become!
> Of *purest spirits* a pure *dwelling-place*
> Symphonious with the planetary spheres,

When man with *changeless* nature coalescing
Will undertake *regeneration's* work,
When its ungenial poles *no longer point*
To the red, and baneful sun,
That faintly twinkles there!

How *"changeless nature"* is to *change*, until the poles change their direction, by a little of man's assistance in removing them, it was not worth Mr. Shelley's while to *stoop* from his flight to inform us; but, setting the absurdity aside, there is in these lines a full recognition of that *superior power* to which the name of God is peculiarly assigned. He employs the same figurative language, and ascribes to this power those attributes which are ascribed to him by the most devout writers. Mr. S. may exceed them in the fervour of his enthusiasm; but he has adopted the basis of all their ideas of divinity. That this Power should have been insulted, by being painted as the "prototype of human misrule," affords no reason for the climax at which Mr. S. afterwards arrives; not by any rational gradation, but by a sudden leap, which is made with such frantic energy as very far to over-shoot its mark.

At p. 57, we have another close imitation of the divinity of Pope:— so close, indeed, as to be a servile copy of the ideas of that poet. And this ushers in the first indication of the peculiar doctrines of our author. This "Spirit of Nature," this "all-sufficing power," is not meant to apply to the ordinary Deity of mankind; but to *"Necessity,"* the *"Mother of the world!"* Mr. S. is simply a *Necessarian!* Every thing is, because it must be; and every thing has been, because it must have been. Those conjurers are perfectly safe, who wait until an event occurs, and then say none other could have happened! This is a species of witch-craft within anybody's reach. But is it worth any thing? Does it explain any thing? Does it help us a jot on our way to truth, or is it available in the pursuit of happiness? I think it is both useless and ridiculous. It seems to me a species of *metaphysical Calvinism!*—and to be as dangerous to morality, as predestination to the interests of religion. We perceive we are in existence—and the Necessarian tells us, very wisely, that we are here of *necessity!* We perceive the varied creation around us replete with life, and plenished with the means of enjoyment, and the Necessitarian wisely tells us, all comes from *necessity!* What an increase to our wisdom, is this information! The world is taken from the back of the elephant, who stands upon the tortoise, and put upon the shoulders of *Dame Necessity*, its august and venerable *mother*, if Mr. Shelley is sufficient authority for this portion of the parentage! The grand secret is merely an exchange of nomenclature. We are not to call the vivifying and superintending principle of creation by the name of God, because impostors have belied his character, and villains have abused his attributes; but we are to get rid of all difficulty and doubt, by hailing "Necessity" as the *"Mother of the world!"* Will it be thought too indecorous by the partizans of Mr. Shelley, if we proceed to make a little enquiry as to the origin of this *prolific necessity?* A necessity is generally defined to be *an effect,* arising out of *a cause!* What cause gave birth to this *Necessity?* What made Necessity the mother of the world? In what manner did Necessity conceive this glorious harmony of "changeless nature?" Whence did Necessity herself arise;—and whence the materials out of which this organization arose? Does the tame, passive, inert word *necessity,* convey any adequate idea of the stupendous creation and its origin? To say that it was necessary, because it exists; and that it owes its existence to necessity, is ringing a childish play on words.

The truth is, that on the question of the nature of the Deity we are utterly at a loss, and there is no means afforded to our reason by which we can arrive at any conception of his being. We are at as great a loss on this subject, as we should be upon the subject of sounds, if we were born deaf; or of colours, if we had no eyes. We are compelled to admit what to our limited senses appears an absurdity; and though we are compelled to admit this, it does not help us in the slightest degree in our researches. We cannot conceive how any thing should be made, without a maker. Nor can we imagine how any maker could make himself. To our reason, an effect must be preceded by an adequate cause. When we talk of a "first cause," we state in fact that our reason cannot begin at any earlier point. The nature of our first cause remains unexplained; for while we are obliged to admit the existence of a power competent to produce the wonders which we see around us, because we do see them, we are equally compelled to confess that we do not know how they could be produced. If we do not know how creation could have been introduced into existence, how can we conceive the nature of the power which has called it into existence? The thing is an utter impossibility. We want a basis for our enquiries which is not afforded us. We only know that there exists a power superior, infinitely superior, to any thing that we see around us, and we call this power GOD! What advantage is obtained by changing the name! This is the Spirit of Nature! before which in all ages the human mind has bent; sometimes in rational worship; sometimes in idle ceremony; sometimes in cruel mockery of devotion.

Revelations, whether real or pretended, afford no light upon the subject of the *nature* of the Divinity. They only describe his attributes, and promulgate the laws by which he governs. And all the fanciful speculators that ever wrote, have not advanced our ideas an iota, as to an *uncaused cause!*—No torch has ever penetrated the thick darkness which surrounds this question; and it still remains as great an enigma as ever, how either the Creator of all should have created himself, or the materials with which he has organized the world. Milton tells us all originated from *Chaos,* and *Old Night.* But whence came Chaos? What produced Old Night? We laugh at the fable of the World being supported by an elephant, and the elephant by a tortoise, while the tortoise stands upon nothing;—but we forget that in pursuing a similar enquiry, our metaphysicians pursue a similar course of illustration. Of all the lame substitutes devised for creation, that of *necessity* seems the most childish, though universally useful

in its application, if it were of any import. So, if we ask Mr. S. how he
could imagine himself removing a difficulty, by introducing an absurdity,
he will tell us it was of *necessity!* If we enquire how he comes to contradict himself, he will say it is of necessity! Or how he comes to lay
down dangerous, and inexplicable doctrines,—it is all of *necessity*, sheer
necessity! But unluckily this *necessity*, which has been aptly described as
the plea of tyrants, and the creed of slaves, is equally applicable to vice, as
to folly. The Inquisition may say, with equal truth, it roasts its victims
out of absolute necessity! The despot may plead he lights up the conflagration of empires, and encreases the miseries of human nature to the most
horrible climax of anguish, by the command of this necessity. The priest
may deceive, the lawyer defraud, and the physician poison, by the same
impulse of necessity. Pickpockets may steal, and ruffians murder, with the
same excuse; and all the evils and horrors of which he complains, are as
much matters of *necessity*, as his condemnation of them. Nor do I see
ought of distinction between necessity and predestination; save that one is
applied to a sectarian definition of the Christian faith, and the other is the
general principle applied to the whole phenomena of nature. I understand
the passage in which Necessity is asserted to be the mother of the world, is
one of those which have been selected for prosecution. Yet the continuation
of the stanza breathes doctrines which would be considered as devout, were
not the opinions of society shocked by the rudeness of substituting *a new*
epithet, for that usually employed when speaking upon such matters.
Allow Mr. Shelley to designate his ruling power by the term Necessity,
and his theology remains as sound as that of other men. He is not an
atheist, even where he fancies himself one. Speaking of the *ruling power*,
he says, in this very stanza,

> . . . the caprice
> Of man's weak will belongs no more to thee;
> Than do the changeful passions of his breast
> To thy unvarying harmony!

Pope himself did not more distinctly draw the line between theism,
and atheism, when he said—

> The *workman* from *the work* distinct was known.

It is true these lines contradict the idea of an ever-ruling necessity, to
which would be of course attributed *the caprice*, and the *changeful passions*
of humanity, as much as the actions which are declared to be absolutely
controlled by this fatal necessity; for he very gravely observes afterwards—

> . . . all that the wide world contains
> Are but thy passive instruments.

I am, however, at some loss to guess why these lines are included in
the indictment. Absurd as they are, I perceive *no* atheism in them. There
is a change of epithets, but little more. He exclaims—

> Spirit of Nature! all sufficing power!

This refers to that principle which regulates the movements of the creation; which he calls—

Necessity, thou mother of the world!

It is an odd phrase, and excites some odd ideas. Had he called Jove the father of the world, no objection would have been taken to the epithet. It is a deviation from the ordinary mode of expression, perhaps without cause, but which might be made without guilt. And when he adds—

Unlike the God of human error, thou
Requirest no prayers, or praises!

he adopts the Epicurean idea, that the gods look with indifference upon the conduct of men, having placed their happiness in their virtue, and leaving their misery to correct their vices. Christians say that God *needs* no prayers, or praises. If he need them not, he *requires* them not;—for he cannot require what he does not need. Nor would they be of any value were they the result of any sense of duty. Where praise is not spontaneously offered, it is better repressed. Unless the heart beat in unison with the tongue, the prayer ought to be disregarded, and the praise is hypocrisy. Besides it would be a strange assumption to single out the Christian deity, as *the* god of human error, when the earth abounds both with false gods, and with false ideas of the divinity. The catholic, who deems the protestants entertain erroneous notions of the Supreme Being, must think the protestant deity a deity of human error. The enmity of Mr. Shelley to the Christian Faith is evident enough; but it is not from this passage I should have expected it to be gathered. In allusion to some god of human error, he says, Necessity (his favourite impulse and origin of all) shall live unchangeable, when the broken altars of this deity shall have bent to the storm of time. What this means, if it mean not that the God of Nature shall triumph over the false opinions of erring humanity, I know not. Mr. S. is so little in agreement with himself, that the charge of this being deism, while he is an atheist, will not be thought of much value. Besides Mr. S. does not profess himself an atheist. He has endeavoured to assimilate his deity to his own imagination, as all enthusiasts do; but though he denies the deities of others, he does not refuse to admit there is one. Nay, more, he attempts to define what the divinity is; and though I cannot but smile at his definition, I am not authorised to dispute his sincerity. All I am disposed to contend for, is that he has made distinctions without difference; and has made people believe him a monster, who would have idolized him, had he been content to express his ideas in ordinary terms.

I now arrive at that appalling declaration, which it was natural to believe would be prosecuted, as throwing down the gauntlet which summons all the feelings of the age to mortal combat. The burning of atheists, (a terrible method of purifying their sentiments) with the natural horror he must have entertained at the idea of such tortures being inflicted upon men for holding opinions which he deemed similar to his own, seems to have taken deep hold upon his fancy. His introduction to the startling declaration, is perhaps the most genuine poetry in the volume. It is simple, affecting, and animated, in a superlative degree. He makes the spirit of Ianthe say—

> I was an infant when my mother went
> To see an atheist burned. She took me there!
> The dark-robed priests were met around the pile,
> The multitude was gazing silently;
> And as the culprit passed with dauntless mien,
> Tempered disdain in his unaltered eye,
> Mixed with a quiet smile, shone calmly forth:
> The thirsty fire crept round his manly limbs!
> His resolute eyes were scorched to blindness soon;
> His death-pang rent my heart! The insensate mob
> Uttered a cry of triumph, and I wept.
> Weep not, child! cried my mother, for that man
> Has said, *There is no God!*

Upon this, Mr. Shelley rushes to the avowal of his faith:—and, because no God could have commanded the sacrifice of a human being, for an error of judgment;—mistaking most unwarrantably the conduct of the murderers for the sanction of the Deity whom they insulted, while they pretended to worship,—he madly exclaims

> . . . There is no God!
> Nature confirms the faith his death-groan sealed.

And then, sinking most miserably from his poetical beauty, in the same proportion as he abandons his reason, he has the following weak and incomprehensible explanation of this unfounded assertion.

> Let heaven and earth, let man's revolving race,
> His ceaseless generations tell their tale;
> Let every part, depending on the chain
> That links it to the whole, point to the hand
> That grasps its term! Let every seed that falls,
> In silent eloquence unfold its store
> Of argument. Infinity within,
> Infinity without, belie creation!
> The *inexterminable spirit* it contains,
> Is nature's ONLY GOD! But human pride
> Is skilful to invent most serious names
> To hide its ignorance. The name of God
> Has fenc'd about all crime with holiness,
> Himself the creature of his worshippers,
> Whose names, and attributes, and passions change,
> Seeva, Budh, Foh, Jehovah, Jove, or Lord!

Much of this rhapsody cannot be met in the way of reason, for it is irrational. The declaration, that there is *no God,* is contradictory to the idea of the *inexterminable spirit,* being *Nature's only God!* But is it not grossly foolish, to shock in this manner the nerves of his ordinary readers—to lead them to imagine he is denying the *existence* of a God, when he is only denying the *mode* of his existence. Had it not been wiser to have said, the idea of a Deity that would order such an act of barbarity, as the burning one of his misjudging creatures, must be erroneous—than thus to start from the real point at issue, and deny the God-head, because those who affect to serve him, degrade his character! The incident imagined is unfortunate, because though we have had executions for alleged atheism, it is questionable whether ever an atheist existed. It was usual for the fanatics to apply this term of reproach to all who differed from them; and from the fact that Vanini, though condemned and executed as an atheist, on his defence took up *a straw,* and said that was sufficient to convince him of the existence of a God, it is evident with what caution the reported profession of atheism should be received. And, while we ought to be cautious in taking atheism upon the credit of fanatics, Mr. S. affords a striking instance that a man is not to be always believed when he professes the creed himself. The wonders of existence that surround us may not sanction the idea of a Deity in human form, or with human passions; but they do point to a power as their origin, separate and distinct from themselves—a power in which they do not participate, and of which they are the creatures, and agents:—and whether this power be called the First Cause, or God, or Necessity, matters not to the fact. In his own words, the hand that grasps the term of animate and inanimate existence—that formed the circle of life and death, is "Nature's God"—no matter what name affectation, caprice, or accident, may have chosen to use as its designation. It is not the seed that is the divinity. The power that called the seed into existence, that implanted its principle of fructification—that bade it through endless ages, reproduce its like—this is the power of the Divinity. Otherwise, Mr. Shelley must applaud the savages who worship stocks and stones;—or if he contend that themselves partaking of the divine power, worship can be due to no other part of it, how will he reconcile the idea of blending the lusts, the ignorance, the caprice, the brutality of man, with that of any portion of the "Spirit of Nature"! Every thing appears to tell us we are not partakers of divinity, not partners in the Divine power, but the creatures of its hands. Infinity is a term as incomprehensible as that of Deity. We cannot conceive what infinity is. Our senses sink in the contemplation of such matters, and our reason cannot help us. We can rationally have no conception of a time when there was no time—yet every thing according to our reason must have had a beginning, and an original cause. We can readily conceive how the phenomena of the world can proceed to eternity. They are in motion; and the same cause may as easily be credited to produce the same effect a million of years forward, as at the present period. But it is not so easy with respect to the past. We want a new sense to comprehend the means by which existence began. One grain of wheat may produce another, because we perceive it has been produced from a former grain. But how came the first grain of wheat into existence? It is no answer to say that it has existed from *infinity*;— or rather this is saying we know nothing about it, which is the truth. But why deny creation because it cannot be comprehended? and substitute another name equally incomprehensible. Does not Mr. Shelley here fall under his own censure, as one of those followers of "human pride," which

> Is skilful to invent most serious names
> To hide its ignorance.

In the total impossibility of deciding correctly, why affect to decide at all? Where is the necessity for a decision? We can reject whatever is unworthy of the Eternal Mind, without denying the existence of a spirit and intelligence which we cannot comprehend. We may refuse our credence to the vulgar errors of attributing the human form or the human passions to the Deity, without denying the existence of a God! And even this denial is only made in words. Mr. Shelley feels there is a power beyond the comprehension of all other men; and to seem wiser than his fellows, he denies their discovery of what cannot be discovered; and talks mysteriously to disguise his own failure, and his close resemblance to themselves. In this dilemma, I think it much the wiser, and the better mode, to take the advice of Pope:—

> Hope humbly then, on trembling pinions soar,
> Wait the great teacher death, and God adore.

Mr. S. may adore Necessity, if he will have necessity to be his Deity. The spirit and author of Nature is the real object of adoration: and it matters little by what epithet he is designated. The errors and absurdities of human creeds can only be charged upon human folly. The Deity is not injured, because his creatures know not what he is, and hit upon ridiculous modes of service. It is true, and it is to be lamented, that

> . . . the name of God
> Has fenc'd about all crime with holiness:

and that madmen, in their ignorance, their interests, and their vices, have made him

> The creature of his worshippers!

The most horrible crimes have been committed in the name of the God of benevolence and love! Murder and bloodshed, and pillage, have been blasphemously sanctioned by his pretended authority. The professing servants of Jehovah have been as barbarous as the followers of Mahomet, and the disciples of the Pagan deities! And had the *same parties* worshipped Necessity, or had no idea of any deity, they would not have wanted other excuses to perform the same acts. It was not the God that led them, but the evil passions that were paramount to the express commands of the God in whose name they spread desolation, and slaughter. This idea is by no means peculiar to Mr. Shelley. One of Shakespeare's heroes could "seem a saint, while most he played the devil." In another place, the dramatist asks—

> . . . In religion,
> What damned error, but some holy cheat,
> Can gloss it over!

Pope to the same effect, tracing the progress of superstition, says—

> Fear made their devils, and weak hope their Gods;
> Gods *partial, changeful, passionate, unjust,*
> Whose attributes were *rage, revenge,* or *lust!*
> Zeal then, not charity, became the guide,
> And hell was built in spite, and heaven in pride.

Some French writer observes that—

> Priests are all for vengeance, force, and fire,
> And only in his thunders act their God!

Thus human passions have contaminated the shrines which human reason should have raised to heaven—and thus, as Mr. Shelley justly remarks,

> . . . Priests babble of a God of peace,
> E'en while their hands are red with guiltless blood!

Thus once the Christian crusaders made a slaughter-house of Turkey, for the conquest of Jerusalem in the name of Christ; and a few weeks since Constantinople has seen the Greek Christians, with their patriarch at their head, murdered to the honor and glory of the god of Mahomet. But is the Great Author of All, the Eternal Immutable Spirit, to be denied, because some beings,

> . . . drest in a little brief authority,
> Play such fantastic tricks before high heaven,
> As make e'en angels weep!

All this folly and barbarity very clearly prove that their authors have neither knowledge, nor fear, of the Deity, before whom they bend in solemn mockery. Did they fear him, they would respect his laws, and imitate his conduct;—did they know him, they would not attribute actions to him of which they are ashamed themselves, and yet perpetrate in the abuse of his authority. But all this does not disprove the existence of a Superior Ruling Power—of that Being with respect to whom the Athenians candidly confessed their ignorance, when they erected an altar to the UNKNOWN GOD! Neither infinity, nor eternity, nor creation, nor necessity, explain the difficulty. He has chosen to shroud himself in mystery, as to his origin, and nature:—but enough of his power and benevolence are known, to induce us to adoration—not because he needs it, but because we cannot possess our reason, and not adore the author of a system which produces so much happiness. That atheism is not capable of removing the

obscurity in which the system of nature is involved—or that Mr. S. is not
an atheist;—must be admitted even by his admirers.

In a note upon the line,

Necessity, thou mother of the world!

he enters into a prose dissertation on this new-found deity, which is to
depose all the ancient and the modern divinities. In this it is attempted to
assimilate the human mind to that part of the creation, in which from
given causes, are produced certain effects. The folly of this reasoning
consists in the want of analogy between the things compared. The material and the moral world are essentially different. There are certain fixed
laws to which the material world is subject, which enable us to speak
with certainty of effects as following causes:—but in the moral world, we
have no such assurance. The disposition of matter depends upon the laws
which regulate matter, which are definite:—but the mind is not governed
by any such determinate principles; nor can we argue that the same causes
shall produce the same effects on the minds of different individuals. If it
be said, if they were exactly in the same circumstances, the same effect
would follow the same cause the reasoning would still fail, for it would
be impossible to find this agreement of circumstances. We can readily
admit the necessity that a grain of wheat shall produce its likeness, when
subjected to the process of vegetation:—or that an acorn should produce
an oak. In these operations, "*nature is uniform,*" and "the constant conjunction of similar events," leads to the "consequent inference of one from
another." But where this evident uniformity ceases, there also ceases the
doctrine of Necessity. Unless you can tell me what I am about to do, as
distinctly as you can predict the expansion of an oak from an acorn, you
cannot apply the same doctrine to the one as to the other. An *inference*
from a certainty, is not an equal certainty; and a supposition from a fact is
entitled to little credit. "Liberty applied to mind," is *not,* as Mr. Shelley
says, "analogous to chance, as applied to matter." There is no greater
analogy between them, than there is between mind, and a dead corpse; or
between the head and the hair which grows upon it; and it is equally wide
of conclusive reasoning to remark, that "the *precise character* and *motives*
of any man, on any occasion, being given, the moral philosopher could
predict his actions with as much certainty, as the natural philosopher could
predict the effects of the mixture of any particular chemical substances."
The "precise character," and the "motives" can *never* be obtained; and
the boast is as idle as that of Archimedes, that *if he had* a place whereon to
place his lever, he could raise the earth. It is a mere sophistical evasion
to demand conditions which cannot be fulfilled, as the data of conclusions
which are to be expected. If the conditions were attainable, the matter
would be *then to be proved.* As it stands, no proof is possible; and the
supposition does not warrant the inference. We know we have never yet
approached the knowledge of mind, if such doctrines are correct. The
"*indisciplinable wanderings of passion,*" of which Mr. Shelley speaks in

his note upon marriage, seem to deride all motive, and to laugh at all rational deductions. The "aged husband-man," is not "more experienced than the young beginner," as Mr. Shelley supposes, "because there *is* a uniform, undeniable necessity in the operations of nature"; but because he has *seen more* of these operations. Now the more we see of the operations of the human mind, the less we are able to comprehend its nature. We are perpetually startled by endless contradictions:—

> The rogue, and fool, by fits, is fair and wise!
> And e'en the best, by fits, what they despise.

Instead of that immutable certainty, which characterises the laws of nature in the material world, we find nothing but uncertainty. "An old statesman" is not always "more skilful than a raw politician." Polonius knew no more of Hamlet's madness than Rosencrantz or Guildenstern. What Mr. Shelley attempts to illustrate by saying, "No farmer carrying his corn to market, doubts the sale of it at market price," I am at a loss to guess. It is of a piece, however, with many other of his illustrations, and can illustrate nothing, because it is a fallacy. If he can sell it in the market at all, he knows he will sell it at the market price! And yet he may have doubts, whether he can effect a sale; and these doubts have often been converted into realities. Such illustrations suit very well with such reasoners as talk about "voluntary actions," and yet tell us "every human being is irresistibly impelled to act precisely as he does act, by a chain of causes generated in the eternity which preceded his birth." An illustration to a similar purpose, states "the master of a manufactory no more doubts that he can purchase the human labour necessary for his purpose, than that his machinery will act as it has been accustomed to act." It is not necessary to have been a manufacturer, to see that this is sometimes a falsehood and must always be a fallacy.

"In the only true sense of the word power," says Mr. Shelley, "it applies with equal force to the *loadstone,* as to the *human will!* Do you think these motives, which I shall present, are powerful enough to rouse him? is a question as common as, Do you think this lever has the power of raising this weight?" This is true; but the answers are not so certain of being similar. We can tell when the lever is powerful enough to raise the weight; but we may in vain endeavour to ascertain the motives that are strong enough to rouse the mind. The difference is, that the weight is passive to the power, and is necessitated to obey its influence. It is the active and determining principle; but the mind bears no similitude to the weight. It may refuse to be acted upon by any motive—the motives we imagine sufficiently powerful to rouse it, may be disregarded; and the motives have not the power of the lever, to enforce the necessity of action. The reason is plain. The mind thinks for itself—the weight obeys the superior impulse of the lever. There is no analogy between them:— and the argument fails from the want of a just degree of comparison.

In this note, however, I find a valuable admission, which sets the supposed atheism of Mr. Shelley entirely at rest. He says, "It is probable that the word GOD was originally only an expression denoting the UNKNOWN CAUSE of the KNOWN EVENTS which men perceived in the universe." This is clear—and the word which Mr. Shelley chooses to employ instead of the word God, to denote the cause of these unknown events, is the word "*Necessity*"! This brings us to the point from which we set out—to the—

> Father of all, in every age
> In every clime ador'd;
> By saint, by savage, and by sage,
> Jehovah, Jove, or Lord.

Mr. Shelley's alteration of the text to "Mother," instead of Father, may strike us as very useless, but we can hardly deem it so wicked, as to deserve, "death here, and hell hereafter." Though Lord Bacon prefers atheism to superstition, and says the former may leave a man to the domestic virtues and to science, while the latter makes a wild beast of him; yet a poetical atheist would have been a most ungracious animal—a sort of traitor to his profession, and a heretic to his creed:—and I am happy to have discovered, that Mr. Shelley is a true worshipper of the divinity, though he refuses to kneel at the ordinary altars, and has endeavoured to frame a liturgy for himself.

I do not give much credit to the motives of the prosecutors of Queen Mab, because it attacks the received notions of a divinity; or because it disputes the authenticity of the Jewish and Christian revelations. The Lord Chief Justice Abbott declares it is *not illegal* to doubt the truth of Christianity, provided such doubts be not expressed in a reviling manner: —but if it be not illegal to doubt, *no mode* of expressing doubt CAN be illegal. It were wiser to leave reviling to neglect. The decision of twelve Christians is no better proof of the truth of Christianity, than the verdict of twelve Mahometans of the truth of the divine mission of Mahomet.

Mr. Shelley, in his Vision of Ahasuerus, the wandering Jew, certainly treats with very little ceremony the Jewish and the Christian revelations:— but *his* objections admit of a most easy reply—one which he himself furnishes. His deity, "Necessity," is to the full as answerable for the deeds of horror committed in the name of any other deity, as the peculiar being whose pretended worship authorized the barbarities. Mr. Shelley declares—

> No atom . . . fulfils
> A vague and unnecessitated act,
> Or acts but as it *must* and *ought* to act.

If this be the case, his charges that "slaves built temples for the Omnipotent,"—that "costly altars smoked with human blood,"—that, "hideous paeans rung through long-drawn aisles,"—are idle, as occurring out of *inevitable necessity;* and it matters little to the barbarities, or the errors, if they are admitted to be so, in what name they were committed, or perpetrated. There is in the language attributed to Ahasuerus, much of what might be called reviling; but the peculiar situation of the party represented will account for much. The dramatist is not answerable for the sentiments of his characters;—he has only to represent them in their proper light. Otherwise the Bible itself might be prosecuted as an atheistical work, because there is in it a declaration that "there is no God." An Attorney-General would have only to omit the context, "the fool hath said in his heart," to make the prophet answerable for the language of the fool.

It may be here remarked, that if the destruction of human life lead Mr. Shelley to reject revelations which attribute such commands to the deity, he ought in like manner to renounce his praises of *Necessity,* from the misery and wreck of human happiness occasioned by such calamities as the overflowings of Etna and Vesuvius—the overwhelming of Pompeii and Herculaneum—the swallowing up of Lisbon—the devastation of tempests—the agony of acute diseases—and the murders committed in the mask of war! These are as much opposed to the benevolence of "Necessity, the mother of the world," as to the wisdom and goodness of any other deity. It matters not to the sufferer, whether the earthquake devour him, the burning lava overwhelm him, or the dagger hasten him to a premature grave.

Mr. Shelley says the present evil is requisite to bring about ulterior good. Of this there is no proof. I cannot tell whether the climate of the poles will ever be so far assimilated to that of the torrid zone, as to make pine apples as plentiful at Nova Zembla, as now in the West Indies. Astronomers may decide that the earth is in its progress to a better state; but I perceive no prospect from *this* of any alteration in the condition of man. His happiness does not depend upon climates or seasons. When the "equator coincides with the ecliptic," and "the nights and days are equal on the earth throughout the year," which Mr. Shelley thinks "exceedingly probable," there will in the same probability be as much error, venality, prejudice, and ignorance, as at present. The happiest climates, instead of producing the happiest and wisest men, afford specimens of the reverse. If it were possible to give into these dreams of a world of endless bliss, which are destined to arise out of the maturity of the universe, what are they to us, who are not destined to approach within centuries upon centuries of their existence?

All these visions are but other views of the millennium, and of those heavens, into which human nature is perpetually endeavouring to pry for that happiness which it cannot find in the present state of things. These idle expectations are the common solace of indolence, the common food of discontent. Mr. Shelley has served up the same dish, varied in the

cooking, and with a more savory sauce;—but equally visionary, unsatisfactory, and unsubstantial:—Those who sit down to the banquet will find
only a feast of air.

FINIS.

RICHARD CARLILE OFFERS A NEW PIRACY

[From The Republican, February 1, 1822 (5:145-148). The Republican was
the longest-lived of several radical periodicals published by Richard Carlile, and
written almost entirely by him. Carlile also published four pirated editions of
Queen Mab. From 1817 to 1834 he was subjected to continuous fines and imprisonment for blasphemous and seditious publications, spending altogether ten years in
prison and continuing his radical activities from jail. Shelley wrote a long letter
protesting against Carlile's second sentence, in 1819. Carlile's periodicals show him
to have been egotistic and domineering, resourceful, and absolutely fearless in his
radicalism. His periodicals show a constant interest in Shelley. He died in 1842.]

This beautiful poem is again in full sale at a reduced price, or at 7s. 6d.
three-fifths only of its first price. The Vice Society, by an indictment, had
succeeded in suppressing its public sale. They are now solicited to try what
they can do again in that respect. If they please, they shall make it as
common as they have made the "Age of Reason."

The present publisher has been called on by a person calling himself
"Consistency" (he hates all anonymous writers, particularly when they
ask questions) to explain how his conduct in publishing Queen Mab corresponds with the objections he has taken to Mr. Benbow's publication of
the Political Works of Paine. If "Consistency" had been consistent in his
views as in his professions, he would have seen no inconsistency on the
part of the present publisher of "Queen Mab": to explain which a short
history of the publication will suffice.

In the summer of 1821, Mr. William Clark, in a shop near St.
Clement's Church in the Strand, published "Queen Mab." The author,
Percy Bysshe Shelley, printed a few copies for his friends a few years back,
but it was never known to be publicly sold until published by Mr. Clark.
Immediately on its appearance the Vice Society pounced upon it with an
indictment, against which the publisher (Mr. Clark) was not proof. He
was arrested, and instead of going to the Bench Prison, or to Newgate, as
he should have done, he offered to compromise the matter with the Society,
and to give up the copies he had by him for their destruction; pleading
ignorance of its being objectionable. This hypocrisy weighed nothing with
Pritchard, the Secretary of the Society, he reminded Mr. Clark that he
needed not to plead ignorance of the quality of the publication, after having
so long served as shopman in Carlile's shop in Fleet Street. "Six Acts"
proved too much for Mr. Clark: he bound himself down to good behaviour, as they call it, and found that he could not move in the sale of
the work, as a second arrest took place because some other person had sold

a copy in his shop. He should not have given recognizances, and he might then have bid them defiance, as has evidently and successfully been done in Fleet Street. By neglecting to do this, "Queen Mab" was suppressed without going to a Jury, without even a struggle on the part of its publisher. Here then it was certainly fair game for any person to take up, particularly for the present publisher, who has suffered from the redoubled violence of the prosecuting gangs occasioned by the scandalous compromises which have been made with them by others.

"Consistency," says, very inconsistently, that Mr. Clark and his family are suffering from the publication of "Queen Mab." It may be wished that it were so, and very happy would have been the writer of this, if the sufferings of Mr. Clark were not from a less honourable source than the publication of "Queen Mab." The whole weight of the expence of paper and printing for "Queen Mab," fell upon the shoulders of others, and not upon those of Mr. Clark, and it is partly to relieve those persons from their loss, that the publication of the same edition with a new imprint has been taken up by its present publisher.

"Consistency" should have looked at the matter before he had complained of inconsistency. He would have seen that Mr. Carlile never complained of Mr. Benbow's publishing the Theological Works of Mr. Paine, although he did express a wish that they had been published publicly. It was the publication of the Theological Works privately, and the Political Works publicly, about which complaint was made.

If Mr. Clark had stood his ground and kept the copies of "Queen Mab" on sale, until a Jury had given a verdict against it, the present publisher would then have taken up the public sale of it in his turn, and this is the way the warfare ought to be carried on. Mr. Clark should have published the "Age of Reason," and Palmer's "Principles of Nature," as well as "Queen Mab," publicly; and after him Mr. Benbow should have done the same openly, instead of clandestinely, and then the matter would have been in a fair train for success, and prosecution would only accelerate the demand. Poor 55, in Fleet Street, has to sustain all the brunt of the battle, whilst others wish to strip it of its feathers and its laurels without assisting to fight in the same foremost rank. This shall not be done. What we earn we will keep and wear. Our comrades shall share our success, but not so with the pirate and the poltroon.

Queen Mab is a philosophical poem in nine cantos, and is remarkably strong in its exposure and denunciation of Kingcraft and Priestcraft. Lord Byron calls it a poem of great strength and wonderful powers of imagination; and, with his Lordship, we differ from some of the Author's metaphysical opinions. However it is upon the principle of free discussion, and upon the principle of giving currency to every thing that is valuable, that the present publisher has taken up the publication. He wrote it twice over during his first imprisonment in the King's Bench Prison, waiting for trial for the Parodies, and in the summer of 1819, he made an effort to obtain the consent of its author to its publication in the Temple of Reason, but did not succeed. Should the Author now wish that the publication should not be proceeded with, the present Publisher would willingly yield to his instructions, in the same manner and disposition as he first hesitated to print without them, although advised to do it by many of the Author's friends and intimate acquaintance.

In addition to the Poem itself, there are Notes by the Author, of equal bulk, equal beauties, and equal merit. Every thing that is mischievous to society is painted in this work in the highest colours. We hesitate before we give assent to the Author's views of marriage, particularly, as he strikes at the contract without modifications, and seems desirous of destroying it without defining a better system. This part of the Notes we understand forms one of the passages selected for indictment, and as war is commenced we would prefer to support the Author without coinciding with all his views, than to give the least encouragement to the hypocrites and villains who would stifle all discussion, and suppress every valuable publication, because it tends to unmask them, and to put a stop to their robberies upon the industrious multitude.

The last Note forms an essay of twenty-two pages, to encourage an abstinence from the use of animal food, and, to our knowledge, it has made a very great impression, upon that point, with many of its readers. Very powerful arguments can be brought forward on both sides of this question, but we hesitate not to say, that the laws of Nature and Necessity determine nothing regular on this point, but vary with climates and seasons. For ourselves we can say that we lean to the use of vegetable food in preference to animal, where its quantity and quality can be rendered sufficient to all the purposes of life and health.

When we say that this volume is replete with beauties, the reader will excuse the hacknied [sic] custom of making selections.

EDITOR.

PIRATED EDITIONS DISCRIMINATED

[From The Republican, December 27, 1822 (6: 978-979), under the title, "Queen Mab." See note to preceding selection.]

There are now no less than four editions of this work on sale, but I would caution my friends against an imperfect edition selling under the imprint of William Clark. I was not aware of it until within the last week. At 5, Water Lane, Fleet Street, perfect copies may be had under my imprint at 7s. 6d. in boards and any other copies selling under my name are not for my profit or under my control.

I have also purchased the whole of the remaining copies of the original edition printed by Mr. Shelley in 1813. There were but 180 copies left, and these will be sold at the same price in sheets to those friends of Mr. Shelley, or others, who may prize an original copy. The difference in the original and in my present edition is, that the notes of the latter are all translated. The imperfections of the copy selling under the imprint of William Clark, consist in the exclusion of all those words and sentences which some simpleton considered libellous. They were sold by the Printer at little better than waste paper price and are now put forth as perfect copies.

RICHARD CARLILE.

WICKEDNESS IS PUT DOWN

[From The Investigator, or Quarterly Magazine, 1822, second part (5: 315-373). The review is headed "Licentious Productions in High Life," and deals with eight books, including Don Juan, Sardanapalus, The Two Foscari, and Cain. Only the section relating to Shelley and Queen Mab is here reprinted. For his vicious personal attack the editor was severely denounced by Leigh Hunt in The Examiner for September 22, in an article entitled "Canting Slander, to the Reverend William Bengo Collyer." It is an ironical fact that Collyer later had to publish a defense of himself against charges of moral degeneracy arising from his congregation.]

To the last part of the painful duty which we have imposed upon ourselves we turn with pleasure, because it is the last, for nothing else could induce us to revert to that most execrable publication, Queen Mab, with any other feelings than those of unmingled horror and disgust. Compared with this Don Juan is a moral poem and Cain a homily. It does not merely question or sneer at revelation, nor is it satisfied with denying it—deism is too mean a flight for its author's wondrous powers—the providence of the Deity too insignificant an object of his attack,—his being therefore is denied, and the atheist-bard confidently assures us, that there is no God. Our blood curdled in our veins as we waded through nine cantos of blasphemy and impiety, such as we never thought that any one, on the outside of bedlam, could have uttered; nor dare we transcribe any portion of it in our pages, save one of the very mildest of its author's attacks upon religion, the slightest of his insults to his God, whom again and again—our hand trembles as we write it—the impious wretch has dared to brand as a tyrant, a murderer, a cheat, a demon, and a fiend.

> How ludicrous the priest's dogmatic roar!
> The weight of his exterminating curse
> How light! and his affected charity,
> To suit the pressure of the changing times,
> What palpable deceit—but for thy aid,
> Religion! but for thee, prolific fiend,
> Who peoplest earth with demons, Hell with men,
> And Heaven with slaves!
>
> Thou taintest all thou look'st upon!
>   *   *   *   *
> But now contempt is mocking thy gray hairs;
> Thou art descending to the darksome grave,

Unhonoured and unpitied, but by those
Whose pride is passing by like thine, and sheds,
Like thine, a glare that fades before the sun
Of truth, and shines but in the dreadful night
That long has lowered above the ruined world.

But we must desist; we cannot quote the shortest passage referring either to the Creator or the Redeemer of mankind, which is not so awfully horrible in its blasphemy, that even to transcribe it for the mere purpose of holding it up to the execrations of mankind, must be in itself a sin. This atheist, like others of a tribe but few in number, and but rarely appearing as monstrosities of their race, dethrones one God, whose attributes are revealed, and whose requirements are known, to set up a strange non-descript something or nothing in his stead, which he passionately invokes as the

> . . . Soul of the Universe,
> Spirit of Nature, all-sufficing Power,
> Necessity!

Of the person, nature, and functions of this old pseudo-divinity newly revived, our readers will, we doubt not, be abundantly satisfied with the following very philosophical and intelligible exposition.

[*Quotes Canto VI, lines 198-226*]

Thus much for the precious jargon of Mr. Shelley's new theology: a word or two ere we leave him upon his morality. The tone and character of this may be easily collected from a single extract, from the representation given by the poet, of how the world should be governed, and would be, were he its governor.

> Then that sweet bondage which is Freedom's self,
> And rivets with sensation's softest tie
> The kindred sympathies of human souls,
> Needed no fetters of tyrannic law:
> Those delicate and timid impulses
> In Nature's primal modesty arose,
> And with undoubted confidence disclosed
> The growing longings of its dawning love,
> Unchecked by dull and selfish chastity,
> That virtue of the cheaply virtuous,
> Who pride themselves in senselessness and frost.

This, one would think, was plain and intelligible enough, but lest it should not be, it is illustrated and expanded in a long, artful, and sophistical note in which we are boldly told that

"Chastity is a monkish and evangelical superstition, a greater foe to natural temperance even than unintellectual sensuality; it strikes at the root of all domestic happiness, and consigns more than half of the human race to misery, that some few may monopolize according to law. A system could not well have been devised more studiously hostile to human happiness than marriage."

The notes of which this extract is a very favourable specimen, as far as their delicacy and morality are concerned, form, in our opinion, the most dangerous part of this wicked and dangerous book, for they are more intelligible than the poem, which is wrapt in an obscurity and mysticism, which neither Madame Quyon nor Jacob Behmen could have surpassed. Their authors, for there were more than one, labour by them to establish and enforce such notable discoveries and propositions as these: "all that miserable tale of the Devil and Eve is irreconcileable with the knowledge of the stars"; "the narrow and unenlightened morality of the Christian religion is an aggravation of the evils of society"; "utility is morality"; "there is neither good nor evil in the universe, otherwise than as the events to which we apply these epithets, have a relation to our own peculiar mode of being"; "the universe was not created, but existed from all eternity"; "Jesus was an ambitious man, who aspired to the throne of Judea"; "had the resolution of Pontius Pilate been equal to his candour, the Christian religion could never have prevailed." Nor is there, according to these new lights of the world "a state of future punishment"; nor, except that sublimely obscure and unintelligible principle, for being it can have none, "necessity, the mother of the world," can there be a God. How they demonstrate these positions to be true and shew all men, except themselves—for we hope and believe there are few other atheists, at least, in the world—to be fools and madmen, two specimens of their candour and their hardihood will more than suffice to shew.

"But even that a man should raise a dead body to life before our eyes, and on this fact rest his claim to being considered the son of God;—the Humane Society restores drowned persons, and because it makes no mystery of the method it employs, its members are not mistaken for the sons of God."

"Lord Chesterfield was never yet taken for a prophet, even by a bishop, yet he uttered this remarkable prediction: 'The despotic government of France is screwed up to the highest pitch; a revolution is fast approaching; that revolution, I am convinced, will be radical and sanguinary.' This appeared in the letters of the prophet long before the accomplishment of this wonderful prediction. Now, have these particulars come to pass, or have they not? If they have, how could the Earl have foreknown them without inspiration?"

Whilst we tremble at the horrid blasphemy of these passages, we cannot suppress a smile at the absurdity of the beardless philosophers, who could think for a moment to gull even their brother freshmen at the university by such ridiculous comparisons.[7] Those who could be gulled by

[7] The reviewer had evidently heard of the Oxford collaboration of Shelley and T. J. Hogg on *The Necessity of Atheism* and confused it with the notes to *Queen Mab*, one of which reprints *The Necessity of Atheism* with a few slight changes.—N.I.W.

them must, indeed, be the veriest fools that ever walked the earth without a keeper. But these boys in reasoning, as in years, are prophets forsooth themselves, as well as interpreters of prophecy; and *arcades ambo,* are drivellers in both. Bear witness the following notable prediction, to the truth of this description.

"Analogy seems to favour the opinion that as, like other systems, Christianity has arisen and augmented, so like them it will decay and perish; that as violence, darkness, and deceit, not reasoning and persuasion, have procured its admission among mankind, so, when enthusiasm has subsided, and time, that infallible controverter of false opinions, has involved its pretended evidences in the darkness of antiquity, it will become obsolete; that Milton's poem alone will give permanency to the remembrance of its absurdities; and that men will laugh as heartily at grace, faith, redemption, and original sin, as they now do at the metamorphoses of Jupiter, the miracles of Romish saints, the efficacy of witchcraft, and the appearance of departed spirits."

To complete the catalogue of absurdities thrown together in glorious confusion, through ninety pages and gleaned from all quarters, all kindreds, and all ages of the system of infidel philosophy, from the "admirable author" of the Inquirer and Political Justice upwards, enforcing the doctrines of equality of property, and an equal division of bodily labour, is followed by a very learned and elaborate note, attributing the origin of evil and all the misery in the world to a non-adherence to vegetable diet, or rather to the pernicious practise of altering our good by fire, the natural conclusion from which is, that it had better be eaten raw. This most elaborate disquisition is enlivened by a new and very ingenious interpretation of the story of Prometheus, whose stealing fire from Heaven means, as is very learnedly shewn, that he was the first cook who "applied that element to culinary purposes," or, in other words, was the inventor of the palatable but most destructive arts of roasting, boiling, frying, and all those et ceteras on which Dr. Kitchener, the Prometheus of modern times, displays so much erudition. We hope that in the next edition of his most popular work, the learned and most appropriately named Doctor will not omit to notice this important discovery, the omission of which, we cannot help thinking, no slight imputation upon his oracular discernment and profound research. This hint for cooks and compilers of cookery-books—in these degenerate days, a most lucrative and honourable employment—what follows concerns divines, who, in all their curious and abstruse speculations upon the fall of man, have not hit, we will undertake to say, upon so novel and ingenious an interpretation as this.

"The allegory of Adam and Eve eating from the tree of evil, and entailing upon their posterity the wrath of God and the loss of everlasting life, admits of no other explanation than the disease and crime that have flowed from unnatural diet."

Who but, after this, must lift up his hands and eyes in astonishment, and exclaim, "A Daniel, Yea, a second Daniel, come to judgment!" But a truce at once with jesting, and commenting of all sorts, on such stuff and nonsense. Of its authors, one was expelled from the University for printing, for private circulation, these atheistical blasphemies, and the other withdrew, to save himself from the disgrace, (for he evidently did not consider it a triumph), of sharing the same fate. The notes, which have a hand appended to them, partly original, but for the greater part extracted from older infidels, are not written by the author of the poem. They have been attributed to his early and constant friend, Lord Byron; but here we are satisfied that rumour does the noble lord some wrong, as they are the production of a much less able and obscurer man. We saw him once some years ago, but whether he is still to be seen or is no more, we know not. To have sat for an hour or two, once in your life, in company with an avowed atheist, is enough, and more than enough for any man who retains the slightest respect for religion, or veneration for the name and attributes of God. These are so habitually and so coarsely blasphemed by the individual in question, as to have shocked even those who make no profession of religion, but who are rather fond than averse to skeptical inquiries, conducted as they ought to be, when entered upon at all, with decency,—with some deference to the opinion of million upon millions of mankind, and with the solemnity due to the awful consequences which they involve. But he disposed of the existence of a God, and a future state, and with the same levity, flippancy, and frivolity as he would dismiss the merits of a play, or the dancing of his partner at last night's ball—and avows—yes, we ourselves have heard him avow, to the disgust of a large assembly—that the only thing worth living for, is the sensual enjoyment in which man participates with brute!—The brute that perishes, we add, and happy would it be for him if he so perished also. But he may yet be—for all we know to the contrary—in the land of the living, and within reach of mercy, and the possibility of repentance. But his wretched friend and co-adjutor, where is he? In the meridian of his days he died not the death of the atheist depictured, by the depraved yet glowing fancy of his youth.

> I was an infant when my mother went
> To see an atheist burned. She took me there:
> The dark-robed priests were met around the pile;
> The multitude was gazing silently;
> And as the culprit passed with dauntless mien,
> Tempered disdain in his unaltering eye,
> Mixed with a quiet smile, shone calmly forth:
> The thirsty fire crept round his manly limbs;
> His resolute eyes were scorched to blindness soon;
> His death-pang rent my heart! the insensate mob
> Uttered a cry of triumph, and I wept.
> "Weep, not, child!" cried my mother," for that man
> Has said, There is no God."

Embarked in a sailing boat on a lovely day upon the waves of the Adriatic, with a chosen companion of his pleasurable excursions, the fisherman marked his sails gallantly unfurled, and glittering in the sun,—he looked again, and in a moment—in the twinkling of an eye, the boat had disappeared, and the atheist had sunk to the bottom of a fathomless abyss, either to rot into annihilation there, or but to deposit the lifeless body for whose gratification he had lived, that his disencumbered spirit might rise to the judgment of his God. That judgment we presume not to pronounce; but this we may, and this we will undertake to say, that he stood not in his presence and before his throne, to utter blasphemies he promulgated upon earth—nor when the dead shall arise—for in spite of his daring assertions and imbecile arguments to the contrary, the dead *shall* arise,—at the great day of final doom, in the face of an assembled universe, and at the bar of him whom as an imposter he villified and despised, will he venture to maintain the creed he adopted for himself, and urged upon others here:—

> There is no God
> Nature confirms the faith his death-groan sealed:
> Let heaven and earth, let man's revolving race,
> His ceaseless generations tell their tale;
> Let every part depending on the chain
> That links it to the whole, point to the hand
> That grasps its term! let every seed that falls
> In silent eloquence unfold its store
> Or argument; infinity within,
> Infinity without, belie creation;
> The exterminable spirit it contains
> Is nature's only God.

Such a death to such a man is awful in the extreme and ought to be impressive—or call it Providence—or call it chance.

"I am acquainted with a lady of considerable accomplishments, and the mother of a numerous family, whom the Christian religion has goaded to incurable insanity. A parallel case is, I believe, within the experience of every physician."

Without attaching any credit to this representation until we have more minute particulars of the case, we can oppose to it a worse illustration of the effects of the philosophy and morality taught by Queen Mab. It had a disciple, the descendant and heir of an ancient, and honourable, and a titled family. That family was disgraced by his vices from youth to his death. These too, with the principles of which they were the natural offspring, most righteously deprived him of the guardianship of his children, but unhappily drove their mother to ruin, prostitution and suicide, whilst he consoled himself for the loss of a wife's society by first seducing one daughter of his friend, and afterwards living in an incestuous connection with another. For his sake we exult not, but rather would weep that he is no more, since nothing short of a greater miracle than those which whilst living he rediculed and rejected, could snatch him from the punishment due to his crimes; but for the sake of the world, we rejoice that both he and the reviver of the principles he adopted, have run their race of impiety and sin.

[*The reviewer here leaves Shelley in order to discuss the projected issue of* The Liberal *by two of Shelley's friends. He warns them that they may partake of Shelley's fate if they continue to insult their maker, and calls on the Society for the Prevention of Vice to prosecute Clark for publishing* Queen Mab.]

IV

THE ALASTOR VOLUME TO THE COURT OF CHANCERY

"SUBLIME OBSCURITY"

[From The Monthly Review, or Literary Journal, April, 1816 (79: 433). This conservative survival of eighteenth-century journalism took notice of nearly every volume published by Shelley over his own name. At first it condemned him for his deviations from traditional, orthodox poetic style; later it condemned his moral and religious heresies, while acknowledging his genius.]

We must candidly own that these poems are beyond our comprehension; and we did not obtain a clue to their sublime obscurity, till an address to Mr. Wordsworth explained in what school the author had formed his taste. We perceive, through the "darkness visible" in which Mr. Shelley veils his subject, some beautiful imagery and poetical expressions: but he appears to be a poet "whose eye, in a fine phrenzy rolling," seeks only such objects as are "above this visible diurnal sphere"; and therefore we entreat him, for the sake of his reviewers as well as of his other readers, (if he has any,) to subjoin to his next publication an *ordo*, a glossary, and copious notes, illustrative of his allusions and explanatory of his meaning.

"PROFOUND STUPIDITY"

[From The British Critic, May, 1816 (N. S. 5: 545-546).]

If this gentleman is not blessed with the inspiration, he may at least console himself with the madness of a poetic mind. In the course of our critical labours, we have been often condemned to pore over much profound and prosing stupidity; we are therefore not a little delighted with the nonsense which mounts, which rises, which spurns the earth, and all its dull realities; we love to fly with our author to a silent nook.

> One silent nook
> Was there. Even on the edge of that vast mountain
> Upheld by knotty roots and fallen rocks
> It overlooked in its serenity
> The dark earth and the bending vault of stars.

Tolerably high, this aforesaid nook, to overlook the stars: but

> Hither the poet came. His eyes beheld
> Their own wan light through the reflected lines
> Of his thin hair, distinct in the dark depths
> Of that still fountain.

Vastly intelligible. Perhaps, if his poet had worn a wig, the case might have been clearer: for then it might have thrown some light on the passage from the ancient legend.

> By the side of a soft flowing stream
> An elderly gentleman sat;
> On the top of his head was his wig,
> On the top of his wig was his hat.

But this aforesaid hair is endowed with strange qualities.

> . . . his scattered hair
> Sered by the autumn of strange suffering,
> Sung dirges in the wind.

This can only be interpreted by supposing, that the poet's hair was entwined in a fiddle stick, and being seared with "the autumn of strange sufferings," alias rosin, "scraped discords in the wind," for so the last line should evidently be read. But, soft—a little philosophy, for our poet is indubitably a vast philosopher.

> Seized by the sway of the *ascending* stream
> With dizzy swiftness round, and round, and round
> Ridge after ridge the straining boat arose,
> Till on the verge of the extremest curve
> Where through an opening of the rocky bank
> The waters overflow, and a smooth spot
> Of glassy quiet, mid those battling tides
> Is left, the boat paused shuddering.

A very animated boat this; something resembling that of an Irishman, which must needs know its way to Greenwich, because it had been down the stream so often. We cannot do sufficient justice to the creative fancy of our poet. A man's hair singing dirges, and a boat pausing and shuddering, are among the least of his inventions; nature for him reverses all her laws, the streams ascend. The power of the syphon we all know, but it is for the genius of Mr. Shelley to make streams run up hill. But we entreat the pardon of our readers for dwelling so long upon this *ne plus ultra* of poetical sublimity.

"MORBID IMAGINATION"

[From The Eclectic Review, October, 1816 (N. S. 5: 391-393). This is the only one of Shelley's books reviewed by the conservative Eclectic Review, but after his death in 1822 it pronounced the regular conservative condemnatory opinion of him.]

It is but justice to Mr. Shelley, to let him give his own explanation of this singular production.

[*Quotes the first paragraph and the first sentence of the second paragraph of Shelley's Preface*]

We fear that not even this commentary will enable ordinary readers to decipher the import of the greater part of Mr. Shelley's allegory. All is wild and specious, untangible and incoherent as a dream. We should be utterly at a loss to convey any distinct idea of the plan or purpose of the poem. It describes the adventures of a poet who "lived" and "died" and "sung in solitude"; who wanders through countries real and imaginary, in search of an unknown and undefined object; encounters perils and fatigues altogether incredible; and at length expires "like an exhalation," in utter solitude, leaving this world inconsolable for a loss of which it is nevertheless unconscious.

The poem is adapted to show the dangerous, the fatal tendency of that morbid ascendency of the imagination over the other faculties, which incapacitates the mind for bestowing an adequate attention on the real objects of this "work-day" life, and for discharging the relative and social duties. It exhibits the utter uselessness of imagination, when wholly undisciplined, and selfishly employed for the mere purposes of intellectual luxury, without reference to those moral ends to which it was designed to be subservient. This could not be better illustrated, than in a poem where we have glitter without warmth, succession without progress, excitement without purpose, and a search which terminates in annihilation. It must surely be with the view of furnishing some such inference as we have supposed, that every indication of the Author's belief in a future state of existence, and in the moral government of God, is carefully avoided, unless the following be an exception.

> O that God,
> Profuse of poisons, would concede the chalice
> Which but one living man has drained, who now,
> Vessel of deathless wrath, a slave that feels
> No proud exemption in the blighting curse
> He bears, over the world wanders forever,
> Lone as incarnate death! (p. 47.)

Our readers will be startled at the profanity of this strange exclamation, but we can assure them that it is the only reference to the Deity in the poem. It was, we presume, part of the Author's plan, to represent his hero as an atheist of that metaphysical school, which held that the universe was God, and that the powers of evil constituted a sort of demonology. He speaks in his Preface of "the poet's self-centered seclusion" being "avenged by the furies of an irresistible passion pursuing him to speedy ruin." "But *that power*," he adds, "which strikes the luminaries of the world with sudden darkness and extinction, by awakening them to too exquisite a perception of its influences, dooms to a slow and *poisonous* decay those meaner spirits which dare to objure its dominion." It is a pity that in his Preface Mr. S. had not avoided such jargon.

We shall enter no further into the Author's theory, nor shall we subject his poetry to minute criticism. It cannot be denied that very considerable talent for descriptive poetry is displayed in several parts. The Author has genius which might be turned to much better account; but such heartless fictions as Alastor, fail in accomplishing the legitimate purposes of poetry. In justice to the Author, we subjoin the following extract.

[*Quotes lines 420-468*]

THE EXAMINER PROPHESIES AND PRAISES

[From The Examiner, December 1, 1816, and January 19, 1817 (no. 466, pp. 761-762, and no. 473, p. 41). These two brief notices mark the beginning of Leigh Hunt's long course of praise, explanation, and defence of Shelley, lasting for many years after the poet's death. With a few possible minor exceptions everything in The Examiner relating to Shelley was written by Hunt, who also wrote about him in The Indicator and in several books. No other person fought as long and as effectively to bring about Shelley's ultimate recognition as a great poet. In reviewing Shelley's works Hunt's aim is primarily sympathetic exposition rather than ardent championship; but in answering hostile reviewers he is a whole-hearted champion, especially on personal matters. It was this connection with Hunt that made many Tory and conservative writers consider Shelley as one of the Cockneys and assail him as such.]

Young Poets

In sitting down to this subject we happen to be restricted by time to a much shorter notice than we could wish; but we mean to take it up again shortly. Many of our readers however have perhaps observed for themselves, that there has been a new school of poetry rising of late, which promises to extinguish the French one that has prevailed among us since the time of Charles the 2d. It began with something excessive, like most revolutions, but this gradually wore away; and an evident aspiration after real nature and original fancy remained, which called to mind the finer times of the English Muse. In fact it is wrong to call it a new school, and still more so to represent it as one of innovation, its only object being to restore the same love of Nature, and of *thinking* instead of mere *talking*, which formerly rendered us real poets, and not merely versifying wits, and bead-rollers of couplets.

We were delighted to see the departure of the old school acknowledged in the number of the *Edinburgh Review* just published,—a candour the more generous and spirited, inasmuch as that work has hitherto been the greatest surviving ornament of the same school in prose and criticism, as it is now destined, we trust, to be still the leader in the new.

We also felt the same delight at the third canto of Lord Byron's *Child Harold*, in which, to our conceptions at least, he has fairly renounced a certain leaven of the French style, and taken his place where we always said he would be found,—among the poets who have a real feeling for numbers, and who go directly to Nature for inspiration. But more of this poem in our next.[1]

[1] By the way, we are authorised to mention, that the person in Cheapside who announces some new publications by his Lordship, and says he has given five hundred guineas for them,

The object of the present article is merely to notice three young writers, who appear to us to promise a considerable addition of strength to the new school. Of the first who came before us, we have, it is true, yet seen only one or two specimens, and these were no sooner sent us than we unfortunately mislaid them; but we shall procure what he has published, and if the rest answer to what we have seen, we shall have no hesitation in announcing him for a very striking and original thinker. His name is PERCY BYSSHE SHELLEY, and he is the author of a poetical work entitled *Alastor, or the Spirit of Solitude.*

[*The remaining two-thirds of the article is devoted to Reynolds and Keats, both of whom are quoted. Shelley is not quoted until January 19, 1817.*]

Hymn to Intellectual Beauty

The following Ode, originally announced under the signature of the *Elfin Knight,* we have since found to be from the pen of the author, whose name was mentioned among others a week or two back in an article entitled "Young Poets." The reader will think with us, that it is alone sufficient to justify what was there observed:—but we shall say more on this subject in a review of the book we mentioned:—

Hymn to Intellectual Beauty

[*Quoted entire. This is its first publication.*]

SHELLEY IN COURT

[From The Examiner, January 26, 1817 (no. 474, p. 60).]

Law Court of Chancery
Friday, Jan. 24
Westbrooke v. Shelley

Sir S. Romilly moved for an order to prevent the defendant exercising any guardianship over his children, on the ground of his Deistical principles. It appeared the defendant had some time since written a book, called *Queen Mab,* which openly avowed the principles of Deism, and in such a case he could certainly not be considered a proper person for educating youth. The interests of society would obviously be endangered were persons of these principles permitted to instil them into their children. Interference in such a case was peremptorily called for, and he (Sir S.) had no doubt, from his Lordship's well-known attention to the duties of parents, and his anxiety respecting every thing where morals were concerned, what his decision in this instance would be.

---

has no warrant whatsoever for so stating. We are sorry to hurt the man's sale, as far as some other booksellers are concerned, who are just as money-getting and impudent in different ways; but truth must be told of one, as it will also be told of others.—(Since writing this note, we find the business noticed in Chancery, and some of the *verses* quoted, which will certainly satisfy the public that the Noble Poet was not the author.)

Sir A. Piggott, on the other hand, contended, that as his client had written this work merely for his own amusement, without the most distant idea of his children seeing it, it was extremely hard that he should be deprived of the exercise of his parental rights, as the work was a mere effusion of imagination.

His Lordship is to give judgment on a future day.

BLACKWOOD'S UNEARTHS PROMISE

[From Blackwood's Edinburgh Magazine, November, 1819 (6: 148-154). By John Wilson. Blackwood's pronounced at length on every book that appeared under Shelley's name except the *Queen Mab* piracies. Shelley read this review in Florence and enjoyed seeing The Quarterly "cut up," as he stated in a letter to Ollier (December 15 or 25). On December 15, 1819, Mary Shelley sent this review to Maria Gisborne, remarking that Blackwood's "takes up arms in Shelley's defence."

In 1826 (Preface to Vol. XIX) Blackwood's reviewed its earlier criticism and took pride in having consistently recognized Shelley's genius. It still condemned his principles, though he was "scarcely in his right mind." If the words of Blackwood's merry men were always to be taken at par value this article would indicate that Walter Scott wrote one or more of the earlier reviews of Shelley, for it claims that Shelley "was proud to know that some of the articles in our work on his poetry were written by a poet whose genius he admired and imitated" (p. xxix). Apparently the Shelleys did suspect that Walter Scott may have written the review of *Alastor*. The letter of Mary Shelley to Maria Gisborne, quoted above (*Shelley Memorials*, p. 142), says, "We half think that . . . it must be Walter Scott, the only liberal man of that faction."

For further discussion of Blackwood's Magazine, see Chapter I.]

We believe this little volume to be Mr. Shelley's first publication; and such of our readers as have been struck by the power and splendour of genius displayed in the Revolt of Islam, and by the frequent tenderness and pathos of "Rosalind and Helen," will be glad to observe some of the earliest efforts of a mind destined, in our opinion, under due discipline and self-management, to achieve great things in poetry. It must be encouraging to those who, like us, cherish high hopes of this gifted but wayward young man, to see what advances his intellect has made within these few years, and to compare its powerful, though still imperfect display, in his principal poem with its first gleamings and irradiations throughout this production almost of his boyhood. In a short preface, written with all the enthusiasm and much of the presumption of youth, Mr. Shelley gives a short explanation of the subject of "Alastor; or, the Spirit of Solitude," which we cannot say throws any very great light upon it, but without which, the poem would be, we suspect, altogether unintelligible to ordinary readers. Mr. Shelley is too fond of allegories; and a great genius like his should scorn, now that it has reached the maturity of manhood, to adopt a species of poetry in which the difficulties of the art may be so conveniently blinked, and weakness find so easy a refuge in obscurity.

[Quotes the first paragraph of Shelley's Preface]

Our readers will not expect, from this somewhat dim enunciation, at all times to see the drift of this wild poem; but we think they will feel, notwithstanding, that there is the light of poetry even in the darkness of Mr. Shelley's imagination.   Alastor is thus first introduced to our notice.

[Quotes lines 67-82]

He is then described as visiting volcanoes, lakes of bitumen, caves winding among the springs of fire, and starry domes of diamond and gold, supported by crystal columns, and adorned with shrines of pearl and thrones of chrysolite—a magnificent pilgrimage no doubt, and not the less so on account of its being rather unintelligible.   On completing his mineralogical and geological observations, and on re-ascending from the interior of our earth into the upper regions, his route is, to our taste, much more interesting and worthy of a poet.

[Quotes lines 107-128]

During the soul-rapt enthusiasm of these mystic and magnificent wanderings, Alastor has no time to fall in love; but we are given to understand that, wherever he roams, he inspires it.   There is much beauty in this picture.

This poor Arabian maid has no power to detain him, and

> The poet wandering on, through Arabie
> And Persia, and the wild Carmanian waste,
> And o'er the aerial mountains which pour down
> Indus and Oxus from their icy caves,
> In joy and exultation held his way.

At last, as he lies asleep in the loneliest and loveliest dell in the Vale of Cashmire, a vision comes upon him, bringing with it a dream of hopes never felt before.

[Quotes lines 151-172]

In an agony of passion, he grasps the beautiful phantom in his arms; but awakening in that delirium, finds himself alone in the now desolate loveliness of nature.   A fire is now in his life's blood, and he is carried along, from clime to clime, on the tempest of his own soul.

[Quotes lines 239-290, omitting 247-272]

Just as he finishes this exclamation, he sees a little shallop floating near the shore, and a restless impulse urges him to embark,

> And meet lone Death on the drear ocean's waste;
> For well he knew that mighty shadow loves
> The slimy caverns of the populous deep.

He sails along in calm or storm, till the shallop is driven into a cavern in the "etherial cliffs of Caucasus."   It is scarcely to be expected that his submontane voyage should be very distinctly described, and we lose sight of Alastor and his pinnace, in dark and boiling caverns, till we joyfully hail his fortunate reappearance.

[*Quotes lines 397-412*]

Here some mysterious influences seem breathed from the spirit of nature over Alastor's soul, and its agitation to sink into a sort of melancholy calm. The following description, though rather too much laboured, in the unsatisfactory prodigality of opulent youth, is, beyond doubt, most highly poetical.

[*Quotes lines 420-468*]

In this sublime solitude, his wornout being is felt to be interfused with that of nature itself, and, at the same time, there blends with his dying delight a profound remembrance of that momentary vision that flashed upon his soul, and filled his longing heart, in the Vale of Cashmire.

> —When his regard
> Was raised by intense pensiveness,—two eyes,
> Two starry eyes, hung in the gloom of thought,
> And seemed with their serene and azure smiles
> To beckon him.

He now feels the dark approaching consciousness of death—and we think the following address to a stream, on whose banks the youth is lying, contains a wild, and solemn, and mysterious foreboding of dissolution.

[*Quotes lines 502-514*]

The beauty of the woods seems now to decay, and there is a gradual but ghastly change all around, which is described by a very fine image.

> For, as fast years flow away,
> The smooth brow gathers, and the hair grows thin
> And white, and where irradiate dewy eyes
> Had shone, gleam stony orbs:—so from his steps
> Bright flowers departed, and the beautiful shade
> Of the green groves, with all their odorous winds
> And musical motions.

The stream, on whose banks he strays, leads him into a dreadful land, where all is wrapped in the dimness and thunder of fear; but the pilgrim's dreary travel ends in peace. For,

> One silent nook
> Was there. Even on the edge of that vast mountain,
> Upheld by knotty roots and fallen rocks,
> It overlooked in its serenity
> The dark earth, and the bending vault of stars.

Soon as his feet fall on the threshold of this green recess, the wanderer feels that his last hour is come. There is scarcely any part of the Poem which does not partake of a character of extravagance—and probably many of our readers may have felt this to be the case in our extracts, even more than ourselves. Be this as it may, we cannot but think that there is great sublimity in the death scene.

> He did place
> His pale lean hand upon the rugged trunk
> Of the old pine. Upon an ivied stone
> Reclined his languid head, his limbs did rest,
> Diffused and motionless on the smooth brink
> Of that obscurest chasm;—and thus he lay,
> Surrendering to their final impulses
> The hovering powers of life. Hope and despair,
> The torturers, slept; no mortal pain or fear
> Marred his repose; the influxes of sense,
> And his own being unalloyed by pain,
> Yet feebler and more feeble, calmly fed
> The stream of thought, till he lay breathing there
> At peace, and faintly smiling:—his last sight
> Was the great moon, which o'er the western line
> Of the great wide world her mighty horn suspended,
> With whose dun beams inwoven darkness seemed
> To mingle. Now upon the jagged hills
> It rests, and still as the divided frame
> Of the vast meteor sunk, the Poet's blood,
> That ever beat in mystic sympathy
> With nature's ebb and flow, grew feebler still:
> And when two lessening points of light alone
> Gleamed thro' the darkness, the alternate gasp
> Of his faint respiration scarce did stir
> The stagnate night:—till the minutest ray
> Was quenched, the pulse yet lingered in his heart.
> It paused—it fluttered. But when heaven remained
> Utterly black, the murky shades involved
> An image, silent, cold, and motionless,
> As their own voiceless earth and vacant air.
> Even as a vapour fed with golden beams
> That ministered on the sunlight, ere the west
> Eclipses it, was now that wondrous frame—
> No sense, no motion, no divinity—
> A fragile lute, on whose harmonious strings
> The breath of heaven did wander—a bright stream
> Once fed with many-voiced waves—a dream
> Of youth, which night and time have quenched for ever,
> Still, dark, and dry, and unremembered now.

Several of the smaller poems contain beauties of no ordinary kind—but they are almost all liable to the charge of vagueness and obscurity.—Mr. Shelley's imagination is enamoured of dreams of death; and he loves to strike his harp among the tombs.

[*Quotes the poem* On Death, *entire*]

There breathes over the following scene, a spirit of deep, solemn, and mournful repose.

A Summer-Evening Church-Yard,
Lechlade, Gloucestershire.

[*Quoted entire*]

Long as our extracts have been, we must find room for one more, from a strange and unintelligible fragment of a poem, entitled "The Daemon of the World." It is exceedingly beautiful.

[*Quotes lines 1-48*]

We beg leave, in conclusion, to say a few words about the treatment which Mr. Shelley has, in his poetical character, received from the public. By our periodical critics he has either been entirely overlooked, or slightly noticed, or grossly abused. There is not so much to find fault with in the mere silence of critics; but we do not hesitate to say, with all due respect for the general character of that journal, that Mr. Shelley has been infamously and stupidly treated in the Quarterly Review. His Reviewer there, whoever he is, does not shew himself a man of such lofty principles as to entitle him to ride the high horse in company with the author of the Revolt of Islam. And when one compares the vis inertiae of his motionless prose with the "eagle-winged raptures" of Mr. Shelley's poetry, one does not think indeed of Satan reproving Sin, but one does think, we will say it in plain words and without a figure, of a dunce rating a man of genius. If that critic does not know that Mr. Shelley is a poet, almost in the very highest sense of that mysterious word, then, we appeal to all those whom we have enabled to judge for themselves, if he be not unfit to speak of poetry before the people of England. If he does not know that Mr. Shelley is a great poet, what manner of man is he who, with such conviction, brings himself, with the utmost difficulty, to admit that there is any beauty at all in Mr. Shelley's writings, and is happy to pass that admission off with an accidental and niggardly phrase of vague and valueless commendation. This is manifest and mean—glaring and gross injustice on the part of a man who comes forward as the champion of morality, truth, faith, and religion. This is being guilty of one of the very worst charges of which he accuses another; nor will any man who loves and honours genius, even though that genius may have occasionally suffered itself to be both stained and led astray, think but with contempt and indignation and scorn of a critic who, while he pretends to wield the weapons of honour, virtue, and truth, yet clothes himself in the armour of deceit, hypocrisy, and falsehood. He *exults* to calumniate Mr. Shelley's moral character, but he *fears* to acknowledge his genius. And therefore do we, as the sincere though sometimes sorrowing friends of Mr. Shelley, scruple not to say, even though it may expose us to the charge of personality from those from whom alone such a charge could at all affect our minds, that the critic shews himself by such conduct as far inferior to Mr. Shelley as a man of worth, as the language in which he utters his falsehood and uncharitableness shews him to be inferior as a man of intellect.

In the present state of public feeling, with regard to poets and poetry, a critic cannot attempt to defraud a poet of his fame, without paying the penalty either of his ignorance or his injustice. So long as he confines the expression of his envy or stupidity to works of moderate or doubtful merit, he may escape punishment; but if he dare to insult the spirit of England by contumelious and scornful treatment of any one of her gifted sons, that contumely and that scorn will most certainly be flung back upon himself, till he be made to shrink and to shiver beneath the load. It is not in the power of all the critics alive to blind one true lover of poetry to the splendor of Mr. Shelley's genius—and the reader who, from mere curiosity, should turn to the Revolt of Islam to see what sort of trash it was that so moved the wrath and the spleen of the Reviewer, would soon feel, that to understand the greatness of the poet, and the littleness of his traducer, nothing more was necessary than to recite to his delighted sense any six successive stanzas of that poem, so full of music, imagination, intellect, and passion. We care comparatively little for injustice offered to one moving majestical in the broad day of fame—it is the injustice done to the great, while their greatness is unknown or misunderstood that a generous nature most abhors, in as much as it seems more basely wicked to wish that genius might never lift its head, than to envy the glory with which it is encircled.

There is, we firmly believe, a strong love of genius in the people of this country, and they are willing to pardon to its possessor much extravagance and error—nay, even more serious transgressions. Let both Mr. Shelley and his critic think of that—let it encourage the one to walk onwards to his bright destiny, without turning into dark or doubtful or wicked ways—let it teach the other to feel a proper sense of his own insignificance, and to be ashamed, in the midst of his own weaknesses and deficiencies and meannesses, to aggravate the faults of the highly gifted, and to gloat with a sinful satisfaction on the real or imaginary debasement of genius and intellect.

And here we ought, perhaps, to stop. But the Reviewer has dealt out a number of dark and oracular denunciations against the Poet, which the public can know nothing about, except that they imply a charge of immorality and wickedness. Let him speak out plainly, or let him hold his tongue. There are many wicked and foolish things in Mr. Shelley's creed and we have not hitherto scrupled, nor shall we henceforth scruple to expose that wickedness and folly. But we do not think that he believes his own creed—at least, that he believes it fully and to utter conviction—and we doubt not but the scales will yet all fall from his eyes. The Reviewer, however, with a face of most laughable horror, accuses Mr. Shelley in the same breath of some nameless act of atrocity, and of having been rusticated, or expelled, or warned to go away from the University of Oxford! He seems to shudder with the same holy fear at the violation of the laws of morality and the breaking of college rules. He forgets that in the world men do not wear caps and gowns as at Oriel or Exeter. He preaches not like Paul—but like a Proctor.

Once more, then we bid Mr. Shelley farewell. Let him come forth from the eternal city, where, we understand, he has been sojourning,—in his strength, conquering and to conquer. Let his soul watch his soul, and listen to the voice of its own noble nature—and there is no doubt that the future will make amends for the past, whatever its errors may have been—and that the Poet may yet be good, great, and happy.

V

THE REVOLT OF ISLAM

THE EXAMINER PRAISES AT LENGTH

[From The Examiner, February 1, February 22, and March 1, 1818 (no. 527, pp. 75-76; no. 530, pp. 121-122; and no. 531, pp. 139-141). This continued review really begins in the issue of January 25, with the quotation (without comment except for italics) of fifty-eight lines of the poem describing Laon's execution, beginning with the last sentence of Canto 12, stanza 2. Seventy-two lines had been previously quoted without comment in the issue of November 30.]

This is an extraordinary production. The ignorant will not understand it; the idle will not take the pains to get acquainted with it; even the intelligent will be startled at first with its air of mysticism and wildness; the livelier man of the world will shake his head at it good naturedly; the sulkier one will cry out against it; the bigot will be shocked, terrified, and enraged; and fall to proving all that is said against himself; the negatively virtuous will resent the little quarter that is given to mere custom; the slaves of bad customs or bad passions of any sort will either seize their weapons against it, trembling with rage or conscious worthlessness, or hope to let it quietly pass by, as an enthusiasm that must end in air; finally, the hopeless, if they are ill-tempered, will envy its hopefulness,—if good tempered, will sorrowfully anticipate its disappointment,—both from self-love, though of two different sorts;—but we will venture to say, that the intelligent and the good, who are yet healthy-minded, and who have not been so far blinded by fear and self-love as to confound superstition with desert, anger and hatred with firmness, or despondency with knowledge, will find themselves amply repaid by breaking through the outer shell of this production, even if it be with the single reflection, that so much ardour for the happy virtues, and so much power to recommend them, have united in the same person. To will them with hope indeed is to create them; and to extend that will is the object of the writer before us.

The story of the "Revolt of Islam" is this. The poet, rising from "visions of despair" occasioned by the late triumphs over the progress of mankind, goes meditating by the sea-shore, and after an awful and prophetic tempest, suddenly sees in the air the extraordinary spectacle of a combat between a serpent and an eagle:—

> The Serpent's mailed and many-coloured skin
> Shone through the plumes its coils were twined within
> By many a swollen and knotted fold; and high
> And far, the neck, receding light and thin,
> Sustained a crested head, which warily
> Shifted and glanced before the Eagle's stedfast eye.

The Serpent is defeated, and falls into the sea, from whence he is received into the bosom of a beautiful woman who sits lamenting upon the shore. She invites the poet to go somewhere across the sea with them in a boat. He consents, more in fear for her than for himself; and in the course of the voyage she tells him that the Serpent and the Eagle are the powers of Good and Evil who combat with each other at intervals; that the Serpent, or Power of Good, has again been defeated; and that she herself is his selected companion, whom in his more radiant shape he appeared to once at night, and announced his having fallen in love with. The Serpent all this while lies still, recovering from the effects of the combat; and at last the voyagers come to a magnificent temple beyond the polar ocean in which

> . . . There sat on many a sapphire throne
> The Great, who had departed from mankind,
> A mighty Senate;—some, whose white hair shone
> Like mountain snow, mild, beautiful, and blind.
> Some female forms, whose gestures beamed with mind;
> And ardent youths, and children bright and fair;
> And some had lyres, whose strings were intertwined
> With pale and clinging flames, which ever there,
> Waked faint yet thrilling sounds that pierced the
>   chrystal air

A magic and obscure circumstance then takes place, the result of which is: that the woman and Serpent are seen no more, but that a cloud opens asunder and a bright and beautiful shape, which seems compounded of both, is beheld sitting on a throne—a circumstance apparently imitated from Milton.

[*Quotes Canto I, lines 640-654, omitting lines 654-657*]

This is a fine Grecian feeling of what may be called the sentiment of shape. The two strangers are the hero and heroine of the poem: and here the more human part of the story commences. *Laon,* the hero, relates it. He was an ardent and speculative youth, born in modern Greece; and grew up with great admiration of the beauties and kindnesses of external nature, and a great horror of the superstitions and other oppressions with which his country and mankind in general were afflicted. A beautiful female orphan under the care of his parents shared these feelings with him; and a mutual love was the consequence. She even speculated upon taking some extraordinary though gentle step to deliver the world from its thraldom; when she was torn away from him by some slaves of the Grand Turk's Seraglio; and he himself, for endeavouring to rescue her, and for taking that opportunity of proclaiming freedom, was shut up in a prison in a rock, where his senses forsook him. The effect of the circumstance however is not lost. He is delivered from his dungeon by an old man, and after a second but milder insanity, is informed by his preserver that the people had been awakened to new ideas, and that there was a maiden who went

about exciting them to a bloodless freedom. It was his love *Cythna,* after
having been made a victim of the tyrant's lust, and having been likewise
imprisoned, and robbed of her senses. A considerable interval elapses while
Laon recovers his reason, but on so doing, and hearing of the exploits of
her whom he justly supposed to be his lovely friend, he takes leave of the
old man, and journeys for Constantinople, or the Golden City, where he
finds the people risen, the tyrant fallen, and *Cythna* the predominant spirit
of the change. He goes with others to the palace, and sees the "sceptered
wretch" sitting silent and sullen on the footstool of his throne,—

> Alone, but for one child, who led before him
> A graceful dance:—*weeping and murmuring*
> *'Mid her sad task of unregarded love,*
> *That to no smiles it might his speechless sadness move.*

She clasps the tyrant's feet, and then stands up when the strangers come
nigh;—

> Her lips and cheeks seemed very pale and wan,
> But on her forehead, and within her eye
> Lay beauty, which makes hearts that feed thereon
> Sick with excess of sweetness; on the throne
> She leaned; the King, with gathered brow and lips
> *Wreathed by long scorn,* did inly sneer and frown
> *With hue like that when some great painter dips*
> *His pencil in the gloom of earthquake and eclipse.*

Laon saves his life from the fury of the crowd; a festival is held at which
Cythna presides like a visible angel, and every thing seems happiness and
security. The Revolters however are suddenly assailed by the allies of
the tyrant; and the fortune of the contest is changed. *Cythna* reaches *Laon*
through the lost battle on a huge black Tartarian horse, "whose path makes
a solitude"; and they fly to a distance through a desolate village, in the
dwellings of which the flames and human beings were now dead:—

> But the wide sky,
> Flooded with lightning, *was ribbed overhead*
> *By the black rafters;* and around did lie
> Women, and babes, and men, slaughtered confusedly.

The only survivor is a female, who has gone mad, and fancies herself the
Plague. The description of her desperate laughter and actions is appalling,
though not without a tendency, we think, to something overwrought and
artificial. When the travellers arrive at a place of rest, *Cythna* tells *Laon*
her adventures. They have been briefly alluded to, and include a finely-
fancied and pathetic account of a child which she had in her dungeon, and
which was taken from her. *Laon* goes out from the retreat occasionally
to get food and intelligence, and finds that Revenge, and subsequently
Pestilence and Famine, have been making terrible havoc in the city. The
tyrant and his slaves, in their terror, make frightened addresses to heaven.

and a priest advises them to expiate its "vengeance" by sacrificing *Laon* and *Cythna*. He accordingly dispatches members to hunt them out; upon which *Laon* comes forward disguised and offers to give up the man provided the woman be spared. They take an oath to do so, and he declares himself; but it is then declared impious to have made the oath; and at last, *Cythna* comes voluntarily forward, and shares the funeral pyre with her beloved friend, from which they find themselves suddenly sailing on a beautiful sea to the Paradise in which the Spirit of Good resides, where *Cythna* meets with her child who had died of the plague; and the poem concludes.

We gave the fine description of the preparation for the sacrifice last week; we shall pursue our criticism next, with further extracts, an account of the particular views of the author, and a summary of the poetical character of the work in general.

*   *   *

We have given the story of this extraordinary book, and some extracts by which the reader can easily judge of its general merits. We have some remarks however to make on the particular qualities of its poetry, and on the deep social interests upon which it speculates; but as we are much pressed for room now the Parliament are sitting, and yet do not wish to pass over the work lightly, we had better occupy our present article at once with some extracts we intended to make from the author's preface. He explains in them the general object of his poem, and touches in a masterly manner upon the great political point of it, and indeed of the age in which we live.

"The poem," says he, "which I now present to the world, is an attempt from which I scarcely dare to expect success, and in which a writer of established fame might fail without disgrace. It is an experiment on the temper of the public mind, as to *how far a thirst for a happier condition of moral and political society survives, among the enlightened and refined, the tempests which have shaken the age in which we live*. I have sought to enlist the harmony of metrical language, the ethereal combinations of the fancy, the rapid and subtle transitions of human passion, all those elements which essentially compose a Poem, in the cause of a liberal and comprehensive morality, and in the view of kindling within the bosoms of my readers, a virtuous enthusiasm for those doctrines of liberty and justice, *that faith and hope in something good*, which neither violence, nor misrepresentation, nor prejudice, can ever totally extinguish among mankind."

After dilating a little more on the subjects of his poem, Mr. Shelley, with the feeling that ever seems to be at the bottom of his warmth, gives the following placid and easy solution of a difficulty, which the world, we believe, is also instinctively solving, but which, as he says, has been the "moral ruin" of some eminent spirits among us. If the Lake School, as they are called, were not as dogmatic in their despair as they used to be in their hope, we should earnestly recommend the passage to their attention.

They might see in it, at any rate, how it becomes an antagonist to talk; and how charitable and consistent the mind can be, that really inquires into the philosophical causes of things. Mr. Shelley does not say that Mr. Southey is "no better than a house-breaker"; nor does he exclaim with Mr. Wordsworth, in the ill-concealed melancholy of a strange piety, which would be still stranger if it were really cheerful, that "Carnage is God's daughter." He is not in the habit, evidently, of begging the question against the low and uneducated; nor has he the least respect for that very sweeping lady, Miss Theodosia Carnage;—but stop; we must not be violating the charity of his philosophy.

"The panic," says our author . . .

[*Quotes, with liberal use of italics, paragraphs four and five of Shelley's Preface, discussing the French Revolution*]

* * *

The reader has seen the fable as well as some passages of this poem, and heard the author's own account of his intentions in extracts from the preface. It remains for us to give a general criticism upon it, interspersed with a few more specimens; and as the object of the work is decidedly philosophical, we shall begin with the philosophy.

Mr. Shelley is of opinion with many others that the world is a very beautiful one externally, but wants a good deal of mending with respect to its mind and habits; and for this purpose he would quash as many cold and selfish passions as possible, and rouse up the general element of Love, till it set our earth rolling more harmoniously. The answer made to a writer, who sets out with endeavours like these, is that he is idly aiming at perfection; but Mr. Shelley has no such aim, neither have nine hundred and ninety-nine out of a thousand of the persons who have ever been taunted with it. Such a charge, in truth, is only the first answer which egotism makes to any one who thinks he can go beyond its own ideas of the possible. If this however be done away, the next answer is, that you are attempting something wild and romantic,—that you will get disliked for it as well as lose your trouble,—and that you had better coquet, or rather play the prude, with things as they are. The worldly sceptic smiles, and says "Hah!"—the dull rogues wonder, or laugh out;—the disappointed egotist gives you a sneering admonition, having made up his mind about all these things because he and his friends could not alter them; the hypocrite affects to be shocked: the bigot anticipates the punishment that awaits you for daring to say that God's creation is not a vile world, nor his creatures bound to be miserable;—and even the more amiable compromiser with superstition expresses alarm for you,—does not know what you may be hazarding, though he believes nevertheless that God is all good and just,—refers you to the fate of Adam, to shew you that because he introduced the knowledge of evil, you must not attempt to do it away again,—and finally, advises you to comfort yourself with *faith*, and to secure a life in the next world because *this* is a bad business, and *that*, of course, you may find a worse. It seems forgotten all this while, that Jesus Christ himself recommended Love as the great law that was to supersede others; and recommended it too to an extreme, which has been held impracticable. How far it has been found impracticable, in consequence of his doctrines having been mixed up with contradictions and threatening dogmas, and with a system of after-life which contradicts all its principles, may be left to the consideration. Will theologians never discover, that men, in order to be good and just to each other, must either think well of a Divine Being, really and not pretendingly or not think of him at all? That they must worship Goodness and a total absence of the revengeful and malignant passions, if not Omnipotence? or else that they must act upon this quality for themselves, and agree with a devout and amiable Pagan, that "it were better men should say there was no such being as Plutarch, than that there was one Plutarch who eat his own children?" Instead of the alarms about searches after happiness being wise and salutary, when the world is confessedly discordant, they would seem, if we believed in such things, the most fatal and ingenious invention of an enemy of mankind. But it is only so much begging of the question, fatal indeed as far as it goes, and refusing in the strangest manner to look after good, because there is a necessity for it. And as to the Eastern apologue of Adam and Eve (for so many Christians as well as others have thought it), it would be merely shocking to humanity and to a sense of justice in any other light; but it is, in fact, a very deep though not wisely managed allegory, deprecating the folly of mankind in losing their simplicity and enjoyment, and in taking to those very mistakes about vice and virtue, which it is the object of such authors as the one before us to do away again. Faith! It is the very object they have in view; not indeed faiths in endless terrors and contradictions, but "a faith and hope," as Mr. Shelley says, "in something good,"—that faith in the power of men to be kinder and happier, which other faiths take so much pains, and professed pains, to render unbelievable even while they recommend it! "Have faith," says the theologian, "and bear your wretchedness, and escape the wrath to come." "*Have* faith," says the philosopher, "and begin to be happier now, and do not attribute odious qualities to any one."

People get into more inconsistencies in opposing the hopes and efforts of a philosophical enthusiasm than on any other subject. They say "use your reason, instead of your expectations"; and yet this is the reverse of what they do in their own beliefs. They say, take care how you contradict custom;—yet Milton, whom they admire, set about ridiculing it, and paying his addresses to another woman in his wife's lifetime, till the latter treated him better. They say it is impossible the world should alter; and yet it has often altered. They say it is impossible, at any rate, it should mend; yet people are no longer burnt at the stake. They say, but it is too old to alter to any great purpose of happiness,—that all its experience goes to the contrary; and yet they talk at other times of the brief life and shortsighted knowledge of man, and of the nothingness of "a thousand years." The experience of a man and an ephemeris are in fact just on a par in all that regards the impossibility of change. But one man,—they say—what can one man do? Let a glorious living person answer,—let Clarkson answer; who sitting down in his youth by a road-side, thought upon the horrors of the Slave Trade, and vowed he would dedicate his life to endeavour at overthrowing it. He was laughed at; he was violently opposed; he was called presumptuous and even irreligious; he was thought out of his senses; he made a noble sacrifice of his own health and strength; and he has *lived* to see the Slave Trade, aye, even the slavery of the descendants of the "cursed" Ham, made a Felony.

We have taken up so much room in noticing these objections, that we have left ourselves none for entering into a further account of Mr. Shelley's views than he himself has given; and we have missed any more quotations at last. But we are sure that he will be much better pleased to see obstructions cleared away from the progress of such opinions as his, than the most minute account given of them in particular. It may be briefly repeated, that they are at war with injustice, violence, and selfishness of every species, however disguised;—that they represent, in a very striking light, the folly and misery of systems, either practical or theoretical, which go upon penal and resentful grounds, and add "pain to pain"; and that they would have men, instead of worshipping tyrannies and terrors of any sort, worship goodness and gladness, diminish the vices and sorrows made by custom only, encourage the virtues and enjoyments which mutual benevolence may realize; and in short, make the best and utmost of this world, as well as hope for another.

The beauties of the poem consist in depth of sentiment, in grandeur of imagery, and a versification remarkably sweet, various, and noble, like the placid playing of a great organ. If the author's genius reminds us of any other poets, it is of two very opposite ones, Lucretius and Dante. The former he resembles in the Daedalian part of it, in the boldness of his speculations, and in his love of virtue, of external nature, and of love itself. It is his gloomier or more imaginative passages that sometimes remind us of Dante. The sort of supernatural architecture in which he delights has in particular the grandeur as well as obscurity of that great genius, to whom however he presents this remarkable and instructive contrast, that superstition and pain and injustice go hand in hand even in the pleasantest parts of Dante, like the three Furies, while philosophy, pleasure, and justice, smile through the most painful passages of our author, like the three Graces.

Mr. Shelley's defects as a poet are obscurity, inartificial and yet not natural economy, violation of costume, and too great a sameness and gratuitousness of image and metaphor, and of image and metaphor too drawn from the elements, particularly the sea. The book is full of humanity; and yet it certainly does not go the best way to work of appealing to it, because it does not appeal to it through the medium of its common knowledges. It is for this reason that we must say something, which we would willingly leave unsaid, both from admiration of Mr. Shelley's genius and love of his benevolence; and this is, that the work cannot possibly become popular. It may set others thinking and writing, and we have no doubt will do so; and those who can understand and relish it, will relish it exceedingly; but the author must forget his metaphysics and sea-sides a little more in his future works, and give full effect to that nice knowledge of men and things which he otherwise really possesses to an extraordinary degree. We have no doubt he is destined to be one of the leading spirits of his age, and indeed has already fallen into his place as such; but however resolute as to his object, he will only be doing it justice to take the most effectual means in his power to forward it.

We have only to observe in conclusion, as another hint to the hopeless, that although the art of printing is not new, yet the Press in any great and true sense of the word is a modern engine in the comparison, and the changeful times of society have never yet been accompanied with so mighty a one. *Books* did what was done before; they have now a million times the range and power; and the Press, which has got hold of Superstition, and given it some irrecoverable wounds already, will, we hope and believe, finally draw it in altogether, and crush it as a steam-engine would a great serpent.

THE MONTHLY MAGAZINE NOTES BRIEFLY

[From The Monthly Magazine and British Register, under Critical Notices of New Books, March, 1818 (45: 154).]

"The Revolt of Islam, a Poem in 12 Cantos, by Percy Bysshe Shelley," proves that the age of simplicity has returned again; but we fear that the experiment, or affectation, of an almost total neglect of harmonious modulation and quantity is carried to a very blameable excess. The following stanzas will convey some idea of the author's style.

[*Quotes the tribute to America, "There is a people, mighty in its youth"—eighteen lines, stanzas 22 and 23 of Canto XI*]

LEIGH HUNT AS A HANDICAP

A

[From The Quarterly Review, May, 1818 (18: 328-329), in the review of Hunt's *Foliage* by J. W. Croker. Shelley is not mentioned by name, but as the person to whom *Foliage* is dedicated and as an author of "disgraceful and flagitious history" whom the writer knew at Eton "setting fire to old trees with burning glasses." The thinly veiled allusions continue as given below.

Shelley read this pleasant picture of himself in Venice, and wrote to Leigh Hunt, "it makes me melancholy to consider the dreadful wickedness of heart which could have prompted such expressions as those with which the anonymous writer exults over my domestic calamities, and the perversion of understanding with which he paints your character."

This article is usually assigned to J. W. Croker, but it should be noted that

Croker was never at Eton, though the author of this article claims to have known
Shelley there, and that John Taylor Coleridge, who wrote the famous *Revolt of Islam*
review in The Quarterly, was at Eton with Shelley.]

. . . We may be very narrow-minded, but we look upon it still as somewhat dishonorable to have been expelled from a University for the monstrous absurdity of a "mathematical demonstration of the non-existence of
a God": according to our understandings, it is not a proof of a very affectionate heart to break that of a wife by cruelty and infidelity; and if we
were told of a man who, placed on a wild rock among the clouds, yet even
in that height surrounded by a loftier amphitheatre of spire-like mountains,
hanging over a valley of eternal ice and snow, where the roar of mighty
waterfalls was at times unheeded from the hollow and more appalling
thunder of the deep and unseen avalanche,—if we were told of a man
who, thus witnessing the sublimest assemblage of natural objects, should
retire to a cabin near and write atheos after his name in the album,[1] we
hope our own feelings would be pity rather than disgust; but we should
think it imbecility indeed to court that man's friendship, or to celebrate his
intellect or his heart as the wisest or warmest of the age.

B

[From The British Critic, July, 1818 (N. S. 10: 94). This passage occurs in a
review of Hunt's *Foliage* and is indexed: Shelley, Mr. P. B. an untouchable subject.]

Mr. Percy Bysshe Shelley—but we will not trust ourselves with this
person; Tacitus has taught us that there are some offences so flagitious in
their nature, that it is necessary, for the benefit of public morals, to conceal
their punishment; we leave them, therefore, to the silent vengeance which
vice sooner or later *must* wreak upon itself.   Mr. John Keats is, we hope,
of another class; and we have already expressed our due sense of his
progress in Mr. Hunt's poetical school.   He is well worthy of the three
sonnets with which he has been graced, for giving Mr. Hunt a "lofty
feeling and a kind," by topping him with leaves.

BLACKWOOD'S PRAISES AND CONDEMNS

[From Blackwood's Edinburgh Magazine, January, 1819 (4: 475-482). By
John Wilson.   Entitled "Observations on the Revolt of Islam."
This review may very well owe a great deal to De Quincey.   It is known that
De Quincey was asked by Wilson to review the book and that he read and praised it
at the time, but declined to review it.   (See *Letters About Shelley*, p. 98.)   George
Gilfillan, a friend of Wilson and a later admirer of Shelley, attributed the review to
Wilson, Edinburgh University Magazine, April, 1839, 1: 48; George Gilfillan, *His-
tory of a Man*, 1856, p. 91; and David Macrae, *George Gilfillan—Anecdotes and
Reminiscences*, 1891, p. 88); but Wilson's habits of picking his friends' minds are so
well established that it is not unlikely that he used some of De Quincey's opinions here.

[1] This story was printed in the following year by both The London Chronicle and The
Commercial Chronicle.   It was probably started by Southey.   See footnote on p. 157.

De Quincey had quoted from the poem a few months earlier in the Westmoreland Gazette. He quoted a motto from it again in 1821 in *The Pains of Opium,* and he praised and quoted the poem to Gilfillan some years later (Frank Henderson's edition of Gilfillan's *Sketches, Literary and Historical,* 1881, pp. 30-31.[2]]

A pernicious system of opinion concerning man and his moral government, a superficial audacity of unbelief, an overflowing abundance of uncharitableness towards almost the whole of his race, and a disagreeable measure of assurance and self-conceit—each of these things is bad, and the combination of the whole of them in the character of any one person might, at first sight, be considered as more than sufficient to render that one person utterly and entirely contemptible. Nor has the fact, in general, been otherwise. In every age, the sure ultimate reward of the sophistical and phantastical enemies of religion and good order among mankind, has been found in the contempt and the disgust of those against whose true interests their weapons had been employed. From this doom the most exquisite elegance of wit, and of words, the most perfect keenness of intellect, the most flattering despotism over contemporary opinion—all have not been able to preserve the inimitable Voltaire. In this doom, those wretched sophists of the present day, who would fain attempt to lift the load of oppressing infamy from off the memory of Voltaire, find their own living beings already entangled, "fold above fold, inextricable coil." Well may they despair:—we can almost pardon the·bitterness of their disappointed malice. Their sentence was pronounced without hesitation, almost without pity—for there was nothing in them to redeem their evil. They derived no benefit from that natural, universal, and proper feeling, which influences men to be slow in harshly, or suddenly, or irrevocably condemning intellects that bear upon them the stamp of power,—they had no part in that just spirit of respectfulness which makes men to contemplate, with an unwilling and unsteady eye, the aberrations of genius. The brand of inexpiable execration was ready in a moment to scar their fronts, and they have long wandered neglected about the earth—perhaps saved from extinction, like the fratricide, by the very mark of their ignominy.

Mr. Shelly [*sic*] is devoting his mind to the same pernicious purposes which have recoiled in vengeance upon so many of his contemporaries; but he possesses the qualities of a powerful and vigorous intellect, and therefore his fate cannot be sealed so speedily as theirs. He is also of the "COCKNEY SCHOOL," so far as his opinions are concerned; but the base opinions of the sect have not as yet been able entirely to obscure in him the character, or take away from him the privileges of the genius born within him. Hunt and Keats, and some others of the School, are indeed men of considerable cleverness, but as poets, they are worthy of sheer and instant contempt, and therefore their opinions are in little danger of being widely or deeply cir-

---

[2] For most of this information about Gilfillan and De Quincey I am indebted to manuscript notes furnished me by Mr. Alan Lang Strout. For Blackwood's on Shelley, see Chapter I; also Mr. Strout's "*Maga,* Champion of Shelley," Studies in Philology, January, 1932 (29: 95-119).

culated by their means. But the system, which found better champions than it deserved even in them, has now, it would appear, been taken up by one, of whom it is far more seriously, and deeply, and lamentably unworthy; and the poem before us bears unfortunately the clearest marks of its author's execrable system, but it is impressed every where with the more noble and majestic footsteps of his genius. It is to the operation of the painful feeling above alluded to, which attends the contemplation of perverted power—that we chiefly ascribe the silence observed by our professional critics, in regard to the Revolt of Islam. Some have held back in the fear that, by giving to his genius its due praise, they might only be lending the means of currency to the opinions in whose service he has unwisely enlisted its energies; while others, less able to appreciate his genius, and less likely to be anxious about suppressing his opinions, have been silent, by reason of their selfish fears—dreading, it may be, that by praising the Revolt of Islam, they might draw down upon their own heads some additional marks of that public disgust which followed their praises of Rimini.

Another cause which may be assigned for the silence of the critics should perhaps have operated more effectually upon ourselves; and this is, that the Revolt of Islam, although a fine, is, without all doubt, an obscure poem. Not that the main drift of the narrative is obscure, or even that there is any great difficulty in understanding the tendency of the undercurrent of its allegory—but the author has composed his poem in much haste, and he has inadvertently left many detached parts, both of his story and his allusion, to be made out as the reader best can, from very inadequate data. The swing of his inspiration may be allowed to have hurried his own eye, *pro tempore,* over many chasms; but Mr. Shelly has no excuse for printing a very unfinished piece—an error which he does not confess,— or indeed for many minor errors which he does confess in his very arrogant preface. The unskillful manner in which the allegory is brought out, and the doubt in which the reader is every now and then left, whether or no there be any allegory at all in the case; these alone are sufficient to render the perusal of this poem painful to persons of an active and ardent turn of mind; and, great as we conceive the merits of Mr. Shelly's poetry to be, these alone, we venture to prophesy, will be found sufficient to prevent the Revolt of Islam from ever becoming any thing like a favourite with the multitude.

At present, having entered our general protest against the creed of the author, and sufficiently indicated to our readers of what species its errors are,—we are very willing to save ourselves the unwelcome task of dwelling at any greater length upon these disagreable parts of our subject. We are very willing to pass in silence the many faults of Mr. Shelly's opinions, and to attend to nothing but the vehicle in which these opinions are conveyed. As a philosopher, our author is weak and worthless;—our business is with him as a poet, and, as such, he is strong, nervous, original; well entitled to take his place near to the great creative masters, whose works have shed its truest glory around the age wherein we live. As a political and infidel treatise, the Revolt of Islam is contemptible;—happily a great part of it has no necessary connexion either with politics or with infidelity. The native splendour of Mr. Shelley's faculties has been his safeguard from universal degradation, and a part, at least, of his genius, has been consecrated to themes worthy of it and of him. In truth, what he probably conceives to be the most exquisite ornaments of his poetry, appear, in our eyes, the chief deformities upon its texture; and had the whole been framed like the passages which we shall quote,—as the Revolt of Islam would have been a purer, so we have no doubt, would it have been a nobler, a loftier, a more majestic, and a more beautiful poem.

We shall pass over, then, without comment, the opening part of this work, and the confused unsatisfactory allegories with which it is chiefly filled. It is sufficient to mention, that, at the close of the first canto, the poet supposes himself to be placed for a time in the regions of eternal repose, where the good and great of mankind are represented as detailing, before the throne of the Spirit of Good, those earthly sufferings and labours which had prepared them for the possession and enjoyment of so blissful an abode. Among these are two, a man and a woman of Argolis, who, after rescuing their country for a brief space from the tyranny of the house of Othman, and accomplishing this great revolution by the force of persuasive eloquence and the sympathies of human love alone, without violence, bloodshed, or revenge,—had seen the fruit of all their toils blasted by foreign invasion, and the dethroned but not insulted tyrant replaced upon his seat; and who, finally, amidst all the darkness of their country's horizon, had died, without fear, the death of heroic martyrdom, gathering consolation, in the last pangs of their expiring nature, from the hope and the confidence that their faith and example might yet raise up successors to their labours, and that they had neither lived nor died in vain.

In the persons of these martyrs, the poet has striven to embody his ideas of the power and loveliness of human affections; and, in there history, he has set forth a series of splendid pictures, illustrating the efficacy of these affections in overcoming the evils of private and of public life. It is in the portraying of that passionate love, which had been woven from infancy in the hearts of Laon and Cythna, and which, binding together all their impulses in one hope and one struggle, had rendered them through life no more than two different tenements for the inhabitation of the same enthusiastic spirit;—it is in the portraying of this intense, overmastering, unfearing, unfading love, that Mr. Shelley has proved himself to be a great poet. Around his lovers, moreover, in the midst of all their fervours, he has shed an air of calm gracefulness, a certain majestic monumental stillness, which blends them harmoniously with the scene of their earthly existence, and realizes in them our ideas of Greeks struggling for freedom in the best spirit of their fathers.—We speak of the general effect—there are unhappily not a few passages in which the poet quits his vantage ground, and mars the beauty of his personifications by an intermixture of thoughts, feelings, and passions, with which, of right, they have nothing to do.

It is thus that Laon narrates the beginning of his love for Cythna,—if, indeed, his love can be said to have had any beginning, separate from that of his own intellectual and passionate life.

[*Quotes Canto II, stanzas 21 through 28, omitting 24*]

While the life of this happy pair is gliding away in day-dreams and night-dreams of delight, the arm of oppression is suddenly stretched forth against them. Their innocent repose is dissolved by the rude touch of savages, who come to bear the beautiful Cythna to the Harem of the tyrant, Othman,—as food

> To the hyena lust, who, among graves,
> Over his loathed meal, laughing in agony, raves,—

Laon, in his phrenzy, slays three of the ravishers, and is forthwith dragged by the rest of them to await the punishment of his violence in a strange prison.

[*Quotes Canto III, stanza 13, line 1218, through stanza 16*]

But the "peace of madness is" of long endurance, and Laon, wakening from thirst and hunger to a sense of his own condition, forgets that again in the remembrance of Cythna. A white sail is set on the bay far below him, and he feels that the vessel is destined to bear the maiden from the shore. The thought of this turns the stream of his mind to a darker channel, and the agonies of fierce madness succeed to the lethargy out of which he had arisen. The fourth day finds him raving on the summit of his pillar, when there arives at the foot of it a venerable hermit, who had heard of the cause of his affliction—of his generous nature and lofty aspirations. This visitor sets him free from his chain, and conveys him to a small bark below, while entirely insensible to what is passing around him; but he learns long afterwards, that the old man's eloquence had subdued his keepers, and that they had consented, at their own peril, to his escape. He is conveyed across the sea to a lonely island, where for seven years he is tended by his aged benefactor, whose kind and compassionate wisdom, and that long space, are not more than sufficient to win back the mind of Laon to entire self-possession.

In the first moments of the patient's perfect recovery, he is informed by the old man, that during the years of his illness the cause of liberty had been slowly gaining ground in the "Golden city"—that he himself would fain assist in the Revolution which had now actually commenced there, but that he felt himself too old and too subdued in his spirit and language to be an effectual leader,—

> While Laon's name to the tumultuous throng
> Were like the star whose beams the waves compel,
> And tempests; and his soul-subduing tongue
> Were as a lance to quell the mailed crest of wrong.

Laon accepts with eagerness the proposal of the old man, and they depart in their bark for the Revolutionized city.

On their arrival they find the work apparently well-nigh completed. An immense multitude of the people—of men weary of political, and women sick of domestic slavery—are assembled in the fields without the walls. Laon and his friend walk into the encampment, and are received as friends. The host already acknowledge a leader and a presiding spirit in the person of a female, whom they reverence under the name of LAONE. Laon and this heroine are attracted to each other by some unknown sympathy; the tones of her voice stir up all the depths of his spirit; but her countenance is veiled, and scarcely dares he wish to have the covering removed. The palace of the tyrant Othman, is, meantime, surrounded by the multitude; and Laon entering it, finds him sitting alone in his hall, deserted by all but one little child, whose affection has been won to him by previous commendations and caresses. Nothing can be more touching than the picture of this innocent. Thus speaks Laon:

[*Quotes Canto V, stanzas 22-23, describing the child*]

The monarch is quietly removed from his palace, none following him but this child; and on this consummation of their triumph, the multitude join in holding a high festival, of which Laone is the priestess. Laon sits near her in her pyramid; but he is withheld, by a strange impulse, from speaking to her, and he retires to pass the night in repose at a distance from where she sleeps.

At break of day, Laon is awakened by sounds of tumults; the multitude, lately so firm and collected, are seen flying in every direction; and he learns that the cause of their disarray is the arrival of a foreign army, sent by some of his brother princes to the relief of Othman. Laon, and a few of the more heroic spirits, withdraw to the side of a hill, where, ill-armed and outnumbered, they are slaughtered till the evening by their enemies. The carnage, and the confidence of the sufferers, are painted with a power and energy altogether admirable; but we have room to quote only the deliverance of Laon.

[*Quotes Canto VI, stanza 18, line 2493—stanza 22, line 2527*]

They take up their abode in a lonely ruin, and many hours are wasted in the transports of a recognition—which, even in such circumstances, to them is joyful.

[*Quotes Canto VI, stanza 32, line 2615—stanza 36, line 2658*]

They remain for some time in this retreat, communicating to each other the long histories of their suffering.—Cythna, according to her own wild tale, being carried away from Laon at the moment when he slew three of the slaves that surrounded her, had been conveyed to the tyrant's palace, and had suffered all the insults, and almost all the injuries to which its inmates were exposed. Her high spirit had, however, offended at last her oppressor, and she was sent to a submarine cavern, near the Symplegades, to which strange dungeon she was borne through the waves by a slave, "made dumb by poison,"

A Diver lean and strong, of Oman's coral sea.

Here she was supplied with a daily pittance of food by an eagle, trained to hover over the only crevice through which the air had access to the captive. She sank into a melancholy phrenzy, and was aroused to consciousness by strange feelings which taught her to expect that she was about to be a mother. It is so, and for a while all the sorrows of her prison are soothed by the caresses of her child; but the child disappears suddenly, and the bewildered mother half suspects that its existence has been but a dream of her madness. At last an earthquake changes the position of the cavern, and Cythna is released by some passing mariners, who convey her to the city of Othman, and are prepared by her discourses during the voyage to take a part in the insurrection, which Cythna arrives in time to lead. But to come to the main story—it is the custom of Laon to ride forth every night on the Tartar horse to procure food for Cythna. By this means their retreat is at last discovered, Laon is seized, led before the tyrant, and sentenced to be burned alive before his eyes, on the very scene of his treason. The guards, the priests, and the slaves, are gathered around the throne of Othman.

[*Quotes Canto XII, stanza 2, line 4465—stanza 8, line 4521, describing Laon's execution*]

This is Cythna come to partake the fate of her lord.

[*Quotes Canto XII, stanza 14, line 5467—stanza 22, line 4647, italicizing the last four and a half lines*]

We forbear from making any comments on this strange narrative; because we could not do so without entering upon other points which we have already professed our intention of waiving for the present. It will easily be seen, indeed, that neither the main interest nor the main merit of the poet at all consists in the conception of his plot or in the arrangement of his incidents. His praise is, in our judgment, that of having poured over his narrative a very rare strength and abundance of poetic imagery and feeling—of having steeped every word in the essence of his inspiration. The Revolt of Islam contains no detached passages at all comparable with some which our readers recollect in the works of the great poets our contemporaries; but neither does it contain any such intermixture of prosaic materials as disfigure even the greatest of them. Mr. Shelly has displayed his possession of a mind intensely poetical, and of an exuberance of poetic language, perpetually strong and perpetually varied. In spite, moreover, of a certain perversion in all his modes of thinking, which, unless he gets rid of it, will ever prevent him from being acceptable to any considerable or respectable body of readers, he has displayed many glimpses of right

understanding and generous feeling, which must save him from the unmingled condemnation even of the most rigorous judges. His destiny is
entirely in his own hands; if he acts wisely, it cannot fail to be a glorious
one; if he continues to pervert his talents, by making them the instruments
of a base sophistry, their splendour will only contribute to render his disgrace the more conspicuous. Mr. Shelly, whatever his errors may have
been, is a scholar, a gentleman, and a poet; and he must therefore dispise
from his soul the only eulogies to which he has hitherto been accustomed—
paragraphs from the Examiner, and sonnets from Johnny Keats. He has
it in his power to select better companions; and if he does so, he may very
securely promise himself abundance of better praise.

MORE PRAISE AND CENSURE

[From The Monthly Review, March, 1819 (88: 323-324). Part of this review
was reprinted in The Fireside Magazine or Monthly Entertainer [Stamford], May
1, 1819 (1: 270), in a department called "Monthly Epitome," consisting of brief
excerpts from contemporary reviews. The part quoted begins with the third
sentence of the second paragraph and extends for three sentences.]

The wild burst of the French Revolution called out ten thousand corresponding fancies and furies in the human heart; and no department of
civil and military life, no branch of science, or region of taste and literature,
was untouched or uninfluenced by this general concussion. Not only were
politics rhapsodized in the course of that tremendous occurrence, but rhapsodies became political; and in the midst of the gravest ratiocination on
the "universal economy," appeared the strangest vagaries of versification,
to answer to the Pindaric flights of some unfledged philosopher in government.

A singular compound of all these qualities is presented in the "Revolt
of Islam." It is lamentable, indeed, to see the waste of so much capability
of better things as the present volume exhibits. The author has many
poetical talents, but he does not seem to have rendered a just account of a
single one. His command of language is so thoroughly abused as to become a mere snare for loose and unmeaning expression; and his facility of
writing, even in Spenser's stanza, leads him into a licentiousness of rhythm
and of rhyme that is truly contemptible. His theories also are pushed to so
extravagant a length, that no "Theophilanthropist" or "Spencean" of the
day would be disposed to follow him into his religious or his political speculations; and his dreams of the perfection of the world, in which the
"eagle of evil" will finally be conquered by the "serpent of good," partake
too much of poetical phrenzy for our comprehension. Mr. Percy Bysshe
Shelley seems to be one of those obdurate dreamers, whose imaginations are
hardened rather than reproved by the frequent exposure of their follies;
and he goes on rhyming without reason, and reasoning without rhyme,
in spite of the manifest advantages of education and society which his work
displays. We subjoin a specimen of this demi-maniac composition:

My brain began to fail when the fourth morn
Burst o'er the golden isles—a fearful sleep,
Which through the caverns dreary and forlorn
Of the riven soul, sent its foul dreams to sweep
With whirlwind swiftness—a fall far and deep,—
A gulph, a void, a sense of senselessness—
These things dwelt in me, even as shadows keep
Their watch in some dim charnel's loneliness,
A shoreless sea, a sky sunless and planetless!

The forms which peopled this terrific trance
I well remember—like a quire of devils,
Around me they involved a giddy dance;
Legions seemed gathering from the misty levels
Of Ocean, to supply those ceaseless revels,
Foul, ceaseless shadows:—thought could not divide
The actual world from these entangling evils,
Which so bemocked themselves, that I descried
All shapes like mine own self, hideously multiplied.

Dii meliora piis.

THE QUARTERLY PASSES SENTENCE

[From The Quarterly Review, April, 1819 (21:460-471), by John Taylor
Coleridge. The review is headed by the full titles of both *Laon and Cythna* and
The Revolt of Islam. Shelley wrote to Leigh Hunt a few months before the review
appeared, "The Quarterly is undoubtedly conducted with talent, great talent, and
affords a dreadful preponderance against the cause of improvement."
  The present review which Peacock later characterized as "one of the most malignant effusions of the *odium theologicum* that ever appeared, even in those days and
in that periodical," is one of the few Shelley is known to have read. Shelley refers to
it several times in his letters with somewhat forced disdain. He drafted, but never
sent, a protest to the editor, and his epistolary contretemps with Southey was partly
due to his supposing, erroneously, that Southey might be the author of this review.
  The copy of *Laon and Cythna* here reviewed is one of the very few copies that
were sent out before the book was suppressed for revision into its later form. The fact
that The Quarterly noticed it at all, knowing it to have been withdrawn, indicates a
special desire to overwhelm the author. Though it gave Shelley only one review
after this, The Quarterly was one of his most determined enemies and was able to
injure him greatly with the large majority who formed opinions at second-hand.
Curiously, even The Quarterly in this review admits that Shelley's genius would be
impressive if properly directed. For further comment on The Quarterly Review, see
Chapter I.]

  This is one of that industrious knot of authors, the tendency of whose
works we have in our late Numbers exposed to the caution of our readers—
novel, poem, romance, letters, tours, critique, lecture and essay follow one
another, framed to the same measure, and in subjection to the same key-
note, while the sweet undersong of the weekly journal, filling up all pauses,
strengthening all weaknesses, smoothing all abruptnesses, harmonizes the
whole strain. Of all his brethren Mr. Shelley carries to the greatest length

the doctrines of the sect. He is, for this and other reasons, by far the least pernicious of them; indeed there is a naïveté and openness in his manner of laying down the most extravagant positions, which in some measure deprives them of their venom; and when he enlarges on what certainly are but necessary results of opinions more guardedly delivered by others, he might almost be mistaken for some artful advocate of civil order and religious institutions. This benefit indeed may be drawn from his book, for there is scarcely any more persuasive argument for truth than to carry out to all their legitimate consequences the doctrines of error. But this is not Mr. Shelley's intention; he is, we are sorry to say, in sober earnest:—with perfect deliberation, and the steadiest perseverance he perverts all the gifts of his nature, and does all the injury, both public and private, which his faculties enable him to perpetrate.

Laon and Cythna is the same poem with the Revolt of Islam—under the first name it exhibited some features which made "the experiment on the temper of the public mind," as the author calls it, somewhat too bold and hazardous. This knight-errant in the cause of "a liberal and comprehensive morality" had already sustained some "perilous handling" in his encounters with Prejudice and Error, and acquired in consequence of it a small portion of *the better part of valour*. Accordingly Laon and Cythna withdrew from circulation; and happy had it been for Mr. Shelley if he had been contented with his failure, and closed his experiments. But with minds of a certain class, notoriety, infamy, anything is better than obscurity; baffled in a thousand attempts after fame, they will still make one more at whatever risk,—and they end commonly like an awkward chemist who perseveres in tampering with his ingredients, till, in an unlucky moment, they take fire, and he is blown up by the explosion.

Laon and Cythna has accordingly reappeared with a new name, and a few slight alterations. If we could trace in these any signs of an altered spirit, we should have hailed with the sincerest pleasure the return of one whom nature intended for better things, to the ranks of virtue and religion. But Mr. Shelley is no penitent; he has reproduced the same poison, a little, and but a little, more mischief at less personal risk to the author, our duty requires us to use his own evidence against himself, to interpret him where he is obscure now, by himself where he was plain before, and to exhibit the "fearful consequences" to which he would bring us, as he drew them in the boldness of his first conception.

Before, however, we do this, we will discharge our duty to Mr. Shelley as poetical critics—in a case like the present, indeed, where the freight is so pernicious, it is but a secondary duty to consider the "build" of the vessel which bears it; but it is a duty too peculiarly our own to be wholly neglected. Though we should be sorry to see the Revolt of Islam in our readers' hands, we are bound to say that it is not without beautiful passages, that the language is in general free from errors of taste, and the versification smooth and harmonious. In these respects it resembles the latter productions of Mr. Southey, though the tone is less subdued, and the copy altogether more luxuriant and ornate than the original. Mr. Shelley indeed is an unsparing imitator; and he draws largely on the rich stores of another mountain poet, to whose religious mind it must be a matter, we think, of perpetual sorrow to see the philosophy which comes pure and holy from his pen, degraded and perverted, as it continually is, by this miserable crew of atheists or pantheists, who have just sense enough to abuse its terms, but neither heart nor principle to comprehend its import, or follow its application. We shall cite one of the passages to which we alluded above, in support of our opinion: perhaps it is that which has pleased us more than any other in the whole poem.

[*Quotes Canto II, stanzas 21 through 24, italicizing as errors the words* aught *in the first stanza and* which *in the last, interpolating* any *in parentheses after* aught]

These, with all their imperfections, are beautiful stanzas; they are, however, of rare occurrence:—had the poem many more such, it could never, we are persuaded, become popular. Its merits and its faults equally conspire against it; it has not much ribaldry or voluptuousness for prurient imaginations, and no personal scandal for the malicious; and even those on whom it might be expected to act most dangerously by its semblance of enthusiasm, will have stout hearts to proceed beyond the first canto. As a whole, it is insupportably dull, and laboriously obscure; its absurdities are not of the kind which provoke laughter, the story is almost wholly devoid of interest, and very meagre; nor can we admire Mr. Shelley's mode of making up for this defect—as he has but one incident where we should have ten, he tells that one so intricately, that it takes the time of ten to comprehend it.

Mr. Shelley is a philosopher by the courtesy of the age, and has a theory of course respecting the government of the world; we will state in as few words as we can the general outlines of that theory, the manner in which he demonstrates it, and the practical consequences, which he proposes to deduce from it. It is to the second of these divisions that we would beg his attention; we despair of convincing him directly that he has taken up false and pernicious notions; but if he pays any deference to the common laws of reasoning, we hope to show him that, let the goodness of his cause be what it may, his manner of advocating it is false and unsound. This may be mortifying to a teacher of mankind; but a philosopher seeks the truth, and has no vanity to be mortified.

The existence of evil, physical and moral, is the grand problem of all philosophy; the humble find it a trial, the proud make it a stumbling-block; Mr. Shelley refers it to the faults of those civil institutions and religious creeds which are designed to regulate the conduct of man here, and his hopes in a hereafter. In these he seems to make no distinction, but considers them all as bottomed upon principles pernicious to man and unworthy of God, carried into details the most cruel, and upheld only by the stupidity of the many on the one hand, and the selfish conspiracy of the few on the other. According to him the earth is a boon garden needing little care or cultivation, but pouring forth spontaneously and inexhaustibly all innocent delights and luxuries to her innumerable children; the seasons have no inclemencies, the air no pestilences for man in his proper state of wisdom and liberty; his business here is to enjoy himself, to abstain from no gratification, to repent of no sin, hate no crime, but be wise, happy and free, with plenty of "lawless love." This is man's natural state, the state to which Mr. Shelley will bring us, if we will but break up the "crust of our outworn opinions," as he calls them, and put them into his magic cauldron. But kings have introduced war, legislators crime, priests sin; the dreadful consequences have been that the earth has lost her fertility, the seasons their mildness, the air its salubrity, man his freedom and happiness. We have become a foul-feeding carnivorous race, are foolish enough to feel uncomfortable after the commission of sin; some of us even go as far as to consider vice odious; and we all groan under a multiplied burthen of crime *merely conventional;* among which Mr. Shelley specifies with great *sang froid* the commission of *incest!*

We said that our philosopher makes no distinction in his condemnation of creeds; we should rather have said, that he makes no exception; distinction he does make, and it is to the prejudice of that which we hold. In one place indeed he assembles a number of names of the founders of religion, to treat them all with equal disrespect.

> And through the host contention wild befell,
> As each of his own God the wondrous works did tell;
> And Oromaze and Christ and Mahomet,[3]
> Moses and Buddh, Zerdusht, and Brahm and Foh,
> A tumult of strange names, &c. (p. 227.)

But in many other places he manifests a dislike to Christianity which is frantic, and would be, if in such a case any thing could be, ridiculous. When the votaries of all religions are assembled with one accord (this unanimity by the bye is in a vision of the *nineteenth* century) to stifle the first breathings of liberty, and execute the revenge of a ruthless tyrant, he selects a Christian priest to be the organ of sentiments outrageously and pre-eminently cruel. The two characteristic principles upon which Christianity may be said to be built are repentance and faith. Of repentance he speaks thus:—

> Reproach not thine own soul, but know thyself;
> *Nor hate another's crime, nor loathe thine own.*
> It is the dark idolatry of self
> Which, when our thoughts and actions once are gone,
> Demands that we should weep and bleed and groan;
> O vacant expiation! be at rest—
> The past is death's—the future is thine own;
> And love and joy can make the *foulest* breast
> A paradise of flowers where peace might build her nest. (p. 188.)

[3] "And Oromaze, Joshua and Mahomet," p. 227. *Revolt of Islam.* This is a very fair specimen of Mr. Shelley's alterations, which we see are wholly prudential, and artfully so, as the blasphemy is still preserved entire. (Reviewer's footnote.)

Repentance then is selfishness in an extreme which amounts to idolatry! but what is Faith? our readers can hardly be prepared for the odious accumulation of sin and sorrow which Mr. Shelley conceives under this word. "Faith is the Python, the Ogress, the Evil Genius, the Wicked Fairy, the Giantess of our children's tales"; whenever any thing bad is to be accounted for, any hard name to be used, this convenient monosyllable fills up the blank.

> Beneath his feet, 'mong ghastliest forms, represt
> Lay Faith, *an obscene worm*. (p. 118.)
> . . . sleeping there
> With lidless eyes lie Faith, and Plague, and Slaughter,
> A ghastly brood conceived of Lethe's sullen water. (p. 220).
> And underneath thy feet writhe Faith and Folly,
> Custom and Hell, and mortal Melancholy. (p. 119).
> Smiled on the flowery grave, in which were lain
> Fear, Faith, and Slavery. (p. 172.)

Enough of Mr. Shelley's theory.—We proceed to examine the manner in which the argument is conducted, and this we cannot do better than by putting a case.

Let us suppose a man entertaining Mr. Shelley's opinions as to the causes of existing evil, and convinced of the necessity of a change in all the institutions of society, of his own ability to produce and conduct it, and of the excellence of that system which he would substitute in their place. These indeed are bold convictions for a young and inexperienced man, imperfectly educated, irregular in his application, and shamefully dissolute in his conduct; but let us suppose them to be sincere;—the change, if brought about at all, must be effected by a concurrent will, and that, Mr. Shelley will of course tell us, must be produced by an enlightened conviction. How then would a skilful reasoner, assured of the strength of his own ground, have proceeded in composing a tale of fiction for this purpose? Undoubtedly he would have taken the best laws, the best constitution, and the best religion in the known world; such at least as they most loved and venerated whom he was addressing; when he had put all these together, and developed their principles candidly, he would have shown that under all favourable circumstances, and with all the best prepensities of our nature to boot, still the natural effect of this combination would be to corrupt and degrade the human race. He would then have drawn a probable inference, that if the most approved systems and creeds under circumstances more advantageous than could ever be expected to concur in reality, still produced only vice and misery, the fault lay in them, or at least mankind could lose nothing by adventuring on a change. We say with confidence that a skilful combatant would and must have acted thus; not merely to make victory final, but to gain it in any shape. For if he reasons from what we acknowledge to be bad against what we believe to be good; if he puts a government confessedly despotic, a religion monstrous and false, if he places on the throne a cruel tyrant, and at the altar a bigoted and corrupt priesthood, how can his argument have any weight with those who think they live under a paternal government and a pure faith, who look up with love and gratitude to a beneficent monarch, and reverence a zealous and upright priesthood? The laws and government on which Mr. Shelley's reasoning proceeds, are the Turkish, administered by a lawless despot; his religion is the Mohammedan, maintained by servile hypocrites; and his scene for their joint operation Greece, the land full beyond all others of recollections of former glory and independence, now covered with shame and sunk in slavery. We are Englishmen, Christians, free, and independent; we ask Mr. Shelley how his case applies to *us?* or what *we* learn from it to the prejudice of our own institutions?

His residence at Oxford was a short one, and, if we mistake not, rather *abruptly* terminated; yet we should have thought that even in a freshman's term he might have learned from Aldrick not to reason from the particular to an universal; and any one of our fair readers we imagine who never heard of Aldrick, would see the absurdity of inferring that all of her own sex were the victims of the lust and tyranny of the other, from the fact, if it be a fact, that young women of Greece were carried off by force to the seraglio of Constantinople. This, however, is the sum and substance of the argument, as far as it attempts to prove the causes of existing evil. Mr. Shelley is neither a dull, nor, considering all his disadvantages, a very ignorant man; we will frankly confess, that with every disposition to judge him charitably, we find it hard to convince ourselves of his belief in his own conclusions.

We have seen how Mr. Shelley argues for the necessity of a change; we must bestow a word or two upon the manner in which he brings that change about, before we come to the consequences which he derives from it. Laon and Cythna, his hero and heroine, are the principal, indeed, almost the sole agents. The latter by her eloquence rouses all of her own sex to assert their liberty and independence; this perhaps was no difficult task; a female tongue in such a cause may be supposed to have spoken fluently at least, and to have found a willing audience; by the same instrument, however, she disarms the soldiers who are sent to seize and destroy her,—

> Even the torturer who had bound
> Her meek calm frame, ere yet it was impaled
> Loosened her weeping then, nor could be found
> One human hand to harm her. (p. 84.)

The influence of her voice is not confined to the Golden City, it travels over the land, stirring and swaying all hearts to its purpose:—

> in hamlets and in towns
> The multitudes collect tumultuously,—
> Blood soon, although unwillingly, to shed. (p. 85.)

These peaceable and tender advocates for "Universal Suffrage and *no* representation" assemble in battle-array under the walls of the Golden

City, keeping night and day strict blockade (which Mr. Shelley calls 'a watch of love,') around the desperate bands who still adhere to the main-tainance of the iron-hearted monarch on the throne. Why the eloquence of Cythna had no power over *them:* or how the monarch himself, who had been a slave to her beauty, and to whom this model of purity and virtue *had borne a child,* was able to resist the spell of her voice, Mr. Shel-ley leaves his readers to find out for themselves. In this pause of affairs Laon makes his appearance to complete the revolution; Cythna's voice had done wonders, but Laon's was still more powerful; the "sanguine slaves" of page 96, who stabbed ten thousand in their sleep, are turned in page 99 to fraternal bands; the power of the throne crumbles into dust, and the united hosts enter the city in triumph. A good deal of mummery follows, of national fêtes, reasonable rites, altars of federation, &c. borrowed from that store-house of cast-off mummeries and abominations, the French revolution. In the meantime all the kings of the earth, pagan and chris-tian, send more sanguine slaves, who slaughter the sons of freedom in the midst of their merry-making; Plague and Famine come to slaughter them in return; and Laon and Cythna, who had chosen this auspicious moment in a ruined tower for the commencement of their 'reign of love,' surrender themselves to the monarch and are burnt alive.

Such is Mr. Shelley's victory, such its security, and such the means of obtaining it! These last, we confess, are calculated to throw a damp upon our spirits, for if the hopes of mankind must depend upon the exertion of super-eminent eloquence, we have the authority of one who had well considered the subject, for believing that they could scarcely depend upon any thing of more rare occurrence. Plures in omnibus rebus, quàm in dicendo admirabiles, was the remark of Cicero a great many ages ago, and the experience of all those ages has served but to confirm the truth of it.

Mr. Shelley, however, is not a man to propose a difficult remedy with-out suggesting the means of procuring it. If we mistake not, Laon and Cythna, and even the sage, (for there is a sort of good stupid Archimago in the poem), are already provided, and intent to begin their mission if we will but give them hearing. In short, Mr. Shelley is his own Laon: this is clear from many passages of the preface and dedication. The lady to whom the poem is addressed is certainly the original of Cythna: we have more consideration for her than she has had for herself, and will either mortify her vanity, or spare her feelings, by not producing her before the public; it is enough for the philanthropist to know that when the season arrives, she will be forthcoming. Mr. Shelley says of himself and her, in a simile picturesque in itself, but laughable in its application,—

> thou and I,
> Sweet friend, can look from our tranquillity,
> Like lamps, into the world's tempestuous night—
> Two tranquil stars, while clouds are passing by
> Which wrap them from the foundering seaman's sight,
> That burn from year to year with unextinguished light. (p. xxxii.)

Neither will the reader be much at a loss to discover what sapient personage is dimly shadowed out in our Archimago; but a clue is afforded even to the uninitiate by a note in the preface, in which we are told that Mr. Malthus by his last edition has reduced the Essay on Population to a commentary illustrative of the unanswerableness of *Political Justice*.

With such instruments doubtless the glorious task will be speedily accomplished—and what will be the issue? this indeed is a serious question; but, as in most schemes of reform, it is easier to say what is to be removed, and destroyed, than what is to be put in its place. Mr. Shelley would abrogate our laws—this would put an end to felonies and misdemeanours at a blow; he would abolish the rights of property, of course there could thenceforward be no violations of them, no heart-burnings between the poor and the rich, no disputed wills, no litigated inheritances, no food in short for sophistical judges, or hireling lawyers; he would overthrow the constitution, and then we should have no expensive court, no pensions or sinecures, no silken lords or corrupt commoners, no slavish and enslaving army or navy; he would pull down our churches, level our Establishment, and burn our bibles—then we should pay no tithes, be enslaved by no superstitions, abused by no priestly artifices: marriage he cannot endure, and there would at once be a stop put to the lamented increase of adulterous connections amongst us, whilst by repealing the canon of heaven against incest, he would add to the purity, and heighten the ardour of those feelings with which brother and sister now regard each other; finally, as the basis of the whole scheme, he would have us renounce our belief in our religion, extinguish, if we can, the light of conscience within us, which embitters our joys here, and drown in oblivion the hopes and fears that hang over our hereafter. This is at least intelligible; but it is not so easy to describe the structure, which Mr. Shelley would build upon this vast heap of ruins. "Love," he says, "is to be the sole law which shall govern the moral world"; but Love is a wide word with many significations, and we are at a loss as to which of them he would have it now bear. We are loath to understand it in its lowest sense, though we believe that as to the issue this would be the correctest mode of interpreting it; but this at least is clear, that Mr. Shelley does not mean it in its highest sense: he does not mean that love, which is the fulfilling of the law, and which walks after the commandments, for he would erase the Decalogue, and every other code of laws; not the love which is said to be of God, and which is beautifully coupled with 'joy, peace, long suffering, gentleness, goodness, faith, meekness, temperance,' for he pre-eminently abhors that religion, which is built on that love and inculcates it as the essence of all duties, and its own fulfilment.

It is time to draw to an end.—We have examined Mr. Shelley's system slightly, but, we hope, dispassionately; there will be those, who will say that we have done so coldly. He has indeed, to the best of his ability, wounded us in the tenderest part.—As far as in him lay, he has loosened the hold of our protecting laws, and sapped the principles of our venerable polity; he has invaded the purity and chilled the unsuspecting ardour of our fireside intimacies; he has slandered, ridiculed and blasphemed our holy religion; yet these are all too sacred objects to be defended bitterly or unfairly. We have learned too, though not in Mr. Shelley's school, to discriminate between a man and his opinions, and while we shew no mercy to the sin, we can regard the sinner with allowance and pity. It is in this spirit, that we conclude with a few lines, which may serve for a warning for others, and for reproof, admonition, and even if he so pleases of encouragement to himself. We have already said what we think of his powers as a poet, and doubtless, with those powers, he might have risen to rsepectability in any honourable path, which he had chosen to pursue, if to his talents he had added industry, subordination, and good principles. But of Mr. Shelley much may be said with truth, which we not long since said of his friend and leader Mr. Hunt: he has not, indeed, all that is odious and contemptible in the character of that person; so far as we have seen he has never exhibited the bustling vulgarity, the ludicrous affectation, the factious flippancy, or the selfish heartlessness, which it is hard for our feelings to treat with the mere contempt they merit. Like him, however, Mr. Shelley is a very vain man; and like most very vain men, he is but half instructed in knowledge, and less than half-disciplined in his reasoning powers; his vanity, wanting the controul of the faith which he derides, has been his ruin; it has made him too impatient of applause and distinction to earn them in the fair course of labour; like a speculator in trade, he would be rich without capital and without delay, and, as might have been anticipated, his speculations have ended only in disappointments. They both began, his speculations and his disappointments, in early childhood, and even from that period he has carried about with him a soured and discontented spirit—unteachable in boyhood, unamiable in youth, querulous and unmanly in manhood,—singularly unhappy in all three. He speaks of his school as "a world of woes," of his masters "as tyrants," of his schoolfellows as "enemies,"—alas! what is this, but to bear evidence against himself? every one who knows what a public school ordinarily must be, will only trace in these lines the language of an insubordinate, a vain, a mortified spirit.

We would venture to hope that the past may suffice for the speculations in which Mr. Shelley has hitherto engaged; they have brought him neither honour abroad nor peace at home, and after so fair a trial it seems but common prudence to change them for some new venture. He is still a young man, and though his account be assuredly black and heavy, he may yet hope to redeem his crime, and wipe it out. He may and he should retain all the love for his fellow-creatures, all the zeal for their improvement in virtue and happiness which he now professes, but let that zeal be armed with knowledge and regulated by judgment. Let him not be offended at our freedom, but he is really too young, too ignorant, too inexperienced, and too vicious to undertake the task of reforming any world, but the little world within his own breast; that task will be a good preparation for the difficulties which he is more anxious at once to encounter. There is a book which will help him to this preparation, which has more poetry in it than Lucretius, more interest than Godwin, and far more philosophy than both. But it is a sealed book to a proud spirit; if he would read it with effect, he must be humble where he is now vain, he must examine and doubt himself where now he boldly condemns others, and instead of relying on his own powers, he must feel and acknowledge his weakness, and pray for strength from above.

We had closed our remarks on Laon and Cythna, when 'Rosalind and Helen' was put into our hands: after having devoted so much more space to the former than its importance merited, a single sentence will suffice for the latter. Though not without some marks of the same ability, which is occasionally manifested in Mr. Shelley's earlier production, the present poem is very inferior to it in positive merit, and far more abundant in faults: it is less interesting, less vigorous and chaste in language, less harmonious in versification, and less pure in thought; more rambling and diffuse, more palpably and consciously sophistical, more offensive and vulgar, more untelligible. So it ever is and must be in the downward course of infidelity and immorality;—we can no more blot out the noblest objects of contemplation, and the most heart-stirring sources of gratitude from the creation without injury to our intellectual and moral nature, than we can refuse to walk by the light of the sun without impairing our ocular vision. Scarcely any man ever set himself in array against the cause of social order and religion, but from a proud and rebel mind, or a corrupt and undisciplined heart: where these are, true knowledge cannot grow. In the enthusiasm of youth, indeed, a man like Mr. Shelley may cheat himself with the imagined loftiness and independence of his theory, and it is easy to invent a thousand sophisms, to reconcile his conscience to the impurity of his practice: but this lasts only long enough to lead him on beyond the power of return; he ceases to be the dupe, but with desperate malignity he becomes the deceiver of others. Like the Egyptian of old, the wheels of his chariot are broken, the path of 'mighty waters' closes in upon him behind, and a still deepening ocean is before him:—for a short time, are seen his impotent struggles against a resistless power, his blasphemous execrations are heard, his despair but poorly assumes the tone of triumph and defiance, and he calls ineffectually on others to follow him to the same ruin—finally, he sinks "like lead" to the bottom, and is forgotten. So it is now in part, so shortly will it be entirely with Mr. Shelley:—if we might withdraw the veil of private life, and tell what we *now* know about him, it would be indeed a disgusting picture that we should exhibit, but it would be an unanswerable comment on our text; it is not easy for those who *read only*, to conceive how much low pride, how much cold selfishness, how much unmanly cruelty are consistent with the laws of this "universal" and "lawless love." But we must only use our knowledge to check the groundless hopes which we were once prone to entertain of him.

LEIGH HUNT TO THE DEFENCE

[From The Examiner, September 26, and October 3 and 10, 1819 (no. 613, pp. 620-621; no. 614, pp. 635-636; no. 615, pp. 652-653), entitled "The Quarterly Review and The Revolt of Islam." Leigh Hunt had warned Shelley that The Quarterly's attack was in preparation and had spoken of donning his "rusty armor" in defence. Shelley read this defence and wrote to Hunt from Florence (November 2, 1819) to express his thanks.]

Since our last paper, we have met with the *Quarterly* Review; and we shall beg our reader's disgust at that publication to be patient a little, while we say something upon its present number.—The *Quarterly Review itself* (for there are one or two deeper articles in it, this time, than usual[4]) ought to be ashamed of the one it has written upon Mr. Shelley. Heavy, and swelling, and soft with venom, it creeps through the middle of it like a skulking toad. The Editor, and the other more malignant writers in this Review, (for we know too much of such publications to confound all the writers together), have grown a little more cunning in their mode of attack. They only missed their aim, and pitched themselves headlong, with their blind fury, in such articles as that on the *Story of Rimini*. They have since undertaken to be more candid and acknowledging; and accordingly, by a ludicrous effort of virtue, they now make a point of praising some *one* thing, or rather giving some *one* extract, which they find rather praiseworthy than otherwise; and then they set to, sharper than ever, and reward their new morals with a double draught of malignity.

They are always too impatient however, not to betray themselves at the outset. They begin their article on Mr. Shelley's *Revolt of Islam* by referring to the same book under another title, which that gentleman suppressed. He suppressed it by the advice of his friends, because in the ardour of his sincerity he had carried one of his theories to an excess which they thought would injure the perusal of it. Perhaps but two or three copies of that first impression were sold. The public at large certainly knew nothing of it. And yet the Quarterly Reviewers, who think these theories so pernicious, drag forth the impression, in order to abuse what he has not used. If on the other hand, he had not suppressed it, then the cry would have been—Surely he ought at least to have suppressed this;— and he would have been reproached for what he did use.

We are not going to nauseate the reader with all the half-sighted and whole-clawed meanness of the article in question. It is, in truth, a dull as well as a malicious endeavour; and to anybody acquainted with the speculations which it undertakes to handle, talks quite as much against

[4] See particularly the article on the Italian Poets, which is the best piece of English criticism we have yet seen upon that subject, as well as a singularly liberal one, in its general remarks, for the Review in question. There is also some deeper writing than ordinary in the article on the Greek comedy and philosophy; though it is edifying enough to see such an elaborate case made out in the *Quarterly Review* for Aristophanes *versus* Socrates. This article seems touched or noted by different hands, as is often the case. If not, we are much mistaken; or some people are strangely acquiescent; some others more strangely improved in writing. (Hunt's footnote.)

itself as for. We will content ourselves with a short specimen or two. Mr. Shelley, in endeavouring to shew the perniciousness of superstition in general, from which the perniciousness of its family members is to be deduced, lays the scene of his philosophical poem among the Mahometans: —upon which the Reviewer after blessing himself upon our present happy government, and expressing his own infinite content with it (which we have no doubt is great) calls upon the author to witness his triumph in the following manner:—

"The laws and government on which Mr. Shelley's reasoning proceeds, are the Turkish, administered by a lawless despot; his religion is the Mohammedan, maintained by servile hypocrites; and his scene for their joint operation Greece, the land full beyond all others of recollections of former glory and independence, now covered with shame and sunk in slavery. We are Englishmen, Christians, free, and independent: we ask Mr. Shelley how his case applies to *us?* Or what *we* learn from it to the prejudice of our own constitution?"—The Reviewer might as well ask what we learnt from any other fiction, which was to apply without being literal. Mr. Shelley is not bound to answer for his critic's stupidity. The reader of Gulliver's Travels might as well ask how the big or little men applied to *him,* he being neither as tall as a church nor as short as a mole-hill. The Editor of the Review himself, for instance, might as well ask how Mr. Hazlitt's appellation of *Grildrig* applied to him,—his name being not *Grildrig,* but *Gifford;* and he never having stood in the hand of an enormous prince, though he has licked the feet of petty ones, and thrown stones at their discarded mistresses' crutches.

Another,—and we have done with specimens. Mr. Shelley, says the Reviewer, "speaks of his school as 'a world of woes,' of his masters as 'tyrants,' of his school-fellows as 'enemies':—Alas! what is this but to bear evidence against himself? Every one who knows what a public school ordinarily must be, can only trace in these lines the language of an insubordinate, a vain, a mortified spirit."[5]

Now, Reader, take the following lines:—

> . . . *Public schools 'tis public folly feeds.*
> *The slaves of custom and establish'd mode,*
> With pack-horse constancy we keep the road,
> Crooked or strait, through quags or thorny dells,
> True to the jingling of our leader's bells.
> To follow foolish precedents, and wink
> With both our eyes, is easier than to think.

*   *   *

Speaking of the worldly views with which even future priests are sent to these schools, the Poet says,

[5] We are much mistaken if anti-despotic opinions have not since taken more root in the school Mr. Shelley was brought up in than these writers are aware. The boys, we are quite sure, will be happier, wiser, gentler, and at the same time more truly courageous, in proportion as they do; though some of their old tyrants may see with alarm and rage their new tyrannies threatened by them. (Hunt's footnote.)

Egregious purpose worthily begun,
In barb'rous prostitution of your son;
Press'd on *his* part by means, that would disgrace
A scriv'ner's clerk, or footman out of place;
And ending, if at last its end be gained,
In sacrilege, in God's own house profan'd.

*   *   *

The *royal letters* are a thing of course;
A King, that would, might recommend his horse;
And Deans,[6] no doubt, and Chapters, with one voice,
As bound in duty,·would confirm the choice.

An lastly:—

Would you your son should be a sot, or dunce,
Lascivious, headstrong, or all these at once;
That in good time the stripling's finished taste
For loose expense, and fashionable waste,
Should prove your ruin, and his own at last,
Train him in public with a mob of boys.

Reader, these are not the profane Mr. Shelley's verses, but the pious Cowper's;—Cowper, the all-applauded as well as the deserving, who in these lines, according to the Quarterly Reviewer, "bears evidence against himself," and proves that there is nothing to be traced in them but the "language of an insubordinate, a vain, a mortified spirit";—Cowper, in short, the independent, the good, and the sensible,—who, because he had not callousness enough to reconcile his faith in the dreadful dogmas of the Church to his notions of the Supreme Goodness, like these reviewing worshippers of power,—nor courage enough to wage war with them, like Mr. Shelley,—finally lost his senses; and withered away in the very imagination of "blasts from hell," like a child on the altar of Moloch.

Our reviewing Scribes and Pharisees beg the question against Mr. Shelley's theories because he does not believe in their own creed. As if they had any creed but that which is established; and the better spirit of which they, and men like them, have ever prevented from appearing! They cannot affect meekness itself, but out of hostility. In the course of an article, full of anger, scandal, and bigotry, they put on little pale-lipped airs of serenity like a vixenish woman; and during one of these they say they would recommend Mr. Shelley to read the Bible, only it is "a sealed book to a proud spirit." We will undertake to say that Mr. Shelley knows more of the Bible, than all the priests who have any thing to do with the Review or its writers. He does not abjure "the pomps and vanities of this wicked world," only to put them on with the greater relish. To them, undoubtedly, the Bible is not a sealed book, in one sense. They open it

[6] We recommend this to the criticism of that illustrious obscure, Dean Ireland, whom Mr. Gifford, in the very midst of his rage against "pretensions" of all sorts, is continually thrusting before the public, and nobody will attend to. (Hunt's footnote.)

to good profit enough. But in the sense which the Reviewer means, they contrive to have it sealed wherever the doctrines are inconvenient. What do they say to the injunctions against "judging others that ye be not judged," —against revenge—against tale-bearing,—against lying, hypocrisy, "partiality," riches, pomps and vanities, swearing, perjury (videlicet, Nolo-Episcopation), Pharisaical scorn, and every species of worldliness and malignity? Was Mr. Canning (the parodist) a worthy follower of him that condoled with the lame and blind, when he joked upon a man's disease? Was Mr. Croker, (emphatically called "the Admiralty Scribe") a worthy follower of him who denounced Scribes, Pharisees, and "devourers of widows' houses," when he swallowed up all those widows' pensions? Was Mr. Gifford a worthy follower of him who was the forgiver and friend of Mary Magdalen, when he ridiculed the very lameness and crutches of a Prince's discarded mistress! Men of this description are incapable of their own religion. If Christianity is compatible with all that they do and write, it is a precious thing. But if it means something much better,—whch we really believe it does mean, in spite both of such men and of much more reverenced and ancient authorities, then is the spirit of it to be found in the aspiration of the very philosophies which they are most likely to ill treat. The Reviewer for instance quotes, with horrified Italics, such lines as these—

> Nor hate another's crime, nor loathe thine own.
> And love of joy can make the foulest breast
> A paradise of flowers, where peace might build her nest.

What is this first passage but the story of the woman taken in adultery? And what the second, but the story of Mary Magdalen, "out of whom went seven devils," and who was forgiven because "she loved much"? Mr. SHELLEY may think that the sexual intercourse might be altered much for the better, so as to diminish the dreadful evils to which it is now subject. His opinions on that matter, however denounced or misrepresented, he shares in common with some of the best and wisest names in philosophy, from Plato down to Condorcet. It has been doubted by Doctors of the Church, whether Christ himself thought on these matters as the Jews did. But be this as it may, it does not hurt the parallel spirit of the passages. The Jews were told "not to hate another's crime." The woman was not told to loathe her sin, but simply not to repeat it; and was dismissed gently with these remarkable words,—"Has any man condemned thee? No, Lord. Neither do I condemn thee." Meaning, on the most impartial construction, that if no man had brought her before a judge to be condemned, neither would he be the judge to condemn her. She sinned, because she violated the conventional ideas of virtue, and thus hazarded unhappiness to others, who had not been educated in a different opinion; but the goodness of the opinion itself is left doubtful. It is to the spirit of Christ's actions and theories that we look, and not to the comments or contradictions even of apostles. It was a very general spirit, if it was any thing, going upon the sympathetic excess, instead of the anti-pathetic—notoriously opposed to existing establishments, and reviled with every term of opprobrium by the Scribes and Pharisees then flourishing. If Mr. Shelley's theological notions run counter to those which have been built upon the supposed notions of Christ, we have no hesitation in saying that the moral spirit of his philosophy approaches infinitely nearer to that Christian benevolence so much preached and so little practised, than any the most orthodox dogmas ever published. The Reviewers with their usual anti-christian falsehood say that he recommends people to "hate no crime" and "abstain from no gratification." In the Christian sense he *does* tell them to "hate no crime"; and in a sense as benevolent, he does tell them to "abstain from no gratification." But a world of gratification is shut out from his code, which the Reviewer would hate to be debarred from; and which he instinctively hates him for denouncing already. Hear the end of the Preface to the *Revolt of Islam*. "I have avoided all *flattery* to those violent and malignant passions of our nature, which are ever on the watch to mingle with and to alloy the most beneficial innovations. *There is no quarter given to Revenge, Envy, or Prejudice.* Love is cel-ebrated every where as the sole law which should govern the moral world." Now, if Envy is rather tormenting to ye, Messieurs Reviewers, there is some little gratification, is there not, in Revenge? and some little gratifying profit or so in Prejudice? "Speak, Grildrig."

Failing in the attempt to refute Mr. Shelley's philosophy, the Re-viewers attack his private life. What is the argument of this? or what right have they to know any thing of the private life of an author? or how would they like to have the same argument used against themselves? Mr. Shelley is now seven and twenty years of age. He entered life about 17; and every body knows, and every candid person will allow, that a young man at that time of life, upon the very strength of a warm and trusting nature, especially with theories to which the world are not ac-customed, may render himself liable to the misrepresentations of the worldly. But what have the Quarterly Reviewers to do with this? What is Mr. Shelley's private life to the *Quarterly Review*, any more than Mr. GIFFORD's or Mr. CROKER's, or any other Quarterly Reviewer's private life is to the *Examiner*, or the *Morning Chronicle*, or to the *Edinburgh Review*,—a work, by the bye, as superior to the *Quarterly*, in all the humanities of social intercourse, as in the liberality of its opinions in gen-eral. The Reviewer talks of what he *"now"* knows of Mr. Shelley. What does this pretended *judge* and actual male-gossip, this willing listener to scandal, this minister to the petty wants of excitement, now know more than he ever knew, of an absent man, whose own side of whatever stories have been told him he has never heard? Suppose the opponents of the *Quarterly Review* were to listen to all the scandals that have been reported of writers in it, and to proclaim this man by name as a pimp, another as a scamp, and another as a place or pulpit-hunting slave made out of a schoolboy tyrant? If the use of private matters in public criticism is not to be incompatible with the decencies and charities of life, let it be proved so; and we know who would be the sufferers. We have experienced, in our own persons, what monstrous misrepresentations can be given of a man, even with regard to the most difficult and unselfish actions of his life, and solely because others just knew enough of delicacy, to avail themselves of the inflexible love of it in others.[7]

We shall therefore respect the silence hitherto observed publicly by Mr. Shelley respecting such matters, leaving him when he returns to England to take such notice or otherwise of his calumniators as may seem best to him. But we cannot resist the impulse to speak of one particular calumny of this Reviewer, the falsehood of which is doubly impressed upon us in consequence of our own personal and repeated knowledge of the reverse. He says Mr. Shelley "is shamefully dissolute in his conduct." We laugh the scandalmonger to scorn. Mr. Shelley has theories, as we have said before, with regard to the regulation of society, very different certainly from those of the Quarterly Reviewers, and very like opinions which have been held by some of the greatest and best men, ancient and modern. And be it observed that all the greatest and best men who have ever attempted to alter the condition of sexual intercourse at *all* have been calumniated as profligates, the devout Milton not excepted. A man should undoubtedly carry these theories into practice with caution, as well as any other new ones, however good, which tend to hurt the artificial notions of virtue, before reasoning and education have prepared them. We differ with Mr. Shelley in some particulars of his theory, but we agree in all the spirit of it; and the consequence has partly been to us, what it has been to him:—those who have only a belief, or an acquiescence, and no real principle at all;—or who prefer being rigid theorists and lax practisers, with the zest of hypocrisy first and penitence afterwards;—or who love to confound conventional agreements and reputations with all that is to be wished for in human nature, and hate, and persecute, and delight to scandalize any body who, with the kindest intentions, would win them out of the hard crust of their egotism, however wretched,—or lastly, those who, having acted with the most abominable selfishness and unfeelingness themselves, rejoice in the least opportunity of making a case out to the world against those they have injured,—these, and such persons as these, have chosen to assume from our theories all which they think the world would least like in point of practice; and because we disdained to notice them, or chose to spare not only the best feelings of others, whom they should have

[7] The Reviewer in question, always true to his paltry trade, is pleased, in speaking of the Editor of this paper, to denounce his "bustling vulgarity, the ludicrous affectation, the factious flippancy, and the selfish heartlessness, which it is hard for the Reviewer's feelings to treat with the mere contempt they merit." Indeed! The saying is a borrowed one, and much the worse for its shabby wear. Oh, good God! how applicable are all these charges but the political one, to some of those we could tell the world! Applied as they are, they have only excited a contemptuous mirth against the Reviewer among the companions of the Editor, who hereby, with a more than exemplary fairness of dealing, repays his mock-contempt with real. (Hunt's footnote.)

been the last to wound, but even their own bad, false, and malignant ones, would have continued to turn that merciful silence against us, had they not unfortunately run beyond their mark and shown their own fear and horror at being called upon to come forward. But to return to Mr. Shelley. The Reviewer asserts that he "is shamefully dissolute in his conduct." We heard of similar assertions, when we resided in the same house with Mr. Shelley for nearly three months; and how was he living all that time? As much like Plato himself, as any of his theories resemble Plato,—or rather still more like a Pythagorean. This was the round of his daily life:—He was up early; breakfasted sparingly; wrote this *Revolt of Islam* all the morning; went out in his boat or into the woods with some Greek author or the *Bible* in his hands; came home to a dinner of vegetables (for he took neither meat nor wine); visited (if necessary) *"the sick and the fatherless,"* whom others gave Bibles to and no help; wrote or studied again, or read to his wife and friends the whole evening; took a crust of bread or a glass of whey for his supper; and went early to bed. This is literally the whole of the life he led, or that we believe he now leads in Italy; nor have we ever known him, in spite of the malignant and ludicrous exaggerations on this point, deviate, notwithstanding his theories, even into a single action which those who differ with him might think blameable. We do not say, that he would always square his conduct by their opinions as a matter of principle: we only say, that he acted just as if he did so square them. We forbear, out of regard for the very bloom of their beauty, to touch upon numberless other charities and generosities which we have known him exercise; but this we must say in general, that we never lived with a man who gave so complete an idea of an ardent and principled aspirant in philosophy as Percy Shelley; and that we believe him, from the bottom of our hearts, to be one of the noblest hearts as well as heads which the world has seen for a long time. We never met in short with a being who came nearer, perhaps so near, to that height of humanity mentioned in the conclusion of an essay of Lord Bacon's, where he speaks of excess in Charity and of its not being in the power of "man or angel to come in danger by it."

"If a man be gracious and courteous to strangers," continues this wise man of the world, in opening the final-stop of his high worship of a greater and diviner wisdom,—"If a man be gracious towards strangers, it shews he is a citizen of the world, and that his heart is no island cut off from other lands, but a continent that joins to them. If he be compassionate towards the afflictions of others, it shews that his heart is like the noble tree that is wounded itself when it gives the balm. If he easily pardons and remits offences, it shews that his mind is planted above injuries, so that he cannot be shot. If he be thankful for small benefits, it shews that he weighs men's minds, and not their trash. But, above all, if he have St. Paul's perfection, that he would wish to be an anathema from Christ, for the salvation of his brethren, it shews much of a divine nature, and a kind of conformity with Christ himself."

We could talk, after this, of the manner in which natures of this kind are ever destined to be treated by the Scribes, Pharisees, and Hypocrites of all times and nations; but what room can we have for further indignation, when the ideas of benevolence and wisdom unite to fill one's imagination?—Blessings be upon thee, friend; and a part of the spirit which ye profess to serve, upon ye, enemies.

VI

ROSALIND AND HELEN

THE EXAMINER EXPLAINS AND PRAISES

[From The Examiner, May 9, 1819 (no. 593, pp. 302-303).]

This is another poem in behalf of liberality of sentiment and the deifica-
tion of love, by the author of the *Revolt of Islam*. It is "not an attempt,"
says the writer, "in the highest style of poetry. It is in no degree calculated
to excite profound meditation; and if, by interesting the affections and
amusing the imagination, it awaken a certain ideal melancholy favourable
to the reception of more important impressions, it will produce in the
reader all that the writer experienced in the composition. I resigned myself, as I wrote, to the impulse of the feelings which moulded the conception of the story; and this impulse determined the pauses of a measure,
which only pretends to be regular inasmuch as it corresponds with, and
expresses the irregularity of the imaginations which inspired it."

Mr. Shelley has eminently succeeded in all that he thus wished to do.
The speakers, who tell each other their stories, are two fine-hearted
women, who have been unhappy in their loves,—the one having seen her
partner in life die of a disappointed sympathy with mankind in consequence
of the late great political changes; and the other, having for the sake of
her reduced family accepted a hard, cold-blooded man for her husband,
after she had been on the eve of marrying a beloved friend, who turned
out at the altar to be her brother. The father

> . . . Came from a distant land
> And with a loud and fearful cry
> Rushed between us suddenly.
> *I saw the stream of his thin grey hair,*
> *I saw his lean and lifted hand,*
> And heard his words,—and live: Oh God!
> Wherefore do I live?—"Hold, hold!"
> He cried,—"I tell thee 'tis her brother!"

The couplet marked in Italics, especially the first line, is very striking and
fearful. He comes between them like a spirit grown old.—There is something very beautiful in the way in which the two heroines meet. It is in
Italy, whither they have both gone, like solitary birds of passage, from a
climate every way colder; and *Rosalind*, who it seems is a legitimate
widow, turns away from her old friend, who had adopted Mary Wollstonecraft's opinion in those matters. This fortune however, coming in

[151]

aid of her former tenderness, melted her heart; and it again ran into that of *Helen* with tears. They unite their fortunes, and have the pleasure of seeing their children, a girl and boy, grow up in love with each other, till in their union they saw

> The shadow of the peace denied to them.

This little publication, in form and appearance resembling the one we criticised last week, presents a curious contrast with it in every other respect. It is in as finer a moral taste, as *Rosalind* and *Helen* are pleasanter names than *Peter Bell*. The object of Mr. Wordsworth's administrations of melancholy is to make men timid, servile, and (considering his religion) selfish;—that of Mr. Shelley's, to render them fearless, independent, affectionate, infinitely social. You might be made to worship a devil by the process of Mr. Wordsworth's philosophy; by that of Mr. Shelley, you might re-seat a dethroned goodness. The Poet of the Lakes always carries his egotism and "saving knowledge" about with him, and unless he has the settlement of the matter, will go in a pet and plant himself by the side of the oldest tyrannies and slaveries;—our Cosmopolite-Poet would evidently die with pleasure to all personal identity, could he but see his fellow-creatures reasonable and happy. He has no sort of respect, real or sullen, for mere power and success. It does not affect him in its most powerful shapes; and he is inclined to come to no compromise with it; he wants others happy, not himself privileged.—But comparisons are never so odious, as when they serve to contrast two spirits who ought to have agreed. Mr. Wordsworth has become hopeless of this world, and therefore would make everybody else so;—Mr. Shelley is superior to hopelessness itself; and does not see why all happiness and all strength is to be bounded by what he himself can feel or can effect.

But we shall again be tempted to transgress the limits of our Literary Notices. We must give some further specimens of the poetry. The following is a passage which will go to every true woman's heart. . . .

> [*Quotes lines 338-370*]

Of *Helen's* lover *Lionel,* in his happier times, it is said that

> A winged band
> Of bright persuasions, which had fed
> On his sweet lips and liquid eyes,
> *Kept their swift pinions half outspread*
> To do on men his least command.

The gentle noise arising from the earth during a still summer evening is thus delightfully described:—but we must go back, and make a larger extract than we intended. *Lionel* comes out of a prison, into which he had been cast for his opinions; and so, says his fond survivor,

> [*Quotes lines 953-976*]

A picture follows, which we were going to say would be appreciated by none but the most delicate minded; but Mr. Shelley can make his infinite earnestness and sincerity understood even by critics of a very different cast, who happen to have no personal pique with him; though we understand also that they take care to abuse him enough, in order to shew the time-serving bigotry of their opinions in general.

To the chief poem succeeds a smaller one entitled "Lines written among the Euganean Hills." Some of them are among the grandest if not the deepest that Mr. Shelley has produced, with a stately stepping in the measure. But we have not space to quote any,[1] not even a noble compliment which he introduces to his friend Lord Byron. We must also abstain from many other passages which tempt us in the poem we have criticised.

Upon the whole, with all our admiration of the *Revolt of Islam*, we think that *Rosalind and Helen* contains, for the size, a still finer and more various, as well as a more popular, style of poetry. The humanity is brought nearer to us, while the abstractions remain as lofty and noble. Mr. Shelley seems to look at Nature with such an earnest and intense love, that at last if she does not break her ancient silence, she returns him look for look. She seems to say to him, "You know me, if others do not." For him, if for any poet that ever lived, the beauty of the external world has an answering heart, and the very whispers of the wind a meaning. Things, with mankind in general, are mere words; they have only a few paltry commonplaces about them, and see only the surface of those. To Mr. Shelley, all that exists, exists indeed,—colour, sound, motion, thought, sentiment, the lofty and the humble, great and small, detail and generality, —from the beauties of a blade of grass or the most evanescent tint of a cloud, to the heart of man which he would elevate, and the mysterious spirit of the universe which he would seat above worship itself.

A DISAPPROVING QUARTET

[From The Commercial Chronicle, June 3, 1819 (no. 2979, p. 1). Identical with the review in The London Chronicle of June 1, 1819. This review also appears in The Gentleman's Magazine, Supplement for 1819 (89: 625-626, part 1) in abbreviated form, as from The New Times. I have been unable to examine the text in The New Times, but that of The Gentleman's Magazine omits from the text here quoted only the quotation entitled "A Mama's Dialogue" (with the following paragraph and short quotation) and the three sarcastically-headed quotations following the paragraph which begins, "The poets of this school. . . ." The only original sentence is the concluding paragraph:

"This work may seem utterly unworthy of criticism, but the character of the School gives importance to the effusions of the writer."]

We speak our sincere opinion in saying, that if we desired to bring a poetic sanction to the basest passions of the human heart, or the most odious, revolting, and unnameable crimes of human society, we should seek it in the works of certain Poets who have lately visited the Lake of Geneva.

[1] The "Lines Written Among the Euganean Hills" is quoted entire in a footnote given at this point.—N.I.W.

Rosalind and *Helen* are two unfortunates, who meet on the shores of another lake, that of Como, a place which appears singularly favored by the unfortunates of the world. But their ill-luck has come upon those weepers in different forms. *Rosalind* was a wife, with a passion for an earlier lover, and *Helen* simply a kept mistress, but of remarkably delicate sentiment, seduced, it is true, but seduceable by only one man in the world, and that man *Lionel,* the laboured portraiture of the 'poetic Peer.' The partners·of both the Ladies have died, and the desolate fair shed tears in deluges—*Helen* for her *protector,* and *Rosalind* to see *Helen* shed tears. In this mournful conference, commen sense points out that they cannot stand for ever, and they accordingly first select a place to sit down in.

> There,
> Let us sit on that grey stone,
> Till our mournful talk be done.

Helen objects to this location for the following weighty reasons:—

> Alas! not there; I cannot bear
> The murmur of this Lake to hear.
> A sound from thee, Rosalind dear,
> Which never yet I heard elsewhere,
> But in our native land, recurs,
> Even here where now we meet, it stirs
> Too much of suffocating sorrow.

Rosalind consents, and they change their position under the guidance of Helen's child.

> *A Mamma's Dialogue*
>
> Henry
>> 'Tis Fenici's seat
> Where are you going? This is not the way,
> Mamma! It leads behind those trees that grow
> Close to the little river.
>
> Helen
>> Yes, I know.
> I was bewildered. Kiss me and be gay,
> Dear boy; why do you sob?
>
> Henry
>> I do not know;
> But it might break any one's heart to see
> You and the lady cry so bitterly.
>
> Helen
> It is a gentle child, my friend. Go home,
> Henry, and play with Lilla till I come.
> We only cried with joy to see each other;
> We are quite merry now. Good night.

This we recommend to all amateurs as one of the most perfect specimens of "lisping in numbers." It is worthy of the purest periods of the nursery. But the Poet knows, that without a terrific story now and then, the cradle republic might lie in "commotion rude," and he has his horror forthcoming with the readiness of a genuine gossip.

> With tremulous lips he told
> That a hellish shape at midnight led
> The ghost of a youth with hoary hair,
> And sate on the seat beside him—there
> When the fiend would change to a lady fair.

The Poets of this school have the original merit of conceiving that the higher emotions of the heart are to be roused in their highest degree by deformity, physical and moral; they have found out a new source of the sublime—disgust; and with them the more sickening the circumstance, the more exquisite the sensibility. The gossip horror is wound up by telling us that the parties were incestuous. But the innocent enthusiasts who perpetrated this poetic crime were unhappily victims to the mob, and that most terrible of manslayers, the priest. The multitude killed the mother and the child,

> But the youth, for God's most holy grace
> A priest saved to burn in the market place.

Infantine Sports

> He was a gentle boy
> And in all gentle sports took joy,
> Oft in a dry leaf for a boat
> With a small feather for a sail,
> His fancy on that spring would float.

Accommodating Sorrow (for the loss of a husband)

> Oh, I could not weep,
> The sources whence such blessings flow
> Were not to be approached by me!
> But I could smile, and I could sleep.

Filial Feelings

> My children knew their Sire was gone,
> But when I told them "he is dead,"
> They laugh'd aloud in frantic glee
> They clapp'd their hands and leap'd about,
> Answering each other's ecstasy
> With many a prank and merry shout.

Rosalind's tale hangs on the favorite and horrid incident of the new school. She has loved a brother, unconscious indeed of the relationship, but the poet could not afford to spare the disgust connected with the simple suggestion. On the altar steps her father forbids the marriage; she is overwhelmed obviously less by the crime than the prohibition, and forthwith neither dies nor goes distracted, but does the last thing that natural feeling would do, and marries another. *Helen's* turn now comes, and she thus disburthens her spirit and her magnanimous contempt for the vulgar opinions against harlotry.

> Thou well
> Rememberest when we met no more,
> And though I dwelt with Lionel,
> That friendless caution pierc'd me sore
> With grief—a wound my spirit bore
> Indignantly.

Lionel, meant as a fac-simile of Lord Byron, for Mr. Shelley writes himself down as the Noble Bard's friend,[2] appears to have started into vigour in that prolific period, the French Revolution, when

> . . . Men dreamed the aged earth
> Was labouring in that mighty birth
> Which many a poet and a sage
> Has aye forseen—the happy age
> When truth and love shall dwell below.

Lionel advances rapidly in his universal love for the happiness of man, and his resolute opposition to the old bug-bears of priestcraft and superstition.

> That poor and hungry men should break
> The laws which wreak them toil and scorn,
> We understand; but Lionel
> We know is rich and nobly born.
> So wondered they: yet all men loved
> Young Lionel, though few approved;
> All but the priests, whose hatred fell
> Like the unseen blight of a smiling day.

Yet we suspect that with all his imagination Mr. Percy Shelley has some slight jealousy of the noble Lord's pen, for this is the description of his poetry:—

> For he made verses wild and queer
> On the strange creeds priests hold so dear,
> Because they bring them land and gold.
> Of devils and saints and all such gear,
> He made tales which whoso heard or read
> Would laugh till he were almost dead.
> So this grew a proverb: "Don't get old
> Till Lionel's 'Banquet in Hell' you hear,
> And then you will laugh yourself young again."
> So the priests hated him, and he
> Repaid their hate with cheerful glee.

---

[2] Lionel is of course based on Shelley himself. The reviewer must have known the story of Byron and Jane Clairmont, and not knowing the story of Mary Shelley and Isabel Baxter, jumped at a false conclusion.—N.I.W.

All this seems to us barbarous nonsense, however jealous it may be; yet Lord Byron may be reconciled by looking on it as the "Puff Preliminary" for his dormant "Il Don Giovanni." Helen then gives the following succint and happy history of her seduction. She and her Lionel had a habit of walking at sunset on the seashore:—

> And so we loved, and did unite
> All in us that was yet divided:
> For when he said, that many a rite,
> By men to bind but once provided,
> Could not be shared by him and me,
> Or they would kill him in their glee,
> I shuddered, and then laughing said—
> "We will have rites our faith to bind,
> But our church shall be the starry night,
> Our altar the grassy earth outspread."

Such, with the wind for the priest, is the formula of a philosophical marriage. But Lionel is captured for the originality of his opinions, and sent to Newgate:

> The ministers of misrule sent,
> Seized upon Lionel, and bore
> His chained limbs to a dreary tower,
> In the midst of a city vast and wide.
> For he, they said, from his mind had bent
> Against their gods keen blasphemy,
> For which, though his soul must roasted be
> In hell's red lakes immortally,
> Yet even on earth must he abide
> The vengeance of their slaves: a trial,
> I think, men call it.

Lionel is released, but dies of a consumption; Rosalind goes the way of all weepers, and is buried on "Chiavenna's precipice," in the hope that her soul may become a "part of its storms." Helen

> Whose spirit is of softer mould,

as is evinced by her greater atrocities and longer life

> Dies among her kindred, being old.

This work may seem utterly unworthy of criticism; but the character of the school gives importance to the nonsense of the writer. Mr. Shelley is understood to be the person who, after gazing on Mont Blanc, registered himself in the Album as Percy Bysshe Shelley, Atheist;[3] which gross and

[3] Southey is probably mainly responsible for the currency of this story, so commonly repeated by hostile reviewers. Byron's letters remark savagely on Southey as the original tale-bearer. In a letter published originally in The Courier and copied by The Examiner of January 13, 1822 (no. 729, p. 28), Southey says that he found at Mont Anvert an avowal of atheism written in Greek, which he copied in his notebook and spoke of on his return. Southey's letter does not mention Shelley by name, but his conversation probably did. Southey disavowed spreading the report of promiscuous relations among the Byron-Shelley party at Geneva.—N.I.W.

cheap bravado he, with the natural tact of the new school, took for a display of philosophic courage;, and his obscure muse has since constantly been spreading all her foulness on those doctrines which a decent infidel would treat with respect, and in which the wise and honourable have in all ages found the perfection of wisdom and virtue."

BLACKWOOD'S ENCOURAGES GENIUS

[From Blackwood's Edinburgh Magazine, June, 1819 (5:268-274). John Wilson ("Christopher North") is supposed to have been the author of this review.]

We have already expressed our belief that Mr. Shelley is a true poet, and that it will be his own fault if his name does not hold a conspicuous place in the literature of his country. With our high hopes of him are mingled, however, many disheartening fears, which, we lament to say, are far from being weakened by the spirit of his new poem. For, while this modern eclogue breathes throughout strong feeling, and strong passion, and strong imagination, it exhibits at the same time a strange perversion of moral principle—a wilful misrepresentation of the influence of the laws of human society on human virtue and happiness—and a fierce and contemptuous scorn of those sacred institutions which nature protects and guards for the sake of her own worth and dignity. Indeed, Mr. Shelley does not write like a conscientious man, sinking into fatal error through the imbecility of his intellect—nor like an enthusiastic man hurried away into fatal error by the violence of his passions—but he often writes like a man angry and dissatisfied with the world, because he is angry and dissatisfied with himself—impotently striving to break those bonds which he yet feels are riveted by a higher power—and because his own headstrong and unhappy will frets and fevers within the salutary confinement of nature's gracious laws, impiously scheming to bring these laws into disrepute, by representing them as the inventions and juggleries of tyranny and priestcraft. We are willing to attribute this monstrous perversity in a man of genius and talents like Mr. Shelley, to causes that are external, and that, therefore, will pass away. We leave it to others to speak of him in the bitterness of anger and scorn—to others again to speak of him in the exultation of sympathy and praise. We claim no kindred with either set of critics—seeing in this highly-gifted man much to admire—nay much to love—but much also to move to pity and to sorrow. For what can be more mournful than the degradation of youthful genius involving in its fall virtue, respectability, and happiness?

Rosalind and Helen are two ladies, whom the events of a disastrous life have driven from their native land, and who, after a long discontinuance of their youthful friendship, meet in their distress, one calm summer evening, on the shore of the lake of Como. They retire into the forest's solitude, to communicate to each other the story of their lives—and in these confessions consist almost the whole poem.

[*Quotes lines 97-111 and 146-154, describing the wood*]

Helen had directed the steps of her friend Rosalind to this spot,

> From the wrecks of a tale of wilder sorrow,
> So much of sympathy to borrow
> As soothed her own dark lot.

And what may be this tale, of power to soften or elevate grief?

> A fearful tale! The truth was worse:
> For here a sister and a brother
> Had solemnized a monstrous curse,
> Meeting in this fair solitude:
> For beneath yon very sky,
> Had they resigned to one another
> Body and soul.

Leaving for the present without any comment on this worse than needless picture of unnatural guilt, let us attend to the heroines.

> Silent they sate, for evening
> And the power its glimpses bring
> Had, with one awful shadow, quelled
> The passion of their grief—

In that profound solitude Rosalind tells the story of her griefs to her melancholy friend. When at the altar stair with her lover, her father, who had come from a distant land, rushed in between them, and forbade the marriage, declaring the youth to be *her brother!*

> Then with a laugh both long and wild
> The youth upon the pavement fell:
> They found him dead! All looked on me,
> The spasms of my despair to see:
> But I was calm. I went away:
> I was clammy-cold like clay!
> I did not weep: I did not speak:
> But day by day, week after week,
> I walked about like a corpse alive!
> Alas! sweet friend, you must believe
> This heart is stone: it did not break.

On her father's death her mother fell into poverty, and Rosalind, for her sake, married a withered, bloodless, cruel miser, whom her heart abhorred. Her description of her joy on feeling that a babe was to be born to comfort her dark and sullen lot, is exceedingly beautiful, and reminds us of the finest strains of Wordsworth.

[*Quotes lines 360-399*]

These fair shadows interposed between her loathing soul and her husband, whom she thus describes. . . .

[*Quotes lines 261-275*]

At last worn out with the feverish and quenchless thirst of gold, and with the selfish cares and cruel thoughts that eat into a miser's heart, this man of sin dies.

[*Quotes lines 436-456*]

Having seen and brooded over his wife's loathing, and disgust, and hatred, the shrivelled miser had laid up revenge in his heart.

> After the funeral all our kin
> Assembled, and the will was read.
> My friend, I tell thee, even the dead
> Have strength, their putrid shrouds within,
> To blast and torture. Those who live
> Still fear the living, but a corse
> Is merciless, and power doth give
> To such pale tyrants half the spoil
> He rends from those who groan and toil,
> Because they blush not with remorse
> Among their crawling worms.

The will imported that, unless Rosalind instantly abandoned her birth-place and her children for ever, they should be disinherited, and all his property go to

> A sallow lawyer, cruel and cold,
> Who watched me, as the will was read,
> With eyes askance, which sought to see
> The secrets of my agony;
> And with close lips and anxious brow
> Stood canvassing still to and fro
> The chance of my resolve, and all
> The dead man's caution just did call.

The effect of this iniquitous last will and testament was to throw over the character of Rosalind the suspicion of adultery and infidelity, the first of which crimes she indignantly denies; but

> As to the Christian creed, if true
> Or false, I never questioned it:
> I took it as the vulgar do:
> Nor my vext soul had leisure yet
> To doubt the things men say, or deem
> That they are other than a dream!!!

Rather than reduce her children to beggary, the widow resolves to endure expatriation and solitary death.

[*Quotes lines 518-535*]

Such is the outline of the Tale of Rosalind, distinguished by great animation and force of passion, and containing much beautiful description of external nature, which we regret it is not possible for us to quote. She then requests Helen "to take up weeping on the mountains wild."

> Yes speak. The faintest stars are scarcely shorn
> Of their thin beams by that delusive morn
> Which sinks again in darkness, like the light
> Of early love, soon lost in total night.

Helen then gives a long, laboured, and to us not very interesting account of her lover, whose whole soul in youth had been absorbed and swallowed up in schemes for the amelioration of the political state of mankind. He seems, first of all, to have revelled in the delight of the French revolution; and finally, if we mistake not, to have fallen into a consumption out of pure grief at the battle of Waterloo and the dethronement of Buonaparte.

[*Quotes lines 732-755, describing Lionel's depression*]

Lionel and Helen now become lovers.

> He dwelt beside me near the sea:
> And oft in evening did we meet,
> When the waves, beneath the starlight, flee
> O'er the yellow sands with silver feet,
> And talked: our talk was sad and sweet.

The progress of their love is then described as terminating in a sort of wedding, without benefit of clergy.

On the very night of these moonlight nuptials, however, Lionel is seized "by the ministers of misrule," and committed to prison. Helen tells this in a very silly manner.

> For he, they said, from his mind had bent
> Against their gods keen blasphemy,
> For which, though his soul must roasted be
> In hell's red lakes immortally,
> Yet even on earth must he abide
> The vengeance of their slaves: *a trial*
> *I think, men call it!!*

With all the fidelity of a wife, and all the passion of a mistress, Helen, who is refused admittance to his cell, takes a lodging beside the prison-gate, and on his release, (whether he had been acquitted, condemned, or not tried at all, we are not told,) accompanies him to the seat of his ancestors.

[*Quotes lines 949-992, describing the journey*]

His imprisonment, however, had entirely destroyed a constitution already shaken by the agitation of so many disappointed passions, and the gradual decay of life is painted by Mr. Shelley with great power and pathos. The closing scene, though somewhat fantastic, as indeed the whole of Helen's history is, could have been written by none but a genuine poet. Lionel's mother had built a temple in memory and honour of a dog (the only saint in her calendar), that had rescued her from drowning, to which we are told she often resorted, and. . . .

[*Quotes lines 1099-1186, describing Lionel's death*]

With all its beauty, we feel that the above passage may, to many minds, seem forced and extravagant, but there can be but one opinion of the following one, than which Byron himself never wrote any thing finer.

[*Quotes lines 1195-1227, describing the effect of Lionel's death on Helen*]

Our extracts have been already long—but it is our anxious desire to bring the genius of this poet fairly before the public, and therefore we quote the conclusion of the poem.

[*Quotes lines 1240-1318*]

Mr. Shelley's writings have, we believe, hitherto had but a very limited circulation, and few of our periodical brethren have condescended to occupy their pages with his poetry. It is one of the great objects of this journal to support the cause of genius and of imagination—and we are confident that our readers will think we have done so in this number, by the full and abundant specimens of fine poetry we have selected from Percy Bysshe Shelley and Barry Cornwall. We trust that the time will soon come when the writings of such men will stand in no need of our patronage.—Meanwhile we give them ours, such as it is worth, and that it is worth more than certain persons are willing to allow, is proved by nothing more decidedly than the constant irritation and fretfulness of those on whom we cannot in conscience bestow it.

But we cannot leave Mr. Shelley without expressing ourselves in terms of the most decided reprobation of many of his principles, if, indeed, such vague indefinite and crude vagaries can, by any latitude of language, be so designated. And, first of all, because priests have been bloody and intolerant, is it worthy of a man of liberal education and great endowments, to talk with uniform scorn and contempt of the ministers of religion? Can any thing be more puerile in taste, more vulgar in feeling, more unfounded in fact, or more false in philosophy? Mr. Shelley goes out of his way—out of the way of the leading passion of his poetry to indulge in the gratification of this low and senseless abuse—and independently of all higher considerations, such ribaldry utterly destroys all impassioned emotion in the hearts of his readers, and too frequently converts Mr. Shelley from a poet into a satirist, from a being who ought, in his own pure atmosphere, to be above all mean prejudices, into a slave, basely walking in voluntary trammels.

From his hatred and contempt of priests, the step is but a short one to something very like hatred and contempt of all religion—and accordingly superstition is a word eternally upon his lips. How many fine, pure, and noble spirits does he thus exclude from his audience? And how many sympathies does he thus dry up in his own heart? If the christian faith be all fable and delusion, what does this infatuated young man wish to substitute in its stead? One seeks, in vain, through his poetry, fine as it often is, for any principles of action in the characters who move before us.

They are at all times fighting against the law of the world, the law of
nature, and the law of God—there is nothing satisfactory in their happiness,
and always something wilful in their misery. Nor could Mr. Shelley's best
friend and most warm admirer do otherwise than confess that he is ever
an obscure and cheerless moralist, even when his sentiments are most lofty,
and when he declaims with greatest eloquence against the delusions of
religious faith. That a poet should be blind, deaf, and insensible to the
divine beauty of Christianity, is wonderful and deplorable, when, at the
same time, he is so alive to the beauty of the external world, and, in many
instances, to that of the human soul. If Mr. Shelley were a settled—a
confirmed disbeliever, we should give him up as a man of whom no high
hopes could rationally be held—but we think him only an inconsiderate
and thoughtless scoffer, who will not open his eyes to a sense of his wickedness and folly—and therefore it is that we express ourselves thus strongly,
not out of anger or scorn, but real sorrow, and sincere affection.

It is also but too evident, from Mr. Shelley's poetry, that he looks
with an evil eye on many of the most venerable institutions of civil polity.
His creed seems to be the same, in many points, as that once held by a
celebrated political writer and novelist, who has lived to abjure it. But in
all that Godwin wrote, one felt the perfect sincerity of the man—whereas
Mr. Shelley seems to have adopted such opinions, not from any deep conviction of their truth, but from waywardness and caprice, from the love
of singularity, and, perhaps, as a vain defence against the reproaches of
his own conscience. His opinions, therefore, carry no authority along with
them to others—nay, they seem not to carry any authority with them to
himself. The finer essence of his poetry never penetrates them—the hues
of his imagination never clothes [sic] them with attractive beauty. The
cold, bald, clumsy, and lifeless parts of this poem are those in which he
obtrudes upon us his contemptible and long-exploded dogmas. Then his
inspiration deserts him. He never stops nor stumbles in his career, except
when he himself seems previously to have laid blocks before the wheels of
his chariot.

Accordingly there is no great moral flow in his poetry. Thus, for
example, what lesson are we taught by this eclogue, Rosalind and Helen?
Does Mr. Shelley mean to prove that marriage is an evil institution, because by it youth and beauty may be condemned to the palsied grasp of
age, avarice and cruelty? Does he mean to shew the injustice of law,
because a man may by it bequeath his property to strangers, and leave his
wife and children beggars? Does he mean to shew the wickedness of that
law by which illegitimate children do not succeed to the paternal and
hereditary estates of their father? The wickedness lay with Lionel and
with Helen, who, aware of them all, indulged their own passion, in violation of such awful restraints—and gave life to innocent creatures for
whom this world was in all probability to be a world of poverty, sorrow,
and humiliation.

But we have stronger charges still—even than these—against this poet. What is it that he can propose to himself by his everlasting allusions to the unnatural loves of brothers and sisters? In this poem there are two stories of this sort—altogether gratuitous—and, as far as we can discover, illustrative of nothing. Why then introduce such thoughts, merely to dash, confound, and horrify? Such monstrosities betoken a diseased mind;—but be this as it may—it is most certain that such revolting passages coming suddenly upon us, in the midst of so much exquisite beauty, startle us out of our dream of real human life, and not only break in upon, but put to flight all the emotions of pleasure and of pathos with which we were following its disturbed discourses. God knows there is enough of evil and of guilt in this world, without our seeking to raise up such hideous and unnatural phantasms of wickedness—but thus to mix them up for no earthly purpose with the ordinary events of human calamity and crime, is the last employment which a man of genius would desire—for there seems to be really no inducement to it, but a diseased desire of degrading and brutifying humanity.

We hope ere long to see the day when Mr. Shelley, having shaken himself free from these faults—faults so devoid of any essential or fundamental alliance with his masterly genius—will take his place as he ought to do, not far from the first poets of his time. It is impossible to read a page of his Revolt of Islam, without perceiving that in nerve and pith of conception he approaches more nearly to Scott and Byron than any other of their contemporaries—while in this last little eclogue, he touches with equal mastery the same softer strings of pathos and tenderness which had before responded so delightfully to the more gentle inspirations of Wordsworth, Coleridge, and Wilson.[4] His fame will yet be a glorious plant if he does not blast its expanding leaves by the suicidal chillings of immorality—a poison that cannot be resisted long by any product of the soil of England.

IMMORAL GENIUS CONDEMNED

[From The Monthly Review, or Literary Journal, October, 1819 (90: 207-209).]

We are here presented with another specimen of the modern school of *poetical metaphysics*. Indistinct, however, and absolutely unmeaning, as Mr. Shelley usually is, he has, in his lucid intervals, a power of composition that raises him much above many of his fellows. We regret, indeed, to see so considerable a portion of real genius wasted in merely desultory fires; and still more do we lament to observe such extensive infidelity in the mind of a writer who is evidently capable of better things. The practical influence, which his scepticism would seem to have on the poet, is a subject of sincere commiseration. We can overlook a few general sallies of a

[4] John Wilson, i.e., "Christopher North," the supposed author of this review.—N.I.W.

thoughtless nature: but, when a man comes to such a degree of perverseness, as to represent the vicious union of two individuals of different sexes as equally sacred with the nuptial tie, we really should be wanting in our duty not to reprobate so gross an immorality.

> We will have rites our faith to bind,
> But our church shall be the starry night,
> Our altar the grassy earth outspread,
> And our priest the muttering wind.

So speaks the Modern *Helen;* who seems about as chaste as her antient namesake and prototype; and this is not the only passage in which such sentiments are clothed in the author's best garb of words, or put into the mouth of some interesting and amiable being.

When this writer speaks of the "bloody faith," we well know *what faith* he means; and to charge the wicked abuses of darker ages, and of false professors of religion, on *the spirit itself* of the mildest of creeds, is no common degree of audacity. We shall not, however, waste any valuable time on an author who, we fear, is quite incorrigible in this respect; and we shall rather turn to his poetical merits; which, with the drawback of obscurity overclouding almost all that he writes, are, on some occasions, of no common stamp.

The following description of a delightful journey, taken by a lover (just released from prison) with his happy love, certainly manifests much force and feeling:

[*Quotes lines 936-977*] ·

We would, in a friendly manner, admonish this poet to *stop in time.*

The death of Lionel is very striking, but occasionally disfigured by extravagant *conceits,* and throughout pervaded by *mysticism.*

In the lines written among the Euganean Hills, (as Mr. Shelley barbarously calls them,—*Euganea quantumvis mollior agna,)* a spirited, handsome, and deserved compliment is paid to Lord Byron. We extract the best part of it. The poet is addressing Venice:

> As the ghost of Homer clings
> Round Scamander's wasting springs;
> As divinest Shakespeare's might
> Fills Avon and the world with light
> Like omniscient power, which he
> Imaged 'mid mortality;
> As the love from Petrarch's urn,
> Yet amid yon hills doth burn,
> A quenchless lamp, by which the heart
> Sees things unearthly; so thou art,
> Mighty spirit: so shall be
> The city that did refuge thee.

A sublime volley of bombast is uttered by the hero, in defiance of his gaolers, at p. 47:

> Fear not, the tyrants shall rule for ever,
> Or the priests of the bloody faith;
> They stand on the brink of that mighty river,
> Whose waves they have tainted with death;
> It is fed from the depths of a thousand dells,
> Around them it foams, and rages, and swells,
> And their swords and their sceptres I floating see,
> Like wrecks in the surge of eternity.

Yield, Nathaniel Lee! and hide thy diminish'd head!

VII

The Cenci

THE EXAMINER PROMISES A REVIEW

[From The Examiner, March 19, 1820 (no. 638, pp. 190-191), under "Literary Notices." Preceded by a paragraph each on Hazlitt's *Lectures on the Literature of the Age of Elizabeth* and Lloyd's *Isabel*.]

OF MR. SHELLEY's tragedy, called *The Cenci*, which to say the least of it, is undoubtedly the greatest dramatic production of the day, we shall speak at large in a week or two. It is founded on a most terrific family story, which actually took place in Italy: but sentiments of the most amiable, and refreshing, and exalting nature nevertheless breathe in a certain under-tone of suggestion through the whole of it, as they always do in the works of this author.—The Correspondents who have written the joint epistle to us, under the signature of *Short and Sweet*, will perceive that we agree with them as to the propriety of criticising this play, however strongly a particular and affectionate circumstance has connected it with our self-love. Nicety is a great thing with us; but a friend is a still greater, especially if he be also a friend to the whole human race.

THE MONTHLY MAGAZINE IS DISGUSTED

[From The Monthly Magazine, or British Register, April 1, 1820 (49:260).]

We observe with pleasure, not unmingled with disgust, a new publication from the pen of Mr. Percy Bysshe Shelley, whose original and extensive genius has so frequently favoured the poetical world with productions of no ordinary merit. In this instance it has assumed a dramatic form, in a singular and wild composition, called *The Cenci*, a family of Italy, whose terrific history seems well adapted to the death-like atmosphere, and unwholesome regions, in which Mr. Shelley's muse delights to tag its wings. We cannot here explain the incestuous story on which it turns; but must content ourselves with observing, that in the attempt to throw a terror over the whole piece, he has transgressed one of the first rules of the master of criticism; and, instead of terror, succeeded only in inspiring us with sentiments of horror and disgust. In the action he has not only "overstepped the bounds of modesty and nature," but absolutely turned sentiment into nonsense, and grief into raving, while we endeavour in vain to persuade ourselves, that such faults can be redeemed by occasional bursts of energy and true poetry.

"A DISH OF CARRION"

[From The Literary Gazette, and Journal of Belles Lettres, Arts, Sciences, etc., April 1, 1820 (no. 167, pp. 209-210).]

Of all the abominations which intellectual perversion, and poetical atheism, have produced in our times, this tragedy appears to us to be the most abominable. We have much doubted whether we ought to notice it; but, as watchmen place a light over the common sewer which has been opened in a way dangerous to passengers, so have we concluded it to be our duty to set up a beacon on this noisome and noxious publication. We have heard of Mr. Shelley's genius; and were it exercised upon any subject not utterly revolting to human nature, we might acknowledge it. But there are topics so disgusting . . . and this is one of them; there are themes so vile . . . as this is; there are descriptions so abhorrent to mankind . . . and this drama is full of them; there are crimes so beastly and demoniac . . . in which The Cenci riots and luxuriates, that no feelings can be excited by their obtrusion but those of detestation at the choice, and horror at the elaboration. We protest most solemnly, that when we reached the last page of this play, our minds were so impressed with its odious and infernal character, that we could not believe it to be written by a mortal being for the gratification of his fellow-creatures on this earth: it seemed to be the production of a fiend, and calculated for the entertainment of devils in hell.

That monsters of wickedness have been seen in the world, is too true; but not to speak of the diseased appetite which would delight to revel in their deeds, we will affirm that depravity so damnable as that of Count Cenci, in the minute portraiture of which Mr. S. takes so much pains, and guilt so atrocious as that which he paints in every one of his dramatic personages, never had either individual or aggregate existence. No; the whole design, and every part of it, is a libel upon humanity; the conception of a brain not only distempered, but familiar with infamous images, and accursed contemplations. What adds to the shocking effect is the perpetual use of the sacred name of God, and incessant appeals to the Saviour of the universe. The foul mixture of religion and blasphemy, and the dreadful association of virtuous principles with incest, parricide, and every deadly sin, form a picture which, "To look upon we dare not."

Having said, and unwillingly said, this much on a composition which we cannot view without inexpressible dislike, it will not be expected from us to go into particulars farther than is merely sufficient to enforce our warning. If we quote a passage of poetic power, it must be to bring tenfold condemnation on the head of the author—for awful is the responsibility where the head condemns the heart, and the gift of talent is so great, as to remind us of Satanic knowledge and lusts, and of "arch-angel fallen."

The story, we are told, in a preface where the writer classes himself with Shakespeare and Sophocles, although two centuries old, cannot be "mentioned in Italian society without awakening a deep and breathless interest." We have no high opinion of the morality of Italy; but we can well believe, that even in that country, such a story must, if hinted at, be repressed by general indignation, which Mr. Shelley may, if he pleases, call breathless interest. It is indeed, as he himself confesses, "eminently fearful and monstrous; any thing like a dry exhibition of it upon the stage would be insupportable" (Preface, p. ix). And yet he presumes to think that that of which even a dry exhibition upon the stage could not be endured, may be relished when arrayed in all the most forcible colouring which his pencil can supply, in all the minute details of his graphic art, in all the congenial embellishments of his inflamed imagination. Wretched delusion! and worthy of the person who ventures to tell us that, "Religion in Italy is not, *as in Protestant countries*, a cloak to be worn on particular days; or a passport which those who do not wish to be railed at carry with them to exhibit; or a gloomy passion for penetrating the impenetrable mysteries of our being, which terrifies its possessor at the darkness of the abyss to which it has conducted him:" worthy of the person who, treating of dramatic imagery, blasphemously and senselessly says, that "imagination is as the immortal God, which should assume flesh for the redemption of mortal passion."

The characters are Count Cenci, an old grey haired man, a horrible fiendish incarnation, who invites an illustrious company to a jubilee entertainment on the occasion of the violent death of two of his sons; who delights in nothing but the wretchedness of all the human race, and causes all the misery in his power; who, out of sheer malignity, forcibly destroys the innocency of his only daughter; and is, in short, such a miracle of atrocity, as only this author, we think, could have conceived. Lucretia, the second wife of the Count, a most virtuous and amiable lady, who joins in a plot to murder her husband; Giacomo, his son, who because his parent has cheated him of his wife's dowry, plots his assassination; Beatrice the daughter, a pattern of beauty, integrity, grace, and sensibility, who takes the lead in all the schemes to murder her father; Orsino, a prelate, sworn of course to celibacy, and in love with Beatrice, who enters with gusto into the conspiracy, for the sound reason, that the fair one will not dare to refuse to marry an accomplice in such a transaction; Cardinal Camillo, a vacillating demi-profligate; two bravos, who strangle the Count in his sleep; executioners, torturers, and other delectable under-parts. The action consists simply of the rout in honour of the loss of two children, of the incest, of the murderous plot, of its commission, and of its punishment by the torture and execution of the wife, son, and daughter. This is the dish of carrion, seasoned with sulphur as spice, which Mr. Shelley serves up to his friend Mr. Leigh Hunt, with a dedication, by way of grace, in which he eulogizes his "gentle, tolerant, brave, honourable, innocent, simple, pure," &c. &c. &c. disposition. What food for a humane, sypathizing creature, like Mr. Hunt! if, indeed, his tender-heartedness be not of a peculiar kind, prone to feast on "gruel thick and slab," which "like a hell-broth boils and bubbles."[1]

We will now transcribe a portion of the entertainment scene, to show how far the writer out herods Herod, and outrages possibility in his personation of villany, by making Count Cenci a character which transforms a Richard III. an Iago, a Sir Giles Overreach, comparatively into angels of light.

[*Quotes Act I, Scene iii, lines 1-99, describing Count Cenci's banquet*]

This single example, which is far from being the most obnoxious, unnatural, and infernal in the play, would fully justify the reprobation we have pronounced. Mr. Shelley, nor no man, can pretend that any good effect can be produced by the delineation of such diabolism; the bare suggestions are a heinous offence; and whoever may be the author of such a piece, we will assert, that Beelzebub alone is fit to be the prompter. The obscenity too becomes more refinedly vicious when Beatrice, whose "crimes and miseries," forsooth, are as "the mask and the mantle in which *circumstances clothed her* for her impersonation on the scenes of world"[2] is brought prominently forward. But we cannot dwell on this. We pass to a quotation which will prove that Mr. Shelley is capable of powerful writing: the description of sylvan scenery would be grand, and Salvator-like, were it not put into the mouth of a child pointing out the site for the murder of the author of her being, "unfit to live, but more unfit to die."

[*Quotes Act III, Scene i, lines 245-274*]

It will readily be felt by our readers why we do not multiply our extracts. In truth there are very few passages which will bear transplanting to a page emulous of being read in decent and social life. The lamentable obliquity of the writer's mind pervades every sentiment, and "corruption mining all within," renders his florid tints and imitations of beauty only the more loathsome. Are loveliness and wisdom incompatible? Mr. Shelley makes one say of Beatrice, that

> Men wondered how such loveliness and wisdom
> Did not destroy each other!

Cenci's imprecation on his daughter, though an imitation of Lear, and one of a multitude of direct plagiarisms, is absolutely too shocking for

---

[1] We are led to this remark by having accidentally read in one of Mr. Hunt's late political essays, an ardent prayer that Buonaparte might be released from St. Helena, were it only to fight another Waterloo against Wellington, on *more equal terms*. A strange wish for a Briton, and stranger still for a pseudo philanthropist, whether arising from a desire to have his countrymen defeated, or a slaughter productive of so much woe and desolation repeated. (Reviewer's footnote.)

[2] Preface, p. xiii, and a sentence, which, if not nonsense, is a most pernicious sophistry. There is some foundation for the story, as the Cenci family were devoured by a terrible catastrophe; and a picture of the daughter by Guido, is still in the Colonna Palace. (Reviewer's footnote.)

perusal; and the dying infidelity of that paragon of parricides, is all we dare to venture to lay before the public.

> Whatever comes, my heart shall sink no more.
> And yet, I know not why, your words strike chill:
> How tedious, false and cold seem all things. I
> Have met with much injustice in this world;
> No difference has been made by God or man,
> Or any power moulding my wretched lot,
> 'Twixt good or evil as regarded me.
> I am cut off from the only world I know,
> From light, and life, and love, in youth's sweet prime.
> You do well telling me to trust in God,
> I hope I do trust in him. In whom else
> Can any trust? And yet my heart is cold.

We now most gladly take leave of this work; and sincerely hope, that should we continue our literary pursuits for fifty years, we shall never need again to look into one so stamped with pollution, impiousness, and infamy.

A COCKNEY WITH POSSIBILITIES

[From The London Magazine and Monthly Critical and Dramatic Review, April, 1820 (1:401-407). In its brief existence this competent magazine gave Shelley three significant encouraging notices, if the present review, partly scornful as it is, may be so characterized. With its successor, The London Magazine and Theatrical Inquisitor, it stands as Shelley's most effective friend among the periodicals of 1820 and 1821, always excepting The Examiner.]

There has recently arisen a new-fangled style of poetry, facetiously yclept the Cockney School, that it would really be worth one's while to enter as a candidate. The qualifications are so easy, that he need never doubt the chance of his success, for he has only to knock, and it shall be opened unto him. The principal requisites for admission, in a literary point of view, are as follows. First, an inordinate share of affectation and conceit, with a few occasional good things sprinkled, like green spots of verdure in a wilderness, with a "parca quod satis est manu." Secondly, a prodigious quantity of assurance, that neither God nor man can daunt, founded on the honest principle of "who is like unto me?," and lastly, a contempt for all institutions moral and divine, with secret yearnings for aught that is degrading to human nature, or revolting to decency. These qualifications ensured, a regular initiation into the cockney mysteries follows as a matter of course, and the novice enlists himself under their banners, proud of his newly-acquired honors, and starched up to the very throat in all the prim stiffness of his intellect. A few symptoms of this literary malady appeared as early as the year 1795, but it then assumed the guise of simplicity and pathos. It was a poetical Lord Fanny. It wept its pretty self to death by murmuring brooks, and rippling cascades, it heaved delicious sighs over sentimental lambs, and love-lorn sheep, apostrophized donkies in the innocence of primaeval nature; sung tender songs to tender nightingales; went to bed without a candle, that it might gaze on the chubby faces of the stars; discoursed sweet nothings to all who would listen to its nonsense; and displayed (horrendum dictu) the acute profundity of its grief in ponderous folios and spiral duodecimos. The literary world, little suspecting the dangerous consequences of this distressing malady, suffered it to germinate in silence; and not until they became thoroughly convinced that the disorder was of an epidemical nature, did they start from their long continued lethargy. But it was then too late! The evil was incurable; it branched out into the most vigorous ramifications, and following the scriptural admonition, "Increase and multiply," disseminated its poetry and its prose throughout a great part of England. As a dog, when once completely mad, is never satisfied until he has bitten half a dozen more, so the Cockney professors, in laudable zeal for the propagation of their creed, were never at rest until they had spread their own doctrines around them. They stood on the housetops and preached, 'till of a verity they were black in the face with the heating quality of their arguments; they stationed themselves by the bye roads and hedges, to discuss the beauties of the country; they looked out from their garrett windows in Grub-street, and exclaimed, "O! rus, quando ego te aspiciam"; and gave such afflicting tokens of insanity, that the different reviewers and satirists of the day kindly laced them in the strait jackets of their criticisms. "But all this availeth us nothing," exclaimed the critics, "so long as we see Mordecai the Jew sitting at the gate of the Temple; that is to say, as long as there is one Cockney pericranium left unscalped by the tomahawks of our Satire." But notwithstanding the strenuous exertions of all those whose brains have not been cast in the mould of this new species of intellectual dandyism, the evil has been daily and even hourly increasing; and so prodigious is the progressive ratio of its march, that the worthy Society for the Suppression of Vice should be called upon to eradicate it. It now no longer masks its real intention under affected purity of sentiment; its countenance has recently acquired a considerable addition of brass, the glitter of which has often been mistaken for sterling coin, and incest, adultery, murder, blasphemy, are among the favorite topics of its discussion. It seems to delight in an utter perversion of all moral, intellectual, and religious qualities. It gluts over the monstrous deformities of nature; finds justification in proportion to the magnitude of the crime it extolls; and sees no virtue, but in vice; no sin, but in true feelings. Like poor Tom, in Lear, whom the foul friend has possessed for many a day, it will run through ditches, through quagmires, and through bogs, to see a man stand on his head for the exact space of half an hour. Ask the reason of this raging appetite for eccentricity, the answer is, such a thing is out of the beaten track of manhood, ergo, it is praiseworthy.

Among the professors of the Cockney School, Mr. Percy Bysshe Shelley is one of the most conspicuous. With more fervid imagination and splendid talents than nine-tenths of the community, he yet prostitutes those talents by the utter degradation to which he unequivocally consigns them. His Rosalind and Helen, his Revolt of Islam, and his Alastor, or Spirit of Solitude, while they possess beauties of a superior order, are lamentably deficient in morality and religion. The doctrines they inculcate are of the most evil tendency, the characters they depict are of the most horrible description; but in the midst of these disgraceful passages, there are beauties of such exquisite, such redeeming qualities, that we adore while we pity— we admire while we execrate—and are tempted to exclaim with the last of the Romans, "Oh! what a fall is *here*, my countrymen." In the modern Eclogue of Rosalind and Helen in particular, there is a pensive sadness, a delicious melancholy, nurst in the purest, the deepest recesses of the heart, and springing up like a fountain in the desert, that pervades the poem, and forms its principal attraction. The rich yet delicate imagery that is every where scattered over it, is like the glowing splendour of the setting sun, when he retires to rest, amid the blessings of exulting nature. It is the balmy breath of the summer breeze, the twilight's last and holiest sigh. In the dramatic poem before us, the interest is of a different nature; it is dark —wild, and unearthly. The characters that appear in it are of no mortal stamp; they are daemons in human guise, inscrutable in their actions, subtle in their revenge. Each has his smile of awful meaning—his purport of hellish tendency. The tempest that rages in his bosom in irrepressible but by death. The phrenzied groan that diseased imagination extorts from his perverted soul, is as the thunder-clap that reverberates amid the cloud-capt summits of the Alps. It is the storm that convulses all Nature—that lays bare the face of heaven—and gives transient glimpses of destruction yet to be. Then in the midst of all these accumulated horrors comes the gentle Beatrice,

> Who in the gentleness of thy sweet youth
> Hast never trodden on a worm, or bruised
> A living flower, but then hast pitied it
> With needless tears.   (p. 50.)

She walks in the light of innocence; in the unclouded sunshine of love-liness and modesty; but her felicity is transient as the calm that precedes the tempest; and in the very whispers of her virtue, you hear the indistinct mutterings of distant thunder. She is conceived in the true master spirit of genius; and in the very instant of her parricide, comes home to our imagination fresh in the spring time of innocence—hallowed in the deepest recesses of melancholy. But notwithstanding all these transcendant quali-ties, there are numerous passages that warrant our introductory observa-tions respecting the Cockney School, and plunge "full fathom five" into the profoundest depths of Bathos. While, therefore, we do justice to the abilities of the author, we shall bestow a passing smile or two on his unfor-tunate Cockney prepensities.

The following are the principal incidents of the play. Count Cenci, the daemon of the piece, delighted with the intelligence of the death of his two sons, recounts at a large assembly, specially invited for the purpose, the circumstances of the dreadful transaction. Lucretia, his wife, Beatrice, his daughter, and the other guests, are of course, startled at his transports; but when they hear his awful imprecations,

> Oh thou light wine whose purple splendour leaps
> And bubbles gaily in this golden bowl
> Under the lamplight, as my spirits do,
> To hear the death of my accursed sons!
> Could I believe thou wert their mingled blood,
> Then would I taste thee like a sacrament,
> And pledge with thee the mighty Devil in Hell,
> Who, if a father's curses, as men say,
> Climb with swift wings after their children's souls,
> And drag them from the very throne of Heaven,
> Now triumphs in my triumph!—But thou art
> Superfluous; I have drunken deep of joy,
> And I will taste no other wine to-night.

their horror induces them to leave the room. Beatrice, in the mean time, who has been rating her parent for his cruelty, is subjected to every species of insult; and he sends her to her own apartment with the hellish intention of prostituting her innocence, and contaminating, as he pithily expresses it, "both body and soul." The second act introduces us to a tete-a-tete between Bernardo (another of Cenci's sons) and Lucretia; when their conference is broken by the abrupt entrance of Beatrice, who has escaped from the pursuit of the Count. She recapitulates the injuries she has received from her father, the most atrocious of which appear to be, that he has given them all "ditch water" to drink, and "buffaloes" to eat. But before we proceed further, we have a word or two respecting this same ditch water, and buffalo's flesh, which we shall mention, as a piece of advice to the author. It is well known, we believe, in a case of lunacy, that the first thing considered is, whether the patient has done anything sufficiently foolish, to induce his relatives to apply for a statute against him: now any malicious, evil-minded person, were he so disposed, might make successful application to the court against the luckless author of the *Cenci, a tragedy in five acts*. Upon which the judge, with all the solemnity suitable to so melancholy a circumstance as the decay of the mental faculties, would ask for proofs of the defendant's lunacy; upon which the plaintiff would produce the affecting episode of the ditch water and buffalo flesh; upon which the judge would shake his head, and acknowledge the insanity; upon which the defendant would be incarcerated in Bedlam.

To return from this digression, we are next introduced to Giacomo, another of Cenci's hopeful progeny, who, like the rest, has a dreadful tale to unfold of his father's cruelty toward him. Orsino, the favoured lover of Beatrice, enters at the moment of his irritation, and by the most artful pleading ultimately incites him to the murder of his father, in which he is to be joined by the rest of his family. The plot, after one unlucky attempt, succeeds; and at the moment of its accomplishment, is discovered

by a messenger, who is despatched to the lonely castle of Petrella (one of
the Count's family residences), with a summons of attendance from the
Pope. We need hardly say that the criminals are condemned; and not
even the lovely Beatrice is able to escape the punishment of the law. The
agitation she experiences after the commission of the incest, is powerfully
descriptive.

[*Quotes Act III, Scene i, line 6 through 23*]

At first she concludes that she is mad, but then parenthetically checks herself saying, "No, I am dead." Lucretia naturally enough enquires into
the cause of her disquietude, and but too soon discovers, by the broken
hints of the victim, the source of her mental agitation. Terrified at their
defenceless state, they then mutually conspire with Orsino against the
Count; and Beatrice proposes to way-lay him (a plot, however, which
fails) in a *deep and dark ravine*, as he journeys to Petrella.

[*Quotes Act III, Scene i, lines 244-266, describing the ravine*]

Giacomo, meanwhile, who was privy to the transaction, awaits the arrival
of Orsino, with intelligence of the murder, in a state of the most fearful
torture and suspense.

[*Quotes Act III, Scene ii, lines 1-31, describing Giacomo's state of mind*]

We envy not the feelings of any one who can read the curses that
Cenci invokes on his daughter when she refuses to repeat her guilt, without
the strongest disgust, notwithstanding the intense vigor of the imprecations.

[*Quotes the curse, Act IV, Scene i, lines 114-167*]

Ohe, jam satis est!!—The minutiae of this *affectionate* parent's curses
remind us forcibly of the equally minute excommunication so admirably
recorded in Tristram Shandy. But Sterne has the start of him; for though
Percy B. Shelley, Esquire, has managed to include in the imprecations of
the Cenci, the eyes, head, lips, and limbs of his daughter, the other has
anticipated his measures, in formally and specifically anathematizing the
lights, lungs, liver, and *all odd joints*, without excepting even the great toe
of his victim.—To proceed with our review; the dying expostulations of
poor Beatrice, are beautiful and affecting, though occasionally tinged with
the Cockney style of burlesque; for instance, Bernardo asks, when they
tear him from the embraces of his sister,

Would ye divide body from soul?

On which the judge sturdily replies—"That is the headman's business."
The idea of approaching execution paralyses the soul of Beatrice, and she
thus frantically expresses her horror.

[*Quotes Beatrice's outbreak of wild despair, Act V, Scene iv, lines 47-67*]

The author, in his preface, observes that he has committed only one
plagiarism in his play. But with all the triumph of vanity, we here stoutly

convict him of having wilfully, maliciously, and despitefully stolen the pleasing idea of the repetition of "down, down, down," from the equally pathetic and instructive ditty of "up, up, up" in Tom Thumb; the exordium or prolegomena to which floweth *sweetly* and *poetically* thus:—

> Here we go up, up, up,
> And here we go down, down, down!

In taking leave of Mr. Shelley, we have a few observations to whisper in his ear. That he has the seedlings of poetry in his composition no one can deny, after the perusal of many of our extracts; that he employs them worthily, is more than can be advanced. His style, though disgraced by occasional puerilities, and simpering affectations, is in general bold, vigorous, and manly; but the disgraceful fault to which we object in his writings, is the scorn he every where evinces for all that is moral or religious. If he must be sceptical—if he must be lax in his human code of excellence, let him be so; but in God's name let him not publish his principles, and cram them down the throats of others. Existence in its present state is heavy enough; and if we take away the idea of eternal happiness, however visionary it may appear to some, who or what is to recompence us for the loss we have sustained? Will scepticism lighten the bed of death?—Will vice soothe the pillow of declining age? If so! let us all be sceptics, let us all be vicious; but until their admirable efficacy is proved, let us jog on the beaten course of life, neither influenced by the scoff of infidelity, nor fascinated by the dazzling but flimsy garb of licentiousness and immorality.

THE THEATRICAL INQUISITOR IS PLEASED

[From The Theatrical Inquisitor and. Monthly Mirror, April, 1820 (16: 205-218), signed B. This is the only notice taken of Shelley by this liberal journal.]

We are not familiar with the writings of Mr. Shelley, and shall therefore discharge a strict critical duty in considering this, "the latest of his literary efforts," upon independent grounds; as neither depreciated nor enhanced by his former productions; but as the offering of a muse that demands our deep, serious, and impartial investigation, to whatever praise or censure it may be ultimately entitled.

This tragedy is founded upon a narrative of facts, preserved in the archives of the "Cenci" palace at Rome, which contains a detailed account of the horrors that ended in the extinction of a rich and noble family of that place, during the pontificate of Clement VIII., in the year 1599. To this manuscript Mr. Shelley obtained access in the course of his travels through Italy, and having found, on his return to Rome, that the story was not to be told in Italian society without a deep and breathless interest, he imbibed his conception of its fitness for a dramatic purpose. The subject of the "Cenci" is, indeed, replete with materials for terrific effect, and when it has been laid before our readers in the words of Mr. Shelley, we feel assured of their adherence to that opinion.

[*Quotes Shelley's summary of the story, from the first paragraph of his Preface*]

From a knowledge of the power inherited by this tale to awaken the sympathy of its hearers, Mr. Shelley determined to clothe it in such language and action as would adjust with the perceptions of his countrymen and "bring it home to their hearts." A dry exhibition of it on the stage, he observes, would be insupportable, and we fully coincide in the justice of that remark. Audiences are universally the dupes of feeling and that feeling is too often a wrong one. Alive only to the intricacies of an elaborate plot, without taste for poetical diction, or judgment for powerful character, their sanction and dissent are equally valueless—can establish no merit, and attribute no distinction. The patent puppet-shows of this mighty metropolis are swayed and supplied by individuals who have no emulation but in the race of gain; rash, ignorant, and rapacious, they have rendered the stage a medium of senseless amusement, and if their sordid earnings could be secured by a parricidal sacrifice of the drama itself, we do not scruple to confess our belief that such a detestable sacrifice would be readily effected. If Mr. Shelley has ever speculated in the remotest manner upon an appeal to the stage, we urge him, most earnestly, to renounce that intention. There is something like latent evidence that the tragedy before us was not meant exclusively for the closet; such a purpose is by no means explicitly avowed; but we are glad, however, to perceive that Mr. Shelley, in the structure of his present poem, has not evinced a single claim to the loathsome honours of play-house approbation.

The Cenci opens with an interview between Count Cenci and Cardinal Camillo, in which the latter alludes to the remission of a great recent offense, on the payment of an enormous forfeiture. In the course of this conversation Count Cenci's appetite for lust and blood are vividly enforced; he spurns the humane counsels of his priestly adviser, who having watched him from his "dark and fiery youth" through "desperate and remorseless manhood" to "dishonoured age" had repeatedly screened him from punishment, and throws out a dark hint of silencing even him by assassination:

> Cardinal,
> One thing, I pray you, recollect henceforth,
> And so we shall converse with less restraint.
> A man you knew spoke of my wife and daughter;
> He was accustomed to frequent my house;
> So the next day his wife and daughter came
> And asked if I had seen him; and I smiled.
> I think they never saw him any more.

This trait of ferocity is still farther heightened by the complete development of Cenci's moral system, which is built up of the most bold and flagitious materials that can help render him a paragon of depravity:

[*Quotes from the opening dialogue of Camillo and Cenci, Act I, Scene i, lines 66-120*]

Cenci appears soon after at a sumptuous feast given to his kindred and many other nobles of Rome. Elated most unnaturally at the intelligence, he communicates to this assembly the death of his two elder sons, Rocco and Cristofano, whom he had removed from Rome to Salamanca,

> Hoping some accident would cut them off,
> And meaning, if he could, to starve them there

In the height of his horrid joy, Cenci thus describes these disastrous events:

> Rocco
> Was kneeling at the mass, with sixteen others,
> When the church fell and crushed him to a mummy,
> The rest escaped unhurt. Cristofano
> Was stabbed in error by a jealous man,
> Whilst she he loved was sleeping with his rival;
> All in the self-same hour of the same night;
> Which shows that Heaven has special care of me.

The guests impute this exaltation to some really agreeable news, till Cenci confirms the tidings he has just delivered, by the following atrocious though sublime ejaculation:

> [*Quotes Act I, Scene iii, lines 77-90, in which Cenci triumphs in the death of his sons*]

Beatrice then steps forward, and adjures the various members of her family to curb the tyranny of Cenci, by removing both her and her step-mother, Lucretia, beyond the reach of his cruel treatment. The effect of Cenci's rigour is thus beautifully illustrated:

> O God! That I were buried with my brothers!
> And that the flowers of this departed spring
> Were fading on my grave!

The danger of exciting Cenci's animosity deters her relatives from inter-fering, and they depart with a sincere but spiritless commiseration of the wrongs it was their duty to relieve. Cenci then revokes his determination of not drinking, and, having quaffed a bowl of wine, bursts into a dark but desperate announcement of some impending villainy, which, under the influence of his exhilarating draught, he rushes out to achieve.

At the opening of Act II., a partial disclosure is made by Beatrice of the execrable crime that her father has resolved to perpetrate, and in ad-vance toward which, he has determined on removing to an ancient castle among the rocks of Apulia. His meditations upon this arrangement are as follows:

> [*Quotes Act II, Scene i, lines 174-193*]

In the meantime Orsino, a wily prelate, who, previous to his embracing a state of sordid celibacy, had won the affections of Beatrice, under the mask of friendship but from designs of a most offensive nature, has urged her to petition the Pope against her father's brutality, which, however, he perpetuates by keeping her petition back, and pretending it has failed. In the same spirit he sympathises with Giacomo, the son and heir of Count

Cenci, whom that hoary sinner by his duplicity and slander has plunged into the deepest shades of domestic distress. The nature and result of Orsino's machinations are unravelled with great adroitness in the following soliloquy:

[*Quotes Act II, Scene ii, lines 147-161*]

The dreadful outrage contemplated by Cenci is at length completed, and Beatrice reels in with the most appalling marks of his incestuous enormity. The circumstances that lead to this crime are not more remarkable for their horror than their extravagance. That "one with white hair and imperious brow" should satiate his hatred by an expedient of this sort, it is impossible to believe, and yet there is something so devilishly malignant in such a consummation, so rashly wicked, and immeasurably fearful, that it contributes more than any other feature of this tragedy to feed the dark splendour and extent of Mr. Shelley's genius. We feel "sick with hate" at this picture of atrocity, and yet what finer compliment can be paid to its power, than the excess of such a painful sensation? We have enjoyed the same gloomy delight while gazing at the works of Spagnoletto, in one of which, the "Flaying of St. Bartholomew," he represents an executioner as he jags down the stubborn skin with a knife between his teeth, from which the blood of the writhing martyr is seen distinctly to drip. It is ridiculous to object that the point of horror is here carried to excess. Horror was the artist's aim, and unless we mean to quarrel at once with the choice of his subject, we have no right to impeach its execution. His volcanic bosom bubbled over in its own way, pouring out columns of smoke and flame without caution or restraint; and gross, indeed, must be the folly that would search for molten gold among its streams of radiant lava.

We are throwing up this ponderous specimen of Mr. Shelley's power, to return most probably with double violence upon our heedless heads and beat us to the very ground from which we have dared urge its ascension. There is something, however, so shudderingly awful in the scene where this mysterious event is described, that we shall make a copious quotation to corroborate our argument:

[*Quotes Act III, Scene i, lines 1-102, Beatrice's outburst of madness and despair following the incest*]

This passage is, perhaps, a fairer specimen of the present drama than any other extract could afford. It has no broken bursts of passion, but proceeds in a tone of fierce equability to the point at which we have concluded. We see the victim of Cenci's destructive hatred rushing from his serpent coil, her veins swollen with the venom of his infectious guilt, her heart bruised in her very bosom by his merciless pressure. She utters no rhapsody of words, though her exclamations are fraught with the strangest phenomena of which nature is susceptible. As her griefs are dark and dreadful, so her lamentation is earnest and excessive; it borders upon frenzy; but when her reason has surmounted the shock that displaced it, she drops at once from the day-dreams of an unsettled fancy, to the sorrows of immovable conviction and the bitterness of unqualified despair. Her thoughts are then devoted to vengeance, and yet could her father's crime be atoned for by the blood he has polluted, she would freely expend it; that, however, cannot happen; and therefore, after a reproachful glance at the laxity of heaven, she resumes her innate piety, and returns to a gloomy speculation of revenge.

Orsino, the crafty tempter to deeds of death, now enters, and, in the true spirit of priestliness, incenses the very passions he ought in duty to allay. The murder of Cenci is concerted to the vindictive delight of Beatrice, and with the timid assent of Lucretia. The approaching journey to Petrella is selected for this purpose, and the spot pointed out for its commission is thus impressively described. . . .

[*Quotes Act III, Scene i, lines 244-265*]

The unscrupulous villainy of the monster thus about to be summarily despatched, is still further blazoned by the injuries of his son, Giacomo, who, having narrated the wrongs he has sustained, accedes to Orsino's plan of retribution. It fails, however, and Cenci reaches his Apulian fort, where fresh and final matters of cruelty engage his attention. . . .

[*Quotes Act IV, Scene i, lines 45-69*]

In this march of mischief he is quickly cut off by Olimpio, the castellan of Petrella, a man who

> hated
> Old Cenci so, that in his silent rage
> His lips grew white only to see him pass;

And Marzio, a common stabber, from whom Cenci, though "well-earned and due," had withheld the guerdon of assassination. These ruffians are loth at first to kill "an old and sleeping man,"

> His veined hands crossed on his heaving breast,

till Beatrice, with unconquerable fierceness, by offering to immolate him herself, incites them to the task. They strangle him and throw his body out of the window where it catches in the branches of a pine-tree, and is speedily discovered. The Pope's legate, Savella, arrives with an order for Cenci's apprehension, and on detecting the manner in which he has been dealt with, leads away Beatrice, Lucretia, and Marzio to Rome, where they are arraigned for his imputed murder. Marzio, subdued by torture, confesses the crime, and · implicates his abettors, upon which Beatrice, with astonishing hardihood, maintains her innocence and succeeds in persuading Marzio to recant his accusation. Giacomo, who had been betrayed by Orsino to facilitate his own escape, and Lucretia are at length tormented to confession, and adjudged to death with Beatrice, who, when her fate is declared, utters this pathetic exclamation: . . .

[*Quotes Act V, Scene iv, lines 48-67*]

Much intercession is used to avert the fulfillment of her sentence, and when counselled to hope for a favorable issue, Beatrice thus repulses the specious delusion. . . .

[*Quotes Act V, Scene iv, lines 97-111*]

Her faithful and devoted brother, Bernardo, who has prayed like a "wreck-devoted seaman" to the pontiff for mercy, now rushes in wildly to proclaim the failure of his hopeless errand. . . .

[*Quotes Act V, Scene iv, lines 121-137*]

Beatrice, turning from the prospect of her premature death and blasted honour, abandons the bitterness, obstinacy, and dissimulation those evils had occasioned. She takes a touching leave of her young and kind brother, does a little familiar office for Lucretia, and placidly follows her guards to the place of execution.

We have now rendered to this tragedy such tokens of our admiration, as a hasty perusal and restricted limits would allow us to afford. The worshippers of old, who with pious inclinations had but imperfect means, when they could not give wine to their gods, offered water, and laid a leaf upon that shrine to which others brought its fruit or its flower. If purity of praise can atone to Mr. Shelley for the rough terms in which it is delivered, we beg him to believe us sincere, though unpolished, in its application. As a first dramatic effort "The Cenci" is unparalleled for the beauty of every attribute with which drama can be endowed. It has few errors but such as time will amend, and many beauties that time can neither strengthen nor abate. The poetical lilies of Mr. Shelley have sprung up much sooner than more common blossoms, and by their blossoms, and by their beauty at the break of the morning, we may speculate upon the fragrance they will yield for the rest of the day.

THE NEW MONTHLY ADMIRES AND DOUBTS

[From The New Monthly Magazine and Universal Register, May 1, 1820 (13: 550-553). Though founded to counteract the very tendencies which Shelley strove to promote, the attitude of this periodical toward Shelley, if somewhat unfavorable, was not altogether unkindly.]

Whatever may be the variety of opinion respecting the poetical genius displayed in this work, there can be but one sentiment of wonder and disgust in every honest heart, at the strange perversity of taste which selected its theme. It is the story of a wretch grown old in crime, whose passions are concentrated at last in quenchless hate towards his children, especially his innocent and lovely daughter, against whom he perpetrates the most fearful of outrages, which leads to his own death by her contrivance, and her own execution for the almost blameless parricide. The narrative, we believe is "extant in choice Italian"; but that is no excuse for making its awful circumstances the groundwork of a tragedy. If such things have been, it is the part of a wise moralist decently to cover them. There is nothing in the circumstance of a tale being true which renders it fit for the general ear. The exposure of a crime too often pollutes the very soul which shudders at its recital, and destroys that unconsciousness of ill which most safely preserves its sanctities. There can be little doubt that the horrible details of murder, which are too minutely given in our public journals, lead men to dwell on horrors till they cease to petrify, and gradually prepare them for that which once they trembled to think on. "Direness familiar to their slaughterous thoughts cannot once start them." One suicide is usually followed by others, because men of distempered imaginations brood over the thoughts of the deed, until their diseased and fevered minds are ready to embrace it. It is sometimes true in more than one sense, that "where there is no law there is no transgression." All know that for many centuries there was no punishment provided at Rome for parricide, and that not an instance occurred to make the people repent of this omission. And may it not be supposed that this absence of crime was owing to the absence of the law—that the subject was thrown far back from the imagination—that the offense was impossible because it was believed so—and that the regarding it as out of all human calculation gave to it a distant awfulness far more fearful than the severest of earthly penalties? We know well, indeed, that crimes like those intimated in the Cenci can never be diffused by any mistaken attempt to drag them forth to the world. But if the mind turns from their loathsomeness, as the sun refused to shine on the horrible banquet of Thyestes, they may still do it irreparable evil. There is no small encouragement to vice in gazing into the dark pits of fathomless infamy. The ordinary wicked regard themselves as on a pinnacle of virtue, while they look into the fearful depth beneath them. The reader of this play, however intense his hatred of crime, feels in its perusal that the sting is taken from offences which usually chill the blood with horror, by the far-removed atrocity which it discloses. The more ordinary vices of the hero become reliefs to us; his cruelties seem to link him to humanity; and his murders are pillows upon which the imagination reposes. It would be well if those who are disposed to exhibit as a spectacle the most awful anomalies of our nature, reflected on the noble reasoning of Sir Thomas Browne in the last chapter of his Enquiries into Vulgar Errors: "For of sins heteroclital, and such as want either name or precedent, there is oft-times a sin even in their histories. We desire no records of such enormities: sins should be accounted new, so that they may be esteemed monstrous. The pens of men may sufficiently expatiate without these singularities of villainy; for as they increase the hatred of vice in some, so do they enlarge the theory of wickedness in all. And this is one thing that may make latter ages worse than the former; for the vicious examples of ages past poison the curiosity of these present, affording a hint of sin unto seduceable spirits, and soliciting those unto the imitation of them, whose heads were never so perversely principled as to invent them. In this kind we recommend the wisdom and goodness of

Galen, who would not leave unto the world so subtle a theory of poisons; unarming thereby the malice of venomous spirits, whose ignorance must be contented with sublimate and arsenic. For surely there are subtler venenations, such as will invisibly destroy, and like the basilisks of heaven. In things of this nature, silence commendeth history; 'tis the veniable part of things lost, wherein there must never rise a Pancirollus,[3] nor remain any register but that of Hell!' "

If the story of the drama before us is unfit to be told as mere matter of historic truth, still further is it from being suited to the uses of poetry. It is doubtless one of the finest properties of the imagination to soften away the asperities of sorrow, and to reconcile by its mediating power, the high faculties of man and the mournful vicissitudes and brief duration of his career in this world. But the distress which can thus be charmed away, or even rendered the source of pensive joy, must not be of a nature totally repulsive and loathsome. If the tender hues of fancy cannot blend with those of the grief to which they are directed, instead of softening them by harmonious influence, they will only serve to set their blackness in a light still more clear and fearful. Mr. Shelley acknowledges that "anything like a dry exhibition of his tale on the stage would be insupportable," and that "the person who would treat such a subject must increase the ideal, and diminish the actual horror of events, so that the pleasure which arises from the poetry which exists in these stupendous sufferings and crimes, may mitigate the pain of the contemplation of the moral deformity from which they spring." But in the most prominent of these sufferings and crimes there is no poetry, nor can poetry do aught to lessen the weight of superfluous misery they cast on the soul. Beauties may be thrown around them; but as they cannot mingle with their essence they will but increase their horrors, as flowers fantastically braided round a corpse, instead of lending their bloom to the cheek, render its lividness more sickening. In justice to Mr. Shelley we must observe that he has not been guilty of attempting to realize his own fancy. There is no attempt to lessen the horror of the crime, no endeavor to redeem its perpetrator by intellectual superiority, no thin veil thrown over the atrocities of his life. He stands, base as he is odious, and, as we have hinted already, is only thought of as a man when he softens into a murderer.

We are far from denying that there is great power in many parts of this shocking tragedy. Its author has at least shown himself capable of leaving these cold abstractions which he has usually chosen to embody, and of endowing human characters with life, sympathy, and passion. With the exception of Cenci, who is half maniac and half fiend, his persons speak and act like creatures of flesh and blood, not like the problems of strange philosophy set in motion by galvanic art. The heroine, Beatrice is, however, distinguished only from the multitude of her sex by her singular beauty and sufferings. In destroying her father she seems impelled by madness rather than will, and in her fate excites pity more by her situation

[3] Who wrote De Antiquis Perditis or of Inventions Lost. (Reviewer's footnote.)

than her virtues. Instead of avowing the deed, and asserting its justice, as would be strictly natural for one who had committed such a crime for such a cause—she tries to avoid death by the meanest arts of falsehood and encourages her accomplice to endure the extremities of torture rather than implicate her by confession. The banquet given by Cenci to all the cardinals and nobles of Rome, in order to give expression to his delight on the violent deaths of his sons, is a wanton piece of absurdity, which could have nothing but its improbability to recommend it for its adoption. The earlier scenes of the play are tame—the middle ones petrifying—and the last scene of all affecting and gentle. Some may object to the final speech of Beatrice, as she and her mother are going out to die, where she requests the companion of her fate to "tie her girdle for her, and bind up her hair in any simple knot," and refers to the many times they had done this for each other, which they should do no more, as too poor and trifling for the close of a tragedy. But the play, from the commencement of the third act, is one catastrophe, and the quiet pathos of the last lines is welcome as breaking the iron spell which so long has bound the currents of sympathy.

The diction of the whole piece is strictly dramatic—that is, it is nearly confined to the expression of present feeling, and scarcely ever overloaded with imagery which the passion does not naturally create. The following beautiful description of the chasm appointed by Beatrice for the murder of her father, is truly asserted by the author to be the only instance of isolated poetry in the drama:

[*Quotes Act III, Scene i, lines 243-265*]

The speeches of Cenci are hardly of this world. His curses on his child—extending, as they do, the view of the reader beyond the subject into a frightful vista of polluting horrors—are terrific, almost beyond example, but we dare not place them before the eyes of our readers. There is one touch, however, in them, singularly profound and sublime to which we may refer. The wretch, debased as he is, asserts his indissoluble relation of father, as giving him a potency to execrate his child, which the universe must unite to support and heaven allow—leaning upon this one sacred right which cannot sink from under him even while he curses! The bewildered ravings of Beatrice are awful, but their subject will not allow of their quotation. We give the following soliloquy of Cenci's son, when he expects to hear news of his father's murder, because, though not the most striking, it is almost the only unexceptionable instance which we can give of Mr. Shelley's power to develope human passion.

[*Quotes Act III, Scene ii, lines 1-30*]

We must make one more remark on this strange instance of perverted genius, and we shall then gladly fly from its remembrance forever. It seems at first sight wonderful that Mr. Shelley, of all men, should have perpetrated this offense against taste and morals. He professes to look almost wholly on the brightest side of humanity—to "bid the lovely scenes at distance hail"—and live in fond and disinterested expectation of a "progeny of golden years" hereafter to bless the world. We sympathize with him in these anticipations, though we differ widely from him as to the means by which the gradual advancement of the species will be effected. But there is matter for anxious inquiry, when one, richly gifted, and often looking to the full triumph of happiness and virtue, chooses to drag into public gaze the most awful crimes, and luxuriates in the inmost and most pestilential caverns of the soul. To a mind, thus strangely inconsistent, something must be wanting. The lamentable solution is, that Mr. Shelley, with noble feelings, with far-reaching hopes, and with a high and emphatic imagination, has no power of religious truth fitly to balance and rightly to direct his energies. Hence a restless activity prompts him to the boldest and most fearful excursions—sometimes almost touching on the portals of heaven, and, at others, sinking a thousand fathoms deep in the cloudy chain of cold fantasy, into regions of chaos and eternal night. Thus will he continue to vibrate until he shall learn that there are sanctities in his nature as well as rights, and that these venerable relations which he despises, instead of contracting the soul, nurture its most extended charities, and cherish its purest aspirations for universal good. Then will he feel that his imaginations, beautiful as ever in shape, are not cold, but breathing with genial life, and that the most ravishing prospects of human improvement, can only be contemplated steadily from those immortal pillars which Heaven has provided Faith to lean upon.

MORE ADMIRATION AND DOUBT

[From The Edinburgh Monthly Review, May, 1820 (3: 591-604).]

In the Colonna palace at Rome, there is a small picture, a masterpiece of Guido, which those who have looked upon it can never forget. It is the portrait of a young pale golden-haired melancholy female—her countenance wears the stamp of settled and mild grief—her hands are folded in the firmness of gentle despair—all around her is black as the night of a prison. It represents Beatrice, a lady of the once illustrious house of Cenci, and was painted two hundred years ago, while she lay under sentence of death for the crime of parricide.

Tradition reports, and those that put any faith in physiognomy will easily believe the tradition, that the crime for which this fair creature suffered the last severity of the law, was alien to her original nature, and that her mind, formed to be of the meekest and most merciful order, had been wrought up to the point of bloody resolution, only by the accumulated horrors of paternal cruelty, continued through all the brief series of her opening years, and terminated at last in one deed of outrage so dark, that it ought forever to be without a name—so atrocious, that if any injury could justify parricide, that worst injury was this.

To choose, as the subject of dramatic embellishment, a story so revolting to all human hearts, as that of which this painting has long been the only memorial—to lavish, in the calm possession of intellectual power, the splendours of a rich and lovely imagination, upon the portraiture of deeds and thoughts so horrible, and the development of characters, so warped from the simplicity of nature as those involved in its delineation—was an idea which, we are firmly persuaded, could never have entered into the head of any man of genius besides Mr. Percy Bysshe Shelley. With the private history of this gentleman we have nothing to do, but we must be permitted to say, that the deliberate conception and the elaborate execution of a tragedy, founded on such a plot, is, to our judgment, an abundant proof that he has embraced some pernicious and sophistical system of moral belief—that he has taught himself to regard, with a sinful indifference, the brightest and darkest places of our frail and imperfect nature—that he delights in deepening, by artificial gloom, those mysteries in the government of this passing world, which it is the part and privilege of Faith alone to lighten—that, confident in the possession of talents which were not given or won to him by himself, he disdains to confess the existence of any thing beyond his reach of understanding, and rashly rejoices, in considering as an arena, whereon to display his own strength, that which, as a man, even if not as a Christian, it might have better become him to contemplate with the humility of conscious weakness. In an evil hour does the pleasure of exhibiting might, first tempt the hand of genius to withdraw the veil from things that ought for ever to remain concealed, and Mr. Shelley should consider (and he has an abundance of time to do so, for he is yet a very young man,) that the perpetration of actual guilt, may possibly be to some natures a pastime of scarcely a different essence from that which is afforded to himself, and some others of his less-gifted contemporaries, by the scrutinizing and anatomizing discovery of things so monstrous. In two poems which have already rendered his name well known to the public, the same lamentable perverseness of thought and belief was sufficiently visible, although the allegorical and mystical strain in which these were composed, prevented the fault from coming before the eye of the reader in the whole of its naked fulness. But now that he has departed from his aerial, and, indeed, not very intelligible impersonations, and ventured to embody the lamentable errors of his system in a plain unvarnished picture of real human and domestic atrocities, we are mistaken in our notion of the British public, if he will not find that he has very far overshot the mark within which some measure of toleration might be permitted to the rashness and intoxication of a youthful fancy. It is absolutely impossible that any man in his sober mind should believe the dwelling upon such scenes of unnatural crime and horror can be productive of any good to any one person in the world—and, when Mr. Shelley has advanced a little farther in life and experience, he will probably learn, that in literature, as in all other human things, that which cannot do good, must, of necessity, tend to do evil. The delicacy of the moral sense of man—what then shall we say of that of woman?—was not a thing made to be tampered with upon such terms of artist-like coolness and indifference as these. He that presumes to make his intellect address a voice to the world, should know that this voice must either harmonize or jar with the universal music of life and wisdom. The lightnings of genius are, indeed, always beautiful, but it should be remembered, that although their business is to purify the air, they may easily, unless reason lift her conducting rod, be converted into the swiftest and surest instruments of death and desolation. In that case, the measure of the peril answers to the brightness of the flash. And had Mr. Shelley's powers appeared to us to be less, we should not have said so much concerning the wickedness of their perversion.

Of a poem the whole essence and structure of which are so radically wrong, it is impossible that we should give any thing like an analysis, without repeating in some sense the offence already committed by its author. Not a few of our contemporaries, however, and some of these not of the lowest authority, seem to us to labor under a foolish timidity, which prevents them from doing justice to the genius, at the same time that they inflict due chastisement on the errors of this remarkable young man. Therefore it is that we think ourselves called upon to justify, by several extracts, the high opinion we have expressed of his capacity, and the consequent seriousness of our reproof. We shall endeavour to select such passages as may give least offence—but this is, in truth, no easy task. The play opens with this conversation between old Cenci, the cruel and brutal father, and Cardinal Camillo, the nephew of the Pope.

[*Quotes the whole of the first scene, 146 lines*]

In the last act—the intervening ones are too full of loathsomeness to be quoted—(although it is there, after all, that the poetry is most powerful—). Beatrice, the injured daughter of the old ruffian—Giacomo her brother—and Lucretia, their step-mother, but to them in all things else a mother, as well as in the participation of their sufferings,—are found guilty of the murder, being betrayed by the weakness of two hired assassins. The fear of death, and the consciousness of original purity of intention, render Beatrice bold in presence of her accuser and her judge.

[*Quotes Act V, Scene ii, lines 81-194*]

Cardinal Camillo intercedes for mercy from the Pope, and Bernardo, a younger brother of Beatrice, is also sent to kneel at his feet; but although the full extent of the provocation is made known, all solicitation is in vain. We give the whole of the last scene.

[*Quotes the last scene entire, 165 lines*]

Mr. Shelley mentions in his preface, that he has only very lately begun to turn his attention to the literature of the drama. From the language of these extracts, beautiful as they are, it might indeed be gathered that he has not yet mastered the very difficult art of English dramatic versification. But that is a trivial matter. His genius is rich to overflowing in all the nobler requisites for tragic excellence, and were he to choose and manage his themes with some decent measure of regard for the just opinions of the world, we have no doubt he might easily and triumphantly overtop all that has been written during the last century for the English stage.

GREAT GENIUS AND BASE MORALS

[From The London Magazine, May, 1820 (1: 546-555). With the possible exception of Blackwood's, The London Magazine was the best English monthly during Shelley's lifetime, though its contemporary importance was hardly on a par with the later distinction of some of its contributors. It recognized Shelley's genius, and while refusing to endorse his principles, showed considerable interest in him.

Though William Hazlitt made casual unfriendly remarks about Shelley in The London Magazine (largely from personal pique, according to Leigh Hunt's conjecture to Shelley) he is hardly to be suspected of this review, since he did not condemn Shelley's principles but only thought of Shelley as jeopardizing them by carrying them too far.]

A miscellaneous writer of the present time urges it, as an objection against some of the second-rate dramatists of the Elizabethan age, that "they seemed to regard the decomposition of the common affections, and the dissolution of the strict bonds of society, as an agreeable study and a careless pastime." On the other hand, he observes, "the tone of Shakespeare's writings is manly and bracing; while theirs is at once insipid and meretricious in the comparison. Shakespeare never disturbs the ground of moral principle; but leaves his characters (after doing them heaped justice on all sides) to be judged by our common sense and natural feeling. Beaumont and Fletcher constantly bring in equivocal sentiments and characters, as if to set them up to be debated by sophistical casuistry, or varnished over with the colours of poetical ingenuity. Or Shakespeare may be said to 'cast the diseases of the mind, only to restore it to a sound and pristine health'; the dramatic paradoxes of Beaumont and Fletcher are, to all appearance, *tinctured with an infusion of personal vanity* and laxity of principle."

We have put in Italics the words at the conclusion of the above paragraph, which appear, to us most completely to indicate the constitutional cause of that unhappy and offensive taste in literary composition, censured by the above author in writers that might be deemed innocent of it, were we to judge of them only by a comparison with some recent and present examples. *Personal vanity* rather than vicious propensity, is the secret source of that morbid irritation, which vents itself in fretfulness against "the strict bonds of society"; which seeks gratification in conjuring up, or presenting, the image or idea of something abhorrent to feelings of the general standard;—which causes the patient to regard with a jaundiced eye the genuine workings of nature in vice as well as in virtue;—which gives to desire the character of rank disease; and so depraves the fancy as to lead it to take mere nuisances for crimes, and hideous or indecent chimaeras for striking objects and incidents. Whatever can in any way be converted into a mirror, to reflect back *self* on the consciousness of him who is thus infatuated, is preferable, in his estimation, to what would turn his admiration to something nobler and better, open fields of speculation that have far wider bounds than his own habits, and a range from which his self-love is excluded. Hence his itch to finger forbidden things; he has these entirely to himself; the disgust of mankind secures him from rivalry or competition. The very fact of a feeling's having been respected, or that a sentiment has prevailed for ages of the world, rouses his anger against it; and, while he cants down all approved practical wisdom, with the offensive protection of philosophy, he would fain make even nature herself truckle to his egotism, by reversing her instincts in the human breast in favour of the triumph of his own absurd systems, or perhaps to mitigate the pain of a certain secret tormenting consciousness. One of this stamp will propose lending his wife to his friend,[4] and expect praises of an enlarged and liberal style of thinking, when he is only insulting decency, and outraging manly feeling, under the influence of a weak intellect, slight affections, and probably currupted appetite. Such persons must evidently be deemed notorious offenders, if they are not recognised for reformers and regenerators; they can only preserve themselves from disgrace, by throwing it on the surest and most sacred of these principles which have hitherto preserved the social union from total dishonour, and on which must be founded that improvement of our social institutions which, in the present day, is so generally desired and expected.

Yet, though thus peculiar in their tastes, these vain sophists are very profuse of compliments, in conversation or in writing, as their opportunities may be. Their friends and associates are all *innocent, and brave, and pure;* and this is saying no little for themselves. We happen at this moment to have on our table Lyly's *Euphues,* which the Monastery has now rendered known by name to many thousands who never before suspected its existence;—it was put there for another purpose, but it will also help to serve our present one. The quaint author excellently describes the trick above-mentioned. "One flattereth another by his own folly, and *layeth cushions under the elbow of his fellow* when he seeth him take a nap with fancie; *and as their wit wresteth them to vice, so it forgeth them* some *feate excuse to cloake* their vanitie." By the same rule, an opponent is ever a rascal, and the most extravagant and absurd assumptions are made with equal readiness, whether the object be to cast lustre on their intimacies, or lay a flattering unction to a wound inflicted by some justly severe hand. All that is foreign, or adverse to themselves, in short, is base, weak, selfish, or mischievous; that is the principle on which are founded their *patient and irreconcilable enmities;* and, on the other hand, the happiness of their *fortunate friendships* is exactly proportionate to the subserviency of these friendships to their habits of indolent self-indulgence,

---

[4] Perhaps the reviewer had seen or heard of the diary of Dr. John Polidori, then unpublished, in which Polidori, shortly after meeting Shelley in Geneva in 1816, said that Shelley wished to share his first wife with a friend, who declined.—N.I.W.

and the intolerance of their roused self-conceit. What ever would annoy their consciousness must, without fail, be proscribed by their *dear friends* as a prejudice or a piece of hyprocrisy; and on these conditions Charles, and James, and John receive each a sonnet apiece, garnished perhaps with a garland. These amiable goings-on, however, form a curious and far from dignified spectacle in the eyes of the public; and most judicious persons are inclined to think, that such fulsome display of parlour-fooleries is as inconsistent with staunchness of sentiment, as it is offensive to good taste. The firm base of independence, and the strong cement of a manly disposition, are wanting to these constructions for the shelter of inferior talent, and the pampering of roughly-treated pretention: they are, therefore, as frail in their substance, as fantastic and ridiculous in their appearance. Disgust is, in a little time, the natural consequence of such an intercourse as we have been describing, where there exists either intellect or feeling enough to be so affected; and infidelity naturally occurs pretty frequently amongst the inferior retainers, who, having been only received because of the tribute they brought, are free, as with some reason they seem to think, to carry it when they please elsewhere.

These remarks are (not altogether) but principally, suggested by the Preface, Poems, and Dedication contained in the volume under our review:[5]—yet it is no more than fair towards Mr. Shelley to state, that the *style* of his writings betrays but little affectation, and that their matter evinces much real power of intellect, great vivacity of fancy, and a quick, deep, serious feeling, responding readily and harmoniously, to every call made on the sensibility by the imagery and incidents of this variegated world. So far Mr. Shelley has considerable advantages over some of those with whom he shares many grave faults. In the extraordinary work now under notice, he, in particular, preserves throughout a vigorous, clear, manly turn of expression, of which he makes excellent use to give force and even sublimity to the flashes of passion and of phrenzy,—and wildness and horror to the darkness of cruelty and guilt. His language, as he travels through the most exaggerated incidents, retains its correctness and simplicity;—and the most beautiful images, the most delicate and finished ornaments of sentiment and description, the most touching tenderness, graceful sorrow, and solemn appalling misery, constitute the very genius of poetry, present and powerful in these pages, but, strange and lamentable to say, closely connected with the signs of a depraved, nay mawkish, or rather emasculated moral taste, craving after trash, filth, and poison, and sickening at wholesome nutriment. There can be little doubt but that *vanity* is at the bottom of this, and that weakness of *character* (which is a different thing from what is called weakness of *talent*) is also concerned. Mr. Shelley likes to carry about with him the consciousness of his own peculiarities; and a tinge of disease, probably existing in a certain part of his constitution, gives to these peculiarities a very offensive cast. This unlucky tendency of his is

---

[5] *The Cenci* contained a dedicatory letter to Leigh Hunt, whose *Foliage* (1818) had contained sonnets to Shelley and Keats.—N.I.W.

at once his pride and his shame; he is tormented by suspicions that the general sentiment of society is against him—and, at the same time, he is induced by irritation to keep on harping on sore subjects. Hence his stories, which he selects or contrives under a systematic predisposition as it were,—are unusually marked by some anti-social, unnatural, and offensive feature:—whatever "is not to be named amongst men" Mr. Shelley seems to think has a peculiar claim to celebration in poetry;—and he turns from war, rapine, murder, seduction, and infidelity—the vices and calamities with the description of which our common nature and common experience permit the generality of persons to sympathise—to cull some morbid and maniac sin of rare and doubtful occurrence, and sometimes to found a *system* of practical purity and peace on violations which it is disgraceful even to contemplate.

His present work (the Cenci) we think a case in point. We shall furnish the reader with the story on which this Drama is founded, as it is given by Mr. Shelley in his preface. . . .

[*Quotes first three paragraphs of Preface*]

In this extract we have considerable incoherency, and more improbability, to begin with. What are we to understand by an old man conceiving "an implacable hatred against his children, which showed itself towards one daughter in the shape of an incestuous *passion*"? A passion resulting from hatred, as well as a hatred showing itself in a passion, must be considered quite new at least. Luckily the language of common sense is not applicable to these monstrous infamies: they are not reducible even to the forms of rational communication: they are so essentially absurd that their very description slides necessarily into nonsense; and a person of talent who has taken to this sort of *fancy*, is sure to stultify himself in committing the atrocious act of insulting the soul of man which is the image of his maker. If it be really true that an individual once existed who really hated his children, and, under the impulse of hatred, committed an outrage on his daughter, that individual was *mad;* and will any who are not the same, or worse, pretend that the horrors of madness, the revolting acts of a creature stripped of its being's best part, can properly furnish the principal interest of a dramatic composition, claiming the sympathy of mankind as a representation of human nature? The author informs us, with reference to his present work, that "the person who would treat such a subject must *increase the ideal, and diminish the actual horror* of the events, so that the *pleasure which arises from the poetry that exists in these tempestuous sufferings and crimes*, may mitigate the pain of the contemplation of the moral deformity from which they spring." Now the necessity which Mr. Shelley here admits finally condemns his attempt; for it is a hopeless one. It is quite impossible to increase the ideal, or to diminish the actual horror of *such* events: they are therefore altogether out of the Muse's province. The Ancients were free to select them, because the superior presence and awful hand of Destiny were visible, all the way through, to the minds at least of the spectators. These could see also, by the help of the Poet's allusions, all Olympus looking on at the terrible but unequal struggle. Man, in their compositions, was not the agent but the sufferer: and the excellence of his endowments, and the noble nature of his faculties only served to give dignity to the scene on which he was played with by Powers whose decrees and purposes were not liable to be affected by his qualities or his will. The woes of the house of Tantalus are the acts of Destiny, not the offspring of human character or conduct:— individual character, in fact, has no concern with them,—and no moral lesson is in any way involved in them, except that of reverencing the gods, and submitting implicitly to the manifestations of their sovereign pleasure. No other question, either practical or philosophical, was mooted: the order and institutions of society were not affected by the representation; it only showed that the thunder of heaven might fall on the fairest edifices of human virtue and fortune. The luckless victim of the wrath of Jove might be lashed to the commission of heart-freezing enormities, without human nature appearing degraded; for it was seen that he was under a direct possession, too powerful for his nature, driving him down a steep place into the abyss of ruin. The only reasonable deduction from this was, that the anger of Jove was to be averted, if possible, by duly respecting the ministers of religion, carefully observing the rites of worship, and keeping the mind in an humble, confiding temper towards the will and interference of heaven. This, at least, is clear,—that no indulgence towards the practise of such denaturalizing depravities, could harbour even in the most secret mental recesses of those who were in the habit of seeing the occurrence represented as the immediate work of howling Furies. It was these latter that scourged the doomed person to the commission of such acts, in despite of himself,—in despite of the shriekings of his soul, and the revoltings of poor human nature! The hissing of preternatural serpents accompanied the perpetration of unnatural acts and thus the human heart was saved from corrupting degradation, and human feeling preserved from being contaminated by a familiarity with evil things.

Mr. Shelley, as author, acts on the principle most immediately opposed to this: his object, he says, is "the teaching the human heart the knowledge of itself," in proportion to the possession of which knowledge every human being is wise, just, sincere, *tolerant*, and kind. p. ix. He therefore considers that his work, The Cenci, is "subservient to a moral purpose." We think he is mistaken in every respect. His work does not teach the human heart, but insults it:—a father who invites guests to a splendid feast, and then informs them of the events they are called together to celebrate, in such lines as the following, has neither heart nor brains, neither human reason nor human affections, nor human passions of any kind:—nothing, in short, of human about him but the external form, which, however, in such a state of demoniac frenzy, must flash the wild beast from its eyes rather than the man.

Oh, thou bright wine whose purple splendour leaps
And bubbles gaily in this golden bowl
Under the lamplight, as my spirits do,
To hear the death of my accursed sons!
Could I believe thou wert their mingled blood,
Then would I taste thee like a sacrament,
And pledge with thee the mighty Devil in Hell,
Who, if a father's curses, as men say,
Climb with swift wings after their children's souls,
And drag them from the very throne of Heaven,
Now triumphs in my triumph!—But thou art
Superfluous; I have drunken deep of joy,
And I will taste no other wine to-night,
Here, Andrea! Bear the bowl around.

In this way Mr. Shelley proposes to *teach* the human heart, and thus to effect "the highest moral purpose!" His precepts are conveyed in the cries of Bedlam; and the outrage of a wretched old maniac, long passed the years of appetite, perpetrated on his miserable child, under motives that are inconsistent with reason, and circumstances impossible in fact, is presented to us as a mirror in which we may contemplate a portion, at least, of our common nature! How far this disposition to rake in the lazar-house of humanity for examples of human life and action, is consistent with a spirit of *tolerance* for the real faults and infirmities of human nature, on which Mr. Shelley lays so much stress, we may discover in one of his own absurd illusions. The murder of the Count Cenci he suggests, in the first quotation we have given from his preface, was punished by the Pope, *chiefly* because the numerous assassinations committed by this insane man were a copious source of papal revenue, which his death dried up forever. The atrocity involved in this supposition is, we hesitate not to say, extravagant and ridiculous. That a Pope of those times might be inclined to make money of a committed murder is not only likely, but consistent with history: but at what epoch, under what possible combination of circumstances of government and society, could it be a rational speculation in the breast of a ruler to preserve a particular nobleman with peculiar care, that his daily murders, committed in the face of the public, he himself, in the meantime, walking about a crowded city, might continue to be a source of personal profit to the sovereign! Nor would the paltriness of such a calculation, contrasted with its excessive guilt, permit it to be seriously made in any breast that can justly be adduced as an example of the heart of man. It would be intolerable to the consciousness of any one invested with the symbols of dignity and the means of authority. It would be for such an one to commit murders himself, not to wait in sordid expectation of the bribery to follow their commission by others. It requires the "enlarged liberality" of Mr. Shelley and his friends to fashion their chimaeras of infamy, and then display them as specimens of Princes, Priests, and Ministers. The truth is, that we see few or no signs of their *toleration*, but in regard to cases of incest, adultery, idleness and improvidence:—towards a class of abuses and enormities, falling too surely within the range of human nature and human history, but from which they are far removed by the circumstances of their conditions in life, and equally so, perhaps, by the qualities of their personal characters, they have neither tolerance nor common sense. Their sympathies then lead them to degrade and misrepresent humanity in two ways: by extenuating the commission of unnatural vices, and aggravating the guilt of natural ones:—and as it forms one of their principal objects to dissipate all the *dogmas* of religion, it is further to be observed, that they thus leave the nature of man bare and defenceless, without refuge or subterfuge—let them call it which they please. They render miserable man accountable for all his acts; his soul is the single source of all that occurs to him; he is forbidden to derive hope either from his own weakness or the strength of a great disposing authority, presiding over the world, and guiding it on principles that have relation to the universe. This is a very different basis from that of the Ancient Drama:—in it, the blackness and the storms suspended over the head of man, and which often discharged destruction on his fairest possessions, *hung from Heaven,* and above them there was light, and peace, and intelligence.

The radical foulness of moral composition, characterizing such compositions as this one now before us, we shall never let escape unnoticed or unexposed, when examples of it offer themselves. It is at once disgusting and dangerous; our duty, therefore, is here at unison with our taste. In The Cenci, however, the fault in question is almost redeemed, by uncommon force of poetical sentiment and very considerable purity of poetical style. There are gross exceptions to the latter quality, and we have quoted one; but the praise we have given will apply generally to the work. The story on which it is founded has already been explained. We shall proceed to give, by some extracts from the Drama itself, an idea of its execution.

The accounts which the hoary Cenci gives of himself—his character, feelings, etc.—are generally overstrained and repulsive: but in the following lines, put into the mouth of one who remonstrates with him, we have a fearful and masterly portrait.

[*Quotes Act I, Scene i, lines 34-56*]

What follows by Cenci himself is not so good.

> I love
> The sight of agony, and the sense of joy,
> When this shall be another's, and that mine.
> And I have no remorse and little fear,
> Which are, I think, the checks of other men.
> This mood has grown upon me, until now
> Any design my captious fancy makes
> The picture of its wish, and it forms none

> But such as men like you would start to know,
> Is as my natural food and rest debarred
> Until it be accomplished.

Beatrice, the unhappy daughter of this man is, almost through the whole of the piece, sustained in beauty, delicacy, and refinement, unsullied by incidents of the most odious and contaminating kind. She is introduced in a lame, ill-executed scene, so far as Orsino, a treacherous priest and her lover, is concerned; but at the conclusion of it we find ourselves powerfully interested by the intimation she gives of what is about to take place in her father's house. . . .

[*Quotes Act I, Scene ii, lines 47-63*]

The banquet scene itself, though strained by the maniac extravagance of Cenci, is yet drawn by the hand of a first-rate master. Lucretia, the miserable wife, flatters herself that these signs of festivity and good humour bode well: the superior intellect of her daughter enables her to divine the truth.

> *Beatr.* Ah! My blood runs cold.
> I fear that wicked laughter round his eye
> Which wrinkles up the skin even to the hair.

Cenci avows the cause of his joy in the hearing of his astounded guests and agonized family.

> Here are the letters brought from Salamanca;
> Beatrice, read them to your mother. God!
> I thank thee! In one night didst thou perform,
> By ways inscrutable, the thing I sought.
> My disobedient and rebellious sons
> Are dead!—Why, dead!—What means this change of cheer?
> You hear me not, I tell you they are dead;
> And they will need no food or raiment more:
> The tapers that did light them the dark way
> Are their last cost. The Pope, I think, will not
> Expect I should maintain them in their coffins.
> Rejoice with me—my heart is wondrous glad.

A movement of indignation makes itself manifest among the company: this part, we think, would *act* with great effect.

> *A Guest (rising).*   Thou wretch!
> Will none among this noble company
> Check the abandoned villain?
> *Camillo.*   For God's sake
> Let me dismiss the guests! You are insane,
> Some ill will come of this.
> *Second Guest.*   Seize, silence him!
> *First Guest.*   I will!
> *Third Guest.*   And I!

Cenci (addressing those who rise with a threatening gesture).
Who moves? Who speaks? *(turning to the company)* 'tis nothing,
Enjoy yourselves.—Beware! For my revenge
Is as the sealed commission of a king
That kills, and none dare name the murderer.

Kean may covet the opportunity that would be afforded him by the words—" 'tis nothing—enjoy yourselves!"

Beatrice, unsuccessful in her appeal to the noble and powerful persons present, for protection for herself and her mother, exclaims, in the bitterness of her heart:

> Oh God! that I were buried with my brothers!
> And that the flowers of this departed spring
> Were fading on my grave! And that my father
> Were celebrating now one feast for all!

The unnatural father gives dark intimation of the dreadful design fermenting in his soul in what follows:

[Quotes Act I, Scene iii, lines 160-178]

The first scene of the second act is so characteristic of the tragedy and so impressive in its ability, that we shall give a long extract from it, as the best method of enabling the reader to judge fairly of Mr. Shelley's power as a poet. . . .

[Quotes lines 1-122 in which Cenci's wickedness is dwelt upon]

The dreadful and disgusting crime on which the tragedy is founded has been perpetrated, when Beatrice again makes her appearance.

[Quotes Act III, Scene i, lines 1-32, showing Beatrice's horror and despair]

We cannot follow step by step the progress of the Drama, suffice it to say, that the murder of Cenci is plotted by his wife and daughter with Orsino, a priest, who has base views on the person of Beatrice and who, after abetting the assassination, withdraws himself from its consequences at the expense of his partners in the act. Cenci retires to his castle of Petrella, where he studies new inflictions of suffering on his wretched victims: the bad taste into which Mr. Shelley inevitably falls, whenever he is led to certain allusions, is strikingly exemplified in the following lines put into his mouth:

> 'Tis plain I have been favoured from above,
> For when I cursed my sons they died.—Ay . . . so . . .
> As to the right or wrong, that's talk . . . repentance . . .
> Repentance is an easy moment's work
> And more depends on God than me. Well . . . well . . .
> I must give up the greater point, which was
> To poison and corrupt her soul.

The scene where the wife and daughter are represented, expecting the consummation of the deed by the assassins, has a creeping horror about it:

Lucretia. They are about it now.
Beatrice.   Nay, it is done.
Lucretia. I have not heard him groan.
Beatrice.   He will not groan.
Lucretia. What sound is that?
Beatrice.   List! 'tis the tread of feet
About his bed.
Lucretia. My God!
If he be now a cold stiff corpse . . .
Beatrice.   O, fear not
What may be done, but what is left undone:
The act seals all.

The means by which the murder was discovered need not be detailed. Beatrice, and her mother, and brother are tortured to extract confession, then condemned; and the tragedy thus concludes. . . .

[*Quotes Act V, Scene iv, lines 141-165*]

Here the Drama closes, but our excited imaginations follow the parties to the scaffold of death. This tragedy is the production of a man of great genius, and of a most unhappy moral constitution.

THE INDICATOR EXPLAINS AND PRAISES

[From The Indicator, July 26, 1820 (no. 42, pp. 329-337). The notices of Shelley in The Indicator were from the pen of his greatest champion, Leigh Hunt, and show the same emphasis as most of The Examiner reviews, upon explaining Shelley's work. Previous to the present review The Indicator had already published one of Shelley's short lyrics. A long article on "The Destruction of the Cenci Family" appeared in the issue preceding the present one (July 19, pp. 321-329), designed to stir up interest in Shelley's tragedy by explaining the story; but since it is confined entirely to the original story and contains no criticism of Shelley it is here omitted, though it forms the first half of this review.]

"The highest moral purpose aimed at in the highest species of the drama, is the teaching the human heart, through its sympathies and antipathies, the knowledge of itself; in proportion to the possession of which knowledge, every human being is wise, just, sincere, tolerant, and kind. If dogmas can do more, it is well: but a drama is no fit place for the enforcement of them. Undoubtedly, no person can be truly dishonoured by the act of another; and the fit return to make to the most enormous injuries is kindness and forbearance, and a resolution to convert the injurer from his dark passions by love and peace. Revenge, retaliation, atonement, are pernicious mistakes. If Beatrice had thought in this manner, she would have been wiser and better; but she would never have been a tragic character: the few whom such an exposition would have interested, could never have been sufficiently interested for a domestic purpose, from the want of finding sympathy in their interest among the mass who surround them. It is in the restless and anatomizing casuistry with which men seek the justification of Beatrice, yet feel that she has done what needs justification; it is in the superstitious horror with which they contemplate alike her wrongs and revenge; that the dramatic character of what she did and suffered, consists."

Thus speaks Mr. Shelley, in the Preface to his tragedy of *The Cenci,*— a preface beautiful for the majestic sweetness of its diction, and still more lovely for the sentiments that flow forth with it.   There is no living author, who writes a preface like Mr. Shelley. The intense interest which he takes in his subject, the consciousness he has upon him nevertheless of the interests of the surrounding world, and the natural dignity with which a poet and philosopher, sure of his own motives, presents himself to the chance of being doubted by those whom he would benefit, casts about it an inexpressible air of amiableness and power. To be able to read such a preface, and differ with it, is not easy; but to be able to read it, and then go and abuse the author's intentions, shews a deplorable habit of being in the wrong.

Mr. Shelley says that he has "endeavoured as nearly as possible to represent the characters as they really were, and has sought to avoid the error of making them actuated by his own conceptions of right or wrong, false or true, thus under a thin veil converting names and actions of the sixteenth century into cold impersonations of his own mind." He has so. He has only added so much poetry and imagination as is requisite to refresh the spirit, when a story so appalling is told at such length as to become a book. Accordingly, such of our readers as are acquainted with our last week's narrative of the Cenci and not with Mr. Shelley's tragedy, or with the tragedy and not with the narrative, will find in either account that they are well acquainted with the characters of the other. It is the same with the incidents, except that the legal proceedings are represented as briefer, and Beatrice is visited with a temporary madness; but this the author had a right to suppose, in probability as well as poetry. The curtain falls on the parties as they go forth to execution,—an ending which would hardly have done well on the stage, though for different reasons, any more than the nature of the main story. But through the medium of perusal, it has a very good as well as novel effect. The execution seems a supererogation, compared with it. The patience, that has followed upon the excess of the sorrow, has put the tragedy of it at rest. "The bitterness of death is past," as Lord Russell said when he had taken leave of his wife.

We omitted to mention last week, that the greatest crime of which Cenci had been guilty, in the opinion of the author of the Manuscript, was atheism. The reader will smile to see so foolish and depraved a man thus put on a level with Spinoza, Giordano Bruno, and other spirits of undoubted genius and integrity, who have been accused of the same opinion. But the same word means very different things to those who look into it; and it does here, though the author of the MS. might not know it. The atheism of men like Spinoza is nothing but a vivid sense of the universe about them, trying to distinguish the mystery of its opinions from the ordinary, and as they think pernicious anthropomorphism, in which our egotism envelopes it. But the atheism of such men as Cenci is the only real atheism; that is to say, it is the only real disbelief in any great and good thing, physical or moral. For the same reason, there is more atheism, to all intents and purposes of virtuous and useful belief, in some bad religions however devout, than in some supposed absences of religion: for the god they propose to themselves does not rise above the level of the world they live in, except in power like a Roman Emperor; so that there is nothing to them really outside of this world, at last. The god, for instance, of the Mussulman, is nothing but a sublimated Grand Signior; and so much the worse, as men generally are, in proportion to his power. One act of kindness, one impulse of universal benevolence, as recommended by the true spirit of Jesus, is more grand and godlike than all the degrading ideas of the Supreme Being, which fear and slavery have tried to build up to heaven. It is a greater going out of ourselves; a higher and wider resemblance to the all-embracing placidity of the universe. The Catholic author of the MS. says that Cenci was an atheist, though he built a chapel in his garden. The chapel, he tells us, was only to bury his family in. Mr. Shelley on the other hand, can suppose Cenci to have been a Catholic, well enough, considering the nature and tendency of the Catholic faith. In fact, he might have been either. He might equally have been the man he was, in those times, and under all the circumstances of his power and impunity. The vices of his atheism and the vices of his superstition would, in a spirit of his temper and education, have alike been the result of a pernicious system of religious faith, which rendered the Divine Being gross enough to be disbelieved by any one, and imitated and bribed by the wicked. Neither his scepticism nor his devotion would have run into charity. He wanted knowledge to make the first do so, and temper and privation to make the second. But perhaps the most likely thing is, that he thought as little about religion as most men of the world do at all times;— that he despised and availed himself of it in the mercenary person of the Pope, scarcely thought of it but at such times, and would only have believed in it out of fear at his last hour. Be this however as it might, still the habitual instinct of his conduct is justly traceable to the prevailing feeling respecting religion, especially as it appears that he "established masses for the peace of his soul." Mr. Shelley, in a striking part of his preface, informs us that even in our own times "religion co-exists, as it were, in the mind of an Italian Catholic, with a faith in that, of which all men have the most certain knowledge. It is adoration, faith, submission, penitence, blind admiration; not a rule for moral conduct. It has no necessary connexion with any one virtue. The most atrocious villain may be rigidly devout; and without any shock to established faith, confess himself to be so. Religion pervades intensely the whole frame of society, and is according to the temper of the mind which it inhabits, a passion, a persuasion, an excuse; never a check." We shall only add to this, that such religions in furnishing men with excuse and absolution, do but behave with something like decent kindness; for they are bound to do what they can for the vices they produce. And we may say it with gravity too. Forgiveness will make its way somehow every where, and it is lucky that it will do so. But it would be luckier, if systems made less to forgive.

The character of Beatrice is admirably managed by our author. She is what the MS. describes her, with the addition of all the living grace and presence which the re-creativeness of poetry can give her. We see the maddened loveliness of her nature walking among us, and make way with an aweful sympathy. It is thought by some, that she ought not to deny her guilt as she does;—that she ought not, at any rate, to deny the deed, whatever she may think of the guilt. But this, in our opinion, is one of the author's happiest subtleties. She is naturally so abhorrent from guilt,—she feels it to have been so impossible a thing to have killed a FATHER, truly so called, that what with her horror of the deed and of the infamy attending it, she would almost persuade herself as well as others, that no such thing had actually taken place,—that it was a notion, a horrid dream, a thing to be gratuitously cancelled from people's minds, a necessity which they were all to agree had existed but was not to be spoken of, a crime which to punish was to proclaim and make real,—any thing, in short, but that a daughter had killed her father. It is a lie told, as it were, for the sake of nature, to save it the shame of a greater contradiction. If any feeling less great and spiritual, any dread of a pettier pain, appears at last to be suffered by the author to mingle with it, a little common frailty and inconsistency only renders the character more human, and may be allowed a young creature about to be cut off in the bloom of life, who shews such an agonized wish that virtue should survive guilt and despair. She does not sacrifice the man who is put to the torture. He was apprehended without her being able to help it, would have committed her by his confession, and would have died at all events. She only reproaches him for including a daughter in the confession of his guilt; and the man, be it observed, appears to have had a light let into his mind to this effect, for her behaviour made him retract his accusations, and filled him so with a pity above his self-interest, that he chose rather to die in torture than repeat them. It is a remarkable instance of the respect with which Beatrice was regarded in Rome, in spite of the catastrophe into which she had been maddened, that Guido painted her portrait from the life, while she was in prison. He could not have done this, as a common artist might take the likeness of a common criminal, to satisfy vulgar curiosity. Her family was of too great rank and importance, and retained them too much in its reverses. He must have waited on her by permission, and accompanied the sitting with all those attentions which artists on such occasions are accustomed to pay to the great and beautiful. Perhaps he was intimate with her, for he was a painter in great request. In order to complete our accounts respecting her, as well as to indulge ourselves in copying out a beautiful piece of writing, we will give Mr. Shelley's description of this portrait, and masterly summary of her character. "The portrait of Beatrice at the Colonna Palace is most admirable as a work of art: it was taken by Guido during her confinement in prison. But it is most interesting as a just representation of one of the loveliest specimens of the workmanship of Nature. There is a fixed and pale composure upon the features: she seems sad and stricken down in spirit, yet the despair thus expressed is lightened by the patience of gentleness. Her head is bound with folds of white drapery, from which the yellow strings of her golden hair escape, and fall about her neck. The moulding of her face is exquisitely delicate; the eyebrows are distinct and arched: the lips have that permanent meaning of imagination and sensibility, which suffering has not repressed, and which it seems as if death scarcely could extinguish. Her forehead is large and clear; her eyes, which we are told were remarkable for their vivacity, are swollen with weeping and lustreless, but beautifully tender and serene. In the whole mien there is a simplicity and dignity, which united with her exquisite loveliness and deep sorrow, are inexpressibly pathetic. Beatrice Cenci appears to have been one of those rare persons, in whom energy and gentleness dwell together without destroying one another: her nature was simple and profound. The crimes and miseries in which she was an actor and a sufferer, are as the mask and the mantle, in which circumstances clothed her from her impersonation on the scene of the world."

The beauties of a dramatic poem, of all others, are best appreciated by a survey of the whole work itself, and of the manner in which it is composed and hangs together. We shall content ourselves therefore, in this place, with pointing out some detached beauties; and we will begin, as in the grounds of an old castle, with an account of a rocky chasm on the road to Petrella.

[*Quotes Act III, Scene i, lines 238-265*]

With what a generous and dignified sincerity does Beatrice shew at once her own character and that of the prelate her lover.

[*Quotes Act I, Scene ii, lines 14-29*]

The following is one of the gravest and grandest lines we ever read. It is the sum total of completeness. Orsino says, while he is meditating Cenci's murder, and its consequences,

> I see, as from a tower, the end of all.

The terrible imaginations which Beatrice pours forth during her frenzy, are only to be read in connexion with the outrage that produced them. Yet take the following, where the excess of the agony is softened to us by the wild and striking excuse which it brings for the guilt.

> What hideous thought was that I had even now?
> 'Tis gone; and yet its burthen remains still
> O'er these dull eyes—upon this weary heart.

O, world! O, life! O, day! O, misery!
    Lucr. What ails thee, my poor child? She answers not:
Her spirit apprehends the sense of pain,
But its cause: suffering has dried away
The source from which it sprung.
    Beatr. (franticly). Like Parricide,
Misery has killed its father.

When she recovers, she "approaches solemnly" Orsino, who comes in, and announces to him, with an awful obscurity, the wrong she has endured. Observe the last line.

Welcome, friend!
I have to tell you, that since last we met,
I have endured a wrong so great and strange
That neither life nor death can give me rest.
Ask me not what it is, for there are deeds
Which have no form, sufferings which have no tongue.
    Ors. And what is he that has thus injured you?
    Beatr. The man they call my father; a dread name.

The line of exclamations in the previous extract is in the taste of the Greek dramatists; from whom Mr. Shelley, who is a scholar, has caught also his happy feeling for compounds, such as "the all-communicating air," the "mercy-winged lightning," "sin-chastising dreams," "wind-walking pestilence," the "palace-walking devil, gold," &c. Gold, in another place, is finely called "the old man's sword."

Cenci's angry description of the glare of day is very striking.

The all-beholding sun yet shines: I hear
A busy stir of men about the streets;
I see the bright sky through the window panes:
It is a garish, broad, and peering day;
Loud, light, suspicious, full of eyes and ears,
And every little corner, nook, and hole
Is penetrated with the insolent light,
Come darkness!

The following is edifying:—

The eldest son of a rich nobleman
Is heir to all his incapacities;
He has wide wants, and narrow powers.

We are aware of no passage in the modern or ancient drama, in which the effect of bodily torture is expressed in a more brief, comprehensive, imaginative manner, than in an observation made by a judge to one of the assassins. The pleasure belonging to the original image renders it intensely painful.

    Marzio. My God! I did not kill him; I know nothing:
Olimpio sold the robe to me, from which

You would infer my guilt.
    2d Judge. Away with him!
    1st Judge. Dare you, with lips yet white from the rack's kiss,
Speak false?

Beatrice's thoughts upon what she might and might not find in the other world are very terrible; but we prefer concluding our extracts with the close of the play, which is deliciously patient and affectionate. How triumphant is the gentleness of virtue in its most mortal defeats!

[*Quotes Act V, scene iv, lines 137-165*]

Mr. Shelley, in this work, reminds us of some of the most strenuous and daring of our old dramatists, not by any means as an imitator, though he has studied them, but as a bold, elemental imagination, and a framer of "mighty lines." He possesses also however, what those to whom we more particularly allude did not possess, great sweetness of nature, and enthusiasm for good; and his style is, as it ought to be, the offspring of this high mixture. It disproves the adage of the Latin poet. Majesty and Love do sit on one throne in the lofty buildings of his poetry; and they will be found there, at a late and we trust a happier day, on a seat immortal as themselves.

GENIUS POORLY EMPLOYED

[From The Monthly Review, February, 1821 (94:161-168).]

As the genius of this writer grows on us, most heartily do we wish that we were able to say, his good sense and judgment grow with it!— but, alas! for the imperfections of the brightest minds, the reverse in this instance is the case; and the extravagance and wildness of Mr. Shelley's first flights yield to the present, not only in their own excentric [*sic*] character but in other most objectionable points.

Without any *mealy-mouthedness*, or pretences to be more delicate than our neighbours, we honestly confess that the story of the Cenci, chosen as a subject for tragedy in the twentieth [*sic*] century, does indeed astonish and revolt us: for it involves incest committed by a father, and murder perpetrated by a daughter. In the early days of our own drama, we know, great atrocities were suffered to form the subjects of some scenes; and whatever natural decency may have been observed in treating such offensive subjects, we cannot but consider the introduction of them in any way as a manifest proof of the rudeness and barbarism of a newly-born, or lately-reviving, literature. In truth, we do not see how any man of sense can view them in any other light, to whatever extent false theories, concerning the sublime awakening of the passions and the deep utterance of the secrets of the human heart, &c. &c. may mislead the vulgar. Yet such a bias towards the older school of poetry, and all its faults, exists at this moment in England, that every champion of common sense, who strives to oppose the prejudice, is at once branded with the imputation of a narrow understanding, a defective imagination, and a French taste. Be it so. The friends of Reason, we are assured, will stand or fall with her; and if she be quite extinct, why then a cheerful good night to her survivors!

Among the most devoted adherents to the style and manner of the antient English drama,—among the persons who, from all that they write, whether as critics or authors, it would seem were afflicted with a sort of *old-play-insanity*,—may be numbered Mr. Percy Shelley. He tells us in his preface that, in order 'to move men to true sympathy, we must use the *familiar language* of men;' and then, as a happy illustration of this profound axiom, he observes that the 'study of the ancient English poets is to incite us to do that for our own age, which they have done for theirs!' He adds that 'it must be the *real language* of men in general, and not of any particular class,' &c. Now what is all this but the exploded *Wordsworthian heresy*, that the language of poetry and the language of real life are the same? and this, too, when the *tragic* drama is in question! Oh, vain Horace, who dreamt of the *"os magna sonaturum,"* as combined with the *"mens sublimior!"* Oh, vain Shakespeare, (for of all poets he is the most *imaginative* in language, in his loftier passages,) who fancied that passion might be poetical when ideally represented; and whose invariable pursuit, when not descending to the sparkling dust that strewed the arena of his *comedy*, was that *ideal beauty*, that charm, which has been embodied by the scenic representations of two and only two performers[6] of our own times! Oh, forgotten Otway and Rowe, condemned to utter neglect and contempt by our wise and worthy contemporaries; because, forsooth, they *occasionally* sin by too much poetry, and too little reality of exhibition; because they, *in a few instances*, fall into misplaced similes and unnatural ornaments of verse!—We talk, however, to the desperately deaf;—we hold colours up for the judgment of the incurably blind;—we display the armour of the warrior in a conclave of *damsels*, among whom lurks no atom of the masculine spirit of old;—of that age which they disgrace by their gross indiscriminate panegyric, and profane by their feeble unhallowed imitation.

Mr. Shelley is worthy of better things: but it is not merely the daemon of bad Taste which is to be laid in his gifted mind. *There* also inhabits, to all visible appearance, a deeper and darker daemon, the joint offspring of Doubt and Vanity:—of Doubt, far from thoroughly exercised in its established process of metaphysical reasoning; of Vanity, venial while young, and merely trying its wings in the atmosphere of its own limbo. Mr. Shelley, like an unfledged and unpractised giant, attempts to scale heaven on a chicken's pinion; and, little only when he is sceptical, he betrays *such* littleness in his attempts to climb and to shake Olympus, that spectators less biassed in his favour than ourselves would cease either to laugh or to behold. His imagination chiefly dwells on some filmy gossamery vision of his own brain, representing an aerial contest between the powers and princes of the

---

[6] Need we mention the great theatrical names of John Kemble and Mrs. Siddons? (Reviewer's footnote.)

air, in which the principle of evil overcomes, for a long and weary time, the principle of good. Such are the Snake and Eagle (if we recollect the *examples* rightly—we are sure of the *precept*,) of his earliest poem; and such are the Jupiter and Prometheus of that *painful* work which we shall next be called to notice.

We now return to the Cenci; and what a return! The spirit of the author will be best seen by a prose-extract, elucidatory of his state of feeling when he published this tragedy. Speaking of the characters of this drama, Mr. Shelley says:

They are represented as Catholics, and as Catholics deeply tinged with religion. To a Protestant apprehension there will appear something unnatural in the earnest and perpetual sentiment of the relations between God and man which pervade the tragedy of the Cenci. It will especially be startled at the combination of an undoubting persuasion of the truth of the popular religion with a cool and determined perseverance in enormous guilt. But religion in Italy is not, as in Protestant countries, a cloak to be worn on particular days; or a passport which those who do not wish to be railed at carry with them to exhibit; or a gloomy passion for penetrating the impenetrable mysteries of our being, which terrifies its possessor at the darkness of the abyss to the brink of which it has conducted him. Religion co-exists, as it were, in the mind of an Italian Catholic with a faith in that of which all men have the most certain knowledge. It is interwoven with the whole fabric of life. It is adoration, faith, submission, penitence, blind admiration; not a rule for moral conduct. It has no necessary connexion with any one virtue. The most atrocious villain may be richly devout, and without any shock to established faith, confess himself to be so. Religion pervades intensely the whole frame of society, and is according to the temper of the mind which it inhabits, a passion, a persuasion, an excuse, a refuge; never a check.

As *Protestants*, we disdain to reply to the insinuations of this passage: but, for our Catholic brethren, we must *protest* against this most uncharitable charge. '*Never a check!*'—We do trust that Mr. Shelley will not be much older ere he regrets this unchristian and unphilosophical remark. How perfectly he falls within the censure of the poet, we need scarcely remind him;

> And deal damnation round the land,
> On each I judge thy foe;

for who is the foe of God like the *religious hypocrite?*

Thus unhappily prepared, Mr. Shelley entered on his dangerous dramatic task, and wonderously has he acquitted himself in it. We cordially hope that *nothing* may ever prevent us from rendering due homage to genius, wherever it be found; for, however man may pervert it, still it bears the indication and retains the sound of the voice of Heaven within us. We grant, then, that a plain proof is afforded of Mr. Shelley's powers in almost every scene of this drama; and one or two such examples we shall endeavour to select.

In the preface, we are thus informed of the story on which the tragedy is founded. . . .

[*Quotes the first five sentences of Shelley's Preface, to the death of the murderers*]

The dreadful display of wickedness at the feast, where the father re-joices in the death of his two sons, we shall omit; as well as the base cow-ardice of the guests, even when invoked by the firm and lovely Beatrice, *La* Cenci; of whose picture Mr. Shelley tells us he possesses a copy, from the original in the Colonna palace:—but we shall present our readers with the impressive scene in which Beatrice first intimates to Lucretia, her inno-cent mother-in-law, the horrors that have passed. Carefully and feelingly touched are these horrors.

[*Quotes Act II, Scene i, lines 28-97*]

The next scene which we can quote without injustice to the course of the story, we think, is the following. Beatrice is condemned to die, for suborning the murder of her execrable father; and thus, in the language of Claudio in "Measure for Measure," (and we say it not in detraction from genius, although in condemnation of taste,) she deplores her fate. . . .

[*Quotes Act V, Scene iv, lines 47-89*]

Here we must take leave of *The Cenci;* earnestly requesting Mr. Shel-ley to consider well the remarks which we have made in the spirit of honest applause and honest censure; and particularly exhorting him to reflect on all the gifts of Providence, and on the last words which we have quoted,

And yet my heart is cold.

CAUTIOUS ADMIRATION

[From The Independent, a London Literary and Political Review, February 17, 1821 (1: 99-103). Since this liberal weekly seems to have succeeded moderately in its announced purpose of avoiding subservience in criticism, the present review may be taken as a fair example of how Shelley's writings impressed the rare unprejudiced reviewer of his day.]

Mr. Shelley writes with vigor, sublimity, and pathos; but we do not admire his train of thought or feeling. He deals too much with abstractions and high imaginings—and forgets the world to which he writes, and by whom he must expect to be read. Abstractions suit not with life—nor are the bulk of readers capable of valuing them. Their value to life and its business is little worth; and when they are coupled with subtractions from our hopes and fears of an hereafter, they become eminently injurious. Mr. Shelley's mind is contemplative: and did he turn his contemplations to the benefit of his fellow men, his superior powers would not be worse than wasted on the world.

The great writers of our time deal too much with the gloomy—they dissect with skill the worst affections of the heart, and dwell too fondly on vicious passions, and aberrations of the mind.

This passion should be checked—its consequences are fearful. We are not sorry that Mr. Shelley is not read, or if read not rewarded. We could pardon much to youth, and make allowance for the first ebullitions of fancy—the first daring of a master mind, even though that daring were, in some degree misdirected. But the systematic abuse of power, and reviling of religion are unpardonable crimes. No man can be insensible to the abandonment of virtue too often visible in rulers and priests: but after all, they are but schoolboy themes, the target for unbearded free thinking to point its arrows at. In manhood we look for something more:—where we find great powers, we look to their development to useful purposes; but extravagance never will pass with us for superior genius. In manhood we may be, as Mr. Shelley says, both cold and subtle; but the coldness results from an exercise of judgment, and the subtlety cannot exist without some power of reflection. Judgment and reflection should lead us to wiser things than the wholesale contempt for power, and the indiscriminate censure of the sacred office. To check the abuses of either, we should not hold them up as useless or criminal. In all cases they are not so; and authors in their vagaries or false estimates too often assume that they are. Did we live in an ideal world it would be quite a different matter. Had we the power of framing and adjusting our faculties and feelings by some Utopian Standard, writers like Mr. Shelley might be tolerated and approved; but did they write till "the last eventful day," while our nature is constituted as it now is, and has been and ever will be, all their efforts would prove nugatory and useless. Perfection is not for man, however much Madame de Stael's philosophy the other way would lead enthusiasts to believe. We can admire this sort of abstract idealism—this system of perfectibility; but our flesh and blood—nature stares us in the face, and we see at once the folly of attempting to regulate it by those simple, yet unknown, rules that govern the rise and fall of the vegetable or mineral world. Philosophy is but wisdom, and the highest wisdom cannot always act with equal power, and bend itself in the same direction. If men were all philosophers, life would be but a dull monotony—and as all men are not equally gifted—as all men are not organized after the same fashion— equal perfectibility is beyond their attainment.

The many are fools and will continue to be so—they think at second hand, and take their faith and their code as they do their inheritances from those who went before them. Perhaps they would be wiser if they did not:—more happy, none but dreamers of wisdom and happiness will imagine. With all our neatness and refinement in literature, common sense still acts its part. The older pedantry may have yielded to modern dandyism; but perfumery and coarseness are equally repulsive to strength of intellect, and correct judgment.

It is impossible to read Mr. Shelley's works without admiration at the richness of his language and the extent of his powers; but we revolt at his doctrines, and our nature shudders at his conclusions. He must evidently forget the great objects of poetry. Improvement and innocent pleasure should be its aim; with our author—gilded atrocity—anointed vice— horror in its gloom—iniquity in its precarious triumph are omnipotent, and omnipresent. The most splendid picturings of crime are not equal to the descriptions of its naked deformity—

> Vice is a monster of such odious mien
> That to be hated—needs but to be seen.

Mr. Shelley's philosophy is objectionable—his reasoning is all directed by the assumption of criminality and passion directing our best actions; and this is making the worse appear the better reason. We cannot argue fairly from abuses to uses; and this is the grand object of this superior young man. He would seem to be unhappy with himself, and, therefore, unreconciled to the world; this is but an imitative feeling. Byron and Maturin tread the same path; but the former mixes life and its scenes with its horrors, he sports and laughs at them; the latter opens the resources of his extraordinary powers in the mention of the terrific—pursues the spectre —anatomizes and disgusts us with his overladen portraitures:—and while we are astonished at his fancy, his language, and his landscape, we loathe and deprecate them all in proportion of our disappointment.

Here we catch ourselves wandering from our more sober duty; but we could not, in justice to ourselves and readers, abstain from entering our humble protest against, we had said, the wanton abuse of powers not given to many men even in this age of intelligence and mind. We think highly of Mr. Shelley—he has nerve and sensibility; his thinking is deep, and his very pathos masculine. His works cannot be read without filling our thoughts—and we could only wish his thoughts had a more human and religious direction. The improvement of morals does not merely result from a condemnation of vice, any more than the advancement of science takes place from the mere exposure of former absurdities. The high colouring of danger will not lead to its avoidance; nor the well-meant eulogy of virtue lead to its general practice. To write successfully authors must proceed on the first principles of justice, religion, and nature. Nature must not be narrowed, religion constrained, nor justice suited to isolated abstract views; the wants, the wishes, and the interests of the many must be consulted; and the many are not of an author's particular day—but they are the people of futurity. In this particular it is, that our modern great men fail. They write for themselves; not for the world; they feel as individuals, not as component parts of a great body. Their closet is their horizon, and not "the visible diurnal sphere." Hence must they fail in their object, however, laudable; and be insecure in reputation or usefulness however well intended their ambitionings may be.

The Cenci is addressed to Mr. Leigh Hunt, and our author gives the following outline of its monstrous history.

[*Quotes Shelley's Preface, paragraphs 1-6*]

It would be impossible for us to convey an adequate idea of this production to our readers; nor could any isolated extracts convey the force of Mr. Shelley's muse. Its mere history as above narrated is its history in verse—without the charm or terror assumed by the latter.   The Cenci is a man monster, as will be seen from the following passage.

[*Quotes Act I, Scene i, lines 77-117, in which Cenci avows his delight in wickedness*]

He seems only to live in others' miseries.   The character of Beatrice his daughter is admirably drawn, and reminds one forcibly of Lady Macbeth. She has all her resolution, more of her amiability; and we pity the evil destiny which prompted her to the very conception of a deed at which humanity revolts.   She depicts the causes of her alienation from her un-natural father in these terms, at a festival given for the purpose of celebrat-ing a monstrous filicide.

[*Quotes Act I, Scene iii, lines 99-125*]

The Cenci, in the second act, charges his wife Lucretia with being the cause of the disturbance at the last night's feast—which she denies; but it rankles in the Cenci's mind, and his purpose of revenge is heightened. His son Giacomo now feels all the weight of his father's ill-treatment—and resolves as the only means of obtaining redress to put him out of the world.   Orsino, a wily prelate, urges him on in his fell purpose—with the hope that his sister Beatrice may be his recompense.   He thus reconciles himself to his own conduct.

[*Quotes Act II, Scene ii, lines 120-161*]

The first scene of the third act is really appalling, its interest is power-fully dramatic and intense,—it is overwhelming.   Beatrice becomes frantic at the thought which has seized possession of her mind—and never was frenzy directed to a terrible dead, but withall a conscience not dead to remorse, more ably pourtrayed than by our author.

[*Quotes Act III, Scene i, lines 137-206*]

Beatrice at length puts Orsino's fidelity to the test, and he pledges himself to obtain the means of taking away the Cenci's life.   In the Apulian Apennines a passage lies toward Petrella, one of the country seats of the Cenci, and a part of the way to it is thus admirably sketched.

[*Quotes Act III, Scene i, lines 243-265*]

Giacomo thus accounts for his hatred to his father, and with this able passage we shall close our extracts.

[*Quotes Act III, Scene i, lines 298-334*]

The death of the Cenci is finally fixed, assassins are hired, but on the first attempt their courage droops.   They are taunted and inspirited to the deed almost in the same breath by Beatrice; they screw their courage to the sticking place, and the parricidal murder is committed.   Just at this moment a legate from the Pope arrives, supposed to be a bearer of a charge against the Cenci.   His murder is discovered—and his wife, daughter, and son are summoned to Rome to abide their trial, together with the actual assassin. Brought before the tribunal, the guilty assassin reveals his crime and his instigators. Confronted, however, with Beatrice, he hesitates—is led to the torture, and declaring himself guilty, dies. The trial of the others is suspended by the interference of Camillo who also wished to espouse the Lady Beatrice, and she is conducted to prison. While in her cell, she is visited by her brother and a judge, who urges her to confess her guilt, and so die at once. We cannot resist extracting the replies of this extraordinary lady to the judge.

[*Quotes Act V, Scene iii, lines 60-92*]

Camillo next visits the cell—his entreaties with the Pope having proved fruitless. The manner in which Beatrice is made to receive the news of her hastening doom, has all the most passionate feeling and awakening interest of Mr. Shelley's highest efforts; the calm resolution with which she prepares to leave this world, is, perhaps, to be considered the less improbable, when we contemplate the whole of a character, which has altogether no parallel in our dramatic annals. There might have been one Beatrice—we scarcely believe another exists or can have existed. The execrable Orsino is seen to have escaped, contrary to all rules of poetic justice.

ILL-WRITTEN BLASPHEMY

[From The British Review and London Critical Journal, June, 1821 (17: 380-389.]

The Cenci is the best, because it is by far the most intelligible, of Mr. Shelley's works. It is probably indebted for this advantage to that class of compositions to which it belongs. A tragedy must have a story, and cannot be conducted without men and women; so that its very nature imposes a check on the vagabond excursions of a writer, who imagines that he can find perfection of poetry in incoherent dreams or in the ravings of bedlam. In speaking of the Cenci, however, as a tragedy, we must add that we do so only out of courtesy and in imitation of the example of the author, whose right to call his work by what name he pleases we shall never dispute. It has, in fact, nothing really dramatic about it. It is a series of dialogues in verse; and mere versified dialogue will never make a drama. A drama must, in the course of a few scenes, place before us such a succession of natural incidents as shall lead gradually to the final catastrophe, and develope the characters and passions of the individuals, for whom our interest or our sympathy is to be awakened: these incidents give occasion to the dialogue, which, in its turn, must help forward the progression of events, lay open to us the souls of the agents, move our feelings by the contemplation of their mental agitations, and soothe us with the charms of poetical beauty. It is from the number and nature of the ends which the poet has to accomplish, as compared with the means which he

employs, that the glory and difficulty of the dramatic art arise. If the
only object of a writer is to tell a story, or to express a succession of various
feelings, the form of dialogue, far from adding to the arduousness of the
task, is the easiest that can be adopted. It is a sort of drag net, which
enables him to introduce and find a place for every thing that his wildest
reveries suggest to him.

The fable of the Cenci was taken from an incident which occurred at
Rome towards the end of the sixteenth century. An aged father committed the most unnatural and horrible of outrages on his daughter; his
wife and daughter avenged the crime by procuring the assassination of the
perpetrator, and became in their turns the victims of public justice. The
incident is still recollected and often related at Rome. Hence Mr. Shelley
infers "that it is, in fact, a tragedy which has already received, from its
capacity of awakening and sustaining the sympathy of man, approbation
and success." It is remembered and related, because it is extraordinary—
because it is horrible—because it is, in truth, *undramatic*. A murder,
attended with circumstances of peculiar atrocity, is scarcely ever forgotten
on the spot where it happened; but it is not for that reason a fit subject for
dramatic poetry. The catastrophe of Marr's family will be long recollected in London; the assassination of Fualdes will not soon be forgotten
in Rhodes; yet who would ever dream of bringing either event upon the
stage? Incestuous rape, murder, the rack, and the scaffold are not the
proper materials of the tragic Muse: crimes and punishments are not in
themselves dramatic, though the conflict of passions which they occasion,
and from which they arise, often is so. The pollution of a daughter by
a father, the murder of a father by his wife and daughter, are events too
disgusting to be moulded into any form capable even of awakening our
interest. Mr. Shelley himself seems to have been aware of this. "The
story of the Cenci," says he, "is indeed eminently fearful and monstrous;
any thing like a dry exhibition of it on the stage would be insupportable.
The person who would treat such a subject must increase the ideal, and
diminish the actual, horror of events, so that the pleasure which arises
from the poetry, which exists in these tempestuous sufferings and crimes,
may mitigate the pain of the contemplation of the moral deformity from
which they spring." Without presuming to comprehend these observations
completely (for we know not what poetry exists in rape and murder, or
what pleasure is to be derived from it) we are sure, that whatever may be
thought as to the possibilities of overcoming by any management the inherent defects of the tale, Mr. Shelley, far from having even palliated its
moral and dramatic improprieties, has rendered the story infinitely more
horrible and more disgusting than he found it, and has kept whatever in it
is most revolting constantly before our eyes. A dialogue in which Cenci
makes an open confession to a Cardinal of a supreme love of every thing
bad merely for its own sake, and of living only to commit murder—a
banquet given by him to the Roman nobility and dignitaries, to celebrate
an event of which he has just received the news,—the death of his two

sons—and declarations of gratuitous uncaused hatred against all his relations, not excepting that daughter whom he resolves to make the victim of
his brutal outrage for no other reason than because his imagination is
unable to devise any more horrible crime, fill up the first two acts. Cenci
has accomplished the deed of horror before the opening of the third act, in
which the resolution to murder him is taken. In the fourth he again comes
before us, expressing no passion, no desire, but pure abstract depravity
and impiety. The murder follows, with the immediate apprehension of
the members of the family by the officers of justice. The last act is occupied with the judicial proceedings at Rome. Cenci is never out of our
sight, and, from first to last, he is a mere personification of wickedness and
insanity. His bosom is ruffled by no passion; he is made up exclusively of
inveterate hatred, directed not against some individuals, but against all
mankind, and operating with a strength proportioned to the love which
each relation usually excites in other men. There is no mode of expressing
depravity in words which Mr. Shelley has not ransacked his imagination to
ascribe to his wretch. His depravity is not even that of human nature;
for it is depravity without passion, without aim, without temptation: it is
depravity seeking gratification, first, in the perpetration of all that is most
repulsive to human feelings, and next, in making a display of its atrocity to
the whole world. The following dialogue, for example, (and it is one of
the gentler passages of the play) takes place in the presence of, and is in
part addressed to, Roman nobles and cardinals assembled at a banquet. . . .

[*Quotes Act I, Scene iii, lines 21-90, showing Cenci's joy at his son's destruction*]

    The first time he alludes to the deed, which constitutes the substance
of the plot, is in the following words addressed to a Cardinal:—

> I am what your theologians call
> Hardened; which they must be in impudence,
> So to revile a man's peculiar taste.
> - - - - - - - - - -
> But that there yet remains a deed to act
> Whose horror might make sharp an appetite
> Duller than mine—I'd do—I know not what.
> (pp. 6, 7.)

    After the unnatural outrage has been committed, he aims at something
still more extravagant in iniquity:

> Might I not drag her by the golden hair?
> Stamp on her? Keep her sleepless till her brain
> Be overworn? Tame her with chains and famine?
> Less would suffice. Yet so to leave undone
> What I most seek! No, 'tis her stubborn will
> Which by its own consent shall stoop as low
> As that which drags it down. (p. 56.)

His wife tries to terrify him by pretending that his death has been announced by a supernatural voice; his reply is in these words:

Why—such things are . . .
No doubt divine revealings may be made.
'T is plain I have been favored from above,
For when I curst my sons they died.—Ay . . . so . . .
As to the right or wrong that's talk . . . repentance . . .
Repentance is an easy moment's work,
And more depends on God than me. Well . . . well . . .
I must give up the greater point, which was
To poison and corrupt her soul. (pp. 57, 58.)

Such blasphemous ravings cannot be poetry for they are neither sense nor nature. No such being as Cenci ever existed; none such could exist. The historical fact was in itself disgustingly shocking; and, in Mr. Shelley's hands, the fable becomes even more loathsome and less dramatic than the fact. It is true that there are tragedies of the highest order (the *Oedipus Tyrannus* for instance) where the catastrophe turns upon an event from which nature recoils; but the deed is done unwittingly; it is a misfortune, not a crime; it is kept back as much as possible from our view; the hopes, the fears, and sufferings of the parties occupy our thoughts, and all that is revolting to purity of mind is only slightly hinted at. Here the deed is done with premeditation; it is done from a wanton love of producing misery; it is constantly obtruded on us in its most disgusting aspect; the most hateful forms of vice and suffering, preceded by involuntary pollution and followed by voluntary parricide, are the materials of this mis-called tragedy. They who can find dramatic poetry in such representations of human life must excuse us for wondering of what materials their minds are composed. Delineations like these are worse than unpoetical; they are unholy and immoral. But "they are as lights," if we believe Mr. Shelley, "to make apparent some of the most dark and secret caverns of the human heart." No, no; they teach nothing; and, if they did, knowledge must not be bought at too high a price. There is a knowledge which is death and pollution. Is knowledge any compensation for the injury sustained by being made familiar with that which ought to be to us all as if it were not? If such feelings, such ideas, exist in the world, (we cannot believe they do, for the Cenci of the Roman tradition is very different from the Cenci of Mr. Shelley) let them remain concealed. Our corporeal frames moulder into dust after death: are putrefying bodies, therefore, to be exposed in the public ways, that, forsooth, we may know what we are to be hereafter? The ties of father and daughter, of husband and wife, ought not to be profaned as they are in this poem. It is in vain to plead, that the delineations are meant to excite our hatred; they ought not to be presented to the mind at all; still less, pressed upon it long and perseveringly.

The technical structure of the piece is faulty as its subject matter is blameable. The first two acts serve only to explain the relative situation of the parties, and do not in the least promote the action of the play; the fifth, containing the judicial proceedings at Rome, is a mere excresence. The whole plot, therefore, is comprised in the incestuous outrage and in the subsequent assassination of the perpetrator; the former enormity occurs in the interval between the second act and third; the latter in the fourth act. The play has, properly speaking, no plot except in the third and fourth acts. But the incurable radical defects of the original conception of this drama render a minute examination of its structure superfluous.

The language is loose and disjointed; sometimes it is ambitious of simplicity, and it then becomes bald, inelegant, and prosaic. Words sometimes occur to which our ears are not accustomed; thus an "unappealable God" means a God from whom there is no appeal. We have a great deal of confused and not very intelligible imagery. A crag is "huge as despair," Cenci

> Bears a gloom duller
> Than the earth's shade or interlunar air;

And he describes his soul as a scourge, which will not be demanded of him till "the lash be broken in its last and deepest wound":

> My soul, which is a scourge, I will resign
> Into the hands of him who wielded it;
> Be it for its own punishment or theirs,
> He will not ask it of me till the lash
> Be broken in its last and deepest wound;
> Until its hate be all inflicted. (p. 58.)

We extract the following lines because we have heard them much admired.

> If there should be
> No God, no Heaven, no Earth in the void world;
> The wide, gray, lampless, deep, unpeopled world!
> If all things then should be . . . my father's spirit,
> His eye, his voice, his touch surrounding me;
> The atmosphere and breath of my dead life!
> If sometimes, as a shape more like himself,
> Even in the form which tortured me on earth,
> Maskt in gray hairs and wrinkles, he should come
> And wind me in his hellish arms, and fix
> His eyes on mine, and drag me down, down, down!
> For was he not alone omnipotent
> On Earth, and ever present? Even tho' dead,
> Does not his spirit live in all that breathe,
> And work for me and mine still the same ruin,
> Scorn, pain, despair? (pp. 99, 100.)

We confess that to us this seems metaphysical jargon in substance, dressed out in much flauntingly half-worn finery.

The following is another of the admired passages in this tissue of versified dialogue.

> *Beatr.* How comes this hair undone?
> Its wandering strings must be what blind me so,
> And yet I tied it fast.—O, horrible!
> The pavement sinks under my feet! The walls
> Spin round! I see a woman weeping there,
> And standing calm and motionless, whilst I
> Slide giddily as the world reels. . . . My God!
> The beautiful blue heaven is fleckt with blood!
> The sunshine on the floor is black! The air
> Is changed to vapours such as the dead breathe
> In charnel pits! Pah! I am choked! There creeps
> A clinging, black, contaminating mist
> About me . . . 'tis substantial, heavy, thick,
> I cannot pluck it from me, for it glues
> My fingers and my limbs to one another,
> And eats into my sinews, and dissolves
> My flesh to a pollution, poisoning
> The subtle, pure, and inmost spirit of life!
> My God! I never knew what the mad felt
> Before; for I am mad beyond all doubt!
> [*More wildly.*] No, I am dead! These putrefying limbs
> Shut round and sepulchre the panting soul
> Which would burst forth into the wandering air! [*A pause.*]
> What hideous thought was that I had even now?
> 'T is gone; and yet its burden remains here
> O'er these dull eyes . . . upon this weary heart!
> O world! O life! O day! O misery!

We say nothing of the conceit of misery killing its own father, because we wish to direct our observations, not to the imperfections of particular passages, but to the general want of fidelity to nature which pervades the whole performance. In the crowd of images here put into the mouth of Beatrice, there is neither novelty, nor truth, nor poetical beauty. Misery like hers is too intensely occupied with its own pangs to dwell so much on extraneous ideas. It does not cause the pavement to sink, or the wall to spin around, or the sunshine to become black; it does not stain the heaven with blood; it does not change the qualities of the air, nor does it clothe itself in a mist which glues the limbs together, eats into the sinews, and dissolves the flesh; still less does it suppose itself dead. This is not the language either of extreme misery or of incipient madness; it is the bombast of a declamation, straining to be energetic, and falling into extravagant and unnatural rant.

[*Quotes Act IV, Scene i, lines 78-111, in which Cenci threatens to continue his tortures of Beatrice*]

This passage exemplifies the furious exaggeration of Mr. Shelley's caricatures, as well as of the strange mode in which, throughout the whole play, religious thoughts and atrocious deeds are brought together. There is something extremely shocking in finding the truths, the threats, and the precepts of religion in the mouth of a wretch, at the very moment that he is planning or perpetrating crimes at which nature shudders. In this intermixture of things, sacred and impure, Mr. Shelley is not inconsistent if he believes that religion is in Protestant countries hypocrisy, and that it is in Roman Catholic countries "adoration, faith, submission, penitence, blind admiration; not a rule for moral conduct, and that it has no necessary connection with any one virtue."—(Preface, p. 13). Mr. Shelley is in an error: men act wrongly in spite of religion; but it is because they have no steady belief in it, or because their notions of it are erroneous, or because its precepts do not occur to them at the moment some vicious passion prevails. A Christian murderer does not amuse his fancy with the precepts and denunciations of his faith at the very moment of perpetrating the deed.

The moral errors of this book prevent us from quarreling with its literary sins.

VIII

PROMETHEUS UNBOUND

A WORK OF IRREGULAR GENIUS

[From The London Magazine, June, 1820 (1:706), under "Literary and Scientific Intelligence."]

MR. SHELLEY's announced dramatic poem, entitled *Prometheus Unbound*, will be found to be a very noble effort of a high and commanding imagination: it is not yet published, but we have seen some parts of it which have struck us very forcibly. The poet may perhaps be accused of taking a wild view of the latent powers and future fortunes of the human race; but its tendency is one of a far more inspiriting and magnanimous nature than that of the Cenci. The soul of man, instead of being degraded by the supposition of improbable and impossible vice, is elevated to the highest point of the poetical Pisgah, from whence a land of promise, rich with blessings of every kind, is pointed out to its delighted contemplation. This poem is more completely the child of the *Time* than almost any other modern production: it seems immediately sprung from the throes of the great intellectual, political, and moral *labour* of nations. Like the Time, its parent, too, it is unsettled, irregular, but magnificent. The following extract from Mr. Shelley's Preface, is, we think, a fine specimen of the power of his prose writings:

"We owe to Milton the progress and development of the same spirit: the sacred Milton was, be it remembered, a republican, a bold enquirer into morals and religion. The great writers of our own age, are, we have reason to suppose, the companions and forerunners of some unimagined change in our social condition, or the opinions which cement it. *The cloud of mind is discharging its collected lightning, and the equilibrium between institutions and opinions is now restoring, or is about to be restored.*"[1]

RIGHTEOUS WRATH FROM THE LITERARY GAZETTE

[From The Literary Gazette, and Journal of the Belles Lettres, September 9, 1820 (no. 190, pp. 580-582). This review furnishes an excellent example of the gap between Shelley's advanced notion of imagery (which he was professedly advancing still further in *Prometheus Unbound*) and the conservative notions of most reviewers on the same subject—an honest difference basically, but probably in many cases exaggerated by hostile bias.]

It has been said, that none ought to attempt to criticise that which they do not understand; and we beg to be considered as the acknowledged

[1] Reviewer's italics.

transgressors of this rule, in the observations which we venture to offer on Prometheus Unbound. After a very diligent and careful perusal, reading many passages over and over again, in the hopes that the reward of our perseverance would be to comprehend what the writer meant, we are compelled to confess, that they remained to us inflexibly unintelligible, and are so to the present hour, when it is our duty to explain them *pro bono publico*. This is a perplexing state for reviewers to be placed in; and all we can do is to extract some of these refractory combinations of words, the most of which are known to the English language, and submit them to the ingenuity of our readers, especially of such as are conversant with those interesting compositions which grace certain periodicals, under the titles of engimas, rebuses, charades, and riddles. To them Mr. Shelley's poem may be what it is not to us *(Davus sum non Œdipus)*—explicable; and their solutions shall, as is usual, be thankfully received. To our apprehensions, Prometheus is little else but absolute raving; and were we not assured to the contrary, we should take it for granted that the author was lunatic—as his principles are ludicrously wicked, and his poetry a melange of nonsense, cockneyism, poverty, and pedantry.

These may seem harsh terms; but it is our bounden duty rather to stem such a tide of literary folly and corruption, than to promote its flooding over the country. It is for the advantage of sterling productions, to discountenance counterfeits; and moral feeling, as well as taste, inexorably condemns the stupid trash of this delirious dreamer. But, in justice to him, and to ourselves, we shall cite his performance.

There is a preface, nearly as mystical and mysterious as the drama, which states Mr. Shelley's ideas in bad prose, and prepares us, by its unintelligibility, for the aggravated absurdity which follows. Speaking of his obligation to contemporary writings, he says, "It is impossible that any one who *inhabits* the same *age*, with such writers as those who stand in the foremost ranks of our own, can conscientiously assure himself, that his language and tone of thought may not have been modified by the study of the productions of those extraordinary intellects." (Mr. S. may rest assured, that neither his language, nor tone of thought, is modified by the study of productions of extraordinary intellects, in the *age* which he *inhabits*, or in any other.) He adds, "It is true, that, not the spirit of their genius, but the forms in which it has manifested itself, are *due* less to the peculiarities of their own minds, than to the peculiarity of the moral and intellectual condition of the minds among which they have been produced. Thus, a number of writers possess the form, whilst they want the spirit of those whom, it is alleged, they imitate; because the former is the endowment of the age in which they live, and the latter must be the uncommunicated lightning of their own mind." We have, upon honour, quoted verbatim: and though we have tried to construe these two periods at least seven times, we avow that we cannot discern their drift. Neither can we collect the import of the following general axiom, or paradox.—"As to imitation, poetry is a mimetic art. It creates, but it *creates* by combination and *representation.*" What kind of creation the creation by representation is, puzzles us grievously. But Mr. Shelley, no doubt, knows his own meaning; and, according to honest Sancho Panza, "that is enough." In his next edition, therefore, we shall be glad of a more distinct definition than this—"*A poet is the combined product of such internal powers as modify the nature of others; and of such external influences as excite and sustain these powers; he is not one but both.*" We fear our readers will imagine we are vulgarly quizzing; but we assure them, that these identical words are to be found at page xiii. In the next page, Mr. S. speaks more plainly of himself; and plumply, though profanely, declares, "For my part, I had rather be damned with Plato and Lord Bacon, than go to heaven with Paley and Malthus."—Poor man! how he moves concern and pity, to supersede the feelings of contempt and disgust. But such as he is, his "object has hitherto been *simply* to familiarise the highly refined imagination of the more select classes of poetical readers with beautiful idealisms of moral excellence"—such, to wit, as the preference of damnation with certain beings, to beatitude with others!

But of this preface, more than enough:—we turn to *Prometheus Unbound;* humbly conceiving that this punning title-page is the soothest in the book—as no one can ever think him worth binding.

The *dramatis impersonae* are Prometheus, Jupiter, Demogorgon, the Earth, the Ocean, Apollo, Mercury, Hercules, Asia, Panthea, Ione, the phantasm of Jupiter, the Spirit of the Earth, Spirits of the Hours, other Spirits of all sorts and sizes, Echoes, substantial and spiritual, Fawns, Furies, Voices, and other monstrous personifications. The plot is, that Prometheus, after being three thousand years tormented by Jupiter, obtains the ascendancy, and restores happiness to the earth—*redeunt Saturnia regna.* We shall not follow the long accounts of the hero's tortures, nor the longer rhapsodies about the blissful effects of his restoration; but produce a few of the brilliant emanations of the mind modified on the study of *extraordinary* intellects. The play opens with a speech of several pages, very argutely delivered by Signior Prometheus, from an icy rock in the Indian Caucacus, to which he is *"nailed"* by *chains* of *"burning cold."* He invokes all the elements, *seriatim,* to inform him what it was he originally said against Jupiter to provoke his ire; and, among the rest—

> Ye icy Springs, *stagnant* with wrinkling frost,
> Which *vibrated* to hear me: and then *crept*
> *Shuddering* through India.
> And ye, *swift* Whirlwinds, who, on *poised* wings
> Hung *mute* and *moveless* o'er yon hushed abyss,
> As thunder, *louder* than your own, made rock
> The orbed world.

This first extract will let our readers into the chief secret of Mr. Shelley's poetry; which is merely opposition of words, phrases, and sentiments, so violent as to be utter nonsense: *ex. gr.* the vibration of stagnant springs, and their creeping shuddering;—the swift moveless (*i.e.* motion-

less) whirlwinds, on poised wings, which hung mute over a hushed abyss
as thunder louder than their own!! In the same strain, Prometheus, who
ought to have been called Sphynx, when answered in a *whisper*, says,

> Tis scarce like sound: it tingles thro' the frame
> As lightning tingles, *hovering ere it strike.*

Common bards would have thought the tingling was felt when it
struck, and not before,—when it was hovering too, of all things for lightening to be guilty of! A "melancholy voice" now enters into the dialogue,
and turns out to be "the Earth." "Melancholy Voice" tells a melancholy
story, about the time—

> When plague had fallen on man, and beast, and worm
> And Famine;

She also advises her son Prometheus to use a spell,—

> ....So the revenge
> Of the Supreme may sweep thro' vacant shades,
> As rainy wind thro' the abandoned *gate*
> Of a fallen *palace.*

Mr. Shelley's buildings, having still gates to them! Then the Furies
are sent to give the sturdy Titan a taste of their office; and they hold as
odd a colloquy with him, as ever we read.
The first tells him,

> Thou thinkest we will rend thee bone from bone,
> And nerve from nerve, working like fire within:

The second,

> Dost imagine
> We will but laugh into thy lidless eyes?

And *the third,* more funnily inclined than her worthy sisters—

> Thou think'st we will live thro' thee
> Like animal life, and though we can obscure not
> The soul which burns within, that we will dwell
> Beside it, like a vain loud multitude
> Vexing the self-content of wisest men—

This is a pozer! and only paralleled by the speech of the "Sixth Spirit,"
of a lot of these beings, which arrive after the Furies. She, for these spirits
are feminine, says,

> Ah, sister! *desolation* is a *delicate thing;*
> It walks not on the earth, it floats not on the air,
> But treads with *silent footsteps,* and fans with silent wing
> The tender hopes which in their hearts the best and gentlest bear;
> Who, soothed to false repose by the fanning plumes above,
> And the *music-stirring motion* of its soft and busy *feet,*
> Dream visions of aerial joy, and call the monster Love,
> And wake, and find the shadow pain.

The glimpses of meaning which we have here, are soon smothered by contradictory terms and metaphor carried to excess. There is another part of Mr. Shelley's art of poetry, which deserves notice; it is his fancy, that by bestowing *colouring* epithets on every thing he mentions, he thereby renders his diction and descriptions vividly poetical. Some of this will appear hereafter; but we shall select one passage, as illustrative of the ridiculous extent to which the folly is wrought.

Asia is longing for her sister's annual visit; and after talking of Spring clothing with *golden* clouds the desert of life, she goes on:

> This is the season, this the day, the hour;
> At sunrise thou shouldst come, sweet sister mine,
> Too long desired, too long delaying, come!
> How like death-worms the wingless moments crawl!
> The point of one *white* star is quivering still
> Deep in the *orange* light of widening morn
> Beyond the *purple* mountains: thro' a chasm
> Of wind-divided mist the *darker* lake
> Reflects it: now it wanes: it gleams again
> As the waves fade, and as the burning threads
> Of woven cloud unravel in *pale* air:
> 'Tis lost! and thro' yon peaks of cloudlike snow
> The *roseate* sun-light quivers: hear I not
> The Æolian music of her *sea-green* plumes
> Winnowing the *crimson* dawn?

Here in seventeen lines, we have no fewer than seven positive colours, and nearly as many shades; not to insist upon the everlasting confusion of this rainbow landscape, with *white* stars quivering in the *orange* light, beyond *purple* mountains; of *fading waves*, and clouds made of *burning threads*, which *unravel* in the *pale* air; of cloudlike snow through which *roseate* sun-light also quivers, and *sea-green* plumes winnowing *crimson* dawn. Surely, the author looks at nature through a prism instead of spectacles. Next to his colorific powers, we may rank the author's talent for manufacturing "villainous compounds." *Ecce signum,* of a Mist.

> Beneath is a wide plain of billowy mist,
> As a *lake,* paving in the morning sky,
> With azure waves which *burst* in *silver* light,
> Some Indian vale. Behold it, rolling on
> Under the curdling winds, and *islanding*
> The *peak* whereon we stand, *midway, around,*
> Encinctured by the *dark* and *blooming* forests,
> Dim *twilight-lawns,* and *stream-illumined* caves,
> And *wind-enchanted* shapes of wandering mist;
> And far on high the keen *sky-cleaving* mountains
> From icy spires of sun-like radiance fling
> The dawn, as lifted Ocean's dazzling spray,
> From some Atlantic islet scattered up,
> Spangles the wind with *lamp-like water-drops.*

> The vale is girdled with their walls, a howl
> Of cataracts from their *thaw-cloven* ravines
> Satiates the listening wind, continuous, vast,
> Awful as silence.

This is really like Sir Sidney Smith's plan to teach morality to Musselmans by scraps of the Koran in kaleidoscopes—only that each scrap has a meaning; Mr. Shelley's lines none.

We now come to a part which quite throws Milton into the shade, with his "darkness visible"; and as Mr. Shelley professes to admire that poet, we cannot but suspect that he prides himself on having out-done him. Only listen to Panthea's description of Demogorgon. This lady, whose mind is evidently unsettled, exclaims,

> I see a *mighty darkness*
> Filling the seat of power, and *rays of gloom*
> Dart round, as *light* from the *meridian sun,*
> *Ungazed upon* and *shapeless—*

We yield ourselves, miserable hum-drum devils that we are, to this high imaginative faculty of the modern muse. We acknowledge that hyperbola, extravagance, and irreconcileable terms, may be poetry. We admit that common sense has nothing to do with "the beautiful idealisms" of Mr. Shelley. And we only add, that if this be genuine inspiration, and not the grossest absurdity, then is farce sublime, and maniacal raving the perfection of reasoning: then were all the bards of other times, Homer, Virgil, Horace, drivellers; for their foundations were laid no lower than the capacities of the herd of mankind; and even their noblest elevations were susceptible of appreciation by the very multitude among the Greeks and Romans.

We shall be very concise with what remains: Prometheus, according to Mr. Percy Bysshe Shelley—

Gave man speech, and *speech created thought*—which is exactly, in our opinion, the cart creating the horse; the sign creating the inn; the effect creating the cause. No wonder that when such a master gave lessons in *astronomy*, he did it thus—

He taught the *implicated orbits woven*

> *Of the wide-wandering stars;* and how the sun
> Changes his *lair*, and by what *secret spell*
> The pale moon is transformed, when *her broad eye*
> Gazes not on the *interlunar sea.*

This, Promethean, beats all the systems of astronomy with which we are acquainted: Shakespeare, it was said, "exhausted worlds and then imagined new"; but he never imagined aught so new as this. Newton was a wonderful philosopher; but, for the view of the heavenly bodies, Shelley double distances him. And not merely in the preceding, but in the following improved edition of his astronomical notions, he describes—

A sphere, which is as many thousand spheres,
Solid as crystal, yet through all its mass
Flow, as through empty space, music and light:
Ten thousand orbs involving and involved,
Purple and azure, white, green, and golden,
Sphere within sphere; and every space between
Peopled with unimaginable shapes,
Such as ghosts dream dwell in the lampless deep,
Yet each inter-transpicuous, and they whirl
Over each other with a thousand motions,
Upon a thousand sightless axles spinning,
And with the force of self-destroying swiftness,
Intensely, slowly, solemnly roll on,
Kindling with mingled sounds, and many tones,
Intelligible words and music wild.
With mighty whirl the multitudinous orb
Grinds the bright brook into an azure mist
Of elemental subtlety, like light;
And the wild odour of the forest flowers,
The music of the living grass and air,
The emerald light of leaf-entangled beams
Round its intense yet self-conflicting speed,
Seem kneaded into one aerial mass
Which drowns the sense.[2]

Did ever the walls of Bedlam display more insane stuff than this?

    When our worthy old pagan acquaintance, Jupiter, is disposed of, his sinking to the "void abyss," is thus pourtrayed by his son Apollo—

        An eagle so caught in some bursting cloud
        On Caucasus, his *thunder-baffled wings*
        Entangled in the whirlwind! &c.

An' these extracts do not entitle the author to a cell, clean straw, bread and water, a strait waistcoat, and phlebotomy, there is no madness in scribbling. It is hardly requisite to adduce a sample of the adjectives in this poem to prove the writer's condign abhorrence of any relation between that part of speech and substantives: sleep-unsheltered hours; gentle darkness; horny eyes; keen faint eyes; faint wings; fading waves; crawling glaciers, toads, agony, time, &c.; belated and noontide plumes; milky arms; many-folded mountains; a lake-surrounding flute; veiled lightening asleep (as well as hovering); unbewailing flowers; odour-faded blooms; semi-vital worms; windless pools, windless abodes, and windless air; unerasing waves; unpavilioned skies; rivetted wounds; and void abysms, are parcel of the Babylonish jargon which is found in every wearisome page of this tissue of insufferable buffoonery. After our quota-

---

[2] This is probably one of the most genuinely difficult passages in the whole poem. It is Shelley's attempt to visualize, in one image, the Earth as it appeared to the science of his day. Professor Carl Grabo (*A Newton Among Poets*, 1930, pp. 140-142) has shown that it conforms closely to Sir Humphrey Davy's theory of matter. But cf. Dante, p. 313 *infra*.— N.I.W.

tions, we need not say that the verse is without measure, proportions, or elegance; that the similes are numberless and utterly inapplicable; and that the instances of ludicrous nonsense are not fewer than the pages of the Drama. Should examples be demanded, the following, additional, are brief. Of the heroic line:—

> Ah me! alas, pain, pain ever, for ever—

Of the simile:—

> We will entangle buds and flowers and beams
> Which twinkle on the fountain's brim, and make
> Strange combinations out of common things,
> *Like* human babes in their brief innocence.—

Of the pure nonsensical:—

> Our *feet* now, every *palm*,
> Are *sandelled* with *calm*,
> And the *dew* of our wings is a rain of balm;
> And *beyond* our eyes,
> The human love lies
> Which makes all it gazes on paradise.

> We'll pass the eyes
> Of the starry skies
> Into the hoar deep to *colonise:*
> Death, Chaos, and Night,
> From the sound of our flight,
> Shall flee, like mist from a tempest's might.

> And Earth, Air, and Light,
> And the Spirit of Night,
> Which drives round the stars in their fiery flight;
> And Love, Thought, and Breath,
> The powers that quell Death,
> Wherever we soar shall assemble beneath.

> And our singing shall *build*
> In the *void's loose field,*
> A world for the Spirit of Wisdom to *wield;*
> We will take our plan
> From the new world of man,
> And our work shall be called the Promethean.

Alas, gentle reader! for poor Tom, whom the foul fiend hath (thus) led o'er bog and quagmire; and blisse thee from whirle-windes, starre-blasting, and taking. Would that Mr. Shelley made it his study, like this his prototype.

How to prevent the fiend, and to kill vermin.

Poor Tom's affected want of wits is inferior to Shelley's genuine wandering with his "father of the hours" and "mother of the months"; and his dialogue of ten pages between *The Earth* and *The Moon,* assuredly the most arrant and gravest burlesque that it ever entered into the heart of man to conceive. We cannot resist its opening

The Earth. The joy, the triumph, the delight, the madness!
The boundless, overflowing, bursting gladness,
The vapourous exultation not to be confined!
    Ha! ha! the animation of delight
    Which wraps me, like an atmosphere of light,
And bears me as a cloud is borne by its own wind.
The Moon. Brother mine, calm wanderer,
            Happy globe of land and air,
Some Spirit is darted like a beam from thee,
    Which penetrates my frozen frame,
    And passes with the warmth of flame,
With love, and odour, and deep melody
    Through me, through me!
The Earth. Ha! ha! the caverns of my hollow mountains,
My cloven fire-crags, sound exulting fountains
Laugh with a vast and inextinguishable laughter,
    The oceans, and the deserts, and the abysses,
    And the deep air's unmeasured wildernesses,
Answer from all their clouds and billows, echoing after.

This is but the first of the ten pages: the sequel, though it may seem impossible to sustain such "exquisite fooling," does not fall of. But we shall waste our own and our readers' time no longer. We have but to repeat, that when the finest specimens of inspired composition may be derived from the white-washed walls of St. Lukes or Hoxton, the author of *Prometheus Unbound,* being himself among these bound writers, and chained like his subject, will have a chance of classing with foremost poets of the place.

HIGH GENIUS AND EVIL PRINCIPLES

[From Blackwood's Edinburgh Magazine, September, 1820 (7:679-687). This review is generally ascribed to John Wilson, but W. S. Lockhart wrote a part or all of it. Miss M. Clive Hilyard's *Lockhart's Literary Criticism* (Oxford, 1931, p. 158) quotes from Lockhart's unpublished letters to Blackwood: "I sent off yest. ev. an article on the Prometheus of Shelley per mail which I hope you have received"; and "I have nothing to add to the Shelley." This does not prove the article as published to have been entirely by Lockhart, as Blackwood's reviews were frequently collaborative. Thus the "Letter of T. Tickler, No. VIII" (Blackwood's, XIV, 213-235, August, 1823) in which Shelley is criticized is credited by Miss Hilyard to Lockhart, on the basis of a convincing letter from Lockhart to Blackwood, which she quotes (pp. 125-126). But Mr. Ralph M. Wardle, of Harvard University, furnishes me with an extract from a letter of William Maginn to Blackwood showing that he was writing the same article at the same time. As published, the article was probably a cento of the two.]

Whatever may be the difference of men's opinions concerning the measure of Mr. Shelley's poetical power, there is one point in regard to which all must be agreed, and that is his Audacity. In the old days of the exulting genius of Greece, Aeschylus dared two things which astonished all men, and which still astonish them—to exalt contemporary men into the personages of majestic tragedies—and to call down and embody into tragedy, without degradation, the elemental spirits of nature and the deeper essences of Divinity. We scarcely know whether to consider the *Persians* or the *Prometheus Bound* as the most extraordinary display of what has always been esteemed the most audacious spirit that ever expressed its workings in poetry. But what shall we say of the young English poet who has now attempted, not only a flight as high as the highest of Aeschylus, but the very flight of that father of tragedy—who has dared once more to dramatise Prometheus—and, most wonderful of all, to dramatise the *deliverance* of Prometheus—which is known to have formed the subject of a lost tragedy of Aeschylus no ways inferior in mystic elevation to that of the Δεσμωτης.

Although a fragment of that perished master-piece be still extant in the Latin version of Attius—it is quite impossible to conjecture what were the personages introduced in the tragedy of Aeschylus, or by what train of passions and events he was able to sustain himself on the height of that awful scene with which his surviving *Prometheus* terminates. It is impossible, after reading what is left of that famous trilogy,[2] to suspect that the Greek poet symbolized any thing whatever by the person of Prometheus, except the native strength of human intellect itself—its strength of endurance above all others—its sublime power of patience. STRENGTH and FORCE are the two agents who appear on this darkened theatre to bind the too benevolent Titan—*Wit* and *Treachery*, under the forms of Mercury and Oceanus, endeavour to prevail upon him to make himself free by giving up his dreadful secret;—but *Strength* and *Force*, and *Wit* and *Treason*, are all alike powerless to overcome the resolution of that suffering divinity, or to win from him any acknowledgment of the new tyrant of the skies. Such was this simple and sublime allegory in the hands of Aeschylus. As to what had been the original purpose of the framers of the allegory, that is a very different question, and would carry us back into the most hidden places of the history of mythology. No one, however, who compares the mythological systems of different races and countries, can fail to observe the frequent occurrence of certain great leading Ideas and leading Symbolisations of ideas too—which Christians are taught to contemplate with a knowledge that is the knowledge of reverence. Such, among others, are unquestionably the ideas of an Incarnate Divinity suffering on account of mankind—conferring benefits on mankind at the expense of his own suffering;—the general idea of vicarious atonement itself—and the idea of the dignity of suffering as an exertion of intellectual might —all of which may be found, more or less obscurely shadowed forth, in the original Μυθοσ of Prometheus the Titan, the enemy of the successful rebel and usurper Jove. We might have also mentioned the idea of a

---

[2] There was another and an earlier play of Aeschylus, Prometheus the Fire-Stealer, which is commonly supposed to have made part of the series; but the best critics, we think, are of opinion, that that was entirely a satirical piece. (Reviewer's footnote.)

deliverer, waited for patiently through ages of darkness, and at last arriving in the person of the child of Io—but, in truth, there is no pleasure, and would be little propriety, in seeking to explain all this at greater length, considering, what we cannot consider without deepest pain, the very different views which have been taken of the original allegory by Mr. Percy Bysshe Shelley.

It would be highly absurd to deny, that this gentleman has manifested very extraordinary powers of language and imagination in his treatment of the allegory, however grossly and miserably he may have tried to pervert its purpose and meaning. But of this more anon. In the meantime, what can be more deserving of reprobation than the course which he is allowing his intellect to take, and that too at the very time when he ought to be laying the foundations of a lasting and honourable name. There is no occasion for going round about the bush to hint what the poet himself so unblushingly and sinfully blazoned forth in every part of his production. With him, it is quite evident that the Jupiter whose downfall has been predicted by Prometheus, means nothing more than Religion in general, that is, every human system of religious belief; and that, with the fall of this, he considers it perfectly necessary (as indeed we also believe, though with far different feelings) that every system of human government also should give way and perish. The patience of the contemplative spirit in Prometheus is to be followed by the daring of the active Demogorgon, at whose touch all "old thrones" are at once and for ever to be cast down into the dust. It appears too plainly, from the luscious pictures with which his play terminates, that Mr. Shelley looks forward to an unusual relaxation of all moral *rules*—or rather, indeed, to the extinction of all moral feelings, except that of a certain mysterious indefinable *kindliness,* as the natural and necessary result of the overthrow of all civil government and religious belief. It appears, still more wonderfully, that he contemplates this state of things as the ideal SUMMUM BONUM. In short it is quite impossible that there should exist a more pestiferous mixture of blasphemy, sedition, and sensuality, than is visible in the whole structure and strain of this poem—which, nevertheless, and notwithstanding all the detestation its principles excite, must and will be considered by all that read it attentively, as abounding in poetical beauties of the highest order—as presenting many specimens not easily to be surpassed, of the moral sublime of eloquence— as overflowing with pathos, and most magnificent in description. Where can be found a spectacle more worthy of sorrow than such a man performing and glorying in the performance of such things? His evil ambition,— from all he has yet written, but most of all, from what he has last and best written, his *Prometheus,*—appears to be no other, than that of obtaining the highest place among those poets,—enemies, not friends, of their species, —who, as a great and virtuous poet has well said (putting evil consequence close after evil cause).

Profane the God-given strength, and *mar the lofty line.*

We should hold ourselves very ill employed, however, were we to enter at any length into the reprehensible parts of this remarkable production. It is sufficient to shew, that we have not been misrepresenting the purpose of the poet's mind, when we mention, that the whole tragedy ends with a mysterious sort of dance, and chorus of elemental spirits, and other indefinable beings, and that the SPIRIT OF THE HOUR, one of the most singular of these choral personages tells us:

> I wandering went
> Among the haunts and dwellings of mankind,
> And first was disappointed not to see
> Such mighty change as I had felt within
> Expressed in other things; but soon I looked,
> And behold! THRONES WERE KINGLESS, and men walked
> One with the other, even as spirits do, &c.

Again—

[*Quotes Act III, Scene iv, lines 164-197, describing perfection resulting from the downfall of kings and priests*]

Last of all, and to complete the picture:—

> And women, too, *frank, beautiful,* and *kind*
> As the free heaven which rains fresh light and dew
> On the wide earth, past; gentle radiant forms,
> From CUSTOM'S evil taint exempt and pure;
> Speaking the wisdom once they dared not think,
> Looking emotions once they dared not feel,
> And *changed to all which once they dared not be,*
> *Yet being now, made earth like heaven; nor pride*
> *Nor jealousy, nor envy, nor ill shame,*
> *The bitterest of those drops of treasured gall,*
> *Spoilt the sweet taste of the Nepenthe, Love!*

It is delightful to turn from the audacious spleen and ill-veiled abominations of such passages as these, to those parts of the production, in which it is possible to separate the poet from the allegorist—where the modern is content to write in the spirit of the ancient—and one might almost fancy that we had recovered some of the lost sublimities of Aeschylus. Such is the magnificent opening scene, which presents a ravine of icy rocks in the Indian Caucasus—Prometheus bound to the precipice—Panthea and Ione seated at his feet. The time is night; but, during the scene, morning slowly breaks upon the bleak and desolate majesty of the region.

[*Quotes Act I, lines 1-210, describing the present state of Prometheus, his desire to recall his curse on Jupiter, and the effects of the curse*]

Or the following beautiful chorus, which has all the soft and tender gracefulness of Euripides, and breathes, at the same time, the very spirit of one of the grandest odes of Pindar.

[*Quotes Act II, Scene ii, lines 1-40, describing the forest through which Asia and Panthea pass*]

We could easily select from the Prometheus Unbound, many pages of as fine poetry as this; but we are sure our readers will be better pleased with a few specimens of Mr. Shelley's style in his miscellaneous pieces, several of which are comprised in the volume. The following is the commencement of a magnificent "VISION OF THE SEA."

[*Quotes* A Vision of the Sea, *lines 1-58 and 66-79*]

There is an "Ode to the West-Wind," another "To a Sky-Lark," and several smaller pieces, all of them abounding in richest melody of versification, and great tenderness of feeling. But the most affecting of all is "The Sensitive Plant," which is the history of a beautiful garden, that after brightening and blossoming under the eye of its lovely young mistress, shares in the calamity of her fate, and dies because she is no more there to tend its beauties. It begins thus. . . .

[*Quotes ten stanzas, lines 1-40*]

Then for the sad reverse—take the morning of the funeral of the young lady. . . .

[*Quotes eleven stanzas, Part III, lines 5-50*]

We cannot conclude without saying a word or two in regard to an accusation which we have lately seen brought against ourselves in some one of the London Magazines; we forget which at this moment. We are pretty sure we know who the author of that most false accusation is—of which more hereafter. He has the audacious insolence to say, that we praise Mr. Shelley, although we dislike his principles, just because we know that he is not in a situation of life to be in any danger of suffering pecuniary inconveniences from being run down by critics; and, *vice versa*, abuse Hunt, Keats, and Hazlitt, and so forth, because we know that they are poor men; a fouler imputation could not be thrown on any writer than this creature has dared to throw on us; nor a more utterly false one; we repeat the word again—than this is when thrown upon us.

We have no personal acquaintance with any of these men, and no personal feelings in regard to any one of them, good or bad. We never even saw any one of their faces. As for Mr. Keats, we are informed that he is in a very bad state of health, and that his friends attribute a great deal of it to the pain he has suffered from the critical castigation his Endymion drew down on him in this magazine. If it be so, we are most heartily sorry for it, and have no hesitation in saying, that had we suspected that young author, of being so delicately nerved, we should have administered our reproof in a much more lenient shape and style. The truth is, we from the beginning saw marks of feeling and power in Mr. Keats' verses, which made us think it very likely, he might become a real poet of England, provided he could be persuaded to give up all the tricks of Cockneyism, and forswear forever the thin potations of Mr. Leigh Hunt. We, therefore, rated him as roundly as we decently could do, for the flagrant affectations of those early productions of his. In the last volume he has published, we find more beauties than in the former, both of language and of thought, but we are sorry to say, we find abundance of the same absurd affectations also, and superficial conceits, which first displeased us in his writings;—and which we are again very sorry to say, must in our opinion, if persisted in, utterly and entirely prevent Mr. Keats from ever taking his place among the pure and classical poets of his mother tongue. It is quite ridiculous to see how the vanity of these Cockneys makes them over-rate their own importance, even in the eyes of us, that have always expressed such plain unvarnished contempt for them, and who do feel for them all, a contempt too calm and profound, to admit of any admixture of any thing like anger or personal spleen. We should just as soon think of being wroth with vermin, independently of their coming into our apartment, as we should of having any feelings at all about any of these people, other than what are excited by seeing them in the shape of authors. Many of them, considered in any other character than that of authors, are, we have no doubt, entitled to be considered as very worthy people in their own way. Mr. Hunt is said to be a very amiable man in his own sphere, and we believe him to be so willingly. Mr. Keats we have often heard spoken of in terms of greater kindness, and we have no doubt his manners and feelings are calculated to make his friends love him. But what has all this to do with our opinion of their poetry? What, in the name of wonder, does it concern us, whether these men sit among themselves, with mild or with sulky faces, eating their mutton steaks, and drinking their porter at Highgate, Hampstead, or Lisson Green? What is there that should prevent us, or any other person, that happens not to have been educated in the University of Little Britain, from expressing a simple, undisguised, and impartial opinion, concerning the merits or demerits of men that we never saw, nor thought of for one moment, otherwise than as in the capacity of authors? What should hinder us from saying, since we think so, that Mr. Leigh Hunt is a clever wrongheaded man, whose vanities have got inwoven so deeply into him, that he has no chance of ever writing one line of classical English, or thinking one genuine English thought, either about poetry or politics? What is the spell that must seal our lips, from uttering an opinion equally plain and perspicuous concerning Mr. John Keats, viz. that nature possibly meant him to be a much better poet than Mr. Leigh Hunt ever could have been, but that, if he persisted in imitating the faults of that writer, he must be contented to share his fate, and be like him forgotten? Last of all, what should forbid us to announce our opinion, that Mr. Shelley, as a man of genius, is not merely superior, either to Mr. Hunt, or to Mr. Keats, but altogether out of their sphere, and totally incapable of ever being brought into the most distant comparison with either of them. It is very possible, that Mr. Shelley himself might not be inclined to place himself so high above these men as we do, but that is his affair, not ours. We are afraid that he shares, (at least with one of them) in an abominable system of belief, concerning Man and the World, the sympathy arising out of which common belief, may probably sway more than it ought to do on both sides. But the truth of the matter is this, and it is impossible to conceal it were we willing to do so, that Mr. Shelley is destined to leave a great name behind him, and that we, as lovers of true genius, are most anxious that this name should ultimately be pure as well as great.

As for the principles and purposes of Mr. Shelley's poetry, since we must again recur to that dark part of the subject, we think they are on the whole, more undisguisedly pernicious in this volume, than even in his Revolt of Islam. There is an Ode to Liberty at the end of the volume, which contains passages of the most splendid beauty, but which, in point of meaning, is just as wicked as any thing that ever reached the world under the name of Mr. Hunt himself. It is not difficult to fill up the blank which has been left by the prudent bookseller, in one of the stanzas beginning:

> O that the free would stamp the impious name,
> Of - - - - into the dust! Or write it there
> So that this blot upon the page of fame,
> Were as a serpent's path, which the light air
> Erases, &c. &c.

but the next speaks still more plainly,

> O that the WISE from their bright minds would kindle
> Such lamps within the dome of this wide world,
> That the pale name of PRIEST might shrink and dwindle
> Into the HELL from which it first was hurled!

This is exactly a versification of the foulest sentence that ever issued from the lips of Voltaire. Let us hope that Percy Bysshe Shelley is not destined to leave behind him, like that great genius, a name for ever detestable to the truly FREE and the truly WISE. He talks in his preface about MILTON, as a "Republican," and a "bold inquirer into Morals and religion." Could any thing make us despise Mr. Shelley's understanding, it would be such an instance of voluntary blindness as this! Let us hope, that ere long a lamp of genuine truth may be kindled within his "bright mind"; and that he may walk in its light the path of the true demigods of English genius, having, like them, learned to "fear God and honour the king."

"A VAST WILDERNESS OF BEAUTY"

[From The London Magazine and Monthly Critical and Dramatic Review, September and October, 1820 (2: 306-308 and 382-391). This long two-part review represents the summit of contemporary admiration of Shelley as a poet.]

This book has made its appearance so extremely late in the month, that, although we profess to give as early and as satisfactory notices of new works as are any where to be met with, it has fairly puzzled even our most consummate ingenuity. "Something must be done, and that right quickly, friend Bardolph"; this is our opinion as well as honest Jack Falstaff's; and with this quotation we buckle to our task. Of "Prometheus Unbound," the principal poem in this beautiful collection, we profess to give no account. It must be reserved for our second series, as it requires more than ordinary attention. The minor pieces are stamped throughout with all the vigorous peculiarities of the writer's mind, and are everywhere strongly impregnated with the alchymical properties of genius. But what we principally admire in them is their strong and healthy freshness, and the tone of interest that they elicit. They possess the fever and flush of poetry; the fragrant perfume and sunshine of a summer's morning, with its genial and kindly benevolence. It is impossible to peruse them without admiring the peculiar property of the author's mind, which can doff in an instant the cumbersome garments of metaphysical speculations, and throw itself naked as it were into the arms of nature and humanity. The beautiful and singularly original poem of The Cloud will evince proofs of our opinion, and show the extreme force and freshness with which the writer can impregnate his poetry.

[*Quotes* The Cloud, *entire, concluding the September review. The remainder of the review as here printed concerns* Prometheus Unbound, *and appeared in the October number*]

This is one of the most stupendous of those works which the daring and vigorous spirit of modern poetry and thought has created. We despair of conveying to our readers, either by analysis or description, any idea of its gigantic outlines, or of its innumerable sweetnesses. It is a vast wilderness of beauty which at first seems stretching out on all sides into infinitude, yet the boundaries of which are all cast by the poet; in which the wildest paths have a certain and noble direction; and the strangest shapes that haunt its recesses, voices of gentleness and wisdom. It presents us with the oldest forms of Greek mythology, informed with the spirit of fresh enthusiasm and youngest hope; and mingles with these the creatures of a new mythology, in which earth and the hosts of heaven, spirits of time and eternity, are embodied and vivified, to unite in the rapturous celebration of the reign of Love over the universe.

This work is not, as the title would lead us to anticipate, a mere attempt to imitate the old tragedy of the Greeks. In language, indeed, there is often a profusion of felicitously compounded epithets, and in the imagery there are many of those clear and lucid shapes, which distinguish the works of Aeschylus and Sophocles. But the subject is so treated that we lose sight of persons in principles, and soon feel that all the splendid machinery around us is but the shadow of things unseen, the outward panoply of bright expectations and theories, which appear to the author's mind instinct with eternal and eternally progressive blessings. The fate of Prometheus probably suggested, even to the heroic bard by whom it was celebrated in older time, the temporary predominance of brute force over intellect; the oppression of right by might; and the final deliverance of the spirit of hu-

manity from the iron grasp of its foes. But, in so far as we can judge
from the mighty fragment that time has spared, he was contented with
exhibiting the visible picture of the magnanimous victim, and with representing his deliverance by means of Hercules as a mere personal event,
having no symbolical meaning. In Mr. Shelley's piece, the deliverance of
Prometheus, which is attended by the dethroning of Jupiter, is scarcely
other than a symbol of the peaceful triumph of goodness over power; of
the subjection of might to right, and the restoration of love to the full
exercise of its benign and all-penetrating sympathies. To represent vividly
and poetically this vast moral change is, we conceive, the design of this
drama, with all its inward depths of mystical gloom, its pregnant clouds
of imagination, its spiry eminences of icy splendours, and its fair regions
overspread by a light "which never was by [sic] sea or land," which con-
secrates and harmonizes all things.

To the ultimate prospect exhibited by that philosophical system which
Mr. Shelley's piece embodies, we have no objection. There is nothing
pernicious in the belief that, even on earth, man is destined to attain a
high degree of happiness and virtue. The greatest and wisest have ever
trusted with the most confiding faith to that nature, with whose best
qualities they were so richly gifted. They have felt that in man were
undeveloped capabilities of excellence; stores of greatness suffered to lie
hidden beneath basest lumber; sealed-up fountains, whence a brighter day
might loosen streams of fresh and ever-living joys. In the worst and
most degraded minds, vestiges of goodness are not wanting; some old
recollections of early virtue; some feeling of wild generosity or unconquerable love; some divine instinct; some fragments of lofty principle;
some unextinguishable longings after nobleness and peace, indicate that
there is good in man which can never yield to the storms of passion or the
decays of time. On these divine instances of pure and holy virtue; on
history; on science; on imagination; on essences of love and hope; we
may safely rest in the expectation that a softer and tenderer light will
ultimately dawn on our species. We further agree with Mr. Shelley,
that Revenge is not the weapon with which man should oppose the erring
and the guilty. He only speaks in accordance with every wise writer on
legislation, when he deprecates the infliction of one vibration of unnecessary pain on the most criminal. He only echoes the feeling of every
genuine Christian, when he contends for looking with deep-thoughted pity
on the vicious, or regarding them tenderly as the unfortunate, and for
striving "not to be overcome of evil, but to overcome evil with good."
He only coincides with every friend of his species, when he deplores the
obstacles which individuals and systems have too often opposed to human
progress. But when he would attempt to realize in an instant his glorious
visions; when he would treat men as though they were now fit inhabitants
of an earthly paradise; when he would cast down all restraint and authority as enormous evils; and would leave mankind to the guidance of passions
as yet unsubdued, and of desires as yet unregulated, we must protest

against his wishes, as tending fearfully to retard the good which he would precipitate. Happy, indeed, will be that time, of which our great philosophical poet, Wordsworth, speaks, when love shall be an "unclouded light and joy its own security." But we shall not hasten this glorious era by destroying those forms and dignities of the social state which are essential to the restraint of the worst passions, and serviceable to the nurture of the kindliest affections. The stream of human energy is gathering strength; but it would only be scattered in vain, were we rashly to destroy the boundaries which now confide it to its deep channel; and it can only be impeded by the impatient attempt to strike the shores with its agitated waters.

Although there are some things in Mr. Shelley's philosophy against which we feel it a duty thus to protest, we must not suffer our difference of opinion to make us insensible to his genius. As a poem, the work before us is replete with clear, pure, and majestical imagery, accompanied by a harmony as rich and various as that of the loftiest of our English poets. The piece first exhibits a ravine of icy rocks in the Indian Caucasus, where Prometheus is bound to the precipice, and Panthea and Ione sit at his feet to soothe his agonies. He thus energetically describes his miseries and calls on the mountains, springs, and winds to repeat to him the curse which he once pronounced on his foe, whom he now regards only with pity.

[*Quotes Act I, Scene i, lines 31-73*]

The voices reply only in vague terms, and the Earth answers that they dare not tell it; when the following tremendous dialogue follows. . . .

[*Quotes Act I, Scene i, lines 131-186*]

At length his mother advises him to call on some phantasm, or shade of a living being, who will be compelled to repeat his curse. He invokes the shade of Jupiter, who delivers his intense execration in the following terms. . . .

[*Quotes the curse, Act I, scene i, lines 262-301*]

Mercury next enters with the Furies sent by Jupiter to inflict new pangs on his victim. This they effect by placing before his soul pictures of the agonies to be borne by that race for whom he is suffering. The Earth afterwards consoles him, by calling up forms who are rather dimly described as

> Subtle and fair spirits
> Whose homes are the dim caves of human thought,
> And who inhabit, as birds wing the wind,
> Its world surrounding ether.

We give part of their lovely chaunt in preference to the ravings of the Furies, though these last are intensely terrible. . . .

[*Quotes Act I, Scene i, lines 694-751*]

The second Act introduces the glorious indications throughout nature of the deliverance of Prometheus from his sufferings. Panthea visits her sister Asia in a lonely vale in the Indian Caucasus, where they relate to each other sweet and mystic dreams betokening the approaching change. When they have ceased Echo calls on them to follow:

> O, follow, follow!
> Thro' the caverns hollow,
> As the song floats thou pursue,
> Where the wild bee never flew,
> Thro' the noontide darkness deep,
> By the odor-breathing sleep
> Of faint night-flowers, and the waves
> At the fountain-lighted caves,
> While our music, wild and sweet,
> Mocks thy gently falling feet,
> Child of Ocean!

The two sisters link their hands and follow the dying voices. They pass into a forest, at the entrance of which two young Fauns are sitting listening, while the Spirits of the Wood in a choral song thus magnificently describe its recesses:

[Quotes Act II, Scene ii, lines 1-63]

Asia and Panthea follow the sounds into the realm of Demogorgon, into whose cave they descend from a pinnacle among the mountains. Here Asia, after an obscure metaphysical dialogue, sets forth the blessing bestowed by Prometheus on the world in the richest colouring, and asks the hour of his freedom. On this question the rocks are cloven and the Hours are seen flying in the heavens. With one of these the sisters ascend in the radiant car; and Asia becomes encircled with lustre, which inspires Panthea thus rapturously to address her. . . .

[Quotes Act II, Scene v, lines 16-47]

Another voice is heard in the air, and Asia bursts into the following strain, which is more liquidly harmonious, and of a beauty more ravishing and paradisaical, than any passage which we can remember in modern poetry. . . .

[Quotes the "enchanted boat" lyric entire, Act II, Scene v, lines 73-110]

In the third act, Jupiter is dethroned by Demogorgon, and Prometheus is unchained by Hercules. The rest of the drama is a celebration of the joyous results of this triumph, and anticipations of the reign of Love. Our readers will probably prefer reposing on the exquisite description given by Prometheus of the cave which he designs for his dwelling, to expatiating on the wide and brilliant prospects which the poet discloses. . . .

[Quotes Act III, Scene iii, lines 10-56]

We have left ourselves no room to expatiate on the minor poems of this volume. The "Vision of the Sea" is one of the most awful pictures which poetry has set before us. In the "Ode to Liberty" there are passages of a political bearing, which, for the poet's sake, we heartily wish had been omitted. It is not, however, addressed to minds whom it is likely to injure. In the whole work there is a spirit of good—of gentleness, humanity, and even of religion, which has excited in us a deep admiration of its author, and a fond regret that he should ever attempt to adorn cold and dangerous paradoxes with the beauties which could only have been produced by a mind instinctively pious and reverential.

PROVINCIAL PRAISE AND CENSURE

[From The Lonsdale Magazine or Provincial Repository. Published at Kirkby Lonsdale, November, 1820 (1:498-501).]

Among all the fictions of early poetry, there was not perhaps a more expressive one than that of the Syrens—they assailed the eye by their beauty, and the ear by the sweetness of their music. But the heedless voyager who was captivated by these allurements, found, when too late, that the most melodious tongue might be connected with the most rapacious heart. As it was in the days of Eneas, it is in our own—those whom Heaven has formed to "wake the living lyre," are too often found to pervert the celestial bounty, and endeavour to allure others by the flowers of rhetoric and music of oratory—to wander from the paths of virtue and innocence—to pursue the bubble, happiness, through the gratifications of sense—to feed on the fancied visions of an ideal perfection, which is to result from an unrestrained indulgence of all our baser passions and propensities—to revel in a prospective state of human felicity, which is to crown the subversion of all social order—and to figure to themselves an earthly paradise, which is to be planted among the ashes of that pure and holy religion which the Deity himself has revealed to his creatures.

Among the pestiferous herd of those who have essayed to destroy man's last and highest hope, some, like Paine, have been so exceedingly low and scurrilous, that even the illiterate could not be induced to drink the filthy poison. Others, like the Edinburgh Reviewers, have been so *exquisitely* absurd, that nothing but the ignorant could possibly be misled by their flimsy sophistry. Others again, like Godwin, have been so metaphysical, that those who were capable of comprehending their sophisms, and developing their complicated hypotheses, were well qualified to confute their logical nonsense, and expose their preposterous philosophy.

But, when writers, like Byron and Shelley, envelope their destructive theories in language, both intended and calculated to entrance the soul by its melodious richness, to act upon the passions without consulting the reason, and to soothe and overwhelm the finest feelings of our nature;— then it is that the unwary are in danger of being misled, the indifferent of being surprised, and the innocent of being seduced.

Mr. Shelley is a man of such poetic powers, as, if he had employed them in the cause of virtue, honour, and truth, would have entitled him to a distinguished niche in the temple of fame. And painful it must be for every admirer of genius and talent, to see one, whose fingers can so sweetly touch the poetic lyre, prostituting his abilities in a manner which must at some future period, embitter the important moment, and throw an awful shade over the gloomy retrospect.

That we may stand justified in the opinion we have given of Mr. Shelley's superior talents as an author, we will quote a few lines from one of his fugitive pieces, entitled "A Vision of the Sea." A piece which for grandeur of expression, originality of thought, and magnificence of description, stands almost unrivalled.

[Quotes lines 1-57, omitting 34-45]

Had all the productions of our author been, like the above, calculated only to "soften and soothe the soul," we should have rejoiced in adding our humble tribute of applause to the numerous encomiums which have greeted him. But alas! he has drunk deeply of the two poisonous and kindred streams—infidelity and sedition. We shall not enter into an analysis of his great work, "Prometheus Unbound," as our principal intention is to *recommend* it to the *neglect* of our readers.—The chief design of the piece, which is a dramatic poem after the manner of the old school, is to charm the unsuspecting heart of youth and innocence, with a luscious picture of the felicities which would succeed the subversion of social, religious, and political order—and which he denominates LIBERTY.

At this happy period when

> Thrones were kingless, and men walked
> One with the other, even as spirits do . . .

After, "Thrones, altars, judgment-seats, and prisons" shall have been destroyed, men shall

> Look forth
> In triumph o'er the palaces and tombs
> Of those who were their conquerors, mouldering around.

Religion, too, will then have vanished, which he characterizes,

> A dark yet mighty faith, a power as wide
> *As is the world it wasted.* . . .

In his ardour to anticipate the joyous period, he breaks out in an exclamation, as though he beheld it present.

> The painted veil. . . . .
> . . . . is torn aside;
> The loathsome mask has fallen; the man remains
> *Sceptreless, free, uncircumscrib'd, but man*
> *Equal, unclass'd, tribeless, and nationless,*
> *Exempt from awe, worship,—the king over himself.*

But this is not all, the very decencies of our nature are to vanish beneath the magic wand of this licentious REFORMER. Every modest feeling, which now constitutes the sweetest charm of society is to be annihilated—and women are to be—*what God and nature never designed them.* But his own description alone can point the lasciviousness of his own heart:—

> And women too, *frank*, beautiful, and kind,
> *As the free heaven,* which rains fresh light and dew
> On the wide earth;—*gentle* radiant form,
> From *custom's evil taint exempt* and pure;
> Speaking the wisdom once they dar'd not think,
> *Looking emotions once they dar'd not feel,*
> And *changed to all which once they dared not be,*
> *Yet being now, make earth like heaven;* nor pride
> Nor jealousy, nor envy, *nor ill-shame,*
> The bitterest of these drops of treasured gall,
> *Spoil the sweet taste of the Nepenthe,* Love.

After having excited his own vicious imagination with this luscious picture of fancied bliss, he seems to have lost all patience with the tardy disciples of this *precious philosophy;* and feels indignant that they do not remove by force the kings and priests and other *trifling* obstacles to the completion of his burning wishes. He thirsts to be transported at once to this ecstatic *Utopia.* For in the same volume, we find an "Ode to Liberty," where he exclaims;—

> O, that the free would stamp the impious name
> Of - - - - into the dust! Or write it there;
> So that this blot upon the page of fame,
> Were as a serpent's path, which the light air
> Erases—
> O, that the wise for their bright minds would kindle
> Such lamps within the dome of the wide world,
> That the pale name of PRIEST might shrink and dwindle,
> Into the HELL from which it first was hurl'd.

Further remarks on sentiments like these, are unnecessary. The beast requires only to be dragged into public light, to meet its merited contempt. We can only express our pity for the author, and regret that so fine a poet should have espoused so detestable a cause.

OBSCURITY, IMPIETY, AND GENIUS

[From The Monthly Review and British Register, February, 1821 (94: 168-173).]

There is an excess of fancy which rapidly degenerates into nonsense: if the *sublime* be closely allied to the ridiculous, the *fanciful* is twin-sister to the *foolish;* and really Mr. Shelley has worthily maintained the relationship. What, in the name of wonder on one side, and of common sense

on the other, is the meaning of this metaphysical rhapsody about the un-
binding of Prometheus? Greek plays, Mr. Shelley tells us in his preface,
have been his study; and from them he has caught—what?—any thing
but the tone and character of his story; which as little exhibits the distinct
imaginations of the heathen mythology as it resembles the virtuous realities
of the Christian faith. It is only *nonsense*, pure unmixed *nonsense*, that
Mr. Shelley has derived from his various lucubrations, and combined in
the laudable work before us.

We are so far from denying, that we are most ready to acknowledge,
the great merit of detached passages in the *Prometheus Unbound:* but this
sort of praise, we fear from expressions in his prose advertisements, the
poet before us will be most unwilling to receive; for he says on one occasion, (preface to the Cenci,) 'I have avoided, *with great care*, in writing
this play, the introduction of what is commonly called *mere poetry;* and I
imagine there will scarcely be found *a detached simile, or a single isolated
description*,'!! &c. Charming prospect, indeed! "I could find it in my
heart," says Dogberry, "to bestow all my tediousness upon your Worship";
and so his anti-type, the author of *Prometheus Unbound*, (which, a punster
might say, will always remain *unbound*,) studiously excludes from his play
everything like 'mere poetry,' *(merum sal,)* or a 'single isolated description.' This speaks for itself; and we should have thought that we had
been reading a burlesque preface of Fielding to one of his *mock tragedies*,
rather than a real introduction by a serious dramatist to one of his *tragic
plays*. We may be told, however, that we must consider the Prometheus
Unbound as a philosophical work. "We cry you mercy, cousin Richard!"
Where are the things, then, "not dreamt of in *our* philosophy?" The
'*Prometheus Unbound*' is amply stored with such things. First, there
is a *wicked supreme deity*.—Secondly, there is a Demogorgon; superior,
in process of time, to that *supreme wickedness*.—Thirdly, there are
nymphs, naids, nereids, spirits of flood and fell, depth and height, the four
elements, and fifty-four imaginary places of creation and residence.—Now,
to what does all this tend? To nothing, positively to nothing. Like
Dandie Dinmont's unproduceable child, the author cannot, in any part of
his work, "*behave distinctly.*" How should he? His Manichean absurdities,
his eternally indwelling notion of a good and an evil principle fighting
like furies on all occasions with their whole *posse comitatus* together, cross
his clearer fancy, and lay the buildings of his better mind in glittering
gorgeous ruins. Let his readers observe the manner in which he talks of
death, and hope, and all the thrilling interests of man; and let us also
attend to what follows:—'For my part I had rather be damned with
Plato and Lord Bacon than go to Heaven with Paley and Malthus.'
Preface to Prometheus, p. 14. This appears to us to be nothing but
hatred of contemporaries; not admiration of the antients. *This* "offence
is rank;—it smells to Heaven."

The benevolent opposition of Prometheus to the oppressive and atrocious rule of Jupiter forms the main object, as far as it can be understood, of

this generally unintelligible work; though some of it can be understood too plainly; and the passage beginning, 'A woful sight,' at page 49, and ending, 'It hath become a curse,' must be most offensive, as it too evidently seems to have been intended to be, to every sect of Christians.

We must cease, however, to expostulate with Mr. Shelley, if we may hope to render him or his admirers any service; and most assuredly we have a sincere desire to be thus serviceable, for he has power to do good, or evil, on an extensive scale;—and whether from admiration of genius, or from a prudent wish to conciliate its efforts, we are disposed to welcome all that is good and useful in him, as well as prepared to condemn all that is the contrary. We turn, then, to other matters, and point out what we think is unexceptionably, or fairly, poetical in the strange book before us.

[*Quotes Act II, Scene iv, lines 7-86, Asia's conversation with Demogorgon*]

The most imaginative of our readers must, we think, be disposed to allow that there is much *nonsense* in all this, however fanciful: yet there is much poetry also,—much benevolent feeling, beautiful language, and powerful versification.

We will take one other extract; and it shall be from the lyric portion of the drama.

[*Quotes Act IV, Scene i, lines 1-55, the song of unseen spirits*]

Such a quotation as this affords ample opportunity for fair judgment; and what is the verdict? With a great portion of uncommon merit, much more absurdity is mixed; and, how great soever the author's genius may be, it is not great enough to bear him out, when he so plainly and heartily laughs in his reader's face as so clever a writer *must do* in this and many other passages.

The "Miscellaneous Poems," which follow Prometheus, display also both his fancy and his peculiarities.

"DRIVELLING PROSE RUN MAD"

[From The Quarterly Review, October, 1821 (26: 168-180). By W. S. Walker. If the accepted attribution of this review to W. S. Walker is correct, and if it was not badly warped by Gifford in the editing, the author changed his opinion of Shelley quite radically by 1824. As E. Haselfoot he is known to have been the author of the notably favorable review of *Posthumous Poems* in Knight's Quarterly Magazine for August, 1824. For Leigh Hunt's guess at the authorship of this article, see p. 310.]

A great lawyer of the present day is said to boast of practising three different modes of writing: one which any body can read; another which only himself can read; and a third, which neither he nor any body else can read. So Mr. Shelley may plume himself upon writing in three different styles: one which can be generally understood; another which can be understood only by the author; and a third which is absolutely and intrinsically unintelligible. Whatever his command may be of the first and second of these styles, this volume is a most satisfactory testimonial of his proficiency in the last.

If we might venture to express a general opinion of what far surpasses our comprehension, we should compare the poems contained in this volume to the visions of gay colours mingled with darkness, which often in child-hood, when we shut our eyes, seem to revolve at an immense distance around us. In Mr. Shelley's poetry all is brilliance, vacuity, and confusion. We are dazzled by the multitude of words which sound as if they denoted something very grand or splendid: fragments of images pass in crowds before us; but when the procession has gone by, and the tumult of it is over, not a trace of it remains upon the memory. The mind, fatigued and perplexed, is mortified by the consciousness that its labour has not been rewarded by the acquisition of a single distinct conception; the ear, too, is dissatisfied: for the rhythm of the verse is often harsh and unmusical; and both the ear and the understanding are disgusted by new and uncouth words, and by the awkward, and intricate construction of the sentences.

The predominating characteristic of Mr. Shelley's poetry, however, is its frequent and total want of meaning. Far be it from us to call for strict reasoning, or the precision of logical deductions, in poetry; but we have a right to demand clear, distinct conceptions. The colouring of the pictures may be brighter or more variegated than that of reality; elements may be combined which do not in fact exist in a state of union; but there must be no confusion in the forms presented to us. Upon a question of mere beauty, there may be a difference of taste. That may be deemed ener-getic or sublime, which is in fact unnatural or bombastic; and yet there may be much difficulty in making the difference sensible to those who do not preserve an habitual and exclusive intimacy with the best models of composition. But the question of meaning, or no meaning, is a matter of fact on which common sense, with common attention, is adequate to decide; and the decision to which we may come will not be impugned, whatever be the want of taste, or insensibility to poetical excellence, which it may please Mr. Shelley, or any of his coterie, to impute to us. We permit them to assume, that they alone possess all sound taste and all genuine feeling of the beauties of nature and art: still they must grant that it belongs only to the judgment to determine, whether certain passages convey any signification or none; and that, if we are in error ourselves, at least we can mislead nobody else, since the very quotations which we must adduce as examples of nonsense, will, if our charges be not well founded, prove the futility of our accusation at the very time that it is made. If, however, we should completely establish this charge, we look upon the question of Mr. Shelley's poetical merits as at an end; for he who has the trick of writing very showy verses without ideas, or without coherent ideas, can contribute to the instruction of none, and can please only those who have learned to read without having ever learned to think.

The want of meaning in Mr. Shelley's poetry takes different shapes.

Sometimes it is impossible to attach any signification to his words; sometimes they hover on the verge between meaning and no meaning, so that a meaning may be obscurely conjectured by the reader, though none is expressed by the writer; and sometimes they convey ideas, which, taken separately, are sufficiently clear, but, when connected, are altogether incongruous. We shall begin with a passage which exhibits in some parts the first species of nonsense, and in others the third.

> Lovely apparitions, dim at first,
> Then radiant, as the mind arising bright
> From the embrace of beauty, whence the forms
> Of which these are the phantoms, casts on them
> The gathered rays which are reality,
> Shall visit us, the immortal progeny
> Of painting, sculpture, and wrapt poesy,
> And arts, tho' unimagined, yet to be. (p. 105.)

The verses are very sonorous; and so many fine words are played off upon us, such as, *painting, sculpture, poesy, phantoms, radiance, the embrace of beauty, immortal progeny,* &c. that a careless reader, influenced by his habit of associating such phrases with lofty or agreeable ideas, may possibly have his fancy tickled into a transient feeling of satisfaction. But let any man try to ascertain what is really said, and he will immediately discover the imposition that has been practised. From beauty, or the embrace of beauty, (we know not which, for ambiguity of phrase is a very frequent companion of nonsense,) certain forms proceed: of these forms there are phantoms; these phantoms are dim; but the mind arises from the embrace of beauty, and casts on them the gathered rays which are reality; they are then baptized by the name of the immortal progeny of the arts, and in that character proceed to visit Prometheus. This *galimatias* (for it goes beyond simple nonsense) is rivalled by the following description of something that is done by a cloud.

> I am the daughter of earth and water,
>   And the nursling of the sky;
> I pass through the pores of the oceans and shores,
>   I change, but I cannot die.
> For after the rain, when with never a stain
>   The pavilion of heaven is bare,
> And the winds and sunbeams with their convex gleams,
>   Build up the blue dome of air.
> I silently laugh at my own cenotaph,
>   And out of the caverns of rain,
> Like a child from the womb, like a ghost from the tomb,
>   I arise and unbuild it again. (pp. 199, 200.)

There is a love-sick lady who "dwells under the glaucous caverns of ocean," and "*wears the shadow of Prometheus' soul,*" without which (she declares) she cannot *go to sleep.* The rest of her story is utterly incomprehensible; we therefore pass on to the *debut* of the Spirit of the earth.

And from the other opening in the wood
Rushes, with loud and whirlwind harmony,
A sphere, which is as many thousand spheres,
Solid as crystal, yet through all its mass
Flow, as through empty space, music and light:
Ten thousand orbs involving and involved,
Purple and azure, white, green, and golden,
Sphere within sphere; and every space between
Peopled with unimaginable shapes,
Such as ghosts dream dwell in the lampless deep,
Yet each inter-transpicuous, and they whirl
Over each other with a thousand motions,
Upon a thousand sightless axles spinning,
And with the force of self-destroying swiftness,
Intensely, slowly, solemnly, roll on,
Kindling with mingled sounds, and many tones,
Intelligible words and music wild.
With mighty whirl the multitudinous orb
Grinds the bright brook into an azure mist
Of elemental subtlety, like light;
And the wild odour of the forest flowers,
The music of the living grass and air,
The emerald light of leaf-entangled beams
Round its intense yet self-conflicting speed,
Seemed kneaded into one aerial mass
Which drowns the sense.

We have neither leisure nor room to develope all the absurdities here accumulated, in defiance of common sense, and even of grammar; whirlwind harmony, a solid sphere which is as many thousand spheres, and contains ten thousand orbs or spheres, with inter-transpicuous spaces between them, whirling over each other on a thousand sightless (alias invisible) axles; self-destroying swiftness; intelligible words and wild music, kindled by the said sphere, which also grinds a bright brook into an azure mist of elemental subtlety; odour, music, and light, kneaded into one aerial mass, and the sense drowned by it!

Oh quanta species! et cerebrum non habet.

One of the personages in the Prometheus is Demogorgon. As he is the only agent in the whole drama, and effects the only change of situation and feeling which befalls the other personages; and as he is likewise employed to sing or say divers hymns, we have endeavored to find some intelligible account of him. The following is the most perspicuous which we have been able to discover:—

. . . A mighty power, which is as darkness,
Is rising out of earth, and from the sky,
Is showered like the night, and from within the air
Bursts, *like eclipse which had been gathered up*
Into the pores of sun-light. (p. 149.)

Love, as might be expected, is made to perform a variety of very extraordinary functions. It fills "the void annihilation of a sceptred curse" (p. 140); and, not to mention the other purposes to which it is applied, it is in the following lines dissolved in air and sun-light, and then folded around the world.

> . . . The impalpable thin air,
> And the all circling sun-light were transformed,
> As if the sense of love dissolved in them,
> Had folded itself around the sphered world. (p. 116.)

Metaphors and similes can scarcely be regarded as ornaments of Mr. Shelley's compositions; for his poetry is in general a mere jumble of words and heterogeneous ideas, connected by slight and accidental associations, among which it is impossible to distinguish the principal object from the accessory. In illustrating the incoherency which prevails in his metaphors, as well as in the other ingredients of his verses, we shall take our first example, not from that great storehouse of the obscure and the unintelligible—the Prometheus, but from the opening of a poem, entitled, "A Vision of the Sea," which we have often heard praised as a splendid work of imagination.

> . . . The rags of the sail
> Are flickering in ribbons within the fierce gale:
> From the stark night of vapours the dim rain is driven,
> And when lightning is loosed, like a deluge from heaven,
> She sees the black trunks of the water-spouts spin,
> And bend, as if heaven was raining in,
> Which they seemed to sustain with their terrible mass
> As if ocean had sunk from beneath them: they pass
> To their graves in the deep with an earthquake of sound,
> And the waves and the thunders made silent around
> Leave the wind to its echo. (p. 174.)

At present we say nothing of the cumbrous and uncouth style of these verses, nor do we ask who this "she" is, who sees the water-spouts; but the funeral of the water-spouts is curious enough: "They pass to their graves with an earthquake of sound." The sound of an earthquake is intelligible, and we suspect that this is what Mr. Shelley meant to say: but an earthquake of sound is as difficult to comprehend as a cannon of sound, or a fiddle of sound. The same vision presents us with a battle between a tiger and a sea-snake; of course we have—

> . . . The whirl and the splash
> As of some hideous engine, whose brazen teeth smash
> The thin winds and soft waves into thunder; the screams
> And hissing crawl fast o'er the smooth ocean streams,
> Each sound like a centipede. (p. 180.)

The comparison of a sound to a centipede would be no small addition to a cabinet of poetical monstrosities: but it sinks into tame common-place before the engine, whose brazen teeth pound thin winds and soft waves into thunder.

Sometimes Mr. Shelley's love of the unintelligible yields to his preference for the disgusting and the impious. Thus the bodies of the dead sailors are thrown out of the ship:

> And the sharks and the dog-fish their grave-clothes unbound,
> And were glutted, like Jews, with this manna rained down
> From God on their wilderness. (p. 177.)

Asia turns her soul into an enchanted boat, in which she performs a wonderful voyage. . . .

[*Quotes Act III, Scene v, lines 73-94*]

The following comparison of a poet to a cameleon has no more meaning than the jingling of the bells of a fool's cap, and far less music.

> Poets are on this cold earth,
>   As camelions might be,
> Hidden from their earthly birth
>   In a cave beneath the sea;
> Where light is camelions change:
>   Where love is not, poets do:
>   Fame is love disguised; if few
> Find either never think it strange
> That poet's range. (p. 186.)

Sometimes to the charms of nonsense those of doggrel are added. This is the conclusion of a song of certain beings, who are called "Spirits of the human minds":

> And Earth, Air, and Light,
> And the Spirit of Might,
> Which drives round the stars in their fiery flight;
> And Love, Thought, and Breath,
> The powers that quell Death,
> Wherever we soar shall assemble beneath.
> And our singing shall build
> In the void's loose field
> A world for the Spirit of Wisdom to wield;
> We will take our plan
> From the new world of man,
> And our work shall be called the Promethean. (p. 130.)

Another characteristic trait of Mr. Shelley's poetry is, that in his descriptions he never describes the thing directly, but transfers it to the properties of something which he conceives to resemble it by language which is to be taken partly in a metaphorical meaning, and partly in no meaning at all. The whole of a long poem, in three parts, called "The Sensitive Plant," the object of which we cannot discover, is an instance of

this.   The first part is devoted to the description of the plants.   The
sensitive plant takes the lead:

> No flower ever trembled and panted with bliss,
> In the garden, the field, or the wilderness,
> Like the doe in the noon-tide with love's sweet want,
> As the companionless sensitive plant. (p. 157.)

Next come the snow-drop and the violet:

> And their breath was mixed with fresh odour, sent
> From the turf, *like the voice and the instrument!*

The rose, too,

> Unveiled the depth of her glowing breast,
> Till, fold after fold, *to the fainting air*
> *The soul of her beauty and love lay bare.*

The hyacinth is described in terms still more quaint and affected:

> The hyacinth, purple, and white, and blue,
> Which flung from *its bells a sweet peal anew,*
> Of music so delicate, soft, and intense,
> It was felt like an odour within the sense.

It is worth while to observe the train of thought in this stanza.   The bells
of the flower occur to the poet's mind; but ought not bells to ring a peal?
Accordingly, by a metamorphosis of the odour, the bells of the hyacinth
are supposed to do so: the fragrance of the flower is first converted into a
peal of music, and then the peal of music is in the last line transformed
back into an odour.   These are the tricks of a mere poetical harlequin,
amusing himself with

> The clock-work tintinnabulum of rhyme.

In short, it is not too much to affirm, that in the whole volume there is
not one original image of nature, one simple expression of human feeling,
or one new association of the appearances of the moral with those of the
material world.

As Mr. Shelley disdains to draw his materials from nature, it is not
wonderful that his subjects should in general be widely remote from every
thing that is level with the comprehension, or interesting to the heart of
man. He has been pleased to call "Prometheus Unbound" a lyrical drama,
though it has neither action nor dramatic dialogue.   The subject of it is
the transition of Prometheus from a state of suffering to the state of happiness; together with a corresponding change in the situation of mankind.
But no distinct account is given of either of these states, nor of the means
by which Prometheus and the world pass from one to the other.   The
Prometheus of Mr. Shelley is not the Prometheus of ancient mythology.
He is a being who is neither a God nor a man, who has conferred supreme

power on Jupiter. Jupiter torments him; and Demogorgon, by annihilating Jupiter's power, restores him to happiness. Asia, Panthea, and Ione, are female beings of a nature similar to that of Prometheus. Apollo, Mercury, the Furies, and a faun, make their appearance; but have not much to do in the piece. To fill up the *personae dramatis*, we have voices of the mountains, voices of the air, voices of the springs, voices of the whirlwinds, together with several echoes. Then come spirits without end: spirits of the moon, spirits of the earth, spirits of the human mind, spirits of the hours; who all attest their super-human nature by singing and saying things which no human being can comprehend. We do not find fault with this poem, because it is built on notions which no longer possess any influence over the mind, but because its basis and its materials are mere dreaming, shadowy, incoherent abstractions. It would have been quite as absurd and extravagant in the time of Aeschylus, as it is now.

It may seem strange that such a volume should find readers, and still more strange that it should meet with admirers. We were ourselves surprised by the phenomenon: nothing similar to it occurred to us, till we recollected the numerous congregations which the incoherences of an itinerant Methodist preacher attract. These preachers, without any connected train of thought, and without attempting to reason, or to attach any definite meaning to the terms which they use, pour out a deluge of sonorous words that relate to sacred objects and devout feelings. These words, connected as they are with all that is most venerable in the eyes of man, excite a multitude of pious associations in the hearer, and produce in him a species of mental intoxication. His feelings are awakened, and his heart touched, while his imagination and understanding are bewildered; and he receives temporary pleasure, sometimes even temporary improvement, at the expense of the essential and even permanent depravation of his character. In the same way, poetry like that of Mr. Shelley presents everywhere glittering constellations of words, which taken separately have a meaning, and either communicate some activity to the imagination, or dazzle it by their brilliance. Many of them relate to beautiful or interesting objects, and are therefore capable of imparting pleasure to us by the associations attached to them. The reader is conscious that his mind is raised from a state of stagnation, and he is willing to believe, that he is astounded and bewildered, not by the absurdity, but by the originality and sublimity of the author.

It appears to us much more surprizing, that any man of education should write such poetry as that of "Prometheus Unbound," than that when written, it should find admirers. It is easy to read without attention; but it is difficult to conceive how an author, unless his intellectual habits are thoroughly depraved, should not take the trouble to observe whether his imagination has definite forms before it, or is gazing in stupid wonder on assemblages of brilliant words. Mr. Shelley tells us, that he imitates the Greek tragic poets: can he be so blinded by self-love, as not to be aware that his productions have not one feature of likeness to what have been deemed classical works, in any country or in any age? He, no doubt, possesses considerable mental activity; for without industry he could never have attained to so much facility in the art of throwing words into fantastical combinations: is it not strange that he should never have turned his attention from his verses to that which his verses are meant to express? We fear that his notions of poetry are fundamentally erroneous. It seems to be his maxim, that reason and sound thinking are aliens in the dominions of the Muses, and that, should they ever be found wandering about the foot of Parnassus, they ought to be chased away as spies sent to discover the nakedness of the land. We would wish to persuade him, if possible, that the poet is distinguished from the rest of his species, not by wanting what other men have, but by having what other men want. The reason of the poet ought to be cultivated with as much care at that of the philosopher, though the former chooses a peculiar field for its exercise, and associates with it in its labours other faculties that are not called forth in the mere investigation of truth.

But it is often said, that though the poems are bad, they at least show poetical power. Poetical power can be shown only by writing good poetry, and this Mr. Shelley has not yet done. The proofs of Mr. Shelley's genius, which his admirers allege, are the very exaggeration, copiousness of verbiage, and incoherence of ideas which we complain of as intolerable. They argue in criticism, as those men do in morals, who think debauchery and dissipation an excellent proof of a good heart. The want of meaning is called sublimity, absurdity becomes venerable under the name of originality, the jumble of metaphor is the richness of imagination, and even the rough, clumsy, confused structure of the style, with not unfrequent violations of the rules of grammar, is, forsooth, the sign and effect of a bold overflowing genius, that disdains to walk in common trammels. If the poet is one who whirls round his reader's brain, till it becomes dizzy and confused; if it is his office to envelop he knows not what in huge folds of a clumsy drapery of splendid words and showy metaphors, then, without doubt, may Mr. Shelley place the Delphic laurel on his head. But take away from him the unintelligible, the confused, the incoherent, the bombastic, the affected, the extravagant, the hideously gorgeous, and 'Prometheus,' and the poems which accompany it, will sink at once into nothing.

But great as are Mr. Shelley's sins against sense and taste, would that we had nothing more to complain of! Unfortunately, to his long list of demerits he has added the most flagrant offences against morality and religion. We should abstain from quoting instances, were it not that we think his language too gross and too disgusting to be dangerous to any but those who are corrupted beyond the hope of amendment. After a revolting description of the death of our Saviour, introduced merely for the sake of intimating, that *the religion he preached is the great source of human misery and vice,* he adds,

—Thy name I will not speak,
It hath become a curse.

Will Mr. Shelley, to excuse this blasphemy against the name *"in which all nations of the earth shall be made blessed,"* pretend, that these are the words of Prometheus, not of the poet? But the poet himself hath told us, that his Prometheus is meant to be "the type of the highest perfection of moral and intellectual excellence." There are other passages, in which Mr. Shelley speaks directly in his own person. In what he calls an ode to Liberty, he tells us that she did

> —groan, not weep,
> When from its sea of death to kill and burn
> The Galilean serpent forth did creep
> And made thy world an undistinguishable heap. (p. 213.)

And after a few stanzas he adds. . . .

[*Quotes* Ode to Liberty, *lines* 211-233]³

At present we say nothing of the harshness of style and incongruity of metaphor, which these verses exhibit. We do not even ask what is or can be meant by *the kneeling of human thought before the judgment throne of its own awless soul:* for it is a praiseworthy precaution in an author, to temper irreligion and sedition with nonsense, so that he may avail himself, if need be, of the plea of lunacy before the tribunals of his country. All that we now condemn, is the wanton gratuitous impiety thus obtruded on the world. If any one, after a serious investigation of the truth of Christianity, still doubts or disbelieves, he is to be pitied and pardoned; if he is a good man, he will himself lament that he has not come to a different conclusion; for even the enemies of our faith admit, that it is precious for the restraints which it imposes on human vices, and for the consolations which it furnishes under the evils of life. But what is to be said of a man, who, like Mr. Shelley, wantonly and unnecessarily goes out of his way, not to reason against, but to revile Christianity and its author? Let him adduce his arguments against our religion, and we shall tell him where to find them answered: but let him not presume to insult the world, and to profane the language in which he writes, by rhyming invectives against a faith of which he knows nothing but the name.

The real cause of his aversion to Christianity is easily discovered. Christianity is the great prop of the social order of the civilized world; this social order is the object of Mr. Shelley's hatred; and, therefore, the pillar must be demolished, that the building may tumble down. His views of the nature of men and of society are expressed, we dare not say explained, in some of those *"beautiful idealisms of moral excellence,"* (we use his own words,) in which the "Prometheus" abounds.

The painted veil, by those who were, called life, which mimicked, as with colours idly spread, all men believed and hoped, is torn aside; the loathsome mask has fallen, the man remains sceptreless, free, uncircumscribed, but man equal, un-classed, tribeless, and nationless, exempt from awe, worship, degree, the king over

³ Leigh Hunt showed that this passage was maliciously misquoted. See p. 310.

himself; just, gentle, wise: but man passionless; no, yet free from guilt or pain, which were for his will made or suffered them, nor yet exempt, tho' ruling them like slaves, from chance and death, and mutability, the clogs of that which else might oversoar the loftiest star of unascended heaven, pinnacled dim in the intense inane. (p. 120.)

Our readers may be puzzled to find out the meaning of this paragraph; we must, therefore, inform them that it is not prose, but the conclusion of the third act of Prometheus verbatim et literatim. With this information they will cease to wonder at the absence of sense and grammar; and will probably perceive, that Mr. Shelley's poetry is, in sober sadness, *drivelling prose run mad*.

With the prophetic voice of a misgiving conscience, Mr. Shelley objects to criticism. "If my attempt be ineffectual, (he says) let the punishment of an unaccomplished purpose have been sufficient; let none trouble themselves to heap the dust of oblivion upon my efforts." Is there no respect due to common sense, to sound taste, to morality, to religion? Are evil spirits to be allowed to work mischief with impunity, because, forsooth, the instruments with which they work are contemptible? Mr. Shelley says, that his intentions are pure. Pure! They may have been so in his vocabulary; for, (to say nothing of his having mistaken nonsense for poetry, and blasphemy for an imperious duty,) vice and irreligion, and the subversion of society are, according to his system, pure and holy things; Christianity, and moral virtue, and social order, are alone impure. But we care not about his intentions, or by what epithet he may choose to characterize them, so long as his words exhale contagious mischief. On his own principles he must admit, that, in exposing to the public what we believe to be the character and tendency of his writings, we discharge a sacred duty. He professes to write in order to reform the world. The essence of the proposed reformation is the destruction of religion and government. Such a reformation is not to our taste; and he must, therefore, applaud us for scrutinizing the merits of works which are intended to promote so detestable a purpose. Of Mr. Shelley himself we know nothing, and desire to know nothing. Be his private qualities what they may, his poems (and it is only with his poems that we have any concern) are at war with reason, with taste, with virtue, in short, with all that dignifies man, or that man reveres.

IX

GENERAL AND INCIDENTAL COMMENT IN 1820 AND 1821

THE BEST OF THE COCKNEYS

[From The Honeycomb, No. IX, Saturday, August 12, 1820 (pp. 65-72), entitled "Portraits of the Metropolitan Poets, No. III, Mr. Percy Byshe [*sic*] Shelley."

The sections of the article here omitted—nearly a third—make no mention of Shelley. They consist of disapproving introductory comments on the "Metropolitans" as a mutual aid society and a concluding attack on the reviewing practice of Blackwood's Magazine, with some excellent sarcastic flings at John Wilson as Professor of Moral Philosophy. The other "Metropolitan Poets" in the series are Hunt and Proctor. There is also an essay on Campbell, but not as a Metropolitan.

Although J. P. Anderson lists this article in his Bibliographical Appendix to William Sharp's *Life of Shelley* (1887) and Dowden borrowed a copy from Bertram Dobell in 1884 and again borrowed or bought it a year later (*Letters of Edward Dowden and His Correspondents*, 1914, pp. 205-206 and 214), he does not mention it in his biography, nor is the Honeycomb listed in any other reference lists or library catalogues I have consulted previous to 1932, when the Duke University Library purchased a bound copy of nos. 1-10 from P. J. and A. E. Dobbell.]

Man is a gregarious animal, else we should have been at a loss to discover for what possible reason Mr. Shelley could have enrolled himself under the banners of Mr. Leigh Hunt. It must surely have been merely for the benefit of company—protection he could not afford him! and the author of the Revolt of Islam should not stoop to require it from the hands of the writer of Rimini. Mr. Shelley is far above his compeers, and he seems only to have associated his name with theirs from personal motives, and not from the consciousness of any poetical approximation. Except on account of some of the principles which he professes, we should never have classed Mr. Shelley with Leigh Hunt, or even with Barry Cornwall, as in power and extent of intellect, richness of imagination, and skill in numbers, he is far their superior. It is only as forming one of the phalanx which we have before described that this poet can be accounted a member of the Metropolitan School. If he cannot be said to be a native soldier, he is yet a very redoubted ally, and from the plains of Italy he trumpets forth the praises of his Sovereign. There is a vignette in Bewick's Beasts, representing two horses in a field kindly scratching one another, by mutually nibbling with their teeth at each other's main [*sic*]. There cannot be a more faithful picture than this of the friendship which exists between Mr. Shelley and Leigh Hunt,

> . . . Friends, how fast sworn,
> Whose double bosoms seem to wear one heart.

[251]

Mr. Shelley dedicates his Tragedy to Mr. Leigh Hunt, assuring the public that he is the most amiable character in the world, and Mr. Leigh Hunt in his Examiner compares Mr. Shelley to an Apostle, while the Quarterly in a mysterious note would make us believe that the latter person more nearly resembles a fallen Angel. But with the personal characters of these gentlemen we have nothing in the world to do; when the pen becomes the instrument of private scandal, and when such an employment of it meets with encouragement from the public, it bespeaks a vitiated state of the public taste. There are indeed some publications which have stooped to pander to this low passion, and which, by the genius and talents wasted in such evil purposes, have rendered their degradation still more conspicuous. To attacks from adversaries like these a wise man will always be insensible, and it did not shew any very high-minded forbearance in Mr. Leigh Hunt when he noticed the personal attacks which were made upon him, in what is said to be a popular periodical work. The venom of a slanderer's tongue must recoil upon himself; and that infamy which he would heap upon his victim's head will be doubled upon his own.—But we wander——

The public do not look with favour on combinations like these; and we question very much whether they do not come within the purview of the statutes which declare all combinations among journeymen illegal. The only difference is, that the journeymen manufacturers conspire to raise the price of their *work*, and the journeymen poets to raise the price of their *works*. There is always something suspicious in this herding together; an appearance of want of confidence in the integrity of a man's own powers; a sort of attempt to carry public opinion by storm and force of numbers, which raises a prejudice in the public mind. When one poet pours forth praises of another, we can in general judge of the coin in which he expects to be repaid.

But while the bards of the metropolis have been securing sweet words from each other's mouths, they have contrived, but with strangely different success, to extort some laudatory articles from some of the reviews. It is we believe well known to whom Mr. Leigh Hunt is indebted for the favourable notice of Rimini in the Edinburgh. On the Quarterly none of these authors have yet made any impression. Mr. Gifford and his coadjutors have poured out the vial of wrath with undistinguishing bitterness on the whole company of them. As an advocate of freedom, and a new system of things, Mr. Shelley has merited their severest vengeance; and the "Endymion" of poor Keats almost withered in their grasp. The mode in which Blackwood's Magazine deals with our little knot of poets is, however, the most curious. With Leigh Hunt they are sworn foes, and we conclude must ever continue so, while Barry Cornwall has elicited praises from them that might make him write "under the ribs of death." Mr. Shelley too, and this is odd enough, has been favoured with sundry high commendations, though we do not believe that his real poetical merits have been the cause of them. The principles which he professes, and the views of things which he takes, so contrary to the principles, if they may so be called, which distinguished that magazine, would be fully sufficient to counterbalance in the minds of the persons who contribute to that work, the harping of an Angel's Lyre. There is therefore undoubtedly some secret machinery of which we are not aware, some friend behind the scenes, or some working of personal interest, which thus induces that magazine for once to throw aside the trammels of party prejudice, and to do justice to a man who even advocates ·the French Revolution. It would be a curious thing if the public could be made acquainted with the history of every review, and see the hidden springs of affection or hatred by which the pen of the impartial critic was moved. The empiricism of patent medicines is nothing to this quackery.

Now let us proceed to examine Mr. Shelley's merits a little more particularly. While Mr. Leigh Hunt has met at the hands of the public about as much encouragement as he deserves, or perhaps too much, and Barry Cornwall has gained certainly a greater reputation than he is entitled to, we think Mr. Shelley has never been duly appreciated. This neglect, for it almost amounts to that, is, however, entirely owing to himself. He writes in a spirit which people do not comprehend: there is something too mystical in what he says—something too high or too deep for common comprehensions. He lives in a very remote poetical world, and his feelings will scarcely bear to be shadowed out in earthly light. There are, no doubt, in the mind of a poet, and they evidently exist in the mind of Mr. Shelley, shades of thought, which it is impossible to delineate, and feelings which cannot be clearly expressed; when, therefore, he attempts to clothe these ideas with words, tho' he may himself perceive the force of them, it will very frequently happen that his readers will not, or that such words at most will only convey a very imperfect idea of the high meanings which the writer attached to them. This is no fault peculiar to Mr. Shelley—the finest geniuses have felt it most, and in reading many passages of Shakespeare, if we were asked to define the exact meaning of some of the most beautiful parts, we should be unable to do so. Expressions of this kind are very frequent in the works of Mr. Shelley, and his sentiments are sometimes equally obscure. The first poem which he published, "Alastor, or the Spirit of Solitude," tho' full of fine writing, abounds with these dimly shadowed feelings, and we seem as we read it, as if we were walking through a country where beautiful prospects extend on every side, which are hidden from us by the mists of evening. Mr. Shelley seems to nurse this wildness of imagination, at the expense of clearness and vigour of style. He has extended the same spirit to the whole composition of his longest poem, the Revolt of Islam, in which he undertakes to teach every great principle—freedom—patriotism—philanthropy—toleration—under an allegory; or as he expresses it, "for this purpose I have chosen a story of human passion in its most universal character, diversified with moving and romantic adventures, and appealing, in contempt of all artificial opinions or institutions, to the common sympathies of every human breast."

So well did Mr. Shelley imagine this poem qualified to accomplish the philanthropic object for which it was written, that we have heard, he actually wished that a cheap edition of it should be printed in order that it might be distributed amongst all classes of persons; certainly one of the very wildest of his imaginations. He should have written intelligibly to common understandings if he wished to become popular.

We wished to give such of our readers as have not access to the volume itself, some idea of the Revolt of Islam; but this we find it impossible to do, both from the nature of the poem itself and the limits to which we are confined. In versification, we consider this poem to be a very high effort of genius. In fact, Mr. Shelley has new-modelled the Spencerian Stanza, and given it a beauty and power of expression which it did not possess before. He manages his pauses very skilfully, and he has introduced double rhymes with fine effects. Of the truth of these remarks the following stanzas selected from the introductory address will afford a sufficient proof.

TO MARY . . . .
So now my summer-task is ended, Mary,
[*Quotes stanzas 1, 2, 3, 4, 7, 8, 9, and 14. The six stanzas omitted are those in which Shelley's radicalism is most evident*]

It will be instantly perceived that in Mr. Shelley's poetry there are none of the puerilities which disgrace the compositions of the persons with whom he has chosen to confound his name. There is no attempt to attain a simplicity out of nature; no determination like Barry Cornwall's "to follow the scent of strong-smelling phrases." He knows that poetry is not composed of the language of common life as Mr. Wordsworth supposes, or its spirit of common feelings,—he knows that the nature of poetry is above the common nature of man, and that in reducing it to that level we are in fact depriving it of all its great characteristics. He knows likewise that one man does not look well in another's clothes, and he refuses, unlike Mr. Barry Cornwall, to wear the cast-off garments of antiquity. In short, Mr. Shelley is essentially, a poet.

There is another feature in the poetical character of Mr. Shelley which favourably distinguishes him from his more imitative and trivial companions —he is an *improving* author. The difference between a superior poet and one of mediocrity consists in the stationary or progressive spirit in which they write. All inferior geniuses and wits display their best efforts at once. They easily find "the length of their tether," and like many other ruminating animals we have seen, sport and amble round the prescribed circle with the delighted consciousness of a little freedom and power. It is the case with all secondary poets; and if our readers will turn to Mr. Barry Cornwall's "Dramatic Scenes," and compare them with his latest production; or to Mr. Leigh Hunt's earliest lucubrations, and his last poetical attempts, they will acknowledge the extraordinary sameness, or even deterioration, which exists between the earliest and most recent writings of these gentlemen. "Can these dry bones live?" We cannot, however, bring a similar

charge against Mr. S.; there is a soul and a fire in his poetical genius which
is not so suddenly burnt out. Without that perpetual straining and eagerness to accomplish something great, which characterizes Mr. B. C., in quiet
and serene strength of spirit he in truth performs much more. Compared
with the dramatic powers of Mr. Shelley, the solitary and mutilated scenes
of Mr. B. C. are insignificant indeed. These possess little claim to originality. The subject, the very names and argument, are borrowed. The
scene is ready sketched to the hand; a little color, and a few *most natural*
touches, and behold a picture, which Mr. C. may as reasonably claim for
his own, as a friseur the head of a poetical coxcomb which he has just
dressed. Yet Mr. Shelley ranks as one of this pigmy race. He is not
ashamed to pander to the reputation of poets like these. An interchange
of fulsome compliments and gross flattery, takes place—their publishers
propagate it, and the public is not yet sickened of this "got up" and ludicrous
scene. We will unfold the secret springs of this poetical pantomine, and
disclose the managers of the puppet show to view. We promise ourselves
no little pleasure, however, in exhibiting it more freely, and exposing it
more clearly to the contempt of an injured and insulted public, which we
know these authors and publishers ridicule behind the scenes. This system
of literary hoaxing was introduced by a convenient and time-serving publication in the North. . . .

HESITANT DISLIKE

[From The Dublin Magazine or General Repertory of Philosophy, Belles
Lettres, and Miscellaneous Information, November, 1820 (1:393-400), entitled
"Critical Remarks on Shelley's Poetry." Shelley had received incidental mention
in The Dublin Magazine several months earlier.]

We have been deterred from before noticing Mr. Shelly's poems by
the obvious difficulty of the task, and it is not without some feelings of dread
that we now approach them. Some credit has, we hope, been given us
for the manner in which we have generally spoken of young poets: we
have done the little we could to encourage and animate them to exertion.
We have ventured to speak of more than one of the number, as if he had
already attained that fame, which it is idle to suppose can be won without
earnest and continual labour; but if our praises have, at times, been exaggerated, they have always been suggested and justified by circumstances
of high promise—by something in the character of the poet or the poem
that claimed affectionate sympathy. Young critics, we declined assuming
the fastidious tone which characterizes, and renders contemptible, most of
the periodical criticism of our day, and which must prevent its becoming
valuable even as a register of contemporary opinion. It is, indeed, painful
to us to speak otherwise than in the language of encouragement: we know
as well as Coleridge the value of literary praise, and agree with him that
suppressing one favorable opinion of a work is an act of positive injustice.
Now the fact is, we think unfavorably of Mr. Shelly; we think his talents

unworthily devoted to evil purposes in his imitations;—and, let him account for the fact as he will, all his poetry is imitative. We see little else than an eloquent use of language, wild and rhapsodical declamation: this very common accomplishment is, no doubt, a valuable one, but while we are listening to this orator, we are often tempted to enquire what is the subject of his discourse. We feel that he has told us nothing, and has nothing to tell us: we would rest the decision of the question—is Mr. Shelly a poet, on the circumstance that, whatever excitement may be felt during the perusal of his works, not one line of them remains on the ear when we have closed the volume; and of all the gorgeous images with which they are loaded, scarcely one is retained in the memory.

It does not strike us as a task by any means difficult to colour the cold speculations of Godwin with the language of poetry, though we think such subjects would be avoided by a poetical mind. That a state of society may be imagined in which men will be "kingless, and tribeless, and nationless," we admit; and even feel that the conception has an imposing and sublime appearance in the same way that the idea of utter desolation is sublime; but we must remember that these notions are put forward by Mr. Shelly, with avowed admiration of the consequences he expects to result from their being applied to the test of experience. Now we must continue to believe that such views are likely to lessen the exercise of the domestic charities; that, when no adequate object is offered to the affections, they will, being left without a support, droop and die in the heart. We believe that man's duty here is something different from comparing phantoms with phantoms: and that whatever his talents, or whatever his professed object may be, no man is justified in giving to the world wild and crude notions, the first effect of which, if reduced to practice, would be the overthrow of all existing institutions, and the substitution of a waste and howling wilderness— the revolutionary Eden, of which the uncontrolled passions of men are to be protecting angels. The facility with which this new philosophy removes the possibility of crime, is one of the most admirable parts of the theory. Murder, as we still call it, is innocent, for it is but diverting a few ounces of blood from their proper channel, and the dead body is soon converted into living beings many times happier than man. Adultery, as Leigh Hunt proved, is founded only on the custom of marriage; and who is there that does not see that we will get rid of it at once by abolishing that odious tyranny. Incest is but a name; we suppose it a crime merely from vulgar prejudices, which, in the new order of things, cannot exist, as when marriage is removed, the degrees of relationship will seldom be strictly ascertained. All those duties, the neglect of which sometimes occasions a little uneasiness to us at present, will no longer be required of a man: prayer is done away with, for we are to live without a God in the world: and repentance is quite idle, for there will be no longer any sin, or if evil is supposed to continue, how can repentance alter the past? and of the future we know nothing. Such is the creed of the enlightened friends of humanity; such are the opinions on man's nature and destiny, which form the groundwork of the "Prometheus Unbound"—the dreams of this enthusiast.

The fact is, however we may wish to conceal it, that infidelity has long been striking its roots deep and wide—that its buds and blossoms are now shining out in rich luxuriance. A few years ago we could have pointed with pride to the poetical literature of England:—voluminous as are the works of Scott, Wordsworth, and Southey, and all the other great men worthy to be named with them, there was not a single line in their writings which could have wounded the chastest ear: but read, as they have of course been by every one, they have taught the world their language; and the manufacture of poetry has become a trade,—a poor and dishonest one. The admirers even of Lord Byron seem to be well aware that he is very indifferent to anything but the sale of his works. The poison he now sells is prepared for the same purposes as that of most other quacks—with him religion is a joke: with Shelly, atheism is a principle. We are afraid to pursue our remarks further, as we cannot, of course, consent to make our pages instrumental in the circulation of the passages which justify these remarks.

We have spoken of Mr. Shelly's poetry as imitation: this is a severe charge, for it is easily made, idly repeated, and with difficulty repelled:—in writers of the same age a resemblance will, perhaps, necessarily exist; nothing is more common than coincidences of thought and expression between writers in such circumstances as preclude the supposition of imitation: passages of striking similarity are found in Homer and the Hebrew poets; but this is not the kind of resemblance on which we found our accusation, to us Mr. Shelly appears in his poetry, like a man speaking a foreign language, translating his thoughts into a dialect in which he does not think—writing under the inspiration of ambition rather than of genius or feeling. His success, if he finally does succeed, will justify Johnson's definition of poetical genius, which he speaks of as the accidental direction of general talents to that particular pursuit. We write hastily, and are not satisfied that our meaning has been clearly expressed; but in these compositions it seems to us that poetical embellishments are often heavily laid on over conceptions essentially unpoetical, which would not actually have excited them; that in all his poetry he is thinking of some other poet with whom he is mentally comparing himself, that the best passages remind us of better in Wordsworth, or Byron, or Aeschylus, which have, we feel, originated those in Shelly; yet while we write down this opinion, we feel it very probable that his active mind is engaged in compositions that will refute all our decisions—be it so.

For the reasons we have alluded to, and because our limits will not permit a particular analysis, we have forborne to give extracts; the following short poems, however, may convey some general idea of his style.

[The Cloud *quoted entire*]
[To a Skylark *quoted entire*]

ENTHUSIASTIC PRAISE

[From The London Magazine, and Theatrical Inquisitor, February, 1821 (3: 122-127), entitled "On the Philosophy and Poetry of Shelley." One of the most enthusiastic appreciations Shelley ever received. There is no evidence of his having heard of it.]

The French Revolution, which trampled into dust the regal tyranny of kingdoms, gave at the same time a new tone to the moral and religious sensibilities of human nature. It shook up the feelings that had so long reposed as a sort of sediment in the depths of the spirit, and by invigorating the inert particles, gave added strength to the intellectual constitution of mankind. Like the winds of heaven, it echoed with its thousand voices through the world, and proclaimed the tidings of salvation to all nature, and by bidding it taste of the sweets of partial liberty, it first taught it to think for itself, and to rely on its own intellect for the furtherance of its lawful claims. The sensibilities of man, that had slept for ages on the stagnant surface of his mind, inert and moveless as is the green weed on the bosom of the standing pool, was roused to sudden exertion by the great call of Freedom. She came upon his imagination as a white-robed Seraph, clothed in the armor of light, and whispered in his ear the words of heaven, bidding him at the same time "Arise, arise, or be forever fallen." France—Europe—the universe roused themselves at the call of genius; they woke the slumbering energies of their souls, and armed valiantly for the day of battle that was at hand. But despotism was yet too strong for the slowly awakened emanations of intellectual freedom. The morning sun shone down indeed from heaven, but was unable wholly to disperse the noxious vapours that clogged the atmosphere. America—France—hailed the light from above, and basked a while in its beam; and the other nations welcomed its splendour, though they felt not its revivifying powers. Unhappily the revolution, while it passed, like a mighty inundation of the Nile, from country to country, and gladdened the fair face of nature by its waters, subsided ere the glebe land was yet fattened by the overflow of its healthful springs. It was dammed up by the dykes of bigotry and prejudice, and compelled once again to return to its original channels. But still, though its inundation has ceased, its effect shall be long felt. It has deposited a fruitful spawn upon the earth; which, fostered by the sun of heaven, and invigorated by the cheering breeze of freedom, shall dawn into a glorious maturity. Mirabeau, with the philosophers and patriots of the French school; Byron, Godwin of our own times; and Shelley, the subject of our article, are the spawn of this mighty revolution. The minutiae of their system, perhaps, may be replete with errors, but its abstract abounds in the most beautiful sensibilities of truth and religion. Shelley in particular seems to have a higher notion of the capability of human nature than any poet or philosopher of his day. He has seen, as from a distance, the glorious truths of divinity, but his mind has not yet embraced the whole. "A bold inquirer," as he himself terms Milton, "into morals and religion," he has

come armed 'as a hero of yore' to the contest, and divested himself of the
dense clouds of prejudice that overhang the mass of mankind, and thicken
the natural obtuseness of their intellect. The ground-work of his system
is of the purest that can be possibly conceived, and well worthy of that
Deity from whom it originally emanated. "Love," says Mr. Shelley in the
preface to his Revolt of Islam, "is the sole tie that should govern the moral
world"; and though the idea is somewhat too Utopian, the basis on which
it rests is divine. It is possible, however, that axioms of this nature may
tend to shock the sensitive feelings of nine-tenths of the community, who
are accustomed to groan over their mental disquietude, while they dread
the application of the axe to the root of their disease. It is possible that
they may be appalled at the convenient latitude of the word "Love"; and
not finding it in the weekly sermons of their spiritual pastors and masters,
may shrewdly exclaim, "I cannot find it—'tis not in the bond." But let
such people consider, that the great and infinitely wise Deity who endowed
man with intellect, and bade him look up to heaven, gave him that intellect, not as a gift that was to be hid like the talent in the earth, until
reclaimed by the donor, but as a largess, that was to be actively and
beneficially employed; and can intellect be better employed, than when
applied to the purposes of religion; in separating the dross from the gold,
and rendering the metal pure and unadulterated? Such are the leading
principles of Mr. Shelley. In endeavoring to restore religion to its primitive
purity, and to render it the voluntary incense of love and brotherly com-
munion, he is performing an acceptable service to the Deity, and a benefit
to society at large. It is not with religion that he bickers, but with the
adulterations that have so long disgraced it. He has discovered that "there's
something rotten in the state of Denmark," and applied his utmost ingenuity to remedy the defect. He has ascertained that religion, in the
common acceptance of the term, has been made a stalking-horse for the
purposes of Mammon, and has become the most intolerant of all creeds.
The "beautiful idealisms of moral excellence," that once shed grace and
splendour on the annals of sacred history, have been blotted with the tears
of martyrs. The vengeance of the bigot has been let loose on society;
religion, like the timid hare, has been chased to and fro; and a loud pack
of evangelical alarmists have been let loose upon her haunches, and she has
been fairly torn in pieces.

In differing from the religious opinions of society, Mr. Shelley is only
sustaining a more elevated tone of feeling, and applying himself to the
fountain-head of devotion, instead of stopping to slake his thirst at the
numerous streamlets that wander by the way-side. He has not bewildered
himself in the folio controversies of Warburton and Lowth; or versed his
mind in the learned disputes of Travis, Porson, and Co. about the credit
of the three witnesses; or puzzled himself with the sage Jesuits of old, as
to the startling fact of ten thousand angels dancing on the point of a
needle, without jostling each other; but he has consulted his own heart;
he has "held converse" with his own reason; and instead of arriving at the

truth by a circumbendibus, has reached it by a straight-forward direction. His principal feeling respecting religion appears to consist in the sentiment of benevolence toward mankind, that strikes home to the heart as an immediate emanation of the Deity. His mind revolts at intolerance and bigotry; and he believes in his devotional creed as one that deserves love as well as admiration. His moral and political principles all spring from the same source, and are founded on the same dignified contempt for bigotry and the "sway of tyranny."

> O that the free would stamp the impious name
>   Of King into the dust! or write it there,
> So that this blot upon the page of fame
>   Were as a serpent's path, which the light air
> Erases, and the flat sands close behind!
>   Ye the oracle have heard.
>   Lift the victory-flashing sword,
> And cut the snaky knots of this foul gordian word,
>   Which, weak itself as stubble, yet can bind
>   Into a mass, irrefragably firm,
>   The axes and the rods which awe mankind;
>   The sound has poison in it, 'tis the sperm
> Of what makes life foul, cankerous, and abhorred;
>   Disdain not thou, at thine appointed term,
>   To set thine armed heel on this reluctant worm.[1]

If these are opinions carried to an extravagant excess, they are at least the excesses of a devotional mind and a generous disposition. They are the excesses of an enthusiastic spirit, soaring above the trammels of superstition, relying on its own capabilities, and asserting the rights of man as a thinking and independent being.

In his dramatic poem of "Prometheus Unbound" Mr. Shelley has given us, in the portraiture of the noble-minded victim, a most "beautiful idealism of moral excellence." He has drawn us Virtue, not as she is, but as she should be,—magnanimous in affliction, and impatient of unauthorized tyranny. Prometheus, the friend and the champion of mankind, may be considered as a type of religion oppressed by the united powers of superstition and tyranny. He is for a time enchained, though not enfeebled, by the pressure of his misfortunes, but is finally triumphant; and by the manful exertions of his own lawful claims frees himself from his ignominious thraldom; and proves the truth of that axiom which is engraved in undying characters on the "fair front of nature"—that right shall always overcome might. This is the leading principle in Mr. Shelley; in its more trifling bearings it is occasionally inconsistent, but exhibits a noble illustration of the intuitive powers and virtues of the human mind. This is the system that he is anxious to disseminate, and a more sublime one was never yet invented. It appeals at once from nature to God, discards the petty bickerings of different creeds and soars upward to the throne of grace as

[1] See Leigh Hunt's comment on this passage, p. 310.

the lark that sings "at heaven's gate" her matin song of thanksgiving. There may be different opinions respecting matters of taste, feeling, and metaphysics, but there can be but one respecting the holiness of benevolence, and universal philanthrophy. Before this great, this important truth, all minor creeds sink into their native insignificance. It is the ladder by which man mounts to Heaven,—the faith which enables him to hear the voice of the Deity welcoming him as he ascends.

In the creed of Mr. Shelley the humanity of religion is so intimately connected with its sacred origin that it is impossible to separate them. He will not, like less humane, but more orthodox, believers, condemn any one for the difference of his creed, or write long books to prove that all who disbelieve in his opinions must be eventually damned. He forms his religion on a more elevated principle,—he makes it a religion of the heart as well as of the head, and by its own virtues proves more strongly the fact of its divine origin:—

> For modes of faith less graceless zealots fight;
> His can't be wrong whose life is in the right.

This opinion of one of England's choicest spirits, followed as it has been and still is by Shelley and others of the same school, is daily gaining ground in the world; and the march of intellect, which day after day is rapidly increasing, threatens the destruction of all civil and religious prejudices.

Men can be no longer hood-winked; they now at least think for themselves; and this strenuous exertion of intellect will eventually prove fatal to fanaticism. It is now as it was fifty years ago, when the piety of the bishops was measured by their circumference, and the devotion of a minister adjudged by the comparative length and drowsiness of his sermon. The waters are out; a fearful ebullition of the human mind is already on the eve of breaking forth; the spirit of the nation heaves, as the ocean billows, from the depth of its own mightiness; and the muttering sound of the distant thunder may be even now heard in the awful pause that precedes the tempest. "The great writers of our age," says Mr. Shelley, "are, we have reason to suppose, the companions and forerunners of some unimagined change in our social condition, or the opinions which cement it. The cloud of mind is discharging its collected lightning, and the equilibrium between institutions and opinions is now restoring, or is about to be restored." Let us hope, then, for the honour of our nature and the advancement of true religion, that the days are not far distant when the Deity shall once again be imaged in the breasts of his creations; when his worship shall be unsullied by the animosity of alarmists, and be considered as benevolence to our fellow-mortals, and love to the being that created us. Let us hope that intolerance, and all the present uncharitableness of the Protestant religion shall be banished from our creed, and that Catholic and Jew, Mahometan and Brahmin, Pagan and Protestant, shall alike vie with each other in the noblest exercises of religion—in love to all around them; and meet with one common purpose, in one temple of concord, to praise the same Deity, whether he be reverenced as Jupiter, Mahomet, Bramah, Jehovah, or God!

Having advanced thus much on the philosophical opinions of Shelley, it remains to say a few words respecting his poetical qualifications. He is perhaps the most intensely sublime writer of his day, and, with the exception of Wordsworth, is more highly imaginative, than any other living poet. There is an air of earnestness, a tone of deep sincerity in all his productions, that give them an electrical effect. No one can read his "Prometheus Unbound" or the magnificent "Ode to Liberty" without a sensation of the deepest astonishment at stupendous mind of their author. The mental visions of philosophy contained in them are the most gorgeous that can be conceived, and expressed in language well suited to the sentiment. They soar with an eagle's flight to the heaven of heavens, and come back laden with the treasures of humanity. But with all the combined attractions of mind and verse, we feel that Mr. Shelley can never become a popular poet. He does not sufficiently link himself with man; he is too visionary for the intellect of the generality of his readers, and is ever immersed in the clouds of religious and metaphysical speculations. His opinions are but skeletons, and he does not sufficiently embody them to render them intelligible. They are magnificent abstractions of mind,—the outpourings of a spirit "steeped to the very full" in humanity and religious enthusiasm.

In intensity of description, depth of feeling, and richness of language, Mr. Shelley is infinitely superior to Lord Byron. He has less versatility of talent, but a purer and loftier imagination. His poetry is always adapted to the more kindly and sublime sensibilities of human nature, and enkindles in the breast of the reader a corresponding enthusiasm of benevolence. It gives him an added respect for the literature of his country, and warms his whole soul, as he marks in the writings of his contemporaries the progressive march of the human intellect to the very perfection of divinity. And well indeed may we rejoice at the exalted character our country still retains in the annals of the world. The national spirit which has been so long enfeebled, is now bursting forth in all its meridian splendour; every day augments the number of our poets and literary characters; and the human mind may soon vie with the Angels of Heaven—in the purity and refinement of its intellect. Great days of light and liberty are on the eve of bursting forth with excessive splendour, and the whole world shall bask in its cheering beams. Byron, Shelley, Godwin, Wordsworth, Hazlitt, and many other such glorious spirits, are the bows of promise that shine in the intellectual atmosphere, to predict the dispersal of gloom, and the restoration of unclouded sunshine. Their example even now produces a generous emulation in the breasts of thousands, who will disseminate their principles and their talents with the improvements that age and circumstance may suggest. In exact proportion to the progress of intellect, is the decay of prejudice and fanaticism. Literature has always the effect of enlightening and humanizing the mind, and dispersing the dense clouds of ignorance that hung around it. Thus then, the glorious example of that "bold enquirer," Shelley, will be followed, at no great lapse of time, by the enthusiasm of his votaries, who in their turn will serve as models to the exertions of others; and thus, from one little seed that was sown in good ground, shall spring up a fruitful crop, destined to overshadow the face of the earth, and fatten the natural increase of the land.

VEGETARIANISM REVIVED

[From The London Magazine and Theatrical Inquisitor, July, 1821 (4: 31-35), entitled "Dinner by the Amateurs of Vegetable Diet (Extracted from an Old Paper)."

This humorous skit is a direct burlesque on Shelley's vegetarian note in *Queen Mab*, the pirated edition of which was being reviewed at this time. The starting-point of the present skit is Shelley's sentence in the original note: "Hopes are entertained that, in April, 1814, a statement will be given that sixty persons, all having lived more than three years on vegetables and pure water, are then in perfect health." The talk of P. B. S. in the present essay is paraphrased from Shelley's original note. Two of the characters are also plainly from Shelley's note, Dr. L. and Mr. N. being respectively Dr. Lambe and Mr. J. F. Newton, both of whom Shelley quotes.

The author might be anyone a little cleverer than the usual magazine writer of the period, inspired by the current interest in *Queen Mab*. Several circumstances, however, point generally in the direction of Thomas Love Peacock or T. J. Hogg.

The wit is Peacockian, and the scene is one such as Peacock loved to describe. The writer, like Peacock, loved to quote Greek. Whether or not Peacock had any connections with this periodical I do not know, but it was a magazine conspicuously friendly to Shelley, so that it would not be unreasonable to suppose it might be in touch with one or two of his friends. Peacock had already treated other oddities of Shelley with good-humored satire in *Nightmare Abbey* (1818) in which J. F. Newton also appears as Mr. Toobad. He tells us himself how he improved Shelley's health at Marlow by prevailing on him to relax his vegetarianism. Moreover, in his earlier novel, *Headlong Hall* (1816), he makes Mr. Escot begin a breakfast-table argument about vegetarianism (Chapter 2) in which the same use of the Prometheus myth is made, and in similar language, as that found in the present essay and in Shelley's note. Peacock's intimacy with Shelley began in 1812, while Shelley was writing *Queen Mab*, and he is generally credited with having suggested the reading of two or three books that influenced the poem. If we suppose Peacock to have been the author, then Mr. G., Mr. H. and Mr. L. H., who sat near him, would reasonably become Godwin, Hogg, and Leigh Hunt, who were precisely the men—with the addition of Peacock himself—who did sit nearest to Shelley between 1811 and 1821. If we suppose the author to have been some one outside the circle of Shelley's friends, he would scarcely have known Shelley's intimates and the initials would become meaningless. Mr. L. H., on evidence contained in the essay, *is* clearly Leigh Hunt, a friend of Peacock's for years, whom it would be as natural for Peacock to make fun of as to make fun of Shelley. I am unable, however, to connect Peacock with The London Magazine and Theatrical Inquisitor. Moreover, Peacock's letter of February 28, 1822, to Shelley, states, "I have published nothing since you left England but *Nightmare Abbey* and *The Four Ages of Poetry.*"

The article may have been written by T. J. Hogg, Leigh Hunt, or Horace Smith, all of whom possessed the requisite knowledge of Shelley and all of whom would have found the humorous style congenial to the subject of Shelley's vegetarianism. Moreover, from the time of Peacock's removal to London in 1819 all three were visitors at his lodgings, where they could have become acquainted with Thomas Taylor, who is one of the characters in the skit (*Works of T. L. Peacock*, ed. H. F. B. Brett-Smith and C. E. Jones, London, 1931, pp. xcv and xcviii). I can connect none of them with The London Magazine and Theatrical Inquisitor. This periodical was a continuation of The London Magazine and Monthly Critical and Dramatic Review, for which some of the authors of Baldwin's London Magazine sometimes wrote. All three men had connections with the latter at the time in question. Horace Smith wrote to Shelley on April 3, 1821 (*Book of Shelley and Mary*, III, 598) that he wrote "principally for Baldwin's London Magazine, under various signatures, but generally "H", and Leigh Hunt, in a letter of October 26, 1822, to John Hunt (Sylva Norman, *After Shelley*, 1934, p. xxi) mentions an arrangement previously made by Hazlitt for Hunt and Hogg to write for Baldwin's.

Of the three, Hogg is the most likely to be the author of the present skit. He had associated for a while with Shelley's vegetarian friends and had, like Peacock, a rather special interest in gastronomic subjects. Almost a whole chapter of his later life of Shelley (Chapter 26) is given over to humorous comment on vegetarianism and Shelley's vegetarian friends, making prominent mention of J. F. Newton as "high-priest" of the cult and incidental comment on "Joe Ritson" as a vegetarian. He also makes a similar application of the Prometheus legend to vegetarianism.

The verse, on the other hand, is hard to accept as by Hogg. Peacock might have written it, but it seems much more proper to Horace Smith, who had been conspicuously successful at the same kind of verse in *Rejected Addresses*. Quite possibly the work is the joint product of one of the occasions on which all four men met at this time, either at Peacock's or Hunt's.

The other characters who appear in the skit may be guessed at as follows: Mr. R., the antiquarian—Joseph Ritson (1752-1803); Sir J. S.—Sir James Stephen, the abolitionist (1789-1859); the Rev. P.—William Paley (1743-1805); Mr. T., the Pythagorean philosopher—Thomas Taylor, the Platonist (1758-1835); Mr. B. of Bible celebrity—Bernard Barton (1784-1849) or, more probably, William Blake (1757-1827). Two of these names have a Peacockian connection. Peacock's *Maid Marian* was based on Ritson's *Robin Hood*, and Thomas Taylor was a frequent visitor at Peacock's lodgings after Peacock moved to London in 1819. They would also be equally à propos, as we have seen, if Hogg were the author.]

Lotophagi and men whose heads are not in their right places.

On the 14th of April, 1814, sixty persons, who had lived for more than three years on vegetables and pure water, met for the purpose of felicitating each other on the circumstances of their still being alive. This singular fact excited such an unusual elation of spirits, that it was unanimously resolved that a solemn dinner should be given, to which all the eaters of vegetable diet in the three kingdoms should be invited. One gentleman present observed, that some qualifying clause was necessary in this resolution, for that as it now was worded, it included all the Scotch and Irish, and a considerable portion of the English peasantry, whose diet was entirely uncontaminated by any carnous admixture. He dwelt largely on the difficulty of bringing such a multitude together; and remarked, that if the whole, or even a considerable part, could be assembled, very great terror would be excited in the good City of London and its environs. That such a multitude, from its herbivorous habits, might justly be regarded as worse than the plague of locusts, for that assuredly they would eat up every green thing. Such a measure, he added, would bring upon its adopters the notice of government, and produce at least a suspension of the Habeas Corpus, and an abolition of the right of public meetings. He therefore humbly moved, that the word "amateurs" should be substituted for "eaters." Mr. L. H. (who, though not a vegetable man, yet thought himself entitled to speak at this meeting, from his fondness for tea, and the lighter kind of meats, etc.) rose to reply. He agreed with the gentleman who spoke last, on the inconvenience that would result from so large a meeting—meetings led him to the right of petition and parliamentary reform. In alluding to the diet of the peasants, he observed, that their privation of animal food was obviously a branch of the borough-mongering system. This to be sure was one of its least pernicious results; but it was a result, and as such to be detested. "Timeo Danaos et dona ferentes."— He dilated much on the amiable character of the peasantry. For the Irish peasant in particular he expressed an enthusiastic admiration: "he was so sweetly serious and unvulgar." To the word "amateurs" he objected, as of French growth; commended his own mode of coining words, as having a kind of freshness and springiness about it. Concluded with recommending the word "appetiters" of vegetable diet, as being at once new, expressive, and unvulgar. The motion, however, passed with the amendment first proposed. The dinner was fixed for the 1st of the ensuing month, and the place for dining was Hampstead Heath, it being considered that the open air harmonized best with vegetable diet, and pure water. Some few were of opinion, that the guests ought to come naked in imitation of the primaeval simplicity of the golden age; but to this the majority very seriously objected. A committee was appointed to cater for the amateurs, and various disputes arose therein, regarding what dishes would be admissible, and what not. The earliness of the season left them no great variety of choice in the vegetable world; some therefore contended, that fish might be allowed upon a solemn occasion of this kind. But this proposal was scouted by the rest with the utmost vehemence. One person held out a good while for oysters; asserting that they were to all intents and purposes vegetables: and Mr. L. H. who was admitted as an honorary member, pleaded hard for shrimps and periwinkles. But their eloquence was spent to no purpose. The Catos of the committee remained unshaken.

On the morning of the 1st of May there was not a vegetable left in Covent Garden Market by nine o'clock: all the greengrocers in the north end of town were speedily disburthened of their wares; and an immense number of families in Hampstead, Highgate, and Kentish Town, were left that day without a single potatoe. An advance took place in the price of vegetables, and a single head of cabbage was known to fetch five shillings. At five o'clock the tables were spread, and the guests assembled on Hampstead Heath. Mr. N. was in the chair. Near him sat Dr. L., Mr. R. the antiquarian, Sir J. S., the Rev. P., and Mr. T. the Pythagorean philosopher. Mr. P. B. S. was vice-president; near him was Mr. G., Mr. H., and Mr. L. H., and many others, whom it would be tedious to enumerate. We were very sorry to see some of the more rigid amateurs looking very pale and thin; but they all declared that they enjoyed the most perfect health.

The dinner was composed of such vegetables as were in season. They were generally boiled, though some few rivals of the gymnosophists preferred their cabbage, etc., in a raw state. One sage in particular we remarked with a dish of clover before him, which he devoured with an avidity worthy of Nebuchadnezzar himself. Like the king of Babylon, he appeared to have served a seven years' apprenticeship to the business. There were not many instances of repletion at this dinner. We are sorry, however, to state that one gentleman was obliged to quit the table very soon, being seized with a fit of the colic, and exhibiting all the symptoms of anasarca, the consequence of an inordinate indulgence in cabbage and toast and water.

After dinner, tea was served up with the dessert; and now began the joyous "rout and revelry." The followers of Pythagoras, however rigid in their adherence to his system of diet, were not very scrupulous observers of his principles of taciturnity. Tongues wagged on all sides, and arguments arose thick, fast, and fiery. The silent heath resounded, and appeared on a sudden to be metamorphosed into the palace of noise, the temple of discord—

> Storming fury rose,
> And clamour such as heard on th' Heath till now
> Was never, tongues on tongues loud chattering brayed
> Horrible discord, and the madding throats
> Of brazen poets raged.

How all this might have ended, it is hard to say, if the noise had not suddenly been interrupted and drowned by a more powerful din from the other side of the Heath. This proceeded from a party of brother-amateurs of the long-ear'd kind, who had just commenced after their dinner concert and jollification. This interruption proved a seasonable corrective to the unphilosophic vociferation of our party, and restored them to a becoming consciousness of their two-legged dignity.

Several toasts were then given and drank; and many appropriate songs sung. The president gave, "A return to nature, or, success to vegetable regimen," drank three times three—Song: "Peas, Beans, and Cabbage." The next toast was, "The cultivation of grain, and may it quickly supersede pasturage." Song: "I wish I was a Brewer's Horse." Several other general toasts were given. Mr. L. H. when called on for a song, gave the following with much effect:—

> It was a very pleasant place,
> And smelt delightfully,
> And all the neighb'rhood wore a face
> Of gay yet tearful glee.
> The floweriness of sweet moss roses
> Was strew'd upon the plain;
> And vast abundance of sweet posies
> Fresh gather'd after rain.
> The tops of the grass look cheerily,
> And little daisies spurted up;
> And the dew-drops gleam'd drearily
> In many a buttercup.
> The leafiness around was roarie,
> With all its dancing bowriness;
> And the wood-tops, half green, half hoary,
> Melted in tender showriness.

Mr. P. B. S. then gave, "the memory of Nebuchadnezzar, and may all kings, like him, be speedily sent to graze with their brother brutes." This toast excited much commotion, but was drank at last, without the adjunct, which it was deemed prudent to omit. Mr. B., of Bible-celebrity, observed, that in supposing Nebuchadnezzar to have fed on grass, we are not borne out by the Hebrew text. This he would prove in his intended translation of the Bible. He also took occasion to declare his opinion, that the longevity of mankind before the flood was owing to their feeding on vegetables, not on raw meat, as had been erroneously supposed; but these were points he trusted would be fully cleared up in his treatise on "Antedeluvian Cherubim." Mr. T., the platonist, proposed as a toast, "The reign of Saturn, and speedy restoration to the worship of Heathen Gods"; which, however, was not drank, as it appeared to infringe upon the principles of religious toleration. Many speeches were made in the course of the evening; but we only have to extract a part of that of the vice-president, who, on his health being drank, after returning thanks, thus proceeded:—

"It is with the most infinite satisfaction that I behold assembled together such an illustrious company of enlightened men; all at least favourable to the principles which dictate an abstinence from animal food, and the majority strict observers of a vegetable regimen. The depravity of man is undoubtedly to be sought for in the indulgence of carnivorous propensities. This has been the persuasion of the enlightened of all ages. This fact has been darkly hinted at in the mythology of all religions. The biblical allegory of the forbidden fruit admits of no explanation but this:—The apple of the fatal tree was nothing, gentleman, but a well-dressed beefsteak, whether plain or with oyster-sauce is doubtful. The serpent is a representative of the brute creation. Man is asserted to have bruised his head, when he devoted the race of animals to death, for the gratification of an unnatural appetite: in return, the heel of man was said to have been bruised by the serpent; that is, the indulgence in flesh-diet deprived him of his energy, and reduced him to torpor, disease, and death. The fable of Prometheus may be similarly explained. Prometheus, gentlemen, was a cook of some ability in his day. The gourmands of that time were so delighted with his culinary preparations, that they declared he must have stolen fire from heaven. But he himself fell the first victim to his own pernicious inventions: a vulture preyed upon his liver; that is, he was afflicted with an incurable hepatitis, which tormented him for many years, and finally put a period to his existence. Such, gentlemen, is the brief but emphatic account of the origin of cookery; that fatal science, which has taught the knowledge of so many ills; that accursed tree, whose fruit is poison, that exhaustless fountain, from which man in every age has drank such copious draughts of perdition. Centuries on centuries have rolled away, since Prometheus discovered his execrable art; and centuries on centuries may roll away again, ere his destructive energies shall have ceased to operate. To this we owe the existence of every evil, of every crime. Animal diet is the parent of madness, madness of criminality and vice. To this, gentlemen, we owe the existence of superstition, the abuse called government, the injustice of law, and the abomination of marriage; and every vice that can result from the perversion of nature in our present distempered state of civilization—

> Διὰ τουτον οὐχ ἀδελφὸς,
> Διὰ τουτον οὐ τοχηἐς.
> Πόλεμος, φόνοι δι' αὐτου.
> Τὸ δὲ χἐρον, ὀλλυμεο οὐχ
> Διὰ τουτου οἱ φιλοῦντες.

Yet I confess I entertain some hopes of at least a partial return to natural diet. When I survey the enlightened assembly around me, I cannot entirely despair. In the countenance of our venerable president, I read the fairest promise of the future dietetic reformation of mankind. As Prometheus was the introducer of cooked flesh into the world, so shall Newton be the illustrious restorer of raw vegetables. 'As in Adam all eat meat, so in Newton shall all eat cabbage.' And who, gentlemen, that looks upon us who have fed on vegetables for the last three years, can doubt for a moment the efficacy of our regimen. In the whole of our animal economy, there is nothing to offend the most fastidious acumen of physiological criticism. Our forms are models for the sculptor. The painter might teach his canvas to glow with a more vivid hue, from a contemplation of the bloom that mantles on our cheeks. Our minds—but I sink beneath that inexhaustible subject. 'De Carthagine melius silere puto, quam parum dicere.'

*　　*　　*

"Yes, Gentlemen, the glorious era is approaching, that will fully develop the perfectibility of our nature. The golden age, in which there shall be no such thing as distinction of property, form of government, institution of law, or establishment of religion. When there shall be neither prostitution nor marriage, crime nor punishment, exchange nor robbery. When every man shall live under his own vine and fig-tree and rise, a gentle being from his meal of roots, to propagate around him his own unperverted feelings. I behold, gentlemen, in our worthy president, the harbinger of that glorious day,—the star in the east for the guidance of the wise,—the John the Baptist of the genuine redemption of mankind. Proceed then, unmoved, illustrious man, in thy frugivorous career—macte virtute tua!

> Te duce, si qua manent, sceleris vestigia nostri
> Irrita perpetua solvent formidine terras.

MODERATE APPRECIATION

[From The Retrospective Review, 1820 (2:204, part 1). A digression on living poets in a review of Wallace's "Various Prospects of Mankind, Nature, and Providence." Shelley read the number in which this notice occurs and found it pleasing, but made no mention of the notice of himself.]

Shelley, too, notwithstanding the odious subject of his last tragedy, evinced in that strange work a real human power, of which there is little trace among the cold allegories and metaphysical splendours of his earlier productions. No one can fail to perceive, that there are mighty elements in his genius, although there is a melancholy want of a presiding power—a central harmony—in his soul. Indeed, rich as the present age is in poetry, it is even richer in promise.

HAZLITT PRONOUNCES

[From an essay "On Paradox and Commonplace," which was published in *Table Talk*, 1821-22. The essay is commented upon in The London Magazine for May, 1821 (3: 549). Hazlitt's opinions of Shelley are more completely expressed in his review of *Posthumous Poems of Percy Bysshe Shelley*, in The Edinburgh Review for July, 1824 (40: 494-514).
Leigh Hunt's letters to the Shelleys show his indignation at Hazlitt's comments on Shelley in The London Magazine. He protested to Hazlitt and even threatened to attack him in print if he persisted.]

The author of the Prometheus Unbound (to take an individual instance of the last character) has a fire in his eye, a fever in his blood, a maggot in his brain, a hectic flutter in his speech, which mark out the philosophic fanatic. He is sanguine-complexioned, and shrill-voiced. As is often observable in the case of religious enthusiasts, there is a slenderness of constitutional *stamina*, which renders the flesh no match for the spirit. His bending, flexible form appears to take no strong hold of things, does not grapple with the world about him, but slides from it like a river—

> And in its liquid texture mortal wound
> Receives no more than can the fluid air.

The shock of accident, the weight of authority make no impression on his opinions, which retire like a feather, or rise from the encounter unhurt, through their own buoyancy. He is clogged by no dull system of realities, no earth-bound feelings, no rooted prejudices, by nothing that belongs to the mighty trunk and hard husk of nature and habit, but is drawn up by irresistible levity to the regions of mere speculation and fancy, to the sphere of air and fire, where his delighted spirit floats in "seas of pearl and clouds of amber." There is no *caput mortuum* of worn-out, thread-bare experience to serve as ballast to his mind; it is all volatile intellectual salt of tartar, that refuses to combine its evanescent, inflammable essence with any thing solid or any thing lasting. Bubbles are to him the only realities:— touch them, and they vanish. Curiosity is the only proper category of his mind, and though a man in knowledge, he is a child in feeling. Hence he puts every thing into a metaphysical crucible to judge of it himself and exhibit it to others as a subject of interesting experiment, without first making it over to the ordeal of his common sense or trying it on his heart. This faculty of speculating at random on all questions may in its overgrown and uninformed state do much mischief without intending it, like an overgrown child with the power of a man. Mr. Shelley has been accused of vanity—I think he is chargeable with extreme levity; but this levity is so great, that I do not believe he is sensible of its consequences. He strives to overturn all established creeds and systems: but this is in him an effect of constitution. He runs before the most extravagant opinions, but this is because he is held back by none of the merely mechanical checks of sympathy and habit. He tampers with all sorts of obnoxious subjects, but it is less because he is gratified with the rankness of the taint, than captivated with the intellectual phosphoric light they emit. It would seem that he wished not so much to convince or inform as to shock the public by the tenor of his productions, but I suspect he is more intent upon startling himself with his electrical experiments in morals and philosophy; and though they may scorch other people, they are to him harmless amusements, the coruscations of an Aurora Borealis, that 'play round the head, but do not reach the heart.' Still I could wish that he would put a stop to the incessant, alarming whirl of his Voltaic battery. With his zeal, his talent, and his fancy, he would do more good and less harm, if he were to give up his wilder theories, and if he took less pleasure in feeling his heart flutter in unison with the panic-struck apprehensions of his readers. Persons of this class, instead of consolidating useful and acknowledged truths, and thus advancing the cause of science and virtue, are never easy but in raising doubtful and disagreeable questions, which bring the former into disgrace and discredit. They are not contented to lead the minds of men to an eminence overlooking the prospect of social amelioration, unless, by forcing them up slippery paths and to the utmost verge of possibility, they can dash them down the precipice the instant they reach the promised Pisgah. They think it nothing to hang up a beacon to guide or warn, if they do not at the same time frighten the community like a comet. They do not mind making their principles odious, provided they can make themselves notorious. To win over the public opinion by fair means is to them an insipid, commonplace mode of popularity: they would either force it by harsh methods, or seduce it by intoxicating potions. Egotism, petulance, licentiousness, levity of principle (whatever be the source) is a bad thing in any one, and most of all, in a philosophical reformer. Their humanity, their wisdom is always "at the horizon." Any thing new, any thing remote, any thing questionable, comes to them in a shape that is sure of a cordial welcome—a welcome cordial in proportion as the object is new, as it is apparently impracticable, as it is a doubt whether it is at all desirable. Just after the final failure, the completion of the last act of the French Revolution, when the legitimate wits were crying out, "The farce is over, now let us go to supper," these provoking reasoners got up a lively hypothesis about introducing the domestic government of the Nayrs into this country as a feasible set-off against the success of the Boroughmongers. The practical is with them always the antipodes of the ideal; and like other visionaries of a different stamp, they date the Millennium or New Order of Things from the Restoration of the Bourbons. Fine words butter no parsnips, says the proverb. "While you are talking of marrying, I am thinking of hanging," says Captain Macheath. Of all people the most tormenting are those who bid you hope in the midst of despair, who, by never caring about any thing but their own sanguine, hair-brained Utopian schemes, have at no time any particular cause for embarrassment and despondency because they have never the least chance of success, and who by including whatever does not hit their idle fancy, kings, priests, religion, government, public abuses or private morals, in the same sweeping clause of ban and anathema, do all they can to combine all parties in a common cause against them, and to prevent every one else from advancing one step farther in the career of practical improvement than they do in that of imaginary and unattainable perfection.

PASSING COMMENT FROM THE LONDON MAGAZINE

A

[From The London Magazine, January, 1821 (3:68), under Town Conversation, headed "Mr. Shelley."]

A friend of ours writes us from Italy, that Mr. Shelley, the author of that powerful drama, "The Cenci," is employed upon an English Historical Tragedy. The title, we believe, is to be *Charles the First;* at any rate, that monarch is the hero or principal person of the story. We hear that Mr. Shelley has expressed his determination to paint a true portrait of the unfortunate English King (it may be made a very captivating one) and to exclude from his work all prejudice, political as well as moral. If so, the reader of poetry may calculate on being acquainted with a high and imperishable production. We differ entirely with the creeds of Mr. Shelley; but we do not on that account refrain from confessing, that he is unquestionably one of the very first of our now living English poets. We wish most heartily that we could bestow on his poetry our praise without qualification; but we cannot.

B

[From The London Magazine, April, 1821 (3:370). From an essay entitled "Table Talk."]

No one (that I know of) is the happier, better, or wiser for reading Mr. Shelley's *Prometheus Unbound.* One thing is that nobody reads it. And the reason for one or both is the same, that he is not a poet, but a sophist, a theorist, a controversial writer in verse. He gives us for representations of things, rhapsodies of words. He does not lend the colours of imagination and the ornaments of style to the objects of nature, but paints gaudy, flimsy, allegorical pictures on gauze, on the cobwebs of his own brain, "Gorgons, Hydras, and Chimaeras dire." He assumes certain doubtful speculative notions, and proceeds to prove their truth by describing them in detail as matters of fact. This mixture of fanatic zeal and poetical licentiousness is not quite the thing.

[*Here follows the essayist's philosophy of what the poet should describe, why and how*]

A VOICE FROM ETON

[From The Etonian, August, 1821 (2:326), entitled "On Etonian Poets."
This paragraph on Shelley is sandwiched between half a page of praise of Milman and two pages praising a poem by E. T. S. Hornsby, entitled "Childhood," the repose of which seems to the author a welcome relief from the "glare and excitement" of *The Cenci*. The article is signed P. C. According to an anonymous, but apparently well-informed writer in The Times Literary Supplement, January 2, 1930 (p. 9), P. C. was W. M. Praed.]

Shall I turn to Shelley?—Yes!—No!—Yes!—I wish that such a mind had not ranked itself among those depraved Spirits, who make it doubtful whether we should more admire their powers, or lament and condemn the abuse of them!—that he had rested contented with the admiration, without extorting the censure, of mankind. He is one of the many whom we cannot read without wonder, or without pain: when I consider his powers of mind, I am proud that he was an Etonian; when I remember their perversion, I wish he had never been one. However, he has made his election; and where Justice cannot approve, Charity can at least be silent!

THE CHAMPION EXPLAINS

[From The Champion, December 23, 1821 (no. 468, p. 815). The idea that Shelley's poetry suffered by being insufficiently objective was shared by Leigh Hunt, John Keats, Horace Smith and Mary Shelley.]

It is our opinion, that the poetical merits of Mr. Percy Byshe [sic] Shelly [sic] have never been duly appreciated by the public. This neglect (for, in reality, it amounts to that) is chiefly to be attributed to himself. He writes in a spirit which the *million* do not comprehend: there is something too mystical in what he says—something too high or too deep for common comprehensions. He lives in a very remote poetical world, and his feelings will scarcely bear to be shadowed out in earthly light. There are, no doubt, in the mind of a poet, and none will be found to deny their existence in the mind of Mr. Shelley, shades of thought which defy the power of delineation, and feelings which it is impossible to lay before the reader in expressions sufficiently lucid; when, therefore, he attempts to clothe these ideas with words, tho he may *himself* perceive the force of them, it will not unfrequently happen, that his readers cannot; or that such words, at most, will only convey a very imperfect and shadowy idea of the lofty meanings which the writer attached to them. This is no fault peculiar to Mr. Shelley—*the finest geniuses have felt it most;* and in reading many passages of Shakespeare, if we were called upon for a definition of the exact meaning of some of his most beautiful sentences, we should be obliged to declare the utter impossibility of doing so. Expressions of this kind not unfrequently occur in the works of Mr. Shelley, and, in our opinion, his sentiments are sometimes equally obscure. The first poem which he published,[2] tho containing many exquisite passages, abounds with these dimly shadowed feelings, and we seem, while perusing it, as if we were walking thro' a country where beautiful prospects extend on every side, which are nearly hidden from us by the mists of evening. Mr. Shelley seems to nurse this wildness of imagination, at the expense of perspicuity and vigour of style. The same spirit appears strikingly manifest in every page of his longest poem,[3] in which he undertakes to teach every great principle—freedom, patriotism, philanthropy, toleration—under an allegory; or, to make use of his own words, "for this purpose I have chosen a story of human passion in its most universal character, diversified with moving and romantic adventures, and appealing, in contempt of all artificial opinions or institutions, to the common sympathies of every human breast."

[2] *Alastor; or, the Spirit of Solitude.* (Reviewer's footnote.)
[3] *The Revolt of Islam.* (Reviewer's footnote.)

So fully convinced was Mr. Shelley, that this poem was qualified to accomplish the philanthropic object for which it was written, that he actually wished that a cheap edition of it should be printed, in order that it might be within the reach of all classes of persons; certainly one of the wildest of his imaginations. If he desired popularity, he should have written in a style intelligible to common understandings.

J. W.

X

EPIPSYCHIDION

THE GOSSIP MIXES PRAISE AND CENSURE

[From The Gossip, June 23, 1821 (n. 17, pp. 129-135).]

THIS IS A very singular production, abounding with poetic beauties, lax morality, and wild incoherent fancies. Of the latter our readers may judge from the following lines. . . .

[*Quotes lines 190-216, describing the poet's ideal "Being"*]

In search of this Being he went forth with hope and fear. . . .

[*Quotes lines 247-266, 321-344, and 75-111, describing the first disappointment in the poet's search, the meeting of Ideal Beauty in Emily, and the effect of Emily's beauty*]

With this lady it was his intention to have gone "to one of the wildest of the Sporades, where he had fitted up the ruins of an old building"; and where they might have possibly lived together for a few weeks in contentment and ecstasy, and then have become as anxious to return to society as they had been to leave it. The island is exquisitely described. . . .

[*Quotes lines 422-423, 435-476, 484-514, and 529-549, describing the island and its mansion*]

The descriptions which follow we must refrain from inserting, as the author's morality and delicacy seem

> Confused in passion's golden purity.

We now arrive at the conclusion of his wishes:

> One hope between two wills, one will beneath
> Two overshadowing minds, one life, one death,
> One Heaven, one Hell, one immortality,
> And one annihilation.

This is his feeling for the moment; but the author appears to be a selfish being, who, with all his professed admiration of female beauty and excellence, has no desire to be confined in his connection.

[*Quotes lines 149-159 and 169-173, Shelley's idea of free love*]

He totally overlooks the vast difference in the situation of the two, on returning to society when tired of each other. To what part could a female turn for protection and respect, after an experiment of this kind?

The author himself, we believe, would not be disposed to extend his protection under such circumstances to one so situated, and appears much too delicate to contemplate the idea of forming any attachment to one whose first love had been bestowed on another. She would be a lone widow in the prime of life, neglected, and scorned; while the sources of pleasure and honour would be open to her companion as freely as ever, and fresh victims ready for his solitudes. As usual, with those who depart from the common rules of life, he affects a contempt for all who do not enter into his feelings, that "certain other class to whom it must ever remain incomprehensible, from a defect of a *common organ of perception* for the ideas of which it treats."

> My Song, I fear that thou wilt find but few
> Who fitly shall conceive thy reasoning,
> Of such hard matter dost thou entertain;
> Whence, if by misadventure, chance should bring
> Thee to base company (as chance may do),
> Quite unaware of what thou dost contain,
> I prithee, comfort thy sweet self again,
> My last delight! tell them that they are dull,
> And bid them own that thou art beautiful.

The genius and feelings of the author will be readily perceived from the extracts we have given; and with high admiration of his poetic talents, we close his poem with a pang of regret that his mind should be harrassed and wasted on such wild and impracticable schemes of happiness, totally at variance with the experience of mankind, and the interests of society.

THE GOSSIP ENJOYS SHELLEY'S STYLE

[From The Gossip, July 14, 1821 (no. 20, pp. 153-159), entitled "Seraphina and Her Sister Clementina's Review of Epipsychidion."]

SIR,

I and my sister Clementina were sitting on the sofa on which we had often sat in days of "childhood innocence," and

> like two artificial gods
> Created with our needles both one flower,
> Both on one sampler, sitting on one cushion;
> Both warbling of one song, both in one key;
> As if our hands, our sides, voices, and minds
> Had been incorporate,—

When a gentleman, who had long been an admirer of Clementina, entered with the Seventeenth Number of the Gossip.

We were reading Goldsmith's delightful poem of the Deserted Village, and had finished that part of it which describes the fond mother who

> Kiss'd her thoughtless babes with many a tear,
> And clasp'd them close, in sorrow doubly dear,

Just as the gentleman made his appearance; and at the same instant the tears which were trembling in Clementina's fine blue eyes, being forced by a gentle sigh to quit their sapphire spheres, fell glistening on her bosom. "What," exclaimed the gentleman, "Clementina in tears!" He might well be surprised, for my lively sister is much more inclined to the laughing than the "melting mood," though she has a heart susceptible of the finest emotions. I explained to him the cause, and desired him to say something pretty and poetical on the occasion. He immediately pronounced the following impromptu:

> I've seen the tear in beauty's eye,
>   Await the sob suppress'd,
> There, shaken by a trem'lous sigh,
>   Fall on the heaving breast.
> Oh! how I've wished that I might kiss
>   The pearly drop away,
> And give the heart a sweeter bliss,
>   The eye a brighter ray.

Clementina put her fan to his lips, bid him hold his saucy tongue, and let her hear what the Gossip had to say, which she was sure would be more entertaining than his nambypamby poetry. He told her it contained extracts from a poem which he believed would excite emotions very different from those produced by the beautiful lines of Goldsmith.

I seized the number, for I am passionately fond of poetry. It contained a review of Epipsychidion. I read the first extract—but did not understand it. "It is poetry *intoxicated*," said Clementina. "It is poetry in *delirium*," said I. "It is a new system of poetry," said the gentleman, "which may be taught by a few simple rules, and when it is learned it may be written by the league." "But in that case," said Clementina, "it would be as well to be provided with a pair of seven-league boots." "It is the poetical currency of the day," said the gentleman.

> A plague on him who did refine it,
> A plague on him who first did coin it,

said Clementina, altering a word in Dryden's couplet. But she is a wild creature, as you well know, from the strange letter which she sent you, and in which she accuses me of making dress my *hobby*. She is a great fibber. Poetry is *my* hobby—yes, poetry, "sweet poetry, dear charming nymph"! But not such poetry as Epipsychidion. "Bless me!" said Clementina," what a number of adjectives, and how strangely coupled with nouns! Only hear—"Odours deep, odours warm, warm fragrance, wild odour, arrowy odour; golden prime, golden purity, golden immortality; living morning, living light, living cheeks; wintry forest, wintry wilderness; blue Ionian weather, blue nightshade, blue heavens; (good Heavens!) wonder-level dream, tremulous floor, unentangled intermixture, crimson pulse, fiery dews, delicious pain; green heart, green immortality, withered hours." "I have not repeated a hundredth part of them," said she, quite out of breath. The gentleman observed, "It is a species of poetry that excites no emotion but that of wonder—we wonder what it means! It lives without the vitality of life; it has animation but no heart; it worships nature but spurns her laws; it sinks without gravity and rises without levity. Its shadows are substances, and its substances are shadows. Its odours may be felt, and its sounds may be penetrated—its frosts have the melting quality of fire, and its fire may be melted by frost. Its animate beings are inanimate things, and its local habitations have no existence. It is a system of poetry made up of adjectives, broken metaphors, and indiscriminate personifications. In this poetry everything must live, and move, and have a being, and they must live and move with intensity of action and passion, though they have their origin and their end in nothing."

"It is a poetical phantasmagoria," said Clementina. "Whatever is possible to our imaginations, or in our dreams," said the gentleman, "is possible, probable, and of common occurrence in this new system of poetry. Things may exchange their nature, they may all have a new nature, or have no nature." "Then they must be non-naturals," said Clementina. "There is a new omnipotence in this poetry," said the gentleman, "things may do impossibilities with, or without impossible powers—this is the *ne plus ultra* of poetical omnipotence."

I read the extract again, with more attention—but, to use the author's phraseology, it was "too deep for the brief fathom-line of thought or sense." It appears that there was a Being whom the spirit oft met on its "visioned wanderings," which it seemed were "far aloft." It met him on fairy isles, and among a great variety of other strange places, "in the air-like waves of wonder-level dream, whose tremulous floor paved her light steps." This is, indeed, metaphor run mad. To pave a person's steps is certainly strange; but for the tremulous floor of wonder-level dream to pave them is wondrous strange indeed. "Steps for path," said the gentleman, "is to me a new metonymy, and the tremulous floor of wonder-level dream is either a new pavior or a new pavement." "It is *immaterial* be it which it may," said Clementina. Did the malapert mean to *pun*, think you? But to proceed—the voice of this Being came to him "through the whispering woods, and from the fountains, and from the *odours* deep of flowers." "How can a voice come from the odour of flowers?" asked Clementina, "can an odour emit, or convey a sound?" "That is one of the possible impossibilities of the omnipotence of this new poetry," said the gentleman. "I do not understand it," said Clementina. "Do you understand metaphysics?" said he. "No," replied she, "but

> I know what's what, and that's as high
> As metaphysicist can fly!

Did you ever know such a giddy creature? I proceeded—this voice came to him from "the breezes, whether low or loud, and from the rain of every passing cloud." "Bless me," said Clementina, "he might have said to this voice what Falstaff says to Prince Henry." "What is that?" said the gentleman. "Something about iteration,"[1] said Clementina. The gentleman laughed. I went on—"the voice came from the singing of the summer birds, and from *all* sounds, and from *all* silence!" "She was the most extraordinary ventriloquist I ever heard of," said Clementina. I now came to the second extract, and read as follows:

> And every gentle passion sick to death
> *Feeding* my *course* with expectation's breath,
> Into the wintry forest of our lives.

Here I could not help asking how a course, or track, could be fed, and that too with expectation's breath. But allowing the incongruous metaphor of feeding a course, how could it be fed into a forest?" "A man may be fed into a fever," said Clementina. "I am inclined to think," said the gentleman, "from the pointing of the passage, the meaning of it is, that while he was diverting his course into the wintry forest, he was feeding it with the breath of expectation." "Well," said Clementina, "you have helped a lame dog over a stile, but he walks as lamely as he did before. Your elucidation of the passage reminds me of La Bruyere's famous French wit, who made it a rule never to be *posed* upon any occasion! and being asked a little abruptly, what was the difference between dryads and hamadryads, answered very readily, 'You have heard of your bishops and your archbishops'." "Dryden," said I, (wishing to put a stop to my sister's pertness) "has been ridiculed for writing the following couplet:

> Yet when that flood in its own depths was drowned,
> It left behind its false and slippery ground.

Here, it has been observed, we have a drowned flood; and what is more extraordinary, a flood so excessively deep that it drowned itself. But in my opinion when a flood, which has overflowed lands, is receding into a greater depth, so as to contract its breadth, and surface, it is not a more extravagant figure of speech to say that it has drowned itself in its own depths, and left its false and slippery ground behind, than it is to talk of feeding a man's course with expectation's breath; the metaphors are equally heterogeneous and extravagant." "Before we employ any figure," said the gentleman, "we should consider what sort of a picture it would make on canvas. How an artist could paint the feeding of a man's course with the breath of expectation, I cannot conceive!" I went on with my reading, and came to one "Whose voice was venomed melody." "Then the creature must have poured poison into the porches of his ears," said Clementina. I went on—"Flame out of her looks into my *vitals* came." "Flame out of her looks!" exclaimed Clementina. "Flame might come out of her mouth, or out of her eyes, or out of her nostrils, as I think it did from that shocking creature's, the Dragon of Wantley; but the looks are a mere modality, and he might as well have said that flame came not from

<hr>

[1] No doubt Clementina's allusion was to Falstaff's saying to Prince Henry, "Thou hast damnable iteration." (Reviewer's footnote.)

her face, but merely from its length, or its breadth. Flame from her looks! they must have been fiery indeed!" I continued—

> And from her living cheeks and bosom flew
> A killing air, which pierced like honey dew
> Into the core of my green heart, and lay
> Upon its leaves.

Here I stopped to ask what he could mean by a *green* heart with leaves. "Oh, he means the heart of a cabbage, to be sure," said Clementina. "But the heart of a cabbage is generally white," said the gentleman. "This green heart with leaves would be a bad figure to paint on canvas." "It would look like an *heart*ychoke," said Clementina. I now read without interruption till I came to those lines—

> And music from her respiration spread
> Like light,—all other sounds were penetrated
> By the small still spirit of that sound.

Bless me! can a sound be penetrated? And what can the spirit of a sound be? "That," said Clementina, "must be the ghost that is said to have appeared in the sound of a drum." I laughed at the oddness of the conceit, and read till I came to the following lines:

> I stood, and felt the dawn of my long night,
> Was penetrating me with living light.

"It is darkness becoming visible," said Clementina. "How can that be?" "Why you know," continued she, "the dawn of day is *light* becoming visible, consequently, the dawn of night must be darkness becoming visible." "But you must observe that this dawn of night was penetrating him with a *living light*." "A living light!—that must have been a *glow-worm* creeping among the leaves of his green heart," said Clementina. I now proceeded to make my way through a crowd of disjointed figures that darkened the subject they were intended to illumine, till I arrived at

> The glory of her being, issuing thence,
> Stains the dead, blank cold air with a warm shade
> Of unentangled intermixture, made
> By love, of life and motion; one intense
> Diffusion, one serene omniprescence,
> Whose flowing outlines mingle in their flowing
> Around her cheeks. . . .

"How can light and motion be so mixed up as to stain the cold night with a warm shade, I do not know," said Clementina, "but the flowing *outlines* of omnipresence must be in the circumference of infinite space." "The circumference of infinite space," said the gentleman, "is nowhere, though its centre is everywhere." But what is a flowing outline in a centre? "An eccentric line," said Clementina. What an eccentric creature! I continued my reading.

> Warm fragrance seems to fall from her light dress—

"Well," said my sprightly sister, "her dress must be much lighter and cooler after the warm fragrance has fallen from it—pray proceed."

> The sweetness seems to satiate the faint wind;
> And in the soul a wild odour is felt
> Beyond the sense.

Here I could not help asking how an odour could be felt. But, allowing the metaphor, what does he mean by its being felt beyond the sense? Does he mean beyond sense of feeling or sense of smelling? "He means beyond *all* sense," said Clementina. I asked what was beyond all sense. "Nonsense, to be sure," said she. But he does not mean nonsense. "I don't pretend to know what he means," said she, "I am now only speaking of what he writes. But he says it is felt in the heart, "like fiery dews that melt in the bosom of the frozen bud." Now admitting that there may be fire-dew as well as honey-dew, I cannot conceive how fire can melt it in frost, though I know from experience that frost will melt in fire. "Dryden," said our visitor, "has produced a similar line as example of excellent imagining:

> Cherubs dissolv'd in Hallelujahs lie.

"Well, I have heard of anchovies dissolved in sauce; but never angels in hallelujahs," said Clementina. But, putting on a serious look, she continued, "when you read such poetry you may say, as the college lad expressed himself by a happy blunder, 'I read six hours a day and no one is the wiser!'" I acknowledged the justness of her remark, threw down the number, and retired to my chamber to write this letter.

SERAPHINA

St. James's Square.

CHRISTOPHER NORTH DETECTS THE AUTHOR

[From Blackwood's Edinburgh Magazine, February, 1822 (11:237-238). The heading is: "Letter from London. Piccadilly, London, February 10, 1822. To C. North, Esq., Edinburgh." The date shows that this number of Blackwood's, as was not uncommon, appeared late.

After two and a half columns of general literary chat the article deals with Shelley as follows.]

You must be careful how you wreak your disdain on the principles of Lord Byron's later poetry, as he will soon have it in his power to make fierce reprisals on you and the other *dissenters*. You have perhaps heard of the Journal which it is to be written by him at Pisa, and sent over here for publication, in order that the balance of critical power may be restored, which has preponderated lately too much on the Tory side. In this great undertaking he has called to himself two allies, namely, Mr. Bysshe Shelley and Mr. Leigh Hunt, the latter of whom has abandoned his suburban villa, (No. 13, Lisson Grove North,) to brave, with his wife and "Little Johnnys," a perilous voyage on the un-cockney ocean. The sphere of this poet's experience will now be nobly enlarged. No one must twist him any more about "poplar rows" and "back gardens." He and his companions will now, like his own Nereids,

turn
And toss upon the ocean's lifting billows,
Making them *banks and pillows*,
Upon whose *springiness* they lean and ride;
Some with an *inward back*; some *upward-eyed*,
Feeling the sky; and some with *sidelong hips*,
O'er which the surface of the water slips.
(*Foliage*, p. xix.)

His lordship of Newstead has sent Leigh a subsidy, and has likewise prepared, in a costly way, the lower part of his Pisan residence for the reception of his London ally. This is certainly very noble on the part of Byron; and if the story be true about the deception he had recourse to the other day, in order to serve a celebrated brother poet, who was invincibly punctilious, it is impossible to extol too highly his munificence and delicacy. I am glad to behold him arming himself, and I hope we shall see a "good fight." Southey does not go the right way to work with him. I have better confidence in your judgment and mettle.

Did it ever fall in your way to see a poem with this title, "Epipsychidion: Verses addressed to the noble and unfortunate Lady Emilia V—, now imprisoned in the convent of ——?" This little pamphlet is a three-fold curiosity, on account of the impenetrable mysticism of its greater portion, the delicious beauty of the rest, and the object of the whole, which I take to be an endeavour to set aside the divine prohibition, that a man may not marry his own sister.[2] The poem was published anonymously,

Our readers will probably suspect, that our correspondent's intention is to attribute the poem in question to Lord Byron; but we venture to say, that there is nobody capable of wasting such poetry on such a theme, except only the unfortunate Mr. Shelley. To this gentleman's genius we have always done justice; and hitherto we have really avoided—what the *Quarterly* (that contained in one Number, a string of filthy stories about him, boy and man) has more recently had the audacity *to say* it has avoided—the smallest allusion to his private character. But Percy Bysshe Shelley has now published a long series of poems, the only object of which seems to be the promotion of ATHEISM and INCEST; and we can no longer hesitate to avow our belief, that he is as worthy of co-operating with the King of Cockaigne, as he is unworthy of co-operating with Lord Byron. Shelley is a man of genius, but he has no sort of sense or judgment. He is merely "an inspired idiot!" Leigh Hunt is a man of talents, but vanity and vulgarity neutralize all his efforts to pollute the public mind. Lord Byron we regard as not only a man of lofty genius, but of great shrewdness and knowledge of the world. What can HE seriously hope from associating his name with such people as these? CAIN is in some parts a reprehensibe performance, but what a gulf profound between it and Queen Mab, or the Cenci, or this Epipsychidion!

Since we have mentioned Cain, we must say that the conduct of the Lord Chancellor, in regard to that poem, has filled us both with wonder and regret. The property of Cain, we humbly think, ought to have been protected. In Mr. Murray's hands, it was a book for gentlemen; but the Benbows will send it on tea-paper into the pothouses, where nothing of it will be properly understood, and much of it absurdly misunderstood. There will now be an opportunity, however, for seeing on what principles the Constitutional Society really acts. C. North.

but as people began to apply it to a certain individual, and make their own inferences, it was, I believe, suddenly withdrawn from circulation. There is no doubt that it comes from the Holy Pisan Alliance; and some of its insulated passages are worthy of the genius which dwells among the members of that body. I read this poem last night at the hushed and sleeping hour of twelve, and never was I so enchanted as in wandering among its strange, etherial, dreamy fancies, some of which contain, in my opinion, the very soul and essence of ideal poesy. The following is the description of the place whither the poet proposes to fly with his mysterious mistress.

It is an isle under Ionian skies,
Beautiful as a wreck of Paradise;
And, for the harbours are not safe and good,
This land would have remain'd a solitude,
But for some pastoral people native there,
Who from the Elysian, clear, and golden air,
Draw the last spirit of the age of gold,
Simple and spirited, innocent and bold.
The blue Aegean girds this chosen home,
With ever-changing sounds, and light, and foam,
Kissing the sifted sands, and caverns hoar;
And all the winds wandering along the shore
Undulate with the undulating tide.
There are thick woods, where sylvan forms abide;
And many a fountain, rivulet, and pond,
As clear as elemental diamond,
Or serene morning air; and, far beyond,
The mossy tracks made by the goats and deer,
(Which the rough shepherd treads but once a-year,)
Pierce into glades, caverns, bowers, and halls,
Built 'round with ivy, which the waterfalls
Illuming, with sound that never fails,
Accompany the noon-day nightingales;
And all the place is peopled with sweet airs;
The light clear element which the isle wears,
Is heavy with the scent of lemon flowers,
  -   -   -   -   -   -   -   -
  -   -   -   -   and from the sky
There fall clear exhalations, soft and bright,
Veil after veil, each hiding some delight,
Which sun or moon or zephyr draw aside,
Till the isle's beauty, like a naked bride,
Glowing at once with love and loveliness,
Blushes and trembles at its own excess.

The poet then describes a house built by some primeval being for the residence of his *"sister and his spouse,"* in which description the following exquisite lines occur:

Parasite flowers illume with dewy gems
The lampless halls, and when they fade, the sky
Peeps through their winter-woof of tracery,
With moonlight patches, or star-atoms keen,
Or fragments of the day's intense serene;—
Working mosaic on their Parian floors.
-   -   -   -   -   -   -   -   -   -
This isle and house are mine, and I have vow'd
Thee to be lady of the solitude;
And I have fitted up some chambers there,
Looking toward the golden eastern air,
And level with the living winds.

[*The remaining two columns are not connected with Shelley.   The letter is signed:*]

Ever yours, my dear Sir,
JOHN JOHNES.

A FOREIGN NOTICE

[From The Paris Monthly Review, March 1822 (1:355), entitled "Extract from a Poem Called 'Epipsychidion'," etc.   It seems also to have been an "extract" from Blackwood's account of the same poem.]

This poem was published anonymously: but as people began to apply it to a certain individual, and make their own inferences, it was suddenly withdrawn.   The following passage is full of delicious beauty, and breathes the very soul and essence of ideal poesy.   It is the description of the place whither the poet proposes to fly with his mysterious mistress.

[*Quotes lines 422-476*]

The poet then describes a house built by some primeval being for the residence of his mistress; in which description the following exquisite lines occur.

[*Quotes lines 502-517, omitting 507-513*]

XI

Adonais and Hellas

I

"TRANSCENDANT MERIT"

[From The Literary Chronicle and Weekly Review, December 1, 1821 (no. 133, pp. 751-754). Shelley sent copies of *Adonais* to the Olliers and to Thomas Love Peacock by his friend John Gisborne, whose arrival in England probably preceded the edition sent by freight. It is probably to one of these men that The Literary Chronicle refers in the first sentence. This is the first publication of *Adonais*.

Shelley was particularly interested in the reception of *Adonais*, but there is no record of any reviews having reached him before his death, unless his letter of April 10, 1822, to John Gisborne, is to be taken as an indication that he had read the unfavorable reviews.]

Through the kindness of a friend we have been favored with the production of a gentleman of no ordinary genius, Mr. Bysshe Shelley. It is an elegy on the death of a youthful poet of considerable promise, Mr. Keats, and was printed at Pisa. As the copy now before us is, perhaps, the only one that has reached England, and the subject is one that will excite much interest, we shall print the whole of it.

It has been often said, and Mr. Shelley repeats the assertion, that Mr. Keats fell a victim to his too great susceptibility of a severe criticism of one of his poems. How far this may have been the case we know not. Cumberland used to say, that authors should not be thin skinned, but shelled like the rhinoceros; but poor Keats was of too gentle a disposition for severity, and to a mind of such exquisite sensibility, we do not wonder that he felt keenly the harsh and ungenerous attack that was made upon him. Besides, we are not without instances of the effects of criticism upon some minds.—Hawkesworth died of criticism: when he published his account of voyages in the South Seas, for which he received £6,000, and innumerable hosts of enemies attacked it in the newspapers and magazines; some pointed out blunders in matters of science, and some exercised their wit in poetical translations and epigrams. "It was," says Dr. Kippis, "a fatal undertaking, and which, in its consequences, deprived him of presence of mind and of life itself."

Tasso was driven mad by criticism; his susceptibility and tenderness of feeling were so great, that when his sublime work, *Jerusalem Delivered*, met with unexpected opposition, the fortitude of the poet was not proof against the keenness of disappointment. He twice attempted to please his ignorant and malignant critics, by recomposing his poem; and, during the

[285]

hurry, the anguish, and the irritation attending these efforts, the vigour of a great mind was entirely exhausted, and, in two years after the publication of his work, the unhappy bard became an object of pity and terror.

Even the mild Newton, with all his philosophy, was so sensible to critical remarks, that Whiston tells us he lost his favour, which he had enjoyed for twenty years, for contradicting Newton in his old age; for, says he, no man was of "a more fearful temper." Whiston declares that he would never have thought proper to have published his work against Newton's chronology during the life of the great philosopher, "because," says he, "I knew his temper so well, that I should have expected it would have killed him."

We have never been among the very enthusiastic admirers of Mr. Keats's poetry, though we allow that he possessed considerable genius; but we are decidedly averse to that species of literary condemnation, which is often practised by men of wit and arrogance, without feeling and without discrimination.

Mr. Shelley is an ardent admirer of Keats; and though he declares his repugnance to the principles of taste on which several of his earlier compositions were modelled, he says that he considers "the fragment of Hyperion as second to nothing that was ever produced by a writer of the same years." Mr. Shelley, in the Preface, gives some details respecting the poet. . . .

[*Quotes all but the first paragraph of Shelley's Preface, footnoting Shelley's reference to "those on whom he wasted the promise of his genius" thus: We do not know to whom Mr. Shelley alludes; but we believe that we may say that the city of London does not boast a bookseller more honorable in his dealings or more liberal to rising genius or indigent merit than the publishers of Mr. Keats's poems.—Ed.*]

Of the beauty of Mr. Shelley's elegy we shall not speak; to every poetic mind its transcendant merits must be apparent.

[*Quotes the whole of* Adonais, *except stanzas 19-24*]

NONSENSE AND IMPIETY

[From The Literary Gazette and Journal of Belles Lettres, December 8, 1821 (no. 255, pp. 772-773).]

We have already given some of our columns to this writer's merits, and we will not now repeat our convictions of his incurable absurdity. On the last occasion of our alluding to him, we were compelled to notice his horrid licentiousness and profaneness, his fearful offences to all the maxims that honorable minds are in the habit of respecting, and his plain defiance of Christianity. On the present occasion we are not met by so continued and regular a determination of insult, though there are atrocities to be found in this poem quite enough to make us caution our readers against its pages.

Adonais is an elegy after *the manner of Moschus,* on a foolish young man, who, after writing some volumes of very weak, and, in the greater part, of very indecent poetry, died some time since of a consumption: the breaking down of an infirm constitution having, in all probability, been accelerated by the discarding his neckcloth, a practice of the cockney poets, who look upon it as essential to genius, inasmuch as neither Michael Angelo, Raphael nor Tasso are supposed to have worn those antispiritual incumbrances. In short, as the vigour of Sampson lay in his hair, the secret of talent with these persons lies in the neck; and what aspirations can be expected from a mind enveloped in muslin. Keats caught cold in training for a genius, and, after a lingering illness, died, to the great loss of the Independents of South America, whom he had intended to visit with an English epic poem, for the purpose of exciting them to liberty. But death, even the death of the radically presumptuous profligate, is a serious thing; and as we believe that Keats was made presumptuous chiefly by the treacherous puffing of his cockney fellow gossips, and profligate in his poems merely to make them saleable, we regret that he did not live long enough to acquire common sense, and abjure the pestilent and perfidious gang who betrayed his weakness to the grave, and are now panegyrising his memory into contempt. For what is the praise of the cockneys but disgrace, or what honourable inscription can be placed over the dead by the hands of notorious libellers, exiled adulterers, and avowed atheists.

Adonais, an Elegy, is the form in which Mr. Shelley puts forth his woes. We give a verse at random, premising that it consists of fifty-five stanzas, which are, to our seeming, altogether unconnected, interjectional, and nonsensical. We give one that we think among the most comprehensible. An address to Urania:—

> Most musical of mourners, weep anew!
> Not all to that bright station dared to climb;
> And *happier they their happiness who knew,*
> *Whose tapers yet burn thro' that night of time*
> *In which suns perish'd;* others more sublime,
> Struck by the *envious* wrath of man or God!!
> *Have sunk extinct in their refulgent prime;*
> And some yet live. . . .

Now what is the meaning of this, or of any sentence of it, except indeed that horrid blasphemy which attributes crime to the Great Author of all virtue! The rest is mere empty absurdity. If it were worth our while to dilate on the folly of the production, we might find examples of every species of the ridiculous within those few pages.

Mr. Shelley summons all kinds of visions round the grave of this young man, who, if he has now any feeling of the earth, must shrink with shame and disgust from the touch of the hand that could have written that impious sentence. These he classifies under names, the greater number as new we believe to poetry as strange to common sense. Those are—

> Desires and *Adorations*,
> Winged *Persuasions* and veiled Destinies,
> *Splendours*, and *Glooms*, and glimmering *Incarnations*
> Of hopes and fears and twilight Phantasies,
> And Sorrow with her family of *Sighs*,
> And Pleasure, *blind with tears!* led by the *gleam*
> Of her own *dying* SMILE instead of eyes!!

Let our readers try to imagine these weepers, and close with *"blind* Pleasure led," by what? "by the *light* of *her own dying smile*—instead of *eyes*!!!"

We give some specimens of Mr. S.'s

> *Nonsense—pastoral.*
> Lost Echo sits amid the voiceless mountains,[1]
> And feeds her grief with his remember'd lay,
> *And will no more reply* to winds and fountains.

> *Nonsense—physical.*
> . . . for whose disdain she (Echo) pin'd away
> Into a *shadow* of all *sounds!*

> *Nonsense—vermicular.*
> Flowers springing from the corpse
> . . . . illumine death
> And *mock* the *merry* worm that wakes beneath.

> *Nonsense—pathetic.*
> Alas! that all we lov'd of him should be,
> But for our grief, as if it had not been,
> And grief itself be mortal! WOE IS ME!

> *Nonsense—nondescript.*
> In the death chamber for a moment Death,
> *Blush'd to annihilation!*

> *Nonsense—personal.*
> A pardlike spirit, beautiful and swift—
> A love in *desolation mask'd,*—a Power
> Girt *round with weakness;*—it can scarce *uplift*
> The *weight* of the *superincumbent hour!*

We have some idea that this fragment of character is intended for Mr. Shelley himself. It closes with a passage of memorable and ferocious blasphemy:—

> He with a sudden hand
> Made bare his branded and ensanguin'd brow,
> Which was like Cain's or CHRIST's!!!

What can be said to the wretched person capable of this daring profanation. The name of the first murderer—the accurst of God—brought into the same aspect image with that of the Saviour of the World! We

---

[1] Though there is *no Echo* and the mountains are *voiceless*, the woodmen, nevertheless, in the last line of this verse hear "a drear murmur between their Songs"!! (Reviewer's footnote.)

are scarcely satisfied that even to quote such passages may not be criminal. The subject is too repulsive for us to proceed even in expressing our disgust for the general folly that makes the Poem as miserable in point of authorship, as in point of principle. We know that among a certain class this outrage and this inanity meet with some attempt at palliation, under the idea that frenzy holds the pen. That any man who insults the common order of society, and denies the being of God, is essentially mad we never doubted. But for the madness, that retains enough of rationality to be wilfully mischievous, we can have no more lenity than for the appetites of a wild beast. The poetry of the work is *contemptible*—a mere collection of bloated words heaped on each other without order, harmony, or meaning; the refuse of a schoolboy's commonplace book, full of the vulgarisms of pastoral poetry, yellow gems and blue stars, bright Phoebus and rosy-fingered Aurora; and of this stuff is Keats's wretched Elegy compiled.

We might add instances of like incomprehensible folly from every stanza. A heart *keeping*, a mute *sleep*, and death *feeding* on a mute *voice*, occur in one verse (page 8); Spring in despair "throws down her *kindling* buds as if she Autumn were," a thing we never knew Autumn do with buds of any sort, the kindling kind being unknown to our botany; a *green lizard* is like an *unimprisoned flame, waking* out of its *trance* (page 13). In the same page the *leprous corpse* touched by the tender spirit of Spring, so as to exhale itself in flowers, is compared to "*incarnations of the stars, when splendour is changed to fragrance!!!*" Urania (page 15) *wounds* the "invisible palms of her tender feet by treading on human hearts as she journeys to see the corpse. Page 22, somebody is asked to "clasp with panting soul the pendulous earth," an image which, we take it, exceeds that of Shakspeare, to "put a girdle about it in forty minutes."

It is so far a fortunate thing that this piece of impious and utter absurdity can have little circulation in Britain. The copy in our hands is one of some score sent to the Author's intimates from Pisa, where it has been printed in a quarto form "with the types of Didot," and two learned Epigraphs from Plato and Moschus. Solemn as the subject is, (for in truth we must grieve for the early death of any youth of literary ambition,) it is hardly possible to help laughing at the mock solemnity with which Shelley charges the Quarterly Review for having murdered his friend with . . . a critique![2] If Criticism killed the disciples of that school, Shelley would not have been alive to write an Elegy on another:—but the whole is most farcical from a pen which, on other occasions, has treated of the soul, the body, life and death agreeably to the opinions, the principles, and the practice of Percy Bysshe Shelley.

BLACKWOOD'S BLOWS UP

[From Blackwood's Edinburgh Magazine, December, 1821 (10: 696-700), entitled "Remarks on Shelley's *Adonais*." William Maginn has generally been

[2] This would have done excellently for a coroner's inquest like that on *Honey*, which lasted *thirty* days, and was facetiously called the "*Honey-moon.*" (Reviewer's footnote.)

credited with this review. The following extracts from his unpublished letters to Blackwood (for which I am indebted to Mr. Ralph M. Wardle, of Harvard University) show that at least the principal culprit was another: Dec. 17, 1821—"Get some good hand—Wilson if possible—to review Shelley's what d'ye call it about Master Clysterpipe the dead poet: and acquit yourself of the murder of that Knight of the burning pestle." Jan. 1, 1882—"Was it Croly who reviewed Shelley's Adonais? I suspect it from the proper names being in Italics—a great trick of his." One might still suspect either Maginn or Lockhart of the derisive verses in the review.

This furious review marks Blackwood's abandonment of any hope of converting Shelley. Perhaps the case would have been handled differently had John Wilson continued in charge of Shelley's case instead of becoming absorbed in his duties as Professor of Moral Philosophy, but his comment on *Epipsychidion* shows his conviction that Shelley was now beyond saving.]

Between thirty and forty years ago, the *Della Crusca* school was in great force. It poured out monthly, weekly, and daily, the whole fulness of its raptures and sorrows in verse, worthy of any "person of quality." It reveled in moonlight, and sighed with evening gales, lamented over plucked roses, and bid melodious farewells to the "last butterfly of the season." The taste prevailed for a time; the more rational part of the public, always a minority, laughed, and were silent; the million were in raptures. The reign of "sympathy" was come again,—poetry, innocent poetry, had at length found out its true language. Milton and Dryden, Pope and the whole ancestry of the English Muse, had strayed far from nature. They were a formal and stiff-skirted generation, and their fame was past and forever. The trumpet of the morning paper, in which those "inventions rich" were first promulgated, found an echo in the more obscure fabrications of the day, and milliners' maids and city apprentices pined over the mutual melancholies of *Arley* and *Matilda*. At length the obtrusiveness of this tuneful nonsense grew insupportable; a man of a vigorous judgment shook off his indolence, and commenced the long series of his services to British literature, by sweeping away, at a brush of his pen, the whole light-winged, humming, and loving population. But in this world folly is immortal; one generation of absurdity swept away, another succeeds to its glories and its fate. The *Della Crusca* school has visited us again, but with some slight change of localities. Its verses now transpire at one time from the retreats of Cockney dalliance in the London suburbs; sometimes they visit us by fragments from Venice, and sometimes invade us by wainloads from Pisa. In point of subject and execution, there is but slight difference; both schools are "smitten with nature, and nature's love," run riot in the intrigues of anemones, daises, and buttercups, and rave to the "rivulets *proud*, and the deep *blushing* stars." Of the individuals in both establishments, we are not quite qualified to speak, from the peculiarity of their private habits; but poor Mrs. Robinson and her correspondents are foully belied, if their moral habits were not to the full as pure as those of the Godwinian colony, that play "the Bacchanal beside the Tuscan sea." But we must do the defunct *Della Crusca* the justice to say, that they kept their private irregularities to themselves, and sought for no reprobate popularity, by raising the banner to all the vicious of the community. They talked nonsense without measure, were simple down to the lowest degree of silliness, and "babbled of green fields" enough to make men sick of summer, but they were not daring enough to boast of impurity; there was no pestilent hatred of everything generous, true, and honourable; no desperate licentiousness in their romance; no daring and fiend-like insult to feeling, moral ties, and Christian principle. They were foolish and profligate, but they did not deliver themselves, with the steady devotedness of an insensate and black ambition, to the ruin of society.

We have now to speak of Mr. P. B. Shelley and his poem. Here we must again advert to the *Della Crusca*. One of the characteristics of those childish persons was, the restless interest which they summoned the public to take in every thing belonging to their own triviality. If Mrs. Robinson's dog had a bad night's repose, it was duly announced to the world; Mr. Merry's accident in paring his nails solicited a similar sympathy; the falling off of Mrs. R.'s patch, at the last ball, or the stains on Mr. M.'s full-dress coat, from the dropping of a chandelier, came before the earth, with praise-worthy promptitude. All within their enchanted ring was perfection; but there the circle of light and darkness was drawn, and all beyond was delivered over to the empire of Dulness and Demogorgon. The New School are here the imitators of those original arbiters of human fame.

The present story is thus:—A Mr. John Keats, a young man who had left a decent calling for the melancholy trade of Cockney-poetry, has lately died of a consumption, after having written two or three little books of verses, much neglected by the public. His vanity was probably wrung not less than his purse; for he had it upon the authority of the Cockney Homers and Virgils, that he might become a light to their region at a future time. But all this is not necessary to help a consumption to the death of a poor sedentary man, with an unhealthy aspect, and a mind harassed by the first troubles of verse-making. The New School, however, will have it that he was slaughtered by a criticism of the Quarterly Review.—"O flesh, how art thou fishified!"—There is even an aggravation in this cruelty of the Review—for it had taken three or four years to slay its victim, the deadly blow having been inflicted at least as long since. We are not now to defend a publication so well able to defend itself. But the fact is, that the Quarterly finding before it a work at once silly and presumptuous, full of the servile *slang* that Cockaigne dictates to its servitors, and the vulgar indecorums which that Grub Street Empire rejoiceth to applaud, told the truth of the volume, and recommended a change of manners and of masters to the scribbler. Keats wrote on; but he wrote *indecently*, probably in the indulgence of his social propensities. He selected from Boccaccio, and, at the feet of the Italian Priapus, supplicated for fame and farthings.

Both halves the winds dispersed in empty air.

Mr. P. B. Shelley having been the person appointed by the *Pisan* triumvirate to canonize the name of this apprentice, "nip in the bud," as he fondly tells us, has accordingly produced an Elegy, in which he weeps "after the manner of Moschus for Bion." The canonizer is worthy of the saint.—"*Et tu, Vitula!*"—Locke says, that the most resolute liar cannot lie more than once in every three sentences. Folly is more engrossing; for we could prove, from the present Elegy, that it is possible to write two sentences of pure nonsense out of every three. A more faithful calculation would bring us to ninety-nine out of every hundred, or,—as the present consists of only fifty-five stanzas,—leaving about five readable lines in the entire. It thus commences:—

> O weep for Adonais—he is dead!
> O, weep for Adonais! though our tears
> *Thaw not the frost* which binds so dear a head!
> And thou, sad hour! selected from all years
> *To mourn our loss,* rouse thy obscure compeers,
> *And teach them thine own sorrow, say with me*
> *Died* Adonais! till the *future does*
> Forget the past. Hit fate and fame shall be
> *An echo and a light!!* unto eternity.

Now, of this unintelligible stuff the whole fifty-five stanzas are composed. Here an hour—a *dead* hour too—is to say that Mr. Keats died *along with it!* yet this hour has the heavy business on its hands of mourning the loss of its *fellow-defunct,* and of rousing all its *obscure compeers* to be taught its *own sorrow,* &c. Mr. Shelley and his tribe have been panegyrized in their turn for power of language; and the man of "Table-talk" swears by all the gods he owns, that he has a great command of words, to which the most eloquent effusions of the Fives Court are *occasionally* inferior. But any man may have the command of every word in the vocabulary, if he will fling them like pebbles from a sack; and even in the most fortuitous flinging, they will sometimes fall in pleasing though useless forms. The art of the modern *Della Cruscan* is thus to eject every epithet that he can conglomerate in his piracy through the Lexicon, and throw them out to settle as they will. He follows his own rhymes, and shapes his subject to the close of his measure. He is a glutton of all names of colours, and flowers, and smells, and tastes, and crowds his verse with scarlet, and blue, and yellow, and green; extracts tears from every thing, and makes moss and mud hold regular conversations with him. "A goosepye talks," —it does more, it thinks, and has its peculiar sensibilities,—it smiles and weeps, raves to the stars, and is a listener to the western wind, as fond as the author himself.

On these principles, a hundred or a hundred thousand verses might be made, equal to the best in Adonais, without taking the pen off the paper. The subject is indifferent to us, let it be the "Golden age," or "Mother Goose,"—"Waterloo," or the "Wit of the Watchhouse,"—"Tom

Thumb," or "Thistlewood." We will undertake to furnish the requisite supply of blue and crimson daises and dandelions, not with the toilsome and tardy lutulence of the puling master of verbiage in question, but with a burst and torrent that will sweep away all his weedy trophies. For example—*Wontner*, the city marshal, a very decent person, who campaigns it once a year, from the Mansion-house to Blackfriars bridge, truncheoned and uniformed as becomes a man of his military habits, had the misfortune to fracture his leg on the last Lord Mayor's day. The subject is among the most unpromising. We will undertake it, however, (premising, that we have no idea of turning the accident of this respectable man into any degree of ridicule).

O Weep for Adonais, &c.

O weep for *Wontner*, for his leg is broke,
O weep for Wontner, though our pearly tear
Can never cure him. Dark and dimly broke
The thunder cloud o'er Paul's enamel sphere,
When his black barb, with lion-like career,
Scatter'd the crowd.—Coquetting Mignonet,
Thou Hyacinth fond, thou Myrtle without fear,
Haughty Geranium, in your beaupots set,
Were then your soft and starry eyes unwet?

The pigeons saw it, and on silver wings
Hung in white flutterings, for they could not fly,
Hoar-headed Thames checked all his crystal springs,
Day closed above his pale, imperial eye,
The silken Zephyrs breathed a vermeil sigh.
High Heavens! ye Hours! and thou Ura-ni-a!
Where were ye then! Reclining languidly
Upon some green Isle in the empurpled Sea
Where laurel-wreathen sprites love eternally.

Come to my arms, &c.

We had intended to call attention by *italics* to the *picturesque* of these lines; but we leave their beauties to be ascertained by individual perspicacity; only requesting their marked admiration of the epithets *coquetting, fond, fearless,* and *haughty,* which all tastes will feel to have so immediate and inimitable an application to mignonet, hyacinths, myrtles, and geraniums. But *Percy Byshe* [*sic*] has figured as a sentimentalist before, and we can quote largely without putting him to the blush by praise. What follows illustrates his power over the language of passion. In the *Cenci,* Beatrice is condemned to die for parricide,—a situation that, a true poet, might awake a noble succession of distressful thought. The mingling of remorse, natural affection, woman's horror at murder, and alternate melancholy and fear at the prospect of the grave, in Percy Byshe works up only this frigid rant:—

> How comes this hair undone?
> Its wandering strings must be what blind me so.
> And yet I *tied it fast!!*
> -   -   -   -   -   -
> The sunshine on the floor is *black!* The air
> Is changed to vapours such as the dead breathe
> In charnel pits! Poh! I am choak'd! There creeps
> A clinging, black, contaminating mist
> About me,—'tis substantial, heavy, thick.
> I cannot pluck it from me, for it glues
> My fingers and my limbs to one another,
> And eats into my sinews, and dissolves
> My flesh to a pollution. . . .

So much for the history of "Glue"—and so much easier it is to rake together the vulgar vocabulary of rottenness and reptilism, than to paint the workings of the mind. This raving is such as perhaps no excess of madness ever raved, except in the imagination of a Cockney, determined to be as mad as possible, and opulent in his recollections of the shambles.

In the same play, we have a specimen of his "art of description." He tells of a ravine—

> And in its depths there is a mighty Rock,
> Which has, from unimaginable years,
> Sustain'd itself with *terror and with toil!*
> Over a gulph, and with the *agony*
> *With which it clings,* seems slowly coursing down;
> Even as a wretched soul, hour after hour,
> Clings to the mass of life, yet clinging *leans,*
> And leaning, makes *more dark* the dread abyss
> In which it fears to fall. Beneath this crag,
> *Huge as despair,* as if *in weariness,*
> The *meloncholy* mountain *yawns* below. . . .

And all this is done by a rock—What is to be thought of the *terror* of this novel sufferer—its *toil*—the *agony* with which so sensitive a personage clings to its paternal support, and from *unimaginable* years? The magnitude of this *melancholy* and injured monster is happily measured by its being the *exact size of despair!* Soul becomes substantial, and *darkens a dread abyss.* Such are Cockney darings before "the Gods, and columns" that abhor mediocrity. And is it to this dreamy nonsense that is to be attached the name of poetry? Yet on these two passages the whole lauding of his fellow-Cockneys has been lavished. But *Percy Byshe* feels his hopelessness of poetic reputation, and therefore lifts himself on the stilts of blasphemy. He is the only verseman of the day, who has dared, in a Christian country, to work out for himself the character of direct ATHE-ISM! In his present poem, he talks with impious folly of "the *envious* wrath of man or God"! Of a

> Branded and ensanguined brow,
> Which was like *Cain's* or CHRIST'S.

Offences like these naturally come before a more effective tribunal than that of criticism. We have heard it mentioned as the only apology for the predominent irreligion and nonsense of this person's works, that his understanding is unsettled. But in his Preface, there is none of the exuberance of insanity; there is a great deal of folly, and a great deal of bitterness, but nothing of the wildness of his poetic fustian. The Bombastes Furioso of these stanzas cools into sneering in the preface; and his language against the *death-dealing* Quarterly Review, which has made such havoc in the Empire of Cockaigne, is merely malignant, mean, and peevishly personal. We give a few stanzas of this performance, taken as they occur.

> O weep for Adonais! He is dead!
> Weep, melancholy mother, wake and weep;
> Yet *wherefore?* quench within their burning bed
> Thy *fiery* tears, and let thy *loud* heart keep
> Like his, a mute and uncomplaining sleep,
> For he is gone, where all things wise and fair
> *Descend!* Oh dream not that the amorous deep
> Will yet restore him to the vital air.
> Death *feeds* on his *mute voice*, and *laughs* at our despair.

The seasons and a whole host of personages, ideal and otherwise, come to lament over *Adonais*. They act in the following manner:

> Grief made the young Spring *wild*, and she threw down
> Her kindling buds, as if she Autumn were,
> Or they dead leaves, since her delight is flown,
> For whom should she have wak'd the sullen year?
> To Phoebus was not Hyacinth so dear,
> Nor to himself Narcissus, as to both,
> Thou, Adonais; wan they stand, and sere,
> Amid the drooping comrades of their youth,
> With dew all turn'd to tears, odour to sighing ruth.

Here is left, to those whom it may concern, the pleasant perplexity, whether the lament for Mr. J. Keats is shared between Phoebus and Narcissus, or Summer and Autumn. It is useless to quote these absurdities any farther *en masse*, but there are flowers of poesy thickly spread through the work, which we rescue for the sake of any future Essayist on the Bathos.

> *Absurdity.*
> The green lizard, and the golden snake,
> Like *unimprison'd* flowers out of their
> trance awake. An hour—
>
> ———————
>
> Say, with me
> Died Adonais, *till the Future dares*
> *Forget the Past*—his fate and fame shall be
> An *echo* and a *light* to all eternity.

Whose *tapers yet* burn through the night of Time,
In which *Sun perish'd!*

Echo,—pined away
Into a *shadow* of all *sounds!*

That mouth whence it was wont to draw the breath
Which gave it strength to pierce the guarded wit!

Comfortless!
As *silent* lightning leaves the starless night.

Live thou whose *infamy* is not thy *fame!*

Thou *noteless* blot on a remembered name!

We in mad trance *strike with our spirit's* knife,
Invulnerable nothings!

Where lofty thought
Lifts a young heart above its mortal lair,
And love, and life, contend in it—for what
Shall be its earthly doom—The dead live there,
And move, like *winds of light*, on dark and stormy air.

Who mourns for Adonais—oh! come forth,
Fond wretch! and know thyself and him aright,
Clasp with thy *panting* soul the *pendulous Earth!*

Dart thy spirit's light
Beyond all worlds, until its *spacious might*
Satiate the *void circumference!*

Then sink
Even to a point within our day and night,
And keep thy heart *light*, lest it make *thee sink*,
When *hope has kindled hope*, and *lured thee to the* brink.

A light is past from *the revolving year;*
And man and women, and what still is dear
Attracts to crush, repels to make thee wither.

That benediction, which th' *eclipsing curse*
Of birth can quench not, that sustaining love,
Which, through *the web of being blindly wove*,
By man, and beast, and earth, and air, and sea!
Burns bright or dim, as each are mirrors of
The *fire* for which all *thirst*.

Death makes, as becomes him, a great figure in this "Lament,"—but in rather curious operations. He is alternately a person, a thing, nothing, &c.

> He is, "The coming bulk of Death,"
> Then "Death feeds on the *mute voice.*"
> A clear sprite
> Reigns over Death—
> Kingly Death
> Keeps his pale court.
> Spreads apace
> The *shadow* of *white* Death.
> The damp Death
> Quench'd its caress—
> Death
> *Blush'd to annihilation!*
> Her distress
> Roused Death. Death rose and smiled—
> He lives, he wakes, 'tis Death is *dead!*

As this wild waste of words is altogether beyond our comprehension, we will proceed to the more gratifying office of giving a whole, unbroken specimen of the Poet's powers, exercised on a subject rather more within their sphere. The following poem has been sent to us as written by Percy Byshe, and we think it contains all the essence of his odiferous, colorific, and daisy-enamoured style. The motto is from *"Adonais."*

Elegy on My Tom Cat.

And others came.—Desires and Adorations,
Wing'd Persuasions, and veil'd Destinies,
Splendours, and Glooms, and glimmering Incantations
Of hopes and fears, and twilight Phantasies;
And Sorrow, with her family of Sighs;
And Pleasure, *blind* with tears, led by the *gleam*
Of her own *dying smile instead of eyes!*

ELEGY.

Weep for my Tomcat! all ye Tabbies weep,
  For he is gone at last! Not dead alone,
In flowery beauty sleepeth he no sleep;
  Like that bewitching youth Endymion!
My love is dead, alas, as any stone,
  That by some violet-sided smiling river
Weepeth too fondly! He is dead and gone,
  And fair Aurora, o'er her young believer,
With fingers gloved with roses, doth make moan,
And every bud its petal green doth sever,
  And Phoebus sets in night for ever, and for ever!
And others come! ye Splendours! and ye Beauties!
  Ye Raptures! with your robes of pearl and blue;
Ye blushing Wonders! with your scarlet shoe-ties;
  Ye horrors bold! with breasts of lily hue;

Ye Hope's stern flatterers! He would trust to you,
     Whene'er he saw you with your chesnut hair,
Dropping sad daffodils; and rosepinks true!
     Ye Passions proud! with lips of bright despair;
Ye Sympathies! with eyes like evening star,
When on the glowing east she rolls her crimson car.

Oh, bard-like spirit! beautiful and swift!
     Sweet lover of pale night; when Luna's lamp
Shakes sapphire dew-drops through a cloudy rift;
     Purple as woman's mouth, o'er ocean damp;
Thy quivering rose-tipped tongue—thy stealing tramp;
     The dazzling glory of thy gold-tinged tail;
Thy whisker-waving lips, as o'er the swamp
     Rises the meteor, when the year doth fail,
Like beauty in decay, all, all are flat and stale.

This poem strikes us as evidence of the improvement that an appropriate subject makes in a writer's style. It is incomparably less nonsensical, verbose, and inflated, than Adonais; while it retains all its knowledge of nature, vigour of colouring, and felicity of language. Adonais has been published by the author in Italy, the fitting soil for the poem, sent over to his honoured correspondents throughout the realm of Cockaigne, with a delightful mysteriousness worthy of the dignity of the subject and the writer.

THE EXAMINER PRAISES AND COUNTER-ATTACKS

[From The Examiner, July 7, 1822 (no. 754, pp. 419-421), entitled "Letters to the Readers of the Examiner, No. 6—On Mr. Shelley's New Poem, Entitled *Adonais*."]

Since I left London, Mr. Shelley's *Adonais, or Elegy on the Death of Mr. Keats,* has, I find, made its appearance. I have not seen the London edition; but I have an Italian one printed at Pisa, with which I must content myself at present. The other was to have had notes. It is not a poem calculated to be popular, any more than the *Prometheus Unbound;* it is of too abstract and subtle a nature for that purpose; but it will delight the few, to whom Mr. Shelley is accustomed to address himself. Spenser would be pleased with it if he were living. A mere town reader and a Quarterly Reviewer will find it *caviare. Adonais,* in short, is such an elegy as poet might be expected to write upon poet. The author has had before him his recollections of Lycidas, of Moschus and Bion, and of the doctrines of Plato; and in the stanza of the most poetical of poets, Spenser, has brought his own genius, in all its etherial beauty, to lead a pomp of Loves, Graces, and Intelligences, in honour of the departed.

Nor is the Elegy to be considered less sincere, because it is full of poetical abstractions. Dr. Johnson would have us believe, that *Lycidas* is not "the effusion of real passion."—"Passion," says he, in his usual conclusive tone, (as if the force of critic could no further go) "plucks no berries from the myrtle and ivy; nor calls upon Arethuse and Mincius, nor tells of rough Satyrs and Fauns with cloven heel. Where there is leisure for fiction, there is little grief." This is only a more genteel common-place, brought in to put down a vulgar one. Dr. Johnson, like most critics, had no imagination; and because he found nothing natural to his own impulses in the associations of poetry, and saw them so often abused by the practice of versifiers inferior to himself, he was willing to conclude, that on natural occasions they were always improper. But a poet's world is as real to him as the more palpable one to people in general. He spends his time in it as truly as Dr. Johnson did his in Fleet-street or at the club. Milton felt that the happiest hours he had passed with his friend had been passed in the regions of poetry. He had been accustomed to be transported with him "beyond the visible diurnal sphere" of his fire-side and supper-table, things which he could record nevertheless with a due relish. (See the *Epitaphium Damonis*.) The next step was to fancy himself again among them, missing the dear companion of his walks; and then it is that the rivers murmur complainingly, and the flowers hang their heads,—which to a truly poetical habit of mind, though to no other, they may literally be said to do, because such is the aspect which they present to an afflicted imagination. "I see nothing in the world but melancholy," is a common phrase with persons who are suffering under a great loss. With ordinary minds in this condition the phrase implies a vague feeling, but still an actual one. The poet, as in other instances, gives it a life and particularity. The practice has doubtless been abused; so much so, that even some imaginative minds may find it difficult at first to fall in with it, however beautifully managed. But the very abuse shews that it is founded in a principle in nature. And a great deal depends upon the character of the poet. What is mere frigidity and affectation in common magazine rhymers, or men of wit and fashion about town, becomes another thing in minds accustomed to live in the sphere I spoke of. It was as unreasonable in Dr. Johnson to sneer at Milton's grief in *Lycidas*, as it was reasonable in him to laugh at Prior and Congreve for comparing Chloe to Venus and Diana, and *pastoralizing* about Queen Mary. Neither the turn of their genius, nor their habits of life, included this sort of ground. We feel that Prior should have stuck to his tuckers and boddices, and Congreve appeared in his proper Court-mourning.

Milton perhaps overdid the matter a little when he personified the poetical enjoyments of his friend and himself under the character of actual shepherds. Mr. Shelley is the more natural in this respect, inasmuch as he is entirely abstract and imaginative, and recalls his lamented acquaintance to mind in no other shape than one strictly poetical. I say acquaintance, because such Mr. Keats was; and it happens, singularly enough, that the few hours which he and Mr. Shelley passed together were almost entirely of a poetical character. I recollect one evening in particular, which they spent with the writer of these letters in composing verses on a given subject.[3] But it is not as a mere acquaintance, however poetical, that Mr. Shelley records him. It is as the intimate acquaintance of all lovely and lofty thoughts, as the nursling of the Muse, the hope of her coming days, the creator of additional Beauties and Intelligences for the adornment and inhabitation of the material world. The poet commences with calling upon Urania to weep for her favourite; and in a most beautiful stanza, the termination of which is in the depths of the human heart, informs us where he is lying. You are aware that Mr. Keats died at Rome:—

> To that high Capital, where kingly Death
> Keeps his pale court in beauty and decay,
> He came;—and bought, with price of purest breath,
> A grave among the eternal—Come away!
> Haste, while the vault of blue Italian day
> Is yet his fitting charnel-roof! while still
> He lies, as if in dewy sleep he lay;
> Awake him not! surely he takes his fill
> Of deep and liquid rest, forgetful of all ill.

"The forms of things unseen," which Mr. Keats's imagination had turned into shape,—the "airy nothings" to which it is the high prerogative of the poet to give "a local habitation and a name," are then represented, in a most fanciful manner, as crowding about his lips and body, and lamenting him who called them into being:

> And others came . . . Desires and Adorations,
> Winged Persuasions and veiled Destinies,
> Splendours, and glooms, and glimmering Incarnations
> Of hopes and fears, and twilight Phantasies;
> And Sorrow, with her family of sighs;
> And Pleasure, blind with tears, led by the gleam
> Of her own dying smile instead of eyes.
> All he had loved, and moulded into thought,
> From shape, and hue, and odour, and sweet sound,
> Lamented Adonais.

A phrase in the first line of the following passage would make an admirable motto for that part of the *Literary Pocket Book*, in which the usual lists of kings and other passing dominations are superseded by a list of **Eminent Men**:

> And he is gathered to *the kings of thought*,
> Who waged contention with their time's decay,
> And of the past are all that cannot pass away.

The spot in which Mr. Keats lies buried is thus finely pointed out. The two similes at the close are among the happiest we recollect, especially the second:

---

[3] Hunt is here referring to the composition by all three of sonnets on the Nile, shortly before Shelley's departure for Italy.—N.I.W.

Go thou to Rome,—at once the Paradise,
The grave, the city, and the wilderness;
And where its wrecks like shattered mountains rise,
And flowering weeds, and fragrant copses dress
The bones of Desolation's nakedness,
Pass, till the Spirit of the spot shall lead
Thy footsteps to a slope of green access,
Where, like an infant's smile, over the dead,
A light of laughing flowers along the grass is spread

And gray walls moulder round, on which dull Time
Feeds, like slow fire upon a hoary brand.

In the course of the poem some living writers are introduced; among
whom Lord Byron is designated as

The Pilgrim of Eternity, whose fame
Over his living head like Heaven is bent
An early but enduring monument!

The poet of Ireland is called, with equal brevity and felicity,

The sweetest lyrist of her saddest wrong:

And among "others of less note," is modestly put one, the description of
whom is strikingly calculated to excite a mixture of sympathy and admiration. The use of the Pagan mythology is supposed to have been worn
out; but in fact, they who say so, or are supposed to have worn it out,
never wore it all. See to what a natural and noble purpose a true scholar
can turn it:—

He, as I guess,
Had gazed on Nature's naked loveliness,
Actaeon-like, and now he fled astray
With feeble steps o'er the world's wilderness,
And his own thoughts, along that rugged way,
Pursued, like raging hounds, their father and their prey.

A pard-like Spirit, beautiful and swift—
A Love in desolation masked;—a Power
Girt round with weakness;—it can scarce uplift
The weight of the superincumbent hour;
It is a dying lamp, a falling shower,
A breaking billow;—even while we speak
Is it not broken? On the withering flower
The killing sun smiles brightly: on a cheek
The life can burn in blood, even while the heart may break.

Ah! te meae si partem animae rapit
Maturior vis!

But the poet is here, I trust, as little of a prophet, as affection and a beautiful climate, and the extraordinary and most vital evergy of his spirit, can
make him. The singular termination of this description, and the useful

reflections it is calculated to excite, I shall reserve for another subject in my next. But how is it, that even that termination could not tempt the malignant common-place of the Quarterly Reviewers to become blind to the obvious beauty of this poem, and venture upon laying some of its noble stanzas before their readers? How is it that in their late specimens of Mr. Shelley's powers they said nothing of the style and versification of the majestic tragedy of *The Cenci,* which would have been equally intelligible to the lowest, and instructive to the highest, of their readers? How is it that they have not even hinted at the existence of this *Elegy on the Death of Mr. Keats,* though immediately after the arrival of copies of it from Italy they thought proper to give a pretended review of a poem which appeared to them the least calculated for their reader's understandings? And finally, how happens it, that Mr. Gifford has never taken any notice of Mr. Keats's *last* publication,—the beautiful volume containing *Lamia,* the Story from Boccaccio, and that magnificent fragment *Hyperion?* Perhaps the following passage of the Elegy will explain:

> Our Adonais has drunk poison!—Oh,
> What deaf and viperous murderer could crown
> Life's early cup with such a draught of woe?
> The nameless worm would now itself disown:
> It felt, yet could escape the magic tone
> Whose prelude held all envy, hate, and wrong
> But what was howling in one breast alone
> Silent with expectation, of the song,
> Whose master's hand is cold, whose silver lyre unstrung.
>
> Live thou, whose infamy is not thy fame!
> Live! fear no heavier chastisement from me,
> Thou noteless blot on a remembered name!
> But be thyself, and know thyself to be!
> And ever at thy season be thou free
> To spill the venom when thy fangs o'erflow:
> Remorse and Self-Contempt shall cling to thee,
> Hot Shame shall burn upon thy secret brow,
> And like a beaten hound tremble thou shalt—as now.

This, one would think, would not have been "unintelligible" to the dullest *Quarterly* peruser, who had read the review of Mr. Keats's *Endymion.* Nor would the following perhaps have been quite obscure:

> Nor let us weep that our delight is fled
> Far from these carrion kites that scream below;
> He wakes or sleeps with the enduring dead;
> Thou canst not soar where he is sitting now.
> Dust to the dust! but the pure spirit shall flow
> Back to the burning fountain whence it came,
> A portion of the Eternal, which must glow
> Through time and change, unquenchably the same,
> While thy cold embers choke the sordid hearth of shame.

However, if further explanation had been wanted, the Preface to the Elegy furnishes it in an abundance, which even the meanest admirers of Mr. Gifford could have no excuse for not understanding. Why then did he not quote this? Why could he not venture, once in his life, to try and look a little fair and handsome; and instead of making all sorts of misrepresentations of his opponents, lay before his readers something of what his opponents say of him? He only ventures to allude, in convulsive fits and starts, and then not by name, to the *Feast of the Poets*. He dares not even allude to Mr. Hazlitt's epistolary dissection of him. And now he, or some worthy coadjutor for him, would pretend that he knows nothing of Mr. Shelley's denouncement of him, but criticises his other works out of pure zeal for religion and morality! Oh these modern "Scribes, Pharisees, and Hypocrites!" How exactly do they resemble their prototypes of old!

"It may well be said," observes Mr. Shelley's Preface, "that these wretched men know not what they do. They scatter their insults and their slanders without heed as to whether the poisoned shaft lights on a heart made callous by many blows, or one, like Keats's, composed of more penetrable stuff. One of their associates is, to my knowledge, a most base and unprincipled calumniator. As to "Endymion," was it a poem, whatever might be its defects, to be treated contemptuously by those who had celebrated with various degrees of complacency and panegyric, "Paris," and "Woman," and a "Syrian Tale," and Mrs. Lefanu, and Mr. Barrett, and Mr. Howard Payne, and a long list of the illustrious obscure? Are these the men, who in their venal good-nature, presumed to draw a parallel between the Rev. Mr. Milman and Lord Byron? What gnat did they strain at here, after having swallowed all those camels? Against what woman taken in adultery, dares the foremost of these literary prostitutes to cast his opprobrious stone? Miserable man! you, one of the meanest, have wantonly defaced one of the noblest specimens of the workmanship of God. Nor shall it be your excuse, that murderer as you are, you have spoken daggers but used none."

Let us take the taste of the Gifford out of one's mouth with the remainder of the Preface, which is like a sweet nut after one with a worm in it.

[*Quotes the fifth paragraph, concluding with Shelley's tribute to Severn*]

Amen! says one who knew the poet, and who knows the painter.

II

A POOR SPECIMEN OF GENIUS

[From The General Weekly Register of News, Literature, Law, Politics, and Commerce, June 30, 1822 (no. 13, pp. 501-503). This weekly, which ran for only thirteen numbers, contains no other notice of Shelley.]

The increase of periodical works cannot be wondered at, considering the multiplicity of new publications that are almost daily issued from the press; the public are nearly sated with the quantity which has been forced upon their attention, and are now satisfied with viewing the generality of works through the medium of reviews.   This attaches a good deal of responsibility to the editors of such works, and imposes not only a strict and candid impartiality, but an opinion unbiased either by party, prejudice, or interest.   The pledge which we have given to the public, it has been our object to redeem, and we trust our readers have found, so far, that we have kept our promise.   Poetry, like states, has been considerably revolutionized, but we fear it has not received much benefit from the change; taste has become subservient to new laws; and public opinion biassed by new principles:—thus a gradual change has been effected, and poetry has assumed a new character.   The modern school of poetasters are not satisfied with following the footsteps of the great masters, but by constantly aiming at novelty and originality they become obscure and unintelligible, and by the misapplication of words, and the misconception of ideas, they lead the imagination into a labyrinth of thought from which it is with difficulty disentangled.   Whether the revolution which poetry has undergone be for the better, it is not for us to determine, but as admirers of the old school we cannot but lament the change.   If harmony, if beauty of expression, if loftiness of idea, and terseness of thought be the constituents of poetry, where can we find them so brilliantly displayed as in Dryden, Pope, Goldsmith, Milton, and the writers of the last century?   In offering these opinions, we do not mean to question the genius of some of our present poets, but we could wish to see poetry flowing in its former channels, and instead of being the enchanting vehicle of sensuality, become again the delightful source of all that is truly beautiful and *sublime*.

Mr. Shelley is one of those writers who seems gifted with a strong imagination, and but little judgment; he is often inharmonious and much too obscure and intricate for the generality of his readers.   In the volume before us, which he calls a mere *improvise*, we find much to censure and but little to admire; the ideas are neither original nor poetical, the language obscure and frequently unpolished, and although the poem undoubtedly possesses some beauties, yet its defects as certainly predominate.   In the first scene Mahmud is discovered sleeping whilst the captive Greek women are chaunting the following wild chorus:

> We strew these opiate flowers
>   On thy restless pillow,—
> They were stript from orient bowers,
>   By the Indian billow.
>   Be thy sleep
>   Calm and deep,
> Like theirs who fell, not ours who weep.

Had Mr. Shelley continued in the manner he commenced, our former observations would have been unnecessary and unjust; but the ear is tired by the monotonous repetition of "keep," "deep," and "sleep," and the senses bewildered in a maze of inexplicable thought: *their panting loud and fast at length awakens Mahmud,* who, starting from his sleep, is strangely moved, and enquires of Hassan concerning an old Jew to whom he wishes to relate a dream which "has thrice hunted him into the troubled day." Hassan gives him the following absurd description of the Israelite, which, for its extravagancy, can, perhaps, scarcely be equalled:

> The Jew of whom I spoke is old; so old
> He seems to have outlived a world's decay;
> The hoary mountains and the wrinkled ocean
> Seem younger still than he;—his hair and beard
> Are whiter than the tempest sifted snow;
> His cold pale limbs and pulseless arteries
> Are like the fibres of a cloud instinct
> With light, and to the soul that quickens them
> Are as the atoms of the mountain-drift
> To the winter-wind;—but from his eye looks forth
> A life of unconsumed thought which pierces
> The present, and the past, and the to come.

The *Pre-Adamite* is described as dwelling *in a sea cavern mid the Demonesi less accessible than the Sultan or God himself;* what is the poet's meaning by this passage we are utterly at a loss to conjecture, and what follows is not less extravagant. After this conversation Mahmud and Hassan retire, meanwhile the chorus of Greek women continues; this is so far from lyric poetry that we hardly consider it worthy the name of poetry at all;—*worlds sinking to decay are compared* to *bubbles bursting on a river;* PORTAL is brought in rhyme with *immortal; Mahomet* with *shall set; spirits are represented as hurrying to and fro thro' the dark chasm of death; brief dust; and the robes cast upon the bare ribs of Death,* are originalities quite beyond our comprehension. The pages which follow are much better, and were Mr. Shelley to confine himself to the dead syllabic verse, he might be more successful; true sublimity consists not in the mere sound of august words, but in brightness and simplicity of idea, and it is this principle upon which the best writers of every age have built their poems. A long dialogue ensues between Mahmud and Hassan in which the former exclaims,

> O miserable dawn after a night
> More glorious than the day which it usurpt!
> O faith in God! O power on earth! O word
> Of the great prophet, whose o'ershadowing wings
> Darkened the thrones and idols of the West,
> Now bright!—For thy sake cursed be the hour,
> Even as a father by an evil child,

> When the Orient moon of Islam rolled in triumph
> From Caucasus to White Ceraunia!
> Ruin above, and anarchy below;
> Terror without, and treachery within;
> The chalice of destruction full, and all
> Thirsting to drink; and who among us dares
> To dash it from his lips? and where is Hope?

This is certainly good poetry, nor are some of the following pages less poetical. Hassan endeavours to rally the spirits of Mahmud by portraying the strength, power, and invincibility of the Turkish arms, to which Mahmud replies,—

> Proud words, when deeds come short, are seasonable;
> Look, Hassan, on yon crescent moon, emblazoned
> Upon that shattered flag of fiery cloud
> Which leads the rear of the departing day;
> Wan emblem of an empire fading now!
> See how it trembles in the blood-red air,
> And like a mighty lamp whose oil is spent
> Shrinks on the horizon's edge, while, from above,
> One star with insolent and victorious light
> Hovers above its fall, and with keen beams,
> Like arrows thro' a fainting antelope,
> Strikes its weak form to death.

Hassan then relates in strong and not unpoetical terms, the events at Wallachia, and the defeat of the Turkish fleet. This conversation is interrupted by a messenger, who informs them of the departure of the Muscovite ambassador from the city, and the treaty of peace at Stromboul; he is succeeded by a second, who after relating the assault of Thebes and Corinth, and a truce brought from Ypsilanti, gives place to a third, who like the comforters of Job, gives place to a fourth; at length an attendant informs Mahmud that the Jew waits to attend him. The chorus is again resumed in the following extraordinary stanza:

> Of the free—
> I would flee
> A tempestuous herald of victory!
> My golden rain
> For the Grecian slain
> Should mingle in tears with the bloody main,
> And my solemn thunder-knell
> Should ring to the world the passing bell
> Of Tyranny!

This is the voice of a *winged cloud*, or spirits who are transformed to clouds; see first stanza. Again

> I hear! I hear!
> The crush as of an empire falling,

> The shrieks as of a people calling
> Mercy! mercy!—How they thrill!
> And then a shout of "kill! kill! kill!"
> And then a small still voice.

Falling and calling certainly rhyme, as do thrill and kill, which in order to make up the line is repeated like fal, lal, lal, in an old ballad to make up the measure; but surely Mr. Shelley does not call this lyric poetry, whose very essence ought to be harmony and easiness of thought.

We are next introduced to Mahmud, and Ahasuerus the old Jew, whose words *"stream like a tempest of drizzling mist within the brain of Mahmud,* and *convulses with wild and wilder thoughts his spirit."* Mahmud is then summoned to a visionary world, and hears the assault of cities, the clash of arms, the blasts of trumpets and other forebodings of the final overthrow of the Turkish empire; he then stretches his eyes and beholds a kingless diadem glittering in the dust, and one of kingly port casting himself beneath the stream of war; ominous signs! After a further disclosure of the *to come,* Ahasuerus conjures up a phantom, which approaching like the ghost of Hamlet, exclaims—

> I come
> Thence whither thou must go! The grave is fitter
> To take the living than give up the dead;
> Yet has thy faith prevailed, and I am here.

To which Mahmud replies,—

> Spirit, woe to all!
> Woe to the wronged and the avenger! Woe
> To the destroyer, woe to the destroyed!
> Woe to the dupe, and woe to the deceiver!
> Woe to the oppressed, and woe to the oppressor!
> Woe both to those that suffer and inflict;
> Those who are born and those who died! But say,
> Imperial shadow of the thing I am,
> When, how, by whom, Destruction must accomplish
> Her consummation?

The imperial shadow tells him to—

> Ask the cold pale Hour,
> Rich in reversion of impending death,
> When he shall fall upon whose ripe gray hairs
> Sit care, and sorrow, and infirmity.

The ghost at the sound of voices vanishes, and Mahmud enquiring whether he lives or wakes, after a little hesitation makes his exit. Meanwhile a voice is heard at intervals exulting in the overthrow of the Greeks, which is answered by a chorus and semi-chorus predicting the revival of the Grecian empire; and the poem concludes with a chorus, which as the author observes in notes, is rather indistinct and obscure. We have given Hellas more attention than it deserves, but the former celebrity of the author occasioned us to dwell so minutely upon the work before us, which upon the whole, though not entirely devoid of merit, is but a bad specimen of Mr. Shelley's powers, and but ill calculated to increase the former fame of its author.

XII

General and Miscellaneous Comment in 1822

LEIGH HUNT FIGHTS BACK

[From The Examiner, January 20, and June 9, 16, and 23, 1822 (no. 770, p. 35; no. 750; pp. 355-357; no. 751, pp. 370-371; and no. 752, pp. 389-390). The first is an incidental defense of Shelley in a general review of The Quarterly. The second is a general attack on The Quarterly for its unfair attitude toward radicals, with special mention of Hazlitt. Shelley is twice mentioned very briefly, in passing, as (according to The Quarterly) "a mere dealer in obscurity and nonsense," and "Mr. Shelley, being a great infidel, is not fond of revenging himself." Considerations of space forbid reprinting the rest of the article here. The last two deal specifically with The Quarterly's treatment of *Prometheus Unbound* and are headed "Letters to Readers of the Examiner—*Prometheus Unbound.*"]

WE HAVE no objection to the review of Mr. Shelley, as far as it merely opposes his opinions and criticises the excess of abstraction and consequent mysticism which form their principal and characteristic defect. In the first particular, they regularly labour in their vocation; and it is the quality rather than the purport of their arguments which can be objected to. The same allowance cannot be made for the literary remarks which are composed precisely in the liberal and agreeable style of those which operated so mercilessly on the too sensitive Keats. It is not, however, the selection of a few cloudy or obscure passages that can always form the requiem of a man of genius, and such is Mr. Shelley even by the specimens produced, and allowing the general justice of much of the objection. The conclusion of this critique is mere rant; the intentions of a writer, it seems, are to be regarded for nothing. Upon certain indications, he must be knocked o'-the-head as a matter of course; and for want of real thunder, the *Quarterly Review* will perform the part of *Salmoneus*, and hurl its bombastic bolts with the most impotent self-importance. All this is folly, even upon its own views; the excursiveness of intellect is not to be bounded by a few hired and bigotted pedants, rancorous in their enmity, but only affected in their indignation—Who publishes *Cain?*[1]

The article in the *Quarterly* alluded to in my last letter, is a pretended review of Mr. Shelley's poem, entitled *Prometheus Unbound*. It does not enter into any discussion of the doctrines contained in that poem. It does not pretend to refute them. It knows very well that it does not dare to enter into the merit of Mr. Shelley's propositions, and answer them as it would answer a treatise by a theological sectarian. And the reason is

[1] The answer, of course, is John Murray, who also published The Quarterly.—N.I.W.

obvious. I do not mean to say that all those propositions are unanswerable; but I say the Quarterly Reviewers, by the very nature of their office, as civil and religious State-hirelings, are not the men to answer them fairly; and accordingly their criticism has all the malice of conscious inability to reply, and eagerness to put down. I am very sincere when I say that I have no knowledge of the writer of the article in question; but if I were asked to guess who it was, I should say it was neither Mr. Gifford with all his bitter common-place, nor Mr. Croker with all his pettifogging, nor Mr. Southey with all his cant; but some assistant clergyman, who is accustomed to beg the question in the pulpit, and who thinks that his undertoned breath of malignity will be mistaken for Christian decorum. What renders this the more probable (though, to be sure, the ordinary readers of the *Quarterly Review* are as much prepared to take things on trust as if they were sitting in pews) is, that the critic thinks it sufficient to quote a passage against priests, in order to have proved its erroneousness. The amount of his reasoning is this:—Here is a rascal! He wishes there were no such things as priests! Upon which all the priests and pluralists shake their well-fed cheeks in a shudder of reprobation, and the poet is confuted. Observe too a little genuine *Quarterly* touch lurking by the way. The Reviewer is collecting passages to prove his author's enmity to the Christian faith,—an enmity, by the bye, which Mr. Shelley always takes care to confine to the violent consequences of faith as contrasted with practice, there being in the latter sense no truer Christian than himself. The poet exclaims—

> O, that the free would stamp the impious name
>   Of **** into the dust! or write it there,
> So that this blot upon the page of fame
>   Were as a serpent's path, which light the air
> Erases, and the flat sands close behind!

These *four* stars, which in fact imply a civil title, and not a religious word, as the allusion to "the page of fame" might evince, are silently turned by the Reviewer into *six* stars, as if implying the name of Christ:—[2]

> O, that the free would stamp the impious name
>   Of ****** into the dust.

I fancy some inexperienced reader doubting whether it be possible even for a Quarterly Reviewer to be guilty of such a meanness, and suggesting that he might have written the stars at random. Alas, my old friends, he does not know the nature of these people as you and I do! Doubtless, when the Reviewer wrote his six stars, he was aware that decent persons, unacquainted with the merits of him and his subject, would make the same good-natured suggestion, had they chanced to observe the difference between the original and the quotation. But when we know the misrepre-

---

[2] See page 249 in this volume. The 1820 and 1839 editions both use four stars. The Boscombe MS and the quotation in The London Magazine and Theatrical Inquisitor (p. 260 in this volume) read *King*.—N.I.W.

sentations which these Reviewers are in the habit of making, when we know how often their mean arts have been exercised and exposed, when we know that they have *put marks of quotation to sentences which are not to be found in the authors they criticise,* have left out parts of a context to *render the remainder absurd,* and have *altered words into words of their own* for the same purpose, nobody will doubt that the writer of the article in question wilfully put down his six stars instead of four, and deserves (like some others who wear as many) to have "the mean heart bared" that "lurks" beneath them. Take another description of similar pettiness. The Reviewer, speaking of one of the most striking passages of the poem, says, "After a revolting description of the death of our Saviour, introduced *merely* for the sake of intimating that *the religion he preached is the great source of human misery and vice,* Mr. Shelley adds,

> Thy name I will not speak,
> It hath become a curse.

Will Mr. Shelley," continues the indignant moralist, "to excuse this blasphemy against the name *in which all the nations of the earth shall be made blessed,* pretend that these are the words of Prometheus, not of the poet?"—No; Mr. Shelley will pretend nothing. He leaves it to the Quarterly Reviewers to pretend, and cant, and commit "pious frauds," in order to make out their case, and act in an unchristian manner in order to prove their Christianity. It is the critic who pretends in this case. He pretends that Mr. Shelley has "added" nothing further; that he has not explained *how* the name in question has become a curse;—and that he has not "intimated," that the religion he preached has been turned against its very essence by those who pretend to preach it in modern times. Who would suppose, from the Reviewer's quotation, that Mr. Shelley, in this very passage, is instancing Christ as a specimen of the fate of benevolent reformers? Yet nothing is more true. Who would suppose, that in this very passage, which they pretend to have quoted entirely, Mr. Shelley puts the consequences which they make him deduce as the only result of the Christian religion, into the mouth of one of the Furies,—not indeed as untrue to a certain extent, but as the only lasting result which she can perceive, and delights to perceive: for in any other sense the whole tenor of Mr. Shelley's poem and speculation is quite the reverse of any such deduction, with reference to what must always *continue* to be. All that he meant in short is this,—that as Christ's benevolence subjected him to the torments he endured, so the uncharitable dogmas produced by those who make a *sine qua non* of the Christian *faith,* have hitherto done more harm than good to mankind; and all the rest of his poem may be said to be occupied in shewing, that it is benevolence, as opposed to faith, which will survive these horrible consequences of its associate, and make more than amends for them. I will quote the whole of the passage in question, that the reader may see what the Reviewer, cunning in his "sins of omission," chose to leave out. Besides, it is very grand and full of matter. Prometheus,—(who is a personification of the Benevolent Principle, subjected for a time to the Phantasm Jupiter, or in other words to that False Idea of the great and beneficent First Cause, which men create out of their own follies and tyrannies)—is lying under the infliction of his torments, patient and inflexible, when two of the Ocean Nymphs, who have come to comfort him, hear a terrible groan, and look out to see what has caused it.

[*Quotes Act I, lines 578-634*]

This is a terrible picture, and doubtless exaggerated, if the latter part is to be taken as a picture of all the good as well as ill which the world contains; but the painter uses his sombre colours to cast a corresponding gravity of reflection on people's minds. I will concede to anybody who requires it, that Mr. Shelley, from the excess of his wishes on this point, is too apt to draw descriptions of the state of mankind without sufficient light on his canvas; but in the lesser extent to which they do apply—(and Heaven knows it is wide enough)—let the reader judge for himself how applicable they are. I will also concede to the Quarterly Reviewer, that Mr. Shelley's poetry is often of too abstract and metaphysical a cast; that it is apt to be too wilful and gratuitous in its metaphors; and that it would be better if he did not write metaphysics and polemics in verse, but kept his poetry for more fitting subjects. But let the reader judge, by this passage out of one of his poems least calculated to be popular, whether "all" his poetry is the nonsense the Reviewer pretends it to be. The Reviewer says that the above picture of the death of Christ is "revolting." The power of exciting pity and terror may perhaps be revolting to the mind of one who cannot "go and do so likewise"; but I will tell him what is a great deal more revolting to the minds of mankind in general, however priest-ridden or pension-ridden,—the feelings that induced the Reviewer to omit the passage which I have marked.

So much for the charges of nonsense and want of decency. In my next, I shall have something edifying to shew you in answer to the charge of nonsense and obscurity, and more assumptions of honesty and candour on the part of the Quarterly critics. Adieu.

As a conclusive proof of Mr. Shelley's nonsense, the Reviewer selects one of his passages which most require attention, separates it from its proper context, and turns it into prose: after which he triumphantly informs the reader that this prose is not prose, but "the conclusion of the third act of *Prometheus verbatim et literatim.*" Now poetry has often a language as well as music of its own, so distinct from prose, and so universally allowed a right to the distinction (which none are better aware of than the versifiers in the *Quarterly Review*), that secretly to decompose a poetical passage into prose, and then call for a criticism of a reader upon it, is like depriving a body of its distinguishing properties, or confounding their rights and necessities, and then asking where they are. Again, to take a passage abruptly from its context, especially when a context is more than usually necessary to its illustration, is like cutting out a piece of shade from a picture, and reproaching it for want of light.   And finally, to select an obscure passage or two from an author, or even to shew that he is often obscure, and then to pretend from these specimens, that he is nothing but obscurity and nonsense, is mere dishonesty.

For instance, Dante is a great genius who is often obscure; but suppose a critic were to pick out one of his obscurest passages, and assert that Dante was a mere writer of jargon. Suppose he were to select one of the metaphysical odes from his *Amoroso Convivio;* or to take a passage from Mr. Cary's translation of his great poem, and turn it into prose for the better mystification of the reader.   Here is a specimen:—

> Every orb, corporeal, doth proportion its extent unto the virtue through its parts diffused. The greater blessedness preserves the more. The greater is the body (if all parts share equally) the more is to preserve. Therefore the circle, whose swift course enwheels the universal frame, answers to that, which is supreme in knowledge and in love. Thus by the virtue, not the seeming breadth of substance, measuring, thou shalt see the heavens, each to the intelligence that ruleth it, greater to more, and smaller unto less, suited in strict and wondrous harmony. (*Paradise,* Canto 28.)

The lines in question from Mr. Shelley's poem are as follows. A spirit is describing a mighty change that has just taken place on earth. It is the consummation of a state of things for which all the preceding part of the poem has been yearning:—

> The painted veil, by those who were, called life,
> Which mimicked, as with colours idly spread,
> All men believed and hoped, is torn aside;
> The loathsome mask is fallen, the man remains
> Sceptreless, free, uncircumscribed, but man
> Equal, unclassed, tribeless, and nationless,
> Exempt from awe, worship, degree, the king
> Over himself; just, gentle, wise: but man
> Passionless; no, yet free from guilt or pain,
> Which were, for his will made or suffered them;
> Nor yet exempt, tho' ruling them like slaves,
> From chance, and death, and mutability,
> The clogs of that which else might oversoar
> The loftiest star of unascended heaven,
> Pinnacled dim in the intense inane.

That is to say,—The veil, or superficial state of things, which was called life by those who lived before us, and which had nothing but an idle resemblance to that proper state of things, which we would fain have thought it, is no longer existing. The loathsome mask is fallen; and the being who was compelled to wear it, is now what he ought to be, one of a great family who are their own rulers, just, gentle, wise, and passionless; no, not passionless, though free from guilt or pain, which were only the consequences of their former wilful mistakes; nor are they exempt, though they turn them to the best and most philosophical account, from chance, and death, and mutability; things, which are the clogs of that lofty spirit of humanity, which else might rise beyond all that we can conceive of the highest and happiest star of heaven, pinnacled, like an almost viewless atom, in the space of the universe:—*The intense inane* implies excess of emptiness, and is a phrase of Miltonian construction, like "the palpable obscure" and "the vast abrupt." Where is the unintelligible nonsense of all this? and where is the want of "grammar," with which the "pride" of the Reviewer, as *Mr. Looney M'Twoulter* says, would "come over" him?

Mr. Shelley has written a great deal of poetry equally unmetaphysical and beautiful. The whole of the tragedy of the *Cenci*, which the Reviewers do not think it to their interest to notice, is written in a style equally plain and noble. But we need not go farther than the volume before us, though, according to the Reviewer, the "whole" of it does not contain "*one* original image of nature, *one* simple expression of human feeling, or *one* new association of the appearances of the moral with those of the material world." We really must apologize to all intelligent readers who know anything of Mr. Shelley's genius, for appearing to give more notice to these absurdities than they are worth; but there are good reasons why they ought to be exposed. The *Prometheus* has already spoken for itself. Now take the following *Ode to a Skylark*, of which I will venture to say, that there is not in the whole circle of lyric poetry a piece more *full* of "original images of nature, of simple expressions of human feeling, and of the associations of the appearances of the moral with those of the material world." You shall have it entire, for it is as fitting for the season, as it is true to the musical and etherial beauty of its subject.

TO A SKYLARK
[*The poem is quoted entire*]

I know of nothing more beautiful than this,—more choice of tones, more natural in words, more abundant in exquisite, cordial, and most poetical associations. One gets the stanzas by heart unawares, and repeats them like "snatches of old tunes." To say that nobody who writes in the *Quarterly Review* could produce any thing half as good (unless Mr. Wordsworth writes in it, which I do not believe he does) would be sorry praise. When Mr. Gifford "sings" as the phrase is, one is reminded of nothing but snarling. Mr. Southey, though the gods have made him more poetical than Mr. Gifford, is always affecting something original, and tiring one to death with common-place. "Croker," as Goldsmith says, "rhymes to joker"; and as to the chorus of priests and virgins,—of scribes and pharisees,—which make up the poetical undersong of the Review, it is worthy of the discordant mixture of worldliness and religion, of faith and bad practice, of Christianity and malignity, which finds in it something ordinary enough to merit its approbation.

One passage more from this immoral and anti-christian volume, that contains "not one simple expression of human feeling," and I will close my letter. It is part of *"An Ode, written October 1819, before the Spaniards had recovered their liberty:"*—

> Glory, glory, glory,
> To those who have greatly suffered and done!
> Never name in story
> Was greater than that which ye shall have won.
> Conquerors have conquered their foes alone,
> Whose revenge, pride, and power they have overthrown:
> *Ride ye, more victorious, over your own.*

Hear that, ye reverend and pugnacious Christians of the *Quarterly!*

> Bind, bind every brow
> With crownals of violet, ivy, and pine:
> Hide the blood-stains now
> With hues which sweet nature has made divine;
> Green strength, azure hope, and eternity;
> But let not the pansy among them be;
> *Ye were injured, and that means memory.*

How well the Spaniards have acted up to this infidel injunction is well known to the whole of wondering Christendom and affords one of the happiest presages to the growth of true freedom and philosophy. Why did not the Reviewer quote such passages as these by way of specimens of the author's powers and moral feeling? Why did his boasted Christianity lead him to conceal these, as well as to omit what was necessary to the one quoted in my last? You pretty well understand why by this time; but I have still further elucidations to give, which are more curious than any we have had yet, and which you shall (soon) see.—I shake your hands.

A GENERAL ESTIMATE

[From The Album, July, 1822 (1 : 222-223). From an article entitled "The Augustan Age in England."]

Besides this host of poets whose names are in everybody's mouth, there are many others of very great—some of the greatest merit, who are, from various causes, less celebrated. There is Mr. Shelley; who possesses the powers of poetry to a degree, perhaps, superior to any of his distinguished contemporaries. The mixing his unhappy philosophical tenets in his writings has prevented, and will prevent, their becoming popular. His powers of thought, too, equally subtle and profound, occasionally lead him beyond the capability of expression, and in those passages he, of course, becomes unintelligible. The recurrence of these has led some readers to stigmatize his works generally as incomprehensible, whereas they are only blemishes which disfigure them, and which are far more than repaid by countless and exquisite beauties. Can any one, indeed, read the Prometheus Unbound with a candid spirit, and not admit it to be a splendid production? We condemn, most unreservedly—for in these days it is necessary to speak with perfect clearness on these subjects—the introduction of his offensive philosophy. We admit the occasional obscurity, sometimes amounting to unintelligibility, of his expression; but we do say that, in despite of these faults, and we fully admit their magnitude, Prometheus Unbound is a production of magnificent poetical power. Did our limits permit us to give extracts, we would place this on indisputable ground. The length, however, to which this paper has already run obliges us to content ourselves with referring our readers to the poem. Nor does Mr. Shelley want sweetness and tenderness when he chooses to display them. The Sensitive Plant is as beautiful a specimen of playful yet melancholy fancy as we remember to have seen. If Mr. Shelley would write a poem in which he would introduce more tenderness and less gloom; never permit his subtlety of thought to run into obscurity; and, above all, totally omit all allusion to his philosophical opinions, we are very sure that it would become universally and deservedly popular. This, to be sure, is asking him to cure himself of all his faults; but where they are those of *com*mission not of *o*mission— where they arise from the misapplication of genius, not from want of it— we always look upon it to be within the power of volition to get rid of them—at least, in a very great degree.

APROPOS OF THE LIBERAL

A

[From Blackwood's Edinburgh Magazine, March, 1822 (11:363). No. 1 of "NOCTES AMBROSIANAE." This article consists of twenty-one pages, in the general rambling manner of "Noctes Ambrosianae." During a discussion of contemporary poety, Keats and Shelley are discussed as follows, on page *363.]

Christopher North, Esquire, *Solus*.
Enter Ensign Morgan Odoherty.[3]

Odoherty.

Hand me the lemons. This holy alliance of Pisa will be a queer affair. The Examiner has let down its price from a tenpenny to a sevenpenny. They say the Editor here is to be one of that faction, for they must publish in London of course.

Editor.

Of course; but I doubt if they will be able to sell many. Byron is a prince; but these dabbling dogglerers destroy every dish they dip in.

Odoherty.

Apt alliteration's artful aid.

Editor.

Imagine Shelley, with his spavin, and Hunt, with his staingalt, going in the same harness with such a caperer as Byron, three abreast! He'll knock the wind out of them both the first canter.

---

[3] William Maginn. The Editor, is, of course, "Christopher North," i.e., John Wilson.

Odoherty.

'Tis pity Keats is dead.—I suppose you could not venture to publish a sonnet in which he is mentioned now? The Quarterly (who killed him, as Shelley says) would blame you.

Editor.

Let's hear it. Is it your own?

Odoherty.

No, 'twas written many months ago by a certain great Italian genius, who cuts a figure about the London routs—one Fudgiolo.

Editor.

Try to recollect it.

Odoherty.

It began

> Signor Le Hunto, gloria di Cocagna
> Chi scrive il poema della Rimini
> Che tutta apparenza ha, por Comini,
> D'esser cantato sopra la montagna
> Di bel Ludgato, o nella campagna
> D'Amstead, o sulle marge Serpentimini
> Com' esta Don Giovanni d'Endyimini
> Il gran poeta D'Ipecacuanha?
> Tu sei il Re del Cocknio Parnasso
> Ed egli il herede appanente
> Tu sei un gran Giacasso ciertamente,
> Ed egli ciertamente Giacasso!
> Tu sei il Signor del Examinero
> Ed egli soave Signor del Glystero.

B

[From The Examiner, October 13, 1822 (no. 768, p. 652). From an advance review of The Liberal.]

A powerful translation from the *May-Day Night* scene of the tragedy of Faust, by Mr. Shelley, is the next in succession. "The poetical reader," says the short notice prefacing it, "will feel with what vivacity he has encountered the ghastly bustle of the revellers,—with what apprehensiveness of tact, yet strength of security, he has carried us into the thick of "the witch element." These are strong terms of praise for a translation; but Mr. Shelley went to his work in a kindred spirit of genius, and Goethe has so completely made his work a work of creation, it seems a thing so involuntary growing out of the world he has got into, like the animated rocks and crags which he speaks of,—that a congenial translator in one's own language seems to step into his place as the abstract observer, and to leave but two images present to one's mind, the work and himself. In other words, he is the true representative of his author. This is the very highest triumph, both of poetry and translation."—This remark spares us additional observation: the friend may possibly temper the critic; but of all men, Mr. Shelley seemed designed by nature and acquirement to combat with the supernatural of Goethe.

C

[From The Country Literary Chronicle and Weekly Review, October 26, 1822 (no. 180, p. 675), conclusion of a review of The Liberal.]

Then comes a translation of the May Day Night scene, in the tragedy of Faust, by that 'seraphic being,' as his friends have called him, Percy Bysshe Shelley. It is ushered in by an extravagant eulogy, in which we are told that 'everybody will like it, who can feel at all what the poet feels most —the secret analogies that abound in all things—the sympathies of which difference, and even antipathy cannot get rid'; a very explicit definition of a poet's feelings certainly. We have always spoken of Mr. Shelley as a man of considerable poetical genius, but of baneful principles; and we now feel sadly disappointed, that one of the very few things from his pen, against which there can be little objection on the latter count, should be so totally destitute of every merit. What, for instance, can be more absurd or less poetic than the following lines:

> But see how swift advance and shift
>   Trees behind trees, row by row,—
> How clift by clift, rocks bend and lift
>   Their frowning foreheads as we go.
>   The giant-snouted crags, ho! ho!
> How they snort, and how they blow!
> The columns of the evergreen palaces
>   Are split and shattered;
> The roots creak, and stretch, and groan;
> And ruinously overthrown,
>   The trunks are crushed and shattered
> By the fierce blast's unconquerable stress.
> Over each other crack and crash they all
> In terrible and intertangled fall;

That this is wretched doggerel and nonsense, we presume few persons will deny; but that Lord Byron, or even Leigh Hunt, should give it his imprimatur, is to us really astonishing, not to say anything of the irreparable injury they are doing the memory of their friend by printing it.

D

[From The Council of Ten, November, 1822 (no. 6, p. 165). The article is entitled "On Liberality, 'The Liberal Verse and Prose from the South,' Postscript to Lord Byron."]

When "The Liberal" was projected, Lord Byron had two coadjutors in the undertaking, Mr. Shelley and Mr. Leigh Hunt. Mr. Shelley, as is well known, was lately lost at sea on a tempestuous night off the coast of

Italy. Mr. Shelley is dead; and in our eyes, except under very particular circumstances, the dead are sacred. Of Mr. Shelley, therefore, and his part in the present publication, we shall say but very little. We believe that he was fearfully and fatally mistaken in his views and opinions: but he might have been honest—and we can pay some respect even to the wildest errors of an honest man. More mature reflection might have taught him, that his principles and notions could not be made practically applicable to the present state of society, or to any future state which is likely to exist upon "this human earth of ours"; and a wider and more confirmed experience might have chastened and sobered down that pride and drunkenness of imagination, which are the too frequent concomitants of youth and enthusiasm. A longer and more comprehensive survey of man, both as he is by nature, and men as they are when brought into communities and trained by political and social institutions, might have demonstrated to him, that something more of caution and steadiness, something of a *charitable tenderness* for established modes of living and thinking, and a disposition to believe, that the faith and practice which have prevailed for ages might *possibly* have some foundation in utility and truth, would rather assist than retard, would be rather cooperative than incompatible with the progress of "philosophy and liberal opinion."

The only thing in the first number of "The Liberal" which is ostensibly written by Mr. Shelley is "May-Day Night," a translation of a short scene in the tragedy of "Faust." By the way, there is a short sentence in the introduction to this translation, which contains the only vestige of pure and temperate reason to be found in the book, and which we would, therefore, especially recommend to the notice and consideration of Lord Byron and his associates. "How we pity Faust in this play, who refines and hardens himself out of his faith in things good, and acquires the necessity of inordinate excitement."

E

ON THE LIBERAL[4]

[From The Edinburgh Magazine and Literary Miscellany (successor to The Scots Magazine, November, 1822 (N. S. 11:563).]

This is a long and bitter article signed "Jonathan Oldmixon," from which I quote as follows: "As to Atheist Shelley, he has gone, with all his imperfections on his head, to his account. . . . He has written himself an Atheist with his own hand; and, dead though he be, we must take the liberty to treat him as such. His share in the present abortion, however, is but small, and the little we have is as silly a piece of mystification as it was possible for a mere translation to be rendered; if indeed a translation it may be called, which translation is none. It is with the account given of him in the preface that we shall at present concern ourselves; and *there*

---

[4] This criticism of Shelley, which escaped my notice, is here reprinted, by the generous permission of Professor Marsh, as it appears in "The Early Reviews of Shelley," by George L. Marsh, in Modern Philology, August, 1929 (27:73-95).

he is described, by that congenial spirit, Hunt, we presume, as 'one of the *noblest of human beings, who had more religion* in his *very differences with religion,* than thousands of your church-and-state men!' Now, we will do Lord Byron the justice to say, that we believe him incapable of inditing such a piece of detestable jesuitical nonsense as this. To place it in its true light, however, it may be necessary to advert to a single passage in the infamous and justly-prohibited *Queen Mab*. In page 61 of that production . . . the Fairy asserts, 'There is no God'; on which we are favoured with a long note, where the nonexistence of a Supreme Being is attempted to be demonstrated *on* what are called, or rather miscalled, *Metaphysical Principles!!!* This, we should imagine, would be decisive of the religious sentiments of Shelley." Then comes mention of the story of Shelley's writing "Atheist" after his name in an inn album, and citation of the passage in *Queen Mab* beginning, "There is no God!" Farther on is the following: "We know something about Shelley's religion, from the best possible authority—himself; but what did this glib-tongued Prefacer *know* about the religion of those whom he dishonours by comparison with an avowed Atheist?. . . . Shelley forsooth, was 'one of the noblest of human beings!' We admit that he has proved one of the most unfortunate, as we have reason to think he was one of the most unhappy. But on what grounds was this 'nobleness' of character attributed to him? Was it because he denied the God that made him, and ridiculed the institution of marriage, with every restraint that opposed the promiscuous intercourse of the sexes? Was it because—but we will not drag forward the life of a man, who has gone to that place where his doubts are already solved, and his state eternally and irrevocably fixed!"

XIII

SHELLEY'S DEATH

ACCOUNT IN THE EXAMINER

[From The Examiner, August 4, 1822 (no. 758, p. 489).]

THOSE WHO know a great mind when they meet with it, and who have been delighted with the noble things in the works of Mr. Shelley, will be shocked to hear that he has been cut off in the prime of his life and genius. He perished at sea, in a storm, with his friend Captain Williams, of the Fusileers, on the evening of the 8th ult., somewhere off Via Reggia, on the coast of Italy, between Leghorn and the Gulf of Spezia. He had been to Pisa, to do a kind action, and he was returning to his country abode at Lerici to do another.—Such was the whole course of his life. Let those who have known such hearts, and have lost them, judge of the grief of his friends. Both he and Capt. Williams have left wives and children. Capt. Williams was also in the prime of life, and a most amiable man, beloved like his friend. The greatest thing we can say in honour of his memory (and we are sure he would think so), is, that he was worthy to live with his friend, and to die with him.—Vale, dilectissime hominum! Vale, dilectissime; et nos ama, ut dixisti, in sepulchro.

ACCOUNT IN THE MORNING CHRONICLE

[From The Morning Chronicle, London, August 12, 1822. The sixth paragraph in a miscellaneous column headed "The Mirror of Fashion." It was copied by both The John Bull and The Republican (*q.v.*). The letter was from Leigh Hunt to Horace Smith and is now in the Ashley Library. It is printed entire in Mr. T. J. Wise's *A Shelley Library*, pp. 106-107. The portions unprinted in the earlier account consist of five short sentences of purely personal interest. Mr. Wise prints "King of the elements" where the present version reads "thing."]

Extract of a Letter from Pisa, Dated July 25, 1822

"I trust that the first news of the dreadful calamity that has befallen us here will have been broken to you by report, otherwise I shall come upon you with a most painful abruptness. But Shelley, my divine-minded friend—your friend—the friend of the Universe—he has perished at sea! He was in a boat with his friend Captain Williams, going from Leghorn to Lerici, when a storm arose, and it is supposed the boat must have foundered. It was on the 8th instant, about four or five in the evening they guess. A fisherman says he saw the boat a few minutes before it went down—he looked again, and it was gone. He saw the boy they had with

[321]

them aloft, furling one of the sails. We hope this story is true, as their passage from life to death will then have been short; and what adds to the hope is, that in S.'s pocket (for their bodies were both thrown on the shore some days afterwards. Conceive our horrible certainty after trying all that we could hope.) a copy of Keats's last volume which he had borrowed of me to read on his passage, was found *open* and doubled back, as if it had been thrust in, in the hurry of a surprise. God bless him! I cannot help thinking of him as if he were alive as much as ever, so unearthly he always appeared to me, and so seraphical a thing of the elements. It has often been feared that Shelley and Captain Williams would meet with some accident, they were so hazardous; but when they set out on the 8th in the morning it was fine. Our dear friend was passionately fond of the sea, and has been heard to say that he should like it to be his death-bed."

OBITUARY NOTICE IN THE COUNTRY LITERARY CHRONICLE

[From The Country Literary Chronicle and Weekly Review, August 10, 1822 (no. 169, p. 504). Under "Biography."]

Mr. Percy Bysshe Shelley, a man of extraordinary but perverted talents, and the author of the Cenci, Queen Mab, and some less censurable productions, has, it appears, lost his life in an aquatic excursion. It has been stated, and we believe with truth, that Lord Byron, Mr. Shelley, and Leigh Hunt, were about establishing a periodical work at Pisa, destined, of course, for England, and which has been looked for with considerable anxiety. The league is now dissolved, and with it, we should think, all thought of the threatened journal. The following notice of the death of Mr. Shelley appeared in the Examiner. It is no doubt authentic as to the fact. . . .

[*Here follows the account given in The Examiner of August 4* (q.v.)]

COMMENT IN THE JOHN BULL

[From The John Bull, August 19, 1822.]

The following paragraph which appeared in the Chronicle of last Monday, relative to the death of Mr. Byshe Shelley, the Author of Queen Mab, savours as much of the ridiculous as any production of the Cockney School, which we happen to have met with, mixed with infinitely more of the positively disgusting.

"Extract from a letter from Pisa, dated July 25, 1822:—

[*For the text of this extract, see above, p. 321.*]

Mr. Shelley is dead, and we have no wish to review his past life and conduct, nor should we have had any desire to allude to his published productions, (the emanations of his "divine mind"), now that he is gone; but when we see the Morning Chronicle descend to the insertion of such nauseating nonsense at this eulogium upon Mr. Shelley's friendship for the universe, and above all *Dare* to invoke the blessing of God upon him, we think it quite a duty to quote a few lines of this very Mr. Shelley's writings, which may serve to shew—first, the loss a Christian country has sustained by his death; secondly, the temerity of the invocation to the Creator; and lastly, the sort of persons the Chronicle considers "divine-minded."—This exposition may be useful to those persons who chance to read in the Chronicle articles touching religion and the Established Church of England.

In Queen Mab, a poem by the "divine-minded—unearthly, seraphical thing of the elements," Mr. Percy Bysshe Shelley, the admiration of the Chronicle, whom God is called upon to bless, are these lines:—

> There is no God:
> Nature confirms the faith his death-groan sealed:
> . . . infinity within,
> Infinity without, belie Creation;
> The exterminable spirit it contains
> Is Nature's only God!
> . . . The name of God
> Has fenced about all crime with holiness—
> *Himself the creature of his worshippers.*
>
> . . . .
>
> Earth groans beneath *religion's iron age,*
> And priests dare babble of a God of Peace.

These lines are selected from amongst others much more appalling, which we literally dared not quote; and it is on the head of this writer that the Chronicle ventures to invoke the blessing of the Almighty, in whom this poem expresses the most unqualified disbelief, and whose very name and attributes are the unvarying theme of its ridicule and invective!

But as the Chronicle has identified its principles with those of this "seraphical thing of the elements," it might be generally useful that Mr. Shelley's notions of affairs in general should be published; so that judging from what it has thus boldly adopted, we may conveniently ascertain the Chronicle's moral and political creed, as well as its religious creed.

The poem we have quoted has announced its author as an Atheist; the following character will evince his faith and feelings in and for Christianity. We dare not insult our readers by naming Him to whom the subjoined lines allude

> . . . . .He led
> The crowd; He taught them justice, truth, and peace,
> In semblance; but He lit within their souls
> The quenchless flames of zeal, and blessed the sword
> He brought on earth to satiate with the blood
> Of truth and freedom His malignant soul.
> At length His mortal frame was led to death.

These lines; the epithet Almighty Tyrant as applied to the Divinity, who in his reigning over us is called "the prototype of human misrule"; the term "senile puerility" used for religion, which is afterwards personified as a "prolific fiend," will satisfy our readers as to the claims of the late Mr. Shelley upon the prayers of Christians and the praises of his country.

The political creed of the Chronicle's "unearthly creature" may be estimated with equal fairness by the following passages:—

> Nature rejects the monarch, not the man;
> The subject, not the citizen; for kings
> And subjects, mutual foes, forever play
> A losing game into each other's hands,
> Whose stakes are vice and misery.
>   The man
> Of virtuous soul commands not, nor obeys.
>   ***   ***   ***
> From kings, and priests, and statesmen, war arose,
> Whose safety is man's deep unbettered woe,
> Whose grandeur his debasement.   Let the axe
> Strike at the root, the poison-tree will fall;
>   ***   ***   ***
> Kings, priests, and statesmen, blast the human flower
> Even in its tender bud; their influence darts
> Like subtle poison through the bloodless veins
> Of desolate society.

Kings are called generally

> —Royal murderers, whose mean thrones
> Are bought by crimes of treachery and gore.

The blasphemy which is mixed up with this abuse of Monarchs and their Governments, as by the law established, in a subsequent passage, is so tremendous that it is impossible to quote it even to shew our readers what the Whig Chronicle enthusiastically admires; but when we state that the most moderate part of the subject is contained in the following description of Heaven, the reader may judge the nature of the rest of it:—

> —Heaven, a meed for those who dare belie
> Their human nature, quake, believe, and cringe
> Before the mockeries of earthly power."
>   . . . .
> Twin sister of Religion, Selfishness,
> Rival in Crime and Falsehood.

And thus we could go on extracting treason and blasphemy from this interdicted book; but we think that we have done enough to shew the merits of the man upheld by the leading Whig paper of England, as an object of admiration, as *the friend of the universe,* as a seraphical thing of the elements, for whom it utters a prayer to the Almighty.

[*The article goes on to comment on The Chronicle's endorsement of Shelley as a "candid avowal of the real principles of the Chronicle," etc. Carlile, the unblushing head of the sect (i.e., atheism), has been commiserated by The Chronicle. The public should notice these avowals, for on this basis "we may fairly estimate the exertions . . . of Hume . . . and Brougham."*]

COMMENT IN THE REPUBLICAN

[From The Republican, August 16, 1822 (6: 380-381), entitled "Death of Percy Bysshe Shelley."]

The celebrated author of "Queen Mab" is no more! We sincerely regret the premature death of so great a genius so well applied. The following account of his death is taken from the "Examiner" of Sunday the 4th inst. We shall seek another opportunity to do our duty by doing justice to his memory.

[*The article then quotes the paragraph which appeared in the August 4 Examiner and concludes by quoting the account of Shelley's death as given in The Morning Chronicle, for which see p. 321 in this volume.*]

COMMENT IN THE BRITISH LUMINARY

[From The British Luminary and Weekly Intelligence, August 18, 1822 (no. 203, p. 685). The quotation from John Bull is from the issue of August 12 (no. 87, p. 693). This item was reprinted entire, without comment, in The Republican for August 23 (6:408) under the title, "From the British Luminary."]

We have no observations to make on Mr. Shelley's opinions; but be they what they may, the following mode of reflecting upon his death by the *John Bull,* is so pure a specimen of the cant which it affects to despise, we cannot help submitting the parody which follows it:

"Mr. Bysshe Shelley, the author of that abominable and blasphemous book called *Queen Mab,* was lately drowned in a storm somewhere in the Mediterranean. His object in visiting that part of the world, it was said, was to coalesce with some others of his opinions to *write down Christianity.* The visitation is, therefore, striking; and the termination of his life (considering his creed) not more awful than *surprising.*" *John Bull.*

Parody

"The Marquis of L—[ondonderry], the author of those detestable measures which gave up the South of Italy to the most coarse and leaden despotism in Europe—delivered Genoa to a tyrant, in the face of a British pledge of honour—and who indemnified the employment of torture in Ireland to extort confession; lost his life on Monday last in a fit of insanity, just as he was about to proceed to the Continent with the object of doing his best for the extinction of dawning freedom in Spain and Greece. The visitation is therefore striking; and the termination of his life (considering *his* creed) not more awful than surprising."

Admirably philosophical in both instances, gentle reader, is it not? and fit to be bound up with the pious tracts which narrate God's Judgment upon Apprentices who hire boats on Sunday. Apprentices are never drowned on any other day, and as no persons lose their lives at sea except authors, like Mr. Shelley, his wreck is, of course, *surprising*. This from the detesters of *Cant*—Gad-a mercy, John!

AN OBITUARY DEFENCE

[From The Paris Monthly Review, August, 1822 (2:392), entitled "Hellas: A Poem. By Percy Bysshe Shelley. London. 1882 (original)." This article was very probably written by Horace Smith, who was in Paris at the time and in communication with Shelley. He was one of the few people—and possibly the only person in Paris at the time—who could speak with special knowledge of Shelley's generosity in financial affairs, since he acted as the poet's financial agent in London. Moreover, the letter quoted at the end of the article is the one written by Leigh Hunt to Smith. And Smith had written to Cyrus Redding only a few days before hearing of Shelley's death: "We have a Paris English magazine. . . . I occasionally give it a lift with my pen" (Cyrus Redding's *Fifty Years' Recollections*, London, 1858, II, 205).

In general tone and in one or two particular expressions the article suggests Smith's letters of the time and his later recollections of Shelley, both published in A. H. Beavan's *James and Horace Smith* (London, 1899). On the other hand, the reviewer categorically denies a personal acquaintance with Shelley and makes such erroneous statements as that Shelley never published a line anonymously and that he printed *Queen Mab* while at college. These errors would have been possible for Smith, though unlikely. It is possible that the article was written by another person with information supplied by Horace Smith.]

While this poem was lying open before us, the pen in our hand, and the heading of our article just written, we received from a Correspondent the following communication, which we lay before our readers in preference to a cold critique. We have determined to let the title of our article stand as it was intended: we could not otherwise well introduce an obituary notice into this department of our work; and we are anxious to record our intention of reviewing the last of Mr. Shelley's productions, before we had heard the fate of the unfortunate author.

Nothing could be more displaced than a series of observations from us on the afflicting catastrophe, which has snatched from English literature a votary of the warmest enthusiasm, blended with the most pre-eminent genius. In that capacity alone did we regard Mr. Shelley—for we knew him not. But, undeterred by calumny or clamour, we should have rejoiced to bring before the circle into which our pages are received, those passages of his works which would have made evident his powers of poetry, without offering violence to feelings or opinions the most remote from his. We should have been pleased to do this in Mr. Shelley's lifetime, because he was the victim of persecution; we shall be proud to do it now that he is dead, because the persecutors still exist, though the victim is no more. From the intention expressed in the following paper, our readers may look for such a performance, we trust at no distant day, and, we promise them, from no incompetent pen.

We shall only further take occasion to observe, that let our own wide difference from Mr. Shelley's doctrines be what it may—let our earlier impressions of his sentiments have been what they might—we have been long since satisfied on the score of his personal character and individual merit; for the hand which traced the tribute we proceed to give our readers, could not have opened to the intimate grasp of unworthiness— the head which dictated it never could have been the dupe of deceit—nor the heart which prompted the effusion, have held fellowship with anything short of virtue.

> Who would not sing for Lycidas? He knew
> Himself to sing, and build the lofty rhime;
> He must not float upon his watery bier
> Unwept, and welter in the parching wind
> Without the meed of some melodious tear.
>   Milton.

Never did the remorseless deep engulph so gentle, so angelic, so melodious a Lycidas, as Percy Bysshe Shelley; and yet never was there a name associated with more black, poisonous, and bitter calumny than his. To explain this apparent solecism, it will suffice to state that he had the misfortune to entertain, from his very earliest youth, opinions, both in religion and politics, diametrically opposed to established systems; and conceiving the happiness of mankind unattainable under the present forms of society, he set about the promulgation of his own theories with all the zeal and conviction of an apostle, and all the generous indiscretion of a boy. Disdaining to hold any compromise with that which he conceived to be fraud and tyranny, he never published a line to which he did not affix his name; and the example of this audacity, in a youth of birth and fortune, not only aggravated the wrath of his theoretical opponents, but afforded them a butt against which they might securely launch all their envenomed shafts.—A certain portion of the English periodical press systematically drags forth the individual from his domestic privacy, when they disapprove his doctrine. The assassins, spies, and informers, who act as purveyors to this literary conspiracy, were subtle and busy in the same proportion that the object of their wiles was incautious and undisguised. In his zeal for the unrestrained liberty of the public press, they knew that he would never claim the protection of the law; and while some invented gross libels upon his private character, and detailed them with a most plausible circumstantiality, others more timid, though not less inveterate, circulated atrocious innuendoes, still keeping on the safe side of prosecution.—It is by no means the object of this hasty notice to exculpate Mr. Shelley from the charge of sometimes adopting crude and rash opinions, but it must be recollected that the most objectionable of his works, "Queen Mab," was never published by him, though printed when he was a boy at College, and distributed among a few friends. A piratical bookseller lately obtained a copy and reprinted it, not only without the consent, but to the great displeasure of the author, then residing at Pisa, who, with his usual candour, avowed that more mature consideration had induced him to retract several of the theories promulgated in that youthful effusion.

Perhaps there never existed a greater enthusiast for the happiness of mankind than Mr. Shelley:—feeling that they were capable of higher destinies, his thoughts were unceasingly employed in the consummation of a political and moral Millennium: and though his romantic visions, and the means which he considered necessary for their accomplishment, may occassionally impugn the solidity of his judgment, they may surely be allowed to testify to the benevolence of his heart. Though too elemental and cosmopolitan in his views to limit his ample love, which embraced the whole world, he was intensely interested in the fate of his native country; and as to individual friendships, he abandoned himself to them with a self-sacrifice which, in so interested and money-worshipping a country as England, not unfrequently entailed upon him the ridicule of worldlings. Those who were incapable of appreciating, still less imitating his noble generosity, found a miserable gratification in adducing it as proof of a disordered intellect. His high, unearthly aspirations, and the melting charities of his heart, occasioned him perhaps to be too regardless of money; and though practising in his own person the most rigid self-denial and economy, he offered in early life the singular spectacle of a man who had involved himself in extensive pecuniary embarrassments, solely for the extrication and assistance of others. From these difficulties he was relieved by large sacrifices of his entail, but continued always to appropriate a considerable portion of his limited income to purposes of benevolence.

As a fact, Mr. Shelley has never had fair play. The outrageous and fierce persecution by which he was assailed, and the malignant libels of which he was the object, had effected their purpose;—his works were scarcely known, except by those objectionable passages which his opponents sedulously obtruded upon the public. In a future Number we may perhaps follow an opposite course, and select a few specimens of such poetical beauties as involve no point of controversy; when, if we mistake not, our readers will admit that he exhibits an unrivalled opulence of harmonious language, and wild exuberance of imagination; though they may regret the absence of that sober judgment, and groundwork of intelligible object, which can alone give full effect to the higher sublimations of the Muse. Under no circumstances, however, could his poems have obtained great popularity:—apart from their questionable theories, they were altogether too flighty and imaginative for vulgar apprehension; and the glimpses of concealed purpose which the author seemed apprehensive of more fully divulging, imparted to the whole an air of abstraction, mystery, and allegory.

His pen, even when it was directed against his revilers, seemed to be guided by the hand of Love, and acrimonious expressions rarely fell from his lips. Could the reader, who has perhaps seen him held up in the pages of the Quarterly Review as a demon, have transported himself to the beautiful Bay of Lerici in the Gulf of Spezzia, and beheld a fragile youth moving about upon the earth like a gentle spirit, imagining incessant plans for promoting the welfare of the great circle of mankind, while he formed the happiness of the little one in which he moved, and recreating himself with music, literature, and poetic reveries while he floated in his "fatal and perfidious bark" upon the blue waves of the Mediterranean—how little would he dream that he was gazing upon the traduced and calumniated Percy Bysshe Shelley!—and how keenly would he regret that such a being, not having yet consummated his thirtieth year, should be "sunk beneath the watery floor," ere the maturing of his great and undoubted genius had enabled him to perfect some imperishable record of his fame; and before the calm appeal of his virtues, and the evidence of his blameless and innocent life had re-established him in the opinions of the candid and the good.

We have only now to copy, with a trembling hand, the particulars of the fatal catastrophe, contained in a letter from one of Mr. Shelley's friends, himself a poet of no mean celebrity, and well competent to appreciate the loss which the whole circle of his associates, and the world at large, have sustained.

[*The article concludes with the often-quoted letter of Leigh Hunt which first appeared in The Morning Chronicle of August 12 (q. v.), p. 321.*]

OBITUARY NOTICE IN THE GENTLEMAN'S MAGAZINE

[From The Gentleman's Magazine, September, 1822 (part 2, 92: 283), entitled "Percy Bysshe Shelley, Esq."]

July 8. Supposed to have perished at sea, in a storm, somewhere off Via Reggia, on the coast of Italy, between Leghorn and the Gulf of Spezia, Percey Bysshe Shelley, Esq. He went out a sailing in a little schooner, in company with his friend Capt. Williams, son of Capt. John Williams, of the Hon. East India Company's Bengal Infantry, and lately exchanged from the 8th Light Dragoons to the 21st Fusileers. He had been to Pisa, and was returning to his country abode at Lerici. The boat has since been found capsized. Mr. Shelley was the eldest son of Sir Timothy Shelley, Bart. M. A. of University College, Oxford, of which Society his son was for a short time a member. He married a daughter of Mr. Godwin by the celebrated Mary Wollstonecraft, and was an intimate friend of Lord Byron and Mr. Leigh Hunt. The wives of Mr. Shelley and Capt. Williams were both at Leghorn overwhelmed with grief.

Mr. Shelley is unfortunately too well known for his infamous novels and poems. He openly professed himself an atheist. His works bear the following titles: "Prometheus Chained." "Alastor, or the Spirit of Solitude; and other Poems, 1816." "Queen Mab." "Cenci."

It has been stated that Mr. Shelley had gone to Pisa to establish a periodical work, with the assistance of Lord Byron and Mr. Leigh Hunt.

OBITUARY NOTICE IN THE MONTHLY MAGAZINE AND THE MONTHLY REPOSITORY

[From The Monthly Magazine and British Register, September, 1822 (54: 178). Copied in The Monthly Repository of Theology and General Literature, September, 1882 (17:577).]

Aged 30, *Percy Bysshe Shelley*, Esq., eldest son of Sir Timothy Shelley, of *Castle Goring*, Bart. He perished at sea, in a storm, with his friend Captain Williams, of the Fusiliers, off Via Reggia, on the coast of Italy. He had been at Pisa, and was returning to his villa at Lerici. Mr. Shelley was the author of "Cenci," a tragedy: "Queen Mab," and several minor pieces, which prove him to have been a man of highly cultivated genius. His last work was "Hellas," a dramatic poem, called forth by the recent events in Greece, in which he took the warmest interest, and dedicated it to Prince Alexander Mavrocordato, whose friendship he enjoyed, and for whom he expressed the highest admiration.

OBITUARY NOTICE IN THE NEW MONTHLY MAGAZINE

[From The New Monthly Magazine, October 1, 1822 (N. S. 6:472), entitled "Biographical Particulars of Celebrated Persons Lately Deceased: Percy Byssche Shelley, Esq." The obvious connection between this article and that in The Paris Monthly Review for August (*q.v.*, and head-note) may indicate Cyrus Redding as the author. Redding was known later as an admirer of Shelley. In 1822 he was the principal working editor of The New Monthly Magazine. Galignani published The Paris Monthly Review, and from 1815-1818 Redding had been editor of Galignani's Paris Weekly Messenger.]

In a storm off Reggia on the 8th of August, P. B. Shelley, Esq., eldest son of Sir Timothy Shelley, Bart. of Castle Goring. He was sailing in a pleasure boat with a friend, Captain Williams of the Fusileers, when the boat overset, and he was drowned. Mr. Shelley was in the 30th year of his age. His last work was "Hellas," a dramatic poem, called forth by the recent events in Greece, in which he took the warmest interest, and dedicated it to Prince Alexander Mavrocordato, whose friendship he enjoyed, and for whom he expressed the highest admiration. Mr. Shelley was a man of talents of a very high order, but they have not been justly appreciated. His opinions were opposed to a strong party in politics, which had he ranked on its side would have made the freedom and openness of those opinions the proof of virtuous honesty, or, at most, the "venial error" of youth. The reverse being the case, however, the latitude of his ideas both prevented his receiving common justice from those who would be thought the impartial literary dictators of the day, and furnished them with a ground of attack which they systemmatically used; without regard to truth or honour, to defame and persecute him. Whatever may be our ideas of Mr. Shelley's sentiments on points on which we cannot agree with him, his private character was most estimable; and he had the merit, and a merit of the very first order in these days it is, of being no hypocrite. Mr. Shelley was an optimist and enthusiast, who imagined in his youthful reveries that man was capable of greater happiness than he seems to enjoy, and a much more worthy being than he will ever be this side the millennium. His notions were often romantic, frequently absurd to the philosopher, but never directed to any object but what he imagined was for the benefit of his fellow-men, to relieve whose distresses he often involved himself in difficulties, and, disregarding the sneer of worldly-minded prudence, looked solely to the good he could effect. Such a disposition would naturally be led into acts that were an aberration from the beaten track of the multitude which always thinks itself in the right. Those matters of opinion which rest between his Creator and him must be left to the beneficence that watches and orders all things and does unerringly what is right. Mr. Shelley has never been fairly treated as a poet; his works are full of wild beauties and original ideas, too much intermixed with fanciful theory, but they display a richness of language and imagination rarely surpassed. He published "Prometheus Unbound," and "Cenci," a tragedy, with some minor poems. "Queen Mab," a poem written when very young, and of which the tendency was most indefensible, was printed for a few friends only. Some years after a copy got into the hand of a sordid and piratical book-seller, who gave notice of publishing it; and, on being remonstrated with and told that it was a youthful production that the author wished to be suppressed, said he did not care; Mr. Shelley could get no injunction from the Chancellor against him, and he should print it. Mr. Shelley had avowed his retractation of several of the theories promulgated in it, the offspring of youthful inexperience and enthusiasm. Mr. Shelley has left a widow and children behind him.

OBITUARY NOTICE IN THE DRAMA

[From The Drama, or Theatrical Pocket Magazine, December, 1822 (3: 387-393), under Dramatic Necrology for 1822, entitled "Sep. 8—Percy Bysshe Shelley, Esq."

John Watson Dalby, author of the verse tribute quoted in this article, was an industrious minor journalist and poet of modern attainments. In 1818-1819 he was editor of a department in The Miniature Magazine. He published frequent contributions in this magazine, in both prose and verse, and in Arliss' Pocket Magazine of Classic and Polite Literature, between 1818 and 1823. He was the author of a poem on Shelley's birthday in The Ladies' Penny Gazette, August 3, 1833, and of one or two poems to Leigh Hunt. He published three volumes of poetry, beginning with *Poems*, in 1822. He died in India in 1832 and received the tribute of a poem in The London Spy entitled "To the Memory of J. W. Dalby."]

Mr. Shelley was the eldest son of Sir John Shelley, Bart. He was educated at Oxford, where his fearless and independent spirit displeased the heads of the university; while, at the same time, his superior abilities,

which were easily evinced, excited no small portion of that universal vice
—envy. Eventually, his want of hypocrisy, and some eccentricities which
are the usual attendants upon extraordinary genius, caused him to be
ejected from the College, a circumstance which reflects less honour upon
it than upon himself, and which, in all probability, had much influence in
causing his mind to take the course which it so steadily pursued. He married while little more than seventeen, and this was an action, which, perhaps more than any other of his life, he had reason to repent. It was one
of those hurried and impetuous resolutions of youth which too frequently
involve the actors in misery. Scandal has been busy in reporting wild and
strange stories relative to this union; but we are sure our readers would
not thank us for repeating tales, horrible and disgusting in themselves, and
the greater part of which have no foundation whatever in truth. By his
first lady Mr. Shelley had two children, whose names (Henry and Ianthe)
he has introduced into that early effusion of his genius "Queen Mab."
After the death of this lady, Mr. Shelley married Mary Woolstoncraft
[*sic*] Godwin, daughter of the celebrated William Godwin, author of "Political Justice," "Caleb Williams," etc. etc. whose wife was the singularly-
gifted author of "The Rights of Women." This marriage, contracted at a
period when his character was formed and his judgment matured, was altogether as productive of happiness, as the former was of the unhappy differences which led to a separation. The present Mrs. Shelley is the daughter
with which Mary Woolstoncraft, then Mrs. Godwin, died in childbirth,
and springing from such a philosophical source, has received an education
and turn of mind, which rendered her, in every respect, a congenial companion for Mr. Shelley. She has acquired great literary celebrity by her
"Frankenstein," and other works, which evince the power and depth of
her imagination, and has now in the press a work around which recent circumstances will throw an intense and extraordinary interest.

Some time after the peace, Mr. Shelley travelled through Switzerland
and France with Lord Byron, and has generally been residing with or
near him ever since.

Mr. Shelley's principal productions were, "Queen Mab," a Philosophical Poem; "Alastor, or the Spirit of Solitude"; "Henry and Ellen," a
Poetical Tale;[1] "The Revolt of Islam"; "Prometheus Unbound," a Lyrical Drama; "The Cenci," a Tragedy; and "Adonais," an elegy on the
death of the young poet Keats, which is one of Mr. Shelley's latest works.

Mr. Shelley perished at sea, in a storm, with his friend, Captain Williams, of the Fusileers, on the evening of the 8th of September, 1822,
somewhere off Via Reggia, on the coast of Italy, between Leghorn and
the Gulf of Spezzia. He was in about the thirtieth year of his age when
he died, and has left children, but we know not how many.

The conflict of wild and terrible emotions which would distract an
ordinary mind almost to annihilation, Shelley could calmly and fearlessly
contemplate, and, like the rock, which offers its unyielding breast to the

---

[1] Meaning probably "Rosalind and Helen."—N.I.W.

ungovernable fury of the world of waters, remain himself "unhurt amid the war of elements." Such was the character of his genius, and it was lucky for him that it was so, as otherwise, he too, like the sensitive Keats, would have fallen beneath the poisoned shafts of his indefatigable and malevolent assailants.   Towering genius and exalted virtue, however much they may attract the veneration of those who are capable of appreciating their worth or emulating their example, are from their lofty situation only the more exposed to the attacks of malice and detraction.

> He who ascends to mountain tops shall find
> The loftiest peaks most wrapt in clouds and snow;
> He who surpasses or subdues mankind,
> Must look down on the hate of all below!

Mr. Shelley has been represented as the *enemy of his species*—his heroism has been termed *lunacy*,—his philosophy *folly*, or worse—his virtue *a cheat*—his religion (and it was the Religion of Love and Nature) a *bubble!*—Yet the life of this calumniated man was spent in doing kind and generous actions, and admitting even that he erred in theory, the most obstinate of bigots could point out no one action of his life at which a Christian would blush; and the most noble men of the age admitted him to their intimate friendship and association.

As a writer Mr. Shelley possessed "*a capacity to comprehend the universe,*" and imagination of the finest and most prolific powers, and a command of language more extensive than that of any author of the day. His "Rosalind and Helen"; his "Revolt of Islam," his "Alastor," and his "Prometheus Unbound," possess beauties of the highest order.   In the modern eclogue of "Rosalind and Helen," in particular, (says a critic by no means favorable to Mr. Shelley, but who, on this occasion, could afford to do justice to his splendid talents) "there is a pensive sadness, a delicious melancholy, nurst in the purest, the deepest recesses of the heart, and springing up like a fountain in the desert, that pervades the poem, and forms its principal attraction. The rich yet delicate imagery that is everywhere scattered over it, is like the glowing splendour of the setting sun, when he retires to rest, amid the blessings of exulting nature. It is the balmy breath of the summer breeze, the twilight's last and holiest sigh."[2] —In the tragedy of the "*Cenci,*" the interest forms a perfect contrast to that we feel in "Rosalind and Helen." It is dark, wild, and unearthly. The characters that appear in it are of no mortal stamp; they are daemons in human guise, inscrutable in their actions, subtle in their revenge. Each has his smile of awful meaning—his purport of hellish tendency. The tempest that rages in his bosom is irrepressible, but by death. The phrenzied groan that diseased imagination extorts from his perverted soul, is as the thunderclap that reverberates amid the cloud capt summits of the Alps. It is the storm that convulses all nature—that lays bare the face of Heaven, and gives transient glimpses of destruction yet to be. Then in the midst of these accumulated horrors comes the gentle Beatrice,

[2] London Magazine and Monthly Critical and Dramatic Review—see p. 173 above.— N.I.W.

> Who in the gentleness of thy sweet youth
> Hast never trodden on a worm, or bruised
> A living flower, but thou hast pitied it
> With needless tears. (Cenci, page 50.)

She walks in the light of innocence; in the unclouded sunshine of loveliness and modesty; but her felicity is transient as the calm that precedes the tempest; and in the very whispers of her virtue, you hear the indistinct mutterings of distant thunder. She is conceived in the true master-spirit of genius; and, in the very instant of her parricide, comes home to our imagination fresh as in the spring-time of innocence—hallowed in the deepest recesses of melancholy. The agitation this lovely but unhappy creature experiences after the commission of the incest, is powerfully descriptive.

[*Quotes Act III, scene i, lines 6-23*]

The idea of approaching execution paralyses the soul of Beatrice, and she thus frantically expresses her horror . . .

[*Quotes Act V, scene iv, lines 48-67*]

The premature and awful death of Mr. Shelley has been celebrated by several poetical pens, friendly and otherwise; among them are those of Mr. Arthur Brooke and Bernard Barton. Our correspondent Mr. J. W. Dalby has also employed his pen upon the subject, and from his poem, which appeared in No. 4 of a Poetical Magazine, entitled the "Troubadour,"[3] we extract the following Stanzas:—

> One more is added to the lengthening list
>   Of the lamented but immortal dead;
> Another glorious Minstrel's harp is missed,
>   And low is laid another laurelled head:
>   The heart that felt,—the hand that wrote are fled;
> The mind that gained poetic strength and gave,
> Hath sunk into the silence of the grave.

> Thou'rt gone! but all who listened to thy songs
>   Feel their true music thrill within them yet;
> And dwelling on thy magic power come throngs
>   Of lofty thoughts, saddened by deep regret,
>   That point (although thy glorious sun is set)
> To the bright promise of a purer time
> When man shall suffer less from care and crime.

> Thou'rt gone! but shall not be forgotten till
>   Hearts cease to feel the force of poet-fire!

---

[3] The title of this poem may be inferred from a note to contributors in The Drama for October, 1822 (3: 209), in which is listed various contributions for which "we cannot spare room yet," including *"Lines to Shakespeare and to Shelley,* by Mr. Dalby, from the Troubadour." The British Museum does not possess The Troubadour, and I have been unable to locate it elsewhere.—N.I.W.

Shelley! each lover of his nature will
   Cherish the bright effusions of a lyre
  Not formed to charm awhile, and then expire,
But destined to illumine after days
And win from juster times more general praise.

Unsparing Ocean! thy wild waves have closed
   Around a breast warmed with a heart that beat
With nature's purest feelings—where reposed
   The social virtues in their native seat;
  Where friendship, honor—found a sure retreat;
Long may thy dark blue waves, wild ocean! roll
Ere thou canst waft to Heaven a nobler soul.

LEIGH HUNT DEFENDS THE DEAD

A

[From The Examiner, November 3, 1822 (no. 771, pp. 690-691). Extract from an article on the suicide of Lord Castlereagh. This article, after flaying Castlereagh for his public actions, admits that his death should silence personal criticism, but flays the conservative press for demanding charity toward Castlereagh while refusing it to radicals.]

When, too, the hypocrites cry out about charity towards the dead, do *they* practise what they preach in regard to *their* opponents? Oh no! The charity which they would construe in so preposterous a sense, in order to shield a bad Minister or a bigot King, is never dreamt of when the memory of a writer, whose only offence is a difference of opinion, is to be reviled and blackened. The *Courier* exulted over the death of one of the most amiable and enthusiastically beloved men that ever existed. Yet PERCY SHELLEY had oppressed and injured none. His crime in the eyes of these ultra declaimers about charity, was having entertained, and promulgated, (as what virtuous and benevolent man could help, if he thought it useful to his fellow-creatures?)—opinions upon politics and religion, which they chose to call seditious and blasphemous. "SHELLEY, the writer of some infidel poetry, has been drowned," says the *Courier; "now* he knows whether there is a God or no;"—meaning, that the writer has the satisfaction of thinking the Divine Being will burn Mr. SHELLEY in everlasting flames for holding the same opinions as Spinoza and Bacon. "So Castlereagh has cut his throat," says the Poet of the *Liberal; "*the worst of this is, that his own was not the first;" meaning, that had he died before, the world would have been saved much bloodshed and sorrow. But the malignant assailant of the drowned Philanthropist is in a perfect fury at the "bare idea of an epigram" on the suicide of the obnoxious Minister. And when reminded, that charity to the dead is not for the sole use and benefit of Tory reputations, he justifies himself in the following passage, which (we beg the reader to remark) occurs in the very article wherein he calls the *Liberal* a "scoundrel-like" publication, for its treatment of George the Third and Lord Castlereagh!

"Of the infidel Shelley we should speak in no compromising terms, were he still capable of future mischief. But he is dead, and the world has no more to do with him. His pernicious writings are the legacy he has left us—and with them we shall deal as freely as we would with the obscenities of Rochester or the impiety of Voltaire."

B

[From The Liberal, or Verse and Prose from the South, 1822 (no. 1, preface, p. xi).]

We will give a specimen of the liberality of these new demanders of liberality. The other day, when one of the noblest of human beings, Percy Shelley, who had more religion in his very differences with religion, than thousands of your church-and-state men, was lost on the coast of Italy, the *Courier* said, that "Mr. Percy Shelley, *a writer of infidel poetry,* was drowned." Where was the liberality of this canting insinuation? Where was the decency or, as it turned out, the commonsense of it? Mr. Shelley's death by the waves was followed by Lord Castlereagh's by his own hand; and then the cry for liberal constructions! How could we not turn such a death against the enemies of Mr. Shelley, if we could condescend to affect a moment's agreement with their hypocrisy? But the least we can do is to let these people see that we know them, and to warn them how they assail us.

INCIDENTAL NOTICES IN REVIEWS OF ELEGIES

A

[From The Literary Chronicle and Weekly Review, October 12, 1822 (no. 178, pp. 643-644). The article is entitled "Percy Bysshe Shelley" and is headed with the titles of both Arthur Brooke's and Bernard Barton's poems.]

Most of our readers are acquainted with our sentiments respecting Mr. Shelley—that he was a man who sacrificed a fine genius at the shrine of infidelity, and that he was consequently dangerous in proportion that his talents were splendid. That such a man should have been suddenly cut off from society by a premature death, may be a subject of regret; but there is nothing in his death that redeems the errors of his life, nor does the grave sanctify that which is in itself unholy. It is painful to speak of the dead except in terms of great charity, but really the friends of Mr. Shelley have outraged all bounds of decency, and ascribed to him what Pope did to Berkeley, "ev'ry virtue under heaven."

Mr. Arthur Brooke is a gentleman of talents, and strongly tinctured with those principles which Mr. Shelley so openly avowed; it is not, therefore to be wondered at, that he should have written an Elegy on this "most distinguished philosopher, philanthropist, and poet," as he calls him. But whatever fellow feeling he might have with Mr. Shelley, his muse appears to have had none; for his elegy is tame and absurd, full of false metaphors and overstrained compliments, and altogether unworthy of Mr.

Brooke's talents; while the principles it would establish are as injurious as those of Mr. Shelley. The last three stanzas will illustrate all we have said of it. . . .

[*Quotes the last three stanzas. See p. 351 in this volume.*]

Mr. Barton's muse has been called forth with a far different feeling; he could not tamely bear to hear Mr. Brooke call Shelley "a most distinguished philosopher and philanthropist," or that his voice was "a living stream of love and wisdom," and he himself "the last defense of a bewilder'd world"; and therefore he has come forth, not to deprecate the talents of Mr. Shelley, but to put his philosophy and philanthropy on their true footing. We have seen many pieces of Mr. Barton's that we liked better, but we admire his zeal in the cause of Christianity against the open and daring attacks of infidelity. The following opening stanzas will give a fair view of the merits and objects of this short poem:—

[*Quotes the first five stanzas, for which see p. 353 in this volume.*]

The commendatory verses to which Mr. Barton alludes are added to the preceeding poem; they are, however, written in the same tone of feeling with regard to Mr. Shelley's principles as the verses on his death.

B

[From The Eclectic Review, November, 1822 (N. S. 18: 476), entitled "On Barton's Stanzas on the Death of Percy Bysshe Shelley."

This criticism of Shelley, which escaped my notice, is here reprinted, by the generous permission of Professor Marsh, as it appears in "The Early Reviews of Shelley," by George L. Marsh, in Modern Philology, August, 1929 (27: 73-95).]

In comment suggested by Barton's poem on Shelley this review suggests that probably not one of Shelley's published works has had purchasers enough to pay the cost of paper and printing; yet everybody has heard of his atheism and his association with "Lord Byron, Leigh Hunt, Hazlitt, and other apostles of the last and lowest school of infidelity. The Quarterly Reviewers lent their aid to lash his publications into notice. But still, his works have remained unread and unreadable." . . . "Poetry, and beautiful poetry, is to be found in his works; though he has never, perhaps, excelled that wild, fanciful brilliant, and absurd allegory which appeared in 1816 under the title of 'Alastor, or the Spirit of Solitude.' But the absence of the sober qualities of common sense and virtuous feeling, the incoherence, savage misanthropy, and daring impiety which disfigure that poem, and which characterize all Mr. Shelley's subsequent productions, deprive his happiest efforts of the power to please, and brand them with worthlessness." The reviewer expresses pity for Shelley in his fate, but makes sarcastic comments on Brooke's eulogy which Barton answers.

C

[From The Monthly Magazine or British Register, October, 1822 (54:255). In Literary and Critical Proemium, entitled "Elegy on the Death of Percy Bysshe Shelley."]

The sudden and afflicting catastrophe, which terminated the career of one of the most original and imaginative of our poets, has excited general sympathy and regret; and the admirers of his brilliant and eccentric genius will not be slow to lament his fate, and commemorate his high endowments. We notice a short, but elegant and feeling tribute to his memory, in an *Elegy on the Death of Percy Bysshe Shelley*, by Arthur Brooke, whose compositions we have heretofore had opportunities of mentioning with deserved approbation.   There is much pathos and poetical spirit in Mr. Brooke's stanzas; and it is an affecting consideration, that the generous poet, who so lately gave "the need of his melodious tear" to the grave of the young and unfortunate Keats, to whom he was personally unknown, should so soon claim the same melancholy offices, and receive them, as in this instance, from stranger hands.   It is not fit that he should "float upon his watery bier unwept," who has "built the lofty rhyme" so often and so well, and from whom, in the maturity of his extraordinary powers, so much more might have been expected.   Nor will the effusion under our notice, though extremely pleasing and creditable to the sentiments and talents of its author, supersede the exertion of the high and acknowledged genius of some of Mr. Shelley's personal friends, on whom the task of raising an honourable and lasting monument to his fame seems naturally to devolve.

D

[From The Gentleman's Magazine and Historical Chronicle (part 2, 92:623), Supplement to 1822 (part 2, 92:623). Entitled "Elegy on the Death of Percy Bysshe Shelley," by Arthur Brooke.]

Mr. Brooke, an enthusiastic young man, who has written some good but licentious verses, has here got up a collection of stanzas, for the ostensible purpose "of commemorating the talents and virtues of that highly-gifted individual, Percy Byssche Shelley" [*sic*] *(Preface).*

Concerning the talents of Mr. Shelley, we know no more than that he published certain convulsive caperings of Pegasus labouring under cholic pains; namely, some purely fantastic verses, in the hubble bubble, toil and trouble style; and as to Mr. Shelley's virtues, if he belonged (as we understand he did,) to a junta, whose writings tend to make our sons profligates, and our daughters strumpets, we ought as justly to regret the decease of the Devil (if that were possible), as of one of his coadjutors.   Seriously speaking, however, we feel no pleasure in the untimely death of this Tyro of the Juan school, that pre-eminent academy of Infidels, Blasphemers, Seducers, and Wantons.   We had much rather have heard, that he and the rest of the fraternity had been consigned to a Monastery of La Trappe, for correction of their dangerous principles, and expurgation of their corrupt minds.   Percy Bysshe Shelley is a fitter subject for a penitentiary dying speech, than a lauding elegy; for the muse of the rope, rather than that of the cypress; the muse that advises us "warning to take by others harm, and we shall do full well."

XIV

ODE

TO THE AUTHOR OF "QUEEN MAB"

[From The Theological Inquirer or Polemical Magazine, July, 1815 (1:380-381). The identity of the author, who signs himself F., is unknown—see note, p. 45.]

I.

O thou! who hast dispelled the shame
That hung about the poet's name,
The poet! rarely seen on that rough shore,
Where the bleak winds of independence roar,
    And brave the nerve of him who loves
    Beyond the orient's spicy groves
To roam with Liberty (in proud disdain
Of Grandeur's palaces) her wild domain.
    But ah! too oft recumbent found
    On the odour-sprinkled ground,
    Trod by the tyrant's footstep base,
    Kindling the liar's incense vase:
O thou! who hast redeemed this load of shame!
A bard obscure invokes thy future fame.

II.

Though *now* defrauded of the praise
    Due to thy truth-supporting lays;
Though noxious prejudice and chilling Sloth
Retard thy blooming chaplet's flowery growth;
    Though *now* a shackled press refuse
    To aid thy nobly-daring muse;
Yet is that time in progress when thy theme
Shall universal spread as day's bright beam.
    Then shall the bloody brand of ire
    Quenched in love and peace expire:
    Their mitres, cowls, and crosiered staves
    Be torn from man-deluding knaves;
The gorgeous canopies of tyrant-might
Sink and o'erwhelm him in eternal night.

III.

O! how thy rich, poetic page
    My growing wonder did engage:
Me thought with Fairy Mab I soared, to trace

The vast immense of universal space.
    While with the pure unspotted soul
    That from Ianthe's bosom stole,
I shed the sacred drops of Feeling's birth,
To view the moral desart of the earth:
    And oft I cursed "th'almighty fiend,"
    Who from his empyrean lean'd
    And poured the venom'd vial of strife
    To damp the hope of human life.
These truths the voice of nations shall proclaim
In coming times, and know, and bless thy name:—
Hail then, immortal bard! hail to thy future fame!

                                                    F.

SONNET

TO THE AUTHOR OF "THE REVOLT OF ISLAM"

[From The Examiner, February 8, 1818 (no. 528, p. 88). This sonnet was republished by the author, Shelley's friend Horace Smith, in his *Amarynthus the Nympholept* (1820) with the third line slightly altered. In reviewing Smith's book in January, 1821, The London Magazine and Theatrical Inquisitor (p. 78) quotes the sonnet entire and pronounces it "excellent."

Smith's friendship with Shelley began shortly before his visit to Marlow in 1817. From then on he was one of the poet's most valuable and disinterested friends. Shelley gives a favorable sketch of his character in his Letter to Maria Gisborne.]

O thou bold Herald of aspirings high,
    No prostituted Muse inspired thy story,
But human Love lent thee his wings to fly
    Forward into a coming age of glory,
    When Tyrannies and Superstitions hoary
Beneath the foot of Liberty shall lie,
    And men shall turn from those oppressors gory
To worship Peace, and Love, and Charity.

The heart that could conceive so bright a day,
    Is proof that it may come;—therefore shall they
        Who live on tears and darkness, steep each tooth
    In poison'd gall to make that heart their prey;
        But thou shalt smile and pity, giving thy youth
        To glorious hopes, and all-defying Truth.

                                                    H.

TO PERCY SHELLEY

ON THE DEGRADING NOTIONS OF DEITY

[From Leigh Hunt's *Foliage*, American edition, 1818, p. 73. The original publication of the sonnet was in the English edition, 1817. The publication of this and the following sonnet attracted unfavorable Tory notice and helped identify Shelley with the Cockneys.]

What wonder, Percy, that with jealous rage
Men should defame the kindly and the wise,
When in the midst of the all-beauteous skies,
And all this lovely world, that should engage
Their mutual search for the old golden age,
They seat a phantom, swelled into grim size
Out of their own passions and bigotries,
And then, for fear, proclaim it meek and sage!
And this they call a light and a revealing!
Wise as the clown, who plodding home at night
In autumn, turns at call of fancied elf,
And sees upon the fog, with ghastly feeling,
A giant shadow in its imminent might,
Which his own lanthorn throws up from himself.

TO THE SAME

[From Leigh Hunt's *Foliage*, American edition, 1818, p. 74. The original publication was in the English edition, 1817. See preceding note.]

Yet, Percy, not for this, should he whose eye
Sees loveliness, and the unselfish joy
Of justice, turn him, like a peevish boy,
At hindrances and thwartings; and deny
Wisdom's divinest privilege, constancy;
That which most proves him free from the alloy
Of useless earth,—least prone to the decoy
That clamours down weak pinions from the sky.
The Spirit of Beauty, though by solemn quires
Hourly blasphemed, stoops not from its calm end,
And forward breathing love, but ever on
Rolls the round day, and calls the starry fires
To their glad watch. Therefore, high-hearted friend,
Be still with thine own task in unison.

STANZAS ADDRESSED TO PERCY BYSSHE SHELLEY

[From *Poems*, by Bernard Barton, 1820. The London Magazine for August, 1820, quotes a part of this poem in reviewing the volume. Barton reprinted the poem in 1822 with his *Verses on the Death of Percy Bysshe Shelley*.

Bernard Barton, often called "the Quaker poet," was one of the dullest and most popular English poets of the 1820's and 1830's. Though a very few of the better periodicals ventured to hint a disparity between his genius and his piety, the provincial press and a large number of London magazines confounded the two and praised him indiscriminately. He was a man of genuine piety and charity, in which he differed from most of the critics whom Shelley's "impiety" offended. His character may be judged from his correspondence with his son-in-law, Edward Fitzgerald, the poet, and his friend, Charles Lamb. Lamb's friendship with Barton was no doubt part of the inspiration for his kindly treatment of Quakers in *Essays of Elia*.]

I.

Forests, and lakes, the majesty of mountains,
  The dazzling glaciers, and the musical sound
Of winds, and waves, or softer gush of fountains;—
  In sights and sounds like these thy soul has found
Sublime delight; but can the visible bound
  Of this small globe be the sole nurse and mother
Of knowledge and of feeling? Look around!
  Mark how one being differs from another;
Yet the world's book is spread before each human brother.

II.

Was this world, then, the parent and the nurse
  Of him whose mental eye outliv'd the sight
Of all its beauties? Him who sang the curse
  Of that forbidden fruit which did invite
Our first progenitors, whom that foul spirite,
  In serpent form, seduc'd from innocence,
By specious promises, that wrong and right,
  Evil and good, when they had gather'd thence,
Should be distinctly seen, as by diviner sense.

III.

They pluck'd, and paid the awful penalty
  Of disobedience: yet man will not learn
To be content with knowledge that is free
  To all. There are, whose soaring spirits spurn
At humble lore, and, still insatiate, turn
  From living fountains to forbidden springs;
Whence having proudly quaff'd, their bosoms burn
  With visions of unutterable things,
Which restless fancy's spell in shadowy glory brings.

IV.

Delicious the delirious bliss, while new;
  Unreal phantoms of wise, good, and fair,
Hover around, in every vivid hue
  Of glowing beauty; these dissolve in air,
And leave the barren spirit bleak and bare
  As Alpine summits! it remains to try
The hopeless task (of which themselves despair)
  Of bringing back those feelings, now gone by,
In making their own dreams the code of all society.

V.

"All fear, none aid them, and few comprehend";
  And then comes disappointment, and the blight
Of hopes that might have bless'd mankind; but end
  In stoic apathy, or starless night:
And thus hath many a spirit, pure and bright,
  Lost that effulgent and ethereal ray,

Which, had religion nourished it, still might
Have shone on, peerless, to that perfect day,
When death's veil shall be rent, and darkness dash'd away.

VI.

Ere it shall prove too late, thy steps retrace:
The heights thy muse has scal'd, can never be
Her loveliest, nor her safest dwelling-place.
In the deep valley of humility,
The river of immortal life flows free
For thee—for all. Oh! taste its limpid wave,
As it rolls murmuring by, and thou shalt see
Nothing in death the Christian dares not brave,
Whom faith in God has given a world beyond the grave.

SONNET

TO THE AUTHOR OF THE REVOLT OF ISLAM

[From The Examiner, November 5, 1820 (no. 671, p. 717). This sonnet was
reprinted in Arthur Brooke's volume, *Retrospection* (1822), and a part of it was
quoted in the review of the volume in The Gazette of Fashion, etc., April 3, 1822.

Arthur Brooke was the pen name of John Chalk Claris. From his poems may
be gleaned the facts that he was born in Canterbury, October 18, 1796, and was
educated at The King's School, Canterbury, and that some time before he published
his volume, *Thoughts and Feelings* (1820), he sojourned in France and Switzerland.
He published six volumes of poetry; viz.: *Juvenile Pieces*, etc., 1816; *Poems*, 1817;
Durovernum, etc., 1818; *Thoughts and Feelings*, 1820; *Retrospection*, 1822; and
(apparently his last) *Elegy on the Death of Shelley*, 1822. The British Museum
possesses only three volumes. The volumes of 1817 and 1818 were somewhat
favorably reviewed in The New Monthly Magazine, October, 1818, and March,
1819. The last volume was extensively noticed. Claris contributed poems under
his pen name to The Thanet Magazine in 1817. His available volumes before 1822
show only a slight trace of Shelleyan influence, mingled with a good deal of Byronic
despondency and a luscious amatory tendency that smacks strongly of Thomas Moore.
In *Durovernum* he shows some Shelleyan contempt of Religion and Custom, but is
principally a philanderer—desperate, gallant, self-pitying, whose "breast is anything
but pure."]

Percy, when from thy wild and mighty lyre
Burst forth that strain which told of Fear and Faith,
And Tyranny and Force and Hate and Death,
Vanquished by Love and Wisdom, the lost fire
Of Hope which flashed from thy electric wire
Burnt in my breast once more, and with hush'd breath
I stood to see Fame's amaranthine wreath
Bound round his brows whose soul could thus aspire.

There shall it rest! and though earth's grovelling throng
Of bat-eyed worldlings, whose enfeebled gaze
Turns back appall'd from Truth's meridian blaze,
See not nor will acknowledge, be thou strong
In self-support, and let thy glorious song
Hold its high course—itself its fittest praise!

THE SPIRIT OF THE STORM

[From The London Magazine and Theatrical Inquisitor, January, 1821 (3:36).
This obvious imitation of Shelley's "The Cloud" was probably inspired by the
quotation of that poem in reviews of the *Prometheus Unbound* volume rather than by
a reading of the volume, which had a very slight sale. Of the author, Leigh Cliffe,
nothing is known.]

> I'm the son of the wind, and I follow behind
>   With swift steps from the sunless shade,
> Like the lightning fleet, each victim I greet,
>   With the havoc my pinions have made.
> On the vessel that glides o'er the boundless tides,
>   With her crew in sweet slumbers bound,
> I love to alight when the mantle of night,
>   Falls in silvery vapours around;
> And parting her sails with my tempest-wing'd gales,
>   To new victims of horror I flee,
> And laugh at their woe as I wantonly go,
>   O'er the boundless expanse of the sea.
> On many a cloud of its beauty proud,
>   I triumphantly ride through the air,
> And then imprecate the water-fiend's hate,
>   To crush every hope with despair.
> O'er land and o'er water, to wreck and to slaughter,
>   I flit like the shade of a dream,
> And on the sea-shore, 'mid the elements' roar,
>   Woo the spirits of death in the stream;
> Then the foamy floods fly, and the water-fiends cry
>   And the sea-mews in agony scream.
> When Earth's beauty is lost in the flower-chilling frost,
>   And her charms like the rainbow decay,
> On snow and on sleet is the trace of my feet,
>   On the rock, on the foam-covered spray;
> And the avalanche falls from its tottering walls,
>   When I rest on its top by the way.
> Then the portals of death are wide-open'd beneath,
>   And the dirge is the plainings of woe,
> And when twilight's pale mist earth's bosom hath kiss'd,
>   My shroud is a mantle of snow.
> In thunders I laugh as with rapture I quaff,
>   The shrieks of despair from the earth,
> Then sullenly die mid the gloom of the sky,
>   Till nature shall give me new birth.

THE ATHEIST

[From The Literary Gazette and Journal of Belles Lettres, June 2, 1821 (no.
228, p. 348). Printed with the statement that "A note from C. informs us that
the following lines were suggested by a review in our number 226." The review was
that of *Queen Mab*, which denounced the passage beginning "There is no God."
The identity of C. is unknown.]

"There is no God," the atheist cried:
And when the daring blasphemy
Ascended from his lips to thee,
Where were thy tardy lightnings, Heaven,
Thy dread reply in thunder given,
To blast him to his native hell,
And in his punishment to tell
 The impious wretch, he lied!
 The lightnings then remained at rest;
No answer to the wretch from high,
In pealing thunder, shook the sky;
For well the Almighty Father knew,
Who pierces Nature with his view,
In all creation's ample round,
So fierce a hell could not be found,
 As glowed within his breast.

       C.

ON MR. SHELLY'S [*sic*] POEM, "PROMETHEUS UNBOUND"

[From John Bull, February 4, 1822, p. 477.]

Shelly [*sic*] styles his new poem *Prometheus Unbound*,
And 'tis like to remain so while time circles round.
For surely an age would be spent in the finding
A reader so weak as to *pay for the binding*.

ON THE DEATH OF MR. SHELLEY

[From The Examiner, August 25, 1822 (no. 761, p. 538). B., the author, may be Elizabeth Kent, Leigh Hunt's sister-in-law, who had spent some time with the Shelleys at Marlow and was known in the Shelley-Hunt circle as "Bessy." Her *Flora Domestica, or the Portable Flower Garden* (1823) quotes from Shelley's poems and gives a warm, friendly sketch of him in the preface.]

'Twas but of late that all the glorious flowers,
Garden'd within thy matchless heart and mind,
Were wreathed into a garland to adorn
Thy brother-poet's grave.[1] In thy full verse
Poesy wept above the young bard's urn,
In sadness-sweetness—strength:—her sigh's soft breath
Swept o'er the chords of thy deep passionate lyre,
And spoke in them the soul of mournfulness!
And, mingled with those gentler sounds, there came
The swell of thine indignant scorn of those
Who had, with bite of reptile-venom, stung
His sensitive soul to death;—and, like the blast
Of the destroying whirlwind in its wrath,

[1] His Verses on the Death of Mr. Keats. (The Examiner's footnote.)

It held them, for a moment, up to scorn,
Then dashed them into atoms in the dust.
Alas! that thou thyself so soon should'st ask
The tribute that thou gav'st!—'twould need a harp
More thickly-gemm'd with gifts than even thine,—
If such there be,—fitly to hymn thy fate.
Death's always dreadful—but, on the fierce wave,
Which swallows up the straining, bursting bark,
And all the shrinking, shuddering souls within,—
Oh God! 'tis fearful then indeed!—And yet 'twas thus
That Shelley was cut off, in all the prime
And lustihood of genius and of heart.
If to behold the promising sapling die
Be cause to grieve, then how much more to see
The full-grown oak uprooted by the storm
In all its pride and luxury of strength!

Oh! who shall speak the grief of those who clung
In ivy-fondness round him?—of that small realm
Of love, which owned him as its only king—
That world of heart of which he was the axis?—
Alas! such sorrow shrinks from every eye,
E'en that of sympathy:—the friendly hand
Should hasten, like the patriarch's son, to throw
The veiling garment o'er its nakedness!

But Genius never dies—it lives beyond
Its owner in his monuments of thought,
More lasting than the broad-based pyramid.
And wilt not *thou* be heard in after time,
Who pour'st the strength of mighty intellect
In the full tide of sweet and solemn sound?
Yes, Shelley, yes—while Genius is admired
And Feeling loved—while Freedom still retains
Amid the waters of Corruption's flood,
An Ararat whereon to rest her foot,—
Thy spirit still will be revered on earth,
And commune with the minds of unborn men.

Farewell!—thy sun is set at noon—
But, like the vestal fire, its light will live
Unquenched—unquenchable:—'twill shed
Its glory on our land—our tongue—our time.
Farewell, thou gifted one!—thy name will rank
Among the giants of our country's thought.
The wave has closed upon thy human weakness,—
But, in the hearts of all who think and feel,
Thy Genius will be ever casketed!

                                        B.

ELEGY ON THE DEATH OF SHELLEY

[From The Bard, being a selection of Original Poetry by F. G. and C. Whiteson, November 16, 1822 (no. 5, pp. 38-40). The identity of F. is unknown.]

> —Tumbled headlong from the height of life
> They furnish matter for the tragic muse.
> Thomson.

In life's gay hour, how little do we think,
    That each swift moment bears us to the grave;
That e'en the next may lead us to the brink,
    From whence nor Fame, nor wealth have power to save?

Yet Pride still springs, still nurtures in the breast,
    And rears its sickly blossoms high in air;
O'er all our blighted schemes, by fate oppress'd,
    The wrecks of love—the ruins of despair—

O Pride! thou foul corruption of the soul,
    To what dread end, thy blind career impels;
The heart, disdaining reason's calm control,
    'Gainst man at first, at last 'gainst God rebels!

Ye sceptic throng! deluded mortals all!—
    Whose self-willed schemes of Providence and Fate,
Are rear'd to hide the demons that appal,
    The dread conviction of a future state!

Come, this exhausted body gather round,
    Whose breast once cherish'd themes as false as thine;
And may reflection in thy bosom sound,
    And echo to the deepest note of mine!

Short was the time—'tis scarce a moment past,
    When fluttering through the giddy range of life,
This clay cold corpse—was busied in the vast
    Important scene of checquer'd joy and strife.—

He dar'd to think—or rather wish'd to find,
    For error's source too often is a sigh,—
That vice and virtue centred in the mind;
    And e'en the soul must with the body die!—

To brave the deep he left his bed of down,
    And as his flowing bark swept o'er the wave,
On heav'n he smiled—but fate returned a frown,
    And in the ocean mark'd him out a grave.

What were his latest thoughts, when sudden sprung
    The vengeful storm that hurried him to death?
What the last word that quiver'd on his tongue?—
    What the last sigh that mock'd his stifled breath?—

O let my pen prophetic truth declare;—
   I see him struggle—yet a moment live—
He looks to heav'n in penitence and prayer;
   And his last words are—"PITY AND FORGIVE!"—

What ray could cheer that conscious bosom, torn
   By doubts more fearful as the truth drew nigh?—
In death, could stoic fortitude, or scorn
   The bless'd tranquillity of Hope supply?—

But 'tis not mine to judge, or to condemn,
   No, while I write, I wipe the falling tear,
And kindred pity even checks my pen,
   Awhile I trace this lesson o'er his bier.

Though riches, youth, and spirits high in health,
   And smiling fortune may inherit pride;
And Pride, disdaining every power but wealth,
   The hand unseen, unfelt, may scorn, deride!

Yet let but sickness, sorrow, or despair,
   O'ertake his wandering thoughts, soon reason flies
O'er all the earth at last to Heaven, and there
   Seeks the relief that nature here denies.
                F.

ELEGY ON THE DEATH OF PERCY BYSSHE SHELLEY

[Published as a separate volume in 1822 and widely noticed. Dedicated to Leigh Hunt, "Companion and Admirer of the Illustrious Deceased,—His friend and fellow-laborer." For a note on its author, Arthur Brooke (John Chalk Claris), see p. 343.]

Advertisement

   This imperfect attempt to commemorate the talents and virtues of the highly gifted individual to whom the following pages refer, was commenced and finished within a few days after the intelligence of his lamented death had reached England: the Author being anxious to shew, if not by the excellence of the performance, at least by priority of effort, his sense of the merits, and his veneration for the memory, of this most distinguished philosopher, philanthropist, and poet.
       Canterbury,
          10th Aug. 1822.

I.

Ye waves! that in your azure calmness kiss,
   Or, lashed by tempest, shake the Ausonian shore;
Ye winds! whose gentle breath wakes love to bliss,
   Or whose wild rage deafens the thunder's roar;

Thou elemental air! and thou abyss
Of waters! where is he whom we deplore?
Spirits of sea and sky! say, do ye hide,
In fondness or in wrath, our joy, our hope, and pride?

II.

But is he lost? and can it be that death
Has quench'd that spirit's most ethereal beam?
Can that most vital thought be held beneath
The sullen deep in unawakening dream?
Could the blind wave, like any common breath,
Stifle that voice which was a living stream
Of Love and Wisdom, whose melodious flow
Was poured on all that is, around, above, below?

III.

Oh for the strains of that soft Grecian reed,
On which Sicilian echoes that had rung
So oft to Bion's lay, refused to feed,
And, sorrowing, round the mountains mutely hung.[2]
Sweet is the classic page! but what the need
Of foreign minstrelsies, if he who sung
Lost Lycidas had left his native lyre,
And there be one who now to strike it dares aspire?

IV.

Who *should* aspire but he who once hath breathed
His dirge sublime o'er Ireland's buried pride?[3]
Nor shall the cypress then for genius wreathed
Be now to genius mightier far denied:
This task the friend, the poet hath bequeathed
By wordless intimation,—best supplied
By the swift promptings of the mutual mind
Of those whom loftier thoughts in holiest brotherhood bind.

V.

If yet once more to Aganippe's spring
With unaccustom'd foot, I, sorrowing, tread,
It is not that my hope be thence to bring
Aught not unworthy the immortal dead;
But, ah! a stranger's hand a flower may fling
Ere kindred grief its costlier gifts hath shed,
And love may claim the privilege to pay
Uncalled, yet unrebuked, such tribute as it may.

[2] See Moschus' Elegy on Bion. (Author's footnote.)
[3] Monody on Sheridan. (Author's footnote.)

VI.

Not for our selves we sorrow, not for those
Who from his presence drew their life's delight,
Not for the bosom friend who soothed the woes
That warped his young heart with their poisonous blight,
Not for his gentle babes whose orphan brows
Their father's fame shall halo, proudly bright;
Not for ourselves, nor these, alone we mourn,—
Such pangs, however keen, could have been better borne.

VII.

But who shall launch the lightning of the mind,
Instinct with aspiration, through the dense
Impalling clouds which slaves and tyrants wind
O'er the bewildered world,—their last defence!
Where now the champion for man's suffering kind,
To raise, unscoffing, his subjected sense,
Unveil foul superstition's idiot faith,
And crush the viperous worm which lurks the mask beneath!

VIII.

But he with intuition's glance looked through
All nature's mysteries; and, kind as wise,
From the green bud that drinks the vernal dew,
To the vast sphere rolling through boundless skies,
From all that lives and moves his spirit drew
The influence of their bland benignities;
And like a new Prometheus brought to men
Lost Hope's abandoned flame;—shall it be quenched again?

IX.

No, no, the spark survives in many a heart,
Kindling from that communicated glow,
Which 'tis the bard's proud privilege to impart,
Which many may receive, but few bestow,—
Ye mighty masters of the Muse's art,
To nobler themes bid nobler numbers flow;
The torch transmitted, o'er the nations raise,
And pass to coming hands with undiminished blaze!

X.

So shall that epoch which his soul fore-shared
Roll, hastening, on its irresistible hour,
And find its path not wholly unprepared,
And Love be Law, and Gentleness be Power,
While Wrong, and Force, and Fear, like vultures scared,
Fly, and their place be found on earth no more;
Freedom, and Truth, and Peace, and guiltless Joy,
Forming no fabulous Age of Gold without alloy.

XI.

Alas, alas! it is a mournful thing
To speak of hope, while bending o'er the bier
Of one so loved, we feel the mortal sting
Of remediless grief;—the bitter tear
That falls, he sees not,—and the sweetest string
That sounds his name he does not, cannot hear;
Unmarked the voice of Friendship as of Fame,
Death sleeps—the living love, hate, praise, and fear, and blame.

XII.

Let calumny, which from the poisonous tongue
Of human reptiles o'er the great and good
Is ever thrown, be on his memory flung;
Such as the blackest of the hideous brood
Have poured till round themselves their foulness clung,
A leprous crust,—while he untainted stood!
His glory is an essence, pure and bright,
Which time shall not obscure nor breath malignant blight.

XIII.

Thou poet's poet! whose sublimer strain
To the extremest verge of human thought
Soared, and the vulgar ken was stretched in vain
To follow, till with baffled powers o'erwrought
They turned their hooded eyes to earth again,
And slandered what themselves had vainly sought;
Effulgent spirit! splendour without peer!
Brief comet of our intellectual hemisphere!

XIV.

And thou art vanished! and the wondrous frame
Wherein the fervour of thy genius burned,
Like centric sunbeams, with intensest flame,
Dissolved, and into common earth returned?
Is all thy being now a bodiless name?
Thy boundless spirit with thy corpse inurned?
Alas, for man, that so divine a ray
Should kindle but to fade, shine but to pass away!

XV.

But he hath bowed to Nature and the power
Of stern Necessity, the One supreme,
Which links impartial with its destined hour
All chance and change; and in whose sightless scheme
A falling nation and a fading flower
Are equal, howso'er to man they seem:
He hath but yielded in obedient awe
Of being, unto that which gives and is its law.

XVI.

Yet shall it be permitted man to mourn
A light departed—an extinguished star—
A glory gone that never shall return!
And sadly pause and ponder from afar
The secrets of that 'dread mysterious bourn'
Which lies between the things which *were* and *are:*
So may the stillness of our sorrows reach
Truths which a happier lore is sometimes so to teach.

XVII.

For me,—alike unknowing and unknown,—
To deck the cenotaph of honouring thought
Where richer flowers shall soon be fitly strown,
These fresh-culled buds,—such as I could,—I brought.
Glory protect his tomb! and if my own
Be left neglected or be sometimes sought,
May those who scorn be such as would not sigh
For him, and those who seek love half so well as I.

The End.

VERSES ON THE DEATH OF PERCY BYSSHE SHELLEY

[This volume was published in 1822 and attracted a considerable amount of notice. For a note on the author, Bernard Barton, see p. 341. The title-page quotes Jeremiah 6:16: "Stand ye in the ways and see, and ask for the old paths, where is the good way, and walk therein; and ye shall find rest for your souls. But they said we will not walk therein." The dedication is "To the Author of 'May You Like It,' whose simple stories strikingly illustrate the beauty and gentleness of Christian principles." Preceding the Preface are seven lines from Cowper importing that God imparts the truth freely to seekers but not "To the proud, uncandid, insincere or negligent."

Charles Lamb, who disapproved of Shelley's radicalism, read and approved this poem. In a letter to Barton (October 9, 1822) he calls it "temperate, very serious, and very seasonable," and adds: "I do not think it will convert the club at Pisa, neither do I think it will satisfy the bigots on our side of the water. Something like a parody on the song of Ariel would please them better:—

> Full fathom five the Atheist lies
> Of his bones are hell dice made, etc.

I want time or fancy to fill up the rest."]

Preface

The Author of the following Verses did not read, without some emotion, the account of Percy Bysshe Shelley's death: yet it was far from his desire publicly to have expressed that feeling. He thought it, indeed, by no means improbable that the zeal of Shelley's friends and admirers might induce one or the other of them to commemorate his powers as a poet; but having himself once freely admitted these, and at the same time lamented their misapplication, the Author hoped to be spared alike the perusal of such eulogies, and the task of commenting on them. It is with regret, however, that he finds silence incompatible with apprehended duty. "An Elegy on the Death of Percy Bysshe Shelley"—in which he is styled "a most distinguished philosopher and philanthropist"; in which his voice is said to have been "a living stream of love and wisdom," and he himself "the last defence of a bewilder'd world,"—a poem of this sort, sent directly to the writer of the following few pages, by its Author,—seemed to render silence on his part criminal: were it only for the sake of a few whom such praise may have a tendency fatally to mislead. Of the gifted visionary whose death has occasioned these brief and hasty verses, their Author trusts he has not spoken, he knows he has not thought, nor felt, with unchristian harshness: by some he may, perhaps, be thought to have erred on the other hand; but, in his view, the better part of those readers whom the productions of sceptical authors are most likely to injure,—the young, the ardent, the aspiring— are not likely to be won to Christianity by a different tone; and for such as these the Author has principally written.

I.

I gave thee praise, while life was thine,
    If weak, at least sincere—
As e'er was offered at the shrine
    To tuneful vot'ries dear;—
I own'd thou hadst no common dower
Of genius, harmony, and power
    To waken hope and fear;
My spirit felt their potent sway,
And mourned to see them cast away.

II.

To see them cast away on themes
    Which ill could recompense
The proud aspirings, lofty dreams,
    Of such intelligence;
I mourn'd to think that gifts so rare,
And rich, should threaten to ensnare
    The Soul's diviner sense;
Should bring a cloud o'er minds unknown,
And fatally mislead thine own.

III.

I felt all this;—and yet a times,
    As through the dark obscure
Of thy wild, visionary rhymes,
    A glimpse of light more pure
Would break in transient lustre forth;
And hopes of more enduring worth
    For thee would then allure;
These too I felt;—was glad to feel;
And hazarded one brief appeal.

IV.

It prov'd in vain;—for thou hadst rear'd
    A fabric of thine own;
And all remonstrance but endear'd
    A structure, which had grown
From airy hopes that dreams invent:
Delusive, from its battlement
    To its foundation-stone;
A BABEL TOWER, by fancy built,
And by her gorgeous sunshine gilt.

V.

I can but grieve, that, in thine eye,
    Such pile—Truth's temple seem'd;
I can but sorrow thou should'st die,
    Nor know thou hast but dream'd;—
I more lament that there should be
Those, who beguil'd, by that, and thee,
    Of both unwisely deem'd:—
Fancied the edifice divine,
And thou the guardian of its shrine.

VI.

And yet my verse—nor shrine, nor priest,
    Again had sought to greet;
If with thy mortal life had ceas'd
    The dangerous counterfeit:—
Had other candidates for fame
But been content to let thy name
    Repose in silence meet;
By me, though thought of with regret,
That name had been unmention'd yet.

VII.

There is a spell by Nature thrown
    Around the voiceless dead,
Which seems to soften censure's tone,
    And guard the dreamless bed
Of those, who, whatsoe'er they *were*,
Wait Heaven's conclusive audit there,
    In silence—dark, and dread!
And with instinctive awe our hearts
Fill all which such a spot imparts.

VIII.

We feel that we ourselves are frail
    In word, in act, in thought,—
And rather wish a kindly veil
    In pity thrown athwart

Errors, and faults, alike gone by;
Than have them to each gazer's eye
    In open daylight brought:
To those who rightly think, and feel,
The dead with eloquence appeal.

IX.

But should their very errors be
    In numbers eulogiz'd;
Their phantasms urg'd—to set us free
    From laws by Virtue priz'd;
If their admirers, not content
Their works should be their monument,
    Would have them canoniz'd;—
It seems a duty to uphold
The faith our sires maintain'd of old.

X.

For thee, departed bard! I feel
    But pity and regret;
And gladly would their anguish heal
    Who mourn thy sun has set:—
More gladly would I hope,—through ONE
Who died for all, that vanish'd sun
    Might rise in glory yet;—
'Tis not for *me* to judge how far
Thy unbelief such hopes must mar.

XI.

With those who think they view in thee
    The champion of their creed,
If their's, in truth, a creed can be
    Who from belief are freed,—
Who view with scorn all modes of faith,
Though seal'd by many a martyr's death,
    With such I fain would plead;
And, in that love which knows no bound,
Once more one brief alarm would sound.

XII.

If Christians err, yourselves admit
    Such error harms them not;—
If you are wrong, and Holy Writ
    No juggling, priestly plot,
But Truth's own Oracle reveal'd;—
Then is your condemnation seal'd,
    And hopeless is your lot!
You DOUBT the Gospel:—keep in view,
What CAN BE DOUBTED—MAY BE TRUE!

XIII.

But O! to YOU,—who halt between
　　The Christian's—sceptic's part:
Who now to Revelation lean,
　　And now to Sophists' art;
As one who many doubts has known,—
Aware what conflicts like your own
　　Awaken in the heart;—
This simple watch-word let me give,
"BELIEVE!—OBEY!—AND YE SHALL LIVE!"

XIV.

What though the Sceptic's lips declare
　　The Christian's hope—a lie;
And pride, that fills the Scorner's chair,
　　The Christian's faith deny;
Be your's that holy hope and faith,
And your's shall be o'er sin and death,
　　The glorious victory;
A victory—not by you obtain'd,
But through your Saviour's triumph gain'd.

XV.

For you THE LAMB was crucified,
　　Enduring every pain;
For you he bled, for you he died,
　　For you he rose again;
And liveth evermore to make
Prompt intercession for your sake,
　　That you with him may reign;
And, through his sacrifice, may prove
The wonders of redeeming Love.

XVI.

Through faith in HIM your sires of old
　　Maintain'd the holy fight
With death and darkness;—and laid hold
　　On Life, and Gospel Light;—
Through faith in him the prophets saw
Beyond the earlier, outward law,
　　To a more glorious rite;—
Beholding with a steadfast eye,
A brighter era drawing nigh.

XVII.

Your pious fathers,—where are they?
　　Ye trust in joy supreme:—
The prophets—live not these for aye
　　Near Life's immortal stream?—
Hope answers "Yes!"—be their's your choice,

Believe THE SPIRIT's teaching voice
   To be no fabled dream;
That so you may, when life be o'er,
Your SAVIOUR and your GOD adore!

NOTE

Stanza III—Page 10

These too I felt,—was glad to feel,
And hazarded one brief appeal.

An allusion having been made, in the preceding Poem, to a former address, that address itself may perhaps form no unsuitable appendage to the Verses now published: it was first suggested by the following stanza in one of Shelley's minor poems.

"This world is nurse of all we know,
   This world is mother of all we feel,
And the evening of death is a fearful blow,
   To a brain unencompass'd with nerves of steel;
When all we know, or feel, or see,
   Shall pass like an unreal mystery."

Has Scepticism no more consolatory views of the termination of existence than this? Christianity, at any rate, carries our hopes further.

[*Here follow* Stanzas Addressed to Percy Bysshe Shelley, *which appeared originally in Barton's* Poems, *1820. The Stanzas, etc. are followed by a sonnet praising religion in English poetry, and by notices of previous volumes by Barton.*]

ON THE DEATH OF PERCY BYSSHE SHELLEY

[From The Hermes, December 14, 1822 (1:55). The identity of J. N. is unknown.]

List to that voice that swells upon the deep;
   It rides upon the billow's roar—
   It comes from Spezzia's rocky shore,
Whispers from where a poet's ashes sleep.
   In the dead silence of the night
   It murmurs from the ruffled wave:
Mark!—who would with rash daring slight
   A warning from a poet's grave?
   That speaks, laid in a watery bed,
   To thee a lesson,—from the dead:
"Art thou a votary to the tuneful muse?
Does feeling, pathos,—breathe in every line?
Send up thy laurels to a purer shrine
Than was my choice! 'twas my rash fate to abuse
Rich gifts, shower'd on me by a Hand divine;
Did poisonous weeds amongst sweet flowers infuse,
And hellish vice in luring garb enshrine!
See, now, how blasted lie those withered bays

That ne'er were won in virtue's nobler praise!
What my mad hand has penn'd; O would it were forgot,
Erased from memory's page, the foul, the erring blot!
  Know loathsome vice—it never can repay
  One soothing hope, in sorrow's blighted day;
  Nor reckless guilt,—but maddens in the brain,
  And tears its victim with increasing pain:
  To memory leaves a name, unlov'd,—forlorn,—
  For some to pity,—others hold in scorn!—
That spirit now recedes again,
Flits swiftly back to whence it came,
Now hovers o'er its deep-sea den,
And plays above that earthly keep,
Where, aye unmoved by praise or blame—
Disturb them not!—a poet's ashes sleep!

J. N. * * * * * *

XV

A Chronological Summary, 1810-1822, Including Shelley's Own Publications

1810

In 1810 Shelley published *Zastrozzi, A Romance*, by P. B. S.; *Original Poetry by Victor and Cazire; A Poetical Essay on the Existing State of Things; Posthumous Fragments of Margaret Nicholson*. The latter were published anonymously. Several poems signed S. and an essay signed P. S., all of which appeared in The Oxford University and City Herald in 1810-11, were possibly written by Shelley.

Zastrozzi was listed in The Monthly Magazine or British Register, May (29: 359), as published in April and in La Belle Assemblée (Supplement to N. S. 2, for 1811) as printed in 1810. It was reviewed in The Gentleman's Magazine, September, 1810 (part 2, 80: 258), and The Critical Review, or Annals of Literature, November (21: 329-331). It was advertised in The Times, June 5 and 12.

Original Poetry by Victor and Cazire was advertised in The Morning Chronicle, September 18; The Morning Post, September 19; The Times, October 12. It is included in the monthly list of publications in The British Critic, September (36: 319), The Literary Panorama, October (8: 1074), and The Monthly Magazine or British Register, November (30: 360). It was reviewed in The Literary Panorama for October (8: 1063-1066). See also Summary for 1811.

Posthumous Fragments of Margaret Nicholson, which was published in November, was listed as just published, by The Oxford University and City Herald, November 17 and 24, but apparently received no notice from periodical reviewers in 1810.

1811

In 1811 Shelley published *St. Irvyne, or The Rosicrucian, A Poetical Essay on the Existing State of Things*, and *The Necessity of Atheism*. The last was published anonymously; the two former as by "A Gentleman of Oxford." There is some evidence (H. B. Forman, *The Shelley Library*, pp. 25-26) that he published a satire on the royal family, which has never been recovered.

Notices of the 1810 publications continued as follows: *Original Poetry by Victor and Cazire* was reviewed in The British Critic, April (37: 408-409), and in *The Poetical Register for 1810-1811* (p. 617). The latter, however, was not published until 1814. *Posthumous Fragments of Margaret Nicholson* was listed among the new publications in The Monthly Magazine or British Register, January (30: 551); and The Edinburgh Annual Register for 1811 (part 2, 4: cxxii).

St. Irvyne was listed under new publications in The Monthly Magazine or British Register for January (30:551); The General Chronicle and Literary Magazine for February (1:181); and The British Review and London Critical Journal for March (1:242); and was advertised in The Times for January 26 and February 11, and in Stockdale's lists appended to his other books of 1811. It was reviewed in The Literary Panorama for February (9:252-253), and in The British Critic, January, 1811 (37:70). Later notices of *St. Irvyne* appeared in 1812 *(q.v.)*.

A Poetical Essay on the Existing State of Things was listed as "just published" in The Oxford University and City Herald, March 9, and under "List of New Books" in The British Review and London Critical Journal, September (2:280). It was advertised in The Times for April 10 and 11. See H. B. Forman, *A Shelley Library*, pp. 20-22.

The Necessity of Atheism seems to have attracted no review before 1822 *(q.v.)*.

1812

In 1812 Shelley published (March 2) *Proposals for an Association,* etc., By Percy Bysshe Shelley; *An Address to the Irish People,* by Percy Bysshe Shelley; *A Letter to Lord Ellenborough; A Declaration of Rights; The Devil's Walk;* the last three anonymously.

Notices of the 1811 publications continued as follows: *St. Irvyne* was reviewed in The Anti-Jacobian Review, January (41:69), and its author was disparagingly characterized in a letter from Oxford in the same journal, February (41:221).

A Declaration of Rights was reprinted by Richard Carlile, in his Republican, September 24, 1819, and was described and condemned in The Brighton Magazine *(q.v.)*, May, 1822.

Shelley's efforts in behalf of the Tremadoc Embankment are reflected in three articles in The North Wales Gazette, viz., October 1, giving the substance of a speech made by Shelley at a meeting of the Corporation of Beaumaris; *ibid.*, a list of subscribers to the Embankment ("Percy B. Shelley £100") with resolutions of thanks; and October 8, correcting the first article above.[1]

Shelley's activities among the Irish radicals during the early part of this year attracted the attention of several Dublin newspapers. His speech at the Fishamble Street Theatre was reported and summarized in The Freeman's Journal for February 29, The Dublin Evening Post for February 29, and Saunders's News Letter for February 29. The Hibernian Journal, or Daily Chronicle of Liberty, for March 2, and Walker's Hibernian Magazine, for February, p. 83, both reprinted the account given in The Freeman's Journal; and The Patriot for March 2 reprinted the account given in Saunders's News Letter. The Weekly Messenger for March 7 published a sketch entitled "Pierce Byshe Shelly, Esq.," and

---

[1] The first and second of these are erroneously printed as one article in the Julian edition of *Shelley's Works*, 7:326-329. The third, overlooked by the Julian editors, is as follows: "We are desired to state that the account of what passed at the Corporation meeting at Beaumaris on the 28th ult. in consequence of Mr. Shelley and Mr. Williams having made a visit there from Tremadoc has been made much more than the real truth would warrant."

The Dublin Journal for March 2 and March 21 contained letters about Shelley's Irish activities signed respectively "An Englishman" and "A Dissenter."

1813

In 1813 Shelley printed, anonymously, *Queen Mab*, and *A Vindication of Natural Diet*.

1814

In 1814 Shelley published *A Refutation of Deism;* and a review of Hogg's *Memoirs of Prince Alexy Haimatoff* for The Critical Review, December (6: 566-574), both anonymously. Neither seems to have attracted any printed notice in 1814, but *A Refutation of Deism* was reprinted in two parts in The Theological Inquirer for March and April, 1815 *(q.v.)*.

Earlier publications were noticed in 1814 as follows: *Original Poetry by Victor and Cazire* was briefly and unfavorably criticized in The Poetical Register and Repository of Fugitive Poetry for 1810-11 (p. 617).

1815

Shelley himself published nothing in 1815, unless the republication of *A Refutation of Deism* in The Theological Inquirer in March and April (pp. 6-24 and 121-131) was by Shelley, as is supposed by Woodberry *(Shelley's Poetical Works*, 1892, I: 411-412). Mr. Bertram Dobell, in a communication to The Athenaeum (London), dated March 7, 1885 (p. 313), says that he has compared this version with Forman's edition of the original and finds that it corrects most of the errors of the original edition, thus suggesting Shelley's connivance at the publication.

During the same year The Theological Inquirer and Polemical Magazine printed a series of articles on *Queen Mab*, March, April, May, and July, signed F. (1: 34-39, 105-110, 205-209, 358-362); a letter on Giordano Bruno, signed Eunomus Wilson, May (1: 164), which praises *Queen Mab* and quotes a passage not quoted by F.; an additional quotation from F., August (1: 446-448); an answer to the *Refutation of Deism*, signed Mary Ann, June (1: 242-247), and an Ode to the Author of Queen Mab, signed F., July (1: 380-381). Without mentioning Shelley's name this mysterious magazine praised him to the skies in both prose and poetry and actually reprinted, within a few months, most of what Shelley had written that might be considered worth reprinting or safe from prosecution.

The only printed mention of Shelley's name that I find in 1815 is in the obituary of his grandfather, Sir Bysshe Shelley, in The Gentleman's Magazine for January (part 1, 85: 93).

1816

In 1816 Shelley published *Alastor, or the Spirit of Solitude, with Other Poems. By Percy Bysshe Shelley.*

This volume was listed under "Works in Press" in The Critical Review, February (3: 205), and is listed among new publications in The

Monthly Magazine or British Register, April (41:256); and again in February, 1818; The New Monthly Magazine, April 1 (5:242); The Eclectic Review, April (5:414); and The British Review and London Critical Journal, May (7:566).

Reviews of the Alastor volume occurred in The Monthly Review, April (79:433); The British Critic, May (5:545-546); and The Eclectic Review, October (N. S. 6:391-393). All assert and vigorously condemn the obscurity of the poem. As yet there is no denunciation of Shelley's radical principles or conduct, except that The Eclectic Review seems to catch a faint whiff of brimstone when it notes only one reference to God or immortality. The Eclectic is the only review to note any signs of genius in the volume. For a more favorable later review, see Blackwood's Edinburgh Magazine, under 1819. The Literary Panorama for May (N. S. 4:297) quotes two translations from the volume, as by Shelley, but without comment or mention of the volume.

The Examiner, in an article entitled *Young Poets,* December 1 (no. 466, p. 761), gives Shelley a slightly guarded endorsement as "a very striking and original thinker."

1817

In 1817 Shelley published the "Hymn to Intellectual Beauty" in The Examiner, January 19 (no. 473, p. 41). In November *Laon and Cythna,* etc., was printed but quickly withdrawn. Eight stanzas from *Laon and Cythna* appeared in The Examiner, November 30 (no. 518, p. 761), which also published Shelley's review of Godwin's *Mandeville,* signed E. K. (December 28, no. 522, pp. 826-827). There also appeared, anonymously, Shelley's joint production, *A History of a Six Weeks' Tour Through a Part of France, Switzerland, Germany, and Holland,* etc.; *An Address to the People on the Death of the Princess Charlotte. By the Hermit of Marlowe,* and *A Proposal for Putting Reform to the Vote. By the Hermit of Marlowe.*

It was in January of this year that the Chancery proceedings of Westbrook *vs.* Shelley took place, with very little newspaper notice, on account of Lord Eldon's discouraging attitude. Yet it gave some publicity to *Queen Mab* and to Shelley's irregular conduct and had an important bearing on the attitude of critics and public toward Shelley after January, 1817.

The Morning Chronicle of January 25 carried an inaccurate account of the proceedings of January 24, which was copied by The Examiner of January 26 (no. 474, p. 60). The same issue of The Examiner contains allusions to the trial presumably written by Leigh Hunt.

The British Museum copy of the 1813 edition of *Queen Mab* contains a clipping from an unnamed newspaper, undated, but probably August 27 or 28, 1817, giving an account of the private hearing of Westbrook *vs.* Shelley, dated Court of Chancery, August 26.

In 1817 Thomas Love Peacock published *Melincourt,* in which Shelley is said to be one of the characters. Shelley's letters show his great admiration for the novel, without revealing any consciousness of his own part in it, nor does my own reading of the novel furnish any clear conviction that any character represents Shelley. That such assumptions cannot be accepted on internal evidence alone is shown by Byron's statement that the principal character of this novel, Sir Oran Outan, was based upon his famous bear, a statement categorically and sarcastically repudiated by Peacock himself.

Leigh Hunt's *Foliage*, published in England in 1817 and in America in 1818 and dedicated to Shelley, contains two laudatory sonnets to Shelley, entitled respectively, "To Percy Bysshe Shelley, on the Degrading Notions of the Deity," and "To the Same." Reviews of this volume (for which see under 1818) contained unfriendly comments on Shelley. The close connection with Leigh Hunt so openly advertised on the eve of the publication of *The Revolt of Islam*, in which Shelley's radicalism is first made apparent over his own name, no doubt intensified the hatred and alarm with which conservative opinion received Shelley's volume.

Shelley's *A Proposal for Putting Reform to the Vote* is listed in the heading of Southey's article on popular disaffection in The Quarterly Review for January (2:158) but without comment and without mention of Shelley's name.

1818

In 1818 Shelley published *The Revolt of Islam*, by Percy Bysshe Shelley. He also published the sonnet, *Ozymandias* (signed Glirastes) in The Examiner, January 11 (no. 525, p. 24). Leigh Hunt's *The Literary Pocket Book* for 1819 published the poem, "Marianne's Dream," without Shelley's name.

The Revolt of Islam was listed under new publications by The British Review and London Critical Journal, May (11:554). It was briefly and colorlessly reviewed in The Monthly Magazine or British Register, March (45:154). The Examiner, January 25 (no. 526, pp. 55-56), printed fifty-eight lines from the poem, without comment and praised it at length in three issues, February 1, February 22, and March 1 (no. 527, pp. 75-76; no. 350, pp. 121-122; and no. 531, pp. 139-141). The Literary Panorama, September (N. S. 8:986), quotes nine stanzas without criticism. For later reviews of the same volume, see under 1819.

The Examiner of February 8 (no. 528, p. 88) contained Horace Smith's admiring sonnet, "To the Author of The Revolt of Islam," republished in 1820 and 1821 *(q.v.)*.

In 1818 the Hunt-Shelley friendship first appears as a handicap to Shelley. Incidental reference to Shelley in connection with "The Cockney School of Poetry" occurs in Blackwood's Edinburgh Magazine, January (2:415). Two reviews of Hunt's *Foliage* contain condemnatory remarks on Shelley, viz., The Quarterly Review, May (18:324, by J. W. Croker or J. T. Coleridge); and The British Critic, July (N. S. 10:94).

Thomas Love Peacock's *Nightmare Abbey*, published in 1818, apparently caricatures Shelley under the name of Scythrop. The caricature was certainly unrecognizable to the general reader of the day, and in fact was never identified with Shelley by Peacock himself; but Shelley's letters to

Peacock indicate that he not only accepted it in this sense, but was amused by it, and Mrs. Shelley in 1840 accepted it as a partial portrait.

1819

In 1819 Shelley published *Rosalind and Helen; a Tale, with Other Poems. By Percy Bysshe Shelley*. Richard Carlile reprinted Shelley's *A Declaration of Rights* in The Republican, September 24 (1:75-78), without mention of Shelley's name.

Earlier publications were noticed in 1819 as follows: *Alastor* was encouragingly reviewed by Blackwood's Edinburgh Magazine, November (6:148-155).

Laon and Cythna was reviewed with *The Revolt of Islam* in The Quarterly Review, April (21:460-471, by John Taylor Coleridge), and condemned on the grounds of dullness, obscurity, and the moral and religious delinquencies of its teachings and of its author. *The Revolt of Islam* is reviewed by Blackwood's Edinburgh Magazine, January (4:475-482), noting Shelley's obscurity, vigorously denouncing his principles, and praising his capabilities. The Monthly Review, March (88:323-324), condemns the poetic style and the principles as a waste of undoubted talents. One paragraph of this review is quoted in The Fireside Magazine or Monthly Entertainer (Stamford), May (1:270). The Examiner, in a series of three articles, September 26, October 3, and October 10 (pp. 620-621, 635-636, 652-653), defends Shelley and *The Revolt of Islam* against the attacks of The Quarterly Review.

Rosalind and Helen is listed under new publications in The British Critic, June (11:668). It is reviewed as follows: The Quarterly, April (21:460-471), condemns it in reviewing *The Revolt of Islam*. The Examiner for May 9 (pp. 302-303) praises it. The London Chronicle, June 1, 1819 (125:521), contains a review which is republished in The Commercial Chronicle, June 3 (no. 2979), and is wholly condemnatory and sarcastic, on moral grounds. Blackwood's Edinburgh Magazine, June (5:268-275), condemns Shelley's principles and asserts his genius. The Monthly Review, October (90:207-209), finds it vague in execution and corrupt in principles, revealing wasted genius. The Gentleman's Magazine (supplement for 1819, part 1, 89:625-626) condemns it unreservedly as an example of the new immorality in poetry.

In the publications of this year begins the important animus against Shelley as the associate of Byron's wickedness. A long anonymous poem called *Don Juan: With a Biographical Account of Lord Byron and his Family, etc., etc.*, contains unfriendly passing mention of Shelley as the author of *Frankenstein:* "The Frankenstein was hatched, the wretch abhorred, whom shuddering Sh———y saw in horrid dream." This passage is quoted in a review of the poem in The Literary Chronicle and Weekly Review, October 23.

The New Monthly Magazine for April (11:944-945) digresses from an account of Byron in Geneva to comment on the Shelleys there.

Blackwood's Edinburgh Magazine again makes incidental reference to Shelley in connection with "The Cockney School of Poetry," September (5: 640).

Leigh Hunt's manuscripts in the British Museum contain several letters addressed to Hunt as editor of The Examiner and referring to Shelley and Byron.

Commonsense, a verse satire published anonymously in Edinburgh (written by Charles Hughes Terrot) attacks Shelley, Byron, Keats, Coleridge, Hunt, etc.

1820

In 1820 Shelley published *The Cenci; Prometheus Unbound;* and *Oedipus Tyrannus, or Swellfoot the Tyrant.* The latter was published anonymously and sold only seven copies before it was suppressed. The "Ode to Naples," which has hitherto been supposed to have been first published by Mrs. Shelley in 1824, appeared without comment over the initials P. B. S. in The Military Register and Weekly Gazette, Historical, Literary, etc., for the Army, Navy, Colonies and Fashionable World, October 1 (1: 433), and (continued) October 8 (1: 464). The periodical was a sixteen-page double-column weekly, owned, printed, edited and published by R. Scott, 3 Pall Mall Court. Between R. Scott and Shelley or any of Shelley's friends, I know of no connection, except that The Military Register, etc. of October 12 carried a friendly review of Hunt's The Indicator. Ingpen gives only one letter from Shelley to an English correspondent (Godwin) between August 25, when the poem was completed, and the date of Scott's publication of it. The presumption must be that the poem was sent directly by Shelley to Scott. Leigh Hunt's *The Literary Pocket Book* for 1821 contained the poem "On a Faded Violet," without Shelley's name.

The Cenci was listed among the new publications by The Monthly Magazine or British Register, April 1 and June 1 (49: 263 and 450); and The New Monthly Magazine, April 1 (13: 487). It was reviewed as follows: The Examiner, March 19 (no. 638, pp. 190-191), praised it as "the greatest dramatic production of the day." The Monthly Magazine or British Register, April 1 and June 1 (49: 260), recognizes Shelley's "original and extensive genius" but condemns the action as disgusting. The Literary Gazette and Journal of Belles Lettres, April 1 (no. 167, pp. 209-211), calls it "a dish of carrion seasoned with sulphur," the "production of a fiend," and the most abominable intellectual perversion of the times, yet inadvertently concedes Shelley's genius. The London Magazine and Monthly Critical and Dramatic Review, April (1: 401-407), starting with an anti-Cockney tirade, finds Shelley guilty of Cockneyisms to the verge of lunacy, cites a number of excellent passages as well as bad ones, and treats Shelley as a real poet who abuses his powers. The Theatrical Inquisitor and Monthly Mirror, April (16: 205-218, signed B.), concludes a long appreciative summary with the judgment that for a first dramatic effort its beauty is unparalleled. The London Magazine, May (1: 546-555), admires and condemns it as the work of "a man of great genius and of a most unhappy moral constitution." The Edinburgh

Monthly Review, May (3:591-604), seeks "to do justice to the genius" while inflicting "due chastisement on the errors of this remarkable young man," quotes admirable passages, and thinks the rich genius of *The Cenci,* rightly employed, might easily "surpass that of the last century." The New Monthly Magazine, May 1 (13:550-553), condemns the horrible subject of the play, and concedes Shelley both genius and noble feelings which are partly thwarted because he lacks religious convictions. The Indicator, July 19 and 26 (pp. 321-329 and 329-337), first answers objections as to the enormity of the Cenci story, retells the story from the old manuscript, then gives a sympathetic and favorable analysis of Shelley's play. At least four other reviews of *The Cenci* appeared in 1821 *(q.v.).*

That Shelley had read at least some of the 1820 reviews of *The Cenci* is shown by his letter of January 20, 1821, to the Olliers: "The reviews of my 'Cenci' (though some of them, and especially that marked 'John Scott,' are written with great malignity) on the whole give me as much encouragement as a person of my habits of thinking is capable of receiving from such a source, which, is inasmuch as they coincided with, and confirm, my own decisions." In the same letter Shelley mentions a friendly review "in your publication." There is no review of *The Cenci* in Ollier's Literary Miscellany, Ollier's only periodical publication at this time. If the review is not one of those listed above, it is an unknown one still to be found. Possible Shelley is referring to the incidental passage in The Retrospective Review *(q.v.,* below), since his letter comments on other articles in the number containing this passage.

Prometheus Unbound is listed among the new publications by The Literary and Scientific Repository and Critical Review (New York), July, (1:270);[2] The London Magazine, September (2:349); The British Review and London Critical Journal, September (16:246); The European Magazine and London Review, September (78:255); and The Monthly Magazine and British Register, November 1 (50:365).

It was reviewed as follows: The London Magazine, June (1:706), gives it a brief enthusiastic notice, as "unsettled, irregular, magnificent." The London Magazine and Monthly Critical and Dramatic Review, September and October (2:306-308 and 382-391) praises first "the extreme force and freshness" of the shorter poems; then, although deprecating Shelley's impatience, summarizes *Prometheus Unbound,* with copious extracts, as "one of the most stupendous . . . works . . . of modern poetry," a "vast wilderness of beauty." The Literary Gazette and Journal of Belles Lettres, September 9 (no. 190, pp. 580-582), is actively hostile, attacking the poem mainly for its obscurity, pronouncing Shelley little better than a lunatic and the poem a "melange of nonsense, cockneyism, poverty, and pedantry." Blackwood's Edinburgh Magazine, September (7:678-688), vigorously denounced the principles of the poem as detes-

---

[2] We must suppose that this July number appeared several months late, which would not be extraordinary. No English notices appeared before September, and the September issue of The London Magazine postpones full consideration of the book until October because it had "just come out that month."

table, but proclaimed its many "poetical beauties of the highest order" and hoped to win from his errors a poet "destined to leave a great name behind him." The Lonsdale Magazine and Provincial Repository, November (1:498-501), acknowledges Shelley's clear genius and talent, but condemns him for teaching sedition and blasphemy.

Thomas Noon Talfourd, who later defended Moxon against a charge of libel for publishing Shelley's works, wrote a favorable review of *Prometheus Unbound* which was presumably never published, since on September 9 he wrote to Ollier that his review of the volume had been rejected by Colburn (because the book was "full of Jacobinism and blasphemy") and that he would try to print it elsewhere, probably in The Champion. The Champion contains no such review. (Cf. T. J. Wise, *A Shelley Library*, p. 101, for Talfourd's letter.) For later reviews of *Prometheus Unbound*, see under 1821.

In 1820 Shelley attracted quite a considerable amount of general and miscellaneous notice. The Dublin Magazine; or General Repertory of Philosophy, Belles Lettres and Miscellaneous Information (Dublin), January (1:56), prints a letter deploring Bryon's effect on the morality of literature and remarking of Shelley: "I need not waste time upon such men as Shelley, men who are too openly virulent to be very dangerous; the wolf may be repelled from the door while the serpent glides in." In November the same magazine (2:393-400) prints an article entitled "Critical Remarks on Shelley's Poetry," rather amusingly hesitant in its unfavorable conclusions. The London Magazine, November (2:516), digresses from a criticism of Blackwood's magazine to call Shelley "a visionary with a weak head and a rich imagination."

What is probably the first American notice of Shelley occurs in The Literary and Scientific Repository and Critical Review (New York), July (no. 1, pp. 223-243), which reprints long extracts from The Quarterly's review of *The Revolt of Islam*, Blackwood's review of *Alastor*, and The New Monthly's review of *The Cenci*. There is no editorial comment except a footnote defending Leigh Hunt from The Quarterly, but the selection and arrangement is very fair to Shelley, since the quotation from Blackwood's, which is the longest of the three, is quite favorable to Shelley and directly answers the strictures of The Quarterly.

The Eclectic Review, September (N. S. 14:169), reviewing Keats's *Lamia* digresses for an instant to link the mythological poetry of Hunt and Shelley with that of Keats as "mere child's play." The Retrospective Review (2:204, no month given), in an enthusiastic digression on living poets, praises both Keats and Shelley. This passage was copied in The Weekly Entertainer and West of England Miscellany (of Sherborne), August 21, under the title, "An Estimate of the Poetry of the Present Age." Ollier's The Literary Miscellany (no. 1, no month given) carried a half-page advertisement of Shelley's books, quoting the first sentence of Blackwood's *Alastor* review. Peacock's "The Four Ages of Poetry," which appeared in this issue, mentions most contemporary poets of note, but somewhat strangely (unless from personal delicacy) omits mention of Shelley and Keats. The Honeycomb, of August 12 (pp. 65-72), published a rather favorable account of Shelley as No. 3 of its "Portraits of Metropolitan Poets."

Poems, by Bernard Barton (published in 1820), contained his dull, well-meant "Stanzas Addressed to Percy Bysshe Shelley," attempting to convert erring genius. This poem is quoted from in the review of the volume in The London Magazine, August (2:196), and was reprinted in 1822 with Barton's "Verses on the Death of Percy Bysshe Shelley."

Horace Smith's Amarynthus the Nympholept, etc., contained a laudatory sonnet "To Percy Bysshe Shelley on his Poems," previously published under the title "To the Author of the Revolt of Islam," in The Examiner (1818). This sonnet is quoted as "exquisite" in The London Magazine and Theatrical Inquisitor, January, 1821 (3:78), in a review of Smith's volume.

The Examiner, November 5 (no. 671, p. 717), prints Arthur Brooke's (John Chalk Claris's) enthusiastic sonnet "To the Author of The Revolt of Islam," marking the accession to Shelley of a young disciple whose "Elegy" (see under 1822) was to attract considerable attention to his hero.

1821

In 1821 Shelley published Adonais, a second edition of The Cenci, and Epipsychidion, the last anonymously. "The Question," one of his shorter poems, was first published in 1821 in Leigh Hunt's The Literary Pocket Book; or Companion for the Lover of Nature and Art for 1822. William Clark brought out two variant piracies of Queen Mab. For Shelley's unsuccessful effort to stop this piracy, see his letters of June 11 to Charles Ollier and June 22 to the editor of The Examiner.

During the same year there also appeared the so-called first American edition of Queen Mab, which both Forman and Ingpen suspect on general grounds of being a London piracy. The ostensible printer is William Baldwin and Co.,[3] Corner of Chatham Street, New York. The Preface concludes with an extract from The Theological Inquirer (1815) article on Queen Mab, and the entire Ode to the Author of Queen Mab, from the same source. Both these productions, originally signed F., are here signed R. C. F.

The Cenci reviews continued in 1821 as follows: The Monthly Review, February (94:161-168), admits that almost every scene contains "plain proof" of Shelley's genius and quotes examples; he is "worthy of

[3] Of the three William Baldwins living in New York at this time, none was a printer, though one, a doctor of medicine, lived on the corner of Chatham Square (not Street) in 1819, but not in 1821. There was, however, a Charles N. Baldwin living on the corner of Chatham Street in 1821, who was a printer and publisher, whose advertisement is one of the most conspicuous ones in Longworth's American Almanack, New York Guide, and City Directory for 1820-21. Obviously, therefore, the New York imprint is fraudulent. It was fabricated, presumably in London, either from Longworth's directory or from memory by someone familiar with New York. Perhaps the cunning culprit was William Benbow, who had just returned from America and had just reviewed Clark's piracy of Queen Mab and who later pirated other Shelley volumes.

better things"; "but it is not merely the demon of bad Taste which is to be laid to his gifted mind," his "Doubt and Vanity" are also to be condemned. The Independent, February 17 (no. 7, pp. 99-103), "thinks highly of Mr. Shelley," who "writes with vigor, sublimity and pathos," but thinks he is rightly little read and little valued, because he wastes "superior powers" in attacking religion and dealing with abstractions and perfectibility. This same issue, incidentally, carries Ollier's advertisement of "Mr. Shelley's Works," with its laudatory quotation from Blackwood's *Alastor* review. The British Review and London Critical Journal, June (17: 380-389), finds *The Cenci* "the best, because by far the most intelligible of Mr. Shelley's works," but finds the subject undramatic, the structure and language faulty, and the speeches "blasphemous ravings" which are both "unholy and immoral." The Literary Chronicle and Weekly Review, December 29 (no. 136, p. 822), refers to a hostile review of the poem in The Advertiser, a periodical which I have been unable to locate. *The Cenci* is also noticed unfavorably, at some length, in Blackwood's review of *Adonais* (*q.v.*, below).

Prometheus Unbound continued to be reviewed as follows: The Monthly Review, February (94: 168-173), denounces the poem as a whole as "*nonsense,* pure, unmixed *nonsense,*" full of obscurity and impiety, but admits Shelley's perverse genius and quotes to show that "there is much poetry also—much benevolent feeling, beautiful language, and powerful versification." The Quarterly Review, October (26: 168-180 by W. S. Walker), develops in detail the poem's "total lack of meaning" and then somewhat illogically condemns its meaning as disgusting and impious, full of immorality and irreligion. Shelley's dull and unoriginal verse is in "sober sadness, drivelling prose run mad."

Epipsychidion was reviewed twice in The Gossip, June 23 and July 14 (no. 17, pp. 129-135, and no. 20, pp. 153-159). In the first it is called "a very singular production, abounding with poetic beauties, lax morality, and wild, incoherent fancies"—all of which are impartially exhibited in quoted passages, the beauties praised (with the customary admission of the author's genius) and the immorality condemned. The second review consists entirely of a light conversation between two poetry-loving sisters and a gentleman friend in which the quotations given in the preceding issue are thoroughly analyzed as examples of the incomprehensible new method in poetry. These reviews were preceded by a passing comment, May 19 (no. 12, p. 91), in a fictitious letter of Byron to Moore: "I have groaned through Southey's *Vision of Judgment* and laughed and wondered through the *Epipsychidion*. Lord have mercy upon us! Della Crusca was intelligible to these!—I dare be sworn on any book in Christendom, that frantic fellow S-ll-y has a finger in the last." For a later criticism of the poem, see Blackwood's Edinburgh Magazine, under 1822.

Adonais was announced as "in the press" by The Literary Gazette and Journal of Belles Lettres, August 18 (no. 239, p. 527). It was reviewed and quoted almost entire in The Literary Chronicle and Weekly Review, December 1 (no. 133, pp. 751-754), as a poem of "transcendent merit" by a poet of "no ordinary genius." This article was based on a copy sent direct from Italy, "perhaps the only one that has reached England," and preceded by eight years the "first English edition" of the poem (Cambridge, 1829). The Literary Gazette and Journal of Belles Lettres, December 8 (pp. 772-773), contemns the poem as an unrelieved farrago of nonsense and impiety, and gives a classification, with excerpts, of six types of nonsense. Blackwood's Edinburgh Magazine, December (10: 696-700) reverses its previous policy of trying to convert Shelley and rains furious denunciation and sarcasm upon his impiety and obscurity, both in The Cenci and Adonais, quoting a whole column of his "absurdities" and offering two contemptuous parodies of Adonais.

The pirated Queen Mab was advertised by the publisher, William Clark, in The Literary Chronicle, May 19 (no. 105, p. 320), with the claim that the 1813 edition had become so scarce that "from 10 to 30 guineas have been offered for a copy."[4] It was reviewed as follows: John Bull's British Journal, March 11 (no. 3, p. 22), gives a sympathetic explanation and summary of the poem and calls it "beautiful and sublime." The London Magazine and Theatrical Inquisitor, March (3: 278-280), gives an appreciative summary and finds the poem proof of a genius that was meant to fulfill a high destiny. The Literary Gazette and Journal of Belles Lettres, December 8 (no. 255, pp. 772-773), finds much beauty and genius in the poem, but assails Shelley's principles and conduct. The Monthly Magazine, June (51: 460-461), calls it a rhapsody without rhyme or reason and condemns the notes for impiety and immorality. The Literary Chronicle and Weekly Review, June 2 (107: 344), treats the author, rather than the poem, as a striking example of perverted genius, powerful, but wicked.

General and miscellaneous printed references to Shelley in 1821 are quite frequent. Blackwood's Edinburgh Magazine, January (8: 397), quotes ten stanzas from "The Sensitive Plant," pronouncing them "exquisite" and "interesting," and in April (9: 93) digresses from praise of Byron's Marino Faliero to praise The Cenci and condemn its subject. The Literary Gazette, or Journal of Criticism, Science, and Arts (Philadelphia), April 28 (no. 17, pp. 285-286), quotes from "The Sensitive Plant" without comment. The London Magazine, January (3: 64-65), in a review of Hunt's The Literary Pocket Book, quotes two unsigned poems from it as by "Mr. Shelley, the author of that most powerful dramatic work, The Cenci." The poems were "Song—On a Faded Violet," and "Grief—A Fragment," which occur in modern editions as lines 9-20 and 28-42 of "The Sunset." The Literary Gazette and Journal of Belles Lettres, June 2 (no. 28, p. 348), printed a poetic attack on Shelley en-

---

[4] This claim seems a little dubious in view of the fact that in December of the next year Richard Carlile was offering the whole remainder of the first edition (180 copies) at 7s. 6d. the copy. See p. 97.

titled "The Atheist," signed C. William Clark, publisher of the first pirated edition of *Queen Mab*, published *A Reply to the Anti-Matrimonial Hypothesis and Supposed Atheism of Percy Bysshe Shelley as Laid Down in Queen Mab*. This work was advertised by Clark as "in the press" in The Literary Chronicle, July 14 (no. 113, p. 448). It was referred to by Clark in his defense against the libel action, as showing his objections to Shelley's views. Quite possibly it was a "lightning-rod" published in anticipation of a prosecution. The London Magazine and Theatrical Inquisitor, February (3: 122-127), published an appreciative general article "On the Philosophy and Poetry of Shelley," and in July (4: 31-34) humorously caricatured the vegetarian ideas of "Mr. P. B. S." in an article entitled "Dinner by the Amateurs of Vegetable Diet."

St. Tammany's Magazine (New York, November 9, no. 1, p. 13) under the heading, "Queen Mab and Its Author: To the Editor of The Examiner," prints Shelley's letter of June 22, protesting against the piracy of *Queen Mab*. The same letter, with the identical heading, appears as a clipping from an unnamed newspaper, presumably English, pasted in the front of the British Museum's copy of the original *Queen Mab*. Since St. Tammany's Magazine consisted largely of extracts from English journals, it is likely that the unnamed journal is the original or that both are copied from a common English original.

The Literary and Scientific Repository and Critical Review (New York, January, 2: 168) reprints the favorable incidental criticism of Shelley in The Retrospective Review (*q.v.*, 1820).

The London Magazine contains four bits of incidental criticism, January, April, May, and July (3: 68; 3: 370; 3: 549; 4: 57). The London Magazine and Theatrical Inquisitor, January (3: 36 and 3: 78), prints an unmistakable imitation of Shelley's "The Cloud," and reprints Horace Smith's sonnet to Shelley in reviewing *Amarynthus the Nympholept*. The same magazine, February (3:172), mentions Shelley as one of the contributors to Hunt's *The Literary Pocket Book*. The Tickler, or Monthly Compendium of Good Things, April 1 (3: 83), reprints Arthur Brooke's sonnet to Shelley from The Examiner of November, 1820.

The Drama, or Theatrical Pocket Magazine, June (1: 189), digressing from a consideration of Byron's *Marino Faliero*, says "The very nature of Mr. Shelley's 'Cenci,' a play still more distinguished by vigorous conception, has banished it from consideration." In the Literary Chronicle and Weekly Review, July 7 (no. 112, p. 426), a letter signed Cantab., on Poetical Coincidences, refers to "Shelley's Queen Mab" and quotes two lines from it. The Etonian, August (2: 326), in an article entitled "On Etonian Poets," and signed P. C., makes a brief, sad comment on Shelley as a great but perverted genius. The Cambro-Britain; and General Celtic Repository, December (3: 121, 123), prints a Welsh translation (signed "Idrison, Hydrev 8, 1821") of stanza 11, canto 5, of *The Revolt of Islam*, followed by the stanza in English.

Hazlitt's essay on Paradox and Commonplace contains a passage adversely criticizing Shelley, and Southey's preface to *A Vision of Judgment*, while not mentioning Shelley by name, plainly has him in mind as one of the Satanic School which Southey condemns.

The Champion, December 23 (no. 468, p. 815), printed some favorable remarks on Shelley.

1822

In 1822 Shelley published *Hellas, a Lyrical Drama;* the May Day Night scene from *Faust* and *Song Written for an Indian Air,* both in The Liberal (no. 1, pp. 123-137 and p. 397); *St. Irvyne; or the Rosicrucian* was reissued as a remainder by the original publisher, J. J. Stockdale; and Richard Carlile issued two pirated editions of *Queen Mab.* Leigh Hunt's *Literary Pocket Book* for 1823 contained five short poems by Shelley, published anonymously.

Earlier publications were reviewed in 1822 as follows: The Examiner in four letters (January 20, no. 730, p. 35; June 9, no. 750, pp. 355-357; June 16, no. 751, pp. 370-371; June 23, no. 752, pp. 389-390) defends Shelley and particularly *Prometheus Unbound,* against the attacks of The Quarterly Review. The Examiner, July 7 (no. 754, pp. 419-421), contains a letter entitled "On Mr. Shelley's New Poem, Entitled Adonais," giving a sympathetic analysis of the poem and condemning The Quarterly reviewers for their treatment of Shelley and Keats. The Brighton Magazine, May (1:540-544), gives unfavorable attention to two early anonymous publications, *The Necessity of Atheism* and *A Declaration of Rights,* definitely ascribing both to Shelley. *Epipsychidion* is described and condemned in Blackwood's Edinburgh Magazine in a letter from London to C. North, February (11:237-238), and is quoted at some length by The Paris Monthly Review, March (1:135).

Hellas was reviewed in The General Weekly Register of News, Literature, Law, Politics, and Commerce, June 30 (no. 13, pp. 501-503), as "not entirely devoid of merit, but a bad specimen of Mr. Shelley's powers." An ostensible review in The Paris Monthly Review, August (2:392), turned into a sympathetic obituary.

Queen Mab (presumably Carlile's piracy) was bitterly assailed by the Rev. Mr. William Bengo Collyer in a collective review entitled "Licentious Productions in High Life," in The Investigator or Quarterly Magazine (no. 10, pp. 315 and 372, no month given).

The numerous general references to Shelley in 1822 center mainly about *Queen Mab,* The Liberal, and Shelley's death. The Examiner, December 22 (no. 778, pp. 805-806), under the heading, "Canting Slander. To the Reverend William Bengo Collyer" (signed H.), administered a stinging rebuke to The Investigator. Richard Carlile in The Republican, February 1 (5:145-148), under the title *Queen Mab* offers his pirated edition, describes the poem, and gives its history. He (*ibid.,* December 27, 6:978-979) describes the four editions of *Queen Mab* then available. The John Bull, December 8 (no. 99, pp. 794-795), in an editorial condemning the prosecutions by the Society for the Suppression of Vice, says they have "resuscitated the atheism of Shelley." The Council of Ten, July (no. 1, p. 196), condemning cheap periodicals, says there is already "a sufficient growth of indigenous irreligion and debauchery, when we have Lord Byron and Mr. Shelley, Don Juan and Queen Mab." The London Christian Instructor, or Congregational Magazine, April (5: 204), condemning Byron's *Cain*, says that Shelley, Byron, and Moore "have ministered to the vile cravings of the pampered and lecherous imagination." The Representative, March 10, in an article entitled "Mr. Carlile," condemns the blasphemy prosecutions as likely to foster blasphemous literature and as sometimes inspired by the love of money or notoriety: "We do long to see Shelley and Byron in the arena with the blasphemous traffickers in religion for filthy lucre's sake." The same journal, October 27, in an article entitled "Conspiracy against Religious and Political Liberty," condemns the "Vice Gang," for the William Clark— *Queen Mab* prosecution (though disclaiming sympathy with Clark and his ilk) and defends Shelley as "honest and candid," whose error was one of understanding and not of feeling. The Monthly Repository of Theology and General Literature, December (17: 717-718), gives a full account of William Clark's trial and conviction for publishing *Queen Mab*.

The apprehension caused in England by the association of Hunt, Byron, and Shelley to publish The Liberal was totally unjustified by the actual nature of the periodical when it appeared, but it was not unnatural, in view of *Cain*, *Don Juan*, and *Queen Mab*, and it no doubt biased in advance most of the conservative critics of that short-lived journal. The "Satanic School" appeared to be actually drawing up articles of confederation in infidelity and sedition.

The European Magazine and London Review, January (81:71), mentions Shelley in connection with the projected Liberal. The Recreative Review (3:21 and 59, no month given) links Shelley and Byron in atheism and refers inaccurately to "the person (now living) who subscribed himself Atheos at Athens." The London Christian Instructor for April (5:204) makes similar incidental comment. An anonymous publication called *Revolutionary Causes: with a Brief Notice of Some late Publications* condemns the revolutionary tendencies of "atheistical poets" and praises The Quarterly's review of *Prometheus Unbound*. John Watkins's anonymous *Memoirs of the Life and Writings of the Right Honorable Lord Byron*, etc. contains a number of unfavorable passing references to Shelley (pp. 268, 403, 405, 410, 411) all in connection with Byron and atheism. The Gazette of Fashion and Magazine of Literature, the Fine Arts and Belles Lettres, March 2 (1:83), announces the forthcoming appearance of The Liberal as the joint work of Byron, Shelley, and Hunt. The Literary Speculum (2:424 and 431, no month given) in reviewing The Liberal makes passing reference to Shelley as the author of *Queen Mab* and of the translation from *Faust*.

An anonymous publication entitled *A Critique of the Liberal*, etc., says that the talents of the three projectors "have long been known" and proceeds to review their present work unfavorably. The Imperial Magazine or Compendium of Religious, Moral, and Philosophical Knowledge (4:1139-1142), without mentioning any author by name, says that The Liberal appears to have been sent into the world as a mental barometer to measure the quantity of vice with which the community is saturated. The Council of Ten, November (no. 6, p. 165), in reviewing The Liberal, gives a page of rather charitable comment on the errors of Shelley, now known to have been lost at sea. Analecta (Rotherham, December 7 [?], no. 3, p. 97) in an unfavorable review of The Liberal expresses disappointment that Byron and Shelley have failed to measure up to its expectations of "something super-excellent." A long, detailed and furious review of No. 1 of The Liberal in The New European Magazine, October (1:354-363), characterizes Shelley's translation from *Faust* as "more insane than the original" and accuses "these three Professors of the Satanic School" of "heartless impiety," "brutal slander," and "awful blasphemies." Shelley's translation is also condemned in The Literary Gazette, October 26 (no. 301, p. 679). The St. James Chronicle, as quoted by The Gentleman's Magazine, October (92:348), says that "blasphemy and impiety of every kind" were expected when the association of Byron, Hunt, and Shelley became known, but that the full atrocity of The Liberal could hardly have been anticipated. The John Bull, October 27 (98:780-781), scornfully rejects "the nonsensical blasphemy of The Liberal"; and snorts that "the wretched Shelley, the fellow who denied his God, and for selling whose infamous writings Clarke was convicted this very week, is called '*the noblest of human beings*' and so on." Shelley's translation from *Faust* is praised in an anticipative review of The Liberal, signed A., in The Examiner, October 13 (no. 768, p. 652). It is mentioned with a slightly favorable implication in the review of The Liberal in The British Luminary and Weekly Intelligencer, October 20 (no. 212, p. 754); and is condemned at some length in The Country Literary Chronicle and Weekly Review, October 26 (no. 180, p. 675). The same periodical, in the preceding number (October 19, no. 179, p. 655), had commented on the effect of Shelley's death on The Liberal. Blackwood's Edinburgh Magazine, March (11:*363), makes passing reference to "the holy alliance at Pisa" scorning Byron for going in the same harness with "Shelley with his spavin and Hunt with his staingalt." This sentiment here uttered by Christopher North, is repeated by William Maginn in the critique on Lord Byron (*ibid.*, April, 11:456-460) who describes Shelley as a fool and "poetico-metaphysical maniac." The Edinburgh Magazine and Literary Miscellany, November (N. S. 11:563), reviewing The Liberal, assails Shelley bitterly.

The Liberal drew other attacks than reviews, e.g., The London Liberal: An Antidote to Verse and Prose from the South, which I have been unable to locate; The Illiberal, a burlesque, which seems never to have been published (see T. J. Wise, *A Shelley Library*, p. 109), introducing

* See original copy.

Shelley's ghost as a character; and a poem of twenty-three stanzas in The Representative, October 13 (no. 41), entitled "An Authentic and Very Marvellous New Ballad, Giving an Account of the Renowned Triple-leagued Champions of Anti-Christendom and Completely Unfolding the Supernatural Mystery of the Holy Trio."

Shelley's death, which is mentioned in a number of the reviews of The Liberal, received considerable independent notice. It is announced in a brief "Extract of a Letter from Pisa," in The Morning Chronicle for August 12. John Bull for August 12 (p. 693) briefly notes Shelley's death as a surprising (and apparently gratifying) visitation of Providence. A brief formal "Death Notice" occurs in The Annual Register (p. 290). Conventional obituaries occur in The Gentleman's Magazine, September (92:283); The Monthly Magazine and British Register, September (54: 178); The Monthly Repository of Theology and General Literature, September (17:577); and The New Monthly Magazine, October 1 (N. S. 6:472), the last of a noticeably kindly tone. Shelley's death is made the occasion for either favorable or unfavorable comment on his life by The Republican, August 16 (6:380-381), in an article by Richard Carlile entitled "Death of Percy Bysshe Shelley," and (ibid., August 23, 6:408) an article entitled "From 'The British Luminary' "; The Liberal (1: xi, preface); The British Luminary and Weekly Intelligencer, August (no. 203, p. 685); The Morning Chronicle, August 12; John Bull, August 19 (no. 87, p. 693); The Literary Chronicle and Weekly Review, August 10 (no. 169, p. 504); The Drama, or Theatrical Pocket Magazine (supplement to vol. 3, pp. 387-392); The Examiner, August 4 and November 3 (no. 758, p. 489, and no. 771, p. 690).

In 1822 Shelley was the subject of nine published poems (including two republications), five of which were occasioned by his death. John Bull, February 4 (p. 477), presented an epigrammatic quatrain, "On Mr. Shelly's Poem, Prometheus Unbound," which could not find "a reader so weak as to pay for the binding." Arthur Brooke (John Chalk Claris) was the author of a sonnet on Shelley which had appeared in The Examiner, November 5, 1820, republished this year in his Retrospection, with Other Poems and quoted in part in the review of the volume in The Gazette of Fashion and Magazine of Literature, the Fine Arts and Belles Lettres, April 13 (1:177). J. W. Dalby published in The Troubadour (probably in September, though I have been unable to find the magazine) a poem called "Lines to Shakespeare and to Shelley" which is mentioned in The Drama, or Theatrical Pocket Magazine, October (3:209), and partly quoted in the same periodical (supplement to vol. 3, pp. 387-392). The Examiner, August 25 (no. 761, p. 538), contains a poem signed B., entitled "On the Death of Mr. Shelley." The Bard, November 16 (1: 38-40), contains an "Elegy on the Death of Shelley," signed F. A previous number, October 26 (no. 2, p. 422), contained a stanza on Shelley in a poem entitled "Rejected Addresses." A poem "On the Death of Percy Bysshe Shelley," signed J. N.xxxxxx, appeared in The Hermes, a

Literary, Moral, and Scientific Journal, December 14 (1:55). *An Elegy on the Death of Percy Bysshe Shelley,* by Arthur Brooke (John Chalk Claris) appeared as a separate, independent publication, as did also Bernard Barton's *Verses on the Death of Percy Bysshe Shelley,* with which was reprinted Barton's earlier poem to Shelley (*q.v.,* under 1820).

Reviews of the volumes by Arthur Brooke and Bernard Barton were numerous and were commonly devoted largely to criticisms of Shelley. The two volumes are reviewed together under the heading, "Persy Bysshe Shelley," in The Literary Chronicle and Weekly Review, October 12 (no. 178, pp. 643-644). Brooke's volume is listed among new publications in The European Magazine and London Review, September (82: 265); and is reviewed in The Monthly Magazine and British Register, October 1 (54:255); The Monthly Review, November (99:326); The Literary Gazette and Journal of Belles Lettres, etc., September 21 (no. 296, p. 591); and The Gentleman's Magazine (supplement to 1822, part 2, 92:623). Barton's volume is listed among recent publications in The Monthly Magazine and British Register, October 1 (54:257); and The European Magazine and London Review, September (82:265). It is reviewed in The Literary Gazette and Journal of Belles Lettres, etc., October 5 (no. 298, p. 626); The Monthly Review, November (99: 327); The Eclectic Review, November (N. S. 18:476-478); The Christian Guardian and Church of England Magazine, December 1 (14: 497-498); The British Review and London Critical Journal, December (pp. 419-420), The Imperial Magazine or Compendium of Religious, Moral, and Philosophical Knowledge (4:1061-1064); and The Evangelical Magazine and Missionary Chronicle (30:522).

Other miscellaneous comment on Shelley occurs in 1822 as follows: The Examiner, January 13 (no. 729, p. 28), reprints a published letter of Southey's in which Shelley's "atheos" inscription in the Mont-Anvert visitor's book is mentioned (without Shelley's name) as an incident which Southey had circulated; The Gridiron, or Cook's Weekly Register, March 23 (no. 1, pp. 23, 24), commenting on Byron's Satanism, condemns Shelley and Hunt as "petty rascals" who should be "whipped at the cart's tail"; The Council of Ten, August (no. 3, p. 391), discussing the state of English drama, asks scornfully, "Is Lord Byron, or Mr. Shelley, to be the founder of a new school?"; The Album, July, 1822 (no. 2, pp. 222-223), in an article on "The Augustan Age in English Poetry," praises Shelley at some length; Blackwood's Edinburgh Magazine, March (11: 345) seems to scorn The Quarterly as "a magazine where you have Milman extolled as a first-rate poet the one number and Shelley run down as no poet at all the next," and in April (11:458) refers the reader to The Quarterly for a correct notion of Shelley. The same magazine, August (12:159), makes passing mention of "Mr. Shelley, bad as he is."

XVI

Summary by Periodicals and Other Publications in Which Shelley Is Noticed, 1810-1822, Including Shelley's Own Publications

The figure (1) indicates a predominantly favorable attitude toward Shelley; (2) indicates a more or less balanced attitude in which Shelley's genius is admitted while his principles and conduct (or both) are condemned; (3) an unfavorable attitude toward Shelley, combining condemnation of his principles and conduct (or both) with denial of his poetic ability. Where the attitude toward Shelley is too cursory or vague to furnish a reasonable inference, no symbol is used. These arbitrary characterizations must not be interpreted too rigidly, however, for it frequently happens that a friendly tone toward Shelley is accompanied by no great perception of his genius, while a very antagonistic critic may at the same time perceive Shelley's greatness as a poet.

Additional remarks on many of the periodicals are given in the head-notes to the first item from each periodical reprinted in this volume.

All items reprinted in this volume are here marked "Reprinted," followed by the page number. Most of the items not reprinted are briefly described in the preceding Chronological Summary.

An Address to the Irish People. By Percy Bysshe Shelley. Published at Dublin, February 25, 1812.

An Address to the People on the Death of the Princess Charlotte. By the Hermit of Marlow. November, 1817.

Adonais, An Elegy on the Death of John Keats, etc. By Percy B. Shelley. 1821.

Alastor; or, the Spirit of Solitude: and Other Poems. By Percy Bysshe Shelley. 1816.

The Album (2). 1822-25. 4 vols. Ed. F. B. B. St. Leger, apparently about 1824; from about 1824 by Robert Sullivan, dramatist and clever friend of Alaric Watts. Moderately conservative.

July 8,1822 (1: 183-234), article "The Augustan Age in England" contains a passage on Shelley, pp. 222-223. Reprinted, p. 315.

Amarynthus, the Nympholept: A Pastoral Drama, in Three Acts. With Other Poems. By Horace Smith. 1820. (1). Contains the sonnet To Percy Bysshe Shelley on his Poems (p. 214). Reprinted, p. 340.

Analecta. (2). Rotherham, nos. 1-5, 1822-23. A fairly able review, at first fortnightly, then monthly, one of whose main purposes was "to exhibit a comprehensive and concentrated view of the Literature of the Age." Its poetical taste seems to run to James Montgomery. Moderately conservative.

No. 3, probably published in December, contains (pp. 97-122) an unfavorable review of No. 1 of The Liberal, with incidental mention of Shelley (p. 97).

The Annual Register, for 1822. 1758—(in progress). Founded by R. Dodsley. Conservative. Its first editor was Edmund Burke. In the death register for August, a brief, colorless statement of Shelley's death (p. 290).

The Anti-Jacobin Review and Magazine, or monthly political and Literary Censor. 1798-1821. Edited by John Gifford (pseud. for John Richards Green, an ad-

venturer who was befriended by William Pitt). Very conservative. Similar to
the old Anti-Jacobin in politics, but less brilliant. (3).

January, 1812 (41:69), review of *St. Irvyne; or the Rosicrucian.* Reprinted,
p. 36.

February, 1812 (41:221), under the title "Salutary Attention to Morals in the
University of Oxford," a letter signed "An Oxford Collegian," on Shelley's Oxford career. In neither of these notices is Shelley's name mentioned. Reprinted,
p. 38.

The Bard, being a selection of original poetry, etc., by F. G. and C. Whiteson. Nos.
1-8. Oct. 19-Dec. 7, 1822. A fugitive "little poetry" magazine of rather commonplace character, consisting of eight pages weekly of "original poetry, rejected
addresses, elegies," etc., published by Chappell and Son, and dedicated (not
inaptly) "To Vanity." (3) Conservative.

October 26, 1822 (no. 2, p. 422), a stanza on Shelley in a poem entitled "Rejected Addresses," by L. B.

November 16, 1822 (no. 5, pp. 38-40), a poem entitled, "Elegy on the Death of
Shelley," signed F. Reprinted, p. 346.

Blackwood's Edinburgh Magazine. Edinburgh. 1817—in progress. During the
life of Shelley brilliant, reckless, often brutal. Tory. Very conservative. Particularly interested in Shelley (see Introduction), whose treatment seems to have
been dominated first by John Wilson and then by a less friendly critic. (2).

January, 1818 (2:415), incidental reference to Shelley in connection with the
"Cockney School of Poetry."

January, 1819 (4: 475-482), *Observations on The Revolt of Islam* [by John
Wilson]. Reprinted, p. 125.

June, 1819 (5:268-275), *Rosalind and Helen* (review) [by John Wilson].
Reprinted, p. 158.

September, 1819 (5: 640), incidental reference to Shelley in connection with the
"Cockney School of Poetry."

November, 1819 (6: 148-155), review of *Alastor* [by John Wilson]. Reprinted,
p. 110.

December, 1819 (6: 241-242), in reviewing Hunt's *Literary Pocket Book* quotes
the whole of Shelley's "Marianne's Dream" with approval.

September, 1820 (7: 678-688), review of *Prometheus Unbound* [by John Wilson or J. G. Lockhart, or both]. Reprinted, p. 225.

January, 1821 (8: 397), quotes the first ten stanzas of "The Sensitive Plant," in
an article entitled "Flores Poetica," with appreciative comment on the lines.

December, 1821 (10:696-700), remarks on Shelley's *Adonais* [by George
Croly?]. Reprinted, p. 289.

February, 1822 (11: 237-238), "A Letter From London, To C. North" contains
remarks on *Epipsychidion*, attributing it to Byron. Footnote on Shelley, signed
C. North. Reprinted, p. 281.

March, 1822 (11: 345), passing reference to Shelley in connection with The
Quarterly. *Ibid.* (11: 363), passing reference to Shelley in connection with The
Liberal. Reprinted, p. 316.

April, 1822 (11:456-460), passing references to Shelley in connection with
Byron and The Liberal.

August, 1822 (12: 159), passing reference to Shelley in connection with Hazlitt
and Keats.

The Brighton Magazine. London. Jan.-Aug., 1822, nos. 1-8. Conservative monthly
of average quality. (3).

May, 1822 (1: 540-544), review of *The Necessity of Atheism* and *A Declaration of Rights*. Reprinted, p. 39.

The British Critic, a new review. 1793-October, 1826. Edited 1793-1813 by W. Beloe and R. Nares; 1814-25 by T. F. Middleton, W. R. Lyall, et al. Conservative monthly, decidedly Tory and High Church. (3).

September, 1810 (36: 319), lists *Original Poetry by Victor and Cazire*.

January, 1811 (37: 70), reviews of *St. Irvyne or The Rosicrucian*. Reprinted, p. 35.

April, 1811 (37: 408-409), reviews *Original Poetry by Victor and Cazire*. Reprinted, p. 31.

May, 1816 (N. S. 5: 545-546), reviews *Alastor, or The Spirit of Solitude*. Reprinted, p. 105.

July, 1818 (N. S. 10: 94), passing comment on Shelley in reviewing Hunt's *Foliage*.

June, 1819 (N. S. 11: 668), lists *Rosalind and Helen*.

The British Luminary and Weekly Intelligencer. May 1821-[?]. Published as The Weekly Intelligencer and British Luminary, July 30, 1820-May, 1821 (nos. 96-139) representing the amalgamation of The Weekly Intelligencer and The British Luminary, both of which seem to have originated in 1817 or 1818. Somewhat radical in political sympathies. (2).

August 18, 1822 (no. 203, p. 685), comment on the treatment of Shelley in John Bull. Reprinted, p. 325.

October 20, 1822 (no. 212, p. 754), passing comment in reviewing The Liberal.

The British Review and London Critical Journal. March, 1811-November, 1825. Conservative monthly. Satirized by Byron as My Grandmother's Review. Described itself in 1824 as having been long considered "a literary work of a character decidedly religious." (3).

March, 1811 (1: 242), lists *St. Irvyne; or The Rosicrucian*.

September, 1811 (2: 280), lists *A Poetical Essay on the Existing State of Things*.

May, 1816 (7: 566), lists *Alastor, or The Spirit of Solitude*.

May, 1818 (11: 554), lists *The Revolt of Islam*.

September, 1820 (16: 246), lists *Prometheus Unbound*.

June, 1821 (17: 380-389), reviews *The Cenci*. Reprinted, p. 210.

December, 1822 (pp. 419-420), passing mention of Shelley in reviewing Barton's *Verses on the Death of Percy Bysshe Shelley*.

The Cambro-Briton; and General Celtic Repository. London. 1819-22. A conservative journal devoted almost entirely to Welsh literature and antiquities. Ed. J. H. Parry, the elder.

December, 1821 (3: 121, 123), a nine-line stanza in Welsh, signed "Idrison, Hydrev 8, 1821," followed (p. 123) by extract from Shelley's *Revolt of Islam*, Canto 5, stanza 11, and a footnote explaining that the stanza is printed as the original of the translation.

The Cenci, A Tragedy in Five Acts. By Percy Bysshe Shelley. 1820.

The Cenci, A Tragedy in Five Acts. By Percy Bysshe Shelley. Second Edition, 1821.

The Champion. Eds. John Scott and later John Thelwall, the "radical" friend of Lamb and Coleridge, who was tried for treason in 1794. Dates uncertain; British Museum has nos. 52-491, January 2, 1814-June 2, 1822. Strongly liberal. (1).

December 23, 1821 (no. 468, p. 815), sympathetic article on Shelley. Reprinted, p. 272.

The Christian Guardian and Church of England Magazine. Bristol and London, 1809-49. (3).

December 1, 1822 (14: 497-498). Passing comment in a review of Barton's *Verses on the Death of Percy Bysshe Shelley.*

The Commercial Chronicle. Dates uncertain; British Museum contains September 28, 1815-March 22, 1823. (3). It was chiefly concerned with news of commercial interest and seldom contained literary notices. Conservative.

June 3, 1819 (no. 2979, p. 1). Review of *Rosalind and Helen.* Identical with that in The London Chronicle, June 1, 1819, The Gentleman's Magazine, and The New Times. Reprinted, p. 153.

The Council of Ten. 1822-23. An intelligent and comparatively charitable Tory publication. (2).

July, 1822 (1: 196), passing comment on Shelley and Byron, in an article on periodical literature.

August, 1822 (3:391), passing comment on Shelley and Byron in an article on English drama.

November, 1822 (2: 165), remarks on Shelley in reviewing The Liberal. Reprinted, p. 318.

The Country Literary Chronicle and Weekly Review—July 1, 1820-May 8, 1823; continued as The Literary Chronicle. A weekly somewhat conservatively liberal. (2). See under Literary Chronicle, etc.

August 10, 1822 (no. 169, p. 504), an obituary account, quoting extensively from that in The Examiner.

October 19, 1822 (no. 179, p. 655), incidental comment on Shelley in announcing The Liberal.

October 26, 1822 (no. 180, p. 675), comment on Shelley and criticism of his translation from *Faust,* in reviewing The Liberal, No. 1. Reprinted, p. 318.

The Critical Review, or Annals of Literature. 1756-1817. Monthly, first edited by Tobias Smollett, a conventional, conservative magazine of rather secondary ability and importance in its last years. (3).

November, 1810 (21: 329-331), a review of *Zastrozzi, a Romance.* Reprinted, p. 33.

December, 1814 (6: 566-574), Shelley's anonymous review of Hogg's *Memoirs of Prince Alexy Haimatoff.*

February, 1816 (3: 205), lists *Alastor, or The Spirit of Solitude.*

A Critique on "The Liberal," etc. Anon. 1822. Passing mention of Shelley, p. 3.

A Declaration of Rights. Anon. (Shelley) 1812.

The Devil's Walk. Anon. (Shelley) 1812.

Don Juan: with a Biographical Account of Lord Byron, etc. Canto III. 1819. (3). Passing comment on Shelley, as the author of *Frankenstein.*

The Drama, or Theatrical Pocket Magazine. 1821-25. A duodecimo fifty-page monthly with few literary interests beyond drama. Published by T. and J. Elvey, Castle St., Holborn. (1).

June, 1821 (1: 89), incidental mention of *The Cenci* as "distinguished by vigorous conception."

October, 1822. (3:209), reference to J. W. Dalby's *Lines to Shakespeare and to Shelley.*

December [?], 1822 (supplement to vol. 3, pp. 387-392), an obituary account, headed "Sept. 8. Percy Bysshe Shelley, Esq." Reprinted, p. 331.

The Dublin Evening Post. Dublin.
> February 25, 29, and March 3, 1812. An advertisement of *An Address to the Irish People*.
> February 29, 1812, an account of Shelley's speech at the Fishamble Street Theatre.

The Dublin Journal. Dublin. Ed. George Faulkner. Conservative. According to D. F. McCarthy's *Shelley's Early Life*, "the government organ of the time." (3).
> March 7, 1812, a letter to the editor, signed An Englishman, commenting sarcastically on Shelley's Fishamble Street Theatre address.
> March 21, 1812, a letter to the editor, signed A Dissenter, of the same tenor as the above.

The Dublin Magazine, or General Repertory of Philosophy, Belles Lettres, and Miscellaneous Information. Dublin. 1820. Conventionally mediocre, conservative and Tory. (2).
> January, 1820 (1:56), incidental comment on Shelley in a letter deploring the immoral effects of Byron's poems.
> November, 1820 (1: 393-400), article entitled "Critical Remarks on Shelley's Poetry." Reprinted, p. 255.

The Eclectic Review. 1805-68. Ed. S. Greatheed, T. Parker, and T. Williams. Dissenting church organ. Conservative quarterly. (3).
> April, 1816 (N. S. 5:414), lists *Alastor; or the Spirit of Solitude*.
> October, 1816 (N. S. 6: 391-393), a review of *Alastor; or the Spirit of Solitude*. Reprinted, p. 106.
> September, 1820 (N. S. 14: 169), incidental reference in reviewing Keats' *Lamia*.
> November, 1822 (N. S. 18: 476-478), a review of Barton's *Verses on the Death of Percy Bysshe Shelley*. Reprinted, p. 335.

The Edinburgh Annual Register. Edinburgh. 1810-28. 1811 (vol. 4, part 2, p. cxxii) lists *Posthumous Fragments of Margaret Nicholson*.

The Edinburgh Magazine and Literary Miscellany. Edinburgh. 1804-26. Formerly (1739-1804) published as The Scots Magazine. (3).
> July, 1820 (N. S. 7: 13), incidental stricture on Shelley in review of Barry Cornwall's *Marcia Colonna*.
> January, 1822 (N. S. 10:110-112), a comparison of *Queen Mab* and *Cain* in a review of Byron.
> November, 1822 (N. S. 11: 563), extended bitter comment on Shelley in a review of The Liberal signed Jonathan Oldmixon. Reprinted, p. 319.

The Edinburgh Monthly Review. Edinburgh. 1819-21. A Tory monthly edited for William Blackwood by Thomas Pringle and James Cleghorn. John Wilson was an important contributor. (2).
> May, 1820 (3: 591-604), a review of *The Cenci*. Reprinted, p. 185.

The Edinburgh Quarterly Review. 1810-11. vol. 17, p. 249. Lists *Original Poetry by Victor and Cazire*.

Elegy on the Death of Percy Bysshe Shelley. By Arthur Brooke [John Chalk Claris]. London, 1822. (1). Reprinted, p. 348.

Epipsychidion. Anon. 1821. (February.)

The Etonian. Windsor. October, 1820-August, 1821. (2).
> August, 1821 (2: 326), brief comment on Shelley in an article entitled "On Etonian Poets," signed P. C. Reprinted, p. 272.

The European Magazine and London Review. 1782-1825. Conservative. September, 1820 (78:255), lists *Prometheus Unbound*.

January, 1822 (81:71), incidental mention of Shelley in connection with The Liberal, which is mentioned only as a project.

September, 1822 (82:265), notice of Brooke's *Elegy on the Death of Percy Bysshe Shelley*.

The Evangelical Magazine and Missionary Chronicle, 1793-1822.

A thoroughly conventional church magazine. (3).

1822 Supplement (30:522), incidental comment on Shelley in reviewing Bernard Barton's *Verses on the Death of Percy Bysshe Shelley*.

The Examiner; a Sunday paper, on politics, domestic economy, and theatricals. 1808-81. Edited successively by Leigh Hunt, Albany Fonblanque, et al. After 1836 the latter part of the title was altered to "Politics, Literature, and Fine Arts" and the size changed from quarto to folio. During Shelley's lifetime, except for part of 1821 and 1822 when it was edited by John Hunt, it was edited by Leigh Hunt. It was radical in politics and liberal in literature. Leigh Hunt's papers in the British Museum (Add. Mss. 38,108, ff., 203, 323, 324) shows that in 1820 The Examiner's receipts from subscriptions were £5948, 10d. and that Hunt's half-share of the profits was £443, 1s., 2¾d. For the first half of 1824 the weekly sales ranged from 3,861 to 5,410 copies, averaging about 5,000. (1).

December 1, 1816 (no. 466, p. 761-762), article entitled "Young Poets." Reprinted, p. 108.

January 19, 1817 (no. 473, p. 41), prints Shelley's "Hymn to Intellectual Beauty." Reprinted, p. 108.

January 26, 1817 (no. 474, p. 60), quotes from The Morning Chronicle a brief report of part of the proceedings in "Westbrook vs. Shelley."

November 30, 1817 (no. 518, p. 761), prints extract from *Laon and Cythna*, eight stanzas.

December 28, 1817 (no. 522, pp. 826-827), Shelley's review of Godwin's *Mandeville*, signed E. K. [Elphin Knight].

January 11, 1818 (no. 524, p. 24), prints "Ozymandias," signed Glirastes.

January 25, 1818 (no. 526, p. ?), extract from *The Revolt of Islam*, fifty-eight lines, without comment.

February 1, 1818 (no. 527, pp. 75-76), notice of *The Revolt of Islam*. Reprinted, p. 00. Also, p. 73, incidental praise of "Ozymandias" by Horace Smith.

February 8, 1818 (no. 528, p. 88), prints Horace Smith's sonnet "To the Author of The Revolt of Islam." Reprinted, p. 340.

February 22, 1818 (no. 530, pp. 121-122), review of *The Revolt of Islam* continued. Reprinted, p. 117.

March 1, 1818 (no. 531, pp. 139-141), review of *The Revolt of Islam*, concluded. Reprinted, p. 117.

May 9, 1819 (no. 593, pp. 302-303), review of *Rosalind and Helen*. Reprinted, p. 151.

September 26, 1819 (no. 613, pp. 620-621), article on The Quarterly Review and its attacks on Shelley. Reprinted, p. 143.

October 3, 1819 (no. 614, pp. 635-636), the same continued. Reprinted, p. 143.

October 10, 1819 (no. 615, pp. 652-653), the same concluded. Reprinted, p. 143.

March 19, 1820 (no. 638, pp. 190-191), notice of *The Cenci*. Reprinted, p. 167.

November 5, 1820 (no. 671, p. 717), Arthur Brooke's sonnet "To the Author of the Revolt of Islam." Reprinted, p. 343.

January 13, 1822 (no. 729, p. 28), copies from The Courier a letter of Southey's referring to Shelley's conduct in Switzerland.

January 20, 1822 (no. 730, p. 35), incidental defense of Shelley, in a review of The Quarterly. Reprinted, p. 309.

June 9, 1822 (no. 750, pp. 355-357), defense of Shelley in an article on The Quarterly Review.

June 16, 1822 (no. 751, pp. 370-371), letters to readers of The Examiner, No. 4, *Prometheus Unbound*. Reprinted, p. 309.

June 23, 1822 (no. 752, pp. 389-390), letters to readers of The Examiner, No. 5, *Prometheus Unbound*. Reprinted, p. 309.

July 7, 1822 (no. 754, pp. 419-421), letters to readers of The Examiner, No. 6, "On Mr. Shelley's New Poem entitled 'Adonais'." Reprinted, p. 298.

August 4, 1822 (no. 758, p. 489), an account of Shelley's death. Reprinted, p. 321.

August 25, 1822 (no. 761, p. 538), a poem, signed B., entitled "On the Death of Mr. Shelley." Reprinted, p. 345.

October 13, 1822 (no. 768, p. 652), incidental praise of Shelley's translation from *Faust*, in an anticipative review of The Liberal, No. 1. Reprinted, p. 317.

November 3, 1822 (no. 771, p. 690), a tribute to Shelley in an article on the death of Lord Castlereagh. Reprinted, p. 335.

December 22, 1822 (no. 778, pp. 805-806), a defense of Shelley in an article entitled "Canting Slander: To the Reverend William Bengo Collyer."

The Fireside Magazine, or Monthly Entertainer. Stamford. 1819. A commonplace provincial magazine.

May 1, 1819 (1:270), in its "Monthly Epitome," quotes a paragraph from The Monthly Review, under the heading "Shelley's Revolt of Islam, a Poem." Reprinted, p. 132.

Foliage. By Leigh Hunt. 1817. Contains two laudatory sonnets to Shelley, entitled "To Percy Shelley, on the Degrading Notions of the Deity," and "To the Same" (pp. 73, 74 in Philadelphia ed., 1818). Reprinted, p. 340.

The Freeman's Journal. Dublin.

February 28, 1812, a brief account of Shelley's speech at Fishamble Street Theatre.

The Gazette of Fashion, and Magazine of Literature, the Fine Arts, and Belles Lettres. 1822. A weekly edited by C. M. Westmacott. Conservative in politics and literature. (3).

March 2, 1822 (1:83), incidental mention of Shelley in announcing The Liberal.

April 3, 1822 (1:177), hostile remarks on Shelley in reviewing Arthur Brooke's *Retrospection.*

The General Chronicle and Literary Magazine, 1811-12.

February, 1811 (1:181), lists *St. Irvyne; or the Rosicrucian.*

The General Weekly Register of News, Literature, Law, Politics, and Commerce. Nos. 1-13. 1822. (2).

June 30, 1822 (no. 13, pp. 501-503), a review of *Hellas, a Lyrical Drama.* Reprinted, p. 303.

The Gentleman's Magazine, or Monthly Intelligencer, January, 1731-1868. Edited from 1792-1826 by J. Nichols. Continued from 1736 as Gentleman's Magazine and Historical Chronicle. Never primarily literary in its interests, it was during Shelley's lifetime a conservative magazine of less literary interest and influence than in the eighteenth century. (3).

September, 1810 (part 2, 80:258), a brief favorable notice of *Zastrozzi*. Reprinted, p. 33.

January, 1815 (85:93), incidental mention of Shelley in obituary notice of Sir Bysshe Shelley.

Supplement for 1819 (89:625-626), review of *Rosalind and Helen*. Reprinted, p. 153.

September, 1822 (part 2, 92:283), obituary notice of Percy Bysshe Shelley, Esq. Reprinted, p. 329.

October, 1822 (part 2, 92:348-351), incidental mention of Shelley in reviewing The Liberal, No. 1.

1822 (supplement to vol. 92, part 2, p. 623), abusive comment on Shelley in a review of Arthur Brooke's *Elegy on the Death of Percy Bysshe Shelley*. Reprinted, p. 338.

The Gossip; a Series of original essays and letters, literary, historical and critical descriptive sketches, etc., nos. 1-24. 1821. A rather sprightly and well-written weekly. (2).

May 19, 1821 (no. 12, p. 91), passing reference to *Epipsychidion*.

June 23, 1821 (no. 17, pp. 129-135), a review of *Epipsychidion*. Reprinted, p. 275.

July 14, 1821 (no. 20, pp. 153-159), Seraphina and her Sister Clementina's *Review of Epipsychidion*. Reprinted, p. 276.

The Gridiron, or Cooke's Weekly Register. Nos. 1-3. 1822. A conservative weekly. (3).

March 23, 1822 (no. 1, pp. 23, 24), incidental scornful reference to Shelley in discussing Byron's Satanism.

Headlong Hall. By Thomas Love Peacock. 1816. One of the characters is said to represent Shelley.

Hellas, A Lyrical Drama. By Percy B. Shelley. 1822. (April?).

The Hermes; a Literary, Moral, and Scientific Journal. Liverpool. Nos. 1-28. 1822-23. Conservative weekly. "We respect religion and morality as the palladium of our country," the editor states in the first number. (2).

December 14, 1822 (1:55), a poem, signed J. N.xxx xxx, entitled "On the Death of Percy Bysshe Shelley." Reprinted, p. 357.

The Hibernian Journal, or Daily Chronicle of Liberty. Dublin.

March 2, 1812, a brief account of Shelley's speech at Fishamble Street Theatre. Identical with those in The Freeman's Journal and in Walker's Hibernian Magazine (*q.v.*)

A History of a Six Weeks' Tour Through a Part of France, Switzerland, Germany, and Holland, etc. Anon. (Shelley and Mary Shelley) 1817.

The Honeycomb. June 17-[August 19?] 1820. Printed by G. Taylor and published by R. Walker, 90, High Holborn. An eight-page two-penny literary weekly that avoided politics and sought to be "new and pleasant." (2).

August 12, 1820 (no. 9, pp. 65-72), "Portraits of the Metropolitan Poets—No. III—Mr. Percy Bysshe Shelley." Reprinted, p. 251.

The Illiberal. 1822. A burlesque by William Gifford in which "the Ghost of Percy B. Shelley" is a character. Apparently suppressed before publication. The only known copy is in the Ashley Library.

The Imperial Magazine, or Compendium of Religious, Moral, and Philosophical Knowledge. Liverpool. 1819-34. Conservative in politics and religion. The earlier numbers show a considerable interest in contemporary writers. (2).

1822 (4: 1061-1064) comment on Shelley in reviewing Bernard Barton's *Verses on the Death of Percy Bysshe Shelley.*

1822 (4: 1139-1142) a review of The Liberal, without mentioning its contributors by name.

The Independent: A London Literary and Political Review, January 6-March 31, 1821. Nos. 1-13. A sixteen-page quarto weekly, liberal in opinions. Printed and published by Nathaniel Bliss, 39 Nelson Square. The editor in the first number condemns the subservience of most literary criticism and aspires to real independence. (2).

February 17, 1821 (1: 99-103), a review of *The Cenci.* Reprinted, p. 206.

February 17, 1821 (1: 112), Ollier's advertisement of "Mr. Shelley's Works," concluding with the opening sentence of Blackwood's review of *Alastor.*

The Indicator. 1819-22. Edited by Leigh Hunt to no. 77 of vol. 2. Liberal essay-weekly. (1).

December 22, 1819 (no. 11, p. 88), prints Shelley's *Love's Philosophy.*

July 19, 1820 (no. 41, pp. 321-329), an article, "The Destruction of The Cenci Family, and Tragedy on that Subject."

July 26, 1820 (no. 42, pp. 329-337), the same, concluded. Reprinted, p. 197.

The Investigator, or Quarterly Magazine. 1820-24. Ed. W. B. Collyer, T. Raffles, and J. B. Brown. Militantly conservative in literary and religious views. (3).

1822 (vol. 5, no. 10, pp. 315-372), a composite review entitled "Licentious Productions in High Life." A bitter attack on Shelley, via *Queen Mab.* Reprinted, p. 98.

John Bull. December 17, 1820-July 16, 1892. Vigorously Tory, carried a crown and a Holy Bible at its mast-head with the legend "For God, the King, and the People." Issued in Sunday and Monday editions. It was established to combat the adherents of Queen Caroline, received a secret subsidy from the Treasury, and was, by his own testimony, the most valuable supporter George IV had. The nominal editor, Shackell, was several times sentenced for libel; but the real guiding genius, the clever and unscrupulous Theodore Hook, managed to keep out of the courts. William Maginn was also a contributor. (3).

February 4, 1822 (p. 477), quatrain sneering at *Prometheus Unbound.* Reprinted, p. 345.

August 12, 1822 (no. 86, p. 693), short hostile notice of Shelley's death.

August 19, 1822 (no. 87, p. 693), editorial condemnation of the Morning Chronicle for charitable remarks on Shelley's death. Reprinted, p. 322.

October 27, 1822 (no. 98, pp. 780-781), incidental condemnation of Shelley in a review of The Liberal. No. 1.

John Bull's British Journal. February 25-March 11, 1821. A radical weekly, published by William Benbow, who also published pirated editions of *Queen Mab.* (1).

March 11, 1821 (no. 3, p. 22), a favorable review of "Queen Mab, a Poem, by Percy Bish Shelley, Esq." Reprinted, p. 52.

La Belle Assemblée. London. N. S. 2, Supplement, 1811, lists *Zastrozzi* among new publications for 1810.

Laon and Cythna; or The Revolution of the Golden City. By Percy B. Shelley. 1818. Quickly withdrawn and re-issued as *The Revolt of Islam.*

A Letter to Lord Ellenborough. Anon. (Shelley). July, 1812.

The Liberal, or Verse and Prose from the South. 1822-23. Nos. 1, 2, 3. Radical, edited in Italy by Hunt, Shelley, and Byron. Leigh Hunt's papers in the British Museum (Add. Mss. 38,108, ff. 257, 258, 323, 324) show that the sales of The Liberal fell below expectations. Of the first number, 7,000 copies were printed and 4,050 sold; of the second number 6,000 were printed and 2,700 sold by September 25, 1823. The first number showed a profit of £377, 16s., od.; the second a loss of £41, 14s., od. The third and fourth numbers showed profits of £2, 11s., 6d. and £14, 6s. 4d. respectively. Among the expenses are listed a total of £96 paid to Mrs. Shelley. (1).

1822 (no. 1, preface, p. xi), incidental rebuke of Tory comment on Shelley's death.

1822 (no. 1, pp. 123-137), Shelley's translation of the May Day Night scene from *Faust*, anon.

1823 (no. 2, p. 397), Shelley's "Song Written for an Indian Air." Anon.

1823 (no. 3, p. 187), Shelley's "Lines to a Critic." Anon., but with a footnote commenting on Shelley as the author.

Lines on a Fete at Carlton House, a lost poem, Shelley's title for which is unknown.

The Literary and Scientific Repository and Critical Review. New York. 1820-22. Consists entirely of reviews, classified as "Original" and "Select." The latter predominate and are taken from English periodicals. (2).

July, 1820 (1:270), lists *Prometheus Unbound*.

July, 1820 (1:223-243), extracts from three English reviews of Shelley.

January, 1821 (2:168), quotes comments on Shelley from Retrospective Review.

The Literary Chronicle and Weekly Review. 1819-28. After July, 1828, incorporated with The Athenaeum, which continued the interest in Shelley. In 1820 it advertised itself as "free from political controversy and particularly suited for the amusement of families and the instruction of the rising generation." A liberal weekly. (2). See under Country Literary Chronicle, etc.

May 19, 1821 (no. 105), announcement of *Queen Mab* in an advertisement by W. Clark.

June 2, 1821 (no. 107, p. 344), review of *Queen Mab*. Reprinted, p. 61.

July 7, 1821 (no. 112, p. 426), incidental mention of Shelley in a letter entitled "Poetical Coincidences," signed Cantab.

July 14, 1821 (no. 113, p. 448), announcement of *An Answer to Queen Mab* as in press, in an advertisement by W. Clark.

December 1, 1821 (no. 133, pp. 751-754), a review of *Adonais*, quoting the entire poem except stanzas 19-24. Reprinted, p. 285.

December 29, 1821 (no. 136, p. 822), reference to a hostile review of *The Cenci* in The Advertiser.

October 12, 1822 (no. 178, pp. 643-644), article entitled "Percy Bysshe Shelley," reviewing the poems on his death by Brooke and Barton. Reprinted, p. 336.

The Literary Gazette and Journal of Belles Lettres, Arts, Sciences, etc., 1817-58. Edited successively by W. Jerdan, S. Phillips, L. Reeve, and J. M. Jephson. New Series, 1858-62; then incorporated with The Parthenon. Weekly. Alaric A. Watts, who was associated with Jerdan on The Literary Gazette for about three years beginning June, 1819, says in his autobiography that the periodical was in general independent and liberal except toward radicals and atheists, against whom "a very powerful clerical pen" thundered. One of its writers in the early 1820's was Dr. William Maginn, who probably had some hand in the later notices of Shelley in Blackwood's. During Shelley's lifetime it was one of the most influential of the weekly publications and one of the bitterest in denouncing Shelley's radicalism. (3).

April 1, 1820 (no. 167, pp. 209-211), a review of *The Cenci*. Reprinted, p. 168.

September 9, 1820 (no. 190, pp. 580-582), a review of *Prometheus Unbound*. Reprinted, p. 217.

May 19, 1821 (no. 226, pp. 305-309), a review of *Queen Mab*. Reprinted, p. 55.

June 2, 1821 (no. 228, p. 348), "The Atheist," a poem attacking Shelley. By C. Reprinted, p. 344.

August 18, 1821 (no. 239, p. 527), announcement and brief description of *Adonais* as in press.

December 8, 1821 (no. 255, pp. 772-773), a review of *Adonais*. Reprinted, p. 286.

September 21, 1822 (no. 296, p. 591), comment on Shelley in reviewing Arthur Brooke's *Elegy on the Death of Percy Bysshe Shelley*.

October 5, 1822 (no. 298, p. 626), comment on Shelley in reviewing Barton's *Verses on the Death of Percy Bysshe Shelley*.

October 26, 1822 (no. 301, p. 679), incidental condemnation of Shelley's translation from *Faust*, in reviewing The Liberal.

The Literary Gazette, or Journal of Criticism, Science, and the Arts. Philadelphia. 1821—?

April 28, 1821 (no. 17, pp. 285-286), quotes without comment a part of Shelley's "The Sensitive Plant."

The Literary Panorama. 1807-19. Incorporated with The New Monthly Magazine after 1819.

October, 1810 (8: 1074), lists *Original Poetry; by Victor and Cazire*.

October, 1810 (8: 1063-1066), a review of *Original Poetry; by Victor and Cazire*. Reprinted, p. 29.

February, 1811 (9: 252-253), a review of *St. Irvyne; or The Rosicrucian*. Reprinted, p. 35.

May, 1816 (N. S. 4: 297), a reprint from the *Alastor* volume of two translations (1) "Sonnet. From the Italian of Dante," (2) "Translated from the Greek of Moschus." The poems are attributed to Shelley without comment and without mention of the *Alastor* volume.

September, 1818 (N. S. 8: 986), quotes nine stanzas from "Mr. Shelley's new work, *The Revolt of Islam*."

The Literary Pocket-Book; or Companion for the Lover of Nature and Art. 1819-23. A sort of pocket memorandum book, published annually by Leigh Hunt, adorned with short literary gems. They were published in the year preceding the dates given.

1819. Shelley's "Marianne's Dream," signed Δ.

1821. Shelley's "On A Faded Violet."

1822. Shelley's "The Question," signed Σ.

1823. Shelley's "To—November 5, 1815," under the title, "November, 1815."

1823. Shelley's "The Sunset" (lines 9-20 and 28-42) as two poems, entitled "Sunset—From an Unpublished Poem" and "Grief, a Fragment."

1823. Shelley's "Sonnet—Ye hasten to the dead." Signed Σ.

1823. Shelley's "Lines to a Reviewer." Signed Σ.

The Literary Speculum. November, 1821-May, 1822. Mediocre combination of monthly and annual.

1822 (2:424 and 431), incidental reference to "the author of the notes to *Queen Mab*" in reviewing The Liberal, and comment on Shelley's translation from *Faust*.

The London Christian Instructor, or Congregational Magazine. 1818-24. Continued as The Congregational Magazine. 1825-45. A well-written, intelligent monthly, rather liberal of its class.

April, 1822 (5:204), incidental comment on Shelley in reviewing Byron's *Cain*.

The London Chronicle. 1757-96, 1798-1802, 1818, April 28, 1823.

June 1, 1819 (125:521), a review of *Rosalind and Helen*. Reprinted, p. 153.

The London Magazine. 1820-29. Sometimes called Baldwin's, from its first publisher. An excellent liberal monthly, to which Lamb, Hazlitt, Hunt, B. W. Proctor, and DeQuincey were contributors. It was regarded by the Tory press as one of the chief Cockney champions. In 1821 its brilliant editor, John Scott, was mortally wounded in a duel resulting from his defence of the Cockneys against Blackwood's Edinburgh Magazine. (2).

May, 1820 (1:546-555), a review of *The Cenci*. Reprinted, p. 188.

June, 1820 (1:706), an announcement and brief preliminary review of *Prometheus Unbound*. Reprinted, p. 217.

August, 1820 (2:196), quotes from "Stanzas Addressed to Percy Bysshe Shelley," in reviewing Bernard Barton's *Poems*.

September, 1820 (2:349), lists Shelley's *Prometheus Unbound*.

November, 1820 (2:516), incidental comment on Shelley in attacking Blackwood's Edinburgh Magazine for its literary criticisms.

January, 1821 (3:64-65), in reviewing *The Literary Pocket Book* quotes from it two poems by Shelley.

January, 1821 (3:68), under "Town Conversation," a note entitled "Mr. Shelley," anticipating his unfinished *Charles the First*. Reprinted, p. 271.

April, 1821 (3:370), about a page of incidental criticism of *Prometheus Unbound*, in an essay entitled "Table Talk." Reprinted, p. 271.

May, 1821 (3:549), incidental comment on Shelley, in reviewing Hazlitt's *Table Talk*.

July, 1821 (4:57), incidental comment on Shelley, in reviewing John Hamilton Reynolds's *The Garden of Florence, and Other Poems*.

September, 1822 (6:42), a brief notice of Shelley's death.

The London Magazine and Monthly Critical and Dramatic Review. 1820. Sometimes called Gold's, from its publisher. Continued as The London Magazine and Theatrical Inquisitor. Whig in politics, partisan of Queen Caroline. Liberal in moral and social views. Although its attitude toward Shelley is so comparatively friendly, it is curious that an essay signed D. N., entitled "An Essay on Poetry, with Observations on the Living Poets" (2:370-374, 470-474, 557-562) makes no mention of Shelley. (2) changing to (1).

April, 1820 (1:401-407), a review of *The Cenci*. Reprinted, p. 171.

September, 1820 (2:306-308), a review of *Prometheus Unbound*. Reprinted, p. 231.

October, 1820 (2:382-391), the same, continued. Reprinted, p. 232.

The London Magazine and Theatrical Inquisitor. 1821. A continuation of The London Magazine and Monthly Critical and Dramatic Review. Liberal monthly. Some numbers have the word Gold's prefixed to the title. (1).

January, 1821 (3:36), a poem, by Leigh Cliffe, entitled "The Spirit of the Storm," an unacknowledged imitation of Shelley's "The Cloud." Reprinted, p. 344.

January, 1821 (3:78), quotes Horace Smith's sonnet to Shelley, in reviewing Smith's *Amarynthus the Nympholept*. Reprinted, p. 340.

February, 1821 (3:122-127), article entitled "On the Philosophy and Poetry of Shelley." Reprinted, p. 263.

February, 1821 (3:172), incidental mention of Shelley in reviewing *The Literary Pocket Book*.

March, 1821 (3:278-280). A review of *Queen Mab*. Reprinted, p. 53.

July, 1821 (4:31-34), a humorous travesty on Shelley's vegetarianism, in an article entitled "Dinner by the Amateurs of Vegetable Diet." Reprinted, p. 262.

The Lonsdale Magazine and Provincial Repository. Kirkby Lonsdale. 1820-22. A provincial monthly of traditional conservative type, with a somewhat charitable critical tendency. Its announced motto was "Ten censure wrong for one who writes amiss." (2).

November, 1820 (1:498-501), a review of *Prometheus Unbound*. Reprinted, p. 236.

Melincourt. By Thomas Love Peacock. 1817. One of the characters is said to represent Shelley.

Memoirs of the Life and Writings of the Right Honorable Lord Byron, with Anecdotes of Some of His Contemporaries. Anon. (John Watkins.) 1822. Incidental criticisms and mentions of Shelley (pp. 268, 402, 408, 410, 411).

The Military Register and Weekly Gazette, Historical, Literary, etc., for the Army, Navy, Colonies, and Fashionable World. 1820-21. A ms note on the file for 1820-21 in the British Museum, says "R. Scott, publisher, printer, editor and proprietor, 3 Pall Mall Court." Announces The Anti-Jacobin as its model, yet deals favorably with Leigh Hunt's The Indicator.

October 1, 1820 (1:433), publishes without comment the first 101 lines of Shelley's "Ode to Naples."

October 8, 1820 (1:464), the same, concluded. (The first publication of this poem, hitherto supposed to have been first published in Mrs. Shelley's *Posthumous Poems of Percy Bysshe Shelley*, 1824.)

The Monthly Magazine and British Register. 1796-1835. Ed. J. A. Herand, (1839-42) B. E. Hill, etc. Continued as Monthly Magazine of Politics, Literature, etc., 1835-38, and as The Monthly Magazine, 1839-43. Monthly. (2). Sir Richard Phillips, who had served sentence for publishing Paine's *The Age of Reason*, was the directing genius of The Monthly Magazine, during Shelley's literary lifetime. It was a liberal magazine, regarded by the Tories as radical. On October 14, 1824, Henry Colburn stated that the maximum rate for The Monthly Magazine was sixteen guineas a sheet and offered to accept articles from Leigh Hunt up to £150 a year. (British Museum Add. Mss. 38,108, f. 331. (2).

May, 1810 (29:359), lists *Zastrozzi, a Romance*.

November, 1810 (30:360), lists *Original Poetry, by Victor and Cazire*.

January, 1811 (30:551), lists *St. Irvyne, or The Rosicrucian*, and *Posthumous Fragments of Margaret Nicholson*.

April, 1816 (41:256), lists *Alastor, or The Spirit of Solitude*.

February, 1818 (45:65), lists *The Revolt of Islam* and *Alastor*.

March, 1818 (45:154), a brief review of *The Revolt of Islam*. Reprinted, p.124.

April, 1820 (49:260), a brief review of *The Cenci*. Reprinted, p. 167.

April, 1820 (49:263), lists *The Cenci*.

June, 1820 (49:450), lists *The Cenci*.

November, 1820 (50:365), lists *Prometheus Unbound*.

June, 1821 (51:460), review of *Queen Mab*. Reprinted, p. 60.

September, 1822 (54:178), obituary notice of Shelley. Reprinted, p. 330.

October, 1822 (54:255), comment on Shelley in reviewing Arthur Brooke's *Elegy on the Death of Percy Bysshe Shelley*.

October, 1822 (54:257), lists Barton's *Verses on the Death of Percy Bysshe Shelley*.

The Monthly Repository of Theology and General Literature. 1806-37. Ed. R. Aspland, W. J. Fox, Leigh Hunt, and R. H. Horne. In 1822 Fox was editor. An ably conducted liberal Unitarian periodical. Fox preached and published a sermon against the prosecution of Richard Carlile for blasphemy. See note on p. 63. (2).

September, 1822 (17:577), an obituary of Shelley.

December, 1822 (17:717-718), a report of the trial of William Clark, for publishing *Queen Mab*.

The Monthly Review, or Literary Journal. 1749-1845. An important Whig journal in the eighteenth century, to which Goldsmith contributed. Edited till 1803 by its founder, Ralph Griffiths, and from 1803-25 by his son. Conservative in literary opinions. A manuscript contract between Thomas Black, owner on January 31, 1814, and William Hone, prospective editor, gives the editor a salary of five guineas monthly and a one-twelfth share in the review provided he can increase the circulation to 1,000 copies. (British Museum Add. Mss. 40,120, f. 32. (2).

April, 1816 (79:433), a brief review of *Alastor*. Reprinted, p. 105.

March, 1819 (88:323-324), a review of *The Revolt of Islam*. Reprinted, p. 132.

October, 1819 (90:207-209), a review of *Rosalind and Helen*. Reprinted, p. 164.

February, 1821 (94:168-173), a review of *Prometheus Unbound*. Reprinted, p. 238.

February, 1821 (94:161-168), a review of *The Cenci*. Reprinted, p. 203.

November, 1822 (99:326), incidental criticism of Shelley in reviewing Arthur Brooke's *Elegy on the Death of Percy Bysshe Shelley*.

November, 1822 (99:327), incidental criticism of Shelley in reviewing Bernard Barton's *Verses on the Death of Percy Bysshe Shelley*.

The Morning Chronicle. December 29, 1770-December 20, 1862. From 1817 till after Shelley's death, The Morning Chronicle was edited by John Black, a fearless advocate of reform. In the first two decades of the nineteenth century it was the principal rival of The Times in circulation and influence.

September 18, 1810, advertisement of *Original Poetry, by Victor and Cazire*.

March 15, 1811, advertisement of *A Poetical Essay on the Existing State of Things*.

March 21, 1811, advertisement of *A Poetical Essay on the Existing State of Things*.

January 25, 1817, a report of Westbrook *vs.* Shelley.

August 12, 1822, a paragraph on Shelley's death, consisting of an "Extract of a letter from Pisa," under the general heading, "The Mirror of Fashion." Reprinted, p. 321.

The Morning Post. November 17, 1772—In progress. Under Daniel Stuart, at the very beginning of the century, The Morning Post was a vigorous liberal newspaper with an able corps of contributors including Lamb, Coleridge, and Wordsworth. After about 1808 it became strongly Tory.

September 18, 1810, lists *Original Poetry, by Victor and Cazire.*

The Museum, or Record of Literature, Fine Arts, Science, etc. 1822-23; continued as The Literary Museum, 1823-24.

October 26, 1822 (1:679), incidental favorable comments on Shelley's translation from *Faust*, in reviewing The Liberal.

The Necessity of Atheism. Anon. February, 1811.

The New European Magazine. 1822-24. Conservative monthly, with a special hatred of Cockneys, as evinced by frequent attacks on Hunt and Hazlitt. (3).

September, 1822 (1:194), unfavorable incidental comment on Shelley's death.

October, 1822 (1:354-363), incidental attacks on Shelley in reviewing The Liberal.

The New Edinburgh Monthly Review. The same as The Edinburgh Monthly Review *(q.v.).*

The New Monthly Magazine and Universal Register. 1814-20. Continued as The New Monthly Magazine and Literary Journal, 1821-84. According to its first editor, Dr. Watkins, the purpose with which The New Monthly was begun was "to counteract the pernicious and anarchical designs of sedition and infidelity." It was especially directed against Sir Richard Phillips and his Monthly Magazine. Alaric A. Watts, a Tory, was an editor from some time in 1818 to about June, 1819. During the 1820's it was nominally edited by Thomas Campbell, but most of the editorial labors from 1821-1830 were performed by Cyrus Redding, a political liberal. (2).

April 1, 1816 (5:242), lists *Alastor, or The Spirit of Solitude.*

April 1, 1819 (11:194-5), brief mention of the Shelley-Byron association in Geneva, under Extract of a Letter from Geneva.

April 1, 1820 (13:487), lists *The Cenci.*

May 1, 1820 (13:550-553), a review of *The Cenci.* Reprinted, p. 181.

October 1, 1822 (N. S. 6:472), a kindly memoir of Shelley. Reprinted, p. 00.

The New Times. Begun as The Day and New Times in 1817 as a rival to The Times, continued 1817-28 as The New Times and merged with The Morning Journal in 1828. A Tory newspaper receiving a subsidy from the government. Edited to 1827 by Dr. John ("Dr. Slop") Stoddart, Hazlitt's brother-in-law.

June [— ?], review of *Rosalind and Helen,* quoted by Gentleman's Magazine.[1] Reprinted, p. 153.

Nightmare Abbey. By Thomas Love Peacock. 1818. The character of Scythrop represents Shelley.

The North Wales Gazette. A weekly newspaper published on Thursdays by John Broster, Bangor, Carnarvonshire.

October 1, 1812 (p. 3), account of a meeting of the Corporation of Beaumaris to support the Tremadoc Embankment, with a speech by Shelley.

October 1, 1812 (p. 3), subscription-list for the Embankment, listing Shelley's subscription, and resolutions of thanks.

October 8, 1812, a correction of the first account above. Reprinted, p. 362, footnote.

Oedipus Tyrannus; or, Swellfoot the Tyrant. Anon. 1820. December.

---

[1] I have been unable to examine The New Times.

Ollier's Literary Miscellany. No. 1. 1820. An excellent ephemeral literary journal published by Shelley's publisher. The most important article it contained was Peacock's "The Four Ages of Poetry."

1820 (no. 1, no further date), contains Ollier's regular advertisement of Shelley's works, with the laudatory sentence quoted from Blackwood's review of *Alastor*.

Original Poetry, by Victor and Cazire. September, 1810.

The Oxford University and City Herald. The set in the British Museum runs, with some breaks, from December, 1806, to February 28, 1815. Very liberal weekly. Printed and published by John Munday, after Jan. 12, 1811, Munday and Slatter (Shelley's printers). It contains an essay signed P. S. and poems signed S. that may have been written by Shelley.

November 17, 1810, lists *Posthumous Fragments of Margaret Nicholson*, as just published.

November 24, 1810, lists *Posthumous Fragments of Margaret Nicholson*, as just published.

March 2, 1811, acknowledges Shelley's contribution to the fund for the relief of Peter Finnerty: "Mr. P. B. Shelley, 1£. 1s. 0d."

March 9, 1811, lists *A Poetical Essay on the Existing State of Things* rather conspicuously.

The Paris Monthly Review, January, 1822 to April, 1823. After February, 1823, known as Galignani's Magazine and Paris Monthly Review. Published by Galignani, the famous Parisian bookseller of the period.[2]

March, 1822 (1: 355), an extract from "Epipsychidion," with a brief introductory comment. Reprinted, p. 284.

August, 1822 (2: 392), a favorable obituary notice, headed as a review of *Hellas*. Reprinted, p. 326.

The Patriot. Dublin.

March 2, 1812, an account of Shelley's speech at Fishamble Street Theatre. Identical with that in Saunder's News Letter (*q.v.*).

Poems, by Bernard Barton. 1820. Contains Stanzas Addressed to Percy Bysshe Shelley. (2). Reprinted, p. 341.

A Poetical Essay on the Existing State of Things. By a Gentleman of the University of Oxford. March, 1811. No copy of this poem has ever been found, though the fact that it was advertised in The Oxford Herald, listed in The Poetical Register and the British Review, described and identified with Shelley in The Dublin Weekly Messenger, seems to establish its existence and authorship.

The Poetical Register and Repository of Fugitive Verse.

1802-14. Consists of brief, undistinguished notices of current books of verse.

1814, Poetical Register for 1810-1811, p. 617. A brief review of *Poems, by Victor and Cazire*. Reprinted, p. 32.

The Posthumous Fragments of Margaret Nicholson. Edited by John Fitzvictor. Anon. 1810.

Prometheus Unbound. August, 1820.

Proposals for an Association, etc. By Percy Bysshe Shelley. March 2, 1812.

A Proposal for Putting Reform to the Vote throughout the Kingdom. By the Hermit of Marlow. March, 1817.

The Quarterly Review, 1809—in progress. Ed. William Gifford, Sir John Taylor Coleridge, John Gibson Lockhart, *et. al.* Gifford was the sole editor during Shel-

[2] For these data I am indebted to Professor George L. Marsh, whose article on "The Early Reviews of Shelley" (Modern Philology, 37: 87) first directed me to the notices of Shelley in this periodical.

ley's lifetime.   The Quarterly was so strongly Tory as to be almost the official spokesman of the government and the church.   Its reviews were generally well informed and well written.   Its influence on public opinion was greater than that of any other periodical, with the possible exception of The Edinburgh Review.   (3).

January, 1817 (published April, 1818, 2:158), Southey's article, "The Rise and Progress of Popular Disaffections," mentions Shelley's pseudonymous *A Proposal for Putting Reform to the Vote Throughout the Kingdom,* without naming Shelley.

May, 1818 (18:324, 328-329), a review of Hunt's *Foliage* (by J. W. Croker or J. T. Coleridge) attacks Shelley without mentioning his name.   Reprinted, p. 124.

April, 1819 (21:460-471), a review of *Laon and Cythna* (by John Taylor Coleridge).   Reprinted, p. 133.

October, 1821 (26:168-180), a review of *Prometheus Unbound.* (by W. S. Walker).   Reprinted, p. 240.

Queen Mab. A Philosophical Poem. By Percy Bysshe Shelley.   Anon.   Privately printed by Shelley in 1813.[3]

Queen Mab. Anon.   1821.   William Clark's pirated edition.   Clark issued a variant of this piracy in the same year.

Queen Mab. A Philosophical Poem. By Percy Bysshe Shelley.   1821.   New York.

Queen Mab. 1822.   Two pirated editions by Richard Carlile.

The Recreative Review.   1821-22.

1822 (3:21, 59), allusions to Shelley in an article entitled "Infidelity."

The Real John Bull.   January 21, 1821-March 21, 1824.   A Whig weekly, not to be confused with John Bull (Tory) or John Bull's British Journal (Radical), with both of which it was in part contemporary.

August 11, 1822 (p. 76), a report of Shelley's death.[4]

December 8, 1822 (no. 99, pp. 794-795), passing mention of Shelley's atheism in an editorial entitled "Religion."

A Refutation of Deism. Anon. (Shelley.)   1814.   Published in the beginning of the year, according to Hogg.

A Reply to the Anti-matrimonial hypothesis and supposed atheism of Percy Bysshe Shelley, as laid down in Queen Mab.   1821.   Printed and published by William Clark.   At his trial for publishing *Queen Mab,* Clark avowed the publication of this Reply, and urged it as proof that he was not in full accord with the libellous and blasphemous parts of the poem.   It is quite possible that it may have been published partly with the intent of providing a defence against a libel prosecution.   Reprinted, p. 62.

The Representative.   January, 1822-April 13, 1823.   A Whig weekly newspaper of liberal sympathies.   Directed by Murdo Young, who also controlled the Sun.   (2).

March 10, 1822 (no. 10), incidental reference to Shelley, in an article entitled "Mr. Carlile."

October 13, 1822 (no. 41), a poem of ninety-two lines, entitled "An Authentic and Very Marvellous *New Ballad,* Giving an Account of the Renowned Triple-

---

[3] Only seventy copies were put into circulation before 1822.   It was Shelley's practise, in giving away copies, to remove his own name and address from the title-page.

[4] Reported in Notes and Queries for July 27, 1912 by Mr. A. G. Potter.   This item was overlooked in my examination of The Real John Bull.   I am indebted to Mr. Alan Strout for my knowledge of it via Notes and Queries.

leagued Champions of Anti-Christendom, and Completely Unfolding the Supernatural Mystery of the Holy Trio." Shelley is not mentioned by name.

October 27, 1822 (no. 43), a paragraph on Shelley in an article entitled "Conspiracies against Religion and Political Liberty."

The Republican. August 27, 1819-Jan. 7, 1826. A weekly, edited by Richard Carlile. Practically all the contents were written by Carlile from Dorchester Gaol, where he was serving his sentence for publishing Paine's *Age of Reason*. It was published, until her own imprisonment, by his wife, Jane Carlile. It is a highly personal organ, containing much about Carlile's own conflicts with the law. There are some items of political interest, such as comments on the trial of Queen Caroline, but the main animus is anti-religious. Whether Carlile ever met Shelley is doubtful, but it is not unlikely that he may have had correspondence with him, though none is known. Carlile says in The Republican for February 1, 1822, that in 1819 he tried to get Shelley's permission to publish *Queen Mab* and that many of Shelley's friends and intimates advised him to publish it over Shelley's refusal. At the time of Carlile's conviction Shelley wrote a long letter to Leigh Hunt protesting against its injustice. (1).

September 24, 1819 (1:75-78), reprints in full, without Shelley's name, *A Declaration of Rights*.

February 1, 1822 (5:145-148), an article by Richard Carlile, entitled *"Queen Mab."* Reprinted, p. 95.

August 16, 1822 (6:380-381), an article entitled "Death of Percy Bysshe Shelley." Reprinted, p. 325.

August 23, 1822 (6:408), an article entitled "From 'The British Luminary'," commenting on Shelley's life and death. Reprinted, p. 325.

December 27, 1822 (6:978-979), an article entitled "Queen Mab," signed Richard Carlile. Reprinted, p. 97.

Retrospection, with Other Poems. By Arthur Brooke (John Chalk Claris). 1822. Contains a sonnet to Shelley and other poems showing Brooke to be a disciple and imitator of Shelley. I could discover no copy of this volume in any of the libraries in Europe and America in which I sought it, but three lines of the sonnet, quoted in a review in The Gazette of Fashion, etc., April 13, 1822, show it to be the same as that published by Claris in The Examiner of November 5, 1820. Reprinted, p. 343.

The Retrospective Review. 1820-28. Ed. H. Southern (later associated with the liberal Westminster Review), N. H. Nichols, etc. Mainly historical in its interests, and devoted to older, rather than contemporary, books. (2).

1820 (vol. 2, part 1, no month, p. 204), incidental praise of Shelley and Keats, in a digression on living poets. Reprinted, p. 269.

The Revolt of Islam. By Percy Bysshe Shelley. January, 1818.

Revolutionary Causes: with a Brief Notice of some Late Publications. Anon. 1822. Incidental condemnation of Shelley as an atheistical poet, and praise of The Quarterly's review of *Prometheus Unbound*.

Rosalind and Helen, A Modern Eclogue; with Other Poems. By Percy Bysshe Shelley. 1819.

St. Irvine; or The Rosicrucian. By a Gentleman of the University of Oxford. December, 1811.

St. Irvyne, etc. 1822. A reissue by J. J. Stockdale, the original publisher.

St. Tammany's Magazine. New York. 1821. Nos. 1-5. A rather cheap journal published by C. S. Winkle, no. 101 Greenwich Street "about once a week." Has no particular personality, and consists mainly of clippings from British journals.

November 9, 1821 (no. 1, p. 13), an article entitled "Queen Mab and Its Author." Consists of a reprint, without comment, of Shelley's letter of June 22, 1821, to the editor of the Examiner, protesting against the pirated edition of *Queen Mab*, by Clark. This article is identical in heading and content with the clipping from an unknown periodical pasted in the front cover of the British Museum's copy of the 1813 *Queen Mab*.

Saunders's News Letter. Dublin.

February 29, 1812, an account of Shelley's speech at Fishamble Street Theatre. See under Patriot.

The Scots Magazine. See under Edinburgh Magazine and Literary Miscellany.

Table Talk. By William Hazlitt. 1821. Contains a criticism of Shelley in the essay, "Paradox and Commonplace." Reprinted, p. 269.

The Theatrical Inquisitor; or, Literary Mirror. By Cerberus. 1812-21. Combined with Gold's London Magazine. Liberal monthly. (1).

April, 1820 (16: 205-218), a review of *The Cenci*, signed B. Reprinted, p. 00.

The Theological Inquirer, or Polemical Magazine. "Being a General Medium of Communication on Religion, Metaphysics, and Moral Philosophy. Conducted by Erasmus Perkins, assisted by Several Eminent Literary Characters." Open to All Parties. March-September, 1815; no more published. (1).

In a prospectus pasted on the inside cover of the British Museum copy, the editor says its success will depend on its being known "to the friends of religious liberty." The Preface, signed E. P., Clarendon Square, Somer's-town, August 30, 1815, says that its purpose is to offer free discussion, all other journals, except The Monthly Repository, being narrowly sectarian and biassed. Two articles signed Varro are attributed in pencil in the British Museum copy to Leigh Hunt. One of these articles, "Remarks on the Illiberality of the Spectator toward Atheists," elicited some eulogistic letters on Giordano Bruno, signed Eunomus Wilson, in which *Queen Mab* is quoted and praised. In the prospectus Erasmus Perkins is called an M. A. and several of his works are listed. But a thorough search fails to find his name among the alumni of British universities or in London directories. Nor could I find any of his works, except one article in Cobbett's Political Register. In 1815 the Repository turned over several articles to The Political Register. See p. 45.

March, 1815 (1: 6-24), a reprint, with some corrections, of Shelley's *A Refutation of Deism, in a Dialogue Between a Deist and a Christian*. Anon. Continued in April number.

March, 1815 (1: 34-39), the first of a series of letters entitled "Queen Mab," signed F. Continued in April, May, and July numbers. Reprinted, p. 45.

April, 1815 (1: 105-110), "Queen Mab," continued. Reprinted, p. 45.

April, 1815 (1: 121-131), "A Refutation of Deism," concluded.

May, 1815 (1: 164), a letter on Giordano Bruno, signed Eunomus Wilson, Pentonville, April 20, 1815, concludes with a tribute to the author of *Queen Mab* and a quotation of fourteen lines not included in the copious quotations given by F. (Canto VII, lines 1-14).

May, 1815 (1: 205-209), "Queen Mab," continued. Reprinted, p. 45.

June, 1815 (1: 242-247), a letter signed Mary Ann, answering *A Refutation of Deism*.

July, 1815 (1: 358-362), "Queen Mab," concluded. Reprinted, p. 45.

July, 1815 (1: 380-381), a poem signed F., entitled "Ode to the Author of 'Queen Mab'." Reprinted, p. 339.

The Tickler; or Monthly Compendium of Good Things. 1818-24. (1).

April 1, 1821 (3:83), Arthur Brooke's sonnet, "To the Author of the Revolt of Islam," previously printed in The Examiner, Nov. 5, 1820.

The Times. January 1, 1785—in progress. Under the ownership of the second John Walters, The Times was just beginning to assert its long ascendancy at the time Shelley began publishing. It was moderately conservative in policy.

June 5 and 12, 1810, advertisement of Zastrozzi, A Romance. By P. B. S.

October 12, 1810, advertisement of Poems by Victor and Cazire.

January 26, 1811, advertisement of St. Irvyne as just published.

February 2, 1811, advertisement of St. Irvyne as just published.

April 10, 1811, advertisement of A Poetical Essay on The Existing State of Things.

April 11, 1811, advertisement of A Poetical Essay on The Existing State of Things.

The Troubadour. An obscure, apparently short-lived magazine of verse in 1822. I have been unable to find it in any library.

Before October, 1822. Contained a poem by J. W. Dalby entitled "Lines to Shakespeare and to Shelley," referred to and quoted in part in The Drama, or Theatrical Pocket Magazine (q.v.), October, 1822.

Verses on the Death of Percy Bysshe Shelley. By Bernard Barton. 1822. Reprinted, p. 352.

A Vindication of Natural Diet. Anon. (Shelley). 1813.

A Vision of Judgment. By Robert Southey. April 11, 1821. The Preface attacks the Satanic School, which clearly includes Shelley, but there is no mention of his name.

Walker's Hibernian Magazine. Dublin. Founded in 1771 as The Hibernian Magazine, or Compendium of Entertaining Knowledge.

February, 1812 (p. 83), a brief account of Shelley's speech at Fishamble Street Theatre.

The Weekly Entertainer; an Agreeable and Instructive Repository, etc. Sherborne. 1784-1825.

August 21, 1820 (N. S. 2:149-151), an extract from The Retrospective Review (q.v.), entitled "An Estimate of the Poetry of the Present Age."

The Weekly Messenger. Dublin. A liberal weekly. (1). Edited at the time of Shelley's Irish adventure by Frederick William Conway. Shelley's friend, John Lawless, later the editor, was a contributor and probably wrote the account of Shelley.

March 7, 1812, an article entitled "Pierce Byshe Shelley, Esq."

March 7, 1812, praise of Shelley (not mentioned by name, but present) in a speech by Thomas Wyse, at the conclusion of the Fishamble Street Theatre meeting.

The Weekly Review. 1821.

1821, May 12 (p. 32), passing comment on Shelley in reviewing Hazlitt's Table Talk.

The Westmoreland Gazette (Kendal). August 29, 1818. Quotes eight stanzas from Canto X of The Revolt of Islam, entitled "Famine and Pestilence." De Quincey was editor at the time.[5]

Zastrozzi, A Romance. By P. B. S., 1810. D. F. MacCarthy, in The Early Life of Shelley, gives the publication date as June 5, but Forman, The Shelley Li-

---

[5] For this information I am indebted to Mr. Alan Strout.

brary, p. 6, quotes Shelley's letter of May 29 to Edward Graham as indicating that the book was then published.

UNIDENTIFIED PERIODICALS

The British Museum copy of the original edition of *Queen Mab* contains, pasted in the front, two cuttings from unnamed newspapers, viz.:

Queen Mab and Its Author. To the Editor of the Examiner. This is Shelley's letter of protest at the Clark edition of 1821. It is identical with the item in St. Tammany's Magazine, listed above. According to Forman (*The Shelley Library*, p. 46) it was cut from The Examiner.

Law Intelligence. Court of Chancery, August 26. Private Hearing—Queen Mab. Westbrook *vs.* Shelley, Esq. This is a fairly detailed account of the proceedings of August 26.

A newspaper cutting, evidently of 1822, inserted in the British Museum copy of *A Vindication of Natural Diet* (1813) commenting on Shelley's funeral pyre. The advertisements on the back of the cutting practically established that the paper was American.